Thinking

An Invitation to Cognitive Science
Daniel N. Osherson, Series Editor

Volume 1: Language
Edited by Lila R. Gleitman and Mark Liberman

Volume 2: Visual Cognition
Edited by Stephen M. Kosslyn and Daniel N. Osherson

Volume 3: Thinking
Edited by Edward E. Smith and Daniel N. Osherson

Volume 4: Conceptual Foundations
Edited by Saul Sternberg and Donald Scarborough

Thinking

An Invitation to Cognitive Science
Second Edition

Volume 3

---

edited by Edward E. Smith and Daniel N. Osherson

A Bradford Book
The MIT Press
Cambridge, Massachusetts
London, England

This book was set in Palatino by Asco Trade Typesetting Ltd., Hong Kong and printed in the United States of America.

Library of Congress Cataloging-in-Publication Data

An invitation to cognitive science.—2nd ed.
p. cm.
"A Bradford book."
Includes bibliographical references and indexes.
Contents: v. 1. Language / edited by Lila R. Gleitman and Mark Liberman—v. 2. Visual cognition / edited by Stephen M. Kosslyn and Daniel N. Osherson—v. 3. Thinking / edited by Edward E. Smith and Daniel N. Osherson.
ISBN 0-262-65045-2 (set),—ISBN 0-262-15043-3 (v. 3 : hardcover).—ISBN 0-262-65043-6 (v. 3 : pbk.).
1. Cognition. 2. Cognitive science. I. Gleitman, Lila R.
BF311:I68 1995
153—dc20 95-10924
CIP

Contents

List of Contributors

Scott Atran
Institute for Social Research
University of Michigan

Ned Block
Department of Linguistics and Philosophy
Massachusetts Institute of Technology

Susan Carey
Department of Brain and Cognitive Sciences
Massachusetts Institute of Technology

Gilbert Harman
Department of Philosophy
Princeton University

Keith J. Holyoak
Department of Psychology
University of California, Los Angeles

John Jonides
Department of Psychology
University of Michigan

Daniel N. Osherson
Istituto San Raffaele
Milan, Italy

Lance J. Rips
Department of Psychology
Northwestern University

Eldar Shafir
Department of Psychology
Princeton University

Edward E. Smith
Department of Psychology
University of Michigan

Norbert Schwarz
Institute for Social Research
University of Michigan

Amos Tversky
Department of Psychology
Stanford University

Foreword

The book you are holding is the third of a four-volume introduction to contemporary cognitive science. The work includes more than forty chapters, written by linguists, psychologists, philosophers, computer scientists, biologists, and engineers. The topics range from muscle movement to human rationality, from acoustic phonetics to mental imagery, from the cerebral locus of language to the categories that people use to organize experience. Topics as diverse as these require distinctive kinds of theories, tested against distinctive kinds of data, and this diversity is reflected in the style and content of the chapters.

The authors of these volumes are united by their fascination with the mechanisms and structure of biological intelligence, especially human intelligence. Indeed, the principal goal of this introductory work is to reveal the vitality of cognitive science, to share the excitement of its pursuit, and to help you reflect upon its interest and importance. You may therefore think of these volumes as an invitation—namely, the authors' invitation to join the ongoing adventure of research into human cognition.

The topics we explore fall into four parts, each corresponding to a separate volume. The parts are: language, visual cognition, thinking, and conceptual foundations. Each volume is self-contained, so they can be read in any order. On the other hand, it is easiest to read the chapters of a given volume in the order indicated. Each chapter concludes with suggestions for further reading and a set of problems to test your understanding.

It remains only to wish you a pleasant and invigorating journey through cognitive science. May it lead to a life-long interest!

Istituto San Raffaele
July 1995

DANIEL N. OSHERSON
SERIES EDITOR

Thinking: Introduction

Edward E. Smith

Thinking is among the most distinctive of all human capacities. Typically, thinking involves mentally representing some aspects of the world (including aspects of ourselves) and manipulating these representations or beliefs so as to yield new beliefs, where the latter may be used in accomplishing some goal. Although all the chapters in this volume deal with thinking, they naturally divide into two sections. Chapters in one group are focused on *concepts and reasoning;* those in the other group concentrate on *memory and problem solving.*

Chapter 1 in the concepts and reasoning section deals with concepts and categorization. *Categorization* refers to the assignment of objects or events to categories; the processes involved in this activity rely on concepts. Concepts and categorization are fundamental to other thought processes because often the latter operate on concepts rather than on individual experiences. Chapter 2 is focused on *judgment,* particularly on our way of judging the probabilities of uncertain events. Such probability judgments figure critically in determining the extent to which our behavior is rational. This concentration on rationality is continued in chapter 3, which deals with *choice,* the means by which we decide among options. Chapter 4 presents a *developmental perspective* on selected issues in concepts and reasoning, particularly on whether development involves qualitative changes in the nature of our concepts. Chapter 5 offers another perspective, that of *cultural variations in cognition.* Here the focus is on concepts of biological kinds and how they figure in inductive reasoning. Chapter 6, last in the concepts and reasoning section, provides still another perspective, that of *philosophy of mind.* In this chapter we return to considerations about human rationality.

In the section on memory and problem solving, chapter 7 surveys the literature on the role of working memory in thought. Working memory seems to be involved in many cases of complex thinking, cases that we refer to as *problem solving.* Problem solving is given fuller treatment in chapter 8, which surveys the various approaches that have been taken in this area. Chapter 9 is focused on a specific class of problems, those that require *deductive reasoning*. Again the emphasis is on the relation between memory and problem-solving processes. Chapter 10 provides a *social cognition* perspective on selected issues in memory and problem solving. The author discusses cases in which the problem consists of generating an impression of another person or some aspect of one's self. Finally, chapter 11 offers a philosophical perspective about the cognitive approach to thinking in general. Its author discusses the computer metaphor that guides most of the research described in this volume, and the possible limitations of this approach.

Thinking

Part One

Concepts and Reasoning

Chapter 1
Concepts and Categorization

Edward E. Smith

We are forever trying to carve nature at its joints, dividing it into categories so that we can make sense of the world. If we see a particular child pet a particular dog at a particular time and a particular place, we code it as just another instance of children liking dogs. In so doing, we reduce a wealth of particulars to a simple relation between the categories of children and dogs. Not only do we free our mental capacities for other tasks, but also we can see the connection between our current situation and our past experience.

To *categorize* some object x is to come to think of it as an instance of a *category* (a class of objects that belong together). How do we do this? Presumably, we have (1) mental representations of various categories, and (2) a means for deciding which of these mental representations provides the best fit to x. These mental representations of categories are the entities psychologists mean by *concepts*. Thus the study of categorization and that of concepts are intimately linked—categories are what concepts are about. Keep in mind, then, that a category usually refers to a group of objects in the world, whereas a concept refers to a mental representation of such a group (Margolis 1994).

We are capable of categorizing many kinds of objects and events in widely varied situations or tasks. There is evidence that different kinds of objects or events are categorized by different means (e.g., Barsalou 1985). Hence, a limited tutorial about categorization, such as this one, must be selective in its coverage, and we focus on just a few kinds of objects in a few kinds of tasks. In particular, we concentrate primarily on categorizing natural kinds and artifacts. By "natural kinds," we mean naturally occurring species of flora and fauna such as daisies and tigers; by "artifacts," we mean person-made objects, such as chairs and shirts. We choose these domains because they are among the most frequent in our lives, among the most

Preparation of this chapter was supported by U.S. Air Force Office of Scientific Research Grant AFOSR No. 91-0225. I thank Daniel Osherson and Lance Rips for helpful comments on an earlier version.

likely to be found in all cultures (see chapter 9 in this volume), and among the most frequently investigated in cognitive studies of categorization.

In examining categorization situations, we deal mainly with variants of two standard *paradigms* (i.e., experimental procedures), one involving visual categorization, the other verbal categorization. In a simple variant of a visual-categorization task, a target category is named (e.g., "Fruit"), and then a pictured object is presented (e.g., a picture of an apple); subjects must decide whether or not it is an instance of the category. A verbal categorization task differs from the preceding only in that the picture is replaced by a term describing or naming the object (e.g., "Macintosh apple"). Examples of the two kinds of tasks are presented in figure 1.1. These two tasks in many ways constitute the simplest possible categorization situations, and hence are useful starting points for analyzing categorization.

With this as background, we can state our agenda for this chapter. In section 1.1 we discuss the major functions of categorization, relying mainly on verbal categorization. We see also that objects in a category tend to be similar to one another, and that this similarity provides a possible basis for categorization (aspects that objects in a category tend to have in common become part of the concept that corresponds to the category). In section 1.2 we discuss alternative means for measuring similarity. We opt for a model in which the similarity of objects is measured in terms of their features. In section 1.3 we apply this model to verbal-categorization tasks and show that it accounts for a variety of empirical findings. In section 1.4 we turn to visual categorization, and see what must be added to our approach to handle results from visual-categorization tasks. In section 1.5 we consider how both verbal and visual categorization break down with certain forms of brain damage. In section 1.6 we consider a somewhat

Visual Categorization Task

"Fruit" - - - - - - - - - - - - - - - - - -  ("yes")

"Fruit" - - - - - - - - - - - - - - - - - -  ("no")

Verbal Categorization Task

"Fruit"- - - - - - - - - - - - - - - - - -Macintosh Apple ("yes")

"Fruit" - - - - - - - - - - - - - - - - - -Oak Tree ("no")

Figure 1.1
Examples of visual and verbal categorization tasks.

more complex categorization task, and demonstrate that categorization is sometimes based on factors other than similarity. Finally, in section 1.7 we summarize our major points, and briefly observe some other issues in research on categorization and concepts.

1.1 Functions of Categorization

The major functions of categorization are coding of experience and licensing of inferences. We discuss these two functions in turn.

1.1.1 Coding of Experience

Categorization is perhaps our primary means for coding experience. We may perceive some complex object as a kind of *chair*, remember it as an instance of *chair*, describe it to others as a "chair," and reason about it as we reason about other chairs.[1] Coding by concept is fundamental to mental life because it greatly reduces the demands on perceptual processes, storage space, and reasoning processes, all of which are known to be limited (see, for example, the discussion of working memory in chapter 7). This coding aspect of categorization is presumably why human languages contain simple terms for categories, such as "tiger," "chair," and "mother"; brief or one-word codes are used for frequently occurring categories.

Concepts vary in the extent to which they are used as codes. Our concepts are often structured into a *taxonomy*—a hierarchy in which successive levels refer to increasingly general kinds of objects—and concepts at an intermediate level are more likely to be used to code experience than are concepts at lower or higher levels (Rosch et al. 1976). Consider the taxonomy for fruits. The concept *fruit* would be at a high or "superordinate" level; *apple* would be at an intermediate level, which psychologists refer to as "basic" level; and *Macintosh apple* would be at a relatively low or "subordinate" level. For objects, the basic level may be identified with the most abstract level that is associated with a specific shape; the superordinate and subordinate levels are simply the levels above and below the basic one. Here, *apple*, which is at the basic level, would be the preferred code, as witnessed by the facts that (1) people in a wide variety of circumstances prefer to name a particular object "apple" rather than "fruit" or "Macintosh apple," and (2) people can decide that a particular apple is an *apple* faster than they can decide that it is a *fruit* or a *Macintosh apple* (Rosch et al. 1976).

1. Throughout the chapter we use italics to indicate concepts (or for special emphasis). Quotation marks are used to indicate words.

1.1.2 Inductive Inferences

Whenever we use a belief to generate a new one, we have drawn an inference. An inference can be perceived to be "deductive," in which case people consider it *impossible* for the new belief to be false if the old one is true, or "inductive," in which case people consider it *improbable* for the new belief to be false if the old one is true (see Skyrms 1986, and chapters 6 and 9 in this volume). An intimate relation connects inductive inferences and categorization; namely, categorizing an object licenses inductive inferences about that object. For example, if we see a round, reddish object on a tree and categorize it as an apple, we can then infer that it is edible and has seeds. Thus categorization is the mental means we have for inferring invisible properties from visible ones.

Similarly, membership in the same category is often taken as justification for inferring that two objects have the same hidden properties. An experimental demonstration used by Gelman and Markman (1986) illustrates this point. On each trial in the experiment subjects were presented three pictures, where the third picture looked like one of the first two but was from the same category as the other picture. For example, on one trial the pictures were of a flamingo, a bat, and a blackbird, where the blackbird resembled the bat. New information was given about the first two pictures, then a question was asked about the third one. For example, regarding the flamingo, subjects were told, "This bird's heart has a right aortic arch only"; regarding the bat, they were told, "This bat's heart has a left aortic arch only"; and regarding the blackbird, they were asked, "What does this bird's heart have?" Subjects responded with "right aortic arch only" almost 90 percent of the time, thus basing their decision on common category membership rather than physical similarity. More surprisingly, when four-year-old children were tested in the same paradigm (though with simpler properties), they based their decision on category membership almost 70 percent of the time. Very early, we know that members of the same category are likely to share many invisible properties even when they do not resemble one another.

Different kinds of concepts and categories differ in the extent to which they support inductive inferences. For one thing, basic and subordinate categories support more inferences than do superordinate categories (Rosch et al. 1976). People will attribute far more properties to an object classified as an apple or a Macintosh apple than to an object classified as a fruit. (There is little difference, though, between the number of inductive inferences supported by basic categories and the number supported by subordinate categories.)

Another distinction among categories that has implications for induction is that between natural kinds and artifact kinds (see, for example, Schwartz 1979). People are more likely to make inductive inferences about invisible properties for natural-kind categories than for artifact categories. Having been told that some chair has a particular nonvisible property—say, that it has lignin all through it—we may be hesitant to conclude that another chair has this property, at least compared to the ease with which we generalize from a flamingo's having a right-aortic-arch heart to another bird's having such a heart (Gelman and O'Reilly 1988).

This discussion of the inductive potential of categories explains another aspect of categories, namely how they differ from most classes of objects. Consider the class of all objects that weigh forty pounds, or the class of all objects that are brown; for both, the objects in the class have some property in common, yet normally the class is not treated as a category. Why not? Presumably because the objects in each of these classes have few salient properties in common other than the one named; in particular, the objects in each of these classes are not assumed to share invisible properties. Hence, the inductive potential of a class may determine whether or not it is treated as a category (Anderson 1991 presents a similar position).[2]

1.2 Similarity

1.2.1 Similarity of Category Members

Now that we have some idea of what categorization is for, we can move on to the principal question of this chapter: How does one assign an object to a category? Perhaps the best known answer hinges on the fact that members of a natural category, particularly a natural-kind category, tend to be perceptually similar to one another though perceptually dissimilar from members of contrasting categories. This relationship applies particularly to categories at the basic level—two apples look like each other yet different from oranges or peaches. Of course, this relationship has limits, as in the earlier example where one bird was less similar to another bird than to a bat. Still, in general, our way of dividing up the world seems to maximize within-category similarity while minimizing between-category similarity (Rosch 1978).

As a consequence, we can assume that categorization is accomplished in roughly this way:

1. Those aspects that are relatively common among members of a category are incorporated into the concept representing that category.

2. In other words, we are distinguishing between two kinds of classes of objects: arbitrary classes, such as the class of all brown objects, and categories, such as birds, where only categories have members that are assumed to share many properties, particularly hidden or deep ones (see Shipley, in press, for discussion).

2. People decide whether or not a novel object belongs to the category by determining whether or not its representation is sufficiently similar to the concept of interest.

Under this view, categorization comes down to assessing the similarity between two mental representations. To flesh out this view, our next order of business is to find a means for measuring precisely the similarity between a pair of representations.

1.2.2 Measurement of Similarity

The two general approaches to the measurement of similarity are the geometric and the featural.

1.2.2.1 Geometric Approach

In the geometric approach, objects or items are represented as points in some multidimensional space such that the metric distance between two points corresponds to the *dissimilarity* between the two items. To illustrate, figure 1.2 represents 20 different fruits, as well as the category of fruit itself, in a two-dimensional space. The shorter the metric distance between a pair of points, the more similar the corresponding fruits. *Apple* is more similar to *plum* than to *date*, but more similar to *date* than to *coconut*.

The space in figure 1.2 was constructed by a systematic procedure developed by Shepard (1962). First, a group of subjects rated the similarity between every possible pair of items (apple–banana, apple–plum, apple–

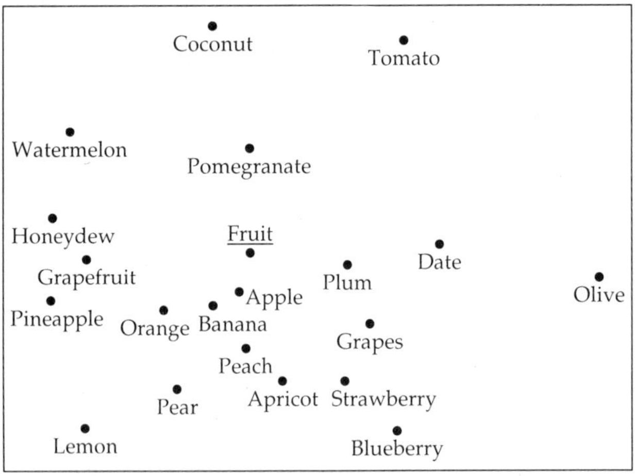

Figure 1.2
A two-dimensional space for representing the similarity relations among 20 instances of fruit and the category of fruit itself. (From Tversky and Hutchinson 1986.)

fruit, and so on—210 distinct pairs in all for the items represented in figure 1.2). The similarity ratings were then input to a computer program that used an iterative procedure to position the items in a space (predetermined to have a certain dimensionality) so that the metric distance between items corresponded as closely as possible to the (inverse of) judged similarity between the items.

An assumption crucial to the representation in figure 1.2 is that psychological distance is "metric" (just as ordinary physical space is). That is, it is assumed there is a function, d, that assigns to every pair of points a nonnegative number, their "distance," in accord with these three axioms:

(1) *Minimality*

$$d(a,b) \geq d(a,a) = d(b,b) = 0$$

(2) *Symmetry*

$$d(a,b) = d(b,a)$$

(3) *Triangle inequality*

$$d(a,b) + d(b,c) \geq d(a,c).$$

Minimality says that the distance between any item and itself is identical for all items, and is the minimum possible. *Symmetry* says that the distance between two items is the same regardless of whether we start at one item or the other. And *triangle inequality* essentially says that the shortest distance between two points is a straight line. All three assumptions are evident in figure 1.2. For example, the distance between *peach* and *date* is (1) greater than that between *peach* and *peach*, (2) equal to that between *date* and *peach*, and (3) less than the sum of the distances between (a) *peach* and *apple* and (b) *apple* and *date*.

The geometric approach has a history of success in representing perceptual objects (for a standard review, see Shepard 1974). Given a two-dimensional representation of color, for example, one can use the distances between the colors to accurately predict the likelihood that a subject in a memory experiment will confuse one color with another. The geometric approach works less well, however, in representing conceptual items, such as categories and their instances. Indeed, for conceptual items, Tversky (1977) produces evidence against each of the metric axioms.

Minimality is compromised because the more we know about an item, the more similar it is judged to itself. A rich, detailed picture seems more similar to itself than does an empty rectangle. A familiar category like that of apples seems more similar to itself than does an unfamiliar category like pomegranates. The axiom of symmetry is undermined by the finding that an unfamiliar category is judged more similar to a familiar or prominent category than the other way around. For example, *pomegranate* is judged more similar to *apple* than *apple* is to *pomegranate.* Although exact violations of the triangle inequality are harder to describe (though see Tversky and Gati 1982), we can capture the gist of them by noting that the axiom implies that if items *a* and *b* are similar to each other and so too are items *b* and *c*, then *a* and *c* cannot be very dissimilar. One counterexample involves countries: Jamaica is similar to Cuba, and Cuba is similar to North Korea, but Jamaica and North Korea are very dissimilar. A milder counterexample appears in the similarity ratings used to construct the space of fruits in figure 1.2: *lemon* was judged similar to *orange*, and *orange* was judged similar to *apricot*, but *lemon* and *apricot* were rated quite dissimilar.

Another problem for the geometric approach involves the notion of a "nearest neighbor" (Tversky and Hutchinson 1986). If we obtain similarity ratings for pairs of items, as in the fruit example, then for each item we can refer to the item rated most similar to it as its "nearest neighbor." We can now characterize an item by how many other items it is nearest neighbor to. When we do this with the similarity ratings for fruits, the category of fruits turns out to be nearest neighbor for 18 of the 20 other terms. This finding is problematic because it is impossible for one item in a metric space to be nearest neighbor to so many other items as long as the space is of relatively low dimensionality. In fact, in a two-dimensional space the maximum number of items to which another item can serve as nearest neighbor is 5. At a minimum, a nine-dimensional space is needed to accommodate *fruit* being nearest neighbor to 18 items. The general problem is that a category serves as nearest neighbor to many of its instances, so many as to call into question the appropriateness of low-dimensional metric representations.

These challenges to the geometric approach are not without their critics. Defenders of the geometric approach argue, for example, that violations of symmetry and the triangle inequality arise more often when similarity is judged directly ("Rate the similarity of *a* to *b*") than when it is judged indirectly (say, by the frequency with which *a* and *b* are confused with one another). This finding suggests that direct judgments require complex decision processes that are the source of the asymmetries (e.g., Krumhansl 1978; Nosofsky 1986). Still, at this moment the weight of evidence points away from geometric representations of natural categories.

1.2.2.2 Featural Approach

In the featural approach, an item is represented as a set of discrete features, such as red, round, and hard, and the similarity between two items is assumed to be an increasing function of the features they have in common and a decreasing function of the features on which they differ. One of the best-known versions of this approach is Tversky's (1977) contrast model. The similarity between the set of features characterizing item *i* (labeled *I*) and the set characterizing item *j* (labeled *J*) is given by (4):

(4) $\text{Sim}(I,J) = af(I \cap J) - bf(I - J) - cf(J - I)$.

Here $I \cap J$ designates the set of features common to the two items, $I - J$ designates the set of features distinct to item i, and $J - I$ designates the set of features distinct to item j. In addition, f is a function that measures the salience of each set of features, and a, b, and c are parameters that determine the relative contribution of the three feature sets.

Table 1.1 illustrates the contrast model with examples drawn from the domain of fruits. Each panel of the table deals with a phenomenon that surfaced in our discussion of the geometric approach. Panel 1 deals with minimality. It includes possible feature sets for the categories of apples and pomegranates. More features appear for *apple* than for *pomegranate* because *apple* is the more familiar concept. This difference will result in *apple* being rated more similar to itself than is *pomegranate*, because the more features an item has the more common features there are when the item is compared to itself. This idea is detailed in the calculations given under each pair, where the contrast model has been used to calculate the similarity between the members of the pair. For simplicity, here and elsewhere, we assume that the function f simply assigns a value of 1 to each feature in a set of common or distinctive features.[3]

Panel 2 deals with symmetry. It compares the similarity of *pomegranate* to *apple* versus that of *apple* to *pomegranate*. As the calculations show, the contrast model is compatible with *pomegranate* being more similar to *apple* than vice versa as long as parameter b exceeds parameter c. In essence, the asymmetry arises because *pomegranate* has fewer distinctive features than *apple*.

Panel 3 demonstrates that the contrast model is compatible with violations of the triangle inequality: *lemon* is similar to *orange* and *orange* is similar to *apricot*, but *lemon* is not similar to *apricot*. As the calculations show, the violation will be pronounced whenever the weight given to common features, a, exceeds that given to either set of distinctive features, b or c, because then similarity will be relatively large for the first two pairs but not for the third.

Panel 4 establishes that the contrast model is compatible with the fact that a concept can serve as nearest neighbor to numerous instances. Among *fruit* instances, *plum* is often rated most similar to *apple*. But as the calculations show, *fruit* is an even closer neighbor to *apple*. The reason is that *fruit* is more abstract than *plum* and hence has fewer distinctive features.

The contrast model therefore offers a satisfactory account of the phenomena that plagued the geometric approach. It is not, however, the

3. These feature sets are derived from the work of Smith, Osherson, Rips, and Keane (1988), who had 30 subjects list features of 15 different instances of fruits (including apple, pomegranate, orange, lemon, and apricot).

Table 1.1
Some illustrations of the contrast model.

Apple	Apple	Pomegranate	Pomegranate
red	red	red	red
round	round	round	round
hard	hard		
sweet	sweet		
trees	trees		
$\text{Sim}(A,A) = a(5) - b(0) - c(0)$		$\text{Sim}(P,P) = a(2) - b(0) - c(0)$	

Pomegranate	Apple	Apple	Pomegranate
red	red	red	red
round	round	round	round
	hard	hard	
	sweet	sweet	
	trees	trees	
$\text{Sim}(P,A) = a(2) - b(0) - c(3)$		$\text{Sim}(A,P) = a(2) - b(3) - c(0)$	

Lemon	Orange	Orange	Apricot	Lemon	Apricot
yellow	orange	orange	red	yellow	red
oval	round	round	round	oval	round
sour	sweet	sweet	sweet	sour	sweet
trees	trees	trees	trees	trees	trees
citrus	citrus	citrus		citrus	
-ade	-ade	-ade		-ade	
$\text{Sim}(L,0) = a(3) - b(3) - c(3)$		$\text{Sim}(O,A) = a(3) - b(3) - c(1)$		$\text{Sim}(L,A) = a(1) - b(5) - c(3)$	

Apple	Plum	Apple	Fruit
red	red	red	red
round	round	round	round
hard	soft	hard	hard
sweet	sweet	sweet	sweet
trees	trees	trees	
$\text{Sim}(A,P) = a(4) - b(1) - c(1)$		$\text{Sim}(A,F) = a(4) - b(1) - c(0)$	

only featural model that can accomplish this explanation. Estes (1994) shows that a "product-rule" model can account for the same phenomena as the contrast model. Whereas in the contrast model, feature matches and mismatches are combined additively, in the product-rule model the matches and mismatches are combined multiplicatively. To illustrate the latter, consider again the representations of *apple* and *pomegranate* in the first panel of table 1.1. According to the product rule: (1) when a pair of features match, a value of t is assigned, and when a pair of features mismatch, a value of s is assigned; and (2) these values are multiplied. Thus, the similarity between *apple* and itself is $t \cdot t \cdot t \cdot t \cdot t = t^5$, whereas the similarity between *pomegranate* and itself is $t \cdot t = t^2$; as long as t is greater than 1, *apple* will be more similar to itself than is *pomegranate*.

We therefore have two (at least) models of similarity that can be used in understanding categorization. It suffices for our purposes to consider just one of them, and we opt for the contrast model. Before applying this model to categorization, though, consider some of its limitations. First, the contrast model does not tell us what an item's features are. For each domain of inquiry, like that of plant categories, researchers need independent procedures for determining the features of the various items (asking people to list features of items is one such procedure, albeit a rough one).

Second, the contrast model offers no theory of the function f that measures the salience of each set of features. Such a theory would have to address issues about the intensity of individual features (for instance, a more saturated color might be assigned greater salience than a less saturated one), as well as issues about the diagnosticity of features (for instance, a feature that discriminates among relevant objects might be assigned higher salience than one that does not). The theory would also have to specify how the salience assigned to a particular feature of an object depends on the context in which that object is embedded. As one example of a context effect, the fact that a cherry is small (for a fruit) seems more salient when it occurs in the context of watermelons than in the context of grapes. (For a discussion of this and related issues about similarity, see Medin, Goldstone, and Gentner 1993; for a discussion of context effects in social categories, see chapter 10 in this volume.)

Third, although the contrast model tells us *what* is computed—measures of sets of common and distinctive features—it says little about the algorithms used to implement the computation. Thus the model does not tell us whether the features of two items are compared simultaneously or sequentially, and if the latter, in what order. As we will see, in applying the contrast model we must add auxiliary assumptions to deal with these limitations.

1.3 Similarity and Verbal Categorization

With these insights into the measurement of similarity, we are in a position to appreciate that similarity underlies some important phenomena in verbal categorization.

1.3.1 Typicality Effects

When verbally presented instances of a category, people can readily order them with respect to how "typical" or "prototypical" or "representative" they are of the category, and different people tend to agree on their orderings. Table 1.2 presents typicality ratings for the categories of fruits and birds. These ratings were obtained by instructing subjects to rate typicality on a 7-point scale, with 7 corresponding to the highest typicality and 1 to the lowest (Malt and Smith 1984). Apples and peaches are considered typical fruits, raisins and figs less typical, and pumpkins and olives atypical. Similar variations are found among the instances of birds. Ratings like these have been obtained for numerous categories and have been shown to be relatively uncorrelated with the frequency or familiarity of the instances (e.g., Malt and Smith 1982).

Table 1.2
Typicality ratings for 15 instances of fruits and birds (from Malt and Smith 1984).

Fruit	Rating	Bird	Rating
Apple	6.25[a]	Robin	6.89
Peach	5.81	Bluebird	6.42
Pear	5.25	Seagull	6.26
Grape	5.13	Swallow	6.16
Strawberry	5.00	Falcon	5.74
Lemon	4.86	Mockingbird	5.47
Blueberry	4.56	Starling	5.16
Watermelon	4.06	Owl	5.00
Raisin	3.75	Vulture	4.84
Fig	3.38	Sandpiper	4.47
Coconut	3.06	Chicken	3.95
Pomegranate	2.50	Flamingo	3.37
Avocado	2.38	Albatross	3.32
Pumpkin	2.31	Penguin	2.63
Olive	2.25	Bat	1.53

a. Ratings made on a 7-point scale, with 7 corresponding to the highest typicality.

The most important aspect about these ratings is that they predict how efficiently people can categorize various instances in a verbal-categorization task. On each trial a subject is given the name of a target category, such as "bird," followed by the test item. The subject must decide as quickly as possible whether the test item names an instance of the target category, such as "robin" or a noninstance, such as "trout." The main data of interest are the decision times for correct categorization. When the test item in fact names a member of the target category, categorization times decrease with the typicality of the test item. With birds as the target category, for example, test items corresponding to robin and swallow are categorized more quickly (by somewhere between 50 and 100 milliseconds) than those corresponding to owl and vulture, which in turn are categorized more quickly (again by 50 to 100 milliseconds) than test items corresponding to flamingo and penguin (see, e.g., Smith, Shoben, and Rips 1974).

These results in no way rest on the specific parameters of the paradigm (e.g., the categories and instances used, or how long the words are presented). Furthermore, to the extent that there is variation in the accuracy of these categorizations, error rates also decrease with the typicality of the test items. These effects are extremely reliable: they have been documented in more than fifty experiments that have used many variants of the verbal-categorization task (for partial reviews, see Smith and Medin (1981) and Chang (1986)). Evidence also shows that categorization depends on typicality in more natural settings. A child developing language acquires the names of typical category members before those of atypical ones (Mervis 1980; Rosch 1978).

1.3.2 Typicality as Similarity

A general interpretation of these findings is that the typicality of an instance in a category is a measure of its similarity to the concept representing this category, and that categorization amounts to determining that an item is sufficiently similar to the relevant concept. We next flesh out this interpretation.

If typicality is really similarity then the contrast model, which measures similarity of instances to concepts, should predict typicality ratings. To test this idea, we proceed through these steps:

1. Select a domain of instances.
2. Estimate the features of the instances and the category (these features comprise the instance representations and concept).
3. Apply the contrast model to each instance–concept pair.
4. See whether this estimate of instance–concept similarity correlates with the rated typicality of the instance in the category.

Table 1.3
How to use listed properties to calculate an instance's similarity to prototype.

Features	Robin	Bluebird	Swallow	Starling	Vulture
Flies	+	+	+	+	+
Sings	+	+	+	+	−
Lays eggs	+	+	+	−	−
Is small	+	+	+	+	−
Nests in trees	+	+	+	+	+
Eats insects	+	+	+	+	−
Similarity to *bird*	$6 - 0 = 6$	$6 - 0 = 6$	$6 - 0 = 6$	$5 - 1 = 4$	$2 - 4 = -2$

Features	Sandpiper	Chicken	Flamingo	Penguin	Bird
Flies	+	−	−	−	+
Sings	+	−	−	−	+
Lays eggs	+	+	−	+	+
Is small	+	−	−	−	+
Nests in trees	−	−	−	−	+
Eats insects	+	−	−	−	+
Similarity to *bird*	$5 - 1 = 4$	$1 - 5 = -4$	$0 - 6 = -6$	$1 - 5 = -4$	

The instances we use as well as their features are from a study by Malt and Smith (1984), in which subjects had 90 seconds to list all the features they could think of for each instance. In the experiment each of 30 subjects was presented 15 instances of birds; they collectively produced more than 50 features, each feature being produced by more than one subject. Table 1.3 covers only 9 of the instances and 6 of the features: flies, sings, lays eggs, is small, nests in trees, and eats insects. The rows in the table list the six features, the columns give the instances in order of decreasing typicality, and the last column represents the concept *bird*. Each entry in the resulting matrix is a + or a −, where + indicates that at least two subjects listed the feature for that instance and − indicates that either one or no subject did. To determine the entries for *bird*, a feature was assigned a + only if a majority of the instances had a + for that feature. This kind of representation is called a "prototype." It is an abstraction about birds; it includes the frequent, salient features of birds, but does not tell us what features, if any, are essential for being a bird.

A simplified version of the contrast model was used to determine the similarity of each instance in table 1.3 to *bird* (the prototype). In making the calculations (given at the foot of the table), it was assumed that (1) all features are equally salient (that is, f assigns a value of 1 to each feature, which means that the salience of a set of common or distinctive features is simply the number of features it includes), and (2) common and distinctive features count equally. The contrast model correctly segregates the instances in table 1.3 into three levels of typicality (3 high, 3 medium, and 3 low), though it makes few distinctions among the instances within each level. Finer distinctions can be made by assuming that features differ in their salience or by considering more features.[4]

You can verify that had the average similarity of an instance to all other instances been computed (rather than its similarity to *bird*), virtually identical similarity scores would have been obtained. Hence the success of the contrast model in predicting typicality does not depend on whether a concept is taken to be an abstract prototype or a set of instances (Estes 1994 further demonstrates the utility of treating a concept as a set of instances when predicting typicality ratings).

Let us now see briefly how the account above could be extended into a model of categorization that explains some of the experimental results mentioned earlier. The general ideas are:

1. The representations of the target category and test item are permanently stored in long-term memory, but once activated they also become part of working memory, where all subsequent processing ensues.
2. An item will be categorized as an instance of a category if and only if its representation exceeds some criterial level of similarity to the concept associated with that category.
3. The time needed to determine that an item exceeds this criterial level of similarity is less the more the item is similar to the concept.

When the latter two assumptions are joined with the claim that an item's typicality in a category reflects its similarity to the concept associated with the category, it follows that more typical items will be categorized faster.

Fleshing out this model requires making specific assumptions about the algorithms used to implement the contrast model. One possibility is to assume that all features of the instance and concept are compared in parallel—with common features incrementing a similarity counter and

4. We have oversimplified things in other ways as well. In particular, the representations in table 2.3 are simple lists of features, and it is well known that such feature lists are too unstructured to account for certain aspects of typicality and categorization. For example, to explain why people generally know that only small birds sing, one needs to include relations between features into the prototype for bird (see Smith 1989 for discussion).

distinctive features decrementing it—and the outcomes of these feature comparisons become available at different times. If an instance is just moderately similar to its concept, the procedure may have to wait for late-arriving feature matches (common features) to reach threshold; consequently categorization will be relatively slow. In contrast, if an instance is highly similar to its concept, the early arriving feature matches may suffice to pass threshold, hence categorization will be relatively rapid.

A related approach is expressed in terms of *spreading activation* (see figure 1.3). When an item representation and concept are activated (e.g., *robin* and *bird*, or *vulture* and *bird*), the activation from these two sources begins to spread to the features associated with them, the activation from each source being subdivided among its features. Once the two sources of activation intersect at some features (common features), a further procedure is undertaken to verify that an instance–category relation holds.

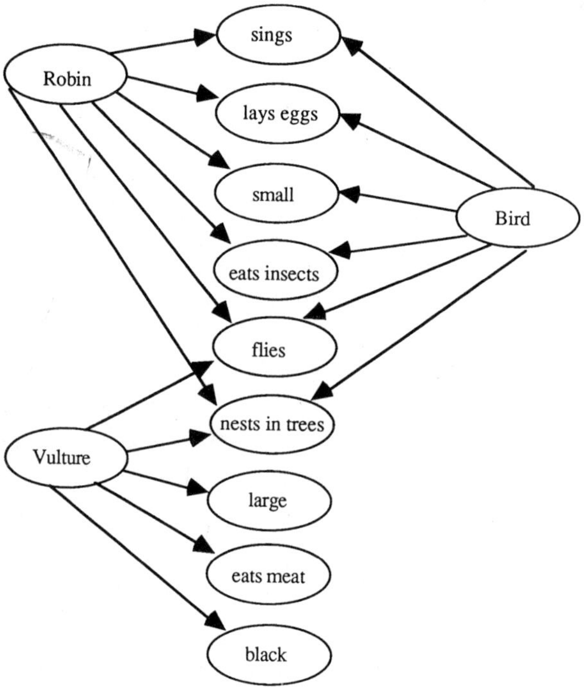

Figure 1.3
Part of a spreading-activation model for concepts of *bird, robin,* and *vulture.* The arrows indicate activation—for example, when *bird* is activated, this activation spreads to sings, lays eggs, is small, and so on. Categorization will be rapid to the extent that activation from the test item and target category intersect at many points.

Because the number of intersecting or common features generally increases with the typicality of an instance to its category, there are more opportunities for an intersection with typical than atypical instances, hence more opportunities for early termination of the process (Collins and Loftus 1975). In this model, features distinct to the concept or item slow the process by thinning the activation from each source.[5]

These models may suffice for the case in which only one category is relevant (as in the experiments described earlier), but often people have to decide which of two or more relevant categories is the correct one (Is this plant a mushroom or a toadstool? Is that car a Chevy or a Ford?). In such cases a categorization model has to consider how an item is related to the categories that contrast with the correct one. Thus, a categorization decision may consider something like the ratio between the similarity of the instance to the target concept versus the similarity of the instance to all contrasting concepts (Nosofsky 1986).

1.4 Similarity and Visual Categorization

What happens if instead of categorizing words, people have to categorize pictures of objects, or drawings of objects, or the objects themselves? To answer this question, numerous experiments have employed a visual-categorization task. On each trial a subject is given the name of a target category, such as "bird," followed by a test picture, photograph, or line drawing; the subject must decide as quickly as possible whether or not the test item pictures an instance of the target category. The general findings from this task are roughly the same as in verbal categorization. When the test item pictures a member of the target category, categorization times decrease with the typicality of the pictured test item (e.g., Smith, Balzano, and Walker 1978; Murphy and Brownell 1984). The model needed to explain these findings differs in important respects from the featural-similarity model we used to explain verbal categorization.

5. Spreading-activation models are related to "connectionist models," which describe cognitive processes in terms of neural-type networks. To convert the spreading-activation model in figure 2.3 into a connectionist model, we treat the existing arrows as excitatory connections, and in addition (1) draw an excitatory connection between any pair of features that tend to be active when the same concept is presented (e.g., between sings and lays eggs); this step will result in a highly interconnected network with the property that once some of a concept's features are activated, the rest also become activated; (2) draw an inhibitory connection between any pair of nodes that are not active at the same time (e.g., between small and large). The resulting network is such that the more typical the instance of the target, the higher the overall level of activation. (See Barsalou 1992 for further discussion of spreading-activation and connectionist models.)

1.4.1 Importance of Shape

Suppose we try to apply the featural-similarity model exemplified in table 1.3 to the visual categorization of birds. A major problem appears. The features that are presumably in the concept—flies, sings, lays eggs, is small, nests in trees, and eats insects—will not be manifested in most pictures of birds! Consequently, the representation of a test picture will not be similar to its corresponding concept, and there will be no basis for categorization. One might protest that the six features above are only a small subset of the features people list for birds, and hence only a small subset of the features of the concept. But even if we use a much larger subset (as in Table 9 of Smith and Medin 1981) the problem remains that most of these features will not be manifested in pictures of birds. To the extent that we use listed features as an estimate of a prototype (hereafter "prototypical features"), they are not sufficient to categorize many pictured objects.

If not features like flies and lays eggs, what do people use to categorize pictured birds? Much evidence shows that in categorizing pictures of both natural kinds and artifacts, we rely heavily on detailed information about the *shape* of the object. Much of this evidence comes from research in perception, particularly studies of *object recognition* (see Biederman's chapter in volume 2).

An experiment by Biederman and Ju (1988) demonstrates the importance of shape in picture categorization. Biederman and Ju tested subjects in a picture-categorization task and varied whether the test items were detailed color photographs of common artifacts, or simple line drawings of the same objects. The photographs had information about color and texture in addition to detailed information about shape; the line drawings, in contrast, contained only relatively global information about shape. The researchers reasoned that if people categorize pictures solely on the basis of shape, then subjects should do as well with the line drawings as with the photographs. This is exactly what happened. The average time to categorize an object was almost identical for line drawings and photographs, 512 msec versus 515 msec, respectively. Also, subjects sometimes made errors in the task, and the average error rate for line drawings, 8.4 percent, was roughly the same as that for photographs, 8.9 percent. Furthermore, Biederman and Ju also compared these same photographs and line drawings in another task—subjects simply had to name the object as quickly as possible. Again, no significant differences appeared between the two kinds of items.[6]

6. In a few domains of objects nonshape information must be used for categorization. One is the category of fruit. Here, different instances can have remarkably similar shapes, and

1.4.2 Typicality as Shape Similarity

The preceding indicates that, rather than relying on prototypical features, picture categorization often relies on detailed representation of shapes. Thus we can readily adapt the model developed for verbal categorization so that it also applies to visual categorization. Specifically:

1. People form a mental representation of the shape of the test object, and determine its similarity to the shape information in the target concept.
2. Only if the similarity in shape exceeds some criterion do people decide that the test item is a member of the target category.
3. The more typical of its category an object is rated, the more similar its shape is to those of other category members, and to the shape information in any prototype of the category.
4. The more similar an instance is to its category, the faster and more accurately it can be categorized.

Thus, we have kept the important notions that typicality in a category reduces to similarity to a concept, but changed the information over which similarity is calculated.

A novel assumption in this proposal is that the typicality of a visual object depends on its shape similarity to other members of the category. A recent study by Kurbat, Smith, and Medin (1994) provides some support for this critical assumption. For each of a few categories, such as birds and fish, subjects were presented pictures of fifteen instances, and asked to rate each for typicality in the category. For each category, the shape similarity of each pictured instance to all other pictured instances in the category was determined in this way:

1. Each instance was normalized for size and orientation.
2. Each instance was overlaid on each of the other category instances, and the amount of shared area was determined in each case.
3. These *area-overlap* scores were averaged, to yield an estimate for each instance of the extent to which it was similar in shape to other members of its category.

According to the similarity model, these area-overlap scores should correlate with typicality. For some of the categories, the correlation between area overlap and typicality was on the order of .7 to .8, which is highly

---

must be distinguished in part by color. Still, even for categories like fruit, the possibility remains that the set of features used in visual categorization differs from that used in verbal categorization.

significant. Furthermore, other studies show that the higher an instance's area-overlap score, the faster and more accurately it can be categorized (Estin, Medin, and Smith 1994). This finding supports the fourth assumption of the model above. Altogether, the evidence just reviewed makes the case that the judged typicality and categorization of a visual object depends critically on that object's shape.[7]

Let us summarize: A concept of a category must include at least two types of information. One type includes the prototypical features discussed in connection with verbal categorization, and the other kind consists of a detailed shape representation. Presumably, when a picture is presented, the shape representation is accessed first, and used as a basis for categorization; then the output of this procedure can be used to access the prototypical features (e.g., Snodgrass 1984).

1.5 Breakdowns of Verbal and Visual Categorization

Like other psychological functions, categorization breaks down with certain forms of brain damage. These breakdowns are referred to as "agnosias." These disorders are often associated with damage to the temporal lobe of the brain (though other regions may also be involved), and result in impairment in the patient's ability to categorize either verbal or pictorial items, even though perceptual functions are mostly intact (see Farah 1990 for a general discussion).

1.5.1 Category-Specific Deficits

These agnosias are particularly interesting because often the deficit is selective, that is, some categories of objects are impaired whereas others are relatively spared. The best known of these *category-specific deficits* is selective loss of ability to categorize or recognize faces (known as *prosopagnosia*). For our purposes, however, the particularly interesting cases are those in which patients are severely impaired in categorizing natural kinds, but not artifacts (such patients often manifest prosopagnosia as well).[8]

To get a feel for these cases, Table 1.4 presents attempts at categorizations by two interesting patients. On all trials the name of a common object was presented, and the patient had to define it (this is a test of verbal categorization). The patients appear quite normal in their definitions

7. Humphreys, Riddoch, and Quinlan (1988) developed a related measure of the shape similarity between two objects. Instead of using the amount of overlap in area, they measure the overlap in contours (boundaries) between two objects. They also found that shape similarity was correlated with categorization performance.

8. The opposite problem—impaired on artifacts but not on natural kinds—also occurs (Warrington and McCarthy 1987), but rarely.

Table 1.4
Performance of two patients with impaired knowledge of living things on definitions task: Examples of definitions

	Name: Definition	Name: Definition
JBR	Parrot: don't know	Tent: temporary outhouse, living home
	Daffodil: plant	Briefcase: small case used by students to carry papers
	Snail: an insect animal	Compass: tools for telling direction you are going
	Eel: not well	Torch: hand-held light
	Ostrich: unusual	Dustbin: bin for putting rubbish in
SBY	Duck: an animal	Wheelbarrow: object used by people to take material about
	Wasp: bird that flies	Towel: material used to dry people
	Crocus: rubbish material	Pram: used to carry people, with wheels and a thing to sit on
	Holly: what you drink	Submarine: ship that goes underneath the sea
	Spider: a person looking for things, he was a spider for his nation or country	

of artifacts (see right-hand side of table 1.4) but seem at a complete loss when trying to define or characterize animals (left-hand side of table 1.4).

These cases focus on verbal categorization or description. Researchers have demonstrated a comparable deficit in visual categorization. Sometimes these researchers have used the standard visual-categorization task, but more often they have simply required the patients to name pictures of common objects. Again the findings indicate a striking dissociation between knowledge of natural kinds versus that of artifacts. One much-studied patient names instances of artifact categories with nearly perfect accuracy, but is only about 20 percent correct in naming familiar animals (Farah, McMullen, and Meyer 1991).

Do we see two different deficits here—one for visual categorization, one for verbal categorization—or does just one deficit impair all kinds of categorization? The evidence thus far supports both possibilities. An occasional patient is profoundly impaired on visual categorization but shows no deficit when the same items are presented verbally (McCarthy and Warrington 1988), whereas other patients show the opposite pattern of results (Damasio 1990), and still other patients show both deficits (Grossman and Mickanin, 1994). These findings are compatible with the framework we developed for normal categorization, which holds that verbal and visual categorization may be qualitatively different.

1.5.2 Two Hypotheses about Category-Specific Deficits

Our framework for normal categorization is also compatible with two current hypotheses about why brain damage tends to selectively impair categorization of natural kinds more than categorization of artifacts. One view, the *structural-similarity* hypothesis, starts from the observation that instances of superordinate, natural-kind categories tend to be more similar in shape than are instances of superordinate, artifact categories (Humphreys, Riddoch, and Quinlan 1988). Thus, the shape similarity of any two fish seems far greater than that of any two pieces of furniture (fish and furniture are superordinate categories). We may thus assume that:

1. The categorization of visual objects first considers just the shape representation (as we postulated earlier).
2. If the shape representation is associated with more than one object (as is likely to happen with a natural-kind category), consideration of shape will not provide a unique categorization of the test object, and additional processing of the details of the shape will be needed.
3. This additional processing is particularly vulnerable to the effects of brain damage.

Perhaps the best evidence for this hypothesis is that if categories are divided on the basis of whether or not their members are similar in shape to one another, the categories with similar members are associated with larger deficits in brain-damaged patients (Humphreys et al. 1988).

The second hypothesis of interest is the *perceptual-functional* hypothesis (Warrington and Shallice 1984). This proposal places the deficit at the level of prototypical features rather than shape descriptions. The key ideas are:

1. Categorizing objects (particularly verbal ones) depends on prototypical features, some of which refer to perceptual aspects (e.g., has large wings), and some of which refer to functional aspects (e.g., can fly for hours).
2. Mainly perceptual features are included in the representation of natural kinds, whereas functional as well as perceptual features figure in the representation of artifacts.
3. Perceptual features are particularly vulnerable to the effects of brain damage.

An unusual sort of evidence for this hypothesis is reported by Farah and McClelland (1991). They first had normal subjects pick out perceptual and functional features in the dictionary definitions of numerous objects. They found, in accordance with assumption (2) above, that about four times as many perceptual features as functional ones appeared in the definitions of natural kinds, whereas roughly the same number of perceptual and functional features occurred in the definitions of artifacts. Farah and McClelland then used these ratios of perceptual to functional features as constraints in constructing representations of natural-kinds and artifact categories that were included as part of a computer program simulating the normal categorization of natural kinds and artifacts. The program was then "damaged" by selectively removing a varying number of its perceptual features. The result was that the program produced category-specific deficits of varying severity, where the deficits resembled in detail those manifested by brain-damaged patients.

What are the implications of this research on category-specific deficits for the framework we have constructed for normal categorization? For one thing, the two hypotheses above further support our earlier proposal that the representation of a category includes shape descriptions as well as prototypical features. Second, the structural-similarity hypothesis suggests that in addition to a comparison of overall shapes, a subsequent process may deal with details of shape. Third, research on the perceptual–functional hypothesis shows us the importance of distinguishing between the two types of prototypical features. And finally, this research with brain-damaged patients tells us something about the neurobiological bases of categorization. For visual categorization, it seems clear that a critical brain region is the inferior part of the temporal lobes, for patients who are impaired in visual categorization often have lesions in this area. This region also is implicated in impaired verbal categorization. Other neurobiological evidence suggests, however, that parts of the frontal lobes may also be involved in verbal categorization (just as they are in working memory for verbal material (see chapter 7 in this volume) and in problem solving (see chapter 8 in this volume)).

1.6 Beyond Similarity

Opening this chapter, we distinguished between categories (sets of objects) and concepts (mental representations of these sets), and throughout we have shown how categorization depends on concepts. Because of this dependence, the findings about categorization reveal something about the nature of concepts. But only *something*. As numerous psychologists and philosophers have argued, by no means do the standard verbal- and visual-categorization paradigms tap *all* the relevant beliefs represented in concepts.

Specifically, the results from these standard paradigms strongly imply that our concepts of natural kinds and artifacts include prototypical features and descriptions of shape, but a moment's thought suggests there must be more to a concept than this. Our concept *bird*, for example, includes not only such features as flies, sings, lays eggs, but also less perceptible (if not invisible) features such as: was born of bird parents, can produce a bird offspring if it mates with another member of its species, has the internal organs common to birds, and has the genetic structure common to birds. These features are more diagnostic about concept membership than are prototypical features, and induction of the former from prototypical features is a major function of categorization. Following current terminology, we refer to these more diagnostic features as *theoretical features*, because the set of such features seems to constitute something like a lay theory of the objects in question (see, e.g., Murphy and Medin 1985).

Increasingly, researchers are altering verbal-categorization paradigms to make them sensitive to theoretical features. Often, researchers present a description of some object, in which most of the descriptors are prototypical features pointing toward one category but at least one is a theoretical feature pointing toward a rival category. For example, subjects might be told about an animal that is black, with a white stripe down its back, which gives off a pungent odor, and which was born of raccoon parents; though the first few features suggest a skunk, the last one unequivocally indicates a raccoon. (Because it is unnatural for prototypical features to indicate one category and theoretical features a different one, the experimenter also provides a cover story about how this unlikely situation came about—e.g., the animal strayed too close to a nuclear power plant.) Adult subjects unsurprisingly categorize the described object as a raccoon, whereas young children initially rely on the prototypical features, but, with development, come to appreciate the decisive diagnostic power of the theoretical feature (e.g., Keil 1989).[9]

This paradigm has also been used by Rips (1989) to demonstrate that when such theoretical features are available, adult categorization is *not* based on similarity. In Rips's experiment, subjects were told about an animal that started out with typical bird properties but suffered an accident that caused many of its properties to resemble those of an insect. Subjects were further told that eventually this animal mated with a normal female of its species, which produced normal young. Subjects rated this creature as more likely to be a bird than an insect, but more similar to an insect

9. Categorization based on theoretical features is reminiscent of the classic view that categorization involves determining whether or not an object satisfies a *definition* (Smith and Medin 1981). Theoretical features, however, do not constitute true definitions. For one thing, a theoretical feature is not fixed as a definition is. Our theory of birds, for example, may involve some mention of genes, but someday scientists may change their theories and genes may be out of favor. Another matter is that the features we are calling theoretical are sometimes too sketchy to qualify as a definition. Thus what we know about bird genes is likely to be quite vague. Rather than trying to specify a precise theory of birds, most of us are content with a vague lay theory plus an indication that experts can fill in the gaps (Putnam 1975).

than a bird. Here we have a situation where similarity and categorization go in opposite directions (Rips and Collins 1993 provide other such demonstrations).

The categorization of natural kinds and artifacts is therefore sometimes theory based rather than similarity based. Such theory-based categorization, however, appears to occur only under special circumstances. Diagnostic features that are usually hidden from view must be made available; and even then the categorizer must sometimes be induced to be reflective (by being required to verbalize the basis for each decision) for theory-based categorization to occur (Smith and Sloman 1994). All this makes theory-based categorization seem like a kind of reasoning; indeed it has sometimes been characterized as a kind of causal reasoning, because the theoretical features are perceived as causing the prototypical ones (Medin 1989). These considerations and others make it unlikely that theory-based categorization is what lies behind our rapid, automatic categorizations of common, everyday objects. Rather, such automatic categorizations are more likely to be the product of a similarity or matching process. Theory-based categorization is important, though, because it tells us something about the underlying concepts that similarity-based categorization does not.

1.7 Summary and Other Issues

1.7.1 Summary

Here is the essential story: Categorization is the mental act of coming to think of some object as an instance of a category. It depends on finding some sort of match between the representation of the object and the representation of some category, where the latter representation is taken to be a concept. For natural kinds and artifacts, this matching of object to concept hinges on determining their similarity.

Detailing the categorization process therefore requires specifying a precise means for computing similarity between a pair of representations. Both geometric and featural approaches to similarity offer such means, but a number of empirical phenomena (such as asymmetries in similarity judgments) indicate that the featural approach, such as Tversky's (1977) contrast model, is best for measuring the similarity among concepts and their instances. Studies show that the similarity of a verbal instance to a concept, with respect to their prototypical features, is part of what lies behind the instance's typicality to its category. An instance's typicality to its category predicts numerous aspects of verbal categorizations, such as its speed and accuracy.

The preceding story is for verbal categorization. In moving to visual categorization, a major change in the model is needed. Now shape information is critical, and categorization is determined by computing the shape similarity of the object to the category. Both visual and verbal categorization break down in comparable ways with certain forms of brain damage. In both cases, categorization of natural kinds is sometimes severely impaired, whereas that of artifacts is relatively spared. The hypotheses advanced to explain these category-specific deficits tend to localize the impairments either to specific kinds of prototypical features or to detailed shape descriptions. Hence, breakdowns of categorization appear to be consistent with our general similarity-based framework for understanding normal categorization. Our framework is limited in that sometimes categorization can be based on factors other than similarity; still, our essential story may cover the multitude of cases of categorization that involve natural kinds and artifacts.

1.7.2 Other Issues

To keep the focus on similarity, we have deemphasized other issues in categorization research. Three such issues deserve at least brief mention.

First, we have seen a couple of times that a concept may be thought of either as an abstract summary—a prototype—or as a set of exemplars. (Our similarity proposals were phrased so that they were noncommittal on this issue.) The concept *bird*, for example, could be specified either by its own set of features or by a set of exemplars (a specific robin that tends to perch on the tree outside your window, your friend's pet canary, and so on), each with its own set of features. Though at first sight it seems more natural to think of a concept as a prototype, it is now clear that an exemplar representation coupled with the right similarity algorithm can account for much of the data in categorization (see, for example, Medin and Schaffer 1978; Estes 1986; Nosofsky 1986).

Experiments on this issue have often employed artificial categories—such as two sets of geometric patterns or schematic faces—to study the learning of concepts as well as their subsequent use in categorization. These studies consistently find that the ease of learning an instance-category relation is better predicted by the similarity of the instance to the other category exemplars than by the similarity of the instance to a prototype representation. Also, the exemplar-similarity models do a superior job of predicting subjects' categorization of novel items (see Estes 1993 for a recent summary). Other considerations, however, favor an abstract summary. Frequently we learn facts about a general class rather than about specific exemplars, such as, "All birds lay eggs," and it seems likely that we store such facts as summary information. Because the evidence on this issue is mixed, some sort of hybrid position (abstraction plus exemplar) may be called for.

Second, we have dealt in this chapter mainly with "simple" categories and concepts—roughly concepts denoted by single words like *apple* and *bird*—and have ignored complex categories, roughly those denoted by more than one word such as *dry apple* and *very large bird*. Because many conjunctive categories are novel combinations and hence cannot be learned from experience, we must have some procedures for combining simple concepts into conjunctive ones.

A number of combinatorial processes have been proposed, particularly for a single modifier applied to a simple concept as in *dry apple*. One of these proposals is an extension of the similarity model advanced earlier for verbal categorization (Smith, Osherson, Rips, and Keane 1988). Roughly, the modifier selectively changes those features of the simple concepts that are mentioned in the modifier (for example, *dry* changes the taste feature of *apple* but not its size feature); then a decision about whether or not an item is an instance of the conjunctive category can be made in exactly the same way as before (by employing the contrast model).

A critical property of this model is that the features attributed to the conjunctive concept are determined entirely by the features of the constituent concepts. Models with this property are said to be "compositional." Other models of conceptual combination (for categories designated verbally) are noncompositional. According to these models, rather than relying on just the features of the constituent concepts, presumably people also bring to bear their general knowledge of the world; because a dry apple may have become so by aging, the feature *old* may be attributed to the concept *dry apple* (see Murphy 1988 for a proposal along these lines).

Third, some of the research presented in this chapter has been used to argue that categories and concepts of natural kinds and artifacts cannot be identified with sets of necessary and sufficient conditions. Although these arguments have been widely accepted in psychology (see, e.g., Smith and Medin 1981), often they have met with sharp criticism in philosophy (see, e.g., Rey's 1983 review of the Smith and Medin book). Some of the difference in opinion may be eliminated by distinguishing between categories and concepts; thus, a natural-kind category may in fact have necessary and sufficient conditions, but because no one knows them, they are not part of anyone's concept (see Rey 1985 and Margolis 1994). Still, a gap remains between the psychological and philosophical work on concepts.

Suggestions for Further Reading

For further discussion of taxonomic levels, see Rosch et al. 1976 and Rosch 1978. For a look at other distinctions between categories, particularly those which have to do with kinds, see Schwartz 1979, and Malt and Johnson 1992.

On the matter of measuring similarity between instances and categories, perhaps the most widely cited paper is Tversky 1977. For a viable alternative way to measure similarity between features sets, see Estes 1994. A discussion of the geometric approach in general is given in Shepard 1974. And a critique of various aspects of similarity theory is provided in Medin et al. 1993.

A psychological perspective on typicality effects and categorization is provided in Smith and Medin 1981. Recent updates on this perspective are given in Barsalou 1992 and Ross and Spalding 1994. For a philosophical perspective on these same issues, see Rey 1983. Murphy and Medin 1985 and Medin 1989 offer a summary of the theory-based approach to concepts and categorization.

The psychological study of concept development is discussed in chapter 4 in this volume. An analysis of concepts is also essential for understanding language, particularly its development, for the meanings of words may be construed as concepts. Language development is the subject of chapter 6 in Volume 1. In addition to psychological studies, there is of course a rich tradition of analyses of concepts in philosophy of mind; here, Margolis 1994, Rey 1983, and Schwartz 1977 provide a useful entry to the literature.

Categorization is also closely related to inductive reasoning. Categorization sometimes involves a kind of inductive reasoning (see the research on theory-based categorization described in section 1.6). In other cases, inductive reasoning reduces to something like similarity-based categorization, and these cases are discussed in chapter 2 in this volume.

Research on how we categorize objects has also proven useful for understanding how we categorize people. For reviews of work on person categorization, see Markus and Zajonc 1985, Hirschfield 1994, and chapter 10 in this volume.

Problems

1.1 Use the contrast model (see sections 1.2 and 1.3) to determine the ordering by typicality of the five vegetables given below (the features are given under the name of each instance). Assume that all features are weighted equally and that $a = 1$, $b = 1/2$, and $c = 1/2$.

String bean	Carrot	Cauliflower	Seaweed	Broccoli	Vegetable
green	orange	white	green	green	green
long	long	round	long	long	long
hard	hard	hard	stringy	bushy	hard

1.2 In question 1.1, what changes occur in the ordering of typicality if color is weighted three times more than the other features?

1.3 We see in section 1.7 that the featural similarity model can be extended to explain categorization with a conjunctive concept like *dry apple*. Can such a feature model be extended to a conjunction like *fake apple*?

1.4 In section 1.5 we describe a measure of shape similarity that amounts to measuring the overlap in area of two objects. We also observe that an alternative is the overlap in borders of two objects (see footnote 7). Provide an example in which area overlap is high and border overlap minimal. Can you specify a general principle about when the two measures of shape similarity will disagree?

1.5 In section 1.6 we consider the perceptual-functional hypothesis, which claims that patients have a deficit only in categorizing natural kinds because the brain damage selectively impairs their knowledge about appearance. How can this hypothesis be extended to account for the occasional patient who has a deficit only in categorizing artifacts?

References

Anderson, J. R. (1991). The adaptive nature of human categorization. *Psychological Review* 98, 409–429.

Barsalou, L. W. (1985). Ideals, central tendency, and frequency of instantiation as determinants of graded structure in categories. *Journal of Experimental Psychology: Learning, Memory, and Cognition* 11, 629–654.

Barsalou, L. W. (1992). *Cognitive psychology: An overview for cognitive scientists.* Hillsdale, NJ: Erlbaum Press.

Biederman, I., and G. Ju (1988). Surface vs. edge-based determinants of visual recognition. *Cognitive Psychology* 20, 38–64.

Chang, T. M. (1986). Semantic memory: Facts and models. *Psychological Bulletin* 99, 199–220.

Collins, A. M., and E. F. Loftus (1975). A spreading-activation theory of semantic processing. *Psychological Review* 82, 407–428.

Damasio, A. R. (1990). Category-related recognition deficits are a clue to the substrates of knowledge. *Trends in Neuroscience* 13, 95–98.

Estes, W. K. (1986). Array models for category learning. *Cognitive Psychology* 18, 500–549.

Estes, W. K. (1993). Models of categorization and category learning. In D. L. Medin, ed., *The psychology of learning and motivation,* Vol. 29. San Diego: Academic Press.

Estes, W. K. (1994). *Classification and cognition.* Oxford: Oxford University Press.

Estin, P., D. L. Medin, and E. E. Smith (1994). Typicality and shape similarity as determinants of the basic-level advantage. Unpublished manuscript. University of Michigan, Ann Arbor, MI.

Farah, M. J. (1990). *Visual agnosia: Disorders of object recognition and what they can tell us about normal vision.* Cambridge, MA: MIT Press.

Farah, M. J., and J. L. McClelland (1991). A computational model of semantic memory impairment. *Journal of Experimental Psychology: General* 120, 339–357.

Farah, M. J., P. A. McMullen, and M. M. Meyer (1991). Can recognition of living things be selectively impaired? *Neuropsychologica* 29, 185–193.

Gelman, S. A., and E. Markman (1986). Categories and induction in young children. *Cognition* 23, 183–209.

Gelman, S. A., and A. W. O'Reilly (1988). Children's inductive inferences with superordinate categories: The role of language and category structure. *Child Development* 59, 876–887.

Grossman, M., and J. Mickanin (1994). Picture comprehension in probable Alzheimer's Disease. *Brain and Cognition* 26, 43–64.

Hirschfield, L. A. (1994). The child's representations of human groups. In D. L. Medin, ed., *The psychology of learning and motivation,* vol. 30. San Diego: Academic Press.

Humphreys, C. W., M. J. Riddoch, and P. T. Quinlan (1988). Cascade processes in picture identification. *Cognitive Neuropsychology* 5, 67–103.

Keil, F. L. (1989). *Concepts, kinds, and cognitive development.* Cambridge, MA: MIT Press.

Krumhansl, C. (1978). Concerning the applicability of geometric models to similarity data: The interrelationship between similarity and spatial density. *Psychological Review* 85, 445–463.

Kurbat, M., E. E. Smith, and D. L. Medin (1994). Categorization, typicality, and shape similarity. *Proceedings* of the Cognitive Science Society Meetings, Atlanta, GA.

Malt, B. C., and E. C. Johnson (1992). Do artifact concepts have cores? *Journal of Memory and Language* 31, 195–217.

Malt, B. C., and E. E. Smith (1982). The role of familiarity in determining typicality. *Memory and Cognition* 10, 69–75.

Malt, B. C., and E. E. Smith (1984). Correlated properties in natural categories. *Journal of Verbal Learning and Verbal Behavior* 23, 250–269.

Margolis, E. (1994). A reassessment of the shift from the classical theory of concepts to prototype theory. *Cognition* 51, 73–89.

Markus, H., and R. B. Zajonc (1985). The cognitive perspective in social psychology. In G. Lindzey and E. Aronson, eds., *The handbook of social psychology*. New York: Random House.

McCarthy, R. A., and E. K. Warrington (1988). Evidence for modality-specific meaning systems in the brain. *Nature* 334, 428–430.

Medin, D. L. (1989). Concepts and conceptual structure. *American Psychologist* 44, 1469–1481.

Medin, D. L., R. Goldstone, and D. Gentner (1993). Respects for similarity. *Psychological Review* 100, 254–278.

Medin, D. L., and M. M. Schaffer (1978). A context theory of classification learning. *Psychological Review* 85, 207–238.

Mervis, C. B. (1980). Category structure and the development of categorization. In R. Spiro, B. C. Bruce, and W. F. Brewer, eds., *Theoretical issues in reading comprehension*. Hillsdale, NJ: L. Erlbaum Associates.

Murphy, G. L. (1988). Comprehending complex concepts. *Cognitive Science* 12, 529–562.

Murphy, G. L., and H. H. Brownell (1985). Category differentiation in object recognition: Typicality constraints on the basic category advantage. *Journal of Experimental Psychology*, 11, 70ff.

Murphy, G. L., and D. L. Medin (1985). The role of theories in conceptual coherence. *Psychological Review* 92, 289–316.

Nosofsky, R. M. (1986). Attention, similarity, and the identification-categorization relationship. *Journal of Experimental Psychology: General* 115, 39–57.

Pinker, S. (1995). Language acquisition. In D. N. Osherson and L. Gleitman, eds., *Language: An invitation to cognitive science*, volume 1. 2nd ed. Cambridge, MA: MIT Press.

Putnam, H. (1975). The meaning of "meaning." In K. Gunderson, ed., *Language, mind, and knowledge*. Minneapolis, MN: University of Minnesota Press.

Rey, G. (1983). Concepts and stereotypes. *Cognition* 15, 237–262.

Rey, G. (1985). Concepts and conceptions: A reply to Smith, Medin, and Rips. *Cognition* 19, 297–303.

Rips, L. J. (1989). Similarity, typicality, and categorization. In S. Voisniadou and A. Ortony, eds., *Similarity, analogy, and thought*. New York: Cambridge University Press.

Rips, L. J., and A. Collins (1993). Categories and resemblance. *Journal of Experimental Psychology: General* 122, 468–486.

Rosch, E. (1978). Principles of categorization. In E. Rosch and B. B. Lloyd, eds., *Cognition and categorization*. Hillsdale, NJ: L. Erlbaum Associates.

Rosch, E., C. Mervis, D. Gray, D. Johnson, and P. Boyes-Braehm (1976). Basic objects in natural categories. *Cognitive Psychology* 3, 382–439.

Ross, B. H., and T. L. Spalding (1994). Concepts and categories. In R. J. Sternberg, ed., *Handbook of Perception and Cognition*, Vol. 12, *Thinking and problem solving*. San Diego: Academic Press.

Schwartz, S. P. (1977). *Naming, necessity and natural kinds*. Ithaca, NY: Cornell University Press.

Schwartz, S. P. (1979). Natural kind terms. *Cognition* 7, 301–315.

Shepard, R. N. (1962). The analysis of proximities: Multidimensional scaling with an unknown distance function. I. *Psychometrika* 27, 125–140.

Shepard, R. N. (1974). Representation of structure in similarity data: Problems and prospects. *Psychometrika* 39, 373–421.

Shipley, E. F. (in press). Categories, hierarchies, and induction. In D. Medin, ed., *The Psychology of Learning and Motivation,* Volume 30. *Representation and processing of categories and concepts.* Orlando, FL: Academic Press.

Skyrms, B. (1986). *Choice and chance: An introduction to inductive logic.* 3rd ed. Belmont, MA: Wadsworth.

Smith, E. E. (1989). Concepts and induction. In M. I. Posner, ed., *Foundations of cognitive science.* Cambridge, MA: MIT Press.

Smith, E. E., and D. L. Medin (1981). *Categories and concepts.* Cambridge, MA: Harvard University Press.

Smith, E. E., D. N. Osherson, L. J. Rips, and M. Keane (1988). Combining prototypes: A modification model. *Cognitive Science* 12, 485–527.

Smith, E. E., E. J. Shoben, and L. J. Rips (1974). Structure and process in semantic memory: A featural model for semantic decisions. *Psychological Review* 81, 214–241.

Smith, E. E., and S. Sloman (1994). Similarity vs. rule-based categorization. *Memory Cognition* 22, 377–386.

Smith, E. E., G. J. Balzano, and J. Walker (1978). Nominal, perceptual, and semantic codes in picture categorization. In J. Cotton and R. L. Klatzky, eds., *Semantic factors in cognition.* Hillsdale, NJ: Erlbaum Associates.

Snodgrass, J. (1984). Concepts and their surface representations. *Journal of Verbal Learning and Verbal Behavior* 23, 3–22.

Tversky, A. (1977). Features of similarity. *Psychological Review* 84, 327–352.

Tversky, A., and I. Gati (1982). Similarity, separability and the triangular inequality. *Psychological Review* 89, 123–154.

Tversky, A., and J. W. Hutchinson (1986). Nearest neighbor analysis of psychological spaces. *Psychological Review* 93, 3–22.

Warrington, E. K., and R. McCarthy (1987). Categories of knowledge: Further fractionation and attempted integration. *Brain* 110, 1273–1296.

Warrington, E. K., and T. Shallice (1984). Category-specific semantic impairments. *Brain* 107, 829–854.

Chapter 2

Probability Judgment

Daniel N. Osherson

2.1 Degrees of Conviction

Examine statements (1a–c), below. The first will strike you as almost certainly true, the second as almost certainly false. By contrast, the truth of the third is not so evident, and you may feel an intermediate degree of conviction about it.

(1) a. It will be hotter in Dallas than in Montreal at noon on July 4, 1999.

b. It will be hotter in Seattle than in Miami at noon on July 4, 1999.

c. It will be hotter in Dallas than in Miami at noon on July 4, 1999.

Your reaction to (1a–c) amounts to a judgment about their respective probabilities. It is this kind of judgment that occupies the present chapter.

One way to express degree of conviction is to attach some definite number to the statement in question, for example, .65 to (1c); the number .65 is then called "your probability" for (1c). Although it is this form of judgment that interests us, in what follows, recognize that our uncertainty about statements cannot always be reduced to a single number. For example, we might feel more comfortable assigning a range of probabilities to (1c) rather than commit ourselves to a specific value, and we might have more confidence in some of these probabilities than in others (see Gärdenfors (1988), Section 2.8 for discussion). It is also important not to confuse the probability invested in a statement with other attitudes we might have about its truth. For example, "accepting" a statement might not be the same as according it high probability (see Cohen 1983, Levi 1980).

Preparation of this chapter was supported by the Swiss National Science Foundation contract #21-32399.91. The author thanks G. Harman, E. Shafir, and E. Smith for comments on earlier versions. Thanks are also due to Larry Stockmeyer, who was kind enough to comment on section 8.

To keep the present discussion manageable, we nonetheless adopt the simplified picture: one statement—one probability. Our concern is the mental origin of these probabilities, and the principles that govern them.

The probability that a person invests in a newly encountered statement depends in part on the information (and misinformation) stored in memory. Statement (1c), for example, is likely to be assigned a different probability by a meteorologist than by a stockbroker. To compare the principles of probability attribution employed by different people we must hold background beliefs constant. This is most easily achieved by posing questions of the following kind, in which all relevant information is stated explicitly.

> *The Three-Card Problem*
> Three cards in a hat. One is red on both sides (the red-red card). One is white on both sides (the white-white card). One is red on one side and white on the other (the red-white card). A single card is drawn randomly and tossed into the air.
>
> a. What is the probability that the red-red card was drawn?
> b. What is the probability that the drawn card lands with a white side up?
> c. What is the probability that the red-red card was drawn, assuming that the drawn card lands with a red side up?

Think carefully about these questions, and write down your answers.

If you gave the answers one-third to (a), one-half to (b), and one-half to (c), then your judgment corresponds to the majority opinion of college undergraduates, as revealed in classroom demonstrations and published data (for example, Bar-Hillel and Falk 1982).[1] In this case it is likely that you will respond with probability one-half to each of the following questions, which are just the contraries of (b) and (c):

> b′. What is the probability that the drawn card lands with a red side up?
> c′. What is the probability that the red-red card was *not* drawn, assuming that the drawn card lands with a red side up?

And surely you would respond with 1 to this query:

> d. What is the probability that the drawn card lands with a red side up, assuming that the red-red card was drawn?

1. Most people reason as follows about (c). The red face excludes only the white-white card. This choice leaves the red-red and red-white cards as the remaining, equiprobable alternatives.

Table 2.1
Probability attributions in the three-card problem.

	Statement	Abbreviation	Judged probability
(a)	The red-red card was drawn.	RR	1/3
(b)	The drawn card lands with a white side up.	W-up	1/2
(b′)	The drawn card lands with a red side up.	R-up	1/2
(c)	The red-red card was drawn assuming that the drawn card lands with a red side up.	RR assuming that R-up	1/2
(c′)	The red-red card was not drawn assuming that the drawn card lands with a red side up.	not-RR assuming that R-up	1/2
(d)	The drawn card lands with a red side up assuming that the red-red card was drawn.	R-up assuming that RR	1

For future reference, table 2.1 summarizes the judgments corresponding to all six questions.

It is an important albeit elementary fact that there is so much agreement about the three-card problem. It suggests considerable uniformity in the mental processes that underlie probability judgment in different people. Another feature of these judgments will emerge once we consider the relation between probability attributions and our willingness to accept wagers at various odds.

2.2 Wagers

2.2.1 Probability Function

We will henceforth conceive of a person's judgment about chance as embodied in a certain kind of function, to be called a *probability function*. A probability function maps pairs of statements into probabilities. Specifically, for each pair (S,A) of statements in its domain, a person's probability function maps (S,A) into the probability that the person attributes to S while assuming the truth of A.[2] For example, if you think the probability is .6 that Mudrunner will finish first, assuming that it rains on the day of the race, then your probability function assigns .6 to this pair of statements:

(2) a. Mudrunner will finish first. $(= S)$

b. It rains on the day of the race. $(= A)$

2. Should A be considered a literal impossibility, then this probability is not defined.

For a given individual I we let "$\mathbf{P}_I$" symbolize I's probability function. For explicitness we write

$$\mathbf{P}_I(S \text{ assuming that } A)$$

instead of $\mathbf{P}_I(S,A)$ or $\mathbf{P}_I(S \mid A)$ (the latter notation is familiar from probability theory).

People often attribute probabilities to statements in the absence of any assumptions at all (or at least, without interesting assumptions not shared by everyone else). Suppose you assign .4 to statement (2a) in this unconditional sense. Now the assumption that $1 + 1 = 2$ is really no assumption at all, and so you surely assign the same .4 probability to statement (2a) while assuming $1 + 1 = 2$. This equivalence leads to the following abbreviation. Given a statement S, we write $\mathbf{P}_I(S)$ instead of $\mathbf{P}_I(S$ assuming that $1 + 1 = 2)$. $\mathbf{P}_I(S)$ may be construed as the probability (without assumptions) that individual I attributes to statement S.

To illustrate our notation, suppose that your probability judgments about the three-card problem conform to table 2.1. Then:

(3) a. $\mathbf{P}_{\text{you}}(\text{RR}) = \frac{1}{3}$

b. $\mathbf{P}_{\text{you}}(\text{W-up}) = \frac{1}{2}$

c. $\mathbf{P}_{\text{you}}(\text{not-RR assuming that R-up}) = \frac{1}{2}$

2.2.2 Fair Bets

A person's probability function helps determine the wagers that she is willing to accept. By a *bet* on a statement S is meant an agreement whereby (1) the bettor is paid a specified sum of money W if S is true and (2) the bettor pays a specified sum of money L if S is false. Such a bet is called *fair* for an individual I just in case $\mathbf{P}_I(S) = L/(W + L)$. This equality holds when $\mathbf{P}_I(S) \times W = (1 - \mathbf{P}_I(S)) \times L$. If we interpret $1 - \mathbf{P}_I(S)$ as I's probability that S is false then the last equation exhibits a bet as fair in case the probabilities of S and not-S are in the same ratio as potential losses and gains.[3] From this it can be seen that, very roughly, a, bet is fair for I if she expects to break even after many repeats of the same bet under similar conditions. In turn, this suggests that I would be equally willing to accept either side of a fair bet, winning in case S or alternatively winning in case not-S. Thus, fair bets are deemed not to be favorable to either party.

3. Why take $1 - P_I(S)$ as I's probability for not-S? The wager on S with winnings W and losses L is the same agreement as the wager on not-S with winnings $-L$ and losses $-W$ (think of "winning" $-L$ as losing L, and "losing" $-W$ as winning W). Hence, if $P_I(S) = L/(W + L)$, then: $1 - P_I(S) = 1 - L/(W + L) = W/(W + L) = -W/(-W - L) = P_I(\text{not-}S)$. (For further discussion, see Skyrms (1986), ch. VI.5.)

To illustrate, suppose that *I* assigns probability $\frac{1}{5}$ to statement (4).

(4) Brazil wins the World Soccer Championship in 2004.

Then any of these bets is fair for *I*:

I wins \$4 if (4) is true; pays \$1 otherwise.
I wins \$8 if (4) is true; pays \$2 otherwise.
Etc.

Next we consider conditional bets. By a *bet* on a statement *S assuming* a statement *A* we mean an agreement whereby (1) the bettor is paid a specified sum *W* of money if both *A* and *S* are true, (2) the bettor pays a specified sum of money *L* if *A* is true but *S* is false, and (3) no money changes hands if *A* is false. As before, such a bet is called *fair* for an individual *I* just in case $\mathbf{P}_I(S \text{ assuming that } A) = L/(W + L)$.[4] To illustrate, suppose that *I* assigns probability $\frac{3}{5}$ to (2a) assuming that (2b). Then the following bet is fair for *I*:

I wins \$2 if it rains on the day of the race and Mudrunner finishes first.
I pays \$3 if it rains on the day of the race and Mudrunner does not finish first.
No payments are made if it does not rain on the day of the race.

For small sums of money people are usually willing to accept bets that are fair or favorable for them and reject the others.[5] Hence, it may be inferred from (3) that you would accept the following bets about the three-card problem.

(5) a. Win \$4.20 if RR; lose \$2.10 otherwise.

[Since $\mathbf{P}_{\text{you}}(\text{RR}) = \frac{1}{3}$.]

b. Win \$2.00 if W-up; lose \$2.00 otherwise.

[Since $\mathbf{P}_{\text{you}}(\text{W-up}) = \frac{1}{2}$.]

c′. Win \$4.00 if R-up and not-RR; lose \$4.00 if R-up and RR; neither win nor lose if not-R-up.

[Since $\mathbf{P}_{\text{you}}(\text{not-RR assuming that R-up}) = \frac{1}{2}$.]

2.2.3 Dutch Books

The bets that you accepted in (5) have an interesting property. *No matter which card is drawn in the three-card problem, and no matter how it lands, you*

4. Provided that *I* does not deem *A* to be an impossibility. See note 2.
5. In contrast, for important sums of money the relation between betting and perceived probability is more complicated. See chapter 3 in this volume.

are guaranteed to lose money. To verify this fact, observe that the draw has exactly three possible outcomes:

> *Possibility 1*
> Some card other than red-red is drawn, and it lands with a white side up, that is, not-RR and W-up.
>
> *Possibility 2*
> Some card other than red-red is drawn, and it lands with a red side up, that is, not-RR and R-up.
>
> *Possibility 3*
> The red-red card is drawn, and it lands (of course) with a red side up—that is, RR and R-up.

It is impossible to obtain the combination RR and not-R-up.

Now if possibility 1 arises, then you lose bet (a), win bet (b), and neither win nor lose bet (c′); overall, you lose $.10. If possibility 2 arises, then you lose bet (a), lose bet (b), and win bet (c′); overall, you lose $.10. If possibility 3 arises, then you win bet (a), lose bet (b), and lose bet (c′); overall you lose $1.80. Thus, you lose no matter what happens.

To recapitulate, your judgment about the three-card problem led you to assign certain probabilities to statements (a), (b), and (c′) in table 2.1. These probability attributions led you to accept as fair bets (a), (b), (c′) of (5). It turns out, however, that the joint outcome of these bets is bound to be unfavorable. In the terminology of probability theory, a *Dutch book* has been made against you.

Most people (including the present author) are lured into Dutch books on first encountering the three-card problem. Let us now see how to avoid them in principle, and then analyze the psychological factors that lead us into situations of this kind.

2.3 How to Avoid Dutch Books

Not every probability function is open to a Dutch book. Those immune to such traps can be characterized with the aid of probability theory.[6] A few preliminary concepts are necessary.

2.3.1 Logical Truth, Exclusion, and Equivalence

Roughly, a *logical truth* is a statement that is true in every conceivable circumstance—for example:[7]

6. Systematic presentations are available in Resnik (1987), Ross (1988), Skyrms (1986).
7. A fuller discussion of logic is available in Allen and Hand (1992). See also chapter 9 in the present volume.

Either all frogs croak or some frog does not croak.

Two statements are called *logically exclusive* just in case there is no conceivable circumstance in which both are true—for example:

The heaviest poodle weighs more than 80 pounds.
The heaviest poodle weighs less than 60 pounds.

Two statements are *logically equivalent* just in case they have the same truth value in every conceivable circumstance—for example:

Not all philosophers like Mozart.
Some philosopher does not like Mozart.

It is assumed in what follows that if S_1, S_2 are statements in the domain of a given probability function, then so too are certain logical combinations of them, namely:

(6) a. not-S_1

b. S_1 or S_2

c. S_1 and S_2

Statement (6c) is called the *conjunction* of S_1 and S_2.

2.3.2 Coherent Probability Functions

Consider a probability function $\mathbf{P}$ such that for all statements S_1, S_2 the following conditions hold.

(7) a. $\mathbf{P}(S_1) \geq 0$.

b. If S_1 is logically true, then $\mathbf{P}(S_1) = 1$.

c. If S_1 and S_2 are logically exclusive, then $\mathbf{P}(S_1 \text{ or } S_2) = \mathbf{P}(S_1) + \mathbf{P}(S_2)$.

d. If $\mathbf{P}(S_2) \neq 0$, then $\mathbf{P}(S_1 \text{ and } S_2) = \mathbf{P}(S_1 \text{ assuming that } S_2) \times \mathbf{P}(S_2)$.

Conditions (7a–d) may be paraphrased:

a. No probability is negative.
b. The probability of a logical truth is 1.
c. The probability that one of two logically exclusive statements is true equals the sum of their respective probabilities.
d. The probability of the conjunction of two statements equals the probability of the first, assuming the second times the probability of the second.

A probability function that satisfies conditions (7) automatically satisfies a variety of other conditions, in particular these (with respect to any statements S_1, S_2):

(8) a. $\mathbf{P}(\text{not-}S_1) = 1 - \mathbf{P}(S_1)$.

b. If S_1 and S_2 are logically equivalent, then $\mathbf{P}(S_1) = \mathbf{P}(S_2)$.

c. If S_1 logically implies S_2, then $\mathbf{P}(S_1) \leq \mathbf{P}(S_2)$.

d. *Bayes's theorem*: If $\mathbf{P}(S_2) \neq 0$ then $\mathbf{P}(S_1 \text{ assuming that } S_2) =$

$$\frac{\mathbf{P}(S_2 \text{ assuming that } S_1) \times \mathbf{P}(S_1)}{\mathbf{P}(S_2)}$$

e. $\mathbf{P}(S_1 \text{ and } S_2) \leq \mathbf{P}(S_1)$.

The deduction of (8) from (7) is problem 2.2 at the end of this chapter. The conditions in (7) are known as *Kolmogorov's axioms* and they suffice to develop the elementary portion of probability theory. Probability functions that satisfy (7) are called *coherent,* the others *incoherent.*

2.3.3 The Dutch Book Theorem

Coherent probability functions stand in the following relation to Dutch books:

(9) *Dutch Book theorem*
Suppose that individual I is willing to accept any bet that is fair for I (in the sense of section 2.2.2). Then a Dutch book can be made against I if and only if $\mathbf{P}_I$ is not coherent.

For proof of the Dutch Book theorem, see Lehman 1955, Kemeny 1955, and the discussion in Gustason 1994, Resnik 1987, and Skyrms 1986. The theorem shows that coherent judgment offers protection against falling for a Dutch book. Conversely, some Dutch book can be contrived against anyone manifesting an incoherent probability function—and willing to accept apparently fair bets. The latter proviso is nontrivial because not everyone likes to wager. The Dutch Book theorem nonetheless provides striking evidence for the reasonableness of the axioms in (7).

Notice that coherent judgment is no guarantee against foolish bets in general. A person may accept an even-money wager that Luciano Pavarotti will finish first in the next Boston Marathon without violating (7a–d). This bet is not a Dutch book. Coherence is protection only against combinations of bets whose logic guarantees a loss.

Now let us return to the three-card problem. From table 2.1 we see that your probability function yields these judgments:

(10) a. $\mathbf{P}_{you}(RR) = \frac{1}{3}$.

b′. $\mathbf{P}_{you}(\text{R-up}) = \frac{1}{2}$.

d. $\mathbf{P}_{you}(\text{R-up assuming that RR}) = 1$.

Plugging these values into Bayes's theorem (8d), we see that $\mathbf{P}_{you}$ is coherent only if

(11) $\mathbf{P}_{you}(\text{RR, assuming that R-up}) =$

$$\frac{\mathbf{P}_{you}(\text{R-up assuming that RR}) \times \mathbf{P}_{you}(\text{RR})}{\mathbf{P}_{you}(\text{R-up})} = \frac{1 \times (1/3)}{1/2} = \frac{2}{3}.$$

However, (c) in table 2.1 reveals that $\mathbf{P}_{you}(\text{RR assuming that R-up}) = \frac{1}{2}$, not $\frac{2}{3}$ as required by (11). We conclude that $\mathbf{P}_{you}$ is not coherent. Theorem (9) thus implies that you are open to a Dutch book. And this is what we saw in section 2.2.3.

2.4 Incoherence or Momentary Illusion?

Incoherence has such far-reaching consequences that we should be cautious about imputing it to ourselves or others. In particular, answers to the three-card problem seem too slender a basis for global evaluation of a person's probability function. Let us therefore consider the possibility that the responses recorded in table 2.1 result from a fleeting illusion that is not typical of our considered judgment.

2.4.1 Illusions in Other Domains

A perceptual analogy may be helpful. Consider the Müller-Lyer illusion in figure 2.1. Although the two horizontal lines are equal in length, the presence of the arrowheads disturbs our perceptual judgment and favors the impression that the top line is longer than the bottom one. Does this

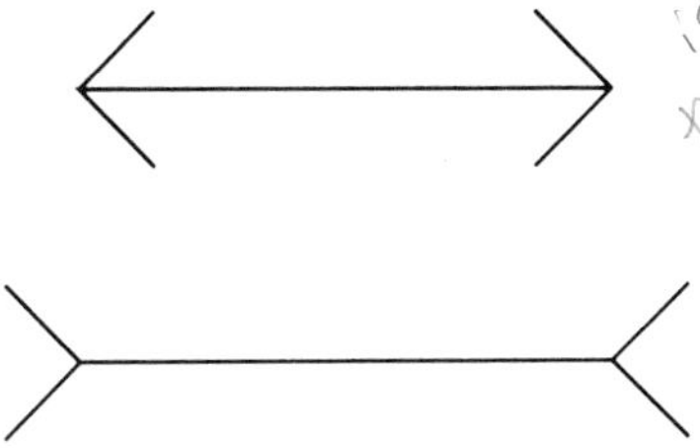

Figure 2.1
The Müller-Lyer illusion.

illusion imply that the human visual system lacks a veridical mechanism for comparing line lengths? The answer must be no, because in the absence of arrowheads we judge the comparative length of parallel lines with great precision.

In the same way, we may qualify as illusory the impression of nongrammaticality engendered by sentences like:

The horse raced past the barn fell.

The sentence is well-formed English, and is perceived as such upon reflection. Its apparent nongrammaticality arises from minor imperfections in human parsing mechanisms.[8] As before, these imperfections ought not to blind us to the existence of mental systems that yield, in usual circumstances, a correct verdict about the grammaticality of sentences.

There are also estimation illusions, such as the following "anchoring" effect discovered by Tversky and Kahneman (1974). These investigators asked people to estimate various quantities stated in percentages. For example, one estimate stated the percentage of African countries in the United Nations. Prior to each estimate, a number between 0 and 100 was determined by spinning a wheel of fortune. Participants were then asked to indicate whether the randomly obtained number was higher or lower than the value of the quantity to be estimated, and finally to estimate the quantity by moving upward or downward from the number given. Despite the evident, arbitrary character of the "anchors," they influenced estimates considerably. For example, the median estimates for the percentage of African countries in the United Nations were 24 and 45 percent for groups that received 10 and 65, respectively, as starting points. The effect of anchoring was not dissipated by offering monetary rewards for accuracy.

A similar phenomenon is reported in Slovic et al. 1980. They describe a study in which people were asked to judge the lethality of various potential causes of death using different, arithmetically equivalent formats. For example, one group of people judged the lethality of heart attacks by responding to question (12a), whereas another group responded to the equivalent question (12b).

(12) a. For each 100,000 people afflicted, how many died?

b. For each person who died, how many were afflicted but survived?

To facilitate comparison of the judgments, answers to (12) were converted into estimates of deaths per 100,000 people afflicted. The average esti-

8. For more on the topic of grammatical parsing, see chapter 8 in volume 1.

mates for the two groups were found to be 13,011 and 131, respectively. Thus, a minor change in wording modified the estimated death rate by a factor of nearly 100. Similar effects arose for other hazards and question formats.

Finally, there are illusions of reasoning, in which apparently sound arguments lead to unacceptable conclusions. An example is the notorious "surprise-quiz paradox," which seems to establish this claim:

(13) It is impossible for the instructor of intelligent students to announce during the first class that there will be a surprise quiz later in the term and then in fact to administer such a quiz.

Here is the "proof" of (13). Suppose the class meets 30 times during the term (we use 30 for concreteness; any other number works as well). It is clear that the instructor cannot administer the quiz at the thirtieth meeting because then it would be no surprise. For, the students (being intelligent) can be expected to reason thus:

(14) "Here we are at the thirtieth and last meeting. No surprise quiz has yet been given, and so it must be given today. Let us therefore expect its occurrence."

It is equally clear that the quiz cannot be administered at the twenty-ninth meeting. For again, its occurrence would be no surprise to intelligent students. This time they would reason thus:

(15) "Here we are at the twenty-ninth and next-to-last meeting. No surprise quiz has yet been given, and so it must be given either today or at the next meeting. Now it can't be given next meeting (which is the last one), because then it would be no surprise [see (14)]. That leaves only today for it to arise. Let us therefore expect its occurrence."

What about giving the quiz at the twenty-eighth meeting? Well, the students (being intelligent) can rely on the reasoning in (14) and (15) to rule out days 30 and 29 for the quiz. This leaves meeting 28 as the only possibility, thereby eliminating any surprise.

By working backward through the class meetings in this way, you can see that there is *no* day on which the instructor can give the quiz without the students expecting it. Statement (13) is thus proved. Right?

2.4.2 Coherent Competence versus Incoherent Performance?

Anchoring and format phenomena constitute illusions inasmuch as people recognize that such influences on their judgment are regrettable and should be avoided where possible. The surprise-quiz paradox is similarly illusory because those caught in its web are persuaded in advance that its proof must be faulty. Returning now to probability judgment, might the three-card problem represent nothing more than a reasoning illusion that masks an underlying, coherent probability function? The illusion in this case would rest on the indiscernability of the two faces of the red-red card. To see the point, refresh your memory of the three-card problem and then examine this argument about the probability of "RR assuming that R-up":

(16) Altogether the three cards have six sides. If the drawn card lands with a red side up, the hidden side can be the white side of the red-white card or *either* side of the red-red card. These are the only possibilities, and they are equally likely. Consequently, the probability in these circumstances of a red underside is 2 out of 3. On the assumption that red comes up, the drawn card has a red underside if and only if it is red-red, and so we conclude that the probability of "RR assuming that R-up" is $\frac{2}{3}$.

Observe that the value $\frac{2}{3}$ matches the calculation (11) given by Bayes's theorem, starting from the judgments recorded in (10). In our experience, most people are convinced by the reasoning in (16). It is thus tempting to conclude that most people's probability functions are coherent after all, despite their answers to tricky questions like the three-card problem (where it is easy to confound the distinct sides of the red-red card). We might therefore wish to claim that human judgment is coherent at the level of *competence* even if coherence is sometimes violated at the level of *performance*.[9]

Despite its reassuring character, the argument for coherent competence cannot be easily reconciled with judgments elicited by other problems, to be presented shortly. Moreover, there is evidence that people make systematic use of reasoning principles that, in certain circumstances, lead inevitably to incoherence. We now examine one such principle in detail.

2.5 Representativeness and Judged Probability

In the present section we describe a principle that people seem often to employ in evaluating probabilities. Its discovery is due to Kahneman and Tversky 1972, Kahneman and Tversky 1973, although formulated somewhat differently here (our discussion draws on Dawes et al. 1993 and Fischhoff and Beyth-Marom 1983).

Consider the category BIRD and its instance **robin**. Knowing that robins are birds predicts many of their salient properties, for example, their

9. For discussion of the competence–performance distinction in linguistics, see chapter 14 in volume 1.

featheredness and the fact that they fly. Other properties of robins (like their size) are not predicted by birdiness, but are not surprising, either—in contrast to the flightlessness of penguins, which *is* surprising given their membership in BIRD. In sum, different properties are more or less predicted by membership in a given category, and different instances leave different, overall impressions of predictability via that category. For example, the properties of **robin** seem more predictable from its membership in BIRD than do the properties of **penguin**.

At issue here is not the objective accuracy of these judgments, but rather the subjective impression that category membership explains the properties of some instances better than others. Under the terminology of "typicality" and "representativeness" such intuitions have been documented and studied extensively (for discussion, see Smith and Medin 1981, Smith 1989, and chapter 1 in this volume). We thus assume that people have a clear impression of the explanatory value of many categories vis à vis their instances, and we say that an instance is *representative* of a category to the extent that the instance's salient properties are predicted by the category.

A more precise model of representativeness might work thus. Given category C and instance i, the properties of i would be evaluated for their saliency and the extent to which they are predicted or counterpredicted by C. Both factors depend on the conceptual structure and background information of the person in question, as well as on the context of judgment (for example, the feathers of birds might have low saliency in culinary contexts compared to hunting). Such variability notwithstanding, overall representativeness can be expected to go up as a function of the number of salient properties that are predicted by membership in C and go down as a function of the number of salient properties that are either unpredicted or counterpredicted—with greater negative impact in the latter case. This idea can be rendered quantitatively precise in various ways (for example, using machinery described in Suppes et al. 1989, sec. 14 or Osherson 1987). We will not need such technicalities, however, for the cases considered here.

We now state a thesis that locates representativeness at the center of a commonly used principle of reasoning.

(17) *Thesis* Let C be a category and let o be an arbitrary object. To judge the probability that o is a member of C, people often rely on their perception of the representativeness of o in C. In particular, o is judged likely to belong to C to the extent that o's salient properties are predicted by membership in C, and it is judged unlikely to belong to C to the extent that o's salient properties are either unpredicted or counterpredicted by membership in C.

Thesis (17) is supported by answers given to probability questions in several psychological experiments, as will be seen in the next section. Because the answers are probabilistically incoherent, the predictive success of the thesis suggests that incoherence is a systematic feature of human judgment, not just a fleeting illusion of reasoning.

2.6 The Thesis Applied

This section is devoted to three experiments whose results are interpretable in light of thesis (17).

2.6.1 The Conjunction Fallacy

2.6.1.1 Basic Finding

Tversky and Kahneman (1983) posed this problem to eighty-nine undergraduates at Stanford University and the University of British Columbia:

(18) Linda is 31 years old, single, outspoken, and very bright. She majored in philosophy. As a student, she was deeply concerned with issues of discrimination and social justice, and also participated in antinuclear demonstrations.

Please rank the following statements by their probability, using 1 for the most probable and 8 for the least probable.

a. Linda is a teacher in elementary school.

b. Linda works in a bookstore and takes yoga classes.

c. Linda is active in the feminist movement.

d. Linda is a psychiatric social worker.

e. Linda is a member of the League of Women Voters.

f. Linda is a bank teller.

g. Linda is an insurance salesperson.

h. Linda is a bank teller and is active in the feminist movement.

A large majority of respondents ranked (18h) as more likely than (18f). Such ranking is incoherent because it has the form

$$\mathbf{P}(S_1 \text{ and } S_2) > \mathbf{P}(S_1),$$

contradicting consequence (8e) of the probability axioms (7). By theorem (9), the door is left open to a Dutch book (see problem 2.4).

Nonrespect of (8e) is known as the *conjunction fallacy*. It is such a flagrant violation of probability theory that one is led to suspect that

Tversky and Kahneman's respondents did not understand the problem put to them. In particular, in the context of alternative (h) of problem (18), it seems possible that subjects understood (f) to mean:

f*. Linda is a bank teller and is *not* active in the feminist movement.

Notice that no fallacy is committed by assigning (h) a higher probability than (f*).

To investigate people's interpretation of (f), Tversky and Kahneman posed the same problem (18) to eighty-eight new respondents. For half the participants, however, the conjunctive statement (h) was deleted from the alternatives, whereas for the other half the conjuncts (c) and (f) were deleted. Thus, no one saw alternative (f) of the original problem in the context of alternative (h). The results of this manipulation were consistent with the original study. The first subgroup's probability rank for "Linda is a bank teller" was lower than that of the second group for "Linda is a bank teller and is active in the feminist movement."

In a further control experiment, Tversky and Kahneman replaced alternative (f) in problem (18) by:

f′. Linda is a bank teller whether or not she is active in the feminist movement.

Alternative (f′) is not open to the unintended interpretation (f*). Only 16 percent of 75 new participants rated (h) as less likely than (f′).

Tversky and Kahneman also investigated the possibility that people simply do not notice the relationship between alternatives (f) and (h) in problem (18). One hundred and forty-two new people were thus shown the same problem with all but alternatives (f) and (h) deleted. They were asked simply to check which of the two alternatives was more likely. Eighty-five percent of the new group committed the conjunction fallacy.

The participants in the foregoing studies had no background in probability or statistics. However, the same fallacy rate was obtained on problem (18) using medical students, graduate students in psychology, and graduate students in education, all of whom had taken one or more courses in statistics. Doctoral students in the Decision Science program of the Stanford University Graduate School of Business also gave essentially identical results. Finally, Tversky and Kahneman present data on medical judgment showing that internists are prone to the same fallacy in judgments about symptomatology.

2.6.1.2 *Explanation via Representativeness*

The representativeness thesis (17) helps us to understand the compelling nature of the conjunction fallacy. Linda may be conceived of as the object *o* designated in the thesis. Linda's salient properties are those given in description (18). The predicates

(19) C_1 is a bank teller
C_2 is a bank teller and is active in the feminist movement

play the role of categories. Now observe that people are likely to find Linda more representative of C_2 than of C_1. For example, Linda's concern for such issues as discrimination and social justice is better predicted by her being a feminist bank teller than by her being simply a bank teller (with no further information). As experimental support for the latter claim, we cite a further manipulation by Kahneman and Tversky. They asked another group of undergraduates to rank alternatives (a)–(h) of (18) by "the degree to which Linda resembles the typical member of the class." The students rated Linda as more similar to a feminist bank teller (alternative (h)) than to a bank teller (alternative (f)).

2.6.1.3 *A Sharper Test of the Representativeness Thesis*

The greater representativeness of Linda in C_2 compared to C_1 is known as the *conjunction effect* (Smith and Osherson 1984).[10] The amplitude of this effect can be measured by obtaining numerical ratings of Linda's typicality for the two categories, and then subtracting the rating for C_1 from the rating for C_2. Larger numbers are associated with larger conjunction effects (negative numbers indicating no effect at all). In the same way, the amplitude of the conjunction fallacy can be defined by subtracting the probability attributed to Linda's membership in C_1 from the corresponding probability for C_2. Larger numbers reflect greater incoherence (in the sense of problem 2.4, below).

In place of C_1 and C_2, now consider these categories:

(20) C_3 is a teacher.
C_4 is a teacher and is active in the feminist movement.

It is shown in Shafir et al. 1990 that the conjunction effect for Linda is smaller with respect to C_3, C_4 than with respect to C_1, C_2. Specifically, fifty-four undergraduates at the University of Michigan rated the typicality of Linda in all four categories on a scale from 0 to 1. The average conjunction effect for the categories in (19) was .18, whereas it was only .09 for (20). According to thesis (17), this difference in conjunction effect predicts a corresponding difference in conjunction fallacy: the conjunction fallacy for C_3, C_4 should be less than for C_1, C_2—with Linda as the instance in both cases. Using a separate group of fifty-six undergraduates, just this result was obtained. The average conjunction fallacy for C_1, C_2 in problem (18) was .16, whereas the average for the corresponding problem with C_3, C_4 was only .07.

10. In contrast to the conjunction fallacy, there is nothing fallacious about the conjunction effect, which just amounts to finding Linda's properties more predictable from the conjunctive category C_2 than from C_1.

More generally, Shafir et al. submitted twenty-eight variants of problem (18) to the two groups of students. The problems involved a variety of instances and categories, rated for typicality by one group of participants and for probability by another. Average conjunction effects ranged from −.20 (hence, no effect) to .33 (a considerable effect). Average conjunction fallacies ranged from −.20 (no fallacy) to .27 (a large fallacy). The two variables were highly correlated, larger conjunction effects being associated with larger conjunction fallacies (across the twenty-eight problems, the Pearson correlation is .83). The correlation provides direct support for the representativeness thesis.

2.6.2 The Inclusion Fallacy

Let us introduce a second application of the representativeness thesis. Suppose you are conducting a survey in a shopping mall and one day you encounter a group of bankers, including some young ones. You are able to determine of each banker whether he or she is in the category of "wealthy persons." How likely do you think it is that every banker you meet that day, without exception, is wealthy? Now focus on just the young bankers. How likely do you think it is that every young banker you meet that day, without exception, is wealthy? Let us record the two statements whose probabilities are at issue:

(21) a. Every banker is wealthy.

b. Every young banker is wealthy.

Whatever exact probabilities are attributed to the statements in (21), thesis (17) suggests that many people will assign (a) a higher probability than (b).

To see how this prediction is obtained, let WEALTHY be category C in thesis (17), and let **banker** and **young banker** be two instances. Although (17) is vague about the matter, let us understand by "**banker** belongs to WEALTHY" that all bankers in some contextually specified group are wealthy, and similarly for **young banker**. The contextually specified group in the present case is the one encountered in the shopping mall. It seems clear that the salient properties of **banker** are better predicted by WEALTHY than are those of **young banker** (in particular, wealth does not predict youth). This judgment is confirmed by typicality ratings provided by forty-seven undergraduates in an experiment reported in Shafir et al. (1990). By thesis (17), this result is enough to conclude that many people will assign higher probability to (21a) than to (21b). In fact, that was the majority response of forty new participants in the same study.

It is easy to see that such a judgment is incoherent. Because (21a) logically implies (21b), consequence (8c) of the probability axioms requires (21b) to be at least as likely as (21a). Incoherent judgments of this kind are known as *inclusion fallacies.* The degree of the fallacy is measured by the difference in probabilities assigned to the two statements.

As in section 2.6.1.3, the judgment that **banker** is more representative of WEALTHY than is **young banker** may be named the *inclusion effect,* and measured by difference in rated representativeness. To illustrate, when "liberal" is substituted for "wealthy" in (21), the inclusion effect diminishes —at least for the forty-seven participants in the Shafir et al. study. It is noteworthy that the inclusion fallacy also declines in these circumstances, as revealed by probability ratings carried out by the same students, as well as by the ratings of an independent group. More generally, Shafir et al. (1990) employed fifteen problems of the foregoing kind and found a systematic relation between the amplitudes of the inclusion effect and fallacy (across the fifteen problems, the Pearson correlation is .87).

Notice the following asymmetry between the inclusion and conjunction fallacies. Committing the former requires attributing lower probability to a statement involving a conjunctive expression (like "young banker"). The latter requires attributing higher probability to such an expression (like "feminist bank teller"). Despite this variation, the representativeness thesis helps predict the occurrence of both kinds of fallacies.

2.6.3 Nonuse of Prior Probability

2.6.3.1 Basic Finding

For a third application of the representativeness thesis, consider these instructions, administered to eighty-five participants in a study performed by Kahneman and Tversky (1973).

(22) A panel of psychologists have interviewed and administered personality tests to 30 engineers of 70 lawyers, all successful in their respective fields. On the basis of this information, thumbnail descriptions of the 30 engineers and 70 lawyers have been written. You will find on your forms five descriptions, chosen at random from the 100 available descriptions. For each description, please indicate your probability that the person described is an engineer, on a scale from 0 to 100.

The same task has been performed by a panel of experts, who were highly accurate in assigning probabilities to the various descriptions. You will be paid a bonus to the extent that your estimates come close to those of the expert panel.

The people who read the foregoing instructions will be called the *low-engineer* group. A different group of 86 participants—the *high-engineer* group—were given identical instructions except that the numbers 70 and 30 were reversed: these people were told that the set from which the descriptions had been drawn consisted of 70 engineers and 30 lawyers.

Participants in both groups were presented with the same five descriptions—for example:

(23) Jack is a 45-year-old man. He is married and has four children. He is generally conservative, careful, and ambitious. He shows no interest in political and social issues and spends most of his free time on his many hobbies, which include home carpentry, sailing, and mathematical puzzles.

The probability that Jack is one of the 30 engineers [or 70 engineers for the high-engineer group] in the sample of 100 is ______ percent.

If the participants manifested coherent judgment, how should the responses of the low- and high-engineer groups to question (23) differ? Let us use these abbreviations:

ENG: The person whose description was drawn randomly from the sample of 100 is an engineer.
DES: This thumbnail description—namely, the one in (23)—happened to be chosen at random from the 100 descriptions prepared by the panel of psychologists.

Then, question (23) amounts to evaluating the conditional probability of ENG assuming that DES. By Bayes's theorem (8d), this probability may be calculated as follows:

(24) $$\mathbf{P}(\text{ENG assuming that DES}) = \frac{\mathbf{P}(\text{DES assuming that ENG}) \times \mathbf{P}(\text{ENG})}{\mathbf{P}(\text{DES})}.$$

We may assume that respondents in both the low- and high-engineer groups assigned the same average value to the term **P**(DES assuming that ENG). For, the number of engineers in the sample of 100 does not affect the probability that a given engineer has the characteristics listed in (23). Likewise, the two groups may be assumed to assign the same value (1 percent, for example) to **P**(DES).

Consider next **P**(ENG), the probability that in advance of any particular information about him, Jack is an engineer. The low-engineer group would be expected to assign probability .3 to this statement, whereas the high-engineer group should assign it .7. To verify this expectation, Kahneman and Tversky posed this problem to all participants:

(25) Suppose now that you are given no information whatsoever about an individual chosen at random from the sample.

The probability that this man is one of the 30 engineers [70 engineers for the high-engineer group] is ______ percent.

As expected, the low- and high-engineer groups gave the appropriate responses of 30 and 70 percent, respectively.

Putting the three terms together, we see that if the participants responded coherently, then the respective estimates of **P**(ENG assuming that DES) by the two groups have these forms:

$$\frac{\mathbf{P}(\text{DES assuming that ENG}) \times .30}{\mathbf{P}(\text{DES})} \qquad \frac{\mathbf{P}(\text{DES assuming that ENG}) \times .70}{\mathbf{P}(\text{DES})}$$

The ratio of these estimates is .3/.7 or .43. In sum, if the participants manifested coherent reasoning, the answers of the low- and high-engineer groups should stand in the ratio of .43. In fact, the ratio obtained was very close to 1. Thus, the low- and high-engineer groups offered essentially identical estimates of **P**(ENG assuming that DES). These results contradict the hypothesis that the participants' judgment is coherent.

The quantity **P**(ENG) is known as the *prior probability* for **P**(ENG assuming that DES). Kahneman and Tversky's respondents apparently ignored prior probability in their deliberations, even though their responses to (25) show that prior probability was not far from consciousness.

2.6.3.2 Explanation via Representativeness

According to the representativeness thesis (17), the judged probability that Jack is an engineer depends on the predictability of Jack's salient characteristics (namely, those in (23)) from his membership in the category ENGINEER, compared to the predictability arising from membership in LAWYER. It seems intuitively clear that most people find Jack's characteristics (for example, his hobbies) to be better explained by his being an engineer than a lawyer. Thesis (17) thus predicts that respondents will assign greater probability in problem (23) to ENGINEER than to LAWYER. Such was the result actually obtained for both the low-engineer and high-engineer groups.

Notice that prior probability does not figure in the predictability of (23) from ENGINEER. Such predictability is represented exclusively by the term **P**(DES assuming that ENG), which is just one component of Bayes's formula (24). In this way the representativeness thesis suggests that respondents will ignore prior probability in evaluating the probability that Jack is an engineer, which is the principal outcome of the study.

What does thesis (17) predict about the judged probability that Dick, described below, is one of the engineers in the sample of 100?

> Dick is a 30-year-old man. He is married with no children. A man of high ability and high motivation, he promises to be quite successful in his field. He is well liked by his colleagues.

Kahneman and Tversky constructed this description to be uninformative about Dick's profession. As a consequence, it is equally predictable from the ENGINEER and LAWYER categories. The representativeness thesis thus implies that both the low- and high-engineer groups will judge the probability that Dick is an engineer to be 50 percent (despite its prior probability of either 30 or 70 percent). Such was the experimental result obtained.

2.7 The Coexistence Thesis

2.7.1 The Case Against Coherent Competence

Let us review the discussion thus far. We saw in section 2.3 that the only defense against Dutch books (aside from refusing bets you deem fair) is to respect condition (7) on probability functions. Such functions were labeled *coherent*, the rest *incoherent*. In section 2.4.2 we articulated the thesis of coherent competence, according to which most people's probability functions are fundamentally coherent even if this fact is sometimes hidden by reasoning illusions of various kinds.

In section 2.6, we presented findings suggesting that if coherent competence exists at all, it lies at a mental level that is often inaccessible to intuition. Moreover, we saw that a reasoning principle based on representativeness provides a convincing account of several experimental findings involving incoherent judgment. It is thus tempting to attribute the latter principle to people's competence in place of inoperative coherent ones.

A strong form of the thesis of coherent competence is therefore difficult to defend. Let us then examine a weaker version according to which coherent reasoning is one of several potentialities that coexist in the competence of most people. On this view, human judgment is expected to manifest coherence in favorable circumstances, but conform to principles like representativeness on other occasions. This new hypothesis may be called the *coexistence thesis*. To defend it, we first underline the diversity of principles that intervene in naive probability judgment and then examine studies that support the coexistence thesis more directly.

As a preliminary, consider again the relation: "Instance *o* is representative of category *C*." Section 2.5 defined it in terms of the predictability of *o*'s properties from membership in *C*. Such predictability amounts to the probability of possessing *o*'s characteristics assuming that *o* belongs to *C*. In contrast, to answer question (18) coherently, the reverse is needed, namely, the probability that *o* belongs to *C* (e.g., BANK TELLER), assuming that *o* has Linda's characteristics. This suggests that the conjunction fallacy might rest upon a small error in reasoning, namely, a reversal of the terms *A* and *B* when attempting to evaluate $\mathbf{P}(A \text{ assuming that } B)$ (as suggested in Braine et al. (1990), Wolford et al. (1990)). The reversal yields judgment in conformity with the incoherent principle of representativeness. Perhaps coherent judgment would result from a gentle reminder not to mix up *A* and *B* in **P**(*A* assuming that *B*)?

2.7.2 The Multiplicity of Reasoning Principles

Representativeness is not sufficient to account for all the peculiarities of human judgment. Consider this problem.

(26) Which of the following events is more probable?

a. That a girl has blue eyes if her mother has blue eyes.

b. That the mother has blue eyes if her daughter has blue eyes.

c. The two events are equally probable.

Tversky and Kahneman (1980) posed this question to 165 college students. Fewer than half judged the two events to be equally probable. Sixty-nine respondents judged alternative (a) to be more likely than alternative (b). Twenty-one students made the contrary judgment. On the other hand, a large majority in another group of 91 students affirmed that the probability of blue eyes in successive generations is equal.

These data suggest that the probability functions of a considerable fraction of college students conform to the following conditions (where MBE = "the mother has blue eyes" and DBE = "the daughter has blue eyes").

(27) a. $\mathbf{P}(\text{DBE assuming that MBE}) > \mathbf{P}(\text{MBE assuming that DBE})$.

b. $\mathbf{P}(\text{DBE}) = \mathbf{P}(\text{MBE})$

Such probability functions are not coherent. Bayes's theorem (8d) yields

(28)
$$\mathbf{P}(\text{DBE assuming that MBE}) = \frac{\mathbf{P}(\text{MBE assuming that DBE}) \times \mathbf{P}(\text{DBE})}{\mathbf{P}(\text{MBE})}.$$

By (27b) the ratio $\mathbf{P}(\text{DBE})/\mathbf{P}(\text{MBE}) = 1$, and so (28) implies that $\mathbf{P}(\text{DBE assuming that MBE}) = \mathbf{P}(\text{MBE assuming that DBE})$, contradicting (27a).

The representativeness thesis (17) does not seem applicable to this problem. It is better explained by appealing to the asymmetry of similarity judgment, as described in chapter 1 of this volume. To summarize, the similarity of *X* to *Y* is often perceived to exceed the similarity of *Y* to *X* if *Y* is a more prominent, important, or central object than *X*, or if *Y* is esteemed to be the cause of *X*. For example, the number 102 seems to resemble 100 more than the reverse, just as portraits resemble their subjects more than vice versa. It is now easy to see that the following assumptions predict (27a).

(29) a. The probability **P**(o_1 belongs to C, assuming that o_2 belongs to C) is often judged according to the similarity of o_1 to o_2.

b. Daughters resemble their mothers more than mothers resemble their daughters.

Further support for principle (29a) is reported in Bar-Hillel 1982 and Tversky and Kahneman 1980.

Yet another reasoning mechanism is responsible for the findings in the following study (Tversky and Kahneman 1983). Respondents were 115 participants in the Second International Congress on Forecasting, held in Istanbul, Turkey, in July 1982. Half the respondents evaluated the probability of (30a), whereas the other half evaluated the probability of (30b).

(30) a. A complete suspension of diplomatic relations between the United States and the Soviet Union, sometime in 1983.

b. A Russian invasion of Poland, and a complete suspension of diplomatic relations between the United States and the Soviet Union, sometime in 1983.

The probability estimates for (30b) were more than three times higher than those for (30a), which is a conjunction fallacy because (30a) is part of (30b). Rather than representativeness, incoherent reasoning in this case seems to hinge on the plausible international scenario depicted in (30b) but absent in (30a). (For discussion, see Thüring and Jungermann 1990 and Tversky and Kahneman 1983.)

The point of these examples is to reveal the multiplicity of principles that underlie human reasoning about chance. Indeed, further factors no doubt influence judgment, such as people's sensitivity to the pragmatic rules that govern cooperative exchange of information (see Politzer and Noveck 1991 for discussion of this theme in connection with the conjunction fallacy, and Macchi 1994, Schwartz et al. 1991 in connection with prior probabilities). Might not coherent mechanisms of probability judgment also lie ready for activation in the right circumstances? In fact, several studies provide direct evidence favoring this possibility.

2.7.3 Glimmers of Coherent Thinking

2.7.3.1 Conjunctions

Tversky and Kahneman (1983) posed this problem to 260 undergraduates at Stanford University and the University of British Columbia.

(31) Consider a regular six-sided die with four green faces and two red faces. The die will be rolled 20 times and the sequence of greens (G) and reds (R) will be recorded. You are asked to select one sequence, from a set of three, and you will win $25 if the sequence you chose appears on successive rolls of the die. Please check the sequence of greens and reds on which you prefer to bet.

1. RGRRR

2. GRGRRR

3. GRRRRR

Because option (1) is a subsequence of option (2), the former is strictly more probable than the latter. Nonetheless, a majority of students chose to bet on (2), perhaps because it has a more random appearance than the others. The same results were obtained in a second experiment in which option (2) was replaced by RGRRRG, which also includes (1) as a subsequence.

These findings, like those discussed in section 2.6.1, suggest insensitivity on the part of college students to the conjunction principle (8e). A different conclusion emerges, however, from a follow-up study carried out by Tversky and Kahneman. Eighty-eight new students were given problem (31) with the third option removed. Instead of selecting a sequence on which to bet, they were asked to indicate which of these arguments, if either, they found to be correct:

Argument 1
The first sequence (RGRRR) is more probable than the second (GRGRRR) because the second sequence is the same as the first with an additional G at the beginning. Hence, every time the second sequence occurs, the first sequence must also occur. Consequently, you can win on the first and lose on the second, but you can never win on the second and lose on the first.

Argument 2
The second sequence (GRGRRR) is more probable than the first (RGRRR) because the proportions of R and G in the second sequence are closer than those of the first sequence to the expected proportions of R and G for a die with four green and two red faces.

A large majority of students chose the probabilistically correct argument 1.[11]

11. Similarly, people's choices in decision situations are reported to often satisfy the standard axioms of rational choice, provided that application of the axioms to the problem at hand is rendered transparent. See Shafir et al. (1993), section 7, and chapter 3 in this volume.

2.7.3.2 *Prior Odds*

Variations on the engineer problem in section 2.6.3 provide additional evidence for the existence of coherent principles of reasoning in everyday thought. Gigerenzer et al. (1988) presented German students with problems of the following kind, whose isomorphism to problem (22) is easy to see.

(32) In the 1978/79 season of the West-German Soccer "Bundesliga," Team A won 10 out of the 34 games. The other games were either drawn or lost. We have selected some of the games of that season randomly and checked their final results as well as their halftime results. For instance, on the 7th day of the season the halftime result was 2:1 in favor of Team A. What is your probability that this game belongs to those 10 games won out of 34?

In different problems, both the halftime score and the overall 1978/79 record were varied. The latter variation involved attributing 7, 10, 15, or 19 wins (out of 34) to the team in question. It is this number that determines the prior probability for winning the game whose halftime score is given; it thus plays the same role as the 30/70 versus 70/30 variation employed in problem (22).

In contrast to the earlier problem, participants in the Gigerenzer et al. study manifested proper appreciation of the role of prior probability in reasoning. For example, the probability attributed in the 15-win version of problem (32) was greater than for the 10-win version, which in turn was greater than for the 7-win version.

More generally, the role of prior probability in human reasoning has given rise to numerous experiments with varying results (see Koehler (1993) for a review of the literature, and Dawes et al. (1993) for methodological discussion). Part of the variation may be due to the difficulty of determining which probabilities a person actually thinks are prior for a given problem. Trying to impose these probabilities via explicit instructions seems not to work in all cases (see Beyth-Marom and Fischhoff 1983).

2.7.3.3 *Sample Size*

Another glimmer of coherent thinking appears in responses to this problem, appearing in Bar-Hillel 1982.

> A certain town is served by two hospitals. In the larger hospital about 45 babies are born each day, and in the smaller hospital about 15 babies are born each day. As you know, about 50 percent of all babies are boys. The exact percentage of baby boys, however, varies from day to day. Sometimes it may be higher than 50 percent,

> sometimes lower. For a period of one year, each hospital recorded the days on which more than 60 percent of the babies born were boys. Which hospital do you think recorded more such days?

In different versions of the problem given to separate groups, the proportion of boys changed from 60 percent to 70 percent, 80 percent, or 100 percent.

The 60 percent version was originally devised by Kahneman and Tversky (1972), who discovered that most respondents ignored the overall number of babies born in each hospital and asserted that the two hospitals recorded the same number of days on which more than 60 percent of babies born were boys. This answer is at variance with the theory of probability—not the elementary theory embodied in (7), but a natural extension of it. On probabilistic grounds we expect that larger samples of babies will tend to show less deviation from 50 percent.

Bar-Hillel's results suggest that, Kahneman and Tversky's original findings notwithstanding, a nascent appreciation of the role of sample size is present in most people. For, compared to the 60 percent version of the problem, more respondents correctly chose the smaller hospital in the 70, 80, and 100 percent versions (with a majority of correct responses in the last case). Related findings are reported in Nisbett et al. 1983.

2.7.4 What Factors Encourage Coherent Reasoning?

The foregoing studies support the coexistence thesis inasmuch as they suggest the presence of coherent reasoning schemes in the competence of people who give incoherent responses to other problems. The coexistence thesis is incomplete, however, without supplementary theses about the kinds of circumstances that evoke one kind of reasoning rather than the other.

To grasp the issue, consider this study, reported in Tversky and Kahneman 1983. Participants read the description (18) of Linda followed by the crucial alternatives of bank teller and feminist bank teller. They were asked to indicate which of these two arguments they found more convincing.

> *Argument 1*
> Linda is more likely to be a bank teller than she is to be a feminist bank teller, because every feminist bank teller is a bank teller, but some women bank tellers are not feminists, and Linda could be one of them.
>
> *Argument 2*
> Linda is more likely to be a feminist bank teller than she is to be a bank teller, because she resembles an active feminist more than she resembles a bank teller.

This study parallels the one involving rolls of a die (see (31)). In the former study, participants usually recognized the persuasiveness of the conjunction principle, once made explicit. In contrast, a majority of respondents in the parallel study about Linda rejected argument 1, based on the conjunction principle, in favor of the similarity-based argument 2. What factors explain people's different responses to these formally parallel problems?

A similar discrepancy between performance in parallel settings emerges from this pair of problems (Tversky and Kahneman 1983).

(33) a. A health survey was conducted in a sample of adult males in British Columbia, of all ages and occupations.
Please give your best estimate of the following values:
— What percentage of the men surveyed have had one or more heart attacks?
— What percentage of the men surveyed both are over 55 years old and have had one or more heart attacks?

b. A health survey was conducted in a sample of 100 adult males in British Columbia, of all ages and occupations.
Please give your best estimate of the following values:
— How many of the 100 participants have had one or more heart attacks?
— How many of the 100 participants both are over 55 years old and have had one or more heart attacks?

Sixty-five percent of people responding to problem (33a) assigned a strictly higher estimate to the second question, thereby committing the conjunction fallacy. In contrast, only 25 percent of the people responding to problem (33b) made the same error.

Several hypotheses have been advanced about the factors leading to coherent versus incoherent reasoning. Nisbett et al. (1983) argue that correct, probabilistic reasoning is encouraged by emphasizing the role of chance in producing the events in question and by clarifying the sampling procedure responsible for the objects or persons actually observed. These factors seem to apply to the two pairs of studies just described, as well as to others reported in Christensen and Beach 1982, Fiedler 1988, Gigerenzer et al. 1988, and Nisbett et al. 1983. Gigerenzer et al. 1988 stress familiarity with the domain in question. Thus, people are likely to have more experience trying to divine the outcome of sporting events than the professions of strangers. This difference may explain greater success with the soccer problem (32) than with the engineer problem (22). More generally, as discussed in Gigerenzer and Murray 1987, coherent judgment appears to be facilitated by casting probabilities as frequencies in a well-defined space of possibilities.

A related hypothesis stems from the distinction between *external* and *internal* uncertainty, formulated in Kahneman and Tversky 1982. We illustrate: People seem inclined to view the uncertainty of a coin toss as due to external, causal mechanisms whose behavior defies prediction. In contrast, a person's uncertainty about the capital of Pakistan reflects internal ignorance. Kahneman and Tversky draw attention to the distinct phenomenologies associated with the two types of uncertainty and suggest that distinct judgmental mechanisms are associated with each. It is tempting to speculate that coherent reasoning is more readily triggered by external uncertainty than by its internal counterpart. (For more discussion, see Curley et al. 1989, Einhorn and Hogarth 1985, and Heath and Tversky 1991.)

Confirming hypotheses like the foregoing would provide additional evidence favoring the coexistence thesis.

2.8 On the Difficulty of Maintaining Coherence

The Dutch book theorem (section 2.3.3) exhibits one advantage of coherent probability functions. Other advantages stem from the role of probability theory in the physical and social sciences (which are more comprehensible to people with coherent intuitions). It is thus fortunate that human judgment is malleable to some degree, and that initiation in statistics and probability leads most people to a more coherent conception of chance. Indeed, several experimental studies point to genuine improvement in probability judgment in the wake of statistics courses or explanations (see Agnoli and Krantz 1989; Baron 1988, ch. 22; Fong et al. 1986; and Holland et al. 1986, ch. 9).

Could study and reflection render our probability functions increasingly coherent with no practical limit? In particular, by meditating the probability axioms and improving our memory and numerical skills, can we hope to avoid incoherency in situations of arbitrary complexity? Although this question is not precise enough to answer definitively, results in the theory of computability and complexity provide grounds for pessimism about the ultimate perfectibility of human judgment in this sense. Some of the results reveal the impossibility of programming a computer to manipulate probabilities in an arithmetical language (as in Gaifman and Snir 1982, theorem 3.7). Others deal with complexity issues that involve program behavior at infinitely many points (Cooper 1987). In contrast, we demonstrate here the practical impossibility of attributing coherent probabilities to a certain finite set of statements. The discussion hinges on a remarkable theorem due to Albert Meyer and Larry Stockmeyer.[12]

12. The remainder of this section is more challenging than preceding material. It may be omitted on a first reading.

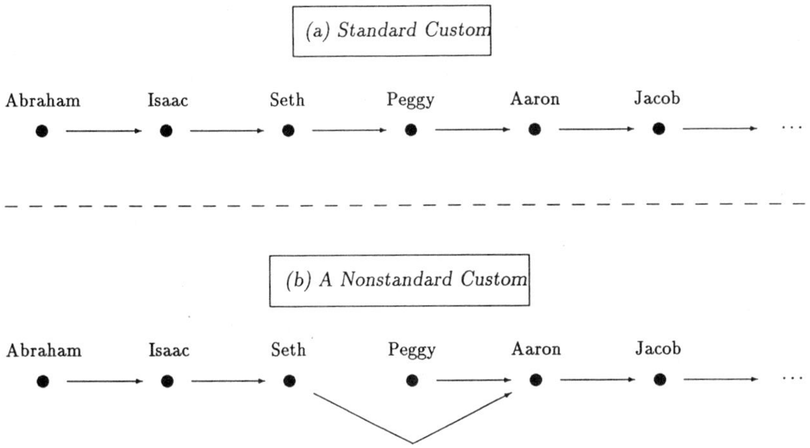

Figure 2.2
Legacy customs.

Imagine that you are an anthropologist investigating legacies among firstborn descendants of a patriarch named "Abraham." Each person in the chain bequeaths his or her wealth to some person of a later generation. You are not sure, however, exactly what the custom is. The situation might be the "standard" one pictured in figure 2.2a, in which each person bequeaths his or her wealth to the immediately succeeding generation. Alternatively, bequests might skip one or more generations, as pictured in figure 2.2b, for example.

Many statements can be formulated about the custom in use, and their truth will depend on whether the actual practice is the standard one or something else. For example, statement (34a) below is true about the custom in figure 2.2a but false about figure 2.2b. The reverse holds for (34b).

(34) a. For any pair of persons, *a*, *b* in the chain, if *a* comes before *b*, then *a*'s inheritor comes before *b*'s inheritor.

b. Some people inherit wealth from more than one ancestor.

The preceding statements refer to individuals in the chain. We also consider statements involving finite sets of individuals, as in:

(35) a. If two finite sets of persons are disjoint (i.e., have no one in common), then they share no inheritor.

b. There exist distinct finite sets of people with identical sets of inheritors.

The first statement is true about figure 2.2a but not figure 2.2b, and vice versa for the second.

A precise idea about statement length will be needed in what follows, and so we revert to a formalized language with symbolic vocabulary. The language in question is denoted **L**. Within **L**, $\in$ denotes set membership, and $>$ denotes succession in the generational chain. We write $a + 1$ to denote a's inheritor, $a + 2$ to denote the inheritor of a's inheritor, and so on; similarly, 0 stands for Abraham, 1 for his inheritor, 2 for 1's inheritor, and so on. Some familiar logical symbols are also used, such as $\neg$, $\wedge$, and $\rightarrow$ for negation, conjunction, and "if ______ then ______." The symbols $\exists$ and $\forall$ allow statements about *some* or *all* members of the chain, or about finite subsets of members. The lowercase letters $a, b \ldots q$ (and their combinations, if needed) are used as temporary names of individuals, as in the statement $\forall a(a < a + 1)$ ("every individual comes before his inheritor"). Similarly, the uppercase letters $A, B \ldots Q$ are temporary names for finite sets, as in the statement $\exists A \forall a(a + 1 \in A)$ ("there is a finite set that contains every inheritor"—which is false for both figure 2.2a and 2.2b).

In all, **L** contains the 62 symbols shown in table 2.2. A rigorous presentation of the language would proceed to an explicit syntax showing how symbols are combined into statements, and then to a semantical apparatus showing how truth values are assigned to statements in the context of customs like those of figure 2.2. However, to avoid technicalities, we shall rely instead on the intuitive interpretation of symbols given above, along with illustrations. For the latter, here are translations of (34) and (35) into **L**.

(34a) $\forall a \forall b(a < b \rightarrow a + 1 < b + 1)$

(34b) $\exists a \exists b \exists c(b \neq c \wedge a = b + 1 \wedge a = c + 1)$

(35a) $\forall A \forall B(\neg \exists a(a \in A \wedge a \in B) \rightarrow$
$\forall a \forall b((a \in A \wedge b \in B) \rightarrow a + 1 \neq b + 1))$

(35b) $\exists A \exists B(A \neq B \wedge \forall c(\exists a(a \in A \wedge c = a + 1) \leftrightarrow$
$\exists b(b \in B \wedge c = b + 1)))$

As an anthropologist, you are interested in which statements characterize the legacy custom in force. You are thus led to assign probabilities to the statements in (34) and (35), among others. It may be supposed, however, that your curiosity does not extend to statements of exceptional length, which are often difficult to comprehend. Therefore let us consider only statements that can be written with at most 616 symbols (the motivation for this number will become apparent shortly). Such a bound is roomy enough to allow expression of many hypotheses about legacies; the longest of the four given above is 42 symbols. Yet it is not so large as to

Table 2.2
The 62 symbols of **L**.

	Symbol	Function
1–2	$\exists, \forall$	quantifiers
3–7	$\neg, \wedge, \vee, \rightarrow, \leftrightarrow$	sentential connectives
8–9	(,)	parentheses
10–11	$\in, \notin$	set membership
12–15	$<, \leq, \geq, >$	order relations
16–17	$=, \neq$	equality
18	+	inheritance
19–35	$a, b \ldots q$	temporary names for individuals
36–52	$A, B \ldots Q$	temporary names for finite sets
53–62	0, 1 ... 9	digits

engender statements that defy interpretation after prolonged study; 616 symbols can easily be written within the confines of a single page. The set of statements in **L** that can be written within the bound is denoted $\mathbf{L}_{616}$.

Examination of fragmentary documents left by Abraham suggests to you that the custom in use is the standard one, represented in figure 2.2a. Thus you assign probability greater than .5 to this hypothesis. Coherence then requires that any statement in $\mathbf{L}_{616}$ that is true of figure 2.2a also be assigned probability greater than .5; the others must be assigned smaller probability. (The deduction of this requirement is discussed below.) You can thus rely upon your probability function to distinguish the true members of $\mathbf{L}_{616}$ from the false, with respect to the standard custom. For this purpose it suffices to determine whether their probabilities exceed one half. It follows that in the situation we have imagined your probability judgment is coherent only if you can perform task (36):

(36) *Task* Given an arbitrary statement S in $\mathbf{L}_{616}$, announce "probable" if S is true about the standard custom; announce "improbable" otherwise.

Probabilistic coherence is therefore a practical impossibility in at least one set of circumstances if neither you nor any other human being is able to perform task (36).

How difficult, then, is task (36)? Is it necessarily beyond the reach of human judgment? Although no conclusive response can be given to this question, it is instructive to consider the resources required to perform (36) using a type of machine whose structure is well understood. The machines in question are *Boolean circuits,* illustrated in figure 2.3. Boolean circuits are

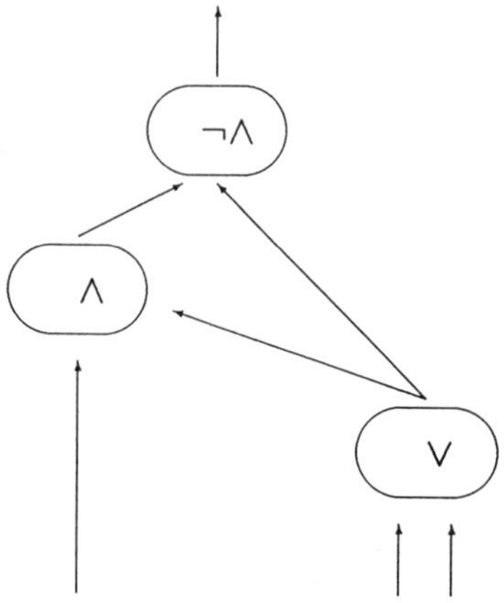

Figure 2.3
A Boolean circuit composed of three gates. There are three input channels and a sole output channel. The components labeled ∧ and ∨ are an AND-gate and OR-gate, respectively. The component labeled ¬∧ maps (x,y) to 1 if at least one of x and y are 0; otherwise, it maps (x,y) to 0.

composed of "gates" each of which accepts two inputs and sends its single output to any number of other gates. Inputs and outputs are restricted to the numbers 0 and 1, and a given gate can implement any of the 16 possible functions within this constraint. For example, the AND-gate maps its input (x,y) into the smaller of x and y, whereas the OR-gate maps (x,y) into the larger. To realize Boolean functions with $n > 2$ inputs, gates are arranged in cascading fashion so that (1) there are no loops in the circuit, (2) there are n free input channels (not coming from gate outputs), and (3) there is one free output channel (not going to a gate input). For example, the circuit of figure 2.3 maps (1,0,1), (1,1,0), and (1,1,1) to 0, and the five other possible triples to 1. (For discussion of circuits, see Cormen et al. 1990, ch. 29.)

To perform task (36) using a Boolean circuit it is necessary to code the members of $\mathbf{L}_{616}$ as strings of 0's and 1's. Our 62 symbols can be represented using six-tuples like 010101, 000111 since there are 2^6 or 64 of them. An arbitrary statement of **L** can then be coded by concatenating the six-tuples associated with its symbols. Any mapping between symbols and six-tuples can be used for coding; the choice does not influence the result cited below. Because our statements have length bounded by 616 symbols, their codes will have length at most 6×616. In fact, we can use one of the two six-tuples left over from the coding to serve as a blank symbol so that all the statements in $\mathbf{L}_{616}$ are padded to length 616. Hence, the desired Boolean circuit will have 6×616 input channels and one output channel. When its inputs are occupied by a coded statement of $\mathbf{L}_{616}$ that is true about the standard custom, the circuit must emit 1 through its sole output channel; in the contrary case, it must emit 0. We thus use 1 and 0 as codes for "probable" and "improbable" (the reverse convention would serve as well).

Because task (36) involves only a finite number of statements, there is guaranteed to be a Boolean circuit that meets the foregoing specifications. Less evident is the minimal number of gates needed for this purpose. If the minimum is large, we have evidence that the task is difficult, perhaps too difficult for any person to perform. In fact, it follows directly from Stockmeyer (1974), theorem 6.1, that any circuit meeting our requirements must have at least 10^{123} gates. To grasp the size of this number, suppose that gates were the size of protons and that the wires connecting them were infinitely thin (taking up no room at all). Then Meyer and Stockmeyer's theorem implies that the circuit required to perform task (36) would nonetheless densely pack the visible universe with gates. (This observation is also from Meyer and Stockmeyer. It assumes that the radius of a proton is 10^{-13} centimeter and that of the universe 11×10^{9} light years.)

Although we shall not attempt to present the proof of the foregoing result, it is important to understand one aspect of it. The theorem was originally formulated in terms of determining the truth and falsity of statements about the standard custom. However, task (36) is an equivalent problem because coherent probability respects logical implication in the sense of (8c). Specifically, because the standard custom was assigned probability greater than .5, all statements implied by the custom must have at least this probability (this is 8c). On the other hand, consider a statement *S* that is not implied by the custom. Then it is easy to see that not-*S* is implied by the custom. Hence, not-*S* has probability greater than .5 and so *S* has probability less than .5 in view of (8a). In this way, truth and falsity about the standard custom are translated into claims about probability. (See also problem 2.7 below.)

To summarize, we have described a set of circumstances that requires probabilistic reasoning about statements in a certain, bounded set. Coherent reasoning in these circumstances implies the ability to perform task (36). However, if circuit complexity is even a rough guide, the task is insuperably difficult. It is thus reasonable to conclude (at least provisionally) that probabilistic coherence is not always a practical possibility, no matter how much effort is devoted to self-improvement and the study of statistics.

2.9 Concluding Remarks

The results of section 2.8 suggest that probabilistic coherence must sometimes be viewed as an unattainable ideal, not only for human beings but for any reasoning agent that can be qualified as "mechanical" in the usual sense. This fact should not discourage us from aiming for coherence, just as the impossibility of drawing perfectly straight lines should not discourage us from determining the area of a pasture as best we can. Indeed, the findings reviewed in section 2.7 indicate that people have implicit awareness of various probability principles, and deploy them spontaneously in favorable circumstances. As computational complexity increases, however, judgmental paralysis can be avoided only by recourse to reasoning "heuristics," that is, to principles that are easy to apply but suboptimal from a theoretical point of view (see Simon 1957). The studies reported in section 2.6 provide evidence that representativeness is one such heuristic for human thought; others are described in section 2.7.2.

Recourse to heuristics is not typically a conscious choice, as if the coherent option were considered and set aside. The result is that heuristics are often applied in situations where coherent reasoning would be both feasible and preferable to all concerned (for examples drawn from medicine, see Arkes et al. 1981, Chapman and Chapman 1971, Eddy 1982, and Lemieux and Bordage 1992). By exposing the character and circumstances of heuristic reasoning in human judgment, and by suggesting means for expanding the domain of coherent thought, cognitive science renders a service to us all. (For general discussion of means for improving human probability judgment, see Klayman and Brown 1993.)

There is also a more positive motive for studying people's reasoning heuristics, namely, to learn about adaptive judgment in the shifting, complex circumstances of ordinary life. Let us not forget that for all its faults and defects, human judgment remains unsurpassed for flexibility and insight. The matter is summarized by Nisbett and Ross 1980, 14:

> Perception researchers have shown that in spite of, and largely because of, people's exquisite perceptual capacities, they are subject to certain perceptual illusions. No serious scientist, however, is led by such demonstrations to conclude that the perceptual system under study is inherently faulty. Similarly, we conclude from our own research that we are observing not an inherently faulty cognitive apparatus but rather, one that manifests certain explicable flaws. Indeed, in human inference as in perception, we suspect that many of people's failings will prove to be closely related to, or even an unavoidable cost of, their greatest strengths.

One challenge for cognitive science is to identify the reasoning mechanisms that allow people to survive and prosper in their environments (when they do), and then to find means of exploiting those mechanisms within the confines of normatively acceptable principles, like the probability axioms (7). Progress along these lines would facilitate development of artificially intelligent systems, offer insight into human psychology, and ultimately stimulate the normative theory of judgment itself.

Suggestions for Further Reading

There are numerous introductions to statistical inference and the theory of probability, including Mendenhall et al. 1986, and Ross 1988. Probability and deductive logic are closely linked. A concise introduction to the latter is offered by Allen and Hand 1992. Inductive logic (including elements of probability) is presented in Gustason 1994, Resnik 1987, and Skyrms 1986. For a psychologically sensitive introduction to the normative theory of judgment and decision, see Dawes 1988 (and also chapter 3 in this volume). A general discussion of rationality, and the difficulty of coherence in particular, is provided by Glymour 1992, part III; see also chapter 6 in this volume. An introduction to the theory of computation and algorithmic complexity is available in Davis and Weyuker 1983 and Papadimitriou 1994.

The history of probability conceptions is discussed in Gigerenzer et al. 1989, Hacking 1975, and Krüger et al. 1990.

An underlying assumption in the present chapter is that degrees of belief can be treated like probabilities and held up to the yardstick of "Bayesian" probability theory. Not everyone agrees. Some alternatives to the Bayesian picture are discussed in Shafer and Pearl 1990. A "frequentist" perspective on human probability judgment is provided in Gigerenzer and Murray 1987. For a dimmer view of the Dutch Book theorem than appears here, see Bacchus et al. 1990; tempered defense of the theorem is available in Howson 1989.

The surprise-quiz paradox (among other conundrums) is discussed in Sainsbury 1988.

A point of entry into the literature on probability judgment is Kahneman et al. 1982. More recent surveys include Baron 1988 and Johnson-Laird and Shafir 1993. Arkes and Hammond 1986 provide readings about the relevance of research on human judgment to social, medical, economic, and political decision making.

An important topic in the theory of confirmation is the influence of new data on the probabilities attributed to prior beliefs. One normative viewpoint is presented in Jeffrey 1983, ch. 11. More general discussion is available in Gärdenfors 1988. Psychological theories on this process are offered in Hogarth and Einhorn 1992, Klayman and Ha 1987, Osherson et al. 1990, Smith et al. 1993, Sloman 1993, and Tubbs et al. 1993.

Reasoning must often be carried out in contexts where not even the probability of events is known. In this case the reasoner might attempt to construct a probability distribution that strikes him or her as a reasonable portrayal of uncertainty in the environment. Discussion of the issues involved in such a process is provided in Osherson et al. 1994c.

Two approaches to exploiting the mechanisms of human probability judgment within a coherent system of reasoning are presented in Osherson et al. 1994b and Osherson et al. 1994a.

Problems

2.1 In our discussion of fair bets (see page 38), it is claimed that $\mathbf{P}_I(S) = L/(W + L)$ if and only if $\mathbf{P}_I(S) \times W = (1 - \mathbf{P}_I(S)) \times L$. Prove this claim.

2.2 Deduce (8a–e) from the probability axioms (7).

2.3 Deduce the following principle from the probability axioms (7). Use the results of problem 2.2.

> (*) Let statements S_1 and S_2 be given. If $\mathbf{P}(S_2) \neq 0$ and $\mathbf{P}(S_2) \neq 1$ then $\mathbf{P}(S_1) = (\mathbf{P}(S_1 \text{ assuming that } S_2) \times \mathbf{P}(S_2)) + (\mathbf{P}(S_1 \text{ assuming that not-}S_2) \times \mathbf{P}(\text{not-}S_2))$.

2.4 Suppose that probability function $\mathbf{P}_I$ is such that

(i) $\mathbf{P}_I(S_1) = .3$
(ii) $\mathbf{P}_I(S_1 \text{ and } S_2) = .4$

a. Show that $\mathbf{P}_I$ is open to a Dutch book. Assume for this purpose that $\mathbf{P}_I(\text{not-}S_2) = 1 - \mathbf{P}_I(S_2)$ (cf. note 2.3).
b. In place of (ii), suppose that:

(ii′) $\mathbf{P}_I(S_1 \text{ and } S_2) = .5$

Notice that the conjunction fallacy associated with (i) and (ii′) is greater than that associated with (i) and (ii) (in the sense of section 2.6.1.3). By the "size" of a bet let us mean the sum of the winnings and losses associated with it. Show that a Dutch bookie faced with (ii′) in place of (ii) can realize greater profits with bets of the same size.

2.5 Casscells et al. (1978) presented 60 students and staff members at the Harvard University Medical School with the following question. (The *prevalence* of a disease is the percentage of the population that has it, and the *false positive rate* of a test for a disease is the probability of a positive outcome in an individual without the disease.)

> If a test to detect a disease whose prevalence is $\frac{1}{1000}$ has a false positive rate of 5 percent, what is the chance that a person found to have a positive result actually has the disease, assuming that you know nothing about the person's symptoms or signs?

Almost half the participants responded with 95 percent. The average answer was 56 percent. The correct response depends on the probability of detecting the disease, if present. Assume that the test is perfect in this respect. What is the answer to the question based on Bayes's theorem (8d)? (For discussion of the Casscells et al. study, see Cosmides and Tooby (1995).)

2.6 A fair coin is tossed three times. You win if at least two of the three tosses end up as "heads." Ask a friend this question:

> Which of these is more likely, or do the two alternatives have the same probability?
>
> a. you end up winning the game, assuming that the first toss comes up heads.
> b. the first toss comes up heads, assuming that you end up winning the game.

What is the correct answer?

2.7 On page 65 it is assumed that the standard custom (figure 2.2a) has probability greater than one half. Write out the proof showing that coherence requires:

a. all statements true about the custom also have probability greater than one half;
b. all statements false about the custom have probability less than one half.

Questions for Further Thought

2.1 Consider this problem, posed by Tversky and Kahneman (1983):

> In four pages of a novel (about 2,000 words), how many words would you expect to find that have the form ----*ing* (seven-letter words that end with -*ing*)? Indicate your best estimate by circling one of the values below:
>
> 0 1–2 3–4 5–7 8–10 11–15 16+

A second version of the question, posed to a different group of participants, requested estimates for words of the form -----*n*-. Even though all words of the first form are also words of the second form, the estimates for ----*ing* words were almost three times higher than the estimates for -----*n*- words.

Is incoherent thought implied by these findings?

2.2 Nisbett, Zukier, and Lemley (1981) asked people in one group to rate the utility of various items of information about college students for predicting the amount of shock that given students would take if they were in an experiment in which they were asked to tolerate as much shock as possible. Such items as "Catholic," "from Detroit," and "3.1 grade point average" were judged to have little or no predictive value in this regard. A second group of people was asked to estimate the amount of shock that would be taken by music majors versus engineering majors. Finally, a third group made the same type of prediction about students described either as "Catholic music majors from Detroit with a 3.1 grade-point average" or "Catholic engineering majors from Detroit with a 3.1 grade-point average."

Here are the results of the study. Engineering majors were predicted to take much more shock than music majors. On the other hand, Catholic engineering majors from Detroit with a 3.1 grade-point average were predicted to take only a little more shock than Catholic music majors from Detroit with a 3.1 grade-point average.

People who accept much shock in the circumstances described above can be called "shocktakers." We may interpret the results of the study as follows:

> a. The participants judged the probability that an engineering major is a shocktaker as considerably higher than the probability that a music major is a shocktaker.
> b. The participants judged the probability that a Catholic engineering major from Detroit with a 3.1 grade-point average is a shocktaker as only slightly higher than the probability that a Catholic music major from Detroit with a 3.1 grade-point average is a shocktaker.

In sum, adding irrelevant attributes seems to "dilute" the influence of the relevant differences in major. How can this dilution effect be explained in terms of the representativeness thesis (17)?

2.3 This problem appears in Nisbett et al. 1983.

> Harold is the coach for a high school football team. One of his jobs is selecting new members for the varsity team. He says the following of his experience: "Every year we add 10–20 younger boys to the team on the basis of their performance at the tryout practice. Usually the staff and I are extremely excited about the potential of two or three of these kids—one who throws several brilliant passes or another who kicks several field goals from a remarkable distance. Unfortunately, most of these kids turn out to be only somewhat better than the rest." Why do you suppose that the coach usually has to revise downward his opinion of players that he originally thought were brilliant?

Formulate your answer as concisely as possible and compare it (when you have the opportunity) with the opinion of a statistician.

2.4 You've been thrust in jail with two other prisoners and informed that one of you has been selected at random to be hanged on the morrow. As if this prospect weren't bad enough, the jailer decides to increase your anxiety with this announcement:

> I shall now privately use a random device to choose one of your two cellmates. If the choice falls on a prisoner to escape hanging, then I shall announce his name; otherwise, I shall announce the name of your other cellmate.

Subsequently the jailer points to one of your cellmates and proclaims: "This man will escape hanging." Sure enough, your anxiety deepens because you become convinced that your chances of hanging have increased from $\frac{1}{3}$ to $\frac{1}{2}$. Is this conviction reasonable? (The puzzle appears in many probability textbooks, for example, Ross (1988), ch. 3, problem 32.)

References

Agnoli, F., and D. Krantz (1989). Suppressing natural heuristics by formal instruction: The case of the conjunction fallacy. *Cognitive Psychology* 21, 515–550.

Allen, C., and M. Hand (1992). *Logic primer.* Cambridge, MA: MIT Press.

Arkes, H., and K. Hammond, eds. (1986). *Judgment and decision making.* Cambridge: Cambridge University Press, 1986.

Arkes, H. R., R. L. Wortmann, P. D. Saville, and A. R. Harkness (1981). Hindsight bias among physicians weighing the likelihood of diagnoses. *Journal of Applied Psychology* 66, 252–254.

Bacchus, F., H. E. Kyburg Jr., and M. Thalos (1990). Against conditionalization. *Synthese* 85, 475–506.

Bar-Hillel, M. (1982). Studies of representativeness. In Kahneman et al. 1982.

Bar-Hillel, M., and R. Falk (1982). Some teasers concerning conditional probabilities. *Cognition* 11, 109–122.

Baron, J. (1988). *Thinking and deciding.* New York: Cambridge University Press.

Beyth-Marom, R., and B. Fischhoff (1983). Diagnosticity and pseudodiagnosticity. *Journal of Personality and Social Psychology* 45, 1185–1197.

Braine, M. D. S., J. Connell, J. Freitag, and D. P. O'Brien (1990). Is the base rate fallacy an instance of asserting the consequent? In K. J. Gilhooly, M. T. G. Keane, R. H. Logie, and G. Erdos, eds. *Lines of thinking,* Vol. 1. Chichester: John Wiley & Sons.

Casscells, W. A., A. Schoenberger, and T. Grayboys (1978). Interpretation by physicians of clinical laboratory results. *New England Journal of Medicine* 299, 999–1000.

Chapman, L., and J. Chapman (1971). Test results are what you think they are. *Psychology Today* November 1971, pp. 18–22, 106–110.

Christensen-Szalanski, J., and L. Beach (1982). Experience and the base-rate fallacy. *Organizational Behavior and Human Performance* 29, 270–278.

Cohen, L. J. (1983). Belief, acceptance, and probability. *The Behavioral and Brain Sciences* 6, 248–249.

Cooper, G. F. (1987). *Probabilistic inference using belief networks is NP-hard.* Memo KSL-87-27, Knowledge Systems Laboratory, Stanford University, May 1987.

Cormen, T. H., C. E. Keiserson, and R. L. Rivest (1990). *Introduction to algorithms.* Cambridge, MA: M.I.T. Press.

Cosmides, L., and J. Tooby (1995). Are humans good intuitive statisticians after all? Rethinking some conclusions of the literature on judgment under uncertainty. *Cognition,* in press.

Curley, S. J., J. F. Yates, and R. Abrams (1989). Psychological sources of ambiguity avoidance. *Organizational Behavior and Human Decision Processes* 38, 230–256.

David, M., and E. Weyuker (1983). *Computability, complexity, and languages.* San Diego: Academic Press.

Dawes, R. M. (1988). *Rational choice in an uncertain world.* Orlando, FL: Harcourt Brace Jovanovich.

Dawes, R. M., H. L. Mirels, Eric Gold, and E. Donahue (1993). Equating inverse probabilities in implicit personality judgments, *Psychological Science* 4(6), 396–400.

Eddy, D. M. (1982). Probabilistic reasoning in clinical medicine: Problems and opportunities. In Kahneman et al. 1982.

Einhorn, H., and R. Hogarth (1985). Ambiguity and uncertainty in probabilistic inference. *Psychological Review* 93, 433–461.

Fiedler, K. (1988). The dependence of the conjunction fallacy on subtle linguistic factors. *Psychological Research* 50, 123–129.

Fischhoff, B., and R. Beyth-Marom (1983). Hypothesis evaluation from a Bayesian perspective. *Psychological Review* 90, 239–260.

Fong, G. T., D. H. Krantz, and R. E. Nisbett (1986). The effects of statistical training on thinking about everyday problems. *Cognitive Psychology* 18, 253–292.

Gaifman, H., and M. Snir (1982). Probabilities over rich languages. *Journal of Symbolic Logic* 47, 495–548.

Gärdenfors, P. (1988). *Knowledge in flux: Modeling the dynamics of epistemic states.* Cambridge: MIT Press.

Gigerenzer, G., W. Hell, and H. Blank (1988). Presentation and content: The use of base rates as a continuous variable. *Journal of Experimental Psychology: Human Perception and Performance* 14(3), 513–525.

Gigerenzer, G., and D. J. Murray (1987). *Cognition as intuitive statistics.* Hillsdale, NJ: L. Erlbaum Associates.

Gigerenzer, G., Z. Swijtink, T. Porter, L. Daston, J. Beatty, and L. Krüger (1989). The empire of chance. Cambridge: Cambridge University Press.

Glymour, C. (1992). *Thinking things through.* Cambridge, MA: MIT Press.

Gustason, W. (1994). *Reasoning from evidence: Inductive logic.* New York: Macmillan.

Hacking, I. (1975). *The emergence of probability.* Cambridge: Cambridge University Press.

Heath, C., and A. Tversky. (1991). Preference and belief: Ambiguity and competence in choice and uncertainty. *Journal of Risk and Uncertainty* 4, 5–28.

Hogarth, R., and H. Einhorn (1992). Order effects in belief updating: The belief-adjustment model. *Cognitive Psychology* 24, 1–55.

Holland, J., K. Holyoak, R. Nisbett, and P. Thagard (1986). *Induction: Processes of inference, learning, and discovery.* Cambridge, MA: MIT Press.

Howson, C. (1989). Subjective probabilities and betting quotients. *Synthese* 81, 1–8.

Jeffrey, R. (1983). *The logic of decision,* 2nd ed. Chicago: University of Chicago Press.

Johnson-Laird, P. N., and E. Shafir, eds. (1993). *Reasoning and Decision Making: Cognition Special Issue* 49, 1–188.

Kahneman, D., P. Slovic, and A. Tversky, eds. (1982). *Judgment under uncertainty: Heuristics and biases.* Cambridge: Cambridge University Press.

Kahneman, D., and A. Tversky (1972). Subjective probability: A judgment of representativeness. *Cognitive Psychology* 3, 430–454.

Kahneman, D., and A. Tversky (1973). On the psychology of prediction. *Psychological Review* 80, 237–251.

Kahneman, D., and A. Tversky (1982). Variants of uncertainty. *Cognition* 11, 143–158.

Kemeny, J. G. (1955). Fair bets and inductive probabilities. *Journal of Symbolic Logic* 20, 263–273.

Klayman, J., and Y.-W. Ha (1987). Confirmation, disconfirmation, and information in hypothesis testing. *Psychological Review* 94, 211–228.

Klayman, J., and K. Brown (1993). Debias the environment instead of the judge: An alternative approach to reducing error in diagnostic (and other) judgment. In Johnson-Laird and Shafir 1993.

Koehler, J. (1993). The base rate fallacy myth. *Psycoloquy* November 9.

Krüger, L., G. Gigerenzer, and M. S. Morgan, eds. (1990). *The probabilistic revolution* vols. 1–2. Cambridge, MA: MIT Press.

Lehman, R. S. (1955). On confirmation and rational betting. *Journal of Symbolic Logic* 20, 251–262.

Lemieux, M., and G. Bordage (1992). Propositional versus structural semantic analyses of medical diagnostic thinking. *Cognitive Science* 16, 185–204.

Levi, I. (1980). *The enterprise of knowledge.* Cambridge: MIT Press.

Macchi, L. (1994). Pragmatic aspects of the base-rate fallacy. Università degli Studi di Milano, Milan.

Mendenhall, W., R. L. Scheaffer, and D. D. Wackerly (1986). *Mathematical statistics with applications.* 3rd ed. Boston: Duxbury Press.

Nisbett, R., H. Zukier, and R. Lemley (1981). The dilution effect: Nondiagnostic information weakens the implications of diagnostic information. *Cognitive Psychology* 13, 248–277.

Nisbett, R., D. Krantz, C. Jepson, and Z. Kunda (1983). The use of statistical heuristics in everyday inductive reasoning. *Psychological Review* 90, 339–363.

Nisbett, R., and Ross, L. (1980). *Human inference: Strategies and shortcomings of social judgment*. Englewood Cliffs, NJ: Prentice-Hall.

Osherson, D. (1987). New axioms for the contrast model of similarity. *Journal of Mathematical Psychology* 31, 93–103.

Osherson, D., E. E. Smith, O. Wilkie, A. Lopez, and E. Shafir (1990). Category based induction. *Psychological Review* 97(2), 185–200.

Osherson, D., K. Biolsi, E. E. Smith, E. Shafir, and A. Gualtierotti (1994). A source of Bayesian priors. *Cognitive Science* in press.

Osherson, D., E. Shafir, and E. E. Smith (1994b). Extracting the coherent core of human probability judgment. *Cognition* 50, 299–313.

Osherson, D., E. Shafir, and E. E. Smith (1993). Ampliative inference. *Cognition* 49, 189–210.

Papadimitriou, C. H. (1994). *Computational complexity*. Reading, MA: Addison-Wesley.

Politzer, G., and I. Noveck (1991). Are conjunction rule violations the result of conversational rule violations? *Journal of Psycholinguistic Research* 15, 47–92.

Resnik, M. D. (1987). *Choices: An introduction to decision theory*. Minneapolis, MN: University of Minnesota Press.

Ross, S. (1988). *A first course in probability*. 3rd ed. New York: Macmillan.

Sainsbury, R. M. (1988). *Paradoxes*. Cambridge: Cambridge University Press.

Schwartz, N., F. Strack, D. Hilton, and G. Naderer (1991). Base rates representativeness, and the logic of conversation: The contextual relevance of "irrelevant" information. *Social Cognition* 9, 67–84.

Shafer, G., and J. Pearl, eds. (1990). *Readings in uncertain reasoning*. San Mateo, CA: Morgan Kaufmann Publishers.

Shafir, E., E. E. Smith, and D. Osherson (1990). Typicality and reasoning fallacies. *Memory and Cognition* 18(3), 229–239.

Simon, H. A. (1957). *Models of man*. New York: Wiley.

Skyrms, B. (1986). *Choice and chance: An introduction to inductive logic*. 3rd ed. Belmont, CA.

Sloman, S. A. (1993). Feature based induction. *Cognitive Psychology* 25(2), 231–280.

Slovic, P., B. Fischhoff, and S. Lichtenstein (1980). Fact versus fears: Understanding perceived risk. In R. Schwing and W. A. Albers, eds., *Societal risk assessment: How safe is safe enough?* New York: Plenum.

Smith, E. E. (1989). Concepts and induction. In M. I. Posner, ed., *Foundations of cognitive science*. Cambridge: MIT Press.

Smith, E. E., and D. L. Medin. (1981). *Categories and concepts*. Cambridge: Harvard University Press.

Smith, E. E., and D. Osherson (1984). Conceptual combination with prototype concepts. *Cognitive Science* 8, 337–361.

Smith, E. E., E. Shafir, and D. Osherson (1993). Similarity, plausibility, and judgments of probability. *Cognition* 49, 67–96.

Stockmeyer, L. J. (1974). *The complexity of decision problems in automata theory and logic*, Ph.D. Thesis, Department of Electrical Engineering, MIT.

Suppes, P., D. H. Krantz, R. D. Luce, and A. Tversky (1989). *Foundations of measurement*, volume II: *Geometrical, threshold, and probabilistic representations*. San Diego: Academic Press.

Thüring, M., and H. Jungermann (1990). The conjunction fallacy: Causality vs. event probability. *Journal of Behavioral Decision Making* 3, 61–74.

Tubbs, R. M., G. J. Gaeth, I. P. Levin, and L. A. Van Osdol (1993). Order effects in belief updating with consistent and inconsistent evidence. *Journal of Behavioral Decision Making* 6, 257–269.

Tversky, A., and D. Kahneman (1974). Judgment under uncertainty: Heuristics and biases. *Science* 185, 1124–1131.

Tversky, A., and D. Kahneman (1980). Causal schemes in judgments under uncertainty. In M. Fishbein, ed., *Progress in social psychology*. Hillsdale, NJ: Erlbaum.

Tversky, A., and D. Kahneman (1983). Extensional versus intuitive reasoning: The conjunction fallacy in probability judgment. *Psychological Review*, 90, 292–315.

Wolford, G., H. A. Taylor, and J. R. Beck (1990). The conjunction fallacy? *Memory and Cognition* 18, 47–53.

Chapter 3

Decision Making

Eldar Shafir and Amos Tversky

3.1 Introduction

Decisions about what to buy, whom to vote for, or where to live, shape many aspects of our lives. The study of decision making is an interdisciplinary enterprise involving economics, political science, and psychology, as well as statistics and philosophy. One can distinguish two approaches to the analysis of decision making, the normative and the descriptive. The normative approach, which underlies much of economic analysis, assumes a rational decision maker, who has well-defined preferences that do not depend on the particular description of the options or on the specific methods for eliciting preference. This conception, which has come to be known as the rational theory of choice, is based primarily on a priori considerations rather than on experimental observation. As a consequence, it has a better claim as a normative account of how decisions ought to be made than as a descriptive theory of how decisions are actually made.

The descriptive approach to individual decision making is based on empirical observation and experimental studies of choice behavior. The experimental evidence indicates that people's choices are often at odds with the assumptions of the rational theory, and suggests some empirical generalizations that characterize people's choices. In this chapter we describe some selected findings and discuss several psychological principles that underlie the decision-making process. In the next section we address the psychological evaluation of gains and losses, and consider people's attitudes toward risk. Section 3.3 demonstrates that alternative descriptions of a decision problem can give rise to predictably different choices. Section 3.4 addresses the asymmetry between the evaluation of gains and losses, known as *loss aversion*. Section 3.5 demonstrates how alternative

Preparation of this chapter was supported by US Public Health Service Grant No. 1-R29-MH46885 from the National Institute of Mental Health, by Grant No. SBR-9408684 from the National Science Foundation, and by a grant from the Russell Sage Foundation. It was completed while the authors were Fellows at the Institute for Advanced Studies and the Center for Rationality and Interactive Decision Theory of The Hebrew University.

methods of eliciting people's preferences give rise to inconsistent decisions. In section 3.6 we address the role of conflict and show how preference among options is altered by the addition of new alternatives. The tension between descriptive and normative conceptions of decision making is addressed in the concluding section. (Further discussion of the relation between normative and descriptive analyses is provided in chapters 2 and 6.)

3.2 Risk and Value

Many decisions in the real world (such as investment, gambling, insurance) are risky in the sense that their outcomes are not known with certainty. To make such decisions, one has to consider two factors, the desirability of the potential outcomes and their probability of occurrence. Indeed, decision theory is concerned with the question of how these factors are, or should be, combined.

Consider a choice between a risky prospect that offers a 50 percent chance to win \$200 (and a 50 percent chance to win nothing) and the alternative of receiving \$100 for sure. Most people prefer the sure gain over the gamble, although the two prospects have the same expected value. The expected value of a gamble is a weighted average where each possible outcome is weighted by its probability of occurrence. The expected value of the gamble above is $.50 \times \$200 + .50 \times 0 = \$100$. A preference for a sure outcome over a risky prospect that has higher or equal expected value is called *risk averse*; a preference for a risky prospect over a sure outcome that has higher or equal expected value is called *risk seeking*.

As illustrated above, people tend to be risk averse when choosing between prospects with positive outcomes. This tendency toward risk aversion can be explained by appealing to the notion of diminishing sensitivity. Just as the impact of a candle is greater when it is brought into a dark room than into a room that is well lit, so the impact of an additional \$100 is greater when it is added to a gain of \$100 than when it is added to a gain of \$800. This principle was first formalized by Daniel Bernoulli and Gabriel Cramer, who proposed early in the eighteenth century that subjective value, or utility, is a concave function of money, as illustrated in figure 3.1. (A function is concave if a line joining any two points on the curve lies entirely below the curve.) Notice that according to such a function the utility difference, $u(\$200) - u(\$100)$, is greater than the utility difference, $u(\$900) - u(\$800)$, though the dollar differences are the same.

Bernoulli and Cramer proposed that a person has a concave utility function that captures his or her subjective value for money, and that prefer-

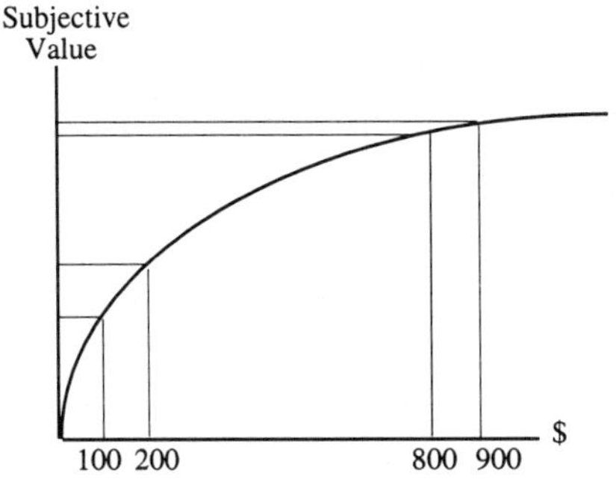

Figure 3.1

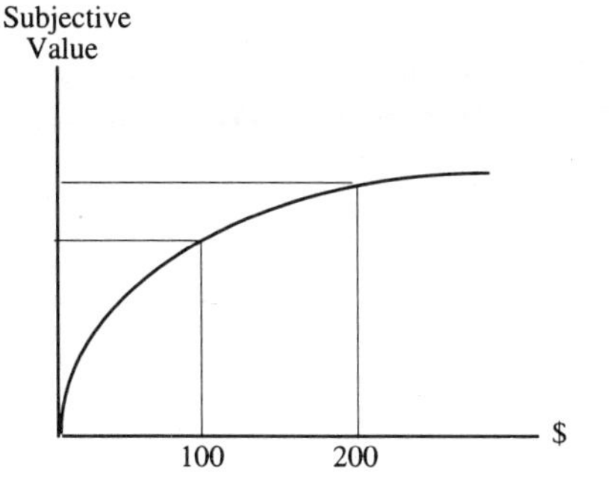

Figure 3.2

ences should be described using expected utility instead of expected value. According to expected utility, the worth of a gamble offering a 50 percent chance to win $200 (and a 50 percent chance to win nothing) is $.50 \times u(\$200)$, where u is the person's utility function. (Assume that $u(0) = 0$.) As can be seen from figure 3.2, it follows from such a function that the subjective value attached to a gain of $100 is more than 50 percent of the value attached to a gain of $200, which entails preference for the sure $100 gain and, hence, risk aversion. Expected utility theory and the assumption of risk aversion play a central role in the standard economic analysis of choice between risky prospects.

Let us turn now to choice involving losses. Suppose you are forced to choose between a prospect that offers a 50 percent chance to lose $200 (and a 50 percent chance to lose nothing) and the alternative of losing $100 for sure. In this problem, most people reject the sure loss of $100 and prefer to take an even chance at losing $200 or nothing. Notice that, as in the choice above involving gains, the prospects have the same expected

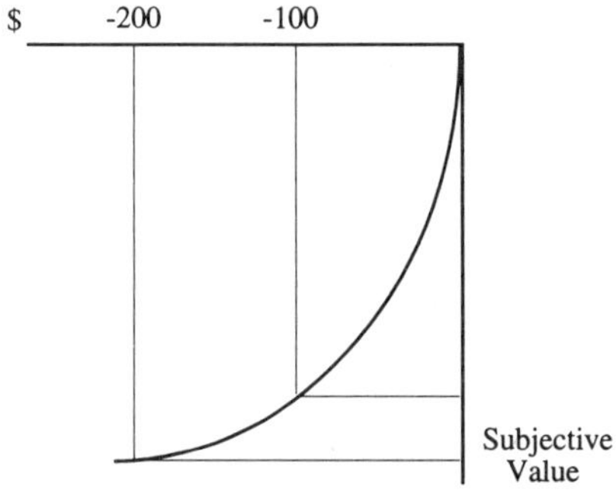

Figure 3.3

value. This preference for a risky prospect over a sure outcome that has the same expected value is an instance of risk seeking. Evidently, risk aversion does not always hold, in contrast to traditional economic analysis. In fact, except for prospects that involve very small probabilities, risk aversion is generally observed in choices involving gains, whereas risk seeking tends to hold in choices involving losses.

The combination of risk aversion for gains and risk seeking for losses can be explained by assuming that diminishing sensitivity applies to negative as well as to positive outcomes. Consequently, the subjective value function for losses is convex, as depicted in figure 3.3. (A function is convex if a line joining any two points on the curve lies entirely above the curve.) According to such a function, the worth of a gamble that offers a 50 percent chance to lose \$200 is greater (that is, less negative) than that of a sure loss of \$100. That is, $.50 \times u(-\$200) > u(-\$100)$. This result implies a risk-seeking preference for the gamble over the sure loss.

By conjoining figures 3.2 and 3.3, we obtain an S-shaped value function that is concave for gains and convex for losses, as illustrated in figure 3.4. This function forms part of a descriptive analysis of choice, known as *Prospect Theory*, which accounts for observed regularities in risky choice (Kahneman and Tversky 1979; Tversky and Kahneman 1992). The value function of Prospect Theory has three important properties: (1) it is defined on gains and losses rather than total wealth, (2) it is steeper for losses than for gains, and (3) it is concave for gains and convex for losses. The first property states that people normally treat outcomes as gains and losses defined relative to a neutral reference point, rather than in terms of total wealth, as we shall illustrate. The second property, called *loss aversion*, states that losses generally loom larger than corresponding gains. Thus, a loss of \$X is more aversive than a gain of \$X is attractive, which is implied by a function that is steeper for losses than for gains, that is, where $u(\$X) < -u(-\$X)$, as in figure 3.4.

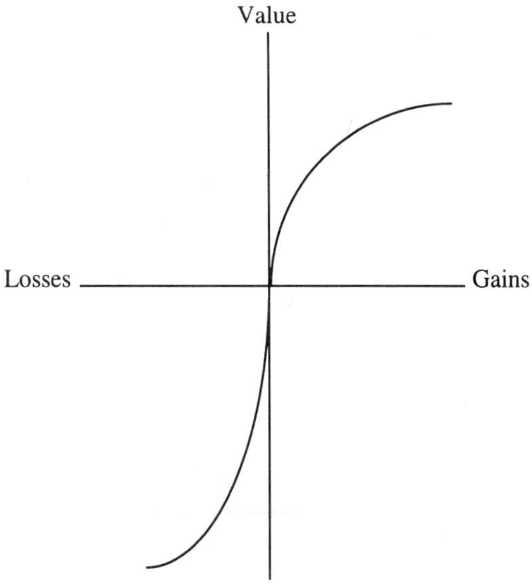

Figure 3.4

The third property of the value function implies the risk attitudes described earlier: risk aversion in the domain of gains and risk seeking in the domain of losses. Although there is a presumption that people are entitled to their own values and each of the attitudes above seems unobjectionable on its own, the combination of the two leads to unacceptable consequences, as we shall show.

3.3 Framing Effects

Consider the following problems (Tversky and Kahneman 1986). The numbers in brackets indicate the percentage of respondents who chose each option. (The number of respondents in each problem is denoted N.)

> *Problem 1* ($N = 126$)
> Assume yourself richer by $300 than you are today.
> You have to choose between
> - a sure gain of $100 [72%]
> - a 50% chance to gain $200 and a 50% chance to gain nothing [28%]
>
> *Problem 2* ($N = 128$)
> Assume yourself richer by $500 than you are today.
> You have to choose between

- a sure loss of $100 [36%]
- a 50% chance to lose nothing and a 50% chance to lose $200 [64%]

In accord with the value function above, most subjects presented with problem 1, which is framed as a choice between gains, are risk averse, whereas most subjects presented with problem 2, which is framed as a choice between losses, are risk seeking. However, the two problems are essentially identical: When the initial payment of $300 or $500 is added to the respective outcomes, both problems amount to a choice between $400 for sure and an even chance at $300 or $500. The different responses to problems 1 and 2 show that subjects did not combine the initial payment with the choice outcomes as required by normative analysis. As a consequence, the same choice problem framed in alternative ways led to systematically different choices. This result is called a *framing effect*.

The combination of risk aversion for gains and risk seeking for losses implied by the value function of figure 3.4 can also lead to violations of dominance, which is perhaps the simplest and most compelling principle of rational choice. The dominance principle states that if option B is better than option A on one attribute and at least as good as A on all the rest, then B should be chosen over A. For example, given a choice between

A: 25% chance to win $240 and 75% chance to lose $760
B: 25% chance to win $250 and 75% chance to lose $750

the dominance principle requires that the decision maker prefer option B to option A, because B offers the same chances of winning more than A and of losing less. Consider, in contrast, the following two choices, one involving gains and the other involving losses (Tversky and Kahneman 1981):

Problem 3 ($N = 150$)
Imagine that you face the following pair of concurrent decisions. First examine both decisions, then indicate the options you prefer.

Decision (i). Choose between
C: a sure gain of $240. [84%]
D: 25% chance to gain $1,000 and 75% chance to gain nothing [16%]

Decision (ii). Choose between
E: a sure loss of $750 [13%]
F: 75% chance to lose $1,000 and 25% chance to lose nothing [87%]

Notice that the expected value of option D is .25 × $1,000 = $250, whereas the expected value of option F is .75 × −$1,000 = −$750. Hence, as the data show, the majority choice in decision (i) is risk averse, and the majority choice in decision (ii) is risk seeking, as predicted by the value function. As it turns out, 73 percent of the subjects chose a combination of the two most popular options, C and F, and only 3 percent of the subjects chose a combination of the two least popular prospects, D and E. Simple calculation, however, shows that the combination of C and F yields prospect A above, whereas the combination of D and E yields prospect B (see problem 3.1). Thus, a great majority of subjects violated dominance and selected an inferior combination of prospects. In contrast, when subjects were presented with a direct choice between A and B, everybody naturally chose the dominant option B. Thus, the principle of dominance is obeyed when its application is transparent, but is often violated when it is not. In particular, the demonstration above shows that the tendency to evaluate prospects in isolation, combined with the common risk attitudes captured by figure 3.4, can lead to the selection of a dominated option.

The effects of framing and the characteristics of the value function are not limited to monetary outcomes, as demonstrated by the following choices between health policies involving human life (Tversky and Kahneman 1981):

> *Problem* 4 ($N = 152$)
> Imagine that the United States is preparing for the outbreak of an unusual Asian disease, which is expected to kill 600 people. Two alternative programs to combat the disease have been proposed. Assume that the exact scientific estimates of the consequences of the programs are as follows:
>
> If Program A is adopted, 200 people will be saved. [72%]
>
> If Program B is adopted, there is 1/3 probability that 600 people will be saved, and 2/3 probability that no people will be saved. [28%]

Notice that both programs have the same expected value in terms of human lives. Because saving people is perceived as a "gain," the majority of subjects made the risk-averse choice of saving 200 people for sure over the chance of saving either 600 people or no one. A second group of subjects was given the same cover story with these descriptions of the alternative programs:

> *Problem* 5 ($N = 155$)
> If Program C is adopted, 400 people will die. [22%]

If Program D is adopted, there is 1/3 probability that nobody will die, and 2/3 probability that 600 people will die. [78%]

Here the outcomes of the two programs are described in terms of lives lost. Accordingly, the majority of subjects made the risk-seeking choice, avoiding the sure loss of 400 lives in favor of the chance to save either all 600 or no one. Subjects again exhibited the familiar pattern of risk aversion in the domain of gains and risk seeking in losses. However, problems 4 and 5 present the same options. In particular, programs A and B are identical, respectively, to programs C and D. They differ only in that the former are framed in terms of number of lives saved, whereas the latter are framed in terms of lives lost.

An essential element in the rational theory of choice is the requirement, known as *description invariance,* that equivalent representations of a choice problem should yield the same preferences. That is, an individual's preference between options should not depend on the manner in which they are described, provided the descriptions convey the same information. The majority preferences expressed in problems 4 and 5, however, violate the principle of description invariance and show that framing the same problem in terms of gains or in terms of losses gives rise to predictably different choices.

Framing effects are pervasive and are often observed even when the same respondents answer both versions of a problem. Furthermore, they are found in the choices of both naive and sophisticated respondents. For example, experienced physicians made markedly different choices between two alternative treatments for lung cancer—surgery and radiation therapy—depending on whether the outcomes of these treatments were described in terms of mortality rates or in terms of survival rates (see problem 3.2). Surprisingly, the physicians were just as susceptible to the effect of framing as were graduate students or clinic patients (McNeil, Pauker, Sox, and Tversky 1982).

The effectiveness of framing manipulations suggests that people tend to adopt the frame presented in a problem and evaluate the outcomes in terms of that frame. Thus, depending on whether a problem is described in terms of gains or losses, people are likely to exhibit risk-averse or risk-seeking behaviors. An interesting class of framing effects arises in the evaluations of economic transactions that occur in times of inflation.

In one study (Shafir, Diamond, and Tversky 1994), subjects were asked to imagine that they worked for a company that produced computers in Singapore, and had to sign a contract for the local sale of new computers in that country. The computers, currently selling for $1,000 apiece, were to be delivered and paid for a year later. By that time, due to inflation, all prices, including production costs and computer prices, were expected to increase by about 20 percent. Subjects had to choose between contract A: selling the computers a year later for the predetermined price of $1,200 (that is, 20 percent higher than the current price), and contract B: selling the computers a year later for the going price at that time. For one group of subjects the options were described relative to the predetermined price of $1,200. In this frame, contract A appears riskless because the computers are guaranteed to sell for $1,200 no matter what, whereas contract B appears risky because the computers' future price will be less than $1,200 if inflation is low, and more than $1,200 if inflation is high. A second group of subjects were presented with the same alternatives described relative to the computers' expected future price. Here, contract B appears riskless because the computers will be sold next year for their actual price then, regardless of the rate of inflation. Contract A, on the other hand, appears risky: the computers are to be sold for $1,200, which may be more than they are worth if inflation is lower than the anticipated 20 percent, and less than they are worth if inflation exceeds 20 percent. Because of loss aversion, the contract that appeared riskless in each frame was relatively more attractive than the one that appeared risky. Thus, contract A was chosen more often in the former case, when it was framed as riskless, than in the latter, when it was framed as risky.

3.4 Loss Aversion

One of the basic observations regarding people's reaction to outcomes is that losses appear larger than corresponding gains. This asymmetry in the evaluation of positive and negative outcomes is called *loss aversion*. Loss aversion gives rise to a value function that is steeper in the negative than in the positive domain, as in figure 3.4. An immediate implication of loss aversion is that people will not accept an even chance to win or lose $X, because the loss of $X is more aversive than the gain of $X is attractive. Indeed, people are generally willing to accept an even-chance prospect only when the gain is substantially greater than the loss. Many people, for example, reject a 50–50 chance to win $200 or lose $100, even though the gain is twice as large as the loss (Tversky and Shafir 1992a).

The example above illustrates loss aversion in decisions involving risky prospects. The principle of loss aversion applies with equal force to riskless choice, between options that can be obtained for certain (Tversky and Kahneman 1991). It entails that the loss of utility associated with giving up a good that is in our possession is generally greater than the utility gain associated with obtaining that good. An instructive demonstration of this effect is provided in an experiment involving the selling of mugs (Kahneman, Knetsch, and Thaler 1990). A class is divided into two groups. Some participants, called *sellers,* are given a decorated mug that they can keep, and are asked to indicate the lowest price for which they would be willing to sell the mug. A second group, called *choosers,* are asked to indicate the amount of money that they would find as attractive as the mug. Subjects in both groups are told that, after they state their price, an official market price $X will be revealed and that each subject will end up with a mug if his or her asking price exceeds $X, or with $X if it is more than the subject's asking price.

Notice that the choosers and the sellers are facing precisely the same decision problem: they will all end up with either some money or a mug, and in effect need to decide how much money they will be willing to take in place of the mug. Hence, standard economic analysis predicts identical asking prices for the two groups. The two groups, however, evaluate the mug from different perspectives: the choosers compare receiving a mug to receiving a sum of money, whereas the sellers compare retaining the mug to giving up the mug in exchange for money. Thus, the mug is evaluated as a potential gain by the choosers and as a loss by the sellers. Consequently, loss aversion, the notion that losses loom larger than corresponding gains, predicts that the sellers will price the mug higher than the choosers. This prediction was confirmed by the data: the median price of the sellers ($7.12) was more than twice as large as the median price for the choosers ($3.12). The difference between these prices reflects an endowment effect, which was produced, instantaneously it seems, by endowing individuals with a mug.

A closely related manifestation of loss aversion is a general reluctance to trade, which is illustrated in the following study (Knetsch 1989). Subjects were divided into two groups: half the subjects were given a decorated mug, and the others were given a large bar of Swiss chocolate. Later, each subject was shown the alternative gift, and offered the opportunity to trade the gift they had received for the other. Because the initial allocation of gifts was arbitrary and the transaction was costless, economic theory predicts that about half the subjects should exchange their gifts. On the other hand, if losses loom larger than gains, then most participants will be reluctant to give up the gift in their possession (a loss) in order to obtain the other (a gain). Indeed, only 10 percent of the participants chose to trade their gifts. This result contrasts sharply with the 50 percent predicted by the standard economic analysis, in which the value of a good does not change when it becomes part of one's endowment.

More generally, loss aversion entails a strong tendency to maintain the status quo, because the disadvantages of departing from it loom larger than the advantages of its alternative. This phenomenon has been demonstrated in several experiments (Samuelson and Zeckhauser 1988). For example, subjects were given this problem: "You have inherited a large sum of money from your great uncle. You are considering different portfolios. Your choices are to invest in (1) a moderate-risk company, (2) a high-risk company, (3) treasury bills, (4) municipal bonds." Four groups of subjects were presented with the same problem, but with one of the four options designated as the status quo. One version, for example, included the statement: "A significant portion of the portfolio you inherited is invested in a moderate-risk company." The data show that designating a particular option as the status quo greatly increased the tendency to choose it (even though transaction costs were said to be insignificant). Although all four groups chose among the same options, subjects tended to stick with the option in which they were already invested.

A striking framing effect that relies on people's tendency to maintain the status quo has been observed in the context of real-world insurance decisions. New Jersey and Pennsylvania have recently introduced the option of a limited right to sue, which entitles automobile drivers to lower insurance rates. The two states differ, however, in what they offer consumers as the default option. New Jersey motorists have to acquire the full right to sue (transaction costs are minimal: one need only sign), whereas in Pennsylvania the full right to sue is the default. When offered the choice, only about 20 percent of New Jersey drivers chose to acquire the full right to sue, but approximately 75 percent of Pennsylvania drivers chose to retain it. The difference in adoption rates due to the different frames had financial repercussions that are estimated at around $200 million (Johnson, Hershey, Meszaros, and Kunreuther 1993).

Recall that loss aversion gives rise to a value function with a steeper slope in the negative than in the positive domain. Beyond the reluctance to depart from the status quo, this result implies that the same difference between two options will be given greater weight when it is viewed as a difference between two disadvantages, or losses (relative to a reference point) than when it is viewed as a difference between two advantages, or gains. This prediction is demonstrated in a study in which subjects compare a combination of a small gain and a small loss with a combination of a larger gain and a larger loss (Tversky and Kahneman 1991). Subjects are asked to suppose that they are looking for employment while their present training job is ending. They are asked to consider two alternative jobs that are like their present job in all respects except for the amount of social contact and the daily commuting time. The relevant information is summarized in the table below. Subjects are divided into two groups: one group is told that they presently hold job A, the second group is told they presently hold job B. Both groups are then asked to choose between job X and job Y. Because their current jobs are said to be ending, maintaining the status quo is not an option.

	Social Contact	*Daily Travel Time*
Present Job A	isolated for long stretches	10 min.
Job X	limited contact with others	20 min.
Job Y	moderately sociable	60 min.
Present Job B	much pleasant social interaction	80 min.

Notice that both X and Y are better than A and worse than B with respect to social contact, and both are worse than A and better than B in terms of commuting time. According to standard economic analysis, the choice between X and Y should not depend on the decision maker's current reference point. On the other hand, if subjects treat their present job as a reference point and if disadvantages relative to this reference point loom larger than corresponding advantages, then subjects are more likely to choose the job with the smaller disadvantage relative to their current job. Thus, subjects who currently hold job A are expected to favor job X, whereas subjects who currently hold job B are expected to favor job Y. The data confirm this expectation: more than two-thirds of subjects in each group chose the predicted option.

Loss aversion, or the asymmetry between the evaluation of gains and losses, emerges as an important empirical generalization that has implications for a wide range of decisions. It promotes stability rather than change by inducing people to maintain their current position. A loss-averse individual at position X would be reluctant to switch to position Y, even though, were she at position Y, she would be reluctant to switch to X. Along these lines, the reluctance to change induced by loss aversion can hinder the negotiated resolution of disputes. If each side to a dispute evaluates the opponent's concessions as gains and its own concessions as losses, then agreement will be hard to reach because each side will perceive itself as relinquishing more than it stands to gain. A skillful mediator may facilitate agreement by framing concessions as bargaining chips rather than as losses.

3.5 Eliciting Preference

Preferences can be elicited by different methods. People can be asked to indicate which option they prefer; alternatively, they can be asked to price each option by stating the amount of money that is as valuable to them as that option. A standard assumption, known as *procedure invariance*, demands that logically equivalent elicitation procedures should give rise to the same preference order. Thus, if one option is chosen over another, it is also expected to be priced higher. Procedure invariance is essential for interpreting both psychological and physical measurement. For example, the ordering of physical objects with respect to mass can be established either by placing each object separately on a scale, or by placing both objects on two sides of a pan balance. Procedure invariance requires that the two methods yield the same ordering, within the limit of measurement error. Analogously, the rational theory of choice assumes that an individual has a well-defined preference order that can be elicited either by choice or by pricing. These alternative methods of elicitation, in turn, should give rise to the same ordering of options.

3.5.1 Compatibility Effects

Despite its appeal as an abstract principle, people sometimes violate procedure invariance. For example, people often choose one bet over another, but price the second bet above the first. In one study, subjects were presented with two prospects of similar expected value. One prospect, the H bet, offered a high probability to win a relatively small payoff (for example, 8 chances in 9 to win $4) whereas the other prospect, the L bet, offered a low probability to win a larger payoff (for example, a 1 in 9 chance to win $40). When asked to choose between these prospects, most subjects chose the H bet over the L bet. Subjects were also asked, on another occasion, to price each prospect by indicating the smallest amount of money for which they would be willing to sell this prospect. Here, most subjects assigned a higher price to the L bet than to the H bet. One recent study that used this pair of bets observed that 71 percent of the subjects chose the H bet, and 67 percent priced L above H (Tversky, Slovic, and Kahneman 1990). This phenomenon, called *preference reversal,* has been observed in numerous experiments using a variety of prospects and incentive schemes. It has also been observed among professional gamblers in a Las Vegas casino (Slovic and Lichtenstein 1983).

What is the cause of preference reversal? Why do people assign a higher monetary value to the low-probability bet, but choose the high-probability bet more often? It appears that the major cause of preference reversal is a differential weighting of probability and payoff in choice and pricing, induced by the required response. In particular, experimental evidence indicates that an attribute of an option is given more weight when it is compatible with the response format than when it is not (Tversky, Sattath, and Slovic 1988). This account suggests that because the price that the subject assigns to a bet is expressed in dollars, the payoffs of the bet, which are also expressed in dollars, will be weighted more heavily in pricing than in choice. As a consequence, the L bet (which has the higher payoff) is evaluated more favorably in pricing than in choice, which can give rise to preference reversals. This account has been supported by the observation that the incidence of preference reversals was greatly reduced for bets involving nonmonetary outcomes, such as a free dinner at a local restaurant, where the outcomes and the subjects' prices are no longer expressed in the same units and are therefore less compatible (Slovic, Griffin, and Tversky 1990).

The compatibility hypothesis does not depend on the presence of risk. Indeed, it predicts a similar discrepancy between choice and pricing in the context of riskless options that have a monetary component. Consider a long-term prospect L, which pays $2,500 five years from now, and a short-term prospect S, which pays $1,600 in one and a half years. Subjects were invited to choose between L and S and to price both prospects by stating the smallest immediate cash payment for which they would be willing to exchange each prospect (Tversky, Slovic, and Kahneman 1990). Because the payoffs and the prices again are expressed in the same units, compatibility suggests that the long-term prospect (offering the higher payoff) will be overvalued in pricing relative to choice. In accord with this hypothesis, subjects chose the short-term prospect 74 percent of the time but priced the long-term prospect above the short-term prospect 75 percent of the time. These observations indicate that different methods of elicitation (for example, choice and pricing) can induce different weightings of attributes that in turn give rise to preference reversals.

3.5.2 Relative Prominence

Another psychological mechanism that leads to violations of procedure invariance involves the notion of relative prominence. In many cases, people agree that one attribute (for instance, safety) is more important than another (such as cost). Although the interpretation of such claims is not entirely clear, there is evidence that the attribute that is judged more important looms larger in choice than in pricing (Tversky, Sattath, and Slovic 1988). This is the *prominence hypothesis*. To illustrate this notion, consider two programs designed to reduce the number of fatalities due to traffic accidents, characterized by the expected reduction in the number of casualties and an estimated cost. Because human lives are regarded as more important than money, the prominence hypothesis predicts that this dimension will be given more weight in choice than in pricing. When given a choice between programs X and Y below, the great majority of respondents favored X, the more expensive program that saves more lives.

	Expected number of casualties	*Cost*
Program X	500	$55 million
Program Y	570	$12 million

However, when the cost of one of the programs is removed and subjects are asked to determine the missing cost so as to make the two programs equally attractive, nearly all subjects assign values that imply a preference for Y, the less expensive program that saves fewer lives. For example, when the cost of program X is removed, the median estimate of the missing cost that renders the two programs equally attractive is $40 million. This choice implies that at $55 million, program X should not be chosen over program Y, contrary to the aforementioned choice. Thus, the prominent attribute (saving lives) dominates the choice but not the pricing. This discrepancy suggests that different public policies will be supported depending on whether people are asked which policy they prefer or how much, in their opinion, each policy ought to cost.

Further applications of the prominence hypothesis were reported in a study of people's response to environmental problems (Kahneman and Ritov 1993). Several pairs of issues were selected, where one issue involves human health or safety and the other protection of the environment. Each issue includes a brief statement of a problem, along with a suggested form of intervention, as illustrated.

> *Problem*: Skin cancer from sun exposure is common among farm workers.
> *Intervention*: Support free medical checkups for threatened groups.
>
> *Problem*: Several Australian mammal species are nearly wiped out by hunters.
> *Intervention*: Contribute to a fund to provide safe breeding areas for these species.

One group of subjects was asked to choose which of the two interventions they would rather support; a second group of subjects was presented with one issue at a time and asked to determine the largest amount they would be willing to pay for the respective intervention. Because the treatment of cancer in human beings is generally viewed as more important than the protection of Australian mammals, the prominence hypothesis predicts that the former will receive greater support in direct choice than in independent evaluation. This prediction was confirmed. When asked to evaluate each intervention separately, subjects, who might have been moved by these animals' plight, were willing to pay more, on average, for safe breeding of Australian mammals than for free checkups for skin cancer. When faced with a direct choice between these options, however, most subjects favored free checkups for humans over safe breeding for mammals. Thus, people may evaluate one alternative more positively than another when each is evaluated independently, but then reverse their evaluation when the alternatives are directly compared, which accentuates the prominent attribute.

3.5.3 Weighing Pros and Cons

Consider having to choose one of two options or, alternatively, having to reject one of two options. Under the assumption of procedure invariance, the two tasks are interchangeable. In binary choice it should not matter whether people are asked which option they prefer, or which they would reject: if people prefer the first they should reject the second, and vice versa. In line with the notion of compatibility, however, we may expect that the positive features of options (their pros) will loom larger when choosing, whereas the negative features of options (their cons) will be weighted more heavily when rejecting. It is natural to select an option because of its positive features, and to reject an option because of its negative features.

This account leads to the following prediction: Imagine two options, an "enriched" option, with many positive and many negative features, and an "impoverished" option, with few positive and few negative features. If positive features are weighed more heavily when choosing than when rejecting and negative features are weighed more heavily when rejecting than when choosing, then an enriched option could be both chosen and rejected more frequently than an impoverished option. Consider, for example, the following problem, which was presented to subjects in two versions that differed only in the bracketed questions (Shafir 1993). Half the subjects received one version, the other half received the other.

Problem 6 ($N = 170$)
Imagine that you serve on the jury of an only-child sole-custody case following a relatively messy divorce. The facts of the case are complicated by ambiguous economic, social, and emotional considerations, and you decide to base your decision entirely on the following few observations. [To which parent would you award sole custody of the child? / To which parent would you deny sole custody of the child?]

		Award	*Deny*
Parent A	average income average health average working hours reasonable rapport with the child relatively stable social life	[36%]	[45%]
Parent B	above-average income very close relationship with the child extremely active social life lots of work-related travel minor health problems	[64%]	[55%]

Parent A, the impoverished option, is quite plain—with no striking positive or negative features. There are no particularly compelling reasons to award or deny this parent custody of the child. Parent B, the enriched option, on the other hand, has good reasons to be awarded custody (a very close relationship with the child and a good income), but also good reasons to be denied sole custody (health problems and extensive absences due to travel). To the right of the options are the percentages of subjects who chose to award and to deny custody to each of the parents. Parent B is the majority choice both for being awarded custody of the child and for being denied it, presumably because this parent provides more compelling reasons both to be awarded as well as denied child custody. As a result, the child is significantly more likely to end up with parent B when we ask whom to award custody to than when we contemplate whom to deny. This discrepancy represents another violation of procedure invariance, in which two logically equivalent tasks give rise to predictably different choices.

3.6 Choice under Conflict

The rational theory of choice assumes that each alternative has a utility or subjective value for the decision maker. Given a set of options, the decision maker selects the alternative with the highest value. This principle of value maximization is routinely assumed in analyzing consumer choice. It implies that the preference between options cannot be reversed by the addition of new alternatives. If you prefer salmon to steak, for example, you should not select steak from a larger menu that includes salmon, unless, of course, other entrées provide some information about the quality of the steak or the salmon. Thus, a nonpreferred option cannot be made preferred by introducing new alternatives. Consequently, the "market share" of an option (that is, the proportion of people who select it) cannot be increased when new options are added. In particular, the proportion of people who choose the option to defer decision should not increase when additional alternatives become available.

Despite the simplicity and intuitive appeal of the principle above, there is evidence that people's preference between two options can depend on the presence or absence of a third alternative. The introduction of a third option can make the decision easier or harder to resolve and thus can affect preference and increase the tendency to defer choice. The making of decisions often creates conflict: we are not sure how to trade off one attribute relative to another or which option would benefit us most. When people are offered a single attractive option, there is little conflict and choice is easy; however, when two or more attractive options are available, each with its advantages and disadvantages, people often experience conflict, which may compel them to delay decision, maintain the status quo, or seek additional information.

The economist Thomas Schelling tells of an occasion on which he had decided to buy an encyclopedia for his children, and was presented at a bookstore with two attractive options. Finding it difficult to choose between them, he ended up buying neither, although had only one encyclopedia been available, he would have happily bought it. More generally, there are situations in which people prefer each of the available alternatives over the status quo but do not have a compelling reason for choosing among the alternatives and, as a result, defer the decision, perhaps indefinitely.

This phenomenon is demonstrated by this pair of problems, which were presented to two groups of students (Tversky and Shafir 1992b).

> *Problem 7* ($N = 121$), *Low Conflict*
> Suppose you are considering buying a compact disc (CD) player, and have not yet decided what model to buy. You pass by a store that is having a one-day clearance sale. They offer a popular SONY player for just $99, well below the list price. Do you?
>
> y. buy the SONY player [66%]
> z. wait until you learn more about the various models [34%]
>
> *Problem 8* ($N = 124$), *High Conflict*
> Suppose you are considering buying a compact disc (CD) player, and have not yet decided what model to buy. You pass by a store that is having a one-day clearance sale. They offer a popular SONY player for just $99, and a top-of-the-line AIWA player for just $169, both well below the list price. Do you?
>
> x. buy the AIWA player [27%]
> y. buy the SONY player [27%]
> z. wait until you learn more about the various models [46%]

The results indicate that people are more likely to buy a CD player in the former, *low conflict*, condition than in the latter, *high conflict*, situation. Both products—the AIWA and the SONY—seem attractive, both are well priced, and both are on a one-day sale. The decision maker needs to determine whether she is better off with a cheaper, popular product, or with a more expensive and sophisticated one. This conflict is not easy to resolve, and compels many subjects to put off the purchase until they learn more about the various products. On the other hand, when the SONY alone is available, there are compelling arguments for its purchase: it is a popular player, it is very well priced, and it is on sale for one day only. In this situation, a greater majority of subjects decide to opt for the CD player rather than delay the purchase.

Adding a competing alternative in the preceding example increased the tendency to delay decision. Adding an option can also have the opposite effect, as illustrated in this problem, in which the original AIWA player was replaced by an inferior model.

> *Problem 9* ($N = 62$), *Dominance*
> Suppose you are considering buying a compact disc (CD) player, and have not yet decided what model to buy. You pass by a store that is having a one-day clearance sale. They offer a popular SONY player for just $99, well below the list price, and an inferior AIWA player for the regular list price of $105. Do you?
>
> x′. buy the AIWA player [3%]
> y. buy the SONY player [73%]
> z. wait until you learn more about the various models [24%]

In this version, the AIWA player is dominated by the SONY: it is inferior in quality and costs more. Thus, the presence of the AIWA does not detract from the reasons for buying the SONY, it actually supplements them: the SONY is well priced, it is on sale for one day only, *and* it is clearly better than its competitor. As a result, in the presence of the inferior AIWA, the SONY is chosen more often. More generally, adding a dominated alternative tends to increase the market share of the dominating option (Huber, Payne, and Puto 1982), contrary to the prediction of value maximization.

In the scenario above, the added options (the superior CD player in one case and the inferior player in the other) may have conveyed some information about the consumer's chances of finding a better deal. This interpretation does not apply to the following demonstrations, in which there is no opportunity to learn about the options, and the decision cannot be delayed. One group of subjects ($N = 106$) was offered a choice between $6 and an elegant Cross pen. The pen was selected by 36 percent of the subjects, and the remaining 64 percent chose the cash. A second group ($N = 115$) was given a choice among three options: $6 in cash, the same Cross pen, and a second pen that was distinctly less attractive. Only 2 percent of the subjects chose the less attractive pen, but its presence increased the percentage of subjects who chose the Cross pen from 36 percent to 46 percent (Simonson and Tversky 1992). Students of marketing recount many instances of the phenomenon above in the marketplace. A common tactic used to induce consumers to purchase a given product is to introduce an inferior option that renders the product in question more attractive. For example, Williams-Sonoma, a mail-order and retail business located in San Francisco, used to offer a bread-baking appliance priced at $275. They then added a second bread-baking appliance, very similar to the first except that it was larger but could not bake whole-wheat bread. The new item was priced at $429, more than 50 percent higher than the original appliance. Not surprisingly, Williams-Sonoma did not sell many units of the new item, but the sales of the less-expensive appliance almost doubled.

The effect of added alternatives is not limited to decisions made by consumers. In one study (Redelmeier and Shafir 1995), 287 experienced physicians were presented with a description of a hypothetical patient suffering from chronic hip pain and about to be referred to orthopedics. Half the physicians were presented with a choice of whether or not to assign this patient a particular medication (Motrin); the other half were presented with two alternative medications (Motrin and Feldene). The proportion of physicians who refrained from assigning any new medication was 53 percent in the former group and 72 percent in the latter. Thus, the availability of a second medication reduced the tendency to assign either. Evidently, the difficulty of deciding which of the two medications was preferable led many physicians to avoid medication altogether.

The experimental evidence shows that, contrary to the principle of value maximization, the availability of additional alternatives can increase conflict and lead the decision maker to maintain the status quo, avoid the decision, or postpone it indefinitely. It is difficult to overestimate the significance of the tendency to delay decision. Many things never get done, not because one has chosen not to do them, but because the person has chosen not to do them *now*. The following demonstration illustrates this point. Students were offered $5 for answering and returning an assigned questionnaire by a given date. One group was given 5 days to complete the questionnaire, a second group was given 3 weeks, and a third group was given no definite deadline. The corresponding rates of return were 60 percent, 42 percent, and 25 percent. Thus, the more time students had to complete the task, the less likely they were to do it. Just as adding a second drug reduces the tendency to administer medication, so too can extending time reduce the likelihood of completing an assignment.

3.7 Discussion

In this chapter we have applied a number of psychological principles to the analysis of individual decision making. We have invoked the notion of diminishing sensitivity to derive the shape of the value function, which reflects people's evaluation of gains and losses. This function accounts for common observations of risk aversion in the domain of gains and risk seeking in the domain of losses. Because the same outcomes can sometimes be described either as gains or as losses, alternative framings of a decision problem can give rise to predictably different choices. We have also considered the principle of loss aversion, according to which losses have a greater impact than the corresponding gains. Loss aversion accounts for a wide range of findings, notably the reluctance to depart from the status quo.

Additional psychological principles were introduced to account for elicitation effects. We suggested that different attributes of options are weighted differently in choice and in pricing, and we invoked the notions of compatibility and prominence to explain the discrepancy between these procedures. Finally, we have appealed to considerations of conflict, or choice difficulty, to explain some effects of the addition of options and the tendency to defer decision.

The psychological principles discussed in this chapter do not form a unified theory, comparable to the rational theory of choice. However, they help explain a wide range of empirical findings that are incompatible with the rational theory. Recall that this theory assumes consistent preferences that satisfy description and procedure invariance. In contrast, the experimental evidence suggests that preferences are actually constructed, not merely revealed, in the elicitation process, and that these constructions depend on the framing of the problem, the method of elicitation, and the available set of options.

We have suggested that the rational theory of choice provides a better account of people's normative intuitions than of their actual behavior. When confronted with the fact that their choices violate dominance or description invariance, people typically wish to modify their behavior to conform with these principles of rationality. Evidently, people's choices are often at variance with their own normative intuitions. The tension between normative and descriptive theories of choice is analogous to the tension between normative and descriptive theories of ethics. A normative ethical account is concerned with the principles that underlie moral judgments. A descriptive ethical account, on the other hand, is concerned with actual human conduct. Both enterprises are essentially empirical; the first addresses people's intuitions, whereas the second focuses on their actual behavior. The two analyses, of course, are interrelated but they do not coincide. For example, people generally agree that one should abstain from lying and contribute to worthy causes, despite the fact they do not always do so. Similarly, people tend to accept the normative force of dominance and description invariance, even though these are often violated in their actual choices. Although the distinction between the normative and descriptive accounts is obvious in the study of ethics, it is somewhat controversial in the study of decision making. This difference may be due to the fact that it is easier to understand violations of ethical norms that stem from self-interest or lack of self-control, than violations of rational norms that stem from the nature of cognitive operations.

Suggestions for Further Reading

Elementary introductions to the field of behavioral decision theory include Bazerman (1992), Dawes (1988), Hogarth (1987), and Yates (1990). von Winterfeldt and Edwards (1986) is an introduction with more of an applied perspective, covering an area known as decision analysis. Thaler (1992) focuses on the role of behavioral theory in interpreting numerous economic anomalies. Shafir, Simonson, and Tversky (1993) consider the role of reasons in the making of decisions. For collections of primary articles relating behavioral decision theory to various domains of inquiry, ranging from economics and the law to engineering and philosophy, see Arkes and Hammond (1986), and Bell, Raiffa, and Tversky (1988). Recent reviews of the field are provided by Camerer (1995), Payne, Bettman, and Johnson (1992), and Slovic, Lichtenstein, and Fischhoff (forthcoming).

Problems

3.1 Show that the majority choice of options C and F in problem 3 is dominated by the unpopular combination of options D and E.

3.2 Consider this statistical information about the outcomes of two treatments for lung cancer—surgery and radiation therapy:

> Surgery: Of 100 people having surgery, 90 live through the postoperative period, 68 are alive at the end of the first year, and 34 are alive at the end of five years.
>
> Radiation therapy: Of 100 people having radiation therapy, all live through the treatment, 77 are alive at the end of one year, and 22 are alive at the end of five years.

Notice that the statistics above are presented in terms of survival rates. Now frame the statistical information about the outcomes above in terms of mortality rates. (Thus, if 68 of 100 are alive at the end of one year, that means 32 die by the end of one year, and so on) Do you have an intuition about whether people's preference between the treatments may differ between the survival and mortality frames, and in what direction?

Questions for Further Thought

3.1 It is suggested in the chapter that although the distinction between normative and descriptive accounts is obvious in the study of ethics, it remains controversial in the study of decision making. Why do you think that may be?

3.2 Loss aversion is shown to generate a strong tendency to maintain the status quo. This is called the "status quo bias," because it sometimes leads people to maintain the status quo in situations where otherwise it would not have been chosen. Can you think of situations in your life, or in that of someone close to you, that may have exhibited a status quo bias?

References

Arkes, H. R., and K. R. Hammond, eds. (1986). *Judgment and decision making*. New York: Cambridge University Press.

Bazerman, M. H. (1992). *Judgment in managerial decision making*. 2nd ed. New York: Wiley.

Bell, D. E., H. Raiffa, and A. Tversky, eds. (1988). *Decision making: Descriptive, normative, and prescriptive interactions.* New York: Cambridge University Press.

Camerer, C. F. (1995). Individual decision making. In J. H. Kagel and A. E. Roth, eds., *Handbook of experimental economics.* Princeton, NJ: Princeton University Press.

Dawes, R. M. (1988). *Rational choice in an uncertain world.* New York: Harcourt Brace Jovanovich.

Hogarth, R. M. (1987). *Judgment and choice.* 2nd ed. New York: Wiley.

Huber, J., J. W. Payne, and C. Puto (1982). Adding asymmetrically dominated alternatives: Violations of regularity and the similarity hypothesis. *Journal of Consumer Research* 9, 90–98.

Johnson, E. J., J. Hershey, J. Meszaros, and H. Kunreuther (1993). Framing, probability distortions, and insurance decisions. *Journal of Risk and Uncertainty* 7, 35–51.

Kahneman, D., J. L. Knetsch, and R. Thaler (1990). Experimental tests of the endowment effect and the Coase theorem. *Journal of Political Economy* 98, 6, 1325–1348.

Kahneman, D., and I. Ritov (1993). Determinants of stated willingness to pay for public goods: A study in the headline method. Working paper, University of California, Berkeley.

Kahneman, D., and A. Tversky (1979). Prospect theory: An analysis of decision under risk. *Econometrica* 47, 263–291.

Knetsch, J. L. (1989). The endowment effect and evidence of nonreversible indifference curves. *American Economic Review* 79, 1277–1284.

McNeil, B. J., S. G. Pauker, H. C. Sox, and A. Tversky (1982). On the elicitation of preferences for alternative therapies. *New England Journal of Medicine* 306, 1259–1262.

Payne, J. W., J. R. Bettman, and E. J. Johnson (1992). Behavioral decision research: A constructive process perspective. *Annual Review of Psychology* 43, 87–131.

Redelmeier, D., and E. Shafir (1995). Medical decision making in situations that offer multiple alternatives. *Journal of the American Medical Association* 273, 4, 302–305.

Samuelson, W., and R. Zeckhauser (1988). Status quo bias in decision making. *Journal of Risk and Uncertainty* 1, 7–59.

Shafir, E. (1993). Choosing versus rejecting: Why some options are both better and worse than others. *Memory and Cognition* 21, 4, 546–556.

Shafir, E., P. Diamond, and A. Tversky (1994). On money illusion. Manuscript, Princeton University.

Shafir, E., I. Simonson, and A. Tversky (1993). Reason-based choice. *Cognition* 49, 2, 11–36.

Simonson, I., and A. Tversky (1992). Choice in context: Tradeoff contrast and extremeness aversion. *Journal of Marketing Research* 29, 281–295.

Slovic, P., D. Griffin, and A. Tversky (1990). Compatibility effects in judgment and choice. In R. Hogarth, ed., *Insights in decision making: Theory and applications,* pp. 5–27. Chicago: University of Chicago Press.

Slovic, P., and S. Lichtenstein (1983). Preference reversals: A broader perspective. *American Economic Review* 73, 596–605.

Slovic, P., S. Lichtenstein, and B. Fischhoff (forthcoming). Decision making. In R. C. Atkinson, R. J. Herrnstein, G. Lindzey, and R. D. Luce, eds., *Steven's handbook of experimental psychology.* 2nd ed. New York: Wiley.

Thaler, R. (1992). *The winner's curse: Paradoxes and anomalies of economic life.* New York: The Free Press.

Tversky, A., and D. Kahneman (1981). The framing of decisions and the psychology of choice. *Science* 211, 453–458.

Tversky, A., and D. Kahneman (1986). Rational choice and the framing of decisions. *Journal of Business* 59, 4, pt. 2, 251–278.

Tversky, A., and D. Kahneman (1991). Loss aversion in riskless choice: A reference dependent model. *Quarterly Journal of Economics* (November), 1039–1061.

Tversky, A., and D. Kahneman (1992). Advances in prospect theory: Cumulative representation of uncertainty. *Journal of Risk and Uncertainty* 5, 297–323.

Tversky, A., S. Sattath, and P. Slovic (1988). Contingent weighting in judgment and choice. *Psychological Review* 95, 3, 371–384.

Tversky, A., and E. Shafir (1992a). The disjunction effect in choice under uncertainty. *Psychological Science* 3, 5, 305–309.

Tversky, A., and E. Shafir (1992b). Choice under conflict: The dynamics of deferred decision. *Psychological Science* 3, 6, 358–361.

Tversky, A., P. Slovic, and D. Kahneman (1990). The causes of preference reversal. *American Economic Review* 80, 204–217.

von Winterfeldt, D., and W. Edwards (1986). *Decision analysis and behavioral research.* Cambridge: Cambridge University Press.

Yates, J. F. (1990). *Judgment and decision making.* Englewood Cliffs, NJ: Prentice-Hall.

Chapter 4
Continuity and Discontinuity in Cognitive Development

Susan Carey

4.1 Introduction

A theory of cognitive development must include both a *descriptive* component and an *explanatory* component. Descriptively, we must characterize the child's conceptual resources at any point and note how these change with age. Insofar as there are changes, the explanatory problem is to characterize the maturational and learning mechanisms causing them.

Here I focus on the descriptive problem—how do young children differ from older children cognitively? Many students of language acquisition and cognitive development argue that the *continuity hypothesis* should be the default, to be defeated only in the face of extraordinary evidence (for example, Pinker 1984; Macnamara 1982). The continuity hypothesis is that young children do *not* differ from adults cognitively in any fundamental way. People who accept the continuity hypothesis agree that young children know less than adults on just about every imaginable topic, but argue that this imbalance is no different from one adult's knowing less than another does about some particular matter.

To even begin exploring the continuity hypothesis, we have to agree on what it means for the child to differ from us in *fundamental* ways. Usually, this is taken to mean that the child lacks some logical or representational capacities that the adult has. To endorse the continuity hypothesis is to assume that the infant has the logical and conceptual resources to represent his or her world as do adults. The continuity hypothesis denies stage changes of the sort envisioned by Piaget. If children's representations are continuous with those of adults, it cannot be that babies' representations are sensory-motor, whereas adults' are conceptual, or that preschool children are incapable of logical thought.

Of course, whether the continuity hypothesis is true or not is an empirical question, and to examine it, one must entertain possibilities as to what types of discontinuities *could* occur in the course of development. If evidence for discontinuities is found, several further questions are then licensed, including what processes cause the change—a maturational process or some kind of learning process by which new representational resources are constructed. A second question is the role of culture in the change. That is, are the new representational resources culturally constructed, and then mastered by each new generation of individual children, or are they constructed by each child independently as he or she interacts with the world?

This chapter is a case study of the continuity hypothesis in the domain of number concepts, as expressed by the integers of the standard counting sequence, "one, two, three ..." and in the expression of number in natural-language syntax. The chapter breaks into three subcases, in two of which evidence is presented for discontinuous changes in representational capacity.

The first subcase concerns a strong version of the continuity hypothesis put forward by Gelman and Gallistel (1978). Gelman and Gallistel have since modified their position (for example, see Gallistel and Gelman 1992; Gallistel 1990). However, I will explore the original Gelman and Gallistel proposal because it is a serious empirical possibility, an examination of which allows us to see what the issues of continuity come to.

4.2 Case 1: Natural-Language Counting Words. The Gelman/Gallistel Continuity Hypothesis and Empirical Evidence Against It

4.2.1 Background: Prelinguistic Representations of Number

There are now many demonstrations that, in at least some situations, both animals and preverbal human babies can base responses on number of objects or events. The animal studies most typically require that the animal make some fixed number of responses to get a reward. To give just one example, a rat may be trained to press one lever a fixed number of times before switching to a second one to be rewarded. Rats can learn to do this act, and have been shown to discriminate numbers up to 49 (the highest that has been tried so far). It is clear that it is number that is being tracked, rather than some other property of the lever pressing correlated with number (such as length of time, amount of effort), because after the behavior has been learned, the levers can be changed in various ways that will change all other parameters of the task. That is, the trial can be arranged so that it is now much harder to press the lever, so that pressing it 49 times will take much longer, and much more effort. The animal still presses 49 times before switching, or 15 times if it has been trained to press 15 times, or as many times as it has been rewarded for (see Gallistel 1990 for an extensive review of studies of animal representations of number).

These studies require keeping the animals very hungry, and highly motivated to learn to get the food. Thousands of trials are required to train the animals. Obviously, these methods cannot be used with human infants.

Research with infants requires a very sensitive, noninvasive measure of how they are representing the world. Over the past fifteen years or so, such a method has been developed and is now very widely used. It relies on babies' ability to control what they attend to. The basic idea is simple. Under most circumstances babies will look longer at what is unfamiliar or unexpected than at what is familiar or expected. Researchers use this fact to diagnose how the baby represents some situation, especially what the baby considers surprising given his or her current state of knowledge.

The two types of studies using this methodology show that babies represent number, at least small numbers from one to three or four. In the first type, babies are simply presented with arrays containing a fixed number of objects, say two of them, one after the other. For example, two cups, followed by two shoes, two bottles, two hats, two pens, and so on. A particular pair of objects is not repeated, and so the arrays have nothing in common but twoness. The baby's looking is monitored. After a while, the baby's attention to each new array decreases, relative to his or her looking time for the first arrays. The baby is getting bored. After looking time has decreased to half its original level, the baby is presented with an array containing one object, or three objects. In both cases, looking time recovers to its original level. The baby notices the difference between two objects, on the one hand, and a single object or three objects, on the other (Starkey and Cooper 1980). A similar result has also been attained with neonates (Antell and Keating 1983).

A second source of evidence that babies represent number derives from data showing that babies can add and subtract. Wynn (1992a) showed 4-month-olds events as in figure 4.1. An object was placed on an empty stage while the baby watched and then a screen was raised that covered

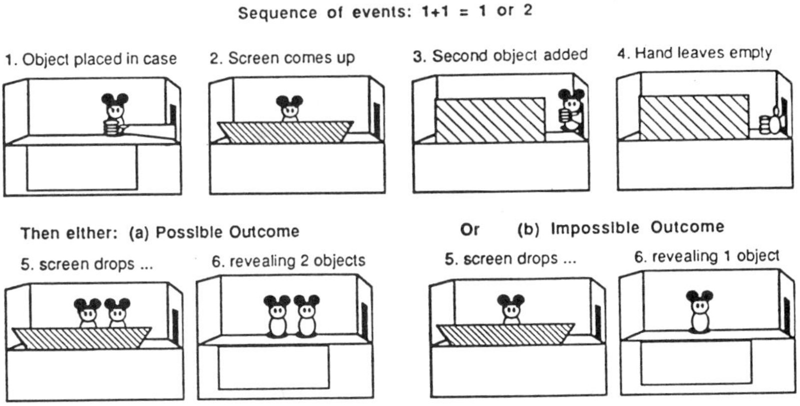

Figure 4.1

the object. A hand carrying a second object was shown going behind the screen and returning empty. The screen was then lowered, revealing either one object (the unexpected outcome, even though that was what the baby had last seen) or two objects (expected outcome, if the baby knows $1 + 1 = 2$). Babies looked longer at the unexpected outcome of one object.

A further experiment showed that babies expected exactly two objects, rather than simply more than one object. In this study, the expected outcome was two objects, as before, but the unexpected outcome was three objects. Again, babies were bored at seeing two objects, and looked longer at the unexpected outcome of three objects.

In sum, there must be some nonlinguistic representation of number; both babies and animals are sensitive to the number of objects and events in their environment.

4.2.2 The Gelman/Gallistel Continuity Hypothesis

At issue, of course, is *how* animals and babies represent number. Gelman and Gallistel (1978) suggested that they establish numerical representations through a counting procedure that works as follows. There is a mentally represented list of symbols &, ~, ∧, *, #. . . . (Of course, we do not know what such symbols might actually be. Given the animal work, the list must be at least 49 items long.) Gelman and Gallistel (1978) dubbed these mentally represented symbols "numerons." Entities to be counted are put in 1–1 correspondence with items on this list, always proceeding in the same order through the list. The number of items in the set being counted is represented by the last item on the list reached, its numerical value determined by the ordinal position of that item in the list. For example, in the list above, "~" represents 2, because "~" is the second item in the list.

This system for representing number should be very familiar to you, for it is exactly how natural languages represent number. This is why the Gelman/Gallistel numeron list hypothesis (hereafter, "the numeron list hypothesis") for nonlinguistic representations of numbers is a paradigm example of continuity over development; the baby's representational system is hypothesized to be exactly the same as the adult's. Learning to count in English, in this view, involves identifying the relevant list ("one, two, . . .") and mapping it to the list of numerons. Learning to count does not require constructing any new types of mental representations.

4.2.3 Evidence for the Numeron List Hypothesis

All natural languages with words for numbers exploit a representational system exactly like the numeron list. For example, in English, the list is "1,

2, 3, 4. . . ." Even languages that employ body-part words as a mnemonic aid to ordering the symbols in the proper sequence (for example, "finger, wrist, elbow, shoulder . . ." might be the words for "one" through "four") employ the same counting principles to establish a numerical representation of a set. This is the technique that would be expected on the continuity hypothesis, because natural languages are merely expressing verbally the system of representation all complex animals, including human beings, are hypothesized to share.

Gelman and Gallistel's major source of evidence for the numeron list hypothesis was their research on very young children (ages 2 to 4) learning to count. They showed that from the very beginning of learning to count, children honor 1–1 correspondence. That is, they attempt to count each item in the set to be enumerated once and only once. And, even if they have not yet mastered the *standard* count list (for example, they might count "one, two, four, seven, eleven . . ."), they always use their *nonstandard* sequence in the same order, emphasizing the last word in the count. All this is consistent with the hypothesis that young children have identified the English counting list as corresponding to the list of numerons, and their knowledge of how to use the numerons to establish a representation of number is guiding their use of the English counting words. The most surprising piece of evidence was the (extremely rare) phenomenon of some children responding to "How many?" by counting with the wrong list: "a, b, c . . ." or "Monday, Tuesday, Wednesday. . . ."

These data are exactly what is expected on the Gelman/Gallistel continuity hypothesis, according to which a nonlinguistic system of numerons is guiding the search for the corresponding list in language, and, once identified, guiding the child in its use. But it is also possible that the early activity of counting is a meaningless game, like patty-cake. Other data support the latter possibility. These data suggest that for about a year children engage in the activity of counting without understanding that the activity of counting "two, three, four" results in a representation of the number of items in the set.

4.2.4 Problems for the Numeron List Hypothesis

Consider first a phenomenon we could call the "recount phenomenon." After children have counted the items in a small array (say, three items), if the experimenter asks how many there were, the child recounts, rather than merely saying "3." Indeed, a 2-year-old will recount as many times as asked, "How many?" This is the behavior that is expected if this question is merely a prompt to engage in this (for the child) meaningless game. This is not a decisive observation, however—after all, the child may suppose he or she must have made a mistake. Otherwise, why is the adult asking again how many there are?

Two other observations confirm that very young counters do not know the numerical meanings of the words in the count sequence. First, if given a pile of objects, and asked to give the adult "two" or "three" or any other number the child can use in the game of counting, most $2\frac{1}{2}$ to $3\frac{1}{2}$-year-olds fail (Wynn 1990, 1992b). Instead the child grabs a random number of objects and hands them to the experimenter. Also, shown two cards, one depicting, for example, two balloons and the other three balloons, and asked to indicate which one has two balloons on it, the child responds at chance. Of course *some* children between ages $2\frac{1}{2}$ and $3\frac{1}{2}$ succeed at these tasks, but these are the children who do not show the recount phenomenon. Rather, these children simply provide the numeral that answers the question, "How many?" when they have just completed a count of a small array. That is, analysis of within-child consistency on these three tasks bolsters the conclusion that young children count for more than a year before they learn what the words in the count sequence *mean*.

There is one more observation of Wynn's that is important to our evaluation of the Gelman/Gallistel continuity hypothesis. Wynn (1990, 1992b) showed that from the beginning of learning to count, children know what "one" means. They can pick *one* object from a pile when asked, and they correctly distinguish a card with "one fish" from a card with "three fish." Further, they know that the other words in the count sequence contrast with one. They always grab a random number of objects greater than one, when asked to hand over "two, three, four ..." objects, and they also successfully point to a card with three fish when it is contrasted with a card with one, even though their choices are random when three is contrasted with two.

The following conclusions can be drawn from this brief empirical review. First, toddlers identify the English count list as relevant to number very early on (younger than age $2\frac{1}{2}$). They know what "one" means and they know that "two, three, four, etc." contrast with "one" and refer to numbers greater than one. They are in this state of knowledge for a full year before they work out how the English count system represents number, that is, before they work out the principle that allows them to determine which number each numeral refers to. But this state of affairs is impossible on the continuity hypothesis: according to this hypothesis, the English count list need only be identified and mapped onto the preexisting nonlinguistic count list, which the infant already uses to represent number.

Let me sum up the argument so far. Some nonlinguistic representation of number must underlie animal and human babies' capacity to respond on the basis of the number of bar presses, or the number of objects in an array. However, there must be some kind of discontinuity between this nonlinguistic representational system and that expressed in natural languages. What might this gap be?

4.2.5 What Kind of Representational Change Might Be Required for Children to Learn the Natural-Language Counting System?

Since Gelman and Gallistel's seminal 1978 book, a model for animals' way of representing number has been proposed by Meck and Church (1983; see Gallistel 1990, for a review of the evidence supporting the Meck and Church model). Meck and Church propose that animals represent number with an analog representational system. The idea is simple—suppose the nervous system has the equivalent of a pulse generator that generates activity at a constant rate, and a gate that can open to allow energy through to an accumulator that registers how much has been let through. When the animal is in a counting mode, the gate is opened for a fixed amount of time (say 200 msec) for each item to be counted. The total energy accumulated will then be an analog representation of number.

The Meck and Church accumulator model serves as a worked-out example of a representational system that is qualitatively different from that expressed in natural languages. In the accumulator model, number is represented by a physical magnitude that is a function of the number of items enumerated, rather than by a list of discrete symbols. In such an analog system, the animal or child does not have to learn *which* number a given state of the accumulator represents because it is an analog mechanism in which its state is a direct linear function of number. If the Church and Meck model captures how nonverbal babies represent number, then mastering natural-language count systems *does* require constructing a new representational resource. Specifically, the child must internalize a system for representing number based on a list of symbols. And the child must learn *which* number the word "two" represents, must learn the rule relating ordinal position in the list and cardinal value of the numeral. The demand from language of expressing each number as a distinct symbol forces construction of a representational system very different from the Church and Meck accumulator model.

I am not claiming that we know for sure that babies represent number with an accumulator system, and that the reason it takes children a full year to learn how natural-language count systems work is that they must construct a qualitatively different representational system. Rather, I offer this case study as an example of a *possible* discontinuity during development, with a specific proposal explaining how the new representational system might differ from the original one. If this account is right, it is most likely to be an example in which the new representational system was culturally constructed, and then mastered by each child as he or she came into contact with the cultural construction. Very interesting further questions remain, such as what mathematical ideas are facilitated by the natural-language count system (infinity, perhaps), and what further representational resources are culturally constructed in the development of mathematics.

4.3 Case 2: Sortal Concepts

As we noted above, the first number word children learn is "one." This is no accident; we cannot count unless we have a way of dividing the world into individuals, and "one" represents a concept closely related to *individual*. The syntax of most world languages marks the distinction between individuated entities and nonindividuated entities; nominal systems distinguish between count nouns (entities that can be counted, such as "table"), and mass nouns (entities that cannot be counted directly, such as "dirt." Notice that we can say "a table, one table, two tables . . . , but not "*a dirt, *one dirt, *two dirts . . ."). The distinction between one and more than one is also commonly marked in syntax as the distinction between singular and plural entities, and of course, only count nouns can be pluralized. Thus, the concept of "one" is fundamental to the syntax of the world's languages and, we might imagine, central to the human conceptual system.

The concept of "one" is at the core of a radical proposal for *noncontinuity* during conceptual development. Quine, an influential modern philosopher, and Piaget, the pioneer in empirical study of cognitive development, have both speculated that the infant's representations of the world are formulated over a perceptual quality space (Quine) or sensorimotor representational system (Piaget). According to these proposals, the baby can register sensory information (colors, shapes), but initially is not capable of formulating any representations with the properties of adult concepts such as *object, dog, table.*

To understand these proposals, we first must explore the properties of adult concepts such as these. Count nouns, such as "object, dog, table . . ." express what philosophers call *sortal concepts*. Sortal concepts provide criteria for individuation (telling where one entity ends and another begins) and identity (sameness in the sense of "same one"). To see the logical role sortals play in our thought, first consider that we cannot simply count what is in this room. Before we begin counting, we must be told what to count. We must supply a sortal (we can count the tables, the dogs, the legs . . .). Next, consider whether a given entity is the same one as we saw before. Again, we must be supplied a sortal to trace identity. When a person dies, that person ceases to exist, but his or her body continues to exist. And so the question of "same one" will receive different answers if posed "same person" or "same body." Both Piaget and Quine claim that the baby lacks the logical resources to represent any sortal concepts. That is, the baby has no capabilities for individuating objects, or for tracing identity over time.

If this claim were correct, it certainly provides us with a case of a radical discontinuity. Seeing the world in terms of enduring objects, individuated from one another, and whose identities can be traced through time, is deeply engrained in human language and thought. This conceptual capacity is required for understanding the count/mass distinction, because it is a distinction between individuated and nonindividuated entities. The quantifiers of natural languages (words like "a, another, one, more, many ...") express concepts related to how entities are individuated. Quine puts his proposal in a way that may be difficult for us to understand, but bear with me and think about it. *If* a radical discontinuity between the baby's representational system and ours exists, it *should* be difficult for us to conceive of how the baby is conceptualizing the world.

Quine's proposal is that the ontology that underlies language is a cultural construction. "Our conceptual firsts are middle-sized, middle-distanced objects, and our introduction to them and to everything comes midway in the cultural evolution of the race" (Quine 1960, 5). Here Quine is granting that we see the world in terms of ordinary objects, but is claiming that the capacity to do so has been constructed culturally, just as natural-language counting sequences were constructed culturally. Before the child has mastered this cultural construction, its conceptual universe consists of representations of histories of sporadic encounters, a scattered portion of what goes on. Quine speculates as to the representations underlying the toddler's uses of the words "water, red," and "Mama." "His first learning of the three words is uniformly a matter of learning how much of what goes on about him counts as the mother, or as red, or as water. It is not for the child to say in the first case, 'Hello, Mama again,' in the second case 'Hello, another red thing,' and in the third case, 'Hello, more water.' They are all on a par: Hello, more Mama, more red, more water" (Quine 1960, 92). The child masters the notion of an object, and of particular kinds of objects, in the course of getting the hang of what Quine calls "divided reference" (the capacity to refer to individuals of a kind). The child achieves this capacity, in Quine's view, through the process of mastering quantifiers and words like "same." "The contextual learning of these various particles goes on simultaneously, we may suppose, so that they are gradually adjusted to one another and a coherent pattern of usage is evolved matching that of one's elders. This is a major step in acquiring the conceptual scheme that we all know so well. For it is on achieving this step, and only then, that there can be any general talk of objects as such" (Quine 1969, 9–10). And in another place he finishes the same idea with a bootstrapping metaphor, underlining the degree of conceptual change he thinks is occurring: "The child scrambles up an intellectual chimney, supporting himself against each side by pressure against the others" (Quine 1960, 93). Quine also states that once the child has mastered the notion of an object, and got the trick of divided reference, he goes back and reanalyzes "Mama," so that it is now the name of a unique, enduring person.

brains designed to see this

why universal

obj thru time

same color not a phys. given

These quotations from Quine introduce two parts of his proposal. First, they give a sense of how he thinks the baby's representational resources differ from the adult's—the baby sees the world in terms of exemplars of sensory experiences. Second, they give a feel for how he thinks the baby's conceptual scheme comes to match that of adults—through learning the schemes for individuation that are expressed in the quantificational systems of human languages.

Quine's view of the baby's world can be schematized as follows. Imagine a portion of bottle experience that we adults would conceptualize as a single bottle. Babies do not conceptualize this as a single bottle. Rather, they respond to an instance of bottle*ness* or bottle*hood*. Babies can learn many things about bottlehood; for instance, he or she can come to associate bottlehood with milk, or with the word "bottle." Now imagine a portion of bottle experience that we would conceptualize as three bottles. The infant would also expect to obtain milk (indeed, more milk) from this bottleness and could also refer to it with the word "bottle." Notice that shape is important to the identification of bottlehood, just as the shape of the individual grains is important for distinguishing rice from spaghetti from macaroni. Similarly, even if Mama is a scattered portion of what goes on, shape is important for distinguishing Mamaness from Roverness or from Papaness. That shape is important for distinguishing what scattered portion of experience constitutes bottlehood does not mean that the baby is capable of representing "a bottle," "two bottles," or "the same bottle I had yesterday."

Representations of shapes presuppose representations of individuals that have those shapes, which might seem to imply that Quine's proposal (at least as construed above) is incoherent. It is not. Please dwell on the spaghetti, macaroni case. It's true that if the contrast between the two types of stuff is based on the shape differences of individual pieces, then some representation of those individual pieces must enter into the representation of *shape*. But our concepts of spaghetti and macaroni (and the words "spaghetti," "macaroni") do not pick out those individuals. Rather, our concepts focus on the stuff, and in English these are mass nouns. We talk about "some macaroni, some more macaroni" not "one macaroni, many macaronis." (This construal of macaroni and spaghetti is not necessary; in Italian these are count nouns.) Similarly, we can represent the shape of a scattered portion of sand, arranged, for example, into an S, and when we refer to it as "a portion" or "an S" we are focusing on that individual. But when we think of it as sand, we are not. Quine's proposal is that the child's *conceptual/linguistic* system has only the capacity to represent the world in terms of concepts like *macaroni, furniture, sand, bottlehood.* Of course the child's perceptual system must pick out individuals in order to represent shape, to determine what to grasp, and so on. At issue is how the child conceptualizes the world.

Piaget, like Quine, believed that baby must construct the concept of enduring objects, but he differed from Quine about the mechanisms he envisioned underlying this construction. As mentioned above, Quine saw the child's mastery of the linguistic devices of noun quantification, the machinery by which natural languages such as English manage to express sortal concepts, as the process through which the child's ontology comes to match his or her elders'. Piaget held that the baby constructs the concept *object* during sensorimotor development by age 18 months or so, and that this construction is the basis for the child's mastery of natural language. Because Piaget did not frame his discussion as an analysis of the logic of sortals, it is not clear when he would attribute full sortals to the child.[1]

The Quine/Piaget conjecture about the baby's representational resources is a serious empirical claim, but as I will show, it is difficult to bring data to bear on it. In the next sections I first consider Quine's views, contrasting his hypothesis that children come to represent sortals only upon learning the linguistic devices of noun quantification with the hypothesis I call "Sortal First." The Sortal First hypothesis is that babies represent sortal concepts, that toddler lexicons include words that express sortals, and that these representations underlie the capacity for learning quantifiers rather than resulting from learning them. The Sortal First hypothesis is a version of the continuity hypothesis; it denies Quine's discontinuity hypothesis. I then turn to early infancy, and explore the contrast between the Quine/Piaget hypothesis and the Sortal First hypothesis as regards the earliest phases of word learning. A preview of my conclusions: Whereas the Sortal First hypothesis is favored (Case 2), evidence is presented for a decidedly Quinian discontinuity in infant conceptual development (Case 3).

4.3.1 The Toddler's Mastery of Count–Mass Syntax

Quine's hypothesis is that the child masters the logic of sortals by adjusting the meanings of nouns and of natural-language quantifiers to one another (scrambling up an intellectual chimney, the walls of which are the child's currently worked-out representations of the quantifiers he or she knows). To address Quine's conjecture experimentally, we must first know when in the child's life the putative scrambling is going on. Even by age 3 the child is not producing all the quantifiers that constitute the walls of Quine's chimney. The very beginnings of the English count/mass distinction are mastered in the months leading up to age $2\frac{1}{2}$. Many children age 2:0 produce nouns with no determiners or plurals, but some have begun

1. For example, Piaget thought that the logical prerequisites for representing the adult concepts *all* and *some* are not acquired until after age 5.

to produce plurals and a few determiners and quantifiers (usually possessives such as "my," plus "a" and "the"). Many 2-year-olds beginning to use determiners do not distribute them differently according to the noun's count–mass status in the adult lexicon. They still omit many determiners (saying things like "give bottle" and "give water") and use others like "the" and "my" that do not differentiate count nouns and mass nouns (saying things like "my bottle" and "my juice"). By $2\frac{1}{2}$, virtually all children distinguish in some ways the syntactic contexts in which words like "table" and "dog" appear from those in which words like "water" and "playdoh" appear (Gordon 1985; Soja et al. 1991). Gordon (1982) showed that between $2\frac{1}{2}$ and 3 years of age the distinction becomes marked in syntax, as the child's speech abruptly comes to reflect the arbitrary rule that determiners are obligatory for singular count nouns, but not for mass nouns (that is, one can say "I like juice," but not *"I like dog").

The developmental facts summarized above determine the relevant ages for an empirical test of Quine's speculations. Data bearing against Quine's claims could be of several types: for example, data showing that children age 2 or under take proper nouns to refer to individuals of a kind or that they take count nouns to refer to kinds of individuals. But, as already mentioned, the trick is in figuring out how we can know whether toddlers' "Mama" refers to an entity babies conceptualize as a unique individual and whether their "bottle" expresses a sortal concept, referring to each individual of a certain kind, as opposed to bottle*hood*.

Another type of evidence could be relevant. If it can be shown that upon first learning "a" or the plural "-s," toddlers interpret them correctly, as signaling an individuated entity of a kind or a plurality of individuals of a kind, respectively, this achievement would provide evidence against Quine because these are the first relevant quantifiers the child learns. If he or she interprets them correctly from the beginning, the interpretation could not have been acquired through an adjustment process involving the entire set of quantificational devices of noun syntax. This last point is important. In the beginnings of language learning, in Quine's view, children will not interpret those few quantifiers in their lexicons as adults do. The scramble will have just begun. Data showing that children use "a" and plurals will not be themselves relevant to Quine's hypothesis; it must be shown that such quantificational devices are doing the same work as they do in the adult language.

4.3.2 Composition of the Toddler Lexicon

A large proportion of the baby's first words are words for middle-sized physical objects, such as "bottle, book, dog, cup," and "banana." But that babies have words in their lexicons that refer to object kinds in the adult lexicon tells us nothing of what these words mean to the babies. Many have argued that the earliest words are often complexive (for example, Bowerman 1978; Dromi 1987; Vygotsky 1962). That is, children appear to extend words to new referents on the basis of any of the salient perceptual properties of the original experiences in which the word was heard. These complexive uses often cut across what are for adults distinct ontological categories, as when "paper" apparently refers to the act of cutting, the act of drawing, to pens and pencils, and to paper (Dromi 1987). If such complexive uses reflect unconstrained (from the point of view of adult lexical categories) projection of word meanings, Quine's views receive support. But it is important to see that such complexive uses are not *necessary* for Quine's conjecture to be correct.

Indeed, others deny that toddlers construct complexive meanings; Huttenlocher and Smiley (1987), for example, present evidence that from the beginning babies use each word for middle-sized objects appropriately: "bottle" to refer to bottles, "book" to books, and so on. But even if Huttenlocher and Smiley are right, this fact does not disconfirm Quine's conjecture. In fact, Quine presupposes that the baby uses the words in contexts adults would. His point is that, even so, the baby might not be individuating the words' referents as we do. The baby could refer only to what *we* conceptualize as bottles when she uses "bottle," but *she* could be referring to bottle*hood*. She could be using the word to refer to a scattered portion of what goes on, determined by perceptual similarity to the portions of her experience when adults use "bottle."

Thus, the fact that infant lexicons include many words that in the adult language are sortals provides no evidence one way or the other for deciding between Quine's hypothesis and the Sortal first hypothesis.

4.3.3 Toddler Sensitivity to Noun Syntax

Children as young as 17 months (at least girls that young) are sensitive to the syntactic context in which a new noun is heard in their decisions about that noun's meaning (Katz et al. 1974; Macnamara 1982). Specifically, if taught a new word in a count noun context, referring to an unfamiliar doll ("See this. This is a dax. Can you touch the dax? Can you put the dax on your head ..."), they assume that other dolls of the same type are also daxes. But if taught in a proper-noun context ("See this. This is Dax. Can you touch Dax. Can you put Dax on your head ..."), they assume that other dolls of the same type are *not* Dax, reserving "Dax" for the original doll only, not a very similar doll of the same kind wearing a different-colored dress and with different-colored hair.

Do these data establish that young children distinguish kinds from individuals, and use count nouns as sortals? They *do* establish that toddlers are sensitive to the syntactic distinction between nouns following determiners and those not following determiners, but this distinction could be signaling a different semantic distinction than that between individuals and kinds. For a sample Quinian interpretation: babies could take nouns without determiners, such as "Dax, Rover," and "Joan," to refer to portions of experience that are more highly similar to the original portion of experience when the word was first heard than is the case for nouns used with determiners. Suppose a Quinian baby, Alice, has a brother whom she hears called both "Rupert" and "a boy." Suppose also that she relies on shape to determine Rupertness and boyness. She could have learned from others' usage of the words that to be called "Rupert," a given portion of experience must be very similar in shape to the original portions of experience to which the term was heard to refer, whereas to be called "a boy, the boy," something need look only somewhat like the original referent. A generalization of this pattern of distinction, across "Alice" and "a baby," "Rover," and "a dog," and so on, could underlie the patterns of projection found by Katz et al. (1974) and subsequent replications.

This interpretation of the Katz et al. data attributes to the baby a meaning for "a" that is different from the adult's as well as different meanings for "bottle, boy, Rupert." This is, of course, Quine's position. In his view, it is only in the course of learning other quantifiers, plural markers, and so on, and adjusting to all the contrasts in usage they mark (the process of scrambling up the intellectual chimney cited above) that the baby works out the meaning of "a," "the," "another," "some," "more", "all," "many," "same," and so on, and in so doing constructs the conceptual distinction between individuals and kinds.

Thus, the demonstration that young toddlers are sensitive to the syntactic distinction between count nouns and proper nouns, and use this distinction to mark a semantic contrast corresponding to that which adults use, is consistent with the Sortal First hypothesis, but is not conclusive evidence for it, for a Quinian interpretation of the data is still available.

4.3.4 Words for Novel Objects and Words for Nonsolid Substances

In several studies, my colleagues and I have attempted to address Quine's proposal by comparing children's representations of solid physical objects, such as cups, with their representations of nonsolid substances, such as sand or gels or creams. Our idea is that because adults conceptualize the former as kinds of individuals (that is, as sortals), but do not conceptualize the latter in this way, we might be able to find evidence that infants and toddlers respect the quantificational distinction between the two as well.

In the first studies, Soja et al. (1991) explored 2-year-olds' learning new words introduced to them as referring either to novel solid physical objects (such as a brass plumbing tee) or novel nonsolid substances (such as a hair-setting gel with Grape Nuts embedded in it). The objects were made of unfamiliar materials and the nonsolid substances were presented formed into distinctive novel shapes. The child was introduced to the novel entity, allowed to handle and play with it, and provided a word for it (such as "blicket" for a novel object; "stad" for a novel nonsolid substance). The child was then presented two new sets of stimuli and asked to give the experimenter the blicket or the stad. For each object trial, the choices consisted of another object of the same shape made of a different material (such as a plastic plumbing tee) or three small pieces of the original material (brass). For each substance trial, the choices consisted of a new substance formed into the original shape, or three small pieces of the original substance. Figure 4.2 shows the design for one trial of each type. There were four object trials and four nonsolid substance trials. Of course, which words were assigned to which entities varied across subjects, but for expository clarity I use "blicket" as my sample object name and "stad" as my sample nonsolid substance name.

Soja et al. carried out two analyses to assess whether children's representations of the referents of the words were influenced by the status of their knowledge of count/mass syntax. We did this to address Quine's hypothesis that only after mastering the quantificational devices of his or her language will the child construct sortal concepts for object kinds. First, we collected production data and assigned each child a value corresponding to the degree to which count nouns and mass nouns appeared in selective syntactic frames (for example, "a table," "tables," "too much dirt"). Scores ran from 0 to nearly 1.0. Second, we introduced the new

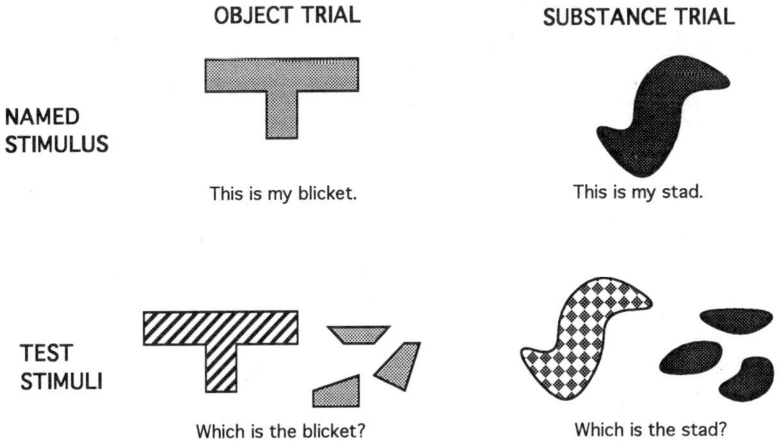

Figure 4.2

words in two ways. In the neutral syntax condition, no syntactic information was provided about the count/mass status of the word. The words were introduced as "my blicket, my stad" and subsequently appeared in the context "the blicket, the stad." In the informative syntax condition, the words were introduced as "a blicket, some stad," and further differentiated syntactically, for instance, "another blicket, some more stad." If this manipulation made a difference to the meaning assigned the word, then we would conclude that the child had already worked out part of the syntax/semantics mapping. If the Sortal First hypothesis is correct, children should be influenced by the status of the entities (objects/nonsolid substances) before we can find any reflection of their command of the syntactic distinction between mass and count nouns.

As figure 4.3 shows, children at age 2:0 and 2:6 used different bases for their projection of words for the two types of entities. They projected "blicket" to the other whole object the same shape as the original referent and they projected "stad" to the scattered portion of substance the same texture and color as the original referent. For object trials, children were sensitive to matches in shape and number; for nonsolid substance trials, children ignored matches in shape and number. Performance was more adultlike on the object trials, but performance on both types of trials was better than chance at both ages. Also apparent in figure 4.3, the syntactic context made no difference. The children were no more likely to interpret "blicket" as the word for a kind of individual when it was heard in a count

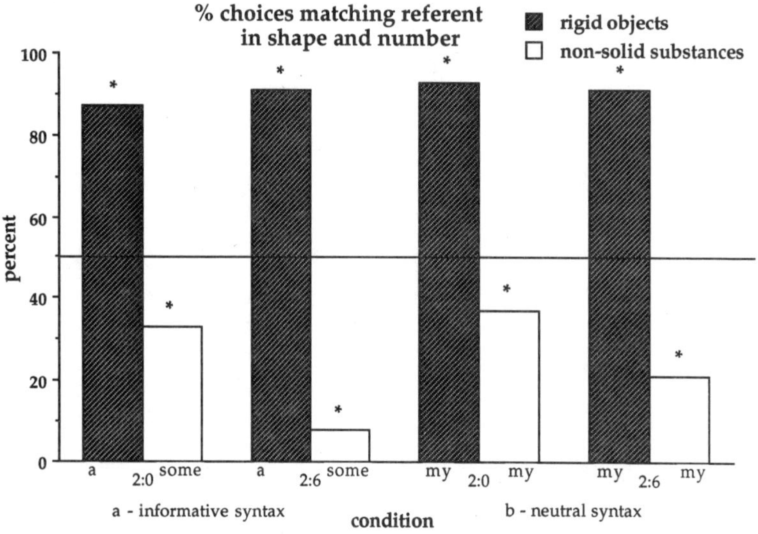

Figure 4.3

noun context. Similarly, hearing "stad" in a mass noun context made them no more likely to conceptualize stad as a substance that can appear either in scattered or singly bounded portions. Further, the child's productive control of count/mass syntax did not influence the pattern of projection: children with differentiation scores of 0 showed the same pattern as those with differentiation scores close to 1. Children of the older ages differentiated the two types of trials significantly more than did children of the younger ages, but even the youngest children (age 2:0) showed this pattern.

We can conclude from these results that an entity's status as a solid physical object (or not) influences which of its properties are salient in determining which other entities are referred to by the same word. We can also conclude that this distinction between objects and nonsolid substances predates mastery of count/mass syntax. These data are consistent with the Sortal First hypothesis, for they are consistent with the child's taking "blicket" to refer to each individual whole object of a kind, and "stad" to refer to a kind of substance, conceptualized as a nonindividuated entity. But the data are also consistent with the following more Quinian interpretation of the child's representations of the blicket and the stad.

Babies, being "body-minded" (Quine 1974) could be sensitive to the perceptual experiences that determine objecthood: boundedness; rigidity, coherence through motion. Whenever these are detected, babies could heavily weight such features as shape in their representation of these experiences. Shape would thus be a salient feature of the blicket, but not of the stad, for nonsolid substances do not maintain their shapes when manipulated. (Remember, the children handled the stimuli.) For nonsolid substances, properties such as texture and color might be salient, for these stay constant over experiences with substances. In other words, the 2-year-old could be using "blicket" to refer to blicketness, and recognize blicketness by shape. Therefore, the differential patterns of projection do not establish that the toddler is using "blicket" to refer to any individual whole object of a certain kind (in Quine's terms that the toddler divides the reference of "blicket").

One detail in the data from figure 4.3 favors the Sortal First over the Quinian interpretation, and that is that toddlers performed more like adults on the object trials than on the substance trials. Quine's interpretation of this finding would have to be ad hoc, perhaps that the baby has had more object experience than substance experience. But the Sortal First hypothesis *predicts* this asymmetry. To see this, suppose the Sortal First hypothesis is true, and suppose that upon first hearing the word "blicket" the child assumes that it refers to each individual object of a certain kind. The choices for testing how the child projects "blicket" included another single object, and three small objects. Even if the child isn't exactly sure which features of the blicket establish its kind, the child can rule out that the three small objects are a blicket, for under no interpretation can they be an individual object of the same kind as the original referent. Children should then be at ceiling on the object trials, which they are. The substance trials are another story. If upon first hearing "stad," the child takes it to refer to the kind of substance of the original referent, then scattered portions have no different status from unitary portions. There is no clue from number of piles which of the choices on the test trials is the stad. If children are not certain what properties of the original sample of stad determines the kind *stad,* they may do worse on the stad trials. And indeed, they do.

The key issue here is the role of number in determining how to project "blicket." If the Quinian interpretation of the data is correct, the baby should project "blicket" on the basis of shape similarity, no matter whether the choice that does not match in shape consists of one object or three objects. That is, the baby should succeed on an object trial as in figure 4.4 as well as on an object trial as in figure 4.2. The Sortal First interpretation predicts that performance on the object trials will fall, perhaps even to the level of performance on the substance trials, if the cue from number is removed. In an object trial such as that in figure 4.4, "blicket" is ostensibly defined as before, but the choices for projection are changed: another blicket of a different material (as before) and another whole object of a different kind made of the same material as the original referent (instead of the three small objects). Now the child has no clues from number of objects as to which is the correct choice. What happened is that performance fell to the level of the substance trials (Soja 1987).

Apparently, the child uses the information provided by number on the object trials, but not on the substance trials. We take this as evidence that

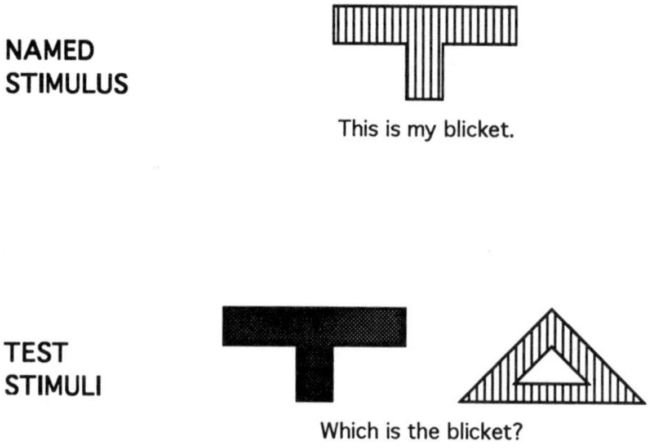

Figure 4.4

the child conceptualizes some entities as individuals (such as kinds of objects) and conceptualizes other entities as nonindividuated (such as kinds of substances). These distinct ways of conceptualizing objects and substances predate mastery of count/mass syntax. Toddlers do not merely project "blicketness" on the basis of shape of individual pieces of blicketness, as we determine whether some pasta is spaghetti on the basis of the shape of individual pieces. Instead, the pattern of projection suggests that toddlers consider "blicket" as a word for a sortal, and take it to refer to any individual of a certain kind.

4.3.5 Toddler's Understanding of "A, Some NOUN_"

I take the data reviewed in the preceding section to show that by age 2:0 children take "blicket" to refer to individual objects of a certain kind and "stad" to refer to nonsolid substances of a kind, and that the toddlers' representations of blickets and stads have the same quantificational structure as would adults'. "Blicket" is a sortal term. These data disconfirm Quine only on the assumption that the baby did not acquire these representations from learning English noun quantifiers. This assumption seems warranted, given that usually toddlers at 2:0 do not produce quantifiers, and given that the pattern of projection was independent of whether the individual subjects produced any noun quantifiers selective for count nouns. A worry, though, is that babies may have better comprehension than production of the quantifiers.

We attempted to address this possibility by manipulating the syntactic context in which the word appeared. As mentioned above, the syntactic environment in which the new word appeared had no effect in the Soja et al. experiments, even at age $2\frac{1}{2}$ when many children did produce quantifiers differentially for what are count and mass nouns in the adult lexicon. The Quinian interpretation of this fact is that quantifiers like "a, another, some NOUN_, some more NOUN_" do not yet signal the distinction between individuated and nonindividuated entities, just as the child is not projecting "blicket" and "stad" on the basis of that distinction. The Sortal First interpretation: objects are naturally construed as individuals of a kind and nonsolid substances are naturally construed as nonindividuated entities, even by toddlers, as shown by performance in the neutral syntax condition. Informative syntax merely reinforces the child's natural construal of the two types of entities.

A study by Soja (1992) decided between these two interpretations, and also established that our production data did not underestimate toddlers' interpretation of the quantifiers. Soja taught toddlers words for the objects and substances in a new condition: contrastive syntax. "Blicket" was introduced in a mass noun context; "stad" in a count noun context. That is, when shown a novel solid object, the child was told, "Here's some blicket.... Would you like to see some more blicket?" And when shown a nonsolid substance fashioned into a distinctive shape, the child was told, "Here's a stad.... Would you like to see another stad?"

Soja found two types of 2-year-olds. Some were not affected by the misleading syntax; these infants responded exactly as did those in the study mentioned above, as predicted by the Sortal First hypothesis. Others, who were producing count/mass syntax, were affected; hearing "a stad" led them to interpret "stad" as an S-shaped pile, rather than as some Nivea with Grape Nuts in it. These data tap the very moment children first learn the meaning of "a." They have only begun the scramble up Quine's chimney, and have not had time to adjust their interpretation of "a" to many other quantifiers. Yet, "a" signals an individuated entity of some kind. Together these data provide converging support for the Sortal First hypothesis. The child naturally construes physical objects as individuals of distinct kinds, and naturally construes nonsolid substances in terms of kinds of nonindividuated entities. These natural construals support adultlike projection of word meaning (figure 4.3), and support adultlike interpretation of newly learned quantifiers like "a, some" and plurals.

4.3.6 Younger Infants

Altogether the data support the Sortal First hypothesis over Quine's conjecture, but they do not establish when the child first begins to represent sortal concepts. As mentioned earlier, it is not clear when Piaget would attribute sortal concepts to children, but it is certain that he would deny them to young infants. The argument I have developed so far does not bear on Piaget's claims about the representational capacities of infants, for it concerns children age 24 months and older. Of course, a demonstration that young infants represent sortal concepts would defeat Quine's conjecture as well as Piaget's characterization of the infants' conceptual resources.

Studies by Cohen and his colleagues (for example, Cohen and Younger 1983) show that quite young babies will habituate when shown, for example, a series of distinct stuffed dogs, and that they generalize habituation to a new stuffed dog and will dishabituate when shown a stuffed elephant. Similarly, when shown a series of distinct stuffed animals, babies of 8 or 9 months habituate, generalize habituation to a new stuffed animal, but dishabituate to a toy truck. Do these data not show that babies of that age represent sortal concepts such as "dog" and "animal"?

Certainly not. Babies may be sensitive to dog shapes or animal shapes; babies may be habituating to dog*hood* or animal*hood*. To credit the baby with sortals such as "dog," or "animal," we must show that such concepts provide the baby with criteria for individuation and identity.

My discussion of this question has two steps. First, I argue that babies represent at least one sortal, *object*. Second, I present some recent data from my lab suggesting that as late as 10 months of age, the baby may have no more specific sortal concepts—not *cup, bottle, truck, dog, animal*.... Thus, a Quinian interpretation of the habituation data above may well be correct.

4.3.7 Principles of Individuation: Younger Infants

Piaget's characterization of infants' cognitive capacities was based on tasks in which the baby had to solve some problem, often involving means–end analysis, and often involving planning (see chapter 8 on problem solving). For example, Piaget's conclusion that babies do not represent objects as continuing to exist when out of view was based on the robust finding that babies under 8 months do not remove a cover to get a hidden object. The babies' failure might be due to their failure to reason that the object still exists, as Piaget thought, or equally might be due to inability to carry out one action (remove a cover) to achieve some other goal. When one uses a reflection of the babies' conceptualization of the world that relies on behaviors well within the repertoires even of neonates, the preferential-looking paradigm discussed above, a very different picture of the baby's conceptualization of objects emerges. There is now ample evidence that even 2-month-olds know that objects continue to exist when out of view (Baillargeon, in press). One famous study is that of Baillargeon, Spelke, and Wasserman (1985). They demonstrated that if a young infant is shown an object placed behind a screen, the infant is surprised if the screen is then rotated down through the space the object should be occupying. This reaction shows that babies know the object is still there and that one object cannot pass through the space occupied by another.

The selective-looking paradigm has been used extensively to probe babies' representations of objects, and the data from a subset of these studies can be recruited to bear on the question at hand. They establish that by 4 months of age the baby represents at least one sortal concept—the concept of a physical object. The baby has criteria for individuation and for numerical identity of objects.

Spelke and her colleagues have shown that babies establish representations of objects on the basis of criteria that individuate them—an object is a coherent, bounded entity that maintains its coherence and boundaries as it moves through space (see Spelke 1990 for a review). The baby predicts the motion of objects according to principles such as that one object cannot pass through the space occupied by another (Spelke et al. 1992; Baillargeon, in press). Most relevant to the present discussion are studies reviewed above showing that babies *count* objects. Whereas these studies were performed to explore the baby's concept of number, they bear on the present question as well. Babies, like anybody else, cannot count unless they have criteria that establish individuals to count. Babies clearly have criteria that establish small physical objects as countable individuals.

4.3.8 Principles of Numerical Identity: Younger Infants

That babies individuate and count objects does not show that they trace identity of objects through time, that they have the representational capacity to distinguish one object seen on different occasions from two numerically distinct but physically similar objects. However, there are now two demonstrations of this capacity in infants age 5 months or younger. Here I describe one (Spelke 1988). Spelke showed 5-month-old babies objects moving behind and reemerging from two separated screens, screen A to the left of screen B (figure 4.5). An object emerged to the right of screen B and returned behind it, and then a second object emerged to the left of screen A and returned behind it. At any given time, at most one object was visible, and no object ever appeared in the space between screens A

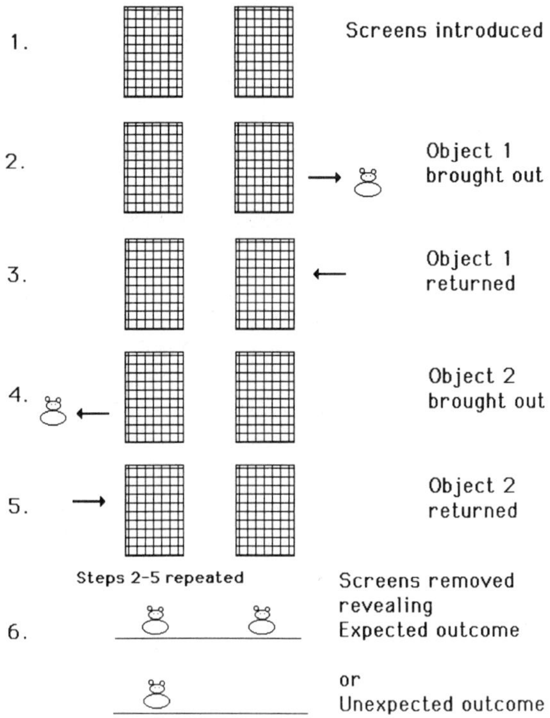

Figure 4.5
Spatiotemporal condition.

and B. Under these conditions, 4-month-olds inferred there must be two objects, as shown by the fact that when the screens were removed, revealing two objects (expected outcome), they looked less than when the screens were removed revealing one object (unexpected outcome). These studies show that babies use two spatiotemporal principles to individuate and trace identity of objects: one object cannot be in two places at the same time, and one object cannot go from one place to another without tracing a spatiotemporally continuous path.

In sum, infants have a concept *physical object* that functions as a sortal. The infant's concept provides criteria for individuation and numerical identity; these criteria are spatiotemporal. These considerations by themselves defeat the Quine/Piaget discontinuity hypothesis and support the Sortal First hypothesis.

4.4 Case 3. A Possible Discontinuity Between Infant and Adult Representations of Sortals

Adults also look longer at the unexpected events in the experiments described above. Further, they ask how the magic tricks are done. They do so because adults use spatiotemporal information in just the same way as do the infants. But adults use other types of information in establishing individuals and tracing their identity through time: property information and membership in kinds more specific than *physical object*. We use property information—if we see a large red cup on a window sill, and later a small green cup there, we infer that two numerically distinct cups are involved, even though we have no spatiotemporal evidence to that effect. And, as discussed above, our identity judgments are relative to sortals more specific than *object* (Wiggins 1980; Hirsch 1982; Macnamara 1986). Imagine a junk car, consigned to the crusher. The process of crushing is a spatiotemporally continuous, gradual process. Any changes in the car's properties are also continuous; it changes shape continuously, for example. Yet at a certain point we say that the car goes out of existence, and is replaced by a lump of metal and plastic. We trace identity relative to kinds more specific than *object*, kinds such as *car, person, table*. Such sortals provide additional criteria for individuation and identity to the spatiotemporal criteria that apply to bounded physical objects in general, and to the general assumption that an object's properties stay stable over time, or change continuously. When a person, Joe Shmoe, dies, Joe ceases to exist, even though Joe's body still exists. The sortal *person* provides the criteria for identity of the entity referred to by the name "Joe Shmoe"; the sortal *body* provides different criteria for identity.

In collaboration with Fei Xu, I have been exploring the question of whether babies represent any sortals more specific than *object*, that is,

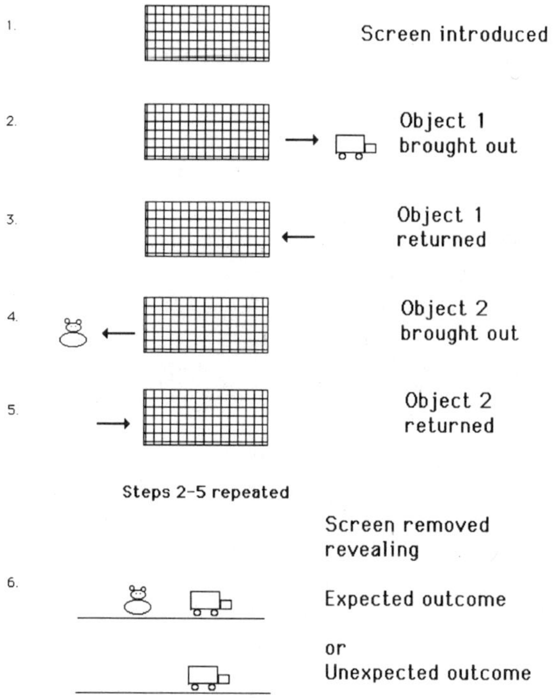

Figure 4.6
Property/kind condition.

whether babies can use property/kind information to individuate and trace identity of objects (Xu and Carey, in press).

Consider the events depicted in figure 4.6. An adult witnessing a truck emerge from behind and then reenter a screen and then witnessing an elephant emerge from behind and then reenter the screen would infer that there are at least two objects behind the screen: a truck and an elephant. The adult would make this inference in the absence of any spatiotemporal evidence for two distinct objects, not having seen two at once or any suggestion of a discontinuous path through space and time. Adults trace identity relative to sortals such as "truck" and "elephant" and know that trucks do not turn into elephants.

Xu and Carey (in press) have carried out four experiments based on this design. Ten-month-old babies were shown screens from which two objects of different kinds (such as a cup and a toy elephant, a ball and a truck) emerged from opposite sides, one at a time. Each object was shown a total of four times. After this familiarization, the screen was removed, revealing either two objects (expected outcome) or one object (unexpected outcome). In all four studies, babies failed to look longer at the unexpected outcome. In fact, they looked longer at the expected outcome (two objects), but this is a baseline preference; there is more to look at in an array of an elephant and a truck than in an array of just an elephant. Babies of 10 months cannot use the difference between a cup and an elephant to infer that there must be two objects behind the screen.

In a crucial control, another group of 10-month-olds was run in a parallel version of this study that differed in just one respect. Before the familiarizations, emergences of each object from either side, *both* objects were brought out together for a few seconds, and thus the child was given spatiotemporal evidence that there were two objects in the array. The experiment then proceeded exactly as in the other condition. In this case, babies significantly overcame their baseline preference for two objects in the test outcomes. That is, they succeeded at the task. This result shows that babies of this age *can* use spatiotemporal information to individuate objects, whereas they *fail* to use the differences in kind between trucks and elephants or between ducks and balls to do so.

We have ruled out several uninteresting interpretations of the failure in the property/kind conditions of these studies. For example, it is not that babies do not notice the difference between the two objects. In one version of the study, babies were allowed to handle each object (one at a time, of course, for we didn't want to provide spatial information that there were two) before beginning the events. This practice made no difference to the results. In another version, we compared looking times in a condition involving two objects of different kinds emerging from the screens (as before) to a condition where only one object emerged from both sides of the screen. In this experiment, we monitored the baby's habituation to the objects during the familiarization emergences (that is, before we took away the screen, revealing either the expected or unexpected outcome). Babies habituated much faster in the condition in which a single object was emerging from the screen. That is, babies noticed that the elephant and the cup were different from each other. After habituation, we removed the screen, revealing either one object or two objects. Babies in both conditions (cup/elephant; elephant/elephant) looked longer at the outcomes of two objects (unexpected in the elephant/elephant condition; expected in the elephant/cup condition). That is, although babies noticed the difference between the elephant and the cup, they simply did not use this information to drive the inference that there must be two numerically distinct objects behind the screen.

It appears, then, that in one sense Quine was right. Very young infants have not yet constructed concepts that serve as adultlike meanings of words like "bottle, ball," and "dog." How *are* the babies representing these events? We can think of two possibilities. First, the babies may actually establish a representation of a single individual object (OBJECTi) moving back and forth behind the screen, attributing to this object the properties of being yellow and duck-shaped at some times and white and spherical at other times. The basis for such a representation could be spatiotemporal: the infants may take the oscillating motion as a single, continuous path.

A second possibility is that the baby is making no commitment at all about whether the objects emerging to the left and right of the screen are the same or different. That is, the baby is representing the event as OBJECT emerging from the left of the screen, followed by OBJECT emerging from the right of the screen, and represents these neither as a single object (OBJECTi) nor as distinct objects (OBJECTi, OBJECTj). Suppose you see a leaf on the sidewalk as you walk to class, and you see a leaf at roughly the same place on the sidewalk as you return from class. That may be the same leaf or it may not; your conceptual system is capable of drawing that distinction, but you leave the question open.

We do not know which possibility is correct. The baby actually may be representing the events as if a duck-shaped object is turning into a ball-shaped object (possibility one) or simply may be failing to establish representations of two distinct objects (possibility two). The take-home message is the same whichever possibility is correct; 10-month-old infants do not use the property/kind differences between a red metal truck and a gray rubber elephant to infer that there must be two numerically distinct objects involved in the event.

These data suggest that a Quinian interpretation of habituation data like that of Cohen and Younger (1983) is correct. Babies habituated to a series of stuffed dogs, and dishabituating to a stuffed horse, are not revealing the concept "dog," but rather are revealing sensitivity to dog shapes, or dogness. The Xu and Carey studies suggest that not until 11 or 12 months will babies use the differences between a stuffed dog and a stuffed horse to establish representations of two numerically distinct objects.

It is significant that babies begin to comprehend and produce object names at about 10 to 12 months of age, the age at which they begin to use the differences between cups and elephants to individuate objects. Again, this pattern of results is consistent with the Sortal First hypothesis. That is, babies do not seem to learn words for bottlehood; they begin to learn words such as "bottle" just when they show evidence for sortal concepts such as *bottle* that provide conditions for individuation and numerical identity. Further studies could explore the relations between specific words understood and success at individuation based on the kinds expressed by those words.

It is not surprising that babies use spatiotemporal information before kind information to individuate and trace the identity of objects. All physical objects trace spatiotemporally continuous paths; no physical object can be in two places at the same time. However, what property changes are possible in a persisting object depends upon the kind. An apparent change of relative location of the handle to the body of a ceramic cup signifies a different cup; an apparent change in relative location of a hand to the body of a person does not signify a different person. It would serve babies well to use spatiotemporal information to establish the individuals in their environment, so that they can then learn which properties covary, and which properties remain constant through time in the face of variation among other properties.

In sum, these data suggest that babies have at least one sortal concept innately—*physical object*. Their object concept provides spatiotemporal conditions for individuation and numerical identity. They can use spatiotemporal information to identify individuals in their environment, and can then learn more specific sortals for kinds of these objects. Exactly how this learning is accomplished is the big question, of course. The present data suggest that they spend most of their first year of life on this accomplishment.

4.5 A Few Concluding Remarks

Where do the case studies presented here leave us vis à vis the continuity assumption? I have argued that there is a discontinuity in children's representation of number; children construct a new representational resource when they master the number-list representational system for integers. Second, I have argued that the major discontinuity posited by Quine and Piaget does not receive support; there is no reason to think that babies lack the logical resources to represent sortals, and indeed, *object* functions as a sortal at least from 4 months on. But if the interpretation of the Xu and Carey data offered above is correct, then an important Quinian discontinuity is supported. Babies may be setting up a representation of an object that sometimes is round, white, and Styrofoam and at other times red, metal, and truck shaped. This is a representational system very different from yours and mine. But because I am convinced that important conceptual changes occur later in life (cf. Carey 1991; Carey and Spelke 1994), I would not be shocked to find interesting discontinuities in the conceptual histories of infants, even in arenas so closely implicated in language as the conceptual underpinnings of number and count nouns.

Problems

4.1 Describe an experiment that could show whether babies understand subtraction. What alternative explanations of the anticipated outcome would you have to control for?

4.2 Show how the Meck and Church accumulator model would explain babies' success in the experiment proposed in exercise 4.1. Explain how the numeron list model would do so.

4.3 Can you think of a third model that might explain success in the experiment proposed in exercise 4.1 that contains *no* symbolic representation of number? That is, can you think of a model that contains no state of an accumulator to represent number and also contains no symbol on a list to represent number?

References

Antell, S., and D. P. Keating (1983). Perception of numerical invariance in neonates. *Child Development* 54, 695–701.

Baillargeon, R. (in press). How do infants learn about the physical world? *Current Directions in Psychological Science.*

Baillargeon, R., E. Spelke, and S. Wasserman (1985). Object permanence in 5-month-old infants. *Cognition* 20, 191–208.

Bowerman, M. (1978). The acquisition of word meaning: An investigation into some current conflicts. In N. Waterson and C. Snow, eds., *Development of communication.* New York: John Wiley & Sons.

Carey, S. (1991). Knowledge acquisition: Enrichment or conceptual change? In S. Carey and R. Gelman, eds., *The epigenesis of mind: Essays in biology and cognition.* Hillsdale, NJ: Erlbaum.

Carey, S., and E. Spelke (1994). Domain specific knowledge and conceptual change. In L. Hirschfeld and S. Gelman, eds., *Mapping the mind: Domain specificity in cognition and culture.* Cambridge: Cambridge University Press, 169–200.

Cohen, L. B., and B. A. Younger (1983). Perceptual categorization in the infant. In E. K. Scholnick, ed., *New trends in conceptual representation.* Hillsdale, NJ: Erlbaum, 197–200.

Dromi, E. (1987). *Early lexical development.* London: Cambridge University Press.

Gallistel, C. R. (1990). *The organization of learning.* Cambridge, MA: MIT Press.

Gallistel, C. R., and R. Gelman (1992). Preverbal and verbal counting and computation. *Cognition* 44, 43–74.

Gelman, R., and C. R. Gallistel (1978). *The child's understanding of number.* Cambridge, MA: Harvard University Press.

Gordon, P. (1982). *The acquisition of syntactic categories: The case of the count/mass distinction.* Unpublished doctoral dissertation, Massachusetts Institute of Technology, Cambridge, MA.

Gordon, P. (1985). Evaluating the semantic categories hypothesis: The case of the count/mass distinction. *Cognition* 20, 209–242.

Hirsch, E. (1982). *The concept of identity.* New Haven: Yale University Press.

Huttenlocher, J., and P. Smiley (1987). Early word meanings: The case of object names. *Cognitive Psychology* 19, 63–89.

Katz, N., E. Baker, and J. Macnamara (1974). What's in a name? A study of how children learn common and proper names. *Child Development* 45, 469–473.

Macnamara, J. (1982). *Names for things: A study of human learning.* Cambridge, MA: MIT Press.

Macnamara, J. (1986). *A border dispute.* Cambridge, MA: MIT Press.

Meck, W. H., and R. M. Church (1983). A mode control model of counting and timing processes. *Journal of Experimental Psychology: Animal Behavior Processes* 9, 320–334.

Pinker, S. (1984). *Language learnability and language development.* Cambridge, MA: Harvard University Press.

Quine, W. V. O. (1960). *Word and object.* Cambridge, MA: MIT Press.

Quine, W. V. O. (1969). *Ontological relativity and other essays.* New York: Columbia University Press.

Quine, W. V. O. (1974). *The roots of reference*. New York: Columbia University Press.

Soja, N. N. (1987). *Ontological constraints on 2-year-olds' induction of word meanings*. Unpublished doctoral dissertation, Massachusetts Institute of Technology, Cambridge, MA.

Soja, N. N. (1992). Inferences about the meanings of nouns: The relationship between perception and syntax. *Cognitive Development* 7, 29–45.

Soja, N. N., S. Carey, and E. S. Spelke (1991). Ontological categories guide young children's inductions of word meaning: Object terms and substance terms. *Cognition* 38, 179–211.

Spelke, E. S. (1988). The origins of physical knowledge. In L. Weiskranz, ed., *Thought without knowledge*. Oxford, UK: Oxford Science Publications, 168–184.

Spelke, E. S. (1990). Principles of object perception. *Cognitive Science* 14, 29–56.

Spelke, E. S., K. Breinlinger, J. Macomber, and K. Jacobson (1992). Origins of knowledge. *Psychological Review* 99, 605–632.

Starkey, P., and R. G. Cooper, Jr. (1980). Perception of number by human infants. *Science*, 210, 1033–1035.

Vygotsky, L. S. (1962). *Thought and language*. Cambridge, MA: MIT Press.

Wiggins, D. (1980). *Sameness and substance*. Cambridge, MA: Harvard University Press.

Wynn, K. (1990). Children's understanding of counting. *Cognition* 36, 155–193.

Wynn, K. (1992a). Addition and subtraction by human infants. *Nature* 358, 749–750.

Wynn, K. (1992b). Children's acquisition of the number words and the counting system. *Cognitive Psychology* 24, 220–251.

Xu, F., and S. Carey (in press). Infant metaphysics: The case of numerical identity. *Cognitive Psychology*.

Chapter 5
Classifying Nature Across Cultures

Scott Atran

Introduction: An Anthropological Perspective

Greek philosophers and historians such as Plato and Herodotus first debated the issue of how people in different cultures think about the world. Herodotus suggested that the different languages people speak, and even the way they may write, makes them think about the world differently. Plato argued that people everywhere have more or less the same "species-memory" of the world, and that cultures differ mainly in what each has "forgotten" (*amnesis*). The issue has provoked more than two millennia of voluminous anecdote and speculation. Progress on it has been meager.

One apparent obstacle to progress has been the theoretical bias to weight the importance of scientific thinking over common-sense thought and belief. This trend began with Aristotle, and has arguably colored the ways in which Western psychologists and sociologists consider how people in other cultures conceive the world around them. But from an anthropological vantage, this curious bias is akin to taking the magical practices of some exotic tribe and using *those* as the standard by which to judge thinking across cultures. For science constitutes a rather specialized activity of thought, one that is hardly required for an apprehension of humankind's immensely rich and varied everyday world. Most people become perfectly

The experimental research reported here is supported by grants from the National Science Foundation (No. SBR-931978) and the French Ministry of Research and Technology as part of a larger project on biological categorization and reasoning across cultures. Participants include Alejandro López (Psychology, Max Planck Institute, Munich), Ximena Lois (Linguistics, CREA-Ecole Polytechnique), Valentina Vapnarsky (Ethnology, Université de Paris X), Douglas Medin (Psychology, Northwestern University), Edward Smith (Psychology, University of Michigan), Lawrence Hirschfeld (Anthropology, University of Michigan), John Coley (Psychology, Northwestern University), Brian Smith (Zoology, University of Texas, Arlington). Alan Gibbard (Philosophy, University of Michigan) helped to prepare the appendix on the logical structure of folk taxonomy.

competent cultural performers without ever knowing about or thinking in line with science.[1]

This is not to deny the cultural importance of science or its power to expand the frontiers of human knowledge. It is only to doubt that scientific thinking and theory are so pertinent to understanding general conceptual development. By contrast, the cognitive structures of ordinary conceptual domains may strongly constrain, and thereby render possible, the initial elaboration of corresponding scientific fields.

The research technique known as "methodological behaviorism" has also been used somewhat abusively in studies of thinking in non-Western societies. Methodological behaviorism aims to extend the laboratory techniques of the natural sciences to the study of people's behavior—for example, by using randomization procedures to justify claims that results apply to the whole population from which samples are drawn. But the "randomized" populations that often serve for the reported experiments are themselves usually far from randomized representatives of the populations to which the results are actually projected. Thus, many, if not most, studies in cognitive and developmental psychology use subjects that are drawn from Western university environments. From these special populations—many of whose members have a long history of being tested on a variety of experimental tasks—context-free generalizations are frequently made to all "Westerners" or "people" (that is, humanity). Such generalizations can be highly dubious, however statistically reliable the results.

Finally, the experimental paradigms that are used may incorporate assumptions which seem self-evident to the experimenter, and perhaps even to other members of the experimenter's own culture, but which are not obvious or acceptable to people in other cultures. As a result, the experimenter may wrongly interpret a rejection of the premises of an experimental design as "failure" on the task, and then take this supposed failure as the *explanandum* for understanding how people in different cultures think. By attending to this issue, cross-cultural researchers may find that rejection of tasks that seem arbitrary or artificial to people can point to ways of thinking that such tasks fail to capture, or capture wrongly.

A case in point is Alexander Luria's (1976) celebrated study of categorization and reasoning among literate and illiterate Russian peasants. Luria argues that his findings show untutored peasants incapable of forming

1. According to a recent Harris poll, for example, only one-fifth of 1,225 American adults randomly questioned scored better than 60 percent on basic science questions about space, the earth, the environment, animals, and the causes of diseases. Assuming that the sample is representative, the majority of Americans do not know that human beings evolved from animal species or that the sun and the earth are in the Milky Way galaxy. Fully one-third believe that human beings and dinosaurs existed at the same time (*The New York Times*, April 21, 1994).

"abstract" taxonomies of objects on the basis of theoretical "similarity" (*ukshaidi*), or of carrying through syllogisms that involve unfamiliar categories or events.[2] For example, they "fail" to segregate *hammer-saw-log-hatchet* into two categories of three items (the instruments: hammer, saw, hatchet) and one item (the patient: log), respectively. This is supposedly because they attend only to the "concrete situation" in which all the items are thematically related (for example, they are all "needed" to build a house). Luria attributes such apparent failure to a lack of "the generalizing function of language"—a function that is supposedly characteristic of "scientific" thinking.

What Luria fails to consider is that the notion of a "generalizing function of language" may itself be a spurious element of ethnocentric theorizing wherein the "primitive" mind is virtually an empty slate (*tabula rasa*) upon which "culture" progressively impresses content and structure through language in advancing to higher stages of "civilization" or "historical consciousness." But what if there were no such thing as a "generalizing function of language" that spans all cognitive tasks and domains? What if all peoples were biologically endowed with distinctly specialized cognitive domains, which "naturally" or "spontaneously" support categorization and reasoning schema in distinctly different ways depending on context?

For example, in an innately determined "default" setting, which is triggered by minimal experience with the actual world, people everywhere may be spontaneously disposed to taxonomically organize and reason about living kinds, but to thematically organize and reason about artifacts. By contrast, in more experientially rich "ecological" contexts, which frame many "traditional" ways of rural life, thematic—that is, purposeful and functional—organizations of living kinds may be learned and thus also readily invoked. Similarly, in more experientially conditioned "educational" contexts, which characterize the widespread influence of formal schooling in urban societies, taxonomic—that is, hierarchical and classificatory—organizations of artifacts may be learned and readily elicited.

All this is not to suggest that scientific method has no place in cross-cultural study. On the contrary, only carefully controlled elicitation or experimentation allows for reliable replication of findings, which focuses comparison and interpretation so that knowledge can be progressively accumulated. It is just that rigorous testing procedures alone do not disallow an ethnocentric bias in the experimental paradigm itself from skewing the interpretation of results.

With this critical stance in mind, the focus of this chapter is on how people the world over formulate and reason from natural categories, such

2. For an anthropological critique of Luria's studies on syllogism, see Cole and Scribner (1974) and Hutchins (1980).

as folk species of animals and plants. There is a summary account of how samples from two different cultural group—American college students and Itza Maya Indians of the Guatemalan rain forest—use these categories to expand knowledge in the face of uncertainty in order to form an integrated appreciation of the biological world. The lesson that emerges is that understanding the possibility and process of cultural variation, including science, requires awareness of the scope and limits of our (evolutionarily) specialized forms of common sense.

5.1 Folk Biology

In this section I adopt a rationalist stance. The argument is that when assessing nondemonstrative (nondeductive) inference within and across cultures, we must take into account evidence that the human mind appears to be endowed with domain-specific schemata, that is, with fundamentally *distinct ways of thinking about the world.* The focus is on one particular natural-category domain: nonhuman living things, that is, kinds of animals and plants.[3] After considering some recent experimental and cross-cultural work on the formation of living-kind categories, I turn in section 5.2 to the issue of how people across cultures spontaneously form hypotheses about the relations between those kinds. The issue has recently been cast as one of "category-based induction," addressed by a case study comparing American students and Itza Maya Indians.

5.1.1 The Concept of Folk Species

Although modern science strives to unify all kinds of causal process under a single system of contingent, mechanical relationships (push/pull, clockwork, and so on), recent work in cognitive anthropology and developmental psychology suggests that even people in our own culture initially do not spontaneously reason in this way, and may never do so. Thus, people from a very early age, and through all their adult lives, seem to think differently about different domains (Atran and Sperber 1991, Wellman and Gelman 1992), including the domains of "naive physics" (Baillargeon 1986, Spelke 1990, Carey et al. 1992), "naive biology" (Atran

3. No culture in the world, except those exposed to Aristotle, considers humans and nonhuman living kinds to belong to the same ontological category. Nor do people ordinarily process information about persons in the same way as they process information about (nonhuman) living kinds. Thus, "For the Kayapó (Indians of the Amazon) all things are divided into 4 categories: (1) things that move and grow, (2) things that grow but do not move, (3) things that neither move nor grow, and (4) man, a creature that is akin to all animals, yet unique and more powerful than most animals because of his social organization" (Posey 1981, 168).

1987, Keil 1989, Gelman and Wellman 1991), "naive psychology" (Leslie 1990, Astington and Gopnik 1991, Avis and Harris 1991), and "naive sociology" (Turiel 1983; Cosmides and Tooby 1992; Hirschfeld, in press). People attribute *contingent* motions to inert object substances; spontaneous actions and *teleological* developments to species of animals and plants (for example, internally directed growth and inheritance of related parts and whole); *intentional* relationships to one another's beliefs, desires, and actions, and group assignments (for instance, kinship, race) that specify a range of *deontological* obligations and contractual actions.

5.1.1.1 *Conceptually Perceiving Living Kinds: The Role of Teleology*

Each of these "conceptual modules"—folk physics, folk biology, folk psychology, and folk sociology—targets a somewhat different database as input in order to structure it in a distinct way as output (that is, as domain-specific representations). For example, categorizing an organism as a kind of living thing, such as a dog, involves selective attention to certain perceptible features of the world. The selected features may involve various aspects of the object's shape, size, movement, texture, sound, and smell.[4] But the selection process itself is driven, at least in part, by a set of causal presumptions to the effect that the living world categorically divides into well-bounded types, regardless of the degree of morphological variation that may actually exist or be observed within or between different kinds: for example, DOG (including puppies, poodles, and huskies), TOAD (including tadpoles), OAK (including saplings and bonsais), and TIGER (including cubs, dwarfs, and three-legged albino mutants).

By constraining input in these ways, such teleological schemata generate categories of living things that more or less correspond to biological species (or genera of closely related species). These teleological presumptions invariably correlate some or all of the following: spontaneous movements, functional relationships between perceptibly heterogeneous parts, canonical patterns of behavioral or morphological change, visibly variable outsides as indicators of less variable but largely imperceptible insides, and reproduction and inheritance of all these. Thus, even very young children

4. The presence of different species triggers different ways of causally weighting the contributions of various sorts of perceptual stimuli in recognizing different living kinds (Boster and D'Andrade 1989). In some cases, movement and shape are secondary or irrelevant: for example, the canopy birds of the rain forest may be recognized and taxonomically diagnosed by their song pattern alone, whereas the intermediate classification of kinds of cactus plants typically involves color, contour, and tactile dimensions rather than size or bounded form (for example, a mature, three-inch-high cactus ball with four-inch spikes may be classed with a three-branched, seven-foot-high, slender cactus with nearly invisible prickles). Even within the visual modality, specific channels for color and shape processing may constitute specialized subcomponents that underlie finer-grained, visually based semantic representations (Warrington and McCarthy 1987).

will tend to attribute the rich characteristic structure of living things to very "abstract," informationally poor stimuli provided they conform to one or more of these teleological "indicators."

For example, they may readily take as representations of living things closed two-dimensional figures that: move irregularly across a screen (as opposed to figures that move regularly), have clusters of symmetrical and repetitively drawn "insides" (as opposed to the randomly drawn arrays that children more readily impute to rocks), and have irregular protruding parts (for example, for a given drawing, children will ask what the protruding part is purposively "for" if they are primed to believe that the drawing represents a prickly plant rather than a prickly mineral). In addition, preschoolers are more likely to attribute biological properties (for example, "has tiny bones inside it") to visually dissimilar but related organisms (such as parent and offspring), but more likely to attribute nonbiological properties (for example, "is very dirty from playing in the mud"), to similar but unrelated organisms (Springer and Keil 1989; cf. Hickling and Gelman 1992, Mandler 1992).

Actual experience or exposure to relevant data thus triggers the inference of a characteristic structure to actual as well as potential data in complex ways that go far beyond the information given. At a limit, one need only once point to one instance of a plant or animal (in the wild, a garden, a zoo, or even a book) to have a child immediately classify it and relationally segregate it from all other (folk) species. In other words, an "automatic" expectation about the organization of the biological world ensures that the thing is essentially of a kind with its species but not essentially of a kind with all other living things.

The cognitive impetus that drives the learner to this "naive" appreciation of the relationship between a largely unknown (and perhaps unknowable) "genotype" and its various "phenotypic" expressions is likely to be a naturally selected endowment of evolution. It enables every person to quickly apprehend particularly salient aspects of the biological reality of how genotypes and their environments jointly produce phenotypes, without that person having to be immediately aware of the precise causal mechanisms involved (an awareness that only now emerges after two millennia of concerted scientific effort). On this account, it is not surprising that urban American children and rural Yoruba children (Nigeria) come to learn about allowable morphological and behavior transformations and variations among animals of a folk species in nearly identical ways and at nearly identical ages (Jeyifous 1985, Walker 1992).

5.1.1.2 *The Presumption of an Underlying Nature*

Children and adults everywhere, regardless of culture, environment, or learning history, spontaneously attribute a living kind's characteristic (and often variable) behavior and morphology to intrinsic, causal processes that they *presume* to be lawful even when hidden (Atran 1987). This presumption that an underlying essence is the cause of the kind that we categorize implies that the kind has an unlimited array of undiscovered (and perhaps undiscoverable) properties that do not follow from the marks by which we distinguish it.

For example, people who have a category for tigers generally believe that tigers are quadrupedal animals that roar and have stripes and tawny fur *because of* their intrinsic species-nature. Nonetheless, most people haven't the foggiest idea of the underlying causal mechanisms that are actually responsible for the tiger's legs, roar, stripes, and fur. Even voiceless, legless albino tigers without stripes can still be generally thought of as roaring, four-legged, striped, tawny animals *by nature*. In such cases, we seek to understand or explain what went wrong with the expected course of causal development. This question sets the stage for a "bootstrapping" program of research, which allows subsequent elaboration and understanding of underlying causal mechanisms (including interactions with the environment), even to the point of assimilating hitherto deviant cases into the normal fold (such as caterpillars to butterflies, bats to mammals).

By contrast, a three-legged table with an undulating surface is not generally thought of as being a flat four-legged artifact "by nature," although most tables may in fact be flat and four-legged. In other words, people do not *infer* four-leggedness as an intrinsically caused characteristic of tables (cf. Schwartz 1978). Indeed, a legless table attached to ceiling cables can be a perfectly good table just as a legless beanbag chair can be a perfectly fine chair, whereas a tiger without "its" four legs or stripes or a cow without "its" four legs or moo is considered deficient or deviant with respect to "its" underlying nature.

People in whatever culture do not expect in their lifetimes, or in any number of lifetimes, to exhaust the common properties of animals and plants, nor do they even suppose them to be exhaustible.[5] By comparison,

5. Again, it was Aristotle who first proposed that both living and inert kinds had essential underlying natures. Locke (1689) deemed these unknowable kinds, nature's "real kinds," and considered that their underlying features could never be completely fathomed by the mind. Mill (1843) referred these kinds to nature's own "limited varieties," and therefore considered them to be the predicates of scientific laws. He dubbed them "natural kinds," including biological species and the fundamental elements of inert substance (such as lead, gold). Cross-culturally, it is not at all clear that inert substances comprise a cognitive domain that is conceived in terms of underlying essences or natures. Nor is it even obvious what the basic elements might be across cultures, for the Greek EARTH, AIR, FIRE, and WATER are not apparently universal. In other words, the conception of "natural kind," which supposedly spans the various sorts of lawful natural phenomena, might turn out not to be a *psychologically real* predicate of ordinary thinking (that is, a "natural kind" of cognitive science). It may be, instead, simply an *epistemic* notion peculiar to Western science and philosophy of science.

there is nothing much common to a class of artifacts, like chairs or clothing, except the functions that we assign them, which put them in the class in the first place. In some cases, such as that of the viola da gamba, the defining criteria may relate to some lost historical context and thus be undiscoverable (cf. Rey 1983). Still, we suppose that such criteria were once readily exhaustible.

Nor do we suppose that all "natural kinds" have such deep and provocative properties. Red things, for example, comprise a superficial natural class; however, such things have little in common except that they are red, and they presumably have few, if any, features that follow from the fact that they are red. True, red objects do share features that relate to the human visual system and human esthetic taste; but we do not presume that these features point to further, lawlike relations that we might hope to discover among *other* properties intrinsic to such objects.

5.1.1.3 The Folk Species Concept: Its Bearing on Cognitive Evolution

All human beings, it appears, classify animals and plants into basic groupings that are "quite as obvious to [the] modern scientist as to a Guaraní Indian" (Simpson 1961, 57). This is the concept of the (folk) species. It provides the primary locus for thinking about biology among layfolk the world over. Historically, it provided a transtheoretical basis for scientific speculation about the biological world in that different biological theories —including evolutionary theory—have sought to account for the apparent constancy of species and for the apparent similarities and differences between species (Wallace 1889, 1; cf. Mayr 1969, 37).

From the standpoint of our own evolution, the concept of such a deep kind represents a balancing act between what our ancestors could and could not afford to ignore about their environment. The concept of the folk species allows us to perceive and predict many important properties that link the members of a biological species *that are actually living together at any one time,* and to categorically distinguish such "nondimensional" species from one another. This description is adequate for understanding the biological makeup of local environments, such as those in which our hominid ancestors evolved and in which many "traditional" cultures have developed.

But from a scientific vantage, the concept of folk species is woefully inadequate for capturing the graded relationships that characterize the evolution of species over geologically vast dimensions of time and space —dimensions for which human minds were not directly designed (naturally selected) to comprehend. Only by painstaking, culturally elaborated conceptual strategies, like those involved in science, can minds transcend the innate bounds of their phenomenal world and begin to grasp nature's graded subtleties. To do so, however, requires continued access to the intuitive categories of common sense, which anchors speculation and allows more sophisticated knowledge eventually to emerge.

5.1.2 Folk Taxonomy

In addition to the spontaneous arrangement of local fauna and flora into specieslike groupings, these basic groupings have "from the most remote period in ... history ... been classed in groups under groups. This classification is not arbitrary like the grouping of stars in constellations" (Darwin 1859, 431). This further taxonomic arrangement of species into higher-order "groups under groups," which is common to folk the world over, provides the principal framework for thinking about the similarities and differences between species and for exploring the varied nature of life on earth (Stross 1973, Dougherty 1979, Hays 1983, Brown 1984).

5.1.2.1 (Folk) Biological Ranks

Ethnobiology is a branch of cognitive anthropology concerned with studying the ways in which members of a culture apprehend and utilize the local flora and fauna. More than a century of ethnobiological research has shown that even within a single culture there may be several sorts of "special-purpose" folk-biological classifications, which are organized by particular interests for particular uses (for example, beneficial versus noxious, domestic versus wild, edible versus inedible) (cf. Hough 1897). Only in the last quarter-century, however, has intensive empirical and theoretical work revealed a cross-culturally universal "general-purpose" taxonomy (Berlin et al. 1973) that supports the widest possible range of inductions about living kinds (Atran 1990).

This classification includes indefinitely many inductions about the plausible distributions of initially unfamiliar biologically related traits over organisms given the discovery of such traits in some organism(s), or the likely correlation of known traits among unfamiliar organisms given the discovery of only some of those traits among the organisms. For example, the discovery of breast cancer in monkeys could warrant the initial induction that mammals are susceptible to breast cancer, but not birds or fish, because only mammals have mammary glands. And the knowledge that wombats have mammary glands would warrant the induction that they also have many of the other external and internal traits associated with mammals, such as fur and warm blood.

This "default" folk-biological taxonomy, which serves as an inductive compendium of biological information, is composed of a fairly rigid hierarchy of inclusive classes of organisms, or *taxa*. At each level of the hierarchy the taxa, which are mutually exclusive, partition the locally perceived biota in a virtually exhaustive manner. Lay taxonomy, it appears, is universally composed of a few absolutely distinct hierarchical levels, or *ranks*, such as the level of *folk kingdom* (for example, ANIMAL, PLANT),[6] *life form* (for example, BUG, FISH, BIRD, MAMMAL, TREE, GRASS, BUSH, MUSHROOM),[7] *folk species* (for example, GNAT, SHARK, ROBIN, DOG, MAPLE, WHEAT, HOLLY, TOADSTOOL),[8] and *folk subspecies* (COLLIE, RETRIEVER; SUGAR MAPLE, RED MAPLE).[9]

Intermediate levels also exist between the levels of the folk species and life form. Taxa at these levels usually have no explicit name (for example, rats + mice but no other rodents), although sometimes they may (for example, felines; legumes). Such taxa—especially unnamed "covert" ones—tend not to be as clearly delimited as folk species or life forms, nor does any one intermediate level always constitute a fixed taxonomic rank that partitions the local fauna and flora into a mutually exclusive and virtually exhaustive set of broadly equivalent taxa. Still, there is a psychologically

6. It makes no difference whether or not these groups are named. English speakers ambiguously use the term "animal" to refer to at least three distinct classes of living things: nonhuman animals, animals including human beings, and mammals (the prototypical animals). The term "beast" seems to pick out nonhuman animals in English, but is seldom used today. The English term "plant" is also ambiguously used to refer to the plant kingdom, or to members of that kingdom that are not trees. Maya languages generally have no name for "plant" as such, although these languages do permit a clear distinction to be made between plants and all other things by other means (for example, by assigning a particular numeral classifier to all and only plants).

7. Life forms may differ somewhat from culture to culture. For example, cultures such as ancient Hebrew or modern Rangi (Tanzania) include the herpetofauna (reptiles and amphibians) with insects, worms, and other "creeping crawlers" (Kesby 1979). Other cultures, such as Itza Maya and (until recently) most Western cultures, include the herpetofauna with mammals as "quadrupeds" (Atran 1994). Some cultures, such as Itza Maya, place phenomenally isolated mammals like the bat with birds, just as Rofaifo (New Guinea) place phenomenally isolated birds like the cassowary with mammals (Dwyer 1976). Whatever the particular constitution of life-form groupings, or *taxa*, the life-form level, or *rank*, universally partitions the living world into broadly equivalent divisions.

8. Botanists and ethnobotanists prefer to emphasize morphological criteria and to identify this basic folk-biological level with the scientific genus (Bartlett 1940, Berlin 1972), whereas zoologists and ethnozoologists tend to emphasize behavioral (especially reproductive) criteria and identify with the species (Diamond 1966, Bulmer 1970). The scientifically "ambivalent" character of basic taxa had led me to dub them *generic-speciemes*—an admittedly unwieldy term that I have replaced here with the less accurate but more convenient notion of *folk species*. Invariably, basic-level groupings are mutually exclusive. They also represent virtually exhaustive partitionings of the local fauna and flora in the sense that hitherto unknown or unfamiliar organisms are generally assigned to a basic taxon when attention is directed toward them.

9. Folk subspecies are generally polynomial, but folk species are usually labeled by a single lexical item. Foreign organisms suddenly introduced into a local environment are often initially assimilated to basic taxa as subgenerics. For example, the Lowland Maya originally labeled the Spanish horse "village tapir," just as they termed wheat "Castilian maize." Similarly, the Spanish referred to the indigenous pacas and agoutis as "bastard hares," just as they denoted the Maya breadnut tree "Indian fig."

evident preference for forming intermediate taxa at a level roughly between that of the scientific family (for example, canine, weaver bird) and order (for example, carnivore, passerine) (Atran 1983, Berlin 1992).

5.1.2.2 *A False Bottom Line: Terminal Contrast*

Many comparisons between folk-biological systems are based on analysis of a specious level of folk taxonomy, called the level of "terminal contrast." Terminal contrast occurs between those named groupings which include no additional named groupings. For example, among folk in Michigan the class of terminal contrast includes: BAT, SQUIRREL, WEASEL, BEAVER, BEAGLE (dog), POODLE (dog), CALICO (cat), SHORTHAIRED TABBY (cat), LONGHAIRED TABBY (cat), and so on.

There is little systematic relation between such terminal folk taxa and corresponding scientific taxa. Thus, BAT corresponds to diverse scientific families, genera, and species in the order Chiroptera, many of which are locally represented in Michigan. SQUIRREL includes different local genera and species of the family Sciuridae. WEASEL encompasses two local species of the genus *Mustela*. BEAVER corresponds to the single local species *Castor canadensis*. BEAGLE and POODLE denote two "varieties" of the species *Canis familiaris*. CALICO refers to a "variety" of *Felis cattus*, whereas SHORTHAIRED TABBY and LONGHAIRED TABBY are (mongrelized) "races" of the species.

Using terminal contrast, then, as the focus of comparison between folk biology and scientific systematics would reveal little relationship. In fact, many studies in psychology and anthropology that purport to compare the "taxonomic structure" of folk and scientific biology use terminal contrast as their basis of analysis (Conklin 1962, Lévi-Strauss 1966, Rosch 1975). This practice is unfortunate, because terminal contrast is a purely (ethno)linguistic feature that has little direct significance for the structure of living-kind taxonomies. As a result, the profound similarities between Linnaean and folk-biological taxonomies have been mostly ignored.

Whereas the notion of "terminal contrast" represents a more or less arbitrary level of analysis, the concept of *rank* does not. But the concept of rank, which people spontaneously *employ*, is not an easy concept to *analyze*. This difficulty should not surprise us, for most of our more powerful and effortless conceptual achievements are difficult to reflect on precisely because they are so "automatic."

5.1.2.3 *The Significance of Rank*

Ranking is a cognitive mapping that places living-kind categories in a structure of *absolute levels*, which may be evolutionarily designed to correspond to fundamentally *different levels of reality*. Thus, the rank of folk kingdom—the level at which organisms are classified as ANIMAL or

PLANT—may be determined, a priori, by our innate ontology (cf. Donnellan 1971). In other words, we can know that something is an organism if and only if we know it is either ANIMAL or PLANT. The rank of folk species—the level at which organisms are classified as DOG, OAK, and so on—corresponds to the level at which morphological, behavioral, and ecological relationships between organisms maximally covary. It is also the rank at which people are most likely to attribute biological properties. This attribution includes characteristic patterns of inheritance, growth, and physiological function as well as more "hidden" properties, such as hitherto unknown organic processes, organs, and diseases.

The life-form level—the level at which organisms are classified as BIRD, TREE, and so on—corresponds to a partitioning of the local ecological landscape, to which we assign species roles in the "economy of nature" as a function of the way their specific morphology and behavior are fitted to those roles. For example, the morphology and behavior of different birds more or less partition the way in which vertebrate life (competitively) accommodates to the air. The morphology and growth pattern of different trees corresponds to a partitioning of the ways in which single-stem plants (competitively) gain access to sunlight. These divisions not only share readily perceptible features and behaviors that are related to habitat, but they also structure inductions about the distribution of underlying properties that presumably relate biology to the local ecology. The rank of folk subspecies—the level at which organisms are classified as BEAGLE, SUGAR MAPLE, and so on—corresponds to ranges of natural variation that human beings are most apt to appropriate and manipulate as a function of their cultural interests.

The lawlike generalizations that hold across taxa of the same rank (that is, a class of classes) are thus of a different logical type than generalizations that apply to only this or that taxon (that is, a class of organisms). Termite, pig, and lemon tree are not lawfully related to one another by virtue of any simple relation of class inclusion or connection to some common taxonomic node, but by dint of their common rank—in this case the level of folk species.

5.1.2.4 The Rank of Folk Species vs. the Basic Level

By far the majority of taxa in any folk-biological classification belong to the level of the folk species. It is this level that people in most societies privilege when they see and talk about biological discontinuities. Comparing the relative salience of folk-biological categories among Tzeltal Maya Indians and other "traditional" societies around the world, anthropologist Brent Berlin and his colleagues (Berlin et al. 1974) find that folk species (genera) are the most basic conceptual groupings of organisms (cf. Hays 1983 for New Guinea). Folk species represent the cuts in nature which Maya children first name and form an image of (Stross 1973), and which Maya adults most frequently use in speech, most easily recall in memory, and most readily communicate to others (Hunn 1976).

Yet, in a series of experiments conducted by psychologist Eleanor Rosch and her colleagues (Rosch et al. 1976), the most salient category cuts in the folk-biological classification of urban American folk do not uniformly correspond to the level of the folk species (cf. Zubin and Köpcke 1986 for Germany). Only folk species of the life form MAMMAL, such as DOG and HORSE, consistently fall within the "one level of abstraction at which the most basic category cuts are made." By contrast, the other life forms tested—TREE, BIRD and FISH—are themselves treated as basic categories. These life-form categories—and not subordinate folk species like OAK, ROBIN, and SHARK—turn out to be the most inclusive category for which a concrete image of the category as a whole can be formed, the first categorization made during perception of the environment, the earliest category named by children (Dougherty 1979), and the categories most codable, most coded, and most prevalent in language (see chapter 1).

Cross-cultural evidence suggests that the most basic level in Rosch's sense is a variable phenomenon that shifts as a function of general cultural significance and individual familiarity and expertise (Dougherty 1978). Thus, urban folk in industrial societies generally have little distinctive familiarity with, knowledge of, and use for various species of trees, fish, and birds. Such folk generally have far fewer named descriptions or images for species than do rural and traditional peoples, who must be intimately aware of the local flora and fauna upon which their lives depend. Only for mammalian species, which retain appreciable cultural importance in industrial societies (often through story books and nature programs on television), is there comparable linguistic, perceptual, and mnemonic saliency across cultures.

The degeneration, or devolution, of folk-biological knowledge in urban societies apparently involves gradual attrition in the cultural saliency of lower levels of taxonomy. The folk species, which is traditionally (and historically) the original basic object level, becomes culturally less significant relative to superordinate categories. Eventually, these more inclusive categories become the most culturally salient. This suggestion that culture conditions the basic level implies that what is most salient for human perceivers in Rosch's sense is not simply determined by the objective structure "out there."

The fact that the basic level cuts across folk-biological ranks in urban societies does not imply that the ranking system is sundered or that the inclusion of a given taxon within a given rank changes. The fact that for some urban Americans both CHICKEN and BIRD are thought of as basic-level categories, although CHICKEN is also thought of as a kind of BIRD, does not indicate confusion of biological rank. It does not because ranks primarily represent *absolute levels of biological significance* and not just *relative levels of linguistic, perceptual, and mnemonic codability*. Thus, it is prima facie more plausible that all oaks or robins will be susceptible to some disease—which will stunt their growth, deform their limbs, or derange their functioning—than are all trees or birds.

For example, whereas urban American or German subjects appear to treat FISH, BIRD and TREE as basic-level categories, Itza and Tzeltal Maya Indians seem to treat them as superordinate to the basic level (see Berlin et al. 1973 and Stross 1973). Nevertheless, in a series of inference studies designed with John Coley, Douglas Medin, and Elizabeth Lynch, American subjects perform much as do Itza subjects in maximizing inductive potential at the folk-species level. Thus, both Americans and Itza are much more likely to infer that, say, oak trees have a disease (or a given enzyme, protein, etc.) that white oak trees have, than to infer that trees have a disease that oak trees have. This result cannot simply be attributed to the fact that subjects are more likely to generalize to a more specific category. Indeed, subjects in both cultures are no more likely to infer that, say, white oak trees have a disease that spotted white oak trees have, than to infer that oak trees have a disease that white oak trees have. The same findings apply in cases of inferences to particular folk species of fish or birds as opposed to inferences to fish or birds in general.

Ranks are domain-specific phenomena peculiar to the biological realm, whereas Rosch's "levels of abstraction" are domain-general heuristics (see chapter 1). The latter can apply to many sorts of objects, including artifacts, and to the same objects in different ways depending on context (for example, TOMATO may be basic when viewed as a type of VEGETABLE but subordinate when perceived as a kind of BUSH). Relative and absolute levels can, and traditionally do, coincide: The most easily accessible criteria for object recognition and communication are the most efficacious indicators of unseen properties of deeper biological significance. But such efficacy is only conditionally necessary, in cultures or contexts where people's lives may depend upon it.

5.1.2.5 *Taxonomic Essentialism*

Taxonomic essentialism is the cognitive principle that recursively weds the presumption that each living kind has an underlying teleological nature to the ranking of living kinds in groups under groups. As we have already seen in section 5.1, the presumption that folk species have essential natures is an inferential principle that underlies the stability of taxonomic types (such as DOG, FROG) despite obvious token variation among exemplars (this Chihuahua and that Saint Bernard, this tadpole and that tailless leaper). This stability, in turn, allows consistent category-based inductions. For example, knowing that a Chihuahua and a Saint Bernard share an internal property is likely to be taken as stronger evidence that all dogs share that property than if only two Chihuahuas are known to share the property.

By recursive application of the perceptual processes and essentialist principles that generate folk species, higher-order folk-biological taxa would also be organized on the basis of clusters of apparent features, with each such cluster separated from others of its rank by a readily perceptible gap where clusters share few, if any, features (Hunn 1976). The clustered features would presumably "go together" because of some shared aspects of underlying essential structure. For example, from the fact that sheep have multichambered stomachs, we may "safely" infer that deer, which are morphologically and behaviorally akin to sheep, also have multichambered stomachs. Making inferences from one category to another (from sheep to deer) enables us to set forth assumptions and predictions, and generalize from the known to the unknown. It is this function of classification that may be considered "the foundation of the scientific method in biology: To most biologists, the 'best' classification must be the one that maximizes the probability that statements known to be true of two organisms are true of all members of the smallest taxon to which they both belong" (Warburton 1967).

Full activation of this principle of category-based induction for all higher-order taxa, and for the whole of the living-kind taxonomy, may require support from a unifying causal theory of the sort science can provide. For example, upon finding that the bacterium *E. coli* shares a hitherto unknown property with turkeys, it may take a Nobel prize-winning insight and belief in the underlying genetic unity of living kinds to "safely" make the inference that all creatures belonging to the lowest-ranked taxon that includes both turkeys and *E. coli* also share that property. In this example, the lowest-ranked taxon just happens to include all organisms.

5.1.3 Section Summary

Readily perceptible properties of taxa (morphotypes) are generally good predictors of deeper, underlying shared properties and may originally provide the basis for living-kind categories. Initially, the underlying essential structures are unknown, and merely presumed to (teleologically) cause the observable regularities in biological categories. Attention to this causal link and a cognitive endeavor to know it better leads to awareness that this correlation between surface and deep features is not perfect. Added knowledge about these deeper properties may then lead to category modification. For example, most adult Americans categorize whales and bats as mammals despite the many superficial properties shared with fish and birds, respectively.

Despite the "boot-strapping" revision of taxonomy implied in this example, notice how much did not change: neither the abstract hierarchical schema furnished by folk taxonomy, nor—in a crucial sense—even the kinds involved. Bats, whales, mammals, fish, and birds did not simply vanish from common sense to arise anew in science like Athena springing from the head of Zeus. Rather, there was a redistribution of affiliations between antecedently perceived kinds. What had altered was the construal of the underlying natures of those kinds, with consequent redistribution of kinds and reappraisal of properties pertinent to reference.

If this scenario is anywhere near correct, then an integrative (folk) biological theory—however rudimentary—*cannot be* the cognitive mechanism responsible for the ontology of living kinds, as some researchers have proposed (Murphy and Medin 1985, Carey 1985, Keil 1989, Gelman and Coley 1991). In other words, it is not the elaboration of a theory of biological causality that progressively distinguishes people's understanding of the (folk) species concept as it applies to (nonhuman) animals and plants, from their understanding of concepts of inert substances, artifacts, or persons. Rather, there seems to be *a universal, a priori presumption* that species constitute "natural kinds" by virtue of their special (initially unknown and perhaps unknowable) teleological natures, and that species further group naturally into ranked taxonomies. This spontaneous arrangement of living things into taxonomies of essential kinds thus constitutes a prior set of constraints on *any and all possible theories* about the causal relations between living kinds. Recent cross-cultural evidence indicates strongly that it does do so in fact.

5.2 A Comparison with Itza Maya Folk Biology

The Itza are the last Maya Indians native to the Petén tropical forest, once the epicenter of Classic Maya civilization. Although the Itza cosmological system was thoroughly sundered by the Spanish conquest and subsequent oppression, Itza folk-biological knowledge—including taxonomic competence as well as practical application—remains strikingly robust. This survival is largely to be expected; for, if the core of any folk knowledge about the biological world is indeed spontaneously emitted and transmitted by minds, then it should be mostly independent of (historically and culturally specific) institutionalized modes of communication.

Itza Maya folk biology thus provides evidence for generalizations about the specific taxonomic structure that delimits the universal domain of folk biology. There is no common lexical entry for the plant kingdom in Itza, but the numeral classifier *tek* is used with all and only plants. Plants generally fall under one of four mutually exclusive life forms: *che'* (trees), *pokche'* (undergrowth = herbs, shrubs, bushes), *ak'* (vines), and *su'uk* (grasses). Each life form is distinguished by a particular stem habit, which is believed to be the natural outgrowth of every primary kind of *pu(k)sik'al* (species-essence) included in that life form. A number of introduced and cultivated plants, however, are not affiliated with any of these life forms, and are simply denoted *jun tek* (literally, "one plant"), as are many of the phylogenetically isolated plants, such as the palms and cacti. Arguably, they may be thought of as *monospecific life forms,* in much the same way as the aardvark is the only known species representing its scientific order. All informants agree that mushrooms (*xikin~che',* literally, "tree-ear") have no *pu(k)sik'al* and are not plants, but take life away from the trees that host them. Lichens and bryophytes (mosses and liverworts) are not considered to be plants, to have an essence, or to live.

The Itza term for animals (*b'a'al~che'* = "forest-thing") polysemously indicates both the animal kingdom as a whole (including invertebrates, birds, and fish), and also a more restrictive grouping of quadrupeds (amphibians = jumping animals, *b'a'al~che' kusiit,* reptiles = slithering animals, *b'a'al~che' kujiltikub'aj* and, most typically, mammals = walking animals, *b'a'al~che' kuximal*). Birds (*ch'iich'*) and fish (*käy*) exhibit patterns of internal structure that parallel those found with the quadrupeds. But for the unlabeled life form of invertebrates, whose morphology and ecological proclivity is very different from that of human beings and other vertebrates, correspondence of folk to modern systematics blurs as one descends the rungs of the scientific ladder, and violations of scientific taxonomy tend to be more pronounced. Still, in this respect as in others, the categorical structure of Itza folk biology differs little from that of any other folk-biological system, including that which initially gave rise to systematics—the science of classifying animals and plants by degrees of biological relatedness.[10]

5.2.1 Cross-Cultural Constraints on Theory Formation

If different cultures have different theories or belief systems about the relations between biological categories, shouldn't there be clear differences in biological reasoning? Not necessarily. Because there are initially universal taxonomic constraints on theories or belief systems about biological categories and their relationships, there should also be some predictable stability and cross-cultural consistency to theory-related inferences. For

10. Thus, for Linnaeus, the Natural System was rooted in "a natural instinct [that] teaches us to know first those objects closest to us, and at length the smallest ones: for example, Man, Quadrupeds, Birds, Fish, Insects, Mites, or firstly the large Plants, lastly the smallest mosses" (Linnaeus 1751, section 153).

example, different cultures may have very different beliefs about reproduction but their judgments about whether or not two species could interbreed may well show the same decreasing function of taxonomic distance.

Thus for Aristotle, offspring are considered "unnatural monsters" to the extent that they fail to resemble their fathers, and in direct proportion to the number of nodes in the "common Greek's" taxonomic tree that must be climbed to encounter a likely progenitor (Atran 1985). Similarly for the Itza Maya, we found a highly structured taxonomy that enjoys a strong cultural consensus and is strongly correlated with notions about the likelihood of mating between animals that do not normally interbreed (Atran 1994). For example, the jaguar's even-headed temperament, the mountain lion's aggressiveness, and the margay's small size generally disallow mating among these three members of the Itza spotted-cat taxon, *b'alum*.

Nevertheless, Itza are readily inclined to believe that even these matings could occur under certain imaginable situations, and which we experimentally manipulated (for example, animals that were caged, dwarfed, or drugged). Given Itza explanations of how reproduction works, actual fulfilment of these conditions can never be empirically confirmed or disconfirmed. For Itza believe offspring are preformed before birth in their same-sex progenitors. Because daughters resemble mothers and sons resemble fathers, there is no empirical counterevidence for unlikely but imaginable crossings. Aristotle's theory of reproduction and generation is markedly different than the Itza's, but the same sorts of taxonomic constraints operate on both. Indeed, evolutionary theory itself initially had to meet much the same conditions.

5.2.2 American and Maya Mammal Taxonomy

As further illustration of the general framework of folk biology, consider recent experimental findings obtained by Alejandro López and myself among University of Michigan students raised in rural Michigan and Itza. Our working hypothesis was that if the same kinds of folk-biological constraints on taxonomies and inductions describe performances of people in such different cultures, then we have reason to believe that the underlying cognitive processes are part of human nature.

What follows is a brief account of findings about all mammals represented in the local environments of the Itza and Michigan groups, respectively. For Itza we included bats, although Itza do not consider them mammals. For the students we included the emblematic wolverine, although it is now extinct in Michigan. Each group was tested in its native language (Itza and English), and included six men and six women. No statistically significant differences between men and women were found on the tasks below, which were designed to probe three general questions.

but v. small N!

5.2.2.1 *To What Extent Are Different Folk-Biological Taxonomies Correlated with One Another and with a Corresponding Scientific (Evolutionary) Taxonomy of the Local Fauna and Flora?*

Elsewhere (Atran 1994), I describe the sorting procedures for eliciting individual taxonomies as well as mathematical techniques for aggregating individual taxonomies into a "cultural model" of the society's folk-biological system. Our results indicate that the individual folk-biological taxonomies of Itza and students from rural Michigan are all more or less competent expressions of comparably robust cultural models of the biological world. To compare the structure and content of cultural models with one another, and with scientific models, we mathematically correlated each group's aggregate taxonomy with an evolutionary taxonomy (for technical details, see Atran 1994, 1995).

The overall correlations were quite high between both evolutionary taxonomy and Itza taxonomy ($r = .81$) and between science and the folk taxonomy of Michigan students ($r = .75$). Somewhat surprisingly, Itza come even closer to a scientific appreciation of the local mammal fauna than do Michigan students. A comparison of higher-order taxa only (that is, excluding folk species) still shows a strong correlation both for Itza ($r = .51$) and Michigan subjects ($r = .48$).

Itza and Michigan folk taxonomic trees at these higher levels compare favorably to one another (figures 5.1 and 5.3) and to science (figures 5.2 and 5.4), both in number of nodes and levels at which nodes are formed. Agreement between the higher-order folk taxonomies and science is maximized at the level of the scientific suborder (that is, mammals grouped at level 4 in figures 5.2 and 5.4), both for Itza and Michigan subjects. On the whole, intermediate taxa formed at this level and below are still somewhat imageable (that is, mammals grouped at level 4 and below in figures 5.1 and 5.3). Thus for the Itza, taxa formed at level 3 in figure 5.1 are not only

Figure 5.1 (see page 150)
Intermediate levels in sample mammal taxonomy for one Itza female subject. As exhibited by average link cluster analysis (the preferred clustering technique in systematics), this tree shows that the folk-biological taxonomy of mammals for the subject has a total of six levels, with only three groups of mammals at level 1: FOX and JAGUARUNDI, JAGUAR and OCELOT, and POCKET MOUSE, RAT, and SHREW. It also shows that MOUNTAIN LION goes together with JAGUAR and OCELOT, at level 2, with MARGAY at level 3, with CAT, FOX, and JAGUARUNDI at level 4, with COYOTE and DOG at level 5, and with the rest of the mammals at level 6 (for example, OTTER). The lowest level at which two given mammals go together in the taxonomy represents the taxonomic distance between them. Thus, low taxonomic distance corresponds to high folk-biological relatedness. In the example, MOUNTAIN LION is closely related to JAGUAR (2), fairly related to CAT (4), and not very related to OTTER (6). Notice that the topological structure of the corresponding scientific tree for Itza mammals in figure 5.2 resembles this individual's tree and that the correlation of "topological distance" between these trees is 0.5.

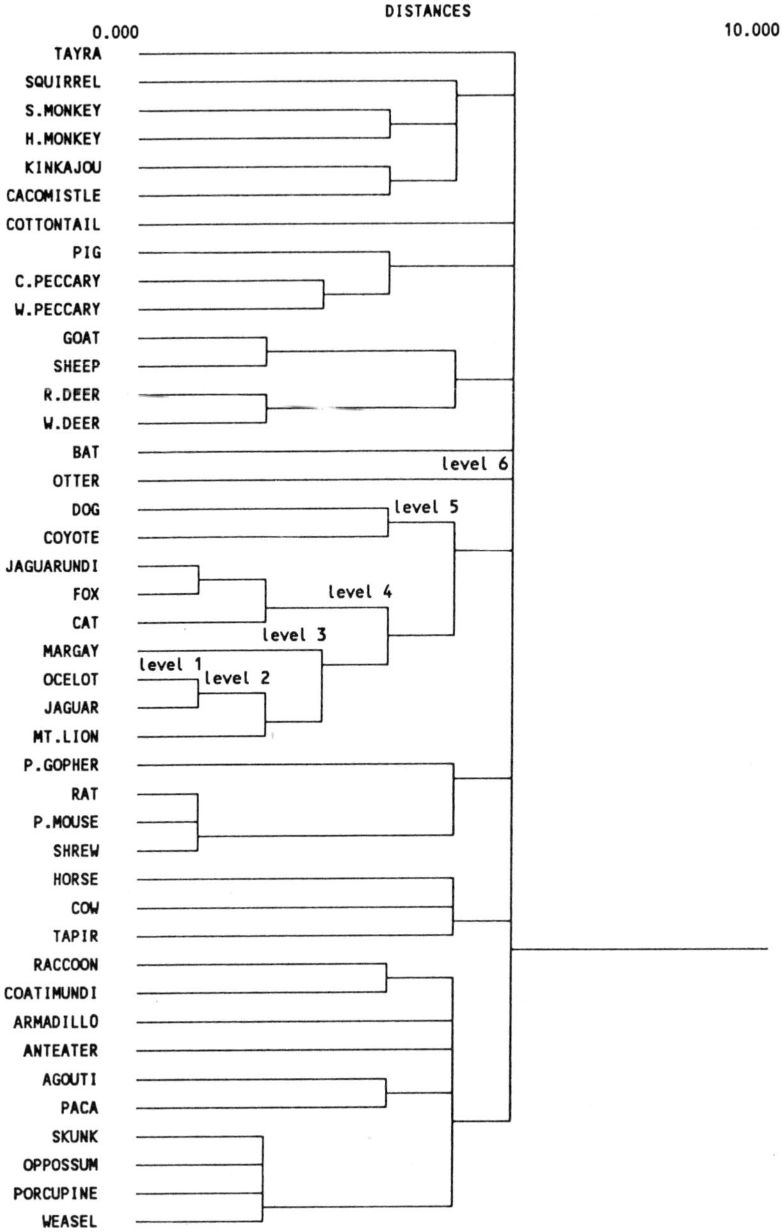
DISTANCES
0.000
10.000
TAYRA
SQUIRREL
S.MONKEY
H.MONKEY
KINKAJOU
CACOMISTLE
COTTONTAIL
PIG
C.PECCARY
W.PECCARY
GOAT
SHEEP
R.DEER
W.DEER
BAT
OTTER
DOG
COYOTE
JAGUARUNDI
FOX
CAT
MARGAY
OCELOT
JAGUAR
MT.LION
P.GOPHER
RAT
P.MOUSE
SHREW
HORSE
COW
TAPIR
RACCOON
COATIMUNDI
ARMADILLO
ANTEATER
AGOUTI
PACA
SKUNK
OPPOSSUM
PORCUPINE
WEASEL
level 1
level 2
level 3
level 4
level 5
level 6

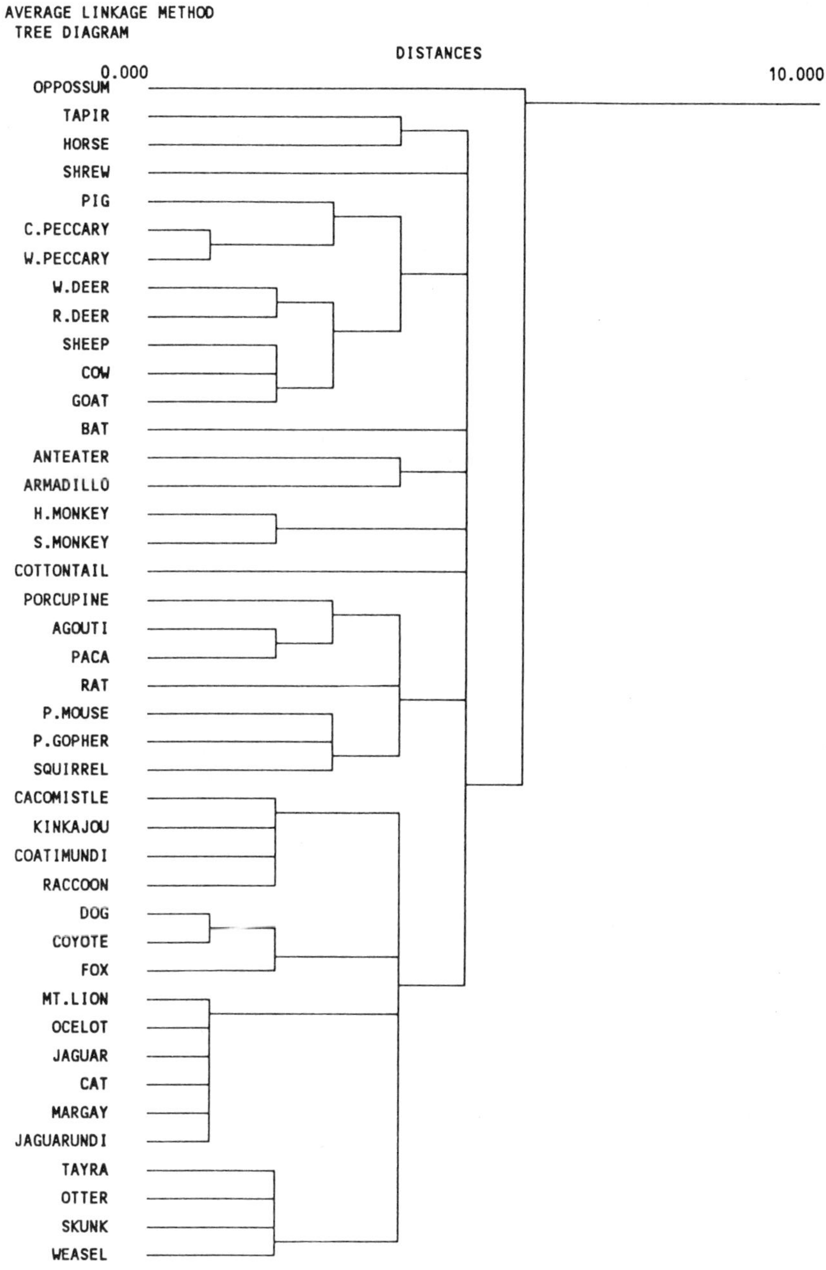

Figure 5.2
Scientific tree for Itza mammals. The six levels represented in the tree from left to right are: Genus, Family, Suborder, Order, Subclass, and Class.

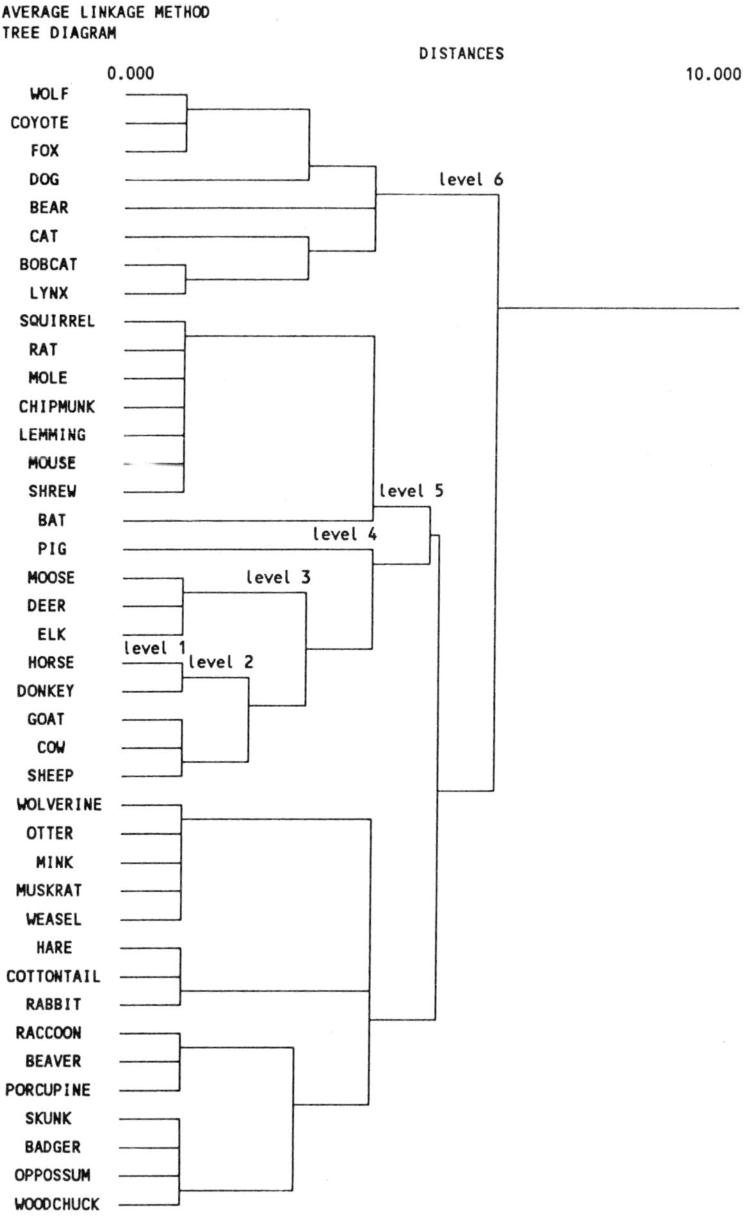

Figure 5.3

Intermediate levels in sample mammal taxonomy for one Michigan male subject. Notice the linkage between OPPOSUM and SKUNK at level 1, whereas in figure 5.4 they are maximally distant in the corresponding scientific tree. The bovids (GOAT, COW, SHEEP) are linked to the equids (HORSE, DONKEY) at level 2, and to the cervids (MOOSE, DEER, ELK) at level 3; scientifically, however, bovids and cervids but not equids are ruminants. The bat is linked to the rodents and SHREW at level 4. Level 5 links this group to all other mammals save canines and felines. Canines and felines are linked at level 4, and with the rest of the mammals at level 6.

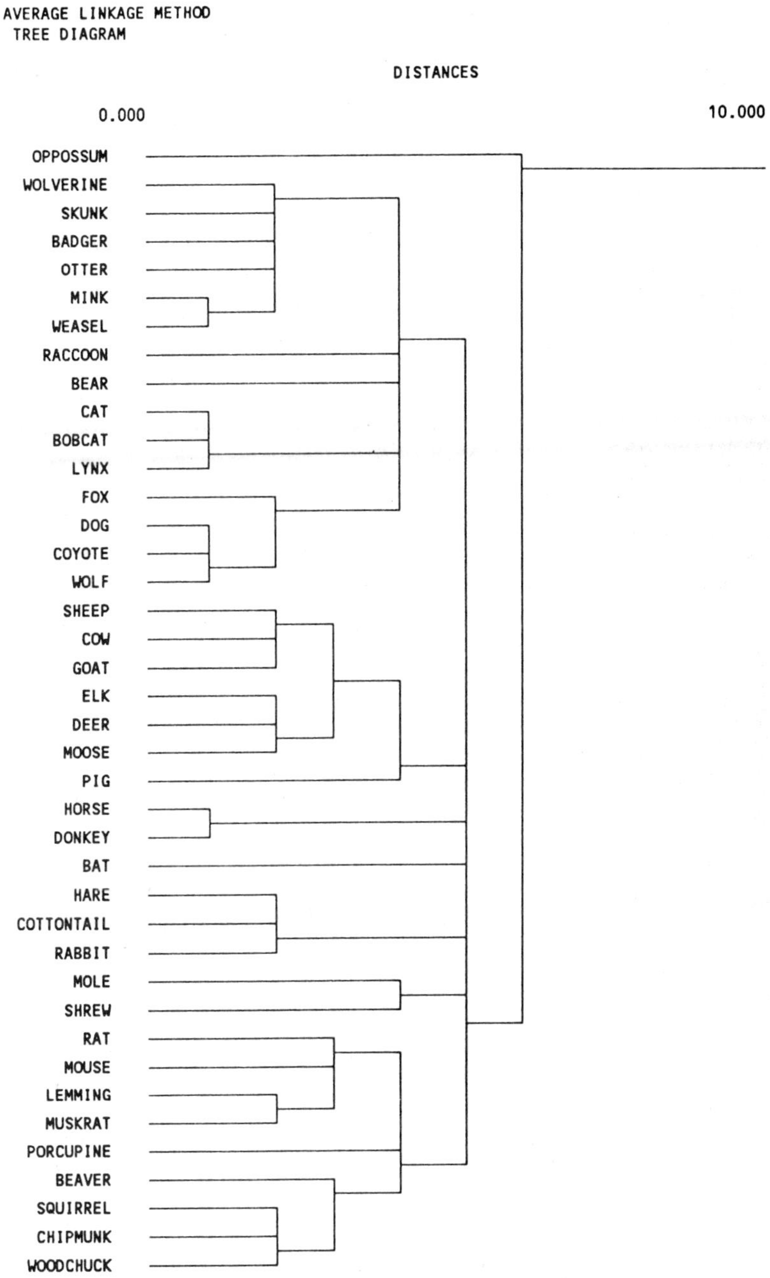

Figure 5.4
Scientific tree for Michigan mammals. The six levels represented in the tree from left to right are: Genus, Family, Suborder, Order, Subclass, and Class.

representable by an abstract image, but are sometimes named as well. At level 3, for example, the named intermediate taxon, *b'alum*, includes the large felines (margay, ocelot, jaguar, and mountain lion). At level 2, *och* includes the skunk, opossum, porcupine, and weasel, which are morphologically and behaviorally close (in figure 5.1) although scientifically distant (in figure 5.2).

To compare Itza and Michigan taxonomies directly, we took the parts of the aggregate taxonomies from each group that have identical scientific trees. Generally, one culture's category is deemed "topologically equivalent" to the other's if there is a node in the scientific tree that includes only those two categories and no others in either culture, although the rule is slightly relaxed in certain cases. We found that the correlation between the partial taxonomics of the two cultures ($r = .57$) proves significantly higher than the correlation between each group's partial taxonomy and the corresponding scientific taxonomy.

This correlation suggests that there are at least some universal cognitive factors at work in folk-biological classification that are mitigated or ignored by science. For example, certain groupings, such as felines + canines, are common to both Itza and Michigan students, although felines and canines are phylogenetically further from one another than either family is from other carnivore families (such as mustelids and procyonids). A multidimensional scaling of taxonomies for each cultural group shows that animals are arrayed along dimensions of size and remoteness from human beings (for Itza) or ferocity (for Michigan students, cf. Henley 1969, Rips et al. 1973). These are dimensions that a corresponding scientific classification of the local fauna does not exhibit.

Other factors in the divergence between folk taxonomies and science are related both to science's incorporation of a worldwide perspective in classifying local biota and to its reliance on biologically "deep," theoretically weighted properties of internal anatomy and physiology. For example, the opossum is the only marsupial present in North and Central America. Both Itza and the students relate the opossum to skunks and porcupines because it shares with them numerous readily perceptible features of morphology and behavior. From a scientific vantage, however, the opossum is taxonomically isolated from all the other locally represented mammals in a subclass of its own. Thus, if we exclude the opossum from the comparison between the folk taxonomies and science, the correlation rises notably for Itza (from $r = .51$ to $r = .60$) and the students (from $r = .48$ to $r = .55$).

One factor mitigating the ability of Itza or Michigan students to appreciate the opossum as scientists do is that there are no other locally present marsupials to relate the opossum to. As a result, the most readily perceptible morphobehavioral difference between the opossum and other local mammals—carrying its young in a pouch—cannot be linked to discoverable differences that would connect the opossum to other marsupials and help to differentiate them from nonmarsupials. The opossum's pouch appears as just another characteristic morphobehavioral feature, like the porcupine's quills or the skunk's smell. Both Michigan students and Itza are apparently unaware of the deeper biological significance of the opossum's lack of a placenta.

5.2.2.2 *To What Extent Do the Culturally Specific Theories and Belief Systems, Such as Science, Shape Folk-Biological Taxonomy?*

A particularly striking folk bias is evident in Itza snake classification. Questioning shows that people fear certain snakes. Only some of these are actually poisonous, but all those feared are nevertheless thought to sprout wings and several heads, and to fly off to the sea with their last victims—a likely cultural survival of the Precolumbian cult of *kukul-kan* ("feathered serpent"). In-depth interviews suggest that supposed danger is an overriding factor in snake sortings, and supports one interpretation of a multidimensional scaling of these sortings.

A first interpretation of the phenomenon might be that in some cases the biological target is determined more by culturally specific interests than by readily perceptible phenotypic gaps in the distribution of local biota. Evidence from biology and social history, however, indicates otherwise. Human beings everywhere, it seems, are emotionally disposed to fear snakes (Seligman 1971) and to socially ritualize this phobia (Marks 1987) in recurrent cross-cultural themes, such as "the cult of the serpent" (Munkur 1983).

The fact that people are spontaneously more inclined to exhibit and express fear of snakes than fear of much more lethal cultural artifacts—like swords, guns, and atom bombs—intimates an evolutionary explanation: such naturally selected phobias to resurgent perils in ancestral environments may have provided an extra margin for survival, whereas there would be no such direct natural selection of cognitive responses to the more recent dangers of particular cultural environments. Upon closer examination, then, it appears that Itza snake classification may be an exception that proves the rule: folk-biological taxonomies are, by and large, naturally selected conceptual structures—"habits of mind"—that are biologically "pretuned" to capture relevant and recurrent contents of those natural environments—"habits of the world"—in which hominid evolution occurred.

The best candidate for the cultural influence of theory in American folk biology is science, of course. Yet, the exposure of Michigan students to science education has little apparent effect on their folk taxonomy. From a scientific view, the students taxonomize no better than do Itza. Science's influence is at best marginal. For example, science may peripherally bear on the differences in the way Itza and Michigan students categorize bats. Itza deem bats to be birds (*ch'iich'*), not mammals (*b'a'al~che'*).

Like Michigan students, Itza acknowledge in interviews that there is a resemblance between bats and small rodents and insectivores. Because Itza classify bats with birds, they consider the resemblance to be only superficial and not indicative of a taxonomic relationship. By contrast, Michigan students "know" from schooling that bats are mammals. But this knowledge can hardly be taken as evidence for the influence of scientific *theory* on folk taxonomy. Despite learning that bats are mammals, the students go on to relate bats to mice and shrews just as Itza might if they did not already "know" that bats are birds. From an evolutionary stand, however, bats are taxonomically no closer to shrews and mice than to other local mammals. The students, it seems, pay little or no attention to the deeper biological relationships science reveals.

The influence of science education on folk induction may also reflect *less actual knowledge* of theory *than willing belief* that there is a scientific theory that supports folk taxonomy. The high concordance between folk taxonomy and science, especially at the level of the folk species, provides Michigan students prima facie support for believing that their folk taxonomy is more or less on a scientific track. Given their belief that science has a causal story to tell, they assume that the same story pretty much holds for their folk taxonomy. This belief steers them into inductive errors, but also to the realization that eliminating such errors leads to a closer accord with science—albeit a modest one.

For example, given that a skunk and opossum share a deep biological property, Michigan students are less likely to conclude that all mammals share the property than if it were shared by a skunk and a bear. From a scientific standpoint, the students are using the right reasoning strategy (that is, diversity-based inference), but reaching the wrong conclusion because of a faulty taxonomy (that is, the belief that skunks are taxonomically further from bears than from opossums). But if *told* that opossums are phylogenetically more distant from skunks than bears are, then the students readily revise their taxonomy to make the correct inference. Still, it would be misleading to claim that the students thereby use theory to revise their taxonomy, although a revision occurs *in accordance with* scientific theory.

5.2.2.3 To What Extent Does Folk-Biological Taxonomy Guide Inferences about the Distribution of Unknown Biological Properties Across Taxa?

We used a model-theoretic technique developed by cognitive psychologists for analyzing substantive claims about reasoning. Called "the similarity-coverage model" (*SCM*, Osherson et al. 1990), it is designed to assess the category-based inductions that people make on the basis of their shared knowledge.

Osherson et al. (1990) identify a set of phenomena that characterize category-based inferences in adults, and formalize a model that predicts the strength of those inferences. Rather than talk about inductive "inferences," Osherson et al. discuss inductive "arguments," in which facts used to generate the inference play the role of premises, and the inference itself plays the role of conclusion. Thus, inferring that all birds have ulnar arteries from the fact that jays and flamingos do, amounts to the argument:

Jays have ulnar arteries.
Flamingos have ulnar arteries.

All birds have ulnar arteries.

This argument is strong to the extent that belief in the premises leads to belief in the conclusion. For all SCM phenomena, the properties (for example, have ulnar arteries) are "blank," that is, plausible but unfamiliar biological properties so as to promote reasoning based solely on the categories.

The Osherson et al. (1990) model endeavors to account for the phenomena of argument strength in terms of two components: similarity and coverage. As an illustration, consider the argument:

Bobcats secrete uric acid crystals.
Cows secrete uric acid crystals.

Foxes secrete uric acid crystals.

Subjects may infer that foxes have secret uric acid crystals because they are somewhat similar to bobcats. Subjects may also infer that foxes share the property because all mammals may have it given that bobcats and cows do. Accordingly, the first component of the model—*similarity*—calculates the maximum similarity of the premise categories to the conclusion category; the greater this similarity, the stronger the argument. The second component—*coverage*—calculates the average maximum similarity of the premise categories to members of the "inclusive category" (average maximum similarity is explained below with reference to the next set of examples). The inclusive category is the lowest category that includes both premise and conclusion categories. For the argument above, the inclusive category is presumably MAMMAL (the relevant sense of "animal" in this case). The greater the coverage of the inclusive category by the premise categories, the stronger the argument.

The model gives the *typicality* of an item (such as species) as the average similarity (such as taxonomic distance) of that item to all other items in the inclusive category (such as life form) (this description is in line with the treatment of typicality in chapter 1). Items that are more typical provide greater coverage of the category than items that are less typical. But a pair of typical items provides *less coverage* than, say, a pair with one item that is typical and another that is atypical. For example:

Horses have an ileal vein.
Donkeys have an ileal vein.
___
All mammals have an ileal vein.

is a weaker argument than:

Horses have an ileal vein.
Gophers have an ileal vein.
___
All mammals have an ileal vein.

Because the average similarity of donkeys to other mammals is about the same as that of horses, donkeys add little to the contribution that horses already make to the computation of average *maximum* similarity. For example, the similarity of horses and donkeys to cows is uniformly high, but the similarity of horses and donkeys to mice is uniformly low. By contrast, the similarity of horses to cows is high, but so too is the similarity of gophers to mice. Consequently, the average maximum similarity of horses and gophers to cows and mice is greater than the average maximum similarity of horses and donkeys to cows and mice.

The model assumes a "default" notion of similarity for each domain of categories. But there may be different notions of similarity within a domain, and different default criteria of similarity for different domains. For example, chickens may be considered somewhat similar to pigs from the standpoint of DOMESTIC ANIMALS, but not from the default standpoint of ANIMALS. In the domain of ARTIFACTS, however, "use" may be a default criterion that treats, say, a metal waste can and a metal stool as dissimilar, although they may be similar from any number of vantages (indeed, they may even be the very same thing, say from the standpoint of a dismayed bartender or artisan who finds her overturned stool used as a waste can).

In addition, "blank" properties may have "default" value as unknown (and possibly unknowable) attributes of a certain kind. In the case of biological categories, "blank" properties are presumptively *essential* properties of living kinds. In fact, if for some reason people are led to believe that the unknown properties attached to living kinds are not essential properties of that which governs what goes on "inside" the organism, then the projection of those properties follows a very different trajectory across categories than presumptively essential properties (Heit and Rubinstein, in press). For example, people may presume that the underlying physiological properties of whales and pigs are essentially alike, but that unknown properties related to what whales eat will be more like those of sharks than pigs.

Accordingly, we used diseases as blank properties and taxonomic distance as a measure of similarity between natural categories for testing the SCM across cultures. Evidence suggests that people reason about diseases much as they do about properties presumed to be biologically essential (Rips 1975, Keil 1994). The typicality gradient is given by the taxonomic structure itself. In other words, mammals that are on the average closest to the other mammals in the taxonomy (that is, with the lowest mean taxonomic distance score) are by definition the most typical as well.

The instructions on the typicality and diversity tasks were:

> In Ontario [*Yucatan*] there is a lake [*noj ja'*] with an island [*peten*] where all the animals [*tulakal b'a'al* ~ *che'*] that live here [*waye'*] also live. Only these animals live on the island and no others and no people [*ma'an krystyaano*]. But on a visit to the island we found that some of the animals on the island have a disease [*koja'anil*]. But we don't know what other animals on the island can have the disease and I want you to tell me which other animals you think can have the disease.

The subjects were then shown cards of all local mammals one by one,[11] and asked if they knew the corresponding animals. The cards they didn't know were set aside, but all the items that were to figure directly in the tests were known to all the subjects. Each subject was tested individually. On the typicality test, members of each pair of items had about the same taxonomic distance between them (to control for diversity effects). On the diversity test, each pair of items had about the same typicality rating (that is, average taxonomic distance to all the other animals).

A table was always between the experimenter and the subject. Beginning with the first set of test items for the first subject, the subject was asked, for example, for typicality:

> Jaguars have a disease and skunks have the same disease that jaguars do. Gophers have another disease and anteaters have the same disease that gophers do. Do you think all the other animals have the

11. A pilot study of sortings used pictures for animals, and dried specimens as herbarium vouchers for plants. But these stimuli often led to misidentifications that do not occur for specimens in natural settings. Surprisingly, we found that name cards work very effectively as stimulus materials. Both literate and illiterate informants are familiarized with name cards (as part of a joint initiative by the community and our team to introduce a standardized transcription of their oral language) and then the sorting is done with these cards.

> same disease that jaguars have with skunks, or the other disease that gophers have with anteaters?

Our findings indicate that both Itza and Michigan subjects find it natural to reason about diseases. Itza informants show typicality just as Michigan informants do. Consistent choice of the more typical pair (for example, for the Itza: jaguars and skunks), indicates that category structure—in particular the typicality of species—influences subjects' hypotheses about how unknown biological properties are likely to be distributed among species.

These results correspond to earlier findings by Rips (1975) for American subjects: "When little is known about the underlying distribution of a property, subjects assume that the distribution mirrors that of the better-known properties." In other words, when people learn that an unknown property is possessed by a typical species, or by a group of fairly typical species (that is, species that share many properties with other members of the same taxonomic category), then they are more likely to generalize than if the same fact had been learned about some atypical species. Consistent use of typicality-based inferences clearly indicates that such mechanisms are built into folk-biological taxonomies themselves.

Following a run through all the typicality items, the subjects were asked the same question about pairs of items (species) that differed in their coverage of the category of mammals, that is, with respect to diversity. On one run, there was no pause between presentation of the typicality and diversity tasks. Another run of diversity (with different items) occurred eight months after another run of typicality (with different items). There were no significant differences in results between runs. There was, however, a significant difference between the Maya and the Americans on the diversity task, of which the following is an example (from the Itza study):

> Squirrels have a disease and tapirs [a relative of the elephant and the horse] have the same disease that squirrels do. Rats have another disease and cheek mice have the same disease that rats do. Do you think all the other animals have the disease that squirrels have with tapirs, or the disease that rats have with cheek mice?

The Michigan students consistently chose the pair of diverse items, whereas the Itza consistently chose the pair of least diverse items. López et al. (1992) tested the SCM with kindergarteners and second-graders, and found that a number of phenomena previously shown only with adults also progressively characterize children's category-based inductions. In particular, children acquire competence early with similarity- and typicality-based reasoning. Only later do they become competent with diversity-based reasoning.

There are, however, significant arguments *against* considering Itza responses to be like those of American children. First, Itza *do* manifest awareness of diversity-based reasoning. Like many swidden (slash-and-burn) farmers, Itza are at the mercy of unpredictable fluctuations in critical agroecological factors, such as precipitation, pest infestation, runaway fires (usually brought on by immigrants unfamiliar with native fire-control techniques), and so on. As a result, they practice a system of risk management by scattering plots over time and space in various portions of the forest. In other words, diversification strategies minimize production risk: spreading the timing of planting, relying on different staple foods and planting several varieties of each, and engaging in both subsistence and small-scale commodity production (Atran 1993; cf. Goland 1993).

Second, it is clear from the Itzas' own explanations of their responses that they were *not accepting the experimenter's premises* on the diversity task; for example:

> *Subject's initial response*: "Squirrels and tapirs can't have the same disease" (*aj ku'uk i tzimin-che' ma' patal yan umiismaj k'oja'anil*); "squirrels live in trees, tapirs no, they are water animals" (*aj ku'uk kukuxtal ti che', tzimin-che' ma', a'lo' b'a'al ~ che'-il ja' i b'a'al ~ che'-il k'aax*).
> *Experimenter*: "But we found that squirrels and tapirs do have the same disease."
> *Subject*: "You, did you see this" (*inteche tawila'*)?
> *Experimenter* [untruthfully]: "Yes."
> *Subject*: "Well I didn't" (*inten ma'*); "I didn't see" (*ma' tinwila'*). "I don't know" (*ma' inwojel*), "maybe a bat bit them and made them sick" (*mya' jun-tul sotz' tuchi'aj uk'oja'anil*). "Bats can go from trees to water" (*aj sotz' patal ub'el ti che' tak ja'*).
> *Experimenter*: "Who did the bat bite and make sick?"
> *Subject*: "Tapir, squirrel" (*tzimin-che', aj ku'uk*).
> *Experimenter*: "And the rat and the cheek mouse?"
> *Subject*: "Yes, they can have the same disease because they go together" (*jaj, patal yan umiismaj k'oja'anil tumen uyet'ok*).
> *Experimenter*: "And the other animals, do they have the disease that the tapir has with the squirrel, or the other disease that the rat has with the cheek mouse?"
> *Subject*: "The rat and cheek mouse" (*aj ch'o' i mumukti'*).
> *Experimenter*: "Why?"
> *Subject*: "They can get sick even with no bat bite" (*patal uk'oja'antal ka'ax ma' uchib'al aj sotz*).

Unlike the American students, who will simply defer to the experimenter's (presumably scientific) knowledge, the Itza will not accept the face value of information they believe to lack independent empirical support. Arguably, the Itza are using their taxonomy to *gauge* the likelihood of an unknown biological property being possessed by different species. The greater the taxonomic distance between species, the less likely it is that those species should share the property. Their first reaction to the experimenter's presentation of such unlikely information is skepticism, followed by discomfort and hesitancy in going on with the task. If prodded to overcome both skepticism and hesitancy in dealing with what they (quite justifiably) believe to be information that is likely to be contrary to fact, they will seek plausible hypotheses that are *ecologically based,* rather than simply category-based.

5.2.3 Section Summary

Human beings everywhere, it appears, have similar folk-biological schema composed of essence-based species and ranked ordering of species into lower-order and higher-order groups. These groups within groups represent the routine products of innate "habits of mind," naturally selected to grasp highly relevant and recurrent "habits of the world." They are not as arbitrary, and therefore not as variable across cultures as, say, the gathering of stars in constellations.

Both Americans and Maya use their folk-biological taxonomies to expand knowledge in the face of uncertainty, but in different ways. American students (deferentially) assume that a surprising finding reported by scientists is, first, a surprising *regularity* within the natural domain (that is, the taxonomy) itself. Given this apparent regularity, which is not predicted by typical morphology and behavior (that is, by familiar properties), Michigan students will do as scientists do and generalize the regularity to the whole inclusive category. This choice requires a leap of faith, which is rooted in deference to the scientist's (often justified) *theoretical presumption* that where there is law anywhere within a natural domain, there is law everywhere. Still, for the students at least, it is the (folk) taxonomy that is driving theoretical speculation rather than the other way around: the greater the taxonomic distance separating species, and the less obvious the property they share, the more likely it is that the property is theoretically motivated and category-general.

By contrast, Itza do not theoretically presume that each life form has a lawlike causal unity, such that every folk species within that life form instantiates that underlying causal pattern to an equal degree. Rather, Itza, like most folk around the world, conceive of superordinate life forms as broad partitions of the local ecology within which folk species are locally connected in causally diverse and complex ways. Folk-biological taxonomy guides speculation (hypothesis formation) about what those causal links might be: the more behaviorally and morphologically different species are, and the less likely they are to share biological properties, the more likely it is that the property is ecologically motivated and category-restricted.

5.3 Conclusion: Science and Common Sense

Specific "modular" habits of mind, it appears, evolved to capture recurrent features of hominid environments relevant to species survival. It is not surprising, therefore, that such core-compatible ideas, once emitted in a cultural environment, will spread "contagiously" through a population of minds. They will be little affected by subsequent changes in a culture's history or institutional ecology. They are learned without formal or informal teaching and, once learned, cannot be easily or wholly unlearned. They remain inordinately stable within a culture, and are by and large structurally isomorphic across cultures.

Aristotle was the first in the West (or anywhere, it seems) to advance the theoretical presumption of overarching causal unity and underlying lawful uniformity for domains of "natural kinds," including biological kinds as well as kinds of inert physical substances. This strategy eventually enabled Western science to extend these "natural" domains from just local relationships among their respective kinds to the whole planet and cosmos. It took more than two thousand years, however, before scientists began to articulate principles that were explicitly designed to go beyond common sense.

In biology (natural history), this beginning did not occur until Linnaeus (1751: sections 153, 209) banned from botany the ecologically "intuitive" and "natural," but "philosophically lubricious," life forms, such as TREE and GRASS. To be sure, TREE constitutes no unitary phyletic line (for example, legumes are variously trees, vines, bushes). Only now are evolutionary theorists beginning to question the "reality" of longstanding zoological life forms such as BIRD and REPTILE, and of the whole taxonomic framework that made biology conceivable in the first place. For example, if the first birds descended from dinosaurs, and if crocodiles but not turtles are also directly related to dinosaurs, it follows that either: crocodiles and birds form a group that excludes turtles; or crocodiles, birds, and turtles form separate groups; or they all form one group. Whatever the arrangement, the traditional separation of the classes BIRD and REPTILE is no longer scientifically tenable.

Yet, Linnaeus no less than any contemporary field biologist would continue to rely on popular life forms like TREE to understand and collect the local arrangements of species. Native people who live intimately with nature can ignore such ecologically salient kinds only at their peril. And even when people become largely ignorant of local ecological relationships, as they do in our urban Western culture, they continue to cling to life forms, such as TREE (BIRD or REPTILE), as unforgettable parts of their lives and the evolutionary history of our species.

Wholesale replacement of "core" common-sense knowledge may even be impossible in some cases. There may be (innately determined) natural limits on assimilation of new knowledge to basic domains when no ready intuitive sense can be made of it. Regarding folk physics, for example, it is doubtful that any complete physical interpretation—much less phenomenal intuition—can be given to the equations of quantum mechanics. In a crucial sense that is unlike the condition for classical mechanics, understanding quantum mechanics just is understanding the mathematics. There is little doubt that people—even quantum physicists—understand and negotiate their interactions with everyday physical objects without ever using, or being able to use, concepts derived from quantum equations. Imagine the paralyzing difficulty of being compelled to *calculate,* in quantum terms, a response to "Could you please pass the salt down the table?"

In certain respects, evolutionary understanding of species is as counterintuitive, and as difficult to teach and understand, as quantum mechanics (Hull 1991). There is no hard and fast rule to categorically distinguish a race or variety from a species in time, although failure to interbreed is a good rule of thumb for distinguishing (some) groups of organisms living in close proximity. There are no laws of molecular or genetic biology that consistently apply to all and only species.

Nevertheless, many philosophers and scientists continue to discuss species taxa as if they were enduring natural kinds. Indeed, some take the notion of the species as a natural kind as a scientific given, and purport to show from this that there is not only a progressive continuity between common sense and science, but that this "scientific" notion of species as natural kind is the ultimate reference for the common-sense meaning of living-kind terms (Kripke 1972, Putnam 1975, Schwartz 1979). If anything, modern science shows as much the reverse: There is marked discontinuity between evolutionary and pre-evolutionary conceptions of species, but the lingering notion of the species as a natural kind in science indicates that certain basic notions in science are more hostage to the dictates of common sense than the other way around.

Such basic "common sense" may remain *psychologically valid* for everyday understanding of the world, but perhaps not *epistemically valid* for the vastly extended or reduced dimensions of modern science. To be sure, our "metacognitive" abilities, which allow us to represent and integrate the outputs of more basic modules, can generate new types of information. Some of this elaborated knowledge can be manipulated so as to meet the input conditions of basic conceptual modules: for example, in the presentation of pictures and stories of animals rather than the animals themselves. By thus altering databases (stimulus inputs) and influencing data structures (representational outputs), even aspects of "core" knowledge may change, but within limits.[12]

The common-sense knowledge underscored by basic cognitive dispositions can—and in the most counterintuitive cases must—remain somewhat separate from more sophisticated scientific conceptions despite the subtle and pervasive interactions between the two kinds of knowledge. These innately determined limits may be such as to preserve enough of the "default" ontology and structure of the core domain to make the notion of domain-specific cross-cultural universals meaningful. This preservation leads to a strong expectation that core principles guide learning in much the same way across cultures. The genesis and understanding of cultural variation, including science, depends on it.

Suggestions for Further Reading

For further discussion of domain-specificity and cognitive "modules" see the interdisciplinary reader, *Mapping the mind,* edited by Hirschfeld and Gelman (1994). For a view of the evolutionary underpinnings of various human cognitive modalities look at the interdisciplinary reader, *The adapted mind,* edited by Barkow, Cosmides, and Tooby (1992).

For distinct views of how basic "naive biology" is to children's minds in comparison to folk physics and folk psychology, see Carey's (1985) *Conceptual change in childhood* and Keil's (1989) *Concepts, kinds, and cognitive development.*

On the finer distinctions and commonalities in the folk-biological classifications of cultures around the world, see Berlin's (1992) *Ethnobiological classification.* For a detailed treatment of the history of biological classification in European science and its relation to folk biology, look at Atran's (1990) *Cognitive foundations of natural history.*

Problems

5.1 Suppose you were to possess the knowledge and tools needed for genetic engineering, but you could apply them only to manipulate familiar features and properties of organisms known to you on an everyday basis. What manipulations, other than those related to reproduction, might convince you and others that you had changed the nature of the organism so that it was no longer the *same kind of* creature that you had started out with?

5.2 Try to name the various folk-biological taxa familiar to you on an everyday basis, and assign them to their proper ranks. You might start with a life form, such as MAMMAL or TREE and think of all (folk) species of mammals and trees there are. What other life forms do you have in mind?

12. Even young children in our society appear to comprehend modern notions of the earth and other heavenly objects as spherelike objects (Vosniadou and Brewer 1987), although they are likely to be unaware that such notions resulted from laborious scientific discoveries involving mathematics. Similarly, our children may believe that whales and bats are mammals, despite only the vaguest awareness of the anatomical insights that made these identifications possible (Medin 1989). Even when there are demonstrable and pervasive effects of metacognitive (for example, scientific) reasoning on basic conceptualization, the effects are not likely to be uniform or such as to have common-sense structures wholly replaced by new structures (for example, theories) (cf. Dupré 1981, diSessa 1988).

5.3 Why are VEGETABLE, FLOWER, and FRUIT not properly taxonomic?

5.4 Consider the following two symbolic relations in regard to the logical structure of folk-biological classification: $\in$ = "is an element of" and K = "is a kind of"; for example,

Fido $\in$ ANIMAL $\in$ Folk Kingdom
K
Fido $\in$ MAMMAL $\in$ Life Form
K
Fido $\in$ DOG $\in$ Folk Species
K
Fido $\in$ SHEEPDOG $\in$ Folk Subspecies

Now, consider how, in the following syllogism, you would replace the placeholding relation "is a" with the appropriate relational symbol in each of the two premises and, if possible, in the conclusion. For example,

Fido is a DOG
DOG is a MAMMAL
____
Hence, Fido is a MAMMAL

should be rendered:

Fido $\in$ DOG
DOG K MAMMAL
____
Fido $\in$ MAMMAL

Of the remaining three syllogisms only one is logically correct. After you have placed an appropriate relational symbol, where possible analyze why the other two syllogisms are wrong:

Fido is a DOG
DOG is a Folk Species
____
Hence, Fido is a Folk Species

DOG is a MAMMAL
MAMMAL is an ANIMAL
____
Hence, DOG is an ANIMAL

DOG is a MAMMAL
MAMMAL is a Life Form
____
Hence, DOG is a Life Form

Match the 3 syllogisms above to their analogs below:

All Greeks are Men
All Men are Mortal
____
All Greeks are Mortal

The Daughters of the American Revolution are Americans
Americans are Numerous
____
The Daughters of the American Revolution are Numerous

Geronimo is an Indian
Indians are Disappearing

Geronimo is Disappearing

5.5 Consider this scenario:

> Mountain lions and moles were found to have the same disease. Skunks and weasels were found to have another disease. Do you think that all the other animals are likely to come down with the disease that the mountain lions have with the moles, or the disease that the skunks have with the weasels?

How do you think a Maya Indian might respond? How would you respond? Why? In what contexts might different answers be considered appropriate?

References

Astington, J., and A. Gopnik (1991). Theoretical explanations of children's understanding of the mind. *British Journal of Developmental Psychology* 9, 7–31.

Atran, S. (1983). Covert fragmenta and the origins of the botanical family. *Man* 18, 51–71.

Atran, S. (1985). Pre-theoretical aspects of Aristotelian definition and classification of animals. *Studies in History and Philosophy of Science* 16, 113–163.

Atran, S. (1987). Constraints on the ordinary semantics of living kinds. *Mind and Language* 2, 27–63.

Atran, S. (1990). *Cognitive foundations of natural history.* Cambridge: Cambridge University Press.

Atran, S. (1993). Itza Maya tropical agro-forestry. *Current Anthropology* 34, 633–700.

Atran, S. (1994). Core domains versus scientific theories. In L. Hirschfeld and S. Gelman, eds., *Mapping the mind: Domain specificity in cognition and culture.* New York: Cambridge University Press.

Atran, S. (1995). Causal constraints on categories and categorical constraints on biological reasoning across cultures. In D. Sperber, D. Premack, and A. Premack, eds., *Causal cognition: A multidisciplinary debate.* Oxford: Oxford University Press.

Atran, S., and D. Sperber (1991). Learning without teaching: Its place in culture. In L. Tolchinsky-Landsmann, ed., *Culture, schooling and psychological development.* Norwood, NJ: Ablex.

Avis, J., and P. Harris (1991). Belief-desire among Baka children. *Child Development* 62, 460–467.

Baillargeon, R. (1986). Representing the existence and location of hidden objects: Object permanence in 6- and 8-month-old infants. *Cognition* 23, 21–41.

Barkow, J., L. Cosmides, and J. Tooby, eds. (1992). *The adapted mind.* New York: Oxford University Press.

Bartlett, H. (1940). History of the generic concept in botany. *Bulletin of the Torrey Botanical Club* 47, 319–362.

Berlin, B. (1972). Speculations on the growth of ethnobotanical nomenclature. *Language and Society* 1, 63–98.

Berlin, B. (1974). Further notes on covert categories. *American Anthropologist* 76, 327–331.

Berlin, B. (1992). *Ethnobiological classification.* Princeton, NJ: Princeton University Press.

Berlin, B., D. Breedlove, and P. Raven (1973). General principles of classification and nomenclature in folk biology. *American Anthropologist* 74, 214–242.

Berlin, B., D. Breedlove, and P. Raven (1974). *Principles of Tzeltal plant classification.* New York: Academic.

Boster, J., and D. D'Andrade (1989). Natural and human sources of cross-cultural agreement in ornithological classification. *American Anthropologist* 91, 132–142.

Bright, J., and W. Bright (1965). Semantic structure in Northwestern California and the Sapir-Whorf hypothesis. In E. Hammel, ed., *Formal semantics*. Washington, DC: American Anthropologist Special Publications, Vol. 67.

Brown, C. (1984). *Language and living things: Uniformities in folk classification and naming*. New Brunswick: Rutgers University Press.

Buck, R., and D. Hull (1966). The logical structure of the Linnaean hierarchy. *Systematic Zoology* 15, 97–110.

Bulmer, R. (1970). Which came first, the chicken or the egg-head? In J. Pouillon and P. Maranda, eds., *Echanges et communications: mélanges offerts à Claude Lévi-Strauss*. The Hague: Mouton.

Carey, S. (1985). *Conceptual change in childhood*. Cambridge, MA: MIT Press.

Carey, S., L. Klatt, and M. Schlaffer (1992). Infants' representations of objects and nonsolid substances. Unpublished manuscript. MIT.

Cole, M., and S. Scribner (1974). *Culture and thought: A psychological introduction*. New York: Wiley.

Conklin, H. (1962). Lexicographical treatment of folk taxonomies. In F. Householder and S. Saporta, eds., *Problems in lexicography*. Indianapolis: Indiana University Press.

Cosmides, L., and J. Tooby (1992). Cognitive adaptations for social exchange. In J. Barkow, L. Cosmides, and J. Tooby, eds., *The adapted mind*. New York: Oxford University Press.

Darwin, C. (1859). *On the origin of species by natural selection*. London: Murray.

Diamond, J. (1966). Zoological classification of a primitive people. *Science* 151, 1102–1104.

diSessa, A. (1988). Knowledge in pieces. In G. Forman and P. Pufall, eds., *Constructivism in the computer age*. Hillsdale, NJ: Erlbaum.

Donnellan, K. (1971). Necessity and criteria. In J. Rosenberg and C. Travis, eds., *Readings in the philosophy of language*. Englewood Cliffs, NJ: Prentice-Hall.

Dougherty, J. (1978). Salience and relativity in classification. *American Ethnologist* 5, 66–80.

Dougherty, J. (1979). Learning names for plants and plants for names. *Anthropological Linguistics* 21, 298–315.

Dupré, J. (1981). Natural kinds and biological taxa. *The Philosophical Review* 90, 66–90.

Dwyer, P. (1976). An analysis of Rofaifo mammal taxonomy. *American Ethnologist* 3, 425–445.

Gelman, S., and J. Coley (1991). Language and categorization: The acquisition of natural kind terms. In S. Gelman and J. Byrnes, eds., *Perspective on language and thought: Interrelations and development*. New York: Cambridge University Press.

Gelman, S., and H. Wellman (1991). Insides and essences: Early understanding of the non-obvious. *Cognition* 38, 214–244.

Goland, C. (1993). Agricultural risk management through diversity. *Culture and Agriculture* 45–46, 8–13.

Gregg, J. (1967). Finite Linnaean structures. *Bulletin of Mathematical Biophysics* 29, 191–206.

Hays, T. (1983). Ndumba folk biology and the general principles of ethnobotanical classification and nomenclature. *American Anthropologist* 85, 489–507.

Heit, R., and J. Rubenstein (1994). Similarity and property effects in inductive reasoning. *Journal of Experimental Psychology* 30, 411–422.

Henley, N. (1969). A psychological study of the semantics of animal terms. *Journal of Verbal Learning and Verbal Behavior* 8, 176–184.

Hickling, A., and S. Gelman (1992). Young children's understanding of seed and plant growth. Paper presented at the Conference of Human Development, Atlanta, GA.

Hirschfeld, L. (in press). The child's representation of human groups. In D. Medin, ed., *The psychology of learning and motivation*, vol. 30. San Diego: Academic Press.

Hirschfeld, L., and S. Gelman, eds. (1994). *Mapping the mind: Domain-specificity in cognition and culture.* New York: Cambridge University Press.

Hough, W. (1897). The Hopi in relation to their plant environment. *American Anthropologist* 10, 33–44.

Hull, D. (1991). Common sense and science. *Biology and Philosophy* 6, 467–479.

Hunn, E. (1976). Toward a perceptual model of folk biological classification. *American Ethnologist* 3, 508–524.

Hutchins, E. (1980). *Culture and inference: A Trobriand case study.* Cambridge, MA: Harvard University Press.

Jeyifous, S. (1985). Atimodemo: Semantic conceptual development among the Yoruba. Ph.D. dissertation, Cornell University.

Keil, F. (1989). *Concepts, kinds, and cognitive development.* Cambridge, MA: MIT Press.

Keil, F. (1994). The birth and nurturance of concepts by domains: The origins of concepts of living things. In L. Hirschfeld and S. Gelman, eds., *Mapping the mind: Domain specificity in cognition and culture.* New York: Cambridge University Press.

Kesby, J. (1979). The Rangi classification of animals and plants. In R. Reason and D. Ellen, eds., *Classifications in their social contexts.* New York: Academic Press.

Kripke, S. (1972). Naming and necessity. In D. Davidson and G. Harman, eds., *Semantics of natural language.* Dordrecht: Reidel.

Lamarck, J.-B., and A.-P. Candolle (1815). *Flore française.* Paris: Desray.

Leslie, A. (1990). Understanding other minds. In *Golem: Special Issue for the 12th Cognitive Science Conference.* Cambridge, MA: MIT Press.

Lévi-Strauss, C. (1966). *The savage mind.* Chicago: University of Chicago Press.

Linnaeus, C. (1751). *Philosophia botanica.* Stockholm: Kiesewetter.

Locke, J. (1848/1689). *An essay concerning human understanding.* London: Tegg.

López, A., S. Gelman, G. Gutheil, and E. Smith (1992). The development of category-based induction. *Child Development* 63, 1070–1090.

Luria, A. (1976). *Cognitive development: its cultural and social foundations.* Cambridge, MA: Harvard University Press.

Mandler, J. (1992). How to build a baby: II. Conceptual primitives. *Psychological Review,* 99, 587–604.

Marks, I. (1987). *Fears, phobias, and rituals.* New York: Oxford University Press.

Mayr, E. (1969). *Principles of systematic zoology.* New York: McGraw-Hill.

Medin, D. (1989). Concepts and conceptual structure. *American Psychologist* 44, 1469–1481.

Mill, J. (1843). *A system of logic.* London: Longmans, Green.

Munkur, B. (1983). *The cult of the serpent.* Albany: State University of New York Press.

Murphy, G., and D. Medin (1985). The role of theories in conceptual coherence. *Psychological Review* 92, 289–316.

Osherson, D., E. Smith, O. Wilkie, A. López, and E. Shafir (1990). Category-based induction. *Psychological Review* 97, 185–200.

Posey, D. (1981). Wasps, warriors and fearless men: Ethnoentomology of the Kayapó Indians of Central Brazil. *Journal of Ethnobiology* 1, 165–174.

Putnam, H. (1975). The meaning of "meaning." In K. Gunderson, ed., *Language, mind and knowledge.* Minneapolis: University of Minnesota Press.

Rey, G. (1983). Concepts and stereotypes. *Cognition* 15, 237–262.

Rips, L. (1975). Inductive judgments about natural categories. *Journal of Verbal Learning and Verbal Behavior* 14, 665–681.

Rips, L., E. Shoben, and E. Smith (1973). Semantic distance and the verification of semantic relations. *Journal of Verbal Learning and Verbal Behavior* 12, 1–20.

Rosch, E. (1975). Universals and cultural specifics in categorization. In R. Brislin, S. Bochner, and W. Lonner, eds. *Cross-cultural perspectives on learning.* New York: Halstead.

Rosch, E., C. Mervis, W. Gray, D. Johnson, and P. Boyes-Bream (1976). Basic objects in natural categories. *Cognitive Psychology* 8, 382–439.
Sartori, G., and R. Job (1988). The oyster with four legs: A neuro-psychological study on the interaction of visual and semantic information. *Cognitive Neuropsychology* 5, 105–132.
Schwartz, S. (1978). Putnam on artifacts. *Philosophical Review* 87, 566–574.
Schwartz, S. (1979). Natural kind terms. *Cognition* 7, 301–315.
Seligman, M. (1971). Phobias and preparedness. *Behavior Therapy* 2, 307–320.
Simpson, G. (1961). *Principles of animal taxonomy*. New York: Columbia University Press.
Spelke, E. (1990). Principle of object perception. *Cognitive Science* 14, 29–56.
Sperber, D. (1975). Pourquoi les animaux parfaits, les hybrides et les monstres sont-ils bons à penser symboliquement? *L'homme* 15, 5–34.
Springer, K., and F. Keil (1989). On the development of biologically specific beliefs. *Child Development* 60, 637–648.
Stross, B. (1973). Acquisition of botanical terminology by Tzeltal children. In M. Edmonson, ed., *Meaning in Mayan languages*. The Hague: Mouton.
Turiel, E. (1983). *The development of social knowledge: Morality and convention*. New York: Cambridge University Press.
van Valen, L. (1964). An analysis of some taxonomic concepts. In J. Gregg and F. Harris, eds., *Form and strategy in science*. Dordrecht: Reidel.
Vosniadou, S., and W. Brewer (1987). Theories of knowledge restructuring in development. *Review of Educational Research* 57, 51–67.
Walker, S. (1992). Supernatural beliefs, natural kinds and conceptual structure. *Memory and Cognition* 20, 655–662.
Wallace, A. (1889). *Darwinism*. London: Macmillan.
Warburton, F. (1967). The purposes of classification. *Systematic Zoology* 16, 241–245.
Warrington, E., and R. McCarthy (1987). Categories of knowledge: Further fractionations and an attempted integration. *Brain* 110, 1273–1296.
Wellman, H., and S. Gelman (1992). Cognitive development: Foundational theories of core domains. *Annual Review of Psychology* 43, 337–375.
Wierzbicka, A. (1984). Apples are not a "kind of fruit." *American Ethnologist* 11, 313–328.
Zubin, D., and K.-M. Köpcke (1986). Gender and folk taxonomy: The indexical relation between grammatical and lexical characterization. In C. Craig, ed., *Noun classes and categorization*. Amsterdam: John Benjamins, Typological Studies in Language 7.

Appendix: The Logical Structure of Folk-Biological Taxonomy

In section 5.1.2.3 on "The Significance of Rank," an implicit distinction was made between taxa conceived as classes of organisms, like CUCKOO and CACTUS, and rank conceived as classes of such taxa, like the folk species. In problem 5.4, this distinction in logical type between taxa as first-order classes and ranks as second-order classes of classes was given quasi-formal expression. This provision was to allow the reader a better grasp of the implications of the distinction between taxa and ranks for reasoning. But a more formally adequate rendition of folk-biological taxonomy in terms of class structures is problematic.

Specifying general criteria (that is, necessary and/or sufficient conditions) of class intension, or meaning, presents formal difficulties that specifying sets does not. For example, a class definition of CUCKOO might be: "birds that by nature repetitively sound the cuckoo call." Nevertheless, should we discover a bird that resembles the cuckoos we know, except that it cannot sound the cuckoo call, we might still consider it to be a cuckoo. Alternatively, we might allow that a bird that does sound the cuckoo call, but does not live with or much resemble the cuckoos we know is not a cuckoo after all.

By contrast, a set is given extensionally, that is, by simple enumeration of its membership. For example, CUCKOO thus denotes the set of all and only those organisms which actually happen to be cuckoo birds, regardless of any intensional criteria we may require to make sense of what it means for an organism to be a cuckoo. Accordingly, what follows is a set-theoretic treatment of the logical structure of folk-biological taxonomy.

A *"kind of"* relation, **K**, is a two-place, acyclic relation with a finite domain. (It is *acyclic* because in no sequence $x_1 \ldots x_n$ of members of its domain do we have x_1 **K** $x_2, \ldots, x_{n-1}$ **K** x_n, x_n **K** x_1. From acyclicity it follows that **K** is irreflexive and asymmetric; these are ruled out by the cases $n = 1$ and $n = 2$.) A *terminal* kind has no subkinds. In other words, x is *terminal* for **K** if and only if x is in the domain of **K** and there is no y such that y **K** x.

A "kind of" relation is *taxonomic* if and only if (i) it is transitive, and (ii) no item is of two distinct kinds unless one is a kind of the other. Our folk categories of animals, for instance, are taxonomic: COLLIE is a kind of DOG and a kind of MAMMAL, but one (namely DOG) is a kind of the other. An instance of a nontaxonomic "kind of" relation is this: one that classifies AVOCADO both as a kind of FRUIT and as a kind of VEGETABLE. This relation is nontaxonomic so long as FRUIT and VEGETABLE are different kinds and neither is a kind of the other.

Formally, let **K** be a "kind of" relation, and let **T** be a subset of the domain **K**. **K** is *taxonomic* over **T** if and only if (i) **K** is transitive over **T** and (ii) **K** satisfies the following:

Taxonomizing Condition
For any members x, y, z of **T** such that x **K** y and x **K** z, either $y = z$ or y **K** z or z **K** y.

Another nontaxonomic relation is this: one that classifies CHAIR as a kind of FURNITURE but not as a kind of VEHICLE, and WHEELCHAIR as a kind of CHAIR and as a kind of VEHICLE. This relation is nontaxonomic because WHEELCHAIR **K** CHAIR and WHEELCHAIR **K** VEHICLE, but neither CHAIR = VEHICLE nor CHAIR **K** VEHICLE nor VEHICLE **K** CHAIR.

Suppose, now, that "kind of" relation **K** is taxonomic over its domain **T***. A member of **T*** is called a *taxon* with respect to **K**. A *taxonomic category* with respect to **K** is a subset of **T*** consisting of a *head* item and everything in **T*** that is a "kind of" this head item. Formally, a subset **T** of **T*** is a *taxonomic category* with respect to **K** if and only if for some $h \in \mathbf{T}^*$, $\mathbf{T} = \{h\} \cup \{x | x \mathbf{K} h\}$; taxon h is then called the *head* of taxonomic category **T**.

A *taxonomic kingdom* with respect to **K** is a maximal taxonomic category with respect to **K**. It follows that the set **T*** of taxa with respect to **K** is partitioned into disjoint taxonomic kingdoms with respect to **K**. The head of a **K**-kingdom stands in relation **K** to no member of **T***. This head is called a *unique beginner*. For example, ANIMAL is a unique beginner, and MAMMAL, BIRD, DOG, and DUCK are taxa of the kingdom headed by ANIMAL.

Let **T** be a subset of the domain of "kind of" relation **K**. A *ranking* of **T** with respect to **K** is a function **R** from set **T** onto a set of consecutive integers $\{m, \ldots, n\}$, with $m < 0$ and $n > 0$, which satisfies the following condition:

$$(\forall x,y \in \mathbf{T})[\text{if } x \mathbf{K} y \text{ then } \mathbf{R}(y) > \mathbf{R}(x)].$$

The integers $m, \ldots, n$ in the range of **R** are called *ranks* with respect to **R**, and $\mathbf{R}(x)$ is called the *rank of x* with respect to **R**.

A rank is *mandatory* if every terminal kind is a subkind of some taxon of that rank. Formally, rank i is mandatory under **R** if and only if:

$$\forall x[x \text{ is terminal} \rightarrow (\mathbf{R}(x) = i \vee \exists y(x \mathbf{K} y \ \& \ \mathbf{R}(y) = i))].$$

It follows that if **T** is a taxonomic category, the maximal rank n of the head of **T** is mandatory. It also follows that if a level is mandatory, it partitions the taxa at that level or lower. That is, let the *level* of a taxonomic category be the rank of its head:

Theorem
Let level i be mandatory with respect to ranking **R** of **T**. Then the taxonomic categories at level i partition the taxa of rank $\leq i$.

Finally, a taxon is *monotypic* if (i) it is not terminal, and (ii) it has only one immediate subkind. Formally, y is an *immediate subkind* of x with respect to **K** if and only if $y \mathbf{K} x$ and not $\exists z(y \mathbf{K} z \ \& \ z \mathbf{K} x)$. A taxon is *monotypic* if and only if x has exactly one immediate subkind.

So far, we have been defining formal structures, without interpretation. Here are some claims about the folk concepts that classify plants and animals. They are classified by a "kind of" relation **K**, which we can read as the "is a kind of" relation as applied to a set **T*** of plants and animals. **K** is taxonomic over its domain $\mathbf{T}^*$. Each kingdom with respect to $\mathbf{K}$ has a special status in the system of folk concepts; call this the status of the *folk kingdom*. For each folk kingdom there is a ranking $\mathbf{R}$, such that each rank with respect to $\mathbf{R}$ has a special conceptual status, with rank 0 the rank of *folk species*. Maximal rank n is the rank of *folk kingdom*, and rank -1 is the rank of folk subspecies. Rank 0, the rank of folk species, is mandatory: Every terminal taxon is either a folk species or a kind of S where S is some folk species:

$$(\forall x \in \mathbf{T})[x \text{ is terminal} \rightarrow \exists y(\mathbf{R}(y) = 0 \;\&\; (x \,\mathbf{K}\, y \vee x = y))].$$

A controversial claim I would like to make is this: Where rank n is the maximal rank under $\mathbf{R}$, the rank of the unique beginner of a folk kingdom, call rank $n - 1$ the rank of a *life form*. The controversial claim is that rank $n - 1$ is mandatory. This requires that some folk life-form taxa are monotypic. For example, suppose that TREE and GRASS (or $\text{PLANT}_{[\text{sense}1]}$) are the first life forms of the folk kingdom $\text{PLANT}_{[\text{sense}2]}$ of which a child is aware. Suppose, further, that the child classifies all folk species she is aware of under one of these two life forms, except perhaps for the folk species CACTUS. If the life-form level is mandatory, then CACTUS must either be classified under some polytypic life form, such as TREE or GRASS, or it must be conceived of as a *monospecific* life form.

Another controversial claim, implicit in some methods for uncovering unnamed intermediate-level taxa (cf. Berlin 1974), is that any intermediate-level taxon is wholly included within some one life-form-level taxon. Formally, the claim is this: Any taxon at rank $n - 2$ is a subkind of some life form; that is,

$$(\forall x \in \mathbf{T})[\mathbf{R}(x) = n - 2 \rightarrow \exists y(x \,\mathbf{K}\, y \;\&\; \mathbf{R}(y) = n - 1)].$$

But there is empirical evidence against this always being the case. For example, Itza Maya discern an intermediate taxon of palms that cross-cuts their life forms TREE (*che'*) and HERB (*pokche'*).

A final point bears on the difference between an intensional class structure and an extensional set-theoretic structure. Conceived as sets, monotypic taxa pose a problem. They do so because the relation between a monotypic taxon and its immediate subkind is apparently one of extensional equivalence. For example, all organisms that actually belong to the folk species CACTUS are also all and only those organisms which belong to the life form CACTUS. From a set-theoretic point of view, such a species constitutes an *improper subset* of its monotypic life form. This condition seems to make the species conceptually identical with its life form.

Notice that for taxa conceived as classes no such problem arises, for the same set of items may be characterized differently by different defining properties. For example, one might choose to characterize a species-level taxon in terms of reproductive criteria and a life-form taxon in terms of ecological criteria. Yet, as noted above, difficulties in specifying general intensional criteria for classes argue against formal substitution of classes for sets.

One set-theoretic solution to the problem of monotypy may be to require that each immediate subkind of a monotypic taxon constitute a *proper subset* of that taxon; that is, there must be at least one individual organism (presumed even if unknown) in the monotypic taxon that is not in its immediate subkind (cf. Gregg 1967). There is, however, no apparent empirical motivation for this formal artifice. Another possible solution is to associate at least one *conditionally empty* immediate subkind to a monotypic taxon in addition to that taxon's one nonempty immediate subkind (cf. van Valen 1964). This result amounts to the idea that any *actually monotypic* taxon is *potentially polytypic.*

There is some empirical motivation for this last maneuver. For example, the Dorzé of Ethiopia appear to accord a singular status to their one snake taxon, *shosh*; however, when a Dorzé travels to the nearby Rift Valley, where many other species of snakes are found, the traveler invariably applies *shosh* to these as well: "this demonstrates that snakes are not a species without a genus [that is, life form], but a genus that contains, *de facto,* a single well-known species and, *de jure,* an indefinite number of species" (Sperber 1975, 15). Eighteenth-century natural historians treated apparently monotypic families, such as Cactaceae, in precisely this way. They argued that future explorations were likely to reveal more types of cactus than were then familiar to Europeans (Lamarck and Candolle 1815). Similarly, modern evolutionary taxonomists do not rule out discovery that the aardvark, which is the only extant species of the monotypic scientific order Tubulidentata, may have ancestral sister species.

The general structure outlined here thus appears to be descriptively adequate for folk-biological taxonomies in all cultures where the issue has been studied in depth. With minor modification, this structure also seems adequate for Aristotelian and finite (that is, *n*-rank) Linnaean taxonomies, including classical evolutionary taxonomies.

Chapter 6

Rationality

Gilbert Harman

6.1 Introduction

What is it for someone to be rational or reasonable, as opposed to being irrational or unreasonable? Think of some examples in which someone is being rational or reasonable as well as examples in which someone is being irrational or unreasonable. What do you think makes the difference?

Think also of some examples in which someone makes a mistake but is not therefore irrational or unreasonable.

6.1.1 Some Examples

Here is one kind of example:

> *Giving in to temptation*
> Jane very much wants to do well in history. There is a crucial test tomorrow and she needs to study tonight if she is to do well in the test. Jane's friends are all going to a party for Bill tonight. Jane knows that, if she goes to the party, she will really regret it. But she goes to the party anyway.

It is irrational for Jane to go to the party, even if it is understandable. The rational thing for her to do is to stay home and study.

Many examples of giving in to temptation involve a bit of irrationality. For example, smoking cigarettes while knowing of the health hazards involved is at least somewhat irrational. The rational thing to do is to give up smoking.

Here is a different sort of example.

> *Refusing to take a remedial course*
> Bob, a college freshman, takes a test designed to indicate whether students should take a useful remedial writing course. Students do not write their names in their examination booklets but write an

The preparation of this chapter was supported in part by a grant from the James S. McDonnell Foundation to Princeton University.

identifying number instead, so that graders will not know the identity of the students whose answers they are grading. Bob does poorly in the test and is told he should take a remedial writing course. He objects to this advice, attributing his poor score on the test to bias on the part of the grader against his ethnic group, and does not take the remedial writing course.

Bob's belief that his score is the result of bias is irrational. It would be more rational for Bob to conclude that he got a poor score because he did poorly on the test.

Refusing a reasonable proposal
Three students, Sally, Ellie, and Louise, have been assigned to a set of rooms consisting of a study room, a small single bedroom, and another small bedroom with a two-person bunk bed. Sally has arrived first and has moved into the single. The other two roommates propose that they take turns living in the single, each getting the single for one third of the school year. Sally refuses to consider this proposal and insists on keeping the single for herself the whole year.

Sally's roommates say she is being unreasonable. (Is she?)

Confusing two philosophers
Frieda is having trouble in her introductory philosophy course. Because of a similarity in their names, she confuses the medieval philosopher Thomas Aquinas with the twentieth-century American philosopher W. V. Quine.

This is a mistake but does not necessarily exhibit irrationality or unreasonableness (although it may).

Failing to distinguish twins
Harry has trouble distinguishing the twins Connie and Laura. Sometimes he mistakes one for the other.

That by itself is not irrational or unreasonable, although it would be unreasonable for Harry to be overly confident in the judgment that he is talking to Connie, given his past mistakes.

Adding mistake
Sam makes an adding mistake when he tries to balance his checkbook.

A mistake in addition need not involve any irrationality or unreasonableness.

Consider the mistakes about probability discussed in chapter 2. Under certain conditions some people assign a higher probability to Linda's being a feminist and a bank teller than to her merely being a bank teller. The probabilities that people assign to certain situations can depend on how the situation is described, even though the descriptions are logically equivalent. Are mistakes of this sort always irrational or unreasonable? Are some of them more like mistakes in addition?

What is the difference between the sort of mistake involved in being irrational or unreasonable and other mistakes that do not involve being irrational or unreasonable? Does it matter what the difference is?

Do you think it is irrational or unreasonable to believe in astrology? To be superstitious? To believe in God? To believe in science? To be moral? To think that other people have mental experiences like your own? To suppose that the future will resemble the past? These questions increasingly raise a question of skepticism. A skeptic about X is someone who takes it to be irrational or unreasonable to believe in X. Is skepticism sometimes itself irrational or unreasonable?

6.1.2 Rationality and Cognitive Science

Issues about rationality have significance for cognitive science. For example, one strategy for dealing with cognition is to start with the assumption that people think and act rationally, and then investigate what can be explained on that basis. Classical economic theory seeks to explain market behavior as the result of interactions among completely rational agents following their own interests. Similarly, psychologists sometimes explain "person perception," the judgments that one makes about others, by taking these judgments to be the result of reasonable causal inferences from the way in which others behave in one's presence. In ordinary life, we often base predictions on the assumption that other people will act rationally (Dennett 1971), as we do when we assume that other drivers will act rationally in traffic.

Such strategies require assumptions about rationality. Economics assumes that the rational agent maximizes expected utility (for example, von Neumann and Morgenstern 1944). Classical attribution theory identifies rationality with the scientific method (for example, Kelley 1967). It is less clear how we identify what is rational in our ordinary thinking. (One possibility is that each person asks what he or she would do in the other person's shoes and identifies that imagined response as the rational one.)

Some of the research described in preceding chapters has been interpreted as showing that people often depart systematically from the ideal economic agent, or the ideal scientist. People often ignore background frequencies, tend to look for confirming evidence rather than disconfirming evidence, take the conjunction of two claims to have a higher probability than one of the claims by itself, and so on.

There is more than one way to try to explain (away) these apparent departures from ideal rationality. One type of explanation (as in chapter 2) points to resource limits.

> *Resource limits*
> Reasoning uses resources and there are limits to the available resources. Reasoners have limited attention spans, limited memories, and limited time. Ideal rationality is not always possible for limited beings. Because of our limits, we may make use of strategies and heuristics, rules of thumb that work or seem to work most of the time, but not always. It is rational for us to use such rules, if we have nothing better that will give us reasonable answers in the light of our limited resources.

A second way to explain apparent departures from rationality is to challenge the view of rationality according to which these are departures even from ideal rationality. If people depart from what is rational according to a particular theory, that may be either because they are departing from rationality or because they are not departing from rationality and that particular theory of rationality is incorrect.

Some of the cases in which people appear to depart from ideal rationality are cases in which people appear to be inconsistent in what they accept. They make logical mistakes or violate principles of probability that they also seem to accept. How could these cases not be cases of irrationality?

Two ways have been suggested. First, it may be that people are not actually being inconsistent in their judgments.

> *Different concepts*
> People may be using concepts in a different way from the experimenter. When people judge that Linda is more likely to be a feminist bank teller than a bank teller, they may be using "more likely" to mean something like "more representative." When people make apparent mistakes in logic, that may be because they mean by "if" what the experimenter means by "if and only if."

Given what they mean by their words, they may not be as inconsistent as they appear to be (Cohen 1981).

Second, even if people are sometimes inconsistent, that does not show they are being irrational.

> *Reasonable inconsistency*
> It is not always irrational or unreasonable to be inconsistent (Pollock 1991, Nozick 1993).

There is an important question about just what connection there is between being inconsistent and being unreasonable or irrational.

In this chapter, we look more closely at rationality and reasonableness. We consider both actions and beliefs. What is it to act rationally or reasonably and what is it to act irrationally or unreasonably? What is it to have rational or reasonable beliefs and what is it to have irrational or unreasonable beliefs?

6.2 Background

6.2.1 Theoretical and Practical Rationality

Let us begin by contrasting two of the examples mentioned above, "Giving in to temptation" and "Refusing to take a remedial course." Jane goes to a party knowing she should instead study for tomorrow's exam. Bob thinks his grade on the writing placement exam is due to prejudice against his ethnic group even though he knows the grader does not have any way to discover the ethnic backgrounds of those taking the exam. One obvious difference is that Jane's irrationality is manifested in a decision to do something, namely, to go to the party, whereas Bob's irrationality is manifested in his belief, whether or not he acts on that belief. Bob does go on to make an irrational decision to refuse to take the writing course that he needs, but the source of that irrational decision is Bob's irrational belief. The source of Jane's irrational decision is not an irrational belief. Jane knows very well that she should stay home and study.

In deciding to go to the party knowing she should instead study for tomorrow's exam, Jane exhibits a defect in practical rationality. In believing that his grade on the writing placement exam is due to prejudice against his ethnic group, Bob exhibits a defect in theoretical rationality. Theoretical rationality is rationality in belief, practical rationality is rationality in action, or perhaps in plans and intentions.

Just as we can distinguish theoretical from practical rationality, we can distinguish theoretical reasoning, which most directly affects beliefs, from practical reasoning, which most directly affects plans and intentions. The upshot of theoretical reasoning is either a change in beliefs or no change, whereas the upshot of practical reasoning is either a change in plans and intentions or no change. Bob's irrationality arises from a problem with his theoretical reasoning. There may be nothing wrong with his practical reasoning apart from that. Jane's irrationality arises entirely from a defect in practical reasoning and not at all from anything in her theoretical reasoning.

Theoretical and practical reasoning are similar in certain respects, but there are important differences. One important difference has to do with the rationality of arbitrary choices.

> *Arbitrary belief*
> Jane is trying to decide which route Albert took to work this morning. She knows that in the past Albert has taken Route A about half the time and Route B about half the time. Her other evidence does not support one of these conclusions over the other. So, Jane arbitrarily decides to believe that Albert took Route A.

Clearly, Jane should suspend judgment and neither believe that Albert took Route A nor believe that he has taken Route B. It is irrational or unreasonable for her to adopt one of these beliefs in the absence of further evidence distinguishing the two possibilities.

On the other hand, consider the practical analogue.

> *Arbitrary intention*
> Albert is trying to decide how to get to work this morning. He could take either Route A or Route B. Taking either of these routes will get him to work at about the same time and the balance of reasons does not favor going one way over going the other way. So, Albert arbitrarily forms the intention of taking Route A.

This arbitrary decision is quite reasonable. In fact, it would be quite irrational or unreasonable for Albert *not* to decide on one route rather than the other, even though his decision in the case must be completely arbitrary. Someone who was unable to make an arbitrary choice of routes would suffer from a serious defect in practical rationality! Arbitrary choices of what to intend can be practically rational in a way that arbitrary choices of what to believe are not theoretically rational.

Another difference between theoretical and practical rationality has to do with the rationality or irrationality of wishful thinking. Wishful thinking is theoretically unreasonable, but practically reasonable. Wishes and desires are relevant to practical reasoning in a way that they are not relevant to theoretical reasoning.

> *Wishful practical thinking*
> Jane's desire to get a good grade on the final exam leads her to study for the exam in order to try to make it true that she will get a good grade on the final exam.

It is rational for Jane to let her desires influence her practical reasoning in this way. But consider the analogous theoretical case.

> *Wishful theoretical thinking*
> After Jane has taken the exam and before she has learned what her grade is, her desire to get a good grade on the exam leads her to conclude that she did get a good grade.

This sort of wishful thinking does not by itself give Jane a reason to believe that she got a good grade. To believe that something is so merely because she wants it to be so is theoretically unreasonable, whereas to decide to try to make something so because she wants it to be so is reasonable practical thinking. Desires can rationally influence the conclusions of practical reasoning in a way that they cannot rationally influence the conclusions of theoretical thinking.

This point has to be carefully formulated. Consider the following case in which desires do rationally influence what theoretical conclusions someone reaches.

> *Goal-directed theoretical reasoning*
> There are various conclusions that Jack could reach right now. He could try to figure out what Albert had for breakfast this morning. He could solve some arithmetical problems. He could work on today's crossword puzzle. He could try to resolve a philosophical paradox that Sam told him the other day. But, at the moment, Jack is locked out of his house and really ought to try to figure out where he left his keys. If Jack thinks about where he left his keys, however, he won't be able at the same time to resolve the philosophical paradox or solve the arithmetical puzzles. Because he wants very much to get into his house, he devotes his attention to figuring out where his keys must be.

Jack's goals can therefore be relevant to what conclusions he reaches. So, it is overly simple to say that one's desires cannot rationally affect what conclusions are legitimately reached in theoretical reasoning. Your desires can rationally affect your theoretical conclusions by affecting what questions you use theoretical reasoning to answer. (See also the discussion of goal-directed reasoning in chapter 9.) The right statement of the constraint on theoretical wishful thinking therefore seems to be something like this: given what question you are using theoretical reasoning to answer, your desires cannot rationally affect what answer you reach to that question. In practical reasoning, on the other hand, your desires can rationally influence not just the questions you consider but also the practical answers you give to those questions.

6.2.1.1 *Practical Reasons for Belief*

However, there are complications. Although wishful theoretical thinking is normally irrational, it is possible to have good practical reasons to believe something.

> *The power of positive thinking*
> Jonathan is sick. He has just read a study showing that people tend to recover more quickly if they believe that they will recover

quickly. So Jonathan takes himself to have a practical reason to believe he will recover quickly.

Loyalty
Mary has been accused of stealing a book from the library. It would be disloyal for her best friend, Fran, to believe the charge against Mary. So, Fran has a practical reason, loyalty, to believe that Mary is innocent.

Group think
Karen has been trying to decide what she thinks about capital punishment. She has noticed that the in crowd at her school all believe that capital punishment for murder is justified and she has also noticed that members of the in crowd do not like people who disagree with them about such things. Karen wants very much to be liked by members of the in crowd. So she takes herself to have a practical reason to believe that capital punishment for murder is justified.

What do you think about this last example? Is there something wrong with Karen if she adapts her opinions to people she wants to please? How does that compare with Fran's belief in Mary's innocence based on loyalty to Mary?

Here are two further examples.

Advertising account
Landon would like very much to get the RST Tobacco advertising account. The RST Tobacco Company will hire only advertisers who believe that cigarette smoking is a healthy pastime. So, Landon takes himself to have a practical reason to believe that cigarette smoking is a healthy pastime.

Pascal's argument for belief in God
Pascal (1678) reasons as follows. "Either there is a God or there is not, and either I believe in God or I do not. So there are four possibilities with the following payoffs: (I) If I believe in God and there is a God, then I go to heaven and have infinite bliss. (II) If I believe in God and there is no God, then my costs are whatever is involved in believing in God. (III) If I do not believe in God and there is a God, then I go to hell and suffer the torments of the damned for eternity. (IV) If I do not believe in God and there is no God, then I have no costs and no gains. Now, the expected value of belief in God is the value of infinite bliss multiplied by the probability that there is a God minus the costs of belief in God multiplied by the probability that there is no God; and the expected value of not believing in God is the negative value of an eternity in hell multi-

plied by the probability that there is a God. No matter how small the likelihood that God exists, the expected value of belief is infinitely greater than the expected value of disbelief. Therefore, I should believe in God."

Here we have what purport to be good practical reasons to believe one thing or another. This conclusion suggests that the difference between practical reasons and theoretical reasons is not just a matter of what they are reasons for, intentions *versus* beliefs.

6.2.1.2 *Epistemic versus nonepistemic reasons for belief*

All but the first of the examples in the preceding section have this feature: the examples mention a reason to believe something that does not make it more likely that the belief is true. Such reasons are sometimes called (for example, by Foley 1987) "nonepistemic reasons" for belief, in contrast with the more usual epistemic reasons for belief that do make the belief more likely to be true.

> *Epistemic reason for belief*
> R is an epistemic reason to believe P only if the probability of P given R is greater than the probability of P given not-R.
>
> *Nonepistemic reason for belief*
> R is a nonepistemic reason to believe P if R is a reason to believe P over and above the extent to which the probability of P given R is greater than the probability of P given not-R.[1]

These definitions leave open the important question whether all practical reasons for belief are nonepistemic reasons, a question we come back to below.

6.2.2 Inference and Reasoning versus Implication and Consistency

Issues about inference and reasoning need to be distinguished from issues about implication and consistency.

1. Suppose that you have assigned probability 1.0 to suitably obvious axioms for number theory and suppose further that N is a nonobvious truth of number theory that follows logically from these axioms. According to standard developments of probability theory, the conditional probability of N given any evidence E is always 1.0, the highest possible value. Given that understanding of probability and these definitions, there is no way you could have an epistemic reason to believe N. But your discovery of a proof can give you an epistemic reason to believe N. What this shows is that the notion of probability formalized in standard probability theory differs from the more ordinary notion of (epistemic) probability as rational degree of belief Before your discovery of the proof of N, the degree of belief it was rational for you to place in N was not 1.0. This point is connected with the discussion of idealizations later in this chapter.

Inference and reasoning are psychological processes leading to possible changes in belief (theoretical reasoning) or possible changes in plans and intentions (practical reasoning). Implication is most directly a relation among propositions. Certain propositions imply another proposition when and only when, if the former propositions are true, so too is the latter proposition.

It is one thing to say

(1) A, B, C imply D

It is quite another thing to say

(2) If you believe A, B, C you should (or may) infer D.

(1) is a remark about implication; (2) is a remark about inference. (1) says nothing special about belief or any other psychological state (unless one of A, B, C has psychological content), nor does (1) say anything normative about what anyone "should" or "may" do (Goldman 1986).

(1) can be true without (2) being true.

> *Rationality versus genius*
> A, B, C imply D. Sam believes A, B, and C. But Sam does not realize that A, B, C imply D. In fact, it would take a genius to recognize that A, B, C imply D. And Sam, although a rational man, is far from a genius.

Here Sam has no reason at all to believe D. (See chapter 9 for a discussion of how people might come to recognize logical implications.) Consider also

> *Discovering a contradiction*
> Sally believes A, B, C and has just come to recognize that A, B, C imply D. Unfortunately, she also believes for very good reasons that D is false. So she now has a reason to stop believing A, B, or C, rather than a reason to believe D.

> *Clutter avoidance*
> Jane believes A, B, C, she recognizes that A, B, C imply D, she does not believe that D is false, and she has no reason to think that D is false. She is also completely uninterested in whether D is true or false and has no reason to be interested. D is the proposition that *either* $2 + 2 = 4$ *or the moon is made of green cheese.* There are many, many trivial consequences like this of her beliefs that she has no reason to infer. She has no reason to clutter her mind with trivial consequences of her beliefs just because they follow from things she believes.

Such examples indicate that, if implication is relevant to what it is reasonable to believe, the connection has to be fairly complex. (We discuss below how implication might be relevant to what it is reasonable to believe.)

Just as issues about implication have to be distinguished from issues about reasonable inference, issues about consistency have to be distinguished from issues about rationality and irrationality. Consistency and inconsistency are in the first instance relations among propositions and only indirectly relations among propositional attitudes. Propositions are consistent when and only when it is possible for them all to be true together. Propositions are inconsistent when and only when it is not possible for them all to be true together.

So, it is one thing to say,

(3) Propositions A, B, C are inconsistent with each other.

It is quite another to say,

(4) It is irrational (or unreasonable) to believe A, B, C.

The first remark (3), unlike (4), says nothing special about belief or other psychological states, nor does it say anything normative. Hence, (3) can be true without (4) being true. Even if A, B, C are actually inconsistent, the inconsistency may have gone unnoticed and may be very difficult to discover. And even if you notice that A, B, C are inconsistent, there may still be reasons to accept each and it may be quite unclear which should be given up. You may not have the time or the ability to work out which should be given up or you may have more urgent matters to attend to before trying to figure out which to give up of A, B, C. In the meantime, it may very well be rational for you to continue to believe all three.

> *Age of the earth*
> In the nineteenth century, Kelvin's calculation of the age of the earth using principles of thermodynamics gave a result that was too small to allow for what was calculated to be the time needed for evolution (Gould 1985). One scientific response was to continue to accept all the relevant principles, despite their leading to this contradiction, while waiting for someone to figure out what was going wrong.

This would seem to have been a rational response to the difficulty.[2]

Someone may show you a paradoxical argument leading to the conclusion that 3 = 1, or a proof that a certain claim, which says of itself that it is not a true claim, is both a true claim and not a true claim.

2. Kelvin's calculations depended on assumptions about sources of energy. The discovery of radioactivity revealed a source he had not allowed for.

Proof that $3 = 1$.
Let $n = 1$.
Then $2n = 2$.
$n^2 + 2n = n^2 + 2$ [adding n^2 to both sides].
$n^2 = n^2 - 2n + 2$ [subtracting $2n$ from both sides].
$n^2 - 1 = n^2 - 2n + 1$ [subtracting 1 from both sides].
$(n + 1)(n - 1) = (n - 1)(n - 1)$ [factoring].
$n + 1 = n - 1$ [eliminating common factor from both sides].
$n + 2 = n$ [adding 1 to both sides].
$3 = 1$ [replacing n with its value, 1].

"Liar paradox"
Let (L) be the claim *that (L) is not true.*
The claim *that (L) is not true* is true if and only if (L) is not true [meaning of "true"].
(L) is true if and only if (L) is not true [substituting].
But that is impossible [logic].

Someone can see that certain assumptions lead to paradox without being able to figure out which assumptions are most plausibly abandoned. In that situation, it may be rational to continue to accept the assumptions in question, trying to avoid the paradoxical patterns of argument.

6.2.3 The Relevance of Goals and Interests

The examples above called "Goal-directed reasoning" and "Clutter avoidance" indicate that what it is rational or reasonable for you to believe can depend upon your needs, goals, and interests in various ways. This is part of what lies behind the

General principle of clutter avoidance
It is not reasonable or rational to fill your mind with trivial consequences of your beliefs, when you have better things to do with your time, as you often do.

If you spend all your time deriving trivial logical implications, for example, you will fail to attend to more important things, like finding food and drink and a place to spend the night.

More generally, whether it is rational to reach a particular conclusion will always depend in part on what questions you want to answer or have reasons to answer. If you need your keys to get into the house and you have data from which you could figure out where your keys are, then you have a reason to use those data to reach a conclusion about where your keys are. If it is urgent that you get into the house, it is not rational for you to spend your time drawing conclusions that do not promise to help you in this task. It is not rational for you to infer trivial consequences of your beliefs, as in "$1 + 1 = 2$; so either $1 + 1 = 2$ or the moon is made of green cheese," even though the disjunctive proposition, "Either $1 + 1 = 2$, or the moon is made of green cheese," has to be true if its first disjunct, "$1 + 1 = 2$" is true.

There is a practical aspect to all reasoning, including theoretical reasoning. What theoretical inferences it is reasonable for you to make depend in part on your needs and goals, because the inferences it is reasonable for you to make depend on what questions you have reasons to answer and what those questions are depends on your needs and goals.

Of course, that is not to say that merely wanting P to be true can give you a reason to believe P (wishful theoretical thinking), although it may give you a reason to find out whether P is true, and it may give you a reason to make P true (wishful practical reasoning).

6.2.4 Ideal Reasoners?

Another point already mentioned is also behind the principle of clutter avoidance. Reasoning is subject to "resource limits" of attention, memory, and time. So, it is not rational to fill your time inferring trivial consequences of your beliefs when you have more important things to attend to.

Some theories of rationality (Stalnaker 1984, Gärdenfors 1988) begin by abstracting away from these limits. Theories of ideal rationality are concerned with an "ideally rational agent" whose beliefs are always consistent and "closed under logical implication."

> *Deductive closure*
> An ideal agent's beliefs are deductively closed, or closed under logical implication, if and only if any proposition logically implied by some of those beliefs is itself also believed.

Other theorists argue that such an idealization appears to confuse rationality, ideal or otherwise, with logical genius or even divinity! And, as we shall see, it is unclear how to relate such an ideal to actual finite human beings, with their resource-limited rationality.

We have already seen that ordinary rationality requires neither deductive closure nor consistency. It does not require deductive closure, because it is not always rational to believe D simply because D is implied by your beliefs in A, B, C. Rationality does not require consistency, because you can be rational even though there are undetected inconsistencies in your beliefs, and because it is not always rational to respond to the discovery of inconsistency by dropping everything else in favor of eliminating that inconsistency.

Now consider an ideal agent with no limitations on memory, attention span, or time, with instantaneous and cost-free computational abilities. It is not obvious whether such an agent would have a reason to infer all the trivial consequences of his or her beliefs. True, it wouldn't cost anything for the agent to draw all those consequences, even all infinitely many of them, let us suppose. But there would also be no need to draw any of those consequences in the absence of a reason to be interested in them, for the agent can effortlessly compute any consequence whenever it may later be needed.

Could an ideal agent's beliefs be inconsistent? If these beliefs were also deductively closed, the agent would then believe everything, because everything follows from inconsistency.

> *Inconsistency implies everything*
> An inconsistent deductively closed agent believes both P and not-P.
> Consider any arbitrary proposition Q.
> P implies (P or Q), so the agent believes (P or Q).
> Not-P and (P or Q) implies Q, so the agent believes Q.
> So an inconsistent deductively closed agent believes every proposition Q.

Now consider rational recovery from inconsistent beliefs.

> *Ordinary recovery from inconsistency*
> An ordinary nonideal rational agent, Tamara, believes that Bill is in his office, but when she looks into the office, no one is there. At least for a moment, Tamara has inconsistent beliefs, believing both that Bill is in his office and that no one is in Bill's office. Tamara quickly and painlessly recovers from this inconsistency by dropping her belief that Bill is in his office, concluding that he must have stepped out for a moment.

Ordinary rational agents deal with this sort of momentary inconsistency all the time, whenever something surprising happens. You are surprised when you believe P but discover Q, realizing that P and Q cannot both be true.

But consider the implications of surprise for an ideal deductively closed agent.

> *A deductively closed agent is unable to recover from inconsistency!*
> If the beliefs of such an agent were even momentarily inconsistent, the agent could never rationally recover, for there would be no trace in the agent's beliefs of how the agent had acquired inconsistent beliefs. Because rational recovery from inconsistency can appeal only to present beliefs, and, because the deductively closed agent has

> exactly the same beliefs no matter how he or she got into inconsistency, there is no way in which the deductively closed agent could use temporal criteria in retreating from inconsistency—the agent would have to recover in exactly the same way, no matter where he or she had started.

An inconsistent, ideally rational, deductively closed cave dweller of 10,000 B.C. and an inconsistent, ideally rational, deductively closed nuclear scientist of A.D. 2000 would have exactly the same beliefs about where he or she had started, for each would believe everything! If any recovery were possible at all, the inconsistent, ideally rational cave dweller and the inconsistent, ideally rational nuclear scientist would have to recover in the same way, ending up with exactly the same beliefs! So, the deductively closed agent had better never have inconsistent beliefs!

It is unclear how ideal rational agents might deal with ordinary surprise. Various possibilities suggest themselves, but we need not explore them here. In what follows, we will be directly concerned with real rather than ideal rational agents.

That's enough background. We now turn to some less obvious and more controversial aspects of rationality.

6.3 Conservatism

The first less obvious aspect of rationality is that ordinary rationality is generally conservative in the following sense. You start from where you are, with your present beliefs and intentions. Rationality or reasonableness then consists in trying to make improvements in your view. Your initial beliefs and intentions have a privileged position in the sense that you begin with them rather than with nothing at all or with a special privileged part of those beliefs and intentions serving as data. So, for example, an ordinary rational person continues to believe something that he or she starts out believing in the absence of a special reason to doubt it.

6.3.1 Special Foundations: Rejection of General Conservatism

An alternative conception of rationality going back at least to Descartes (1637) might be called "special foundationalism." In this view, your beliefs are to be associated with your reasons or justifications for them. These justifications appeal to other beliefs of yours, themselves to be associated with justifications, and so on. Circular justifications of belief are ruled out, so the process of justification ultimately rests on special foundational beliefs that are self-justifying and need no further justification. Special foundational beliefs include beliefs about immediate experience, such as headaches and perceptual experiences, obvious logical and mathematical axioms, and similar beliefs. In other words, you start from your evidence: those things that are evident to you. Rationality or reasonableness then consists in accepting only what can be justified from your evidence basis, in this view.

> *Ted's justification for believing that this is a piece of paper*
> It is thin, flexible, and white, with printing on it; it has the feel of paper rather than plastic. This evidence is best explained on the supposition that it is a piece of paper. Ted's justification for believing it is white: it looks white to him and the circumstances of perception are such that something's looking white is best explained by the supposition that it is white. Ted needs no justification for believing that this looks white, because that is a foundational belief....

According to recent versions of special foundationalism (for example, Foley 1987, Alston 1989, Chisholm 1982), foundational beliefs do not have to be guaranteed to be true. In the absence of specific challenges to them, they are justified, but their initial justified status might be overridden by special reasons to doubt them.

> *Defeating a foundational belief*
> Omar is terrified as he sits in the dentist's chair about to have a tooth drilled. When the dentist begins, Omar yells. The dentist stops and asks what's wrong. "That hurt!" exclaims Omar, quite sincerely. "But I haven't yet touched the drill to your teeth," says the dentist. "Oh!" says Omar after a pause, "I guess I was confusing my anticipation of pain with actual pain." Omar's initial foundational belief that he feels pain is overridden by the further consideration that nothing had happened that could have caused pain. Beliefs about pain are foundational, but can be overridden by special reasons.

There are similar examples involving seemingly obvious logical or definitional truths.

> *Defeating a definitional belief*
> Paula is quite confident that all women are female, something she takes to be true by definition. Quinn objects, "Wasn't a woman disqualified by the Olympic Committee for having the wrong chromosomes? Didn't they decide that she was not female?" Paula is set back by this question. "I don't remember that case, but now that you mention that possibility, I can see that there could be a woman who is not, strictly speaking, female."[3]

3. I am indebted to Robert Schwartz for this example, which he mentioned to me many years ago.

Paula's confidence that she has intuited a definitional truth is shaken by the awareness of a possibility she had not previously considered. Seemingly obvious axioms or definitions are foundational but their justification can be overridden by special considerations.

We can describe each of the competing theories (foundationalism, conservatism) in the terminology of the other theory. So, we can say that the special foundations theory is conservative about all foundational beliefs but only foundational beliefs. And we can say that general conservatism treats all beliefs as foundational.

6.3.2 Objections to Special Foundationalism as a Theory of Rationality

One problem for special foundationalism is to explain why special foundational beliefs should have the relevant sort of special status. What distinguishes foundational beliefs from others that would justify applying conservatism to the foundational beliefs but not other beliefs?

A second, and perhaps more serious problem is that people tend not to keep track of their reasons for their nonfoundational beliefs. But, according to special foundationalism, if you don't associate a complete enough justification with a nonfoundational belief, then it is not rational or reasonable for you to continue to believe it. This realization may undermine a great many of your beliefs.

General beliefs with forgotten justifications

Foundationalist: What country is Athens in?
Maureen: That's easy, Greece. Everyone knows that!
F: But what reason do you have for thinking Athens is in Greece? Can you remember a specific occasion on which you learned that information?
M: Well, no; but I'm sure if you just ask anyone. . . .
F: But what grounds do you have now before you ask someone else?
M: I can't put my finger on anything specific, but I am sure.
F: If you don't have a justification that goes beyond the mere fact that you believe it, you are not justified in continuing to believe it.
M: Oh dear!

Specific beliefs originally based on perception

Foundationalist: Was Paul at the meeting yesterday?
Maureen: Yes, he was, although he didn't say anything.
F: Can you remember your perceptual evidence for thinking he was there?
M: Well, I remember seeing him.
F: Was he wearing a tie?

M: I don't recall.

F: Can you remember what he looked like?

M: Not in detail, but I do remember seeing him there.

F: If you no longer recall the sensory evidence on which that conclusion is based, you should abandon it.

M: That's ridiculous!

Originally, Maureen's belief was based on the evidence of her senses. But she almost immediately lost track of exactly what her sensory evidence was. Now she has at best the memory (another belief) that her belief was justified without any special justification for it that would distinguish it from her other nonfoundational beliefs.

Special foundationalism implies that she should abandon such a belief as no longer justified. Because most of her nonfoundational beliefs are in the same position with respect to justification, almost all her nonfoundational beliefs should be abandoned as unjustified, according to special foundationalism. Special foundationalism implies that it is not reasonable or rational for her to continue to believe most of the things she currently believes! Some foundationalists are happy to endorse that sort of skeptical conclusion, but it is an extreme one and we will try to avoid such extremes in our discussion.

6.3.3 The Burden of Proof

The issue between general conservatism and special foundationalism amounts to a question about the burden of proof, or (better) the burden of justification. According to special foundationalism, the burden of justification falls on continuing to believe something, at least for nonfoundational beliefs. Any nonfoundational belief requires special justification.

Foundational beliefs do not require special justification. For them, what requires justification is failing to continue to believe them. Sometimes there is a reason to abandon a foundational belief, but such abandonment requires such a special reason.

According to general conservatism, the burden of justification is always on changing beliefs or intentions. You start with certain beliefs and intentions and any change in them requires some special reason. Any sort of change in belief or intention requires special justification. Merely continuing to believe what you believe or intend requires no special justification in the absence of a specific challenge to that belief or intention.

Which of these views, general conservatism or special foundationalism, best fits ordinary judgments about rationality and irrationality? (What do you think?) Not special foundationalism, for that view implies that it is irrational or unreasonable to continue to believe most of what you believe. So general conservatism fits better.

We now turn to a different issue, the relation between deduction and induction. (See also chapter 1.)

6.4 Induction and Deduction

It is important to notice that deduction and induction are not two kinds of reasoning. In fact, induction and deduction are not two kinds of anything.

Deduction is concerned with certain relations among propositions, especially relations of implication and consistency. Induction is not concerned with those or any similar sort of relation among propositions. Induction is a kind of reasoning. But, as we will see, deduction is not a kind of reasoning.

6.4.1 Induction and Deduction as Two Kinds of Reasoning

Consider this misleading account (based on Black 1958) of the relation between induction and deduction.

> *Deductive model of inference*
> Deductive logic is presented via a certain notion of "proof" or "argument." A proof or argument has premises, intermediate steps, and a final conclusion. Each step must follow logically from prior steps in accordance with one or another specific rule, sometimes called a "rule of inference." Such a proof or argument is an instance of "deductive reasoning." Deductive reasoning in this sense is contrasted with "inductive reasoning," which is said to take a similar form, with premises, maybe intermediate steps, and final conclusion, but with the following difference: deductive steps are always truth preserving, whereas inductive steps are not.

This picture is very misleading. First, consider the reasoning that goes into the construction of a deductive proof or argument. Except in the simplest cases, the best strategy is not to expect to start with the premises, figure out the first intermediate step of the proof, then the second, and so on until the conclusion is reached. Often it is useful to start from the proposition to be proved and work backward. It is useful to consider what intermediate results might be useful. (See chapter 9.)

The so-called deductive rules of inference are not rules that you follow in constructing the proof. They are rules that the proof must satisfy in order to be a proof.

In other words, there is a difference between reasoning about a proof, involving the construction of a proof that must satisfy certain rules, and reasoning that proceeds temporally in the same pattern as the proof in accordance with those rules. You do not reason deductively in the sense that you reason in the pattern of a proof. You can reason about a deductive proof, just as you can reason about anything else. But your reasoning is not well represented by anything like a proof or argument in the sense above.

6.4.2 Implication and Consistency: Deduction

Deduction is not a kind of inference or reasoning, although you can reason about deductions. Deduction is implication. A deduction or proof or argument exhibits an implication by showing intermediate steps.

Logic, the theory of deduction, is not by itself a theory of reasoning. In other words, it is not by itself a theory about what to believe (or intend); it is not a theory concerning how to change your view.

It is true that deductions, proofs, arguments do seem relevant to reasoning. It is not just that you sometimes reason about deductions in the way you reason about the weather or how much tax you owe. It is an interesting and nontrivial problem to say just how deductions are relevant to reasoning, a problem that is hidden by talk of deductive and inductive reasoning, as if it is obvious that some reasoning follows deductive principles.

The answer must be that it is often useful to construct deductions in reasoning about ordinary matters, and not just when you are explicitly reasoning about deductions or proofs. But why should it be useful to construct deductions? What role do they play in our reasoning?

Sometimes we do accept a conclusion because we have constructed a proof of it from other things we accept. But there are other cases in which we construct a proof of something we already accept in order to see what assumptions might account for it. In such a case, the conclusion that we accept might be a premise of the proof. The connection between proofs and reasoning is complex.

6.4.3 Kinds of Induction

The term "induction" is sometimes restricted to "enumerative induction."

> *Enumerative induction*
> Given that all observed F's are G's, you infer that all F's are G's, or at least that the next F is a G.

But often the term "induction" is used more widely so as to include also inference to the best explanation of the evidence.

> *Inference to the best explanation*
> Holmes infers the best explanation for the footprints, the absence of barking, the broken window: "The butler wears size 10 shoes,

is known to the dog, broke the window to make it look like a burglary. . . ."

Scientific hypothetic induction
Scientists infer that Brownian motion is caused by the movement of invisible molecules.

What makes one hypothesis better than another for this purpose is something we must discuss later.

6.4.4 Problem of Induction

It is sometimes said that there is a "problem of induction" (Bonjour 1992).

(Alleged) problem of induction
When your beliefs logically imply the conclusion you come to accept, your conclusion cannot be wrong unless your premises are. Your premises guarantee your conclusion. This is not so in inductive reasoning, where your prior beliefs do not logically imply your conclusion. A question therefore arises whether you can be justified in drawing a conclusion that is not guaranteed by your premises.

But it is not clear what the problem of induction is supposed to be. Premises in an argument are to be distinguished from the starting points in reasoning, as we have already observed. The conclusion of an argument is not to be identified with the conclusion of reasoning, in the sense of what you end up with or "conclude" after reasoning. Even when reasoning culminates in the construction of an argument, the conclusion of the *argument* may be something you started off believing, and the conclusion of your *reasoning* may be to accept something that is a premise of an explanatory argument constructed as a result of inference to the best explanation.

Clearly, it would be stupid—indeed, highly irrational—not to engage in inductive reasoning. You would no longer be able to learn from experience. You would have no basis for any expectations at all about the future, for your evidence entirely concerns the past.

So, it would seem that the "problem of induction" is a creation of confusion about induction and deduction, arising out of the deductive model of inference. Again, it is important to see that there are not two mutually exclusive kinds of reasoning, deductive and inductive. Deduction has to do with implication and consistency and is only indirectly relevant to what you should believe.

6.4.5 Nonmonotonic Reasoning

Unclarity about the relation between deduction and induction may be responsible for the occasional description of induction as "nonmonotonic reasoning" in alleged contrast with deduction, which is described as "monotonic."

The terms "monotonic" and "nonmonotonic" are borrowed from mathematics.

> *Monotonic function*
> A monotonic (or "monotonically nondecreasing") function $f(x)$ is a function whose value does not decrease as x increases. [A monotonic nonincreasing function is one whose value does not increase as x increases.] A nonmonotonic function is one whose value sometimes increases as x increases and sometimes decreases as x increases.

Deductive implication is monotonic in this sense:

> *Deductive implication is monotonic*
> Everything deductively implied by a set of propositions is also implied when additional propositions are added to a set. So, the deductive implications of a set of premises do not decrease in any respect as new premises are added. If A and B logically imply Z, so do A, B, and C, and so do A, B, C, and D, and so on.

On the other hand, reasoning is nonmonotonic in this sense:

> *Reasoning is nonmonotonic*
> Conclusions that are reasonable on the basis of specific information can become unreasonable if further information is added. Given the announced schedule for your course, your experience of the last few weeks, and that today is Monday, it may be reasonable for you to believe that your course will meet at 11:00 this morning. But if you are also given the further information that there is a sign on the classroom door saying that the 11:00 meeting of the course is canceled today because your professor is ill, it is no longer reasonable for you to believe that your course will meet at 11:00 A.M. Now it is reasonable for you to believe that your course will not meet at 11:00 A.M. And, given the further information that the sign on the classroom door is a hoax by a student, it will be no longer reasonable to believe your course will not meet. New information can make old conclusions unreasonable, whereas additional premises in a deductive argument do not affect what conclusions follow deductively.

This aspect of inductive reasoning has been described in various ways. For example, it is sometimes said that inductive reasoning is "defeasible." Considerations that support a given conclusion can be *defeated* by additional information.

Sometimes this is described as "default" reasoning. Given your original information, your *default assumption* is that the course will meet on Monday at 11:00 A.M Additional information can override that default.

Default assumptions need not even be the usual case, as long as you can expect to find out when they do not hold. A default assumption might therefore take the form, "Assume P, unless you hear otherwise."

One use of default assumptions is sometimes called "negation from failure."

> *Negation from failure*
> The idea is to assume that something is not so unless you find information that it is so. Suppose, for example, you are interested in whether there are any direct flights from Newark, New Jersey, to Lincoln, Nebraska. You do a computer search trying to locate such flights. When the computer does not find any, you conclude that there are none. The failure to find positive information leads you to accept a negative conclusion.

A number of attempts have been made to develop "nonmonotonic logics" to capture these aspects of reasoning. Results have been fairly limited (Ginsberg 1987). Some of these attempts are due to thinking of induction and deduction as two things of the same sort, the thought being that, because we have a deductive logic for deductive reasoning, we should develop an inductive logic for inductive reasoning. We have already seen what is wrong with this idea, namely, that deductive logic is concerned with deductive implication, not deductive reasoning. All reasoning is inductive.

It will be useful to develop an inductive or nonmonotonic logic only as an account of a kind of implication: default implication. Whether this development leads to any results that are useful to a theory of reasoning is still unclear.

There has been some discussion of the logic of conditionals, that is, statements of the form, "If A, B." At least some conditionals have the following sort of nonmonotonic property. "If A, B" can be true, when "If C and A, B" is not true.

> *Nonmonotonic conditionals*
> "If you turn the key, the engine will start" can be true even though "if I disconnect the battery and you turn the key, the engine will start" is not true.

Horty and Thomason (1991) observe that research on the logic of conditionals comes together with research in nonmonotonic logic if we associate "A default implies B" with "if A, B."

6.5 Coherence

The nonmonotonic aspect of inductive reasoning means that everything you believe is at least potentially relevant to the conclusions you can reasonably draw. Rationality is a matter of your overall view, including your beliefs and your intentions.

If it is reasonable to change your view in a certain way, we might say that your view would be more rationally "coherent" if changed in that way. We can describe principles of rationality as principles of rational coherence.

Adopting this terminology, we can (following Pollock 1979) distinguish two sorts of coherence, positive and negative.

6.5.1 Negative Coherence

Negative coherence is the absence of incoherence. This is the sort of coherence discussed in chapter 2. Beliefs and intentions are incoherent to the extent that they clash with each other, for instance, through being inconsistent. Incoherence is something to be avoided, if possible, although we have seen that it isn't always possible to avoid incoherence. Your beliefs might be inconsistent without your knowing that they are. And, even if you are aware of inconsistency, you may not know of a sufficiently easy way to get rid of it.

> *Principle of negative coherence*
> To the extent that you are aware of incoherence in your view, you have a reason to modify your view in order to get rid of the incoherence, if you can do so without too much expense.

Here is one way in which deductive logic is relevant to the theory of rationality, through providing an account of (one kind of) incoherence or inconsistency.

6.5.2 Positive Coherence

There is positive coherence among your beliefs (and intentions) to the extent that they are connected in ways that allow them to support each other. We can only speculate about what provides positive coherence. Some of the factors that seem relevant are the following.

> *Explanatory connections*
> A set of unrelated beliefs seems to be less coherent than a tightly organized conceptual scheme that contains explanatory and other principles that make sense out of most of your beliefs. This is why inference to the best explanation is an attractive pattern of inference.

Causal connections are a special case of coherence giving explanatory connections:

> *Causal connections*
> Belief in two events seems to be more coherent if one is seen as a cause of the other. When the lights go out in one room in her house, it makes more sense for Zelda to conclude that the fuse for that room has blown than to suppose that the fuse in a neighbor's house has blown. She easily envisions a causal connection between the fuse for that room blowing and the lights in the room going out. She does not as easily envision a causal connection between the fuse in her neighbor's house blowing and the lights in her room going out.

To be sure, Zelda can envision a complex causal connection between the fuse in her neighbor's house and the lights in her room. But to believe in that complicated connection would presumably offend against conservatism, which would seem to favor minimal changes in belief in order to obtain explanatory coherence. Also, without evidence of such complication, adding a belief in such a complication would actually decrease the overall coherence of her view.

Causation is not the only thing that would seem to bring explanatory coherence. Connecting generalization is another.

> *Coherence from connecting generalization*
> All the emeralds Steve has observed are green. Steve infers that emeralds tend to be green, or even that all emeralds are green. This is an instance of enumerative induction.

We might think of enumerative induction as inference to the best explanation, taking the generalization to explain its instances. But then we must recognize that this is a different kind of explanation from causal explanation. A general correlation does not cause its instances!

Implication is an important kind of connector among beliefs.

> *Coherence from implication*
> Teri believes that Jack is either in his office or at home. She finds that his office is empty. She concludes that he is at home. This conclusion is implied by her prior beliefs.

Here is a second way in which deductive logic can be relevant to rationality. It is relevant to implication, and implication is a coherence-giving connection.

In trying to develop an account of rational coherence, we might try to reduce some of the factors mentioned to others in a substantive way. One idea would be to try to treat all factors as special cases of explanatory coherence. That idea is not very plausible for many cases like the last one, in which a conclusion is accepted because it is implied by other beliefs. What is the relevant explanation in that case? One might say that the premises of Teri's argument "explain why its conclusion is true." But that seems to stretch the notion of explanation.

Another idea would be to try to reduce all coherence to that involved in implication. That has some plausibility for certain explanations. And strict generalizations are related to their instances by implication. Often explanations in physics work via implication. Recognition of this fact gave rise to the so-called deductive nomological model of explanation (Hempel 1965), which works for many scientific explanations, but not for all.

One class of exceptions appeals to default principles that hold, other things being equal.

> *Explanation without implication*
> A certain substance dissolved in a certain liquid because it is sugar placed in water, and sugar normally dissolves in water. We have to say "normally" because sugar does not always dissolve in water. It does not dissolve if there is already a supersaturated solution in the water, or if there is wax covering the outside of the sugar, or indefinitely many other things haven't occurred.

Here a general default principle helps to explain the dissolving in this case without guaranteeing that the sugar will dissolve. So, this explanatory connection is not based on strict implication.

6.6 Simplicity

In trying to explain some data, it is reasonable to consider a very limited range of the infinitely many logically possible explanations. The rational inquirer restricts attention to the set of relatively simple hypotheses that might account for most of the data.

This is not to say very much, for it amounts to using the term "simple" for whatever the relevant factors are that restrict rational attention to a certain few hypotheses. Furthermore, we are concerned with *relative* simplicity in this sense. A hypothesis that is too complicated as compared with other available hypotheses at one time, can have a different status at another time if those other hypotheses have been eliminated. The first hypothesis might then be among the simplest of available hypotheses.

So, to say that the rational inquirer is concerned to find a simple hypothesis is not to say that the rational inquirer is committed to believing that "reality is simple," whatever that might mean.

Let us now try to say more about simplicity in this sense, understanding that our discussion must be even more speculative than what has gone before. First, let us see how the relevant kind of simplicity might be involved in a famous philosophical "riddle."

6.6.1 Goodman's "New Riddle of Induction"

Goodman (1965) discusses the following example. Suppose that Fran has a test for emeralds that does not depend on color, she has examined various emeralds for color, and she has found that each was green at least when she examined it. This evidence rationally supports the hypothesis

(H1) All emeralds are green.

Using the terminology of the preceding section, the evidence supports (H1) because it consists of instances of (H1) that are made more coherent if (H1) is true.

But there are many other hypotheses that are generalizations of the evidence, where the evidence consists of instances of each of these hypotheses. For example:

(H2) All emeralds are: either green if first examined before A.D. 2000 or blue if not first examined before A.D. 2000.

Goodman suitably defines the term "grue" to stand for the predicate after the colon in (H2), so that the hypothesis can be abbreviated as follows:

(H2) All emeralds are grue.

Notice that (H2) conflicts with (H1) regarding any emeralds not first examined by A.D. 2000. According to (H1) those emeralds are green. According to (H2) they are blue.

Goodman points out that hypotheses like (H2) are not taken seriously. His "new riddle of induction" asks what the difference is between (H1) and (H2).

Clearly, there is a sense in which Fran's (and our) preference for (H1) is due to its being a much simpler hypothesis than (H2). But what sort of simplicity is in question and why is it relevant?

6.6.2 Using Simplicity to Decide Among Hypotheses That Are Taken Seriously

It is very important to see that using simplicity to rule hypotheses out of consideration is to be distinguished from using simplicity as an explicit consideration in theory choice. Sometimes a scientist will say that a particular theory is better than another because the first theory assumes the existence of fewer objects, fewer basic principles, or whatever. When a scientist argues in some such way he or she is arguing in favor of one rather than another hypothesis that is being taken seriously. As Sober (1988) observes, such appeals to simplicity are often quite controversial. That is, it is controversial whether simplicity in one or another respect is a relevant consideration in choosing among hypotheses.

But, even where there are deep controversies in a subject, reasonable disputants will still take seriously only a very few of the infinitely many possible hypotheses. We are concerned with whatever it is that leads reasonable people to disregard most of the hypotheses as too "silly" to be considered.

(To repeat an earlier point, silliness is a relative matter. Hypothesis (H2) is silly because (H1) has not been ruled out. We can imagine a situation in which (H2) becomes acceptable.)

Let's call the sort of simplicity we are concerned with "basic simplicity." Because the phenomenon of ruling out crazy or silly hypotheses occurs in all domains, let us assume that there is a single domain-independent notion of simplicity for this purpose.

6.6.3 Speculation: Basic Simplicity Has to Do with How Easy It Is to Use Hypotheses

The basic simplicity of a hypothesis seems to have something to do with the simplicity of its representation. But it is always possible to represent any hypothesis simply, so the matter is a bit more complex.

> *Simple representation of a complex hypothesis*
> We have already seen that the complex hypothesis (H2), *All emeralds are: either green if first examined before* A.D. *2000 or blue if not first examined before* A.D. *2000*, can be given a much simpler representation, if a suitable predicate is defined: *all emeralds are grue.*

In fact, any hypothesis can be abbreviated by a single symbol, so simplicity of representation cannot be taken at face value.

Now, if a hypothesis like *All emeralds are grue* is used to explain the data, it has to be expanded to its more complex form, *All emeralds are: either green if first examined before* A.D. *2000 or blue if not first examined before* A.D. *2000.* This expansion is required so on the assumption that we are more interested in accounting for the colors of objects, like whether they are blue or green, as opposed to their "cholers," like whether they are grue or bleen! If instead we were more interested in explaining why emeralds were grue, we could use the hypothesis *All emeralds are grue* without having to expand it, and the hypothesis that *All emeralds are green* would require elaboration in terms of grue and bleen in order to provide the desired explanation.

So, perhaps the thing to look at is not so much the mere statement of the hypothesis but also how complicated it is to use the hypothesis to explain the data and predict new observations of a sort in which we are interested. (Here again theoretical rationality would depend on practical concerns.)

Simplicity as ease of use
In considering possible explanations of given data, it is rational and reasonable to ignore hypotheses that are much harder to use in explanation and prediction than other available hypotheses that in other respects account equally well for the data.

6.6.4 Parasitic Theories

A parasitic theory says that, as far as evidence goes, it is as if some other theory were true.

Descartes's Demon Hypothesis
Your sensory experience is the result of a powerful evil demon, giving you experiences as if of a world of physical objects.

Scientific instrumentalism
Scientific theories can be used as devices for calculating observations, but should not be treated as saying anything about the real nature of the world. All that can be rationally believed is that it is as if this or that scientific theory holds (van Fraassen 1989).

In the classroom, it may be unclear how you can reject Descartes's Demon Hypothesis. But it would be crazy to take that hypothesis seriously in ordinary life. Similarly, outside the philosophy classroom it makes sense to take scientific instrumentalism seriously only when the theory can be accepted only as an instrument, for example, when the theory is known not to be wholly true. In that case, it makes sense to consider instrumentalist hypotheses.

Newton's laws as instruments
Relativity theory tells us that Newton's laws are not completely accurate, but they hold as good approximations at speeds much less than the speed of light. Under those conditions, it is as if Newton's laws were correct.

We don't take parasitic theories seriously unless we have reason to reject the theories on which they are parasitic. In other words, parasitic theories are treated as "less simple" than the theories on which they are parasitic.

This result fits our tentative suggestion that simplicity be measured by how easy it is to use a hypothesis to explain data and make new predictions. A parasitic theory is normally more complicated according to this suggestion than is the theory on which it is parasitic, because to use the parasitic theory, you have to do everything you do when using the nonparasitic theory and you have to do something more. You first calculate what is to be expected on theory T, then use the principle that what will happen is what is expected according to theory T. So, there is an additional step to the use of the parasitic theory that is not part of the original theory T.

> *Nonparasitic explanation*
> Why does E occur? Because of initial conditions C, and laws L. Given C and L and the following calculation ..., we expect E.
>
> *Parasitic explanation*
> Why does E occur? According to theory T, it is because of initial conditions C, and laws L. Given C and L and the following calculation ..., we would on theory T expect E. Our theory is that things will occur as if T is true. So, we expect E also.

The explanation of E from the nonparasitic explanation occurs as a part of the parasitic explanation. So, the parasitic explanation has to be somewhat more complicated than the nonparasitic explanation.

6.7 Practical Rationality and Reasonableness

So far, all that has been said about practical rationality is that your goals play a role in practical rationality that they do not play in theoretical rationality. The negative part of this remark, concerning theoretical rationality, may require qualification, given the apparent role of simplicity and conservatism in theoretical rationality, if these factors have a practical justification. We will discuss the possible need for such a qualification in the next section of this chapter. In the present section, we say something more about the way in which goals are relevant to practical rationality.

One issue is whether there is a single category of goal, or perhaps a single measure of "utility," as opposed to a variety of functionally different things: desires, values, goals, intentions, commitments, principles, rules, and so on. A related issue is whether we need to allow for a structure within goals in which some goals depend on others.

But let us begin with a few remarks about the mathematical decision theory that is often used as a model of rationality in economics.

6.7.1 Decision Theory

In its simplest form (for example, von Neumann and Morgenstern 1944), mathematical decision theory applies when you are faced with a decision between two or more exclusive acts. Each act has one or more possible outcomes to which you assign certain values or "utilities." Let us use $u(A)$ to represent the utility of act A. You also assign conditional probabilities, prob(O,A), to each possible outcome O in relation to a given act A. Then the "expected gain" of a given outcome O of an act A is $u(O) \times$

prob(O,A). The "expected utility" of each act A is the sum of the expected gains of each possible consequence of that act. Finally, the theory holds that rationality requires doing either the act with the highest expected utility or, if there is a tie for highest, one of the acts with highest expected utility.

The principles of decision theory are like principles of logic in being principles of consistency or coherence. It would be a mistake to identify decision theory with a full theory of practical rationality, just as it is a mistake to identify the theory of theoretical rationality with logic.

Some decision theorists argue that it is useful for individuals faced with hard practical problems to think of them in decision theoretic terms. Such individuals are advised to consider carefully what their possible acts are, what possible consequences each act might have, what utility they assign to each possible consequence, and how likely they think a given act would be to have a given consequence. They should then calculate expected utilities and choose that act with the highest calculated expected utility.

Is that good advice? That's an empirical question: Do people do better using such a method or not? The suggested method is not obviously good advice. Given a poor enough assignment of utilities and probabilities, you could be led very wrong by your calculation.

6.7.2 Derivative Goals

Some goals are derivative from others in a way that is important for practical rationality. You want A. B is a means to A. So you want B. That is, you want B as a means to A. If you get A in some other way, you no longer have the same reason to want B. Or if you discover that B is not going to lead to A you no longer have the same reason to want B. It is irrational to continue to pursue an instrumental goal after your reason for wanting it has lapsed.

Also, consider the problem of deciding what to do when you have several goals. If you do A, you will satisfy goals G1, G2, and G3. If you do B, you will satisfy goals G4, G5, and G6. It is not easy to say how a rational person reaches an overall evaluation of acts A and B by combining his or her evaluation of the outcomes of each act. One idea (Franklin 1817) is to try to reduce the lists by trying to match outcomes of A with equivalent outcomes of B, canceling these equivalent goals out, and then considering only the remaining advantages of each course of action. That can still leave difficult choices.

But one thing can be said: Do not count the satisfaction of two goals as distinct advantages of an act if your only reason for one of the goals is that it will enable you to attain the other.

Choosing a career
Mabel is trying to decide between a career in business and a career in Academia. These careers are associated with different life-styles, and she considers which life-style she would prefer. She also considers the difference in income and wealth associated with the two choices, forgetting that income and wealth are means to the life-styles associated with the choices.

Mabel is irrationally counting the same consideration (style of life) twice when she treats income as a separate consideration.

6.7.3 Nonultimate, Noninstrumental Desires

You can care about things that are neither ultimate ends nor instrumental toward getting other things you want.

Good news
Jack has been tested to see whether he has a fatal disease D. The test is quite reliable. Jack desperately wants the results of the test to be negative, indicating that he does not have the disease. Jack's desire is not an ultimate end of his, nor is it for something that might be instrumental in obtaining something else that Jack desires. He desires a negative result because of what it indicates about him, not because of what it might lead to.

Notice that Jack's desire in this case is not for something that he could rationally treat as a goal. It would be irrational for Jack to bribe a lab technician to guarantee that the test yields a negative result. That wouldn't have any effect on whether Jack has disease D, which is (after all) what Jack is basically concerned with.

6.7.4 Intentions

Does a rational person always reason directly from current goals, always figuring out the best ways to maximize satisfaction of current goals? That would resemble special foundationalism with respect to theoretical reasoning.

It ignores the role of long-term intentions. Such intentions record the decisions already made. These decisions are not irrevocable, but they carry considerable weight and should not be frivolously discarded. A person incapable of maintaining long-term intentions would be incapable of long-term planning and would have at best only a low level of rationality (Bratman 1987).

Intentions are not reducible to desires and beliefs, but put constraints on current planning of a special kind. A person's actual goals, as contrasted with things merely valued or desired, might be identified with what that person intends.

Intentions are directly related to action in ways not fully understood. Some authors think there are special intentions to do something *now*, constituting acts of will or volitions, these serving as the immediate cause of action.

6.7.5 Strength of Will

Our initial example of irrationality was an example of practical irrationality: Jane goes to the party rather than study for her exam. Jane finds the immediate pleasure of an evening more attractive than the longer-term considerations involved in doing well in her history course.

It is not that Jane temporarily overvalues the immediate pleasure of the party and undervalues the longer-term gains of study. She remains aware of the relative importance of these things. Her desires conflict with her evaluations.

In such a case, rationality requires sticking with her previously formed intentions, staying with her principles and resisting temptation. This is a matter of having good character, good habits. Jane's irrationality on this occasion derives from a character defect.

6.7.6 Reasonable Cooperation

Finally, consider our earlier example of unreasonable negotiation, which I repeat:

> *Refusing a reasonable proposal*
> Three students, Sally, Ellie, and Louise, have been assigned to a set of rooms consisting of a study room, a small single bedroom, and another small bedroom with a two-person bunk bed. They discuss the proposal that they should take turns, each getting the single for one third of the school year. Sally refuses to consider this proposal and insists on keeping the single for herself the whole year.

When her roommates say that Sally is being unreasonable, they seem to be making a moral judgment about Sally. She is not being "fair" (Miller 1992).

Notice that her roommates say that Sally is being "unreasonable" and would not say that she is being "irrational." Similarly, a teenager asking for permission to use the family car might plead with his mother by saying, "Be reasonable, Mom!" and not by saying, "Be rational, Mom!"

6.8 Theoretical Rationality and Philosophical Pragmatism

Earlier I said that goals are relevant to practical rationality in a way in which they are not relevant to theoretical rationality. Although your goals are relevant to what questions it is rational for you to be interested in answering, they are not relevant to determining the answer you should accept through theoretical reasoning in the way in which your goals can be relevant to determining what it is rational for you to decide to do through practical reasoning. Wishful thinking is theoretically irrational even as it is practically okay.

We mentioned the possibility of good practical reasons to believe certain things and were therefore led to distinguish epistemic or theoretical reasons to believe something from nonepistemic practical reasons to believe something. Evidence that John was elsewhere at the time of the crime is an epistemic or theoretical reason to believe him innocent. On the other hand, loyalty to John provides a nonepistemic, practical reason to believe him innocent.

The possibility of philosophical pragmatism complicates this picture. Everyone can agree that practical considerations are relevant to the choice of a notation for developing a theory.

> *Roman numerals*
> It would be hard to balance your bank account if you had to use Roman numerals rather than the more standard Arabic decimal notation. There are good practical reasons to use the one notation rather than the other.

Philosophical pragmatism argues against any sharp distinction between choice of theoretical hypothesis and choice of notation (Quine 1976). Pragmatists stress such practical features as we have already mentioned—simplicity, ease of use, and conservatism, for example—in deciding what to believe about any subject.

But then what happens to the distinction between theoretical and practical reasoning or, more precisely, the distinction between epistemic and nonepistemic reasons?

Pragmatists can still allow for this last distinction, defined as we defined it earlier.

> *Epistemic reason for belief*
> R is an epistemic reason to believe P only if the probability of P given R is greater than the probability of P given not-R.

> *Nonepistemic reason for belief*
> R is a nonepistemic reason to believe P if R is a reason to believe P over and above the extent to which the probability of P given R is greater than the probability of P given not-R.

Considerations of simplicity and conservatism are reflected in our probability judgments in a way that more specific practical considerations are not. For example, of the hypotheses that explain the evidence, we treat the simpler hypotheses as more likely to be true than the less simple hypotheses, given that evidence. On the other hand, a rational advertising agent should not suppose that it would be evidence that cigarettes do not cause cancer (in the sense of making that conclusion more likely to be true) if a tobacco company were willing to give advertising accounts only to agents who believe that smoking cigarettes does not cause cancer, even though that consideration might provide the rational advertising agent with a reason to have that belief.

So pragmatism seems to be compatible with distinguishing epistemic from nonepistemic reasons, allowing some practical considerations to fall on the epistemic side of this distinction.

6.9 Concluding Remarks

Despite the clear intuitive distinction we must make between theoretical and practical reasoning, theoretical and practical considerations are rationally intertwined in more than one way. Theoretical reasoning is goal directed in the sense that goals are relevant to the questions to be considered theoretically and there are practical reasons behind the role of conservatism and simplicity in reasoning.

At present, there is no mathematically elegant account of all aspects of rationality. Formal theories of implication and consistency are possible, but these are only part of the subject. Conservatism, simplicity, and coherence are important aspects of rationality, with explanation, implication, and consistency being relevant to coherence. Our ordinary judgments about rationality and reasonableness are often sensitive to these considerations, but also to strength of will and even fairness.

Logic and probability theory are not directly theories of rationality and reasonableness and, furthermore, it is a misuse of language to say that violations of principles of logic and probability theory are indications of irrationality or unreasonableness. We do not normally consider someone to be "irrational" or "unreasonable" simply because of a mistake in arithmetic, or probability theory, or logic. Instead we use the words "irrational" and "unreasonable" in a rather different way, for example, for those who refuse to accept "obvious" inductions, or for those who jump to conclusions on insufficient evidence, or for those who act knowing that they are frustrating their own purposes, or for those who are uncooperative.

Suggestions for Further Reading

Philosophers approach the study of rationality under the heading of "epistemology." Dancy and Sosa (1992) is an encyclopedia of the whole subject, with references to the philosophical literature. Nozick (1993) provides a rich, original, and highly suggestive discussion of many aspects of rationality with references to research in cognitive science and philosophy.

Harman (1986) discusses many of the considerations mentioned in this chapter. Goldman (1986, 1992) develops in detail an account of rationality and other aspects of philosophical epistemology with special attention to the reliability of information-gathering techniques. Stich (1990) criticizes reliability approaches and advocates pragmatism.

Goodman (1965) presents the "new riddle of induction" and provides a good discussion. A number of recent essays discussing the "new riddle" are collected in Stalker (1993). Lipton (1991) is a useful account of various aspects of inference to the best explanation. Sober (1988) discusses the role of explicit appeals in evolutionary biology to simplicity.

Bratman (1987) is an excellent introduction to certain issues involved in practical reasoning. Mele (1992) provides a somewhat different view of the same subject.

Problems

6.1 Assess Pascal's argument for belief in God, discussed above. Does Pascal try to offer an epistemic reason or a reason of some other kind? Does his argument overlook any relevant possibilities?

6.2 Assess the "proof" that 3 = 1. Does the proof purport to provide an epistemic reason or a reason of some other kind? What mistake if any does the proof make?

6.3 Assess the "proof" of the liar paradox.

6.4 The chapter argues that special foundationalism would require Maureen to abandon too many of her beliefs. Assess this response in defense of special foundationalism:

> *Attempted defense of special foundationalism*
>
> Even if Maureen has forgotten her original reasons, she knows that she believes P and can suppose it likely that she had a good reason when she first believed P. She is therefore justified in thinking that there is good reason to believe P and so is justified in continuing to believe P.

6.5 Assess this argument against "conservatism."

> *Objection to conservatism*
>
> Suppose that Mabel's reasons do not favor hypothesis 1 over hypothesis 2. Her reasons are equally balanced between these two competing hypotheses. Mabel does not realize this and supposes wrongly that she has more reason to believe hypothesis 1. And so, Mabel comes to believe hypothesis 1. Conservatism implies that once she believes hypothesis 1, she is justified in continuing to believe it in the absence of a special challenge to it. But surely Mabel is no more justified in believing hypothesis 1 after she starts to believe it than she was before she started to believe it!

Questions for Further Thought

6.1 Can you simply decide to believe something in the way that you can simply do something? Of course, there would have to be limits in both cases. You cannot simply decide to run a three-minute mile or believe that you can do so. But if someone tells you something, you may have to decide whether to believe it.

6.2 In the light of considerations in this chapter, particularly the discussion of conservatism, what can be said about belief in astrology? Is it unreasonable for someone to believe in astrology? Under what conditions would such a belief be reasonable or unreasonable?

References

Alston, W. (1989). *Epistemic justification: Essays in the theory of knowledge.* Ithaca, NY: Cornell University Press.

Black, M. (1958). Self-supporting inductive arguments. *Journal of Philosophy* 55, 718–725.

Bonjour, L. (1992). Problems of induction. In J. Dancy and E. Sosa, eds., *A companion to epistemology.* Oxford, England: Basil Blackwell, 391–395.

Bratman, M. (1987). *Intention, plans, and practical reason.* Cambridge, MA: Harvard University Press.

Chisholm, R. (1982). *The foundations of knowing.* Minneapolis, MN: University of Minnesota Press.

Cohen, J. (1981). Can human irrationality be experimentally demonstrated? *Behavioral and Brain Sciences* 4, 317–370.

Dancy, J., and E. Sosa (1992). *A Companion to Epistemology.* Oxford, England: Blackwell.

Dennett, D. C. (1971). Intentional systems. *Journal of Philosophy* 68, 87–106.

Descartes, R. (1637). *Discours de la méthode.* Paris.

Foley, R. (1987). *The theory of epistemic rationality.* Cambridge, MA: Harvard University Press.

Franklin, B. (1817). *Private correspondence I.* London: Colburn.

van Fraassen, B. (1989). *Law and symmetry.* Oxford, England: Oxford University Press.

Gardenfors, P. (1988). *Knowledge in flux.* Cambridge, MA: MIT Press.

Ginsberg, M., ed. (1987). *Readings in nonmonotonic reasoning.* Los Altos, CA: Morgan Kaufmann.

Goldman, A. (1986). *Epistemology and cognition.* Cambridge, MA: Harvard University Press.

Goldman, A. (1992). *Liaisons: Philosophy meets the cognitive sciences.* Cambridge, MA: MIT Press.

Goodman, N. (1965). *Fact, fiction and forecast.* Indianapolis, IN: Bobbs-Merrill.

Gould, S. J. (1985). *The flamingo's smile.* New York: W. W. Norton.

Harman, G. (1986). *Change in view: Principles of reasoning.* Cambridge, MA: MIT Press.

Hempel, C. G. (1965). *Aspects of scientific explanation.* New York: Free Press.

Horty, J. F., and R. H. Thomason (1991). Conditionals and artificial intelligence. *Fundamenta Informaticae* 15, 301–323.

Kelley, H. H. (1967). Attribution theory in social psychology. *Nebraska Symposium on Motivation* 14, 192–241.

Lipton, R. (1991). *Inference to the best explanation.* London: Routledge.

Mele, A. (1992). *The springs of action.* New York: Oxford University Press.

Miller, R. W. (1992). *Moral differences: Truth, justice and conscience in a world of conflict.* Princeton, NJ: Princeton University Press.

von Neumann, J., and O. Morgenstern (1944). *Theory of games and economic behavior.* Princeton, NJ: Princeton University Press.

Nozick, R. (1993). *The nature of rationality.* Princeton, NJ: Princeton University Press.

Pascal, B. (1678). *Pensées.* Paris.

Pollock, J. (1979). A plethora of epistemological theories. *Justification and knowledge,* George Pappas, ed., Dordrecht, Holland: Reidel, 93–114.

Pollock, J. (1991). OSCAR: A general theory of rationality. *Philosophy and AI: Essays at the interface,* edited by R. Cummins and J. Pollock, Cambridge, MA: MIT Press, 189–213.

Quine, W. V. (1976). Carnap and logical truth. *The ways of paradox and other essays.* Revised and enlarged edition. Cambridge, MA: Harvard University Press, 107–132.

Sober, E. (1988). *Reconstructing the past.* Cambridge, MA: MIT Press.

Stalker, D. (1993). *Grue: The new riddle of induction.* Peru, IL: Open Court.

Stalnaker, R. C. (1984). *Inquiry.* Cambridge, MA: MIT Press.

Stich, S. (1990). *The fragmentation of reason.* Cambridge, MA: MIT Press.

Part Two

Problem Solving and Memory

Chapter 7

Working Memory and Thinking

John Jonides

In all its various forms, thinking recruits a complex set of mental processes. These processes differ, of course, depending on what sort of thinking is involved. Trying to decide whether two objects belong to the same category involves mental operations different from those which are critical to working out the solution to a problem in chess. The former may depend on judging the similarity of the objects to each other and the similarity of each to some mental representation of the category in question (see chapter 1). By contrast, solving a chess problem may rely on assessing the difference between your current board position and your desired board position, in the light of what you know about the rules of chess and the likely outcomes of various moves (see chapter 8 for more on problem-solving strategies). As different as these examples seem on the face of it, they nonetheless illustrate that there is an important role for memory in thinking, whether it involves categorization, problem solving, deduction, or whatever. You wouldn't be able to decide whether an object belonged in some category unless you had stored some representation of that category in memory. Likewise, you wouldn't be able to make a decision about a move in chess unless you had stored at least the rules of chess. In fact, memory comes into play in thinking in even subtler ways than these. To see this extensive influence, let us examine three quite different cases of human reasoning to illustrate not only the critical role of memory in many complex cognitive tasks, but also the varied forms of memory that are required.

7.1 Thinking and Memory

7.1.1 Raven Progressive Matrices

Anyone reading this chapter has taken one or more tests of basic cognitive skills, such as an IQ test. One of the most demanding of these is the Raven

The preparation of this chapter was supported in part by a Fellowship from the McDonnell-Pew Program in Cognitive Neuroscience, and in part by a grant from the Office of Naval Research. Address correspondence to John Jonides, Department of Psychology, University of Michigan, Ann Arbor, Michigan 48109. Electronic mail: John.Jonides@um.cc.umich.edu

Progressive Matrices Test, an instrument that is used to measure problem-solving and reasoning skills in the face of novel information (Raven 1962). The Raven test is especially interesting because it is impressively correlated with measures of achievement, and it correlates well with a host of other basic tests of intelligence.

The test itself is best understood by considering an example problem, such as that shown in figure 7.1 (from Carpenter, Just, and Shell 1990). Test takers are given a problem like the one in the box at the top of the figure together with eight alternative answers shown at the bottom of the figure. Their task is to examine the 3 × 3 matrix of geometric forms in

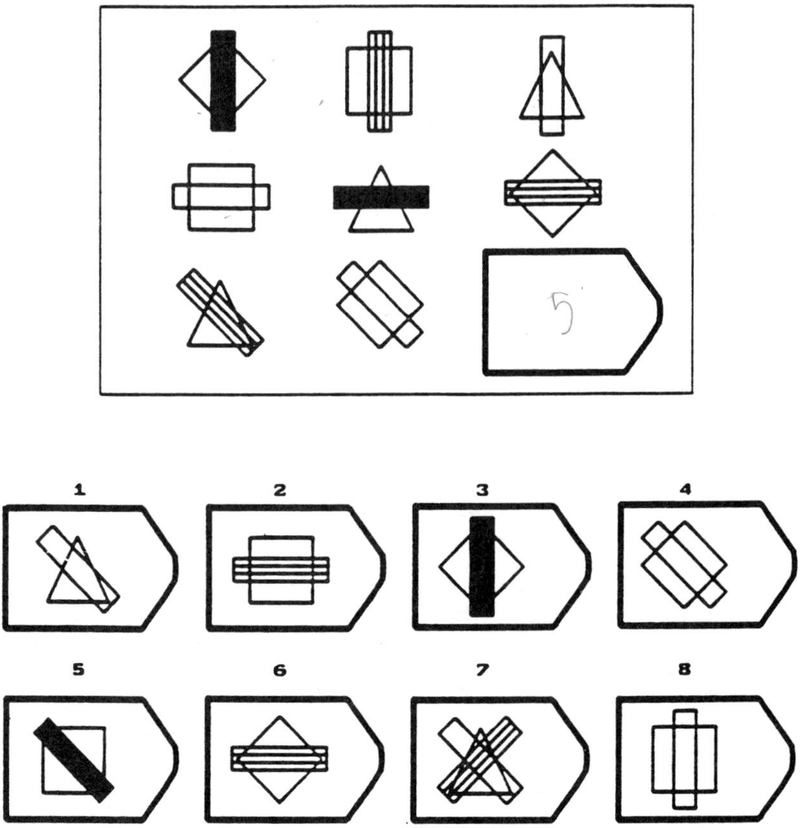

Figure 7.1
An example of a problem that is similar to ones on the Raven Progressive Matrices Test. This problem is not on the actual test, to preserve the test's security. As described in the text, the goal is to choose one of the eight alternatives that best fits in the missing cell to complete the matrix (from Carpenter et al. 1990, fig. 2, 407).

the box and to determine what figure should fall in the missing box at the bottom right of the matrix in order to fit properly within the matrix. The instructions tell test takers to examine the figures in the matrix to determine what rules govern the orderliness of figures along the rows and columns, and then to use the rules they have determined to pick the missing entry. Before reading on, try to solve the problem in figure 7.1.

Here is one line of reasoning that will yield a solution to this problem. Notice that each of the top two rows contains three geometric forms. In the top row, they are a diamond, a square, and a triangle, reading from left to right. In the second row they are a square, a triangle, and a diamond. The third row has two of these figures, a triangle, and a diamond. And so, if this row is to follow the same rule as the top two, the final item must contain a square. Notice also that the top row has a bar through each of the figures in the same orientation in each. In the left figure it is solid, in the middle one it is striped, and in the right one it is clear. Likewise, the second row shows three parallel bars, in the order clear, solid, and striped. To follow the same rule, the last row must also have three bars in the same orientation, with the first striped, the second clear, and the third solid. Thus the figure required to complete the matrix must be a square with a solid diagonal bar through it; this is alternative 5 among the choices.

You can see from this example that the Raven test is not trivial in its cognitive demands (the actual test has yet more difficult problems). Carpenter, Just, and Shell (1990) proposed an analysis of the test that includes component processes required to complete it successfully. For example, one component process involves identifying the elements in each cell of the matrix that correspond to each other. In figure 7.1, this identification amounts to noticing that the three bars, for example, are the critical figures to compare with respect to one another in each row, and likewise that the three geometric forms are the relevant figures to compare. Carpenter et al. (1990) found that a component critical to successful performance was ability to keep track of the characteristics of figures in each problem and of the rules that had been tentatively determined. Introspection about the problem in figure 7.1 reveals this relation also. Solving the problem requires storing the rule about variation in the shape of figures at the same time as one is working through the variation in the shading of the bars.

What is meant by "keeping track" in this analysis? Clearly, we need a memory that will store partial information about figures and rules for a brief period while still allowing computation of the remaining information needed to solve the problem. We shall call this "working memory," in keeping with current cognitive literature. Carpenter et al. (1990) used this concept of working memory in developing computational models to account for performance in the Raven test. Their computer models included a working-memory component in which information from figures is stored and used as the basis of further computations about a problem. In fact, Carpenter et al. (1990) argued that much of the variation in problem difficulty, and in differences among people in solving a particular Raven problem, is due to differences in working memory ability.

Success in solving Raven problems involves a very different type of memory as well, which is called long-term memory. This is the memory that allows the problem solver to comprehend the instruction that attention to row and column regularities is what is needed to be successful. To comprehend this instruction, the test taker must rely on his or her knowledge of what a row and a column is, and what it means to compare one figure to another. You may take this memory for granted because it seems so natural and automatic, but long-term knowledge on the part of the problem solver is clearly a necessary condition for any skillful problem-solving performance. The present discussion of memory will not concentrate on the long-term system largely because it is not the major source of variation in skilled performance in problems like those due to Raven. That is, differences between one person and another in Raven performance are not due largely to differences in ability to comprehend the instructions and to understand the concept of comparison. Likewise, differences in performance within an individual between one problem and another are not due to the long-term memory demands of the task. Rather, these differences are mainly a function of our ability to juggle the information at hand in each individual problem. This is not to say that long-term memory is unimportant in thinking. Indeed, there would be no thinking without it. For the present, though, what is of most interest is identifying the nature of working memory that seems to be at the heart both of differences among individuals in thinking and of differences among thinking activities that are difficult versus those that are relatively easy.

7.1.2 Thinking About Spatial Relations

Let us now examine a second case in which working memory plays a role in human reasoning. There are many times in normal life when we need to reason about spatial relations. For example, giving directions from one place to another or working out a travel route are tasks in which there is direct need to manipulate spatial information in the service of solving a problem. The study of spatial reasoning has taken many forms in the psychological literature, but one form especially highlights the role of memory. The task in question is one in which a respondent has to solve a problem that requires working out the spatial relations among various elements. Consider this problem, for example (after Byrne and Johnson-Laird 1989):

A is on the right of B
C is on the left of B
D is in front of C
E is in front of B

Where is D with respect to E?

There are a number of ways to solve problems like this one, and, indeed, people may adopt different strategies depending on one factor or another. One strategy seems to appear quite often, however, and it makes use of an internal representation of both the elements and the spatial relations in a kind of image that is presumably stored in working memory. For the problem above, you might have created an image that looked something like this:

```
C   B   A
D   E
```

This representation could then be used to answer the question in the problem by reading off the inference that D must be to the left of E.

The evidence that people at least sometimes solve spatial problems in this way is compelling. For example, the farther two terms are from each other in the image, the easier it is to judge their relative spatial locations, just as it would be easier to judge the spatial relations between two objects if they were clearly separated in the visual field (for example, it would be easier to make a judgment about the relation between A and C than between B and C; see Potts 1974 and Scholz and Potts 1974 for discussion). Another effect is illustrated by this problem:

B is on the right of A
C is on the left of B
D is in front of C
E is in front of B

Where is D with respect to E?

Using the same sort of layout as in the first problem, we might represent this problem in working memory as follows:

```
C   A   B
D       E
```

This representation allows us to answer that D is to the left of E. But notice that this is not the only representation that is possible. The following also properly follows from the stated premises:

```
A   C   B
    D   E
```

Notice that in either case, we can conclude that D is to the left of E. But also notice that we have to consult two internal representations in order to conclude this. The complication here is that more work needs to be done internally to represent both versions of the second problem than to represent the single version of the first problem. The additional work is due to both the processes required to create the representations and the memory required to store and retrieve them. Indeed, the evidence is that problems of the second sort are solved less accurately than problems of the first sort, presumably due to the extra work required and to the possibility of error that may come about with that extra work (Byrne and Johnson-Laird 1989).

If you compare your introspections in solving spatial problems of this sort to those in solving Raven problems, you may come to the conclusion that something quite similar is involved. In both cases, there seems to be a working-memory system that is being taxed both to store information for a brief time and to operate on this information in a way that will yield a problem solution. Before turning to the details of this system, let us consider yet one more example to see how broadly working memory is involved in cognition.

7.1.3 Mental Arithmetic

Try this mental addition problem and think about the strategy you use to solve it. Read the problem and then look away as you solve it:

$$\begin{array}{r} 434 \\ +87 \\ \hline \end{array}$$

Most people report a strategy that involves stages of calculation (Hitch 1978). One common strategy is to divide the problem into parts, adding the units digits, followed by the tens digits, followed by the hundreds digits. Notice that for a strategy like this to be effective, a memory system that can hold various pieces of information must be involved. For example, in this problem you have to store the entire problem, pick out the units digits (4 and 7), store the sum of these, retrieve the tens digits (3 and 8), retrieve the fact that a 1 has to be carried from the units digits, and so on. Obviously, a memory is required for the numerical material and partial results, and a computational mechanism is required to carry out the arithmetic in an orderly way. The memory component, furthermore, is a fragile one. If you had used the units-tens-hundreds strategy that is fairly common for this problem but had been constrained to write your answer from left to right rather than from right to left, you would have made more errors in writing the units part of your answer (Hitch 1978).

Working memory is not the only sort that is required for this task, of course. There has to be a long-term memory from which you can retrieve such things as the units-tens-hundreds strategy that you might have used, the facts of mental addition such as that $4 + 7 = 11$, the concept of carrying and how to execute it, and so on. This library of knowledge and skills is part of your long-term store, and it is integrally involved in this and many other tasks.

We can get our first sense of how working memory and long-term memory interact by examining a flow model for mental arithmetic in this

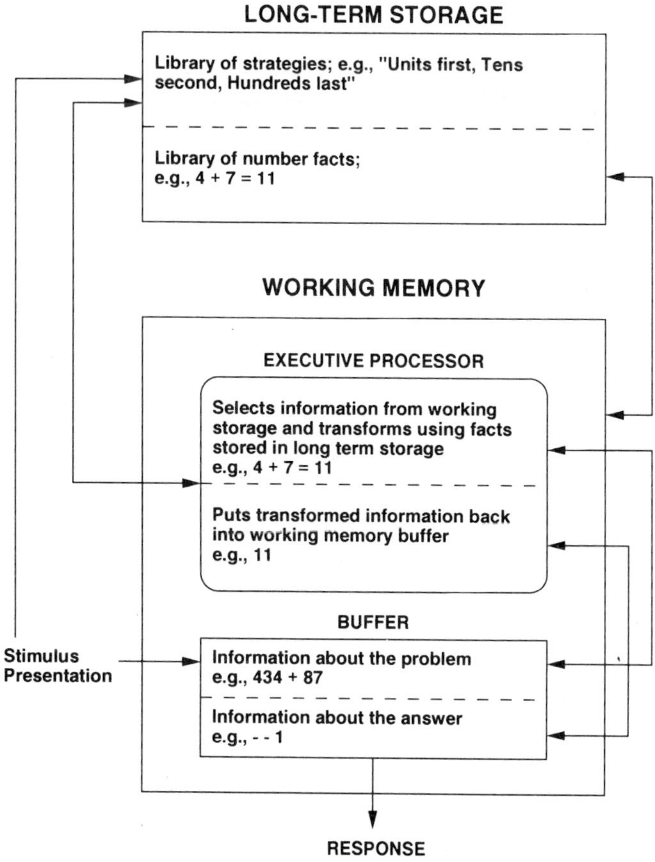

Figure 7.2
A model to account for the processes involved in mental arithmetic. Notice that both long-term and working memory are needed in mental arithmetic tasks, as the text describes. Working memory is indicated by two structures, the executive processor and the working-memory buffer. The model shows the interplay of memory and executive processes necessary to solve a mental arithmetic problem (after Hitch 1978, fig. 7, 320).

task (Hitch 1978). It is presented in figure 7.2. According to this flow model, the presentation of a mental addition problem causes representations to be created in both long-term memory and working memory. Long-term memory supplies the knowledge, strategies, and skills that are needed to execute a solution. The actual computation is done by an executive processor, making use of partial information stored in a working-memory buffer. The partial results are also stored in the buffer awaiting a response when the entire problem is complete (or one digit at a time, if you are permitted to give your response in that way).

Let's step back from the details of this model and consider its general implications. The important features of this model for the present are three: First, it includes two very different types of memory systems. Second, it shows that interactions among these systems are the driving force of thinking processes. And third, the working-memory system itself is more than just a memory; it includes processing capability as well. Before exploring the characteristics of the working-memory component in this model in more detail, let us briefly consider the two types of memory that are implied by this model.

7.2 Working Memory and Long-Term Memory

What is clear from the study of mental arithmetic, spatial reasoning, and performance on the Raven test is this: Thinking requires memory. It is also compelling that the type of memory required is not unitary in character. There is need for both a long-term memory system that holds knowledge and skills and a working-memory system that can hold information briefly for present purposes. Introspection tells us this. But there is more than introspection that we can use to justify thinking of memory as having a dual character. Various sorts of other evidence also indicate that there is a dissociation between long-term memory and working memory.

7.2.1 Neurobiological Evidence About Long-Term and Working Memory

Perhaps the most convincing evidence pointing to the existence of more than one memory system comes from studies of patients who have suffered brain injury that has a detrimental effect on their memory—patients who suffer from amnesia. Amnesia is itself not a unitary phenomenon, and, in fact, two quite different forms are relevant to the dissociation of long-term and working memory.

Consider first a phenomenon called anterograde amnesia. This type can be caused by a variety of brain insults. Perhaps the most famous case of anterograde amnesia is a patient whose initials are H. M., studied in detail by Milner and her colleagues (for example, Milner, Corkin, and Teuber 1968). This patient underwent surgery in 1953 to remove the hippocampus bilaterally; this was an extreme measure to alleviate intractable epileptic seizures. The surgery was successful in relieving H. M. of his seizures, but the unexpected side effect was quite devastating cognitively: H. M. was rendered largely unable to learn any new information after his surgery. This is the hallmark of anterograde amnesia, the inability to learn new information. By contrast, H. M. was perfectly able to recall information that he had learned prior to his surgery: He knew facts of his life prior to surgery (such as events from his school days), he had preserved language skills, he recognized people whom he had known before the operation, and so on. He could not, however, identify people whom he met after the surgery, even after repeated meetings with the same people. And even very salient events that occurred after his trauma, such as the hospitalization of his mother for surgery, were ones that H. M. could not remember, even on the same day they occurred. He was only dimly aware of the sudden death of his father, or of the job that he was doing at a new place of employment, even after working at it for six months. (Interestingly, H. M. and other anterograde amnesics have relatively spared memory for motor skills, classical conditioning, and other tasks that do not require explicit retrieval of information for successful performance.) By contrast to these startling memory deficits in long-term acquisition, H. M. has a normally functioning working memory. For example, his performance on the digit span test (memory for a series of random digits that is read to the subject) is close to that of normal subjects. This performance is true of other anterograde amnesics who have been studied as well, ones whose amnesia was the result of disease such as Korsakoff's syndrome or Alzheimer's disease. The dissociation between the inability to learn new information that is remembered for long periods and the normal ability to remember new information for brief periods supports the distinction between long-term and working memory.

This distinction is also supported by examining cases of amnesia for working, but not long-term memory. One such case, a patient with the initials K. F., who suffered a closed head injury, has been studied in great detail by Elizabeth Warrington and her colleagues (for example, Warrington and Shallice 1969). K. F.'s deficit was first recorded by Warrington while administering him the Wechsler Adult Intelligence Scale, which has a number of subtests that tap various cognitive skills. K. F. performed quite normally on most of the subtests except for a test of digit span. On this test, K. F.'s digit span was only 1 item, far inferior to the normal digit span of 7 or so items. Succeeding tests of K. F. revealed that his deficit on working-memory tasks extended well beyond memory for digits; he was consistently below average on all tests of working memory, as are a number of other patients who have been studied. Yet even in the face of their severe deficits in working-memory tasks, these patients have a quite normal level of performance on tasks that involve long-term memory. For example, they can recall a short story, learn word lists when the lists are presented repeatedly, and perform quite well on long-term recognition tests for lengthy lists of items.

Let us summarize, then, what we know from patients who have amnesic symptoms. On the one hand, there are patients such as H. M. who suffer from inability to place new information into long-term memory in a way that will allow later retrieval, yet have reasonably normal working-memory performance. On the other hand, we have patients such as K. F. who have severely impaired working-memory performance, but can engage in long-term memory tasks with little difficulty. This pattern of results presents us with what is known as a "double dissociation."

To understand the implication of a double dissociation for a theory of memory, consider the following line of reasoning. Suppose there are two memory systems, one responsible for the long-term retention of information and one responsible for the retention of information for a short period. If these two systems are separate in their function and in their representation in the brain, then it may be possible to find a person with a brain injury that insulted the long-term system, but not working memory, and likewise a patient who suffered injury to the working-memory system, but not the long-term one. This pattern of results is what constitutes a double dissociation when it comes to the study of brain injury and its effect on cognition. Thus, the two patients cited above, H. M. and K. F., constitute a double dissociation for working and long-term memory. The fact that patients exist who show the symptoms that they do lends credence to the theoretical notion that memory consists of at least two components. Notice in passing that more components may be involved than just two. For example, the working-memory system may itself be composed of separable subsystems. Establishing this composition, however, would require yet more double dissociations, in this case between, say, two types of working-memory disturbance. This issue is elaborated below.

7.2.2 Behavioral Evidence About Long-Term and Working Memory

Neuropsychological evidence is not the only means to dissociate working from long-term memory. It is supplemented by evidence of a purely behavioral nature. Suppose, for example, that people are given a list of 30 nouns to memorize and recall in any order. The probability of recall will not be uniform as a function of the position of an item in the list (for example, Deese and Kaufman 1957). Rather, items at the beginning and end of the list have a higher probability of recall than do items in the middle. These are called "primacy" and "recency" effects respectively, indicating that the first and last parts of a list enjoy better retrieval than the middle. Why? One influential theory about this result is that recall at the two ends of the list is drawn from two memory systems. Items at the end, being most recent in their presentation, are still stored temporarily in a working store. Items at the beginning, however, have had time to be coded into a more lasting representation in a long-term store. This theory is supported by several lines of evidence. For example, if you simply observe subjects as they are engaged in a free-recall task, immediately after presentation of a list they typically begin their recall with the last items, as if they need to get these out before they are forgotten. This sequence is just what one would expect if these items are stored in a fragile working memory.

More evidence comes from experiments that systematically manipulated variables having different effects on the long-term and working memories. Postman and Phillips (1965) conducted one such set of experiments. They either allowed subjects to begin their recall directly after a list had been presented, or they enforced a delay before recall by requiring subjects to count backward for a 30-second interval. When there was no delay between list presentation and recall, there was a substantial recency effect. That is, items at the end of the list were recalled with higher probability than items in the middle; but this was not the result when a delay was enforced between presentation and recall. This is as it should be if the end of the list is stored in working memory; when items reside there too long, as in the delay condition, they are forgotten. Delay has essentially no effect on recall of the early part of a list, though.

By contrast, Glanzer and Cunitz (1966) have demonstrated that it is possible to influence the primacy effect without touching the recency effect. In their experiment, they presented 20-word lists to subjects at either a fast or a slow rate. They found that the slow rate improved the primacy and middle portions of the serial position curve but had little or no effect on the recency portion. This result is consistent with the claim that items in the primacy and middle portions have been coded into a long-term representation, but those at the end of the list have not had this opportunity. A slower rate of presentation provides subjects greater opportunity to engage in long-term coding and results in a higher accuracy rate.

Notice that the pattern of behavioral evidence just reviewed constitutes another double dissociation, similar to the one that was suggested by examining patients with amnesias. The double dissociation comes about because different behavioral variables have different effects on the serial position curve. One affects the recency portion of the curve but leaves the primacy portion intact. The other affects the primacy portion but leaves the recency portion intact. This pattern suggests that two different mechanisms are at work in determining the shape of the serial position curve. One interpretation is that these two mechanisms are two memory systems, one responsible for working-memory retention and the other for long-term retention.

The weight of evidence such as we have just reviewed indicates a distinction between working and long-term memory. (Even more recent evidence suggests that long-term memory may itself be composed of more than one system: for example, Squire 1992, Schacter, Chiu, and Ochsner 1993.) Let us concentrate now on the features of the working-memory system that is suggested by this analysis and on its role in thinking.

Reflect on the Raven, mental-arithmetic, and spatial-reasoning tasks with which this chapter begins. In all three of these tasks, it seemed introspectively compelling that working memory was required for successful performance. In the Raven problems, this memory is needed to remember hypotheses about critical features that might describe any row or column. In mental arithmetic, working memory is necessary to store the problem at hand and intermediate solutions. In spatial reasoning, working memory is needed to store the spatial relationships that are specified, so that new ones can be deduced. These introspections are real and valuable in leading to the conclusion that working memory is an integral part of thinking. But there is more than this as well. Evidence comes from two behavioral sources about the involvement of working memory in thinking, the study of individual differences and the study of interference effects. Examining these two sources of evidence implicates working memory in various thinking tasks and possibly in language comprehension as well.

7.3 Working Memory in Thinking

People differ in their thinking skills, sometimes dramatically. The causes of these individual differences are undoubtedly many. One factor that has been implicated repeatedly is differences in working memory.

Consider first one of the model tasks described above, the Raven test. The test is designed, as are all tests of basic cognitive skills, to reveal differences among individuals. What is required in this test is an extensive program of managing information in working memory about attributes and about rules that relate these attributes to the figures, which Carpenter et al. (1990) call goal and subgoal management. This is what taxes working memory in these problems. If success on Raven's problems comes about because of success in goal and subgoal management, then the same subjects who do well on Raven's problems should do well on other problems that involve the same sort of goal and subgoal skills. Indeed, they do.

Carpenter et al. (1990) compared the performance of subjects on Raven's problems and on another problem that involves extensive subgoal management, called the Tower of Hanoi (see chapter 9 for more about this problem). In this problem, subjects are presented three pegs, with three disks of different sizes stacked on one of the pegs, the smallest on the top and the largest on the bottom. The task is to move the pyramid of disks from the source peg to a goal peg, one disk at a time, never stacking a larger disk on a smaller one. The third peg can be used to solve the problem. Extensive research with this task shows that a frequent strategy is to set up goals of disk movement in working memory that are nested within one another. For example, you might set the goal of moving the largest disk from the source peg to the goal peg. This sequence requires first moving the two disks above it, which in turn can be analyzed as a problem in moving the larger of these to a goal peg, and so on. It is easy to see that creating and managing subgoals is the hallmark of this strategy. Thus, it is of interest that performance on the Tower of Hanoi problem correlates highly with performance on the Raven test ($r = .77$: Carpenter et al. 1990), suggesting that the two tests recruit the same sorts of processes in working memory.

The claim that working memory is involved in performance of Raven's problems is confirmed by the study of adult age-related differences in Raven's test scores and age-related differences in working memory. Salthouse (1992) reviewed a number of studies of age differences in performance on Raven's test, finding that the correlation of Raven's score and age averaged $r = -.61$ among adults. That is, as age increased among adults, Raven's score decreased. Why? One possibility suggested by analyzing the working-memory requirements of Raven's test is that older adults are impaired in their use of working memory compared to younger adults. Indeed, evidence from a wide range of tests supports this general assertion (see Salthouse 1990, for a review of relevant evidence). Furthermore, it is well established that there is a strong relationship between several measures of working memory and performance on Raven's test (Larson, Merritt, and Williams 1988, Larson and Saccuzzo 1989, Salthouse 1993). Perhaps most telling, however, is the evidence that Salthouse (1993) presents showing that when variation in working memory performance is statistically controlled (by multiple regression), the correlation between Raven's performance and age essentially disappears. This result confirms that working memory plays a leading role in producing variation among people in Raven's performance, hence it is reasonable to conclude that working memory is an important component in successfully solving Raven's problems.

The study of individual differences in reasoning allows us to extend our conclusion about the role of working memory in reasoning beyond the confines of Raven's task. It seems clear that performance on a number of reasoning tasks relies to a significant extent on working-memory skill (see, for example, Carpenter et al. 1990). Kyllonen and Christal (1990) present an argument that this relationship may be mediated by speed of processing. That is, success in tasks that rely on working memory may depend on how quickly subjects can process the information involved in the task. Perhaps this is because the faster the processing, the less likely it is that the material in working memory will be forgotten. Indeed, Salthouse (1992) has shown that the differences among adults of different ages in working-memory ability may be due in large part to differences in processing speed.

One natural implication of these studies of individual differences in reasoning is that interfering with working memory in an individual should interfere with that individual's ability to reason and solve problems. This is a sound inference, but difficult to test. The problem is this: Many tasks will interfere not only with working memory, but with other psychological processes required in reasoning as well. Suppose, for example, that we had a subject write her answers to some problem with her nondominant hand. This would surely lengthen problem-solving time, but probably not because we had interfered with working-memory capacity.

Gilhooly, Logie, Wetherick, and Wynn (1993) provide one example of careful application of the logic of interference. In their study, the task of interest was syllogistic reasoning. Syllogisms are deductive-reasoning problems that involve presenting two premises that are presumed true, from which a valid conclusion may follow (see chapter 9 for more on these problems). A simple example is:

All A's are B's
All B's are C's
Therefore . . . ?

It is not hard to see that one can properly conclude that all A's are C's. Syllogisms vary a good deal in how easily a conclusion can be drawn from the premises. Consider this example:

Some B's are not A's
All B's are C's
Therefore . . . ?

A proper conclusion is that "Some C's are not A's"; however, reaching this conclusion takes some work. Indeed, Johnson-Laird and Bara (1984) found that a sample of subjects nearly all successfully solved the first of these two examples, whereas none solved the second.

Two pieces of evidence from the study by Gilhooly et al. (1993) implicate working memory in syllogistic reasoning. One is that presenting problems orally (versus visually) depressed accuracy in solving the problems. Oral presentation requires one to store the premises and the computations on these premises as the problems are solved, but visual presentation allows the problem to be always at hand, making the working-memory requirement relatively lighter. The second result of interest is that a secondary task in which subjects were required to generate numbers from the set 1–5 in random order reliably decreased accuracy in the reasoning task, whereas simply repeating the numbers 1–5 over and over again did not. Randomly generating numbers is a task that places heavy demands on working memory. To generate a string that appears random, one must store the previously generated numbers and compare the present candidate against that string to see if it conforms to a seemingly random pattern. By contrast, repeating a fixed string over and over again does not impose much of a memory burden on the subject. Random generation is a task that engages executive processes that are part of working memory, leaving them relatively less available to work on the syllogistic-reasoning problems.

To summarize, the weight of evidence from studies of individual differences, from effects of competing tasks, from computational studies of reasoning performance, and from our own introspections leads to the conclusion that working memory plays an important role in a variety of reasoning tasks. Were this the only role of working memory in thought it would be significant. However, there is evidence that working memory is involved in language comprehension as well.

7.4 Working Memory in Language Comprehension

In his insightful 1908 book, *The Psychology and Pedagogy of Reading,* Huey recognized that working memory must be recruited in the service of language comprehension. His hypothesis, as indicated in the following quotation, was that working memory (which he and others at that time called "primary memory") was required to store words early in a sentence so that later words could be integrated with them to form a coherent meaning:

> The initial subvocalization seems to help hold the word in consciousness until enough others are given to combine with it in touching off the unitary utterance of the sentence which they form.... It is of the greatest service to the reader or listener that at each moment a considerable amount of what is being read should hang suspended in the primary memory of the inner speech. It is doubtless true that without something of this there could be no comprehension of speech at all.

If working memory is involved in language comprehension, as Huey suspected, there could be two functions it would serve. First, it might store partial information about an utterance or a piece of printed text while the remainder of that utterance or text was encoded. Second, comprehension processes might work with the information being temporarily stored to produce a coherent meaning for an entire utterance or a piece of text. Huey's assertions about the role of working memory come alive when one tries to comprehend this sentence from a study by Daneman and Carpenter (1983):

> There is a sewer near our home who makes terrific suits.

The beginning of the sentence appears to be about the network of pipes and the like that collect water from a street. However, a reinterpretation is necessitated by the balance of the sentence. Huey's argument is that comprehending this sentence requires interpreting the words as they are read and storing them as well, so that a proper *reinterpretation* of them can occur as necessary. There is evidence from several sources which confirms Huey's view of language comprehension but which also shows the boundary conditions within which working memory may play a role.

One implication of Huey's view is that people with better working memories should be better at language comprehension. This implication was evaluated in a line of research by Daneman and Carpenter (1980, 1983). They developed a measure of working memory that includes its capacity to store information for brief periods and to perform computations on that information. The measure is quite simple: They presented subjects with a sequence of sentences, after which the subjects had to recall the last word in each sentence. This task requires both storage of the words and comprehension of the meanings of the sentences because subjects were queried about the meanings. "Working memory span" was defined as the number of sentence-final words that subjects could recall correctly as the number of sentences was increased from two to six. In different tests with this measure, Daneman and Carpenter (1980) found that it correlated with a separate test of reading comprehension from $r = .72$ to $r = .90$. Lest you worry that the high correlations come about because the working-memory span and the reading-comprehension tests both involve a comprehension component, Turner and Engle (1989) confirmed the finding with a working-memory measure that included solving arithmetic problems (rather than reading sentences) coupled with storage of a set of words for later recall. The correlations between working-memory span and comprehension are bolstered by the demonstration that subjects with relatively small working-memory spans are worse at interpreting sentences such as the one above about the "sewer" than subjects with relatively large spans (Daneman and Carpenter 1983).

Individual differences in comprehension are not the only reason to think that working memory may play a role in language comprehension. A very different line of evidence from Hardyck and Petrinovich (1970) shows that suppressing working memory causes a reduction in the comprehension of text that is relatively difficult to comprehend under ordinary circumstances, but not text that is easy to understand. Thus, it may be that working memory is engaged when significant effort is required for language comprehension to be successful. One might think of such instances as problem-solving episodes, times when the seemingly automatic processes of language comprehension are not sufficient to analyze a linguistic construction; rather, other processes, such as those of working memory, must be engaged as well.

What of subjects who have pathologically deficient working memories? A direct implication of the work with normal individuals is that such patients should be substantially worse at language comprehension due to their inability to use working memory as effectively. The evidence on this issue is mixed. On the one hand, there are patients such as P. V., described by Vallar and Baddeley (1984, 1987). P. V. is a right-handed woman who at age twenty-three had a stroke that caused extensive damage to the left hemisphere of her brain. One of P. V.'s presenting symptoms was a severely reduced memory span, much like the patient K. F., discussed in section 7.2.1 above. P. V. also showed difficulty in interpreting sentences with complex syntactic constructions, even though she had little difficulty comprehending either short or long simple sentences. This and similar evidence has led to the hypothesis that working memory is involved in sentence comprehension, but only when sentence structure is sufficiently complex that many words have to be held in memory while the remainder of the sentence is perceived.

This hypothesis has been called into question, however, by contrary evidence from other patients who also show working-memory deficits, but who do not show significant sentence-comprehension difficulties. One such patient is E. A., a woman who has a recorded memory span of just two items. Even with this limited working-memory ability, E. A. appears to be quite close to normal in her comprehension of sentences that have complex relative-clause structures (Martin 1993). Moreover, E. A. is not the only such patient with reduced working memory but nearly normal language comprehension; others have been documented (see, for example, Waters, Caplan, and Hildebrandt 1991).

The resolution of whether pathology in working memory produces deficits in comprehension is not yet at hand. It may be that the discrepant results from different patients will be resolved by finer-grained analyses of the deficits that each patient has and of the locus of each patient's lesions. Perhaps, for example, patients who show both deficient working memory and deficient comprehension are ones whose brain injury has damaged not only the storage component of working memory but also the processing component. Patients who show deficient working memory with little deficiency in language comprehension may be ones with deficits in only a storage component. Because the jury is still out on the data from patients with working-memory pathologies, one must be cautious in interpreting these results. Nevertheless, the evidence certainly suggests some sort of link between working memory and verbal comprehension.

Even if there *is* such a link, however, it has boundaries. Perhaps the most obvious is that it does not apply to the comprehension of relatively simple language constructions. This has been demonstrated in a variety of contexts. As one illustration, Baddeley and his colleagues have shown that comprehension of relatively simple sentences is not interfered with by a secondary task that taxes working memory significantly. For example, in one experiment subjects had to judge the truth or falsehood of sentences such as: "Canaries have wings" or "Cats have gills" (Baddeley 1986). Subjects had to make judgments of this sort while they stored from zero to eight random digits in memory. The experiment was designed to maximize interference between the two tasks because subjects were first given the digits to store, then they were presented a sentence about which they had to make a judgment, and finally they had to recall the digits that had been presented. What is remarkable about performance in this experiment is that judging whether the sentences were true or false was affected only modestly by the number of digits that subjects stored.

Another example comes from a bit more demanding language-comprehension task. This is a study by Hitch and Baddeley (1976). They had subjects solve reasoning problems in which short sentences were presented with letter pairs, and subjects had to verify whether the sentences accurately described the letter pairs. Examples are:

A is preceded by B	AB
A follows B	BA
B does not follow A	BA
A is not preceded by B	AB

A subject who successfully solved these problems would answer, "false, true, true, true." Half the subjects in Hitch and Baddeley's experiment had to solve these problems, after which they had to memorize and recall a string of six letters. The other half of the subjects had to listen to a string of six letters, then solve a problem, then recall the letters. This second group was therefore responsible for holding the letters in memory while they were problem solving. The result was straightforward: There was little interference from storing six letters in memory while making judgments about the sentences. As with the experiment involving verification of simple sentences, a working-memory requirement did not seem to intrude much on this language-comprehension task.

These data tell us that comprehension of relatively simple linguistic constructions is not mediated by a significant involvement of working memory. As discussed above, however, when sentence constructions become more complex, working memory may play a more significant role in comprehension.

There has been a common theme in all the studies implicating working memory in thinking, whether in explicit problem solving or in comprehension of language. In all the cases we have considered, information must be stored for a brief period while processes operate on this information for purposes of the task at hand. This implies that a comprehensive theory of working memory must distinguish storage from processing components. A major theory of this sort is due to Alan Baddeley and his colleagues. We consider it next.

7.5 A Working-Memory Theory

Recognizing that a proper theory of working memory must include both storage and processing components, Alan Baddeley and colleagues (1986, 1992, Baddeley and Hitch 1974) developed a view of the working-memory system that is schematized in figure 7.3. The major feature of this view is that working memory consists of a central executive that is responsible for computational operations on information and for scheduling the allocation of attention to various tasks at hand. Acting in the service of this central executive are two storage devices, called the phonological loop and the visuospatial buffer. The first of these is responsible for storing information that is speechlike in form, and the second is responsible for storing visual information. Of course, Baddeley's list of storage devices is incomplete. It does not include a facility, for example, for nonlinguistic auditory information (for example, the sound of a passing truck). Also, the two buffers, tied as they are to speech and visuospatial codes, are not assumed to store information about the meaningful or propositional content of the speech or visual information in question. Thus, for example, the phonological loop

Figure 7.3
The working-memory theory of Baddeley (1986, 1992). The theory has two major components: a central executive and two buffer systems that serve the executive.

may store a speechlike code for the sentence, "Mary bashed Jack on the neck with her umbrella," but nothing is assumed in the theory about storing the various aspects of the meaning of this sentence (for example, who did the bashing, what the instrument was, what the likely effect was on Jack).

However incomplete, Baddeley's theory helps us understand such tasks as mental arithmetic. Indeed, Hitch's (1978) analysis of mental arithmetic, reviewed in figure 7.2, explicitly distinguishes storage from processing. Reexamining that figure will show that Hitch has made explicit use of the concepts of storage and processing that are central to Baddeley's theory. In Hitch's version, the central executive is the seat of mental-arithmetic operations, drawing on information stored temporarily in a buffer that holds the numerical facts of the problem at hand (as well as drawing on a long-term memory system, of course). This and other models of thinking and reasoning (for example, Carpenter et al. 1990) have made good use of the sort of view that Baddeley has developed.

In light of the growing use of this view of working memory in theories of thinking, it is appropriate to examine the evidence that supports it as a basis for a working-memory system. Let's start with the case for multiple storage buffers as part of a working-memory system. Available evidence confirms the proposal of two storage systems, and it provides some specification of the characteristics of each. It also suggests that the number of memory systems may even be more than two.

7.5.1 The Phonological Loop

Imagine picking up a telephone book and looking up a randomly selected number. If you had the opportunity to dial the number immediately, you'd have the number available in memory while you were dialing. If you had to store the number in memory for a few seconds while you went to the phone, you'd still have the number available in memory for dialing, but, to keep it fresh, you would have to engage a rehearsal process that involves internally repeating the number until you dialed it. This example highlights the assertion that there are two components to the phonological loop. One is a memory, called the phonological buffer or store, that is responsible for storing the information. The other component is a rehearsal process that is responsible for recirculating the contents of the phonological store.

As its name implies, the phonological loop is responsible for coding linguistic information in phonological form. This procedure is as opposed, for example, to coding in a form that represents meaning, visual qualities, or some other aspect of the memory trace. As we shall see shortly, the evidence for phonological coding is quite strong. If storage is by way of a phonological code, there must be the capability to create such a code for information that is not directly presented in auditory form. By assumption, the rehearsal process is charged with this responsibility. Thus, for example, if a list of words is presented auditorily, the phonological code for this material is, by hypothesis, created directly by the perceptual system responsible for auditory input, and this code can be directly deposited in the phonological buffer. If a list is presented visually, the visual code that is created during perception of the list is then translated into a phonological code (by the rehearsal process) for storage in the phonological buffer.

The foregoing picture embodies some noteworthy assumptions. For example, we have assumed that the code for verbal information is phonological in form, that the memory in question has limited capacity for storing information, that there is a rehearsal process that keeps information in verbal working memory fresh, that this presumed rehearsal process is distinct from the phonological store itself, and that auditory presentation of verbal information is handled somewhat differently than visual presentation. In fact, there is evidence in favor of each of these assumptions, as we'll now see.

7.5.1.1 Phonological Coding

The nature of the code stored in the phonological loop was first described by Conrad (1964). The task he gave his subjects was ordered recall of strings of six letters. What was critical in his experiment was the set of letters from which the six were drawn on each trial. This set included the letters B C P T V F M N S X. Notice that the first five letters in this set are acoustically confusable because they end in the sound "ee," and the last five are confusable because they all begin with the sound "eh." Notice also that letters in one subset of five are acoustically different from those in the other subset of five. Conrad chose this set of ten letters so that he could assess whether subjects were likely to make acoustic confusion errors in their recall. He did this by examining cases in which subjects correctly recalled all but one of the six letters in a sequence. In those cases, he asked whether the letter that was misrecalled was more likely to come from the confusable subset than from the other subset. For example, if the letter B was included in one series and was not correctly recalled, was it more likely that subjects would substitute a letter from the similar-sounding subset (that is, C P T V) than from the dissimilar-sounding subset (that is, F M N S X)? Indeed it was. In the case of the letter B, for example, it was four times more likely that subjects would substitute a confusable than a nonconfusable letter. And the same held true for the other letters as well. These confusions indicate that the code in which information is held in working memory must have some property of the sound of the letters. If so, then partial forgetting of a letter leaves some trace of part of its sound, leading to possible confusion with a similar-sounding alternative letter.

We can be even more specific about the nature of phonological coding. In a follow-up experiment, Conrad (1970; see also 1972) tested profoundly deaf schoolboys, some of whom were better than others at producing speech. The test was recall of words. The words were drawn from either a set of phonologically similar or phonologically dissimilar words. The results of this experiment are interesting because they are counterintuitive: The subjects who were better at producing speech were worse in their recall of the phonologically similar words than the subjects who were poorer in producing speech. This was the result that Conrad predicted because he reasoned that the subjects who could articulate more proficiently ought to be more confused by the articulatory similarity between words like "way" and "weigh" (two of the words in the confusable set); the subjects who were relatively poor at articulation would not be as confused by articulatory similarity (perhaps because they would store the words using a visual representation). Thus, Conrad's evidence suggests that the coding used by the phonological loop is partly articulatory in character. This hypothesis makes sense of our introspection about remembering a telephone number that must be dialed after a delay; we feel as if we are internally articulating the number to keep it in memory.

There follows from this conclusion a quite simple implication: Hindering someone from creating an articulatory code should cause a decline in working-memory performance if the person tried to use an articulatory representation even in the face of interference. Testing this implication requires the kind of dual-task methodology introduced earlier. Applied to the present case, the logic is to have a secondary task interfere with subjects' creation of an articulatory code for material that is presented visually (visual presentation is necessary so that the phonological code is not inherent in the stimulus, but must be created). An experiment by Murray (1968) illustrates this technique. He had subjects memorize visually presented letters while they had to articulate some irrelevant material. Subjects were presented with lists of letters to memorize that varied in the extent to which the letters were confusable with one another in sound. In one condition, subjects studied the lists, rehearsing the letters silently. In another, they had to say the word "the" with the presentation of each letter in a sequence. In general, having to articulate the irrelevant word "the" (called "articulatory suppression") hurt performance, as predicted if the internal code that needs to be created in the phonological loop is articulatory. An additional result from Murray's (1968) experiment supports this conclusion: Without articulatory suppression, similar-sounding letters were remembered more poorly than letters that differed in sound. But this effect all but disappeared when articulatory suppression was added, suggesting again that suppression prevented creation of an articulatory code for the letters in the list.

7.5.1.2 *Storage Capacity*

How much can be stored in the phonological loop? This issue has been under debate since a classic paper by George Miller (1956) proposed a limitation on the capacity of what we now call working memory. Miller's argument was that the limitation of working memory was best characterized as a limitation in the number of chunks of information that could be stored. The definition of a chunk is not altogether clear, but intuitively it amounts to any coherent unit of information. A single word would typically qualify as a chunk in a list of words, or a syllable might if the list were composed of isolated syllables. Perhaps even a short phrase might be a chunk if a list of these was presented. Miller's point was that, however measured, the fundamental capacity of working memory was limited, and this limitation was approximately constant when measured in chunks.

More recent experiments suggest that this view needs modification. Among the more interesting experiments motivating reanalysis are those of Baddeley, Thomson, and Buchanan (1975). They had subjects memorize lists all of which were composed of two-syllable words, but some of the words were relatively quickly articulated (such as "bishop" or "pectin") while others took longer to articulate (such as "harpoon" or "voodoo"). Baddeley et al. (1975) found that more of the words like "bishop" could be remembered than the words like "harpoon." Furthermore, Baddeley et al. (1975) made this effect of word length disappear by using articulatory suppression, suggesting that articulatory suppression has its effect by interfering with the operation of rehearsal. An important implication of the effect of pronunciation length on recall is that the capacity of the phonological loop cannot simply be measured in chunks (for example, words if the stimuli are words), otherwise it would have been constant regardless of the length of pronunciation of a word. This experiment raises the hypothesis that the length of a stimulus may be a determinant of the capacity of the loop.

How could both the number of chunks and the length of the stimulus have an effect on capacity? One plausible hypothesis is that there are two limits on the capacity of working memory, not just one (see, for example, Longoni, Richardson, and Aiello 1993). One is the limit imposed by the size of the phonological store, which may be best measured in constant items, such as chunks. The other is the limit imposed by the rehearsal process, which may be best measured by time rather than by items. Suppose, by analogy, that the rehearsal component of the phonological loop, like a tape-recorder loop, can store a fixed time-slice of information. Anything that can be represented in that time-slice can be stored, but the time-slice is approximately fixed, so that representations that exceed it (such as longer words) will not be accommodated.

The effect of word length (for example, length of pronunciation) on memory capacity—as distinct from the effect of sheer number of items—points to a time-based account of the capacity of rehearsal. According to this account, the phonological loop stores whatever can be articulated within a fixed span of time, by some estimates about two seconds. This relation explains why people who naturally speak quickly have a larger working-memory capacity for verbal material than people who speak slowly (Baddeley et al. 1975). It also explains why languages that have relatively longer words result in relatively poorer working-memory spans measured word by word (Ellis and Hennelly 1980; Naveh-Benjamin and Ayres 1986). Thus, there is considerable consistency among results in leading to the conclusion that time is the limiting commodity in determining the capacity of rehearsal. This evidence can be added to the evidence summarized by Miller (1956), among others, that there is also a fundamental limit on the capacity of verbal working memory as measured in number of items or chunks. The best presumption is that the latter limit is a limit in the capacity of the phonological buffer, added to the time limitation of about two seconds that apparently constrains rehearsal.

7.5.1.3 *Rehearsal*

We have been constructing a model of the phonological loop, including the assumption that it is composed of two parts: a phonological storage buffer and a rehearsal component. Rehearsing verbal material from the buffer is assumed to refresh the strength of the memory trace. If material is not rehearsed, as might be the case if something distracted the memorizer from her task, the material would be subject to forgetting. All this leads directly to the implication that the phonological loop should make heavy use of language processes to store information and recirculate it; hence there should be evidence that the language centers in the brain are engaged and active during working-memory tasks. Recently, it has become possible to investigate this implication using neuroimaging techniques. Positron emission tomography (PET) and functional magnetic resonance imaging (fMRI) are techniques that allow one to see brain activation that accompanies neural activity, and they have been used to examine the circuitry involved in storage and rehearsal. These techniques make possible measurement of regional blood flow in the brain with little or no invasion of the tissue in question. Since the classic work of Roy and Sherrington (1890), it has been known that when neural activity increases in a portion of the brain, there is an accompanying increase in the flow of blood in that portion. This phenomenon makes possible the use of neuroimaging techniques to make inferences about neural activity in brain regions: Where blood flow increases regionally there is assumed to be an underlying increase in neural activity.

An example of research that has been used to identify rehearsal processes in working memory comes from a study by Paulesu, Frith, and Frackowiak (1993). In one of their experiments they had English-speaking subjects remember a series of six items after which a probe item was presented; subjects had to judge whether the probe was identical to one of the six previous items. In one condition, the items were letters of the English alphabet. In the other, they were letters of the Korean alphabet, with which the subjects were not familiar. In the first condition, subjects were instructed to use rehearsal to store the items and in the second condition they were told to store them visually. The logic of the experiment was that many of the processes in the two conditions would be similar (for example, a decision to say Yes or No, preparation of a motor response, perception of the visually presented items), and so if the images of the control condition (with Korean letters) were subtracted from those of the English-letter condition, the resulting subtraction image should contain evidence of brain activation that accompanies working memory for verbal material in one's own language. Subtracting one image from another (that is, subtracting the brain activation at each point in one image from the activation at a corresponding point in the other) is a standard technique in neuroimaging studies of this sort. In the Paulesu et al. (1993) experiment, subtraction resulted in several sites of activation, among them an area in the front of the brain, with the largest activation in the left hemisphere. This area, called Broca's area after the neurophysiologist who first documented it, is known to participate in the production of spoken speech (see chapter 13 by E. Zurif in Volume 1 of this series). It is reasonable to surmise, then, that Broca's area plays a role in working memory for letters by being the seat of processes that are involved in rehearsing the letters while they are held in memory. This and similar evidence (for example, Koeppe, Minoshima, Jonides, Smith, Awh, and Mintun 1993) supports the proposal that one of the components of working memory is a rehearsal process that makes use of internal processes much like the processes used in overt language production. Thus, rehearsal can be characterized as inner speech in the service of memory maintenance.

7.5.1.4 Distinguishing the Buffer and Rehearsal

The preceding section provides evidence that rehearsal is important to working memory. Let us now ask whether rehearsal is distinct from the phonological buffer. Perhaps, by counterargument, there is no need to assume two components; rehearsal by itself may be sufficient to account for working-memory phenomena for verbal material.

The issue is whether two components are involved or just one. This issue can be addressed by testing the effects of different experimental variables on working memory. The logic is this: If there are two working-memory components (a buffer and a rehearsal process), one might be able to identify two experimental variables, one of which influences storage of information in the buffer but not rehearsal, and the other of which influences rehearsal but not storage in the buffer. Each variable would have an effect on working-memory performance, but the two effects would be independent of each other—that is, the influence of one variable would not modulate the influence of the other. In the case of the phonological buffer and rehearsal, this kind of experimental logic has been applied by several investigators, perhaps most impressively by Longoni, Richardson, and Aiello (1993). In a series of carefully designed experiments, these investigators teased apart the buffer from rehearsal by testing the joint effects of articulatory suppression, phonemic similarity, and word length in a working-memory task. The task involved memory for word lists that were presented by ear to eliminate any possible influence the rehearsal process might have in creating a phonological code to begin with. The words in a list could be phonemically similar or not; they could be long or short in length; and subjects had to memorize them under silent study conditions, or under articulatory suppression, that is, while saying "one, two, three" to themselves over and over (they did this in Italian, being Italian university students). In a pair of experiments, the results were quite clear: First, as others had found, longer words were remembered more poorly than shorter words. Second, phonemically similar words were remembered more poorly than phonemically distinct words. What was striking in the experiments was that articulatory suppression abolished the effect of word length, but had no such influence on the effect of phonemic similarity. This result suggests that articulatory suppression and word length both affect the same psychological process, different from the one affected by phonemic similarity. It is reasonable to presume that the common site for word-length and suppression effects is rehearsal, and the site for the phonemic similarity effect is the phonological buffer.

In another experiment, these authors took advantage of another variable known to affect verbal working memory: the presentation of irrelevant speech during presentation of the stimulus materials. It has been documented that irrelevant speech damages performance in verbal working-memory tasks (for example, Salame and Baddeley 1982). Longoni et al. (1993) composed an experiment in which they simultaneously varied whether irrelevant speech was presented for word stimuli that were either short or long. In that experiment, they found that both variables had an effect on memory: Memory performance was worse when presentation of the words was accompanied by irrelevant speech, and it was worse with long words. But these two effects were quite independent of each other, suggesting that they had their influences on different processes. If, as discussed above, word length has its effect on rehearsal processes, then it is reasonable to conclude that the effect of irrelevant speech was on another process, the phonological buffer.

This behavioral evidence for two components of the phonological loop is supported by studies of brain-injured patients as well. One of these is P. V., the patient whom we considered in section 7.4. One of P. V.'s presenting symptoms was a significant deficit in tests of verbal working memory, but her deficit was largely limited to auditory presentation (Basso, Spinnler, Vallar, and Zanobio 1982). For example, when presented sets of three letters to recall, she was able to get only 20 percent of the sets correct when they were presented auditorily, but she was completely successful in recalling all the sets when they were presented visually (Vallar and Baddeley 1984). Now consider some aspects of P. V.'s performance. First, she shows a phonemic similarity effect in her recall; that is, phonemically similar material is recalled more poorly. Second, this similarity effect appears only when material is presented auditorily, not when it is presented visually. Third, when given articulatory suppression during a memory test, she showed no interference when material was presented visually, in contrast to what happens to normal subjects. Finally, P. V. shows no effect of word length in her memory performance, yet another difference from normal subjects. The absence of a word-length effect confirms damage to her rehearsal process; as shown above, the word-length effect is one sign of intact rehearsal.

What can we conclude about P. V.'s working memory from these results? She certainly shows evidence of a phonological buffer when material is presented by ear, as if auditory presentation gains obligatory access to this store. To be sure, her performance with auditory presentation is not nearly normal in quantity, but the presence of a similarity effect does indicate that there is some semblance of a phonological buffer mediating performance. With visual presentation, however, there is no similarity effect, indicating that she does not create a phonological representation from the visually presented material. This result indicates that one of the functions of rehearsal is deficient, the ability to create a phonological code from visual material. Further evidence of damage to rehearsal comes from the result that she is not affected by articulatory suppression. This result would be expected if rehearsal was not a functional process for her; she should not be adversely affected by inhibiting rehearsal with articulatory suppression. The absence of a word-length effect confirms damage to rehearsal; as reviewed above, the word-length effect is one of the hallmarks of a normally working rehearsal process.

Overall, P. V.'s results confirm the conclusions based on studies of normals. P. V. shows a dissociation between a phonological buffer and a rehearsal process. She has a functioning phonological buffer (although it is not functioning completely normally), but evidence of significant rehearsal is absent. Likewise, normal subjects also show a dissociation between these components when they are tested on the effects of variables such as word length, phonological similarity, and irrelevant speech. Taken together, these results inspire confidence in the view that the phonological loop is a two-part mechanism, both parts of which are important to its function in working memory.

7.5.2 The Visuospatial Buffer

Think back to one of the problems with which this chapter begins:

A is on the right of B
C is on the left of B
D is in front of C
E is in front of B

Where is D with respect to E?

Various lines of evidence suggest that problems of this sort require construction of an internal representation that preserves the spatial relations among elements. There are many circumstances in which creation and manipulation of a representation that preserves spatial features is critical to normal thinking. Examples are as varied as giving and comprehending directions from one location to another, remembering where you left car keys in your house, solving geometry problems, mentally rotating a statue to imagine how it looks from the other side, and imagining someone else's perspective in viewing a scene. These are all tasks that may depend on use of an internal representation that includes spatial information. Solving tasks of this sort requires ability to store spatial information as well as ability to manipulate it when needed. In this way, the requirements for spatial reasoning are much the same as the requirements for verbal reasoning: a working-memory system that can both store and operate on information. What differs, of course, is the nature of the code that is involved. No kind of phonological coding will allow you to deduce the correct solution to the spatial problem above, for example. A very different sort of representation is needed, and allowance for this has been made in Baddeley's (1986, 1992) model of working memory.

That model includes a structure, the visuospatial buffer, that is presumed to store information in a visuospatial code for use by central executive processes. Although Baddeley's model does not provide detail on the interplay between the visuospatial representation and executive processes, this detail is available in other theories. The most prominent among these is that of Kosslyn (1980, 1981), who describes a theory in which a working-memory component is specialized for using visuospatial information. This component can retrieve information from a propositional code in long-term memory and can create from it an internal representation that is perceptlike; or it can represent information coming in from the senses, creating from it an imaginal representation. According to the theory, to form a visuospatial representation in working memory is to construct a representation that shares similarities with a percept that would be formed if we were viewing a scene that contained the imagined objects. Indeed, evidence from PET studies of mental imagery suggest that much the same neural machinery is used for imagery as for visual perception (Kosslyn, Alpert, Thompson, Maljkovic, Weise, Chabris, Hamilton, and Buonanno 1993). Once formed, the representation is similar to a percept of a scene: it can be inspected, scanned, rotated, enlarged, shrunk, and so on. This is just the sort of representation one would need to solve spatial-relations problems, to give directions from information in long-term memory, to take another's perspective on a scene, or to accomplish any of the other skills that require visuospatial manipulation (see Kosslyn's chapter in volume 2 of this series).

Apart from intuitive appeal and computational sufficiency, what evidence is there that such a representation is part of the working-memory system? Is there evidence of a double dissociation between the visuospatial buffer and the phonological buffer, for which there is already well-established empirical support? Indeed, there is, and it comes from both behavioral and neuropsychological sources.

7.5.2.1 *Visuospatial vs. Phonological Buffers: Behavioral Evidence*

Consider first two tasks from a classic experiment by Brooks (1968). For the visual task, subjects were briefly shown a block capital letter such as

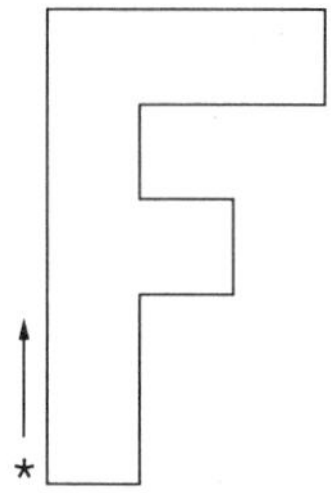

Figure 7.4
An example stimulus from the experiment of Brooks (1968). Subjects had to imagine the block letter, begin at the vertex marked by an asterisk, and mentally trace around it in the direction indicated by the arrow.

the one in figure 7.4. From memory, subjects had to begin at a comer marked by an asterisk and move around the letter mentally in a direction indicated by an arrow. As they encountered each vertex, if it was at the top or bottom of the figure, they responded, Yes; if it was in the middle, they responded No. These responses were given in one of two ways that are relevant here: In one condition, they said the words Yes and No aloud. In the second condition, they pointed to a Y or an N on an answer sheet in which the Y's and N's were haphazardly arranged, forcing subjects to scan the sheet for the spatial location of their desired response before pointing to it. The second task in Brooks's experiment was verbal. Subjects were presented a sentence on each trial that they held in memory. They then had to retrieve the sentence, going from left to right, indicating for each word whether it was a noun or not. Again, Yes and No responses were given in one of two ways, as in the visual task. The rationale behind the experiment hinged on the predicted selective interference of each response mode on each memory task. The visuospatial buffer used to store and work on the block letters should show selective interference from the pointing task, which is also visuospatial in form, because of the layout of the letters on the answer sheet. The verbal buffer should show selective interference from the vocal responding required, in that this response mode introduced irrelevant speech to interfere with the required memory for the sentence.

The results of the experiment establish a double dissociation of verbal from visuospatial working memory. For the visual task, having to give responses by pointing to the Y's and N's on the answer sheet produced worse performance than having to say Yes and No aloud. By contrast, for the verbal task, verbal responding produced worse performance than pointing. The experiment supports the distinction between two buffer systems of working memory, one for visuospatial information and one for verbal information.

7.5.2.2 *Visuospatial vs. Phonological Buffers: Biological Evidence*

Recent evidence from studies of the biological basis of working memory in human beings adds to the evidence from behavioral studies by offering glimpses of the circuitry that may underlie the verbal and spatial working-memory systems. What is revealed in these studies is a different pattern of brain activation that accompanies spatial versus verbal working-memory tasks. Two experiments from our laboratory illustrate this difference in activation.

One task is illustrated in figure 7.5. The illustration shows a series of stimulus presentations of single letters that each subject saw while being scanned with PET. The task is to report for each letter presented whether it matches the letter that appeared two items before in the sequence. The

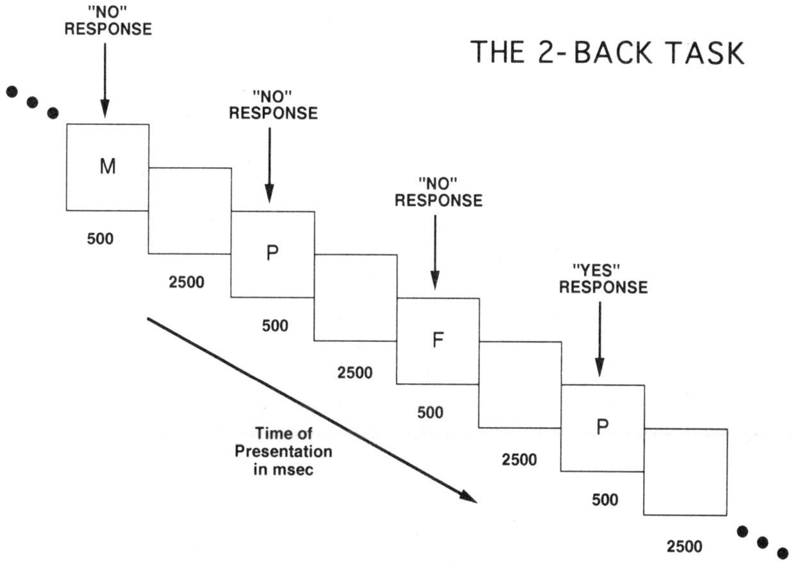

Figure 7.5
A schematic of the events in the "two-back" task. A sequence of single letters appears, and subjects must respond to each depending on whether each matches the letter that appeared two letters back. A correct response to each letter is shown above it.

figure illustrates the proper response for the example sequence shown. It is easy to see that this task is demanding of working memory. Subjects need to keep a constant stream of at least three letters in mind: the present one, plus the two that appeared previously. Then they must match the present one with its "two-back" counterpart, after which they have to update the contents of working memory in preparation for the next letter. The rate of presentation, one letter every three seconds, leaves time to do the updating and to rehearse the sequence that is relevant at any given time. In this way, this task ought to recruit both the phonological loop and the rehearsal process, in addition to adding a central executive component involved in the updating. In order to isolate the working-memory processes of interest from other processes involved in the task (encoding of the letters, response execution, and so on), we included another task in which subjects simply responded for each letter whether it matched a constant target letter for that sequence. This control task minimized the load on working memory because the target letter was constant for an entire sequence, while including perceptual and motor processes in common with the memory condition shown in figure 7.5.

The results of this experiment are consistent with the evidence reviewed in section 7.5.1.3 about the biological basis of rehearsal, and they add to those data a view of the rest of the circuitry involved in working memory. The data on rehearsal by Paulesu et al. (1993) and others implicates the language-production centers of the frontal lobes, principally Broca's area in the left hemisphere. Likewise, our verbal working-memory experiment also shows activation in this area, indicating that subjects are applying rehearsal processes to the task of keeping in mind and updating the letters they are required to store. In addition, the "two-back" task shows marked activation in another area of the frontal lobe, different from Broca's area, an area that we shall see shortly is similar to one found in studies of working memory in monkeys. The final major focus of activation in the "two-back" task is in the parietal lobe at the back part of the brain, principally in the left hemisphere. Many have suggested on the basis of evidence from brain-injured patients that this area is involved in working memory. For example, this is the site of damage of the patient K. F., whose deficits in working memory have been extensively documented.

Notice that the major foci of activation in the two-back study and in other studies of verbal working memory are in the left hemisphere. This placement contrasts with the results of a study by Jonides, Smith, Koeppe, Awh, Minoshima, and Mintun (1993) on a spatial working-memory task. The task and its control are illustrated in figure 7.6. The memory task shown in that figure involved presentation of three dots at seemingly random locations around the circumference of an imaginary circle centered on a fixation cross. These were presented briefly, following which a retention interval of three seconds intervened. Then a single outline circle was presented. Subjects were to decide whether the outline circle encircled a location previously occupied by a dot or not. If so, they made one response; if not, another. This task required faithful memory of the locations of the three dots because if the outline did not fall directly over a dot, it fell quite close to one. Thus, subjects had to encode and store the dot locations quite accurately to perform well. Subjects engaged in this task while PET measurements were taken. Notice that the major portion of this task was occupied by the retention interval, and so activation patterns revealed by PET should have resulted largely from processes during this interval. In order to subtract out perceptual and motor processes, a control condition, also illustrated in figure 7.6, was included. In the control, subjects were also shown three dots, but they did not have to commit them to memory because the probe display included a re-presentation of the dots together with the probe outline. Again, subjects indicated whether the outline probe encircled a dot location or not, and activation patterns were collected from this condition and subtracted from the memory condition.

There were four major foci of activation in this task, two in the frontal lobe, one in the parietal lobe, and one in the occipital lobe. One hypothesis consistent with these activation sites is that subjects create a mental image

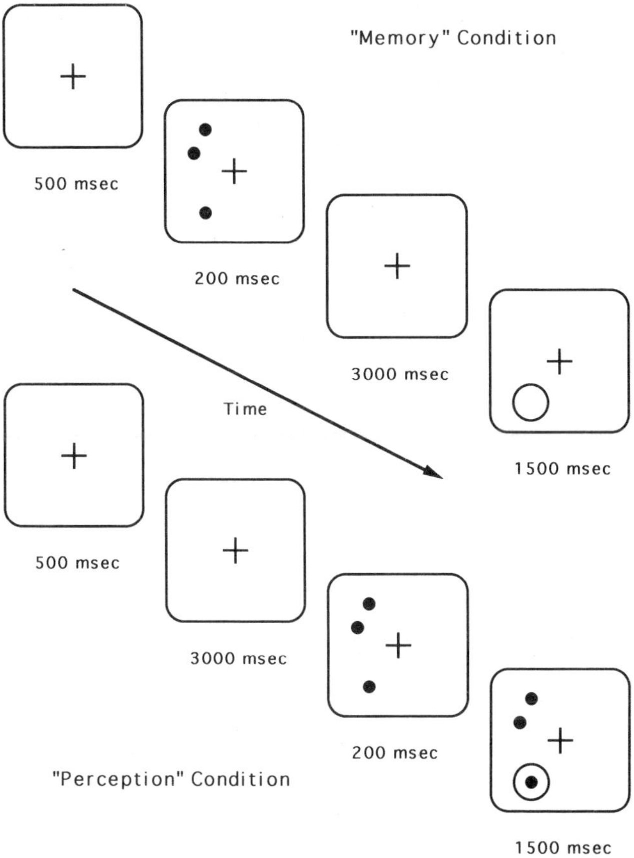

Figure 7.6
A schematic of the events in the Memory and Control tasks of the experiment by Jonides et al. (1993). In the Memory condition, subjects had to store the dot locations in memory for three seconds before the probe appeared. In the Control condition, the dots and probe appeared simultaneously and so no memory was needed to succeed in the task.

of the dot locations, using processes of the occipital lobe. They encode the locations of the dots from this image using processes of the parietal lobe, and they then store these encoded locations using frontal mechanisms. Whether this or another interpretation ultimately proves true, one feature of the data from the spatial task is critical: All the significant activations were discovered in the right hemisphere; none were found to be reliable in the left hemisphere. Take these data together with those of the two-back task, and you see a clear dissociation between working memory for phonological and spatial information respectively. The phonological task recruits processes largely of the left hemisphere, and the spatial task recruits those of the right hemisphere. These data, then, are consistent with the behavioral data of Brooks (1968) and others showing a distinction between working memory for verbal and spatial information.

7.5.2.3 *Neurophysiological Studies of the Visuospatial Buffer*

The imaging data on working memory in human beings have limited usefulness in revealing the details of processes. Partly, this limitation is because the techniques that have been used have limited spatial resolution, so that only fairly large areas of brain tissue can be resolved (on the order of multiple cubic millimeters). Partly, this is because the techniques do not allow one to cleanly isolate just the memory processes in tasks of interest; some other processes undoubtedly remain even after activations from control conditions are subtracted. Thus, there is great interest in examining more precise data from experiments on nonhuman animals. In such experiments the localization and details of working-memory processes can be studied with greater precision. There is a long tradition of such experiments, beginning with those of Jacobsen (1936), many of which have implicated mechanisms of the frontal lobes (among other loci) in mediating working-memory effects. The most recent developments in this tradition are especially exciting because they have uncovered mechanisms of working-memory processes at the level of single neurons in the cortex. This research has been led by Patricia Goldman-Rakic and her collaborators (Goldman-Rakic 1987).

A representative result from these experiments is illustrated in a report by Funahashi, Bruce, and Goldman-Rakic (1989). They had three monkeys engage in a working-memory task for spatial location that is illustrated schematically in figure 7.7. The monkeys were trained to fixate on a small spot at the center of a screen, illustrated by the FP in the figure, indicating the fixation point. After achieving fixation on a trial, a monkey would be briefly presented with a small square presented at an unpredictable one of eight locations surrounding the fixation point, as indicated in figure 7.7. The animals were trained to maintain their fixation during the presentation of this square and during a three-second delay period that ensued. At the end of the delay, the fixation point disappeared, and this was the cue to the animal to shift its gaze to the location of the previously presented square. The animals were quite accurate in moving their eyes to the position of the square even after a delay. Of interest is the pattern of response that was discovered in single neurons in the frontal cortex whose activity was recorded during the trial events.

Although different neurons exhibited different characteristics, a substantial number had the pattern shown in figure 7.7. The figure shows the responsiveness of a single neuron in the right hemisphere of a monkey to stimuli that appeared at each of the eight positions tested. Each of the

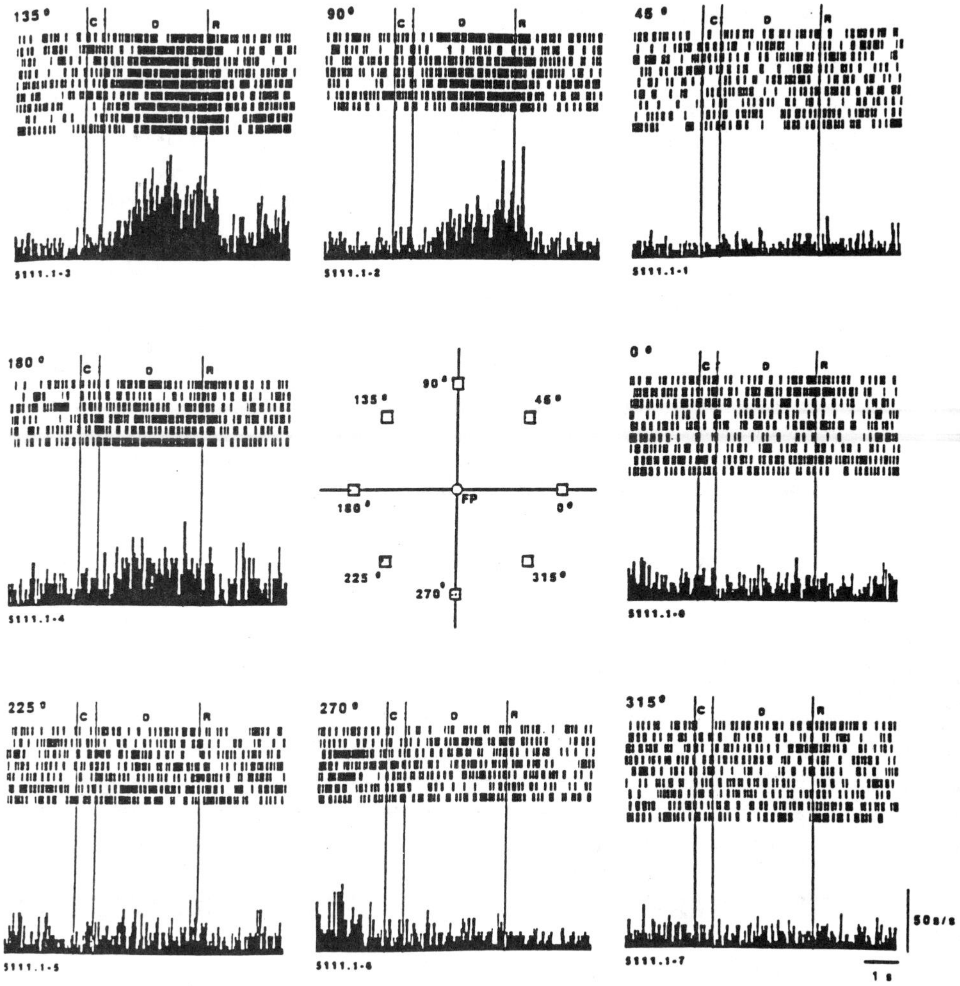

Figure 7.7
A schematic of the stimuli from the experiment by Funahashi et al. (1989) together with data from a neuron and its responses to stimuli that appeared at each of the eight possible stimulus locations. Notice that this neuron was selectively responsive largely during the delay period of each trial, and it responded best to stimuli in the vicinity of 135 degrees from the fixation point (from Funahashi et al. 1989, fig. 4, 335).

eight graphs plots the number of spikes per second of activity shown by that neuron to stimuli presented at that position, and each position is marked by a degree label, to show its location relative to the fixation spot. Each graph also includes vertical lines to mark off the period between trials (in the first epoch), the period during which the small square is presented (marked by a C to denote the cue), the delay interval between the cue and the response (marked with a D), and the response interval (indicated with an R). Consider the 315-degree position first. Notice that when the cue is presented at this position, the cell of interest does not reliably change its level of response during the entire task. That is, its activity during the presentation of the cue, the delay, and the response interval is about the same as its activity before the trial begins. Now consider the activity of the cell when a stimulus is presented at the 135-degree position. The cell begins with a low spontaneous level of activity, which continues when the cue is presented. However, during the delay interval, its activity increases sharply, falling off again when a response is required and given. This is a quite different pattern than that shown for a 315-degree cue. You will also notice that the cell provides a pattern of activity somewhat similar to the 135-degree pattern when a cue is presented at either 90 degrees, or at 180 degrees, but it is largely unresponsive to stimuli at the other positions. Although this is not the only pattern of activation found for cells in this region, it is not by any means an isolated example, either. Many cells in this region were selectively responsive to some locations but not others, and they responded during the delay interval, but not at other times. Notice that different cells were responsive to different locations, so that across a population of cells, all the locations were represented by selectively responsive neurons.

This overall pattern invites the following interpretation: This cell is wired to code a memory of a particular stimulus position during a retention interval. The cell does not respond noticeably during the time when the cue stimulus is presented, nor does it respond as strongly when the animal is moving its eye to the proper location. Its major responsiveness occurs during the delay interval, when the animal is charged with remembering the location of the cue for the upcoming response. Thus, one can conclude that this cell is part of the circuitry involved in memory for location, and its involvement is quite well specified: It stores information about the particular spatial location of a previously presented stimulus. Other studies show that this circuitry involves neurons in the parietal lobe of the cortex as well, a finding that is consistent with the human imaging studies reviewed above.

These and other data from the study of working memory in humans and other animals begin to lay out the circuitry of the working-memory system responsible for spatial information. They also allow us to make a distinction that we have not made heretofore. The theory due originally to Baddeley (1986) about working memory assumed that there were but two buffer systems involved, a phonological one and a visuospatial one. However, quite recent evidence from both monkeys and human beings suggests that more than two stores are implicated. This new evidence allows us to distinguish between a buffer responsible for spatial information (shown in the studies by Funahashi et al. 1989, and by Jonides et al. 1993 reviewed here) and one responsible for visual information that is not spatial in character.

7.5.3 The Visual Buffer

In retrospect, notice that the evidence marshaled to support the claim of a visuospatial buffer has been based on tasks requiring storage of spatial information, yet it is quite clear that not all visual information need be spatial in character. Color and shape, for example, are dimensions of visual stimuli that are not spatial. In principle, then, one need not conflate spatial and visual processing when considering working memory. This observation raises the following question: Are spatial and visual information coded by the same buffers in working memory or are they treated separately? Evidence from recent studies of the biological basis of working memory invites the conclusion that there are separate buffers for these two dimensions.

The first documentation of a distinction between visual and spatial memory coding was by Wilson, O Scalaidhe, and Goldman-Rakic (1993). They paired a test of spatial memory much like the one described in the preceding section with a test of visual memory for shape, both administered to monkeys. The spatial task involved presenting stimuli for a short duration to the left or right of a fixation point while the monkeys fixated on that point. As in the experiment by Funahashi et al. (1989), the monkeys were trained to shift their gaze to the location of the stimulus after a delay interval. The visual-memory task involved brief presentation of a pattern at the center of a screen following which there was a delay. The monkeys were trained to shift their gaze to the left or right after the delay depending on which of two patterns had been presented. This pair of tasks presents the animals with quite different memory requirements, yet with the same response requirement. In the first task, they must maintain memory of the spatial location of the stimulus, but in the second, they must maintain a representation of the stimulus's shape. In both cases, though, they are required to make a left or right eye movement as the response, thus equating the motor task.

As in other experiments, individual neurons were found that were responsive largely during the delay interval of each task. The spatial-memory task led to activation of neurons in the same area that had been previously documented by other studies (for example, Funahashi et al. 1989). This area is in the frontal cortex. The pattern memory task also led to activation of neurons during the delay interval, but the neurons that showed this activation were in a different area, just below the ones found active during the spatial task. It was also largely the case that the neurons active during the spatial task were not active during the pattern task, and vice versa. Thus, this experiment documents a double dissociation between spatial and pattern memory by documenting different brain areas active during these two tasks.

This pattern of dissociation is not limited to monkeys, as research by Smith and Jonides (1994) shows. In their study of working memory in humans using PET, they also showed a dissociation between working memory for location and working memory for object shape. For humans, the major dimension of difference in brain activation patterns was left versus right hemisphere. The right hemisphere was engaged in a spatial working-memory task while the left hemisphere was active during an object-memory task. Thus, research on humans and other primates leads to the view that it is best to consider the working-memory system for visuospatial information as having two components, visual and spatial respectively, not just one.

7.5.4 The Conceptual Buffer

This brings the number of buffers involved in working memory to at least three: a phonological loop, a spatial buffer, and a visual buffer. But this view of working memory must be incomplete. We know from the sort of research reviewed at the beginning of this chapter that working memory is an integral component of many thinking tasks, tasks that require meaningful codes for the information that is being processed, not just sensory codes. How could this be so if the only information stored in working memory is a code defined by only phonological, spatial, or visual characteristics? We also know that there are some patients who can process complex language constructions quite well even though they show profound deficits in their phonological working-memory capacities (for example, Martin 1993). Because language processing must involve some working memory capability (as reviewed in section 7.4), these patients must be using a working-memory system that goes beyond simple phonological storage. Indeed, this and other examples raise the issue of how semantic information is extracted from codes stored in working memory. Two possibilities suggest themselves.

One possibility is that although the three modality-tied buffer systems (phonological, visual, and spatial) store information according to their three respective codes, central executive processes that use this information create a meaningful code for what is stored every time it is used. This might seem inefficient because if each of the buffers themselves stored a meaningful code, there would be no need to do a translation of this information every time it had to be used in the service of some reasoning task. However, the sensory systems are known to be involved in coding by these three formats, and so storage of information according to these formats may just be an inevitable consequence of how the information flows from the sensory systems to systems responsible for using the information (see, for example, Wilson et al. (1993), for an argument of this type related to the storage of information of a spatial or visual sort).

Another quite different possibility is that there is a separate storage buffer in working memory that is designed precisely to store information in a modality-free way, in terms of its conceptual properties. Potter (1993) argues that such a buffer might receive information from encoding processes that allow a direct semantic code to be stored in parallel with the storage of a phonological, spatial, or visual code for the same information. If so, then executive processes that need to make use of the semantic content of some incoming information could have direct access to it, rather than just having access to a modality-specific code for that information.

Compelling as it seems that there must be some conceptual code for information in working memory, there has been surprisingly little research to uncover how this information is stored and accessed by central executive processes. There are, however, a series of reports that make plausible the notion that some sort of semantic code is stored in working memory (see Shulman 1971 for a partial review). Hintzman (1965) found, for example, that in a working-memory task in which letters and digits were the stimuli, not only were errors in recall explainable by acoustic confusions, in addition there was some tendency for subjects to confuse items within the same class (letter or number), as if the class of the items had been coded in addition to the phonological characteristics of each. Also, blocking items in a working-memory task by their conceptual category (words versus digits) improves recall for the items versus intermingling them (Schwartz 1966).

The study of forgetting from working memory has also produced evidence supporting the view that a conceptual code may be stored as well as modality-specific codes. Dale and Gregory (1966) demonstrated that introducing retroactively interfering material during a retention interval caused forgetting, and that this interference was accentuated by conceptual similarity of the interfering material to the material that had to be remembered. Wickens, Born, and Allen (1963) also implicated a conceptual code in their studies of release from proactive inhibition. In these studies, subjects engaged in a series of trials of a working-memory task. The material to be remembered was of the same conceptual type (for example, consonant strings), with occasional switches to another conceptual type (for example, digit strings). Performance on successive trials with the same type of material gradually declined, but it then recovered when the type of material was changed. This recovery suggests that part of the code for the items included information about their conceptual category, and similarity of category gradually increased interference for the items themselves.

These and other results raise the possibility of a semantic or conceptual code as part of working memory. Exactly how this code is stored in relation to the modality-specific codes is not yet clear, however, and deserves further empirical research. All that is presently clear is that a conceptual code of some sort is needed in order to make working memory useful in the stream of information processing, for it is a conceptual code that is often used by executive processes, which we examine next.

7.5.5 Central Executive Processes

The central executive in working memory is often discussed as if it is a unitary processing mechanism, but it is perhaps better characterized as a *set* of operations that can process information in the buffers of working memory in the service of one task or another. To appreciate this structure, think again about the reasoning tasks with which this chapter began. Solving problems on the Raven test involved executive processes that can extract the critical dimensions of the stimuli, compare these dimensions among members of a row or column, and extrapolate the values of these dimensions to predict the missing member of the matrix. Solving mental arithmetic involves a quite different set of operations, which manipulate numerical information. Different again from these examples are the processes required by the spatial reasoning tasks of Byrne and Johnson-Laird (1989), in which arrays of symbols must be created with the spatial relations among them well specified. It is easy to see that the processes involved in these varied tasks are quite different from one another. In short, understanding the nature of central executive processes will involve studying myriad processes in myriad tasks. It is perhaps for this reason that it is widely recognized that progress in understanding central executive processes has lagged behind progress in understanding the buffer systems that report to these processes (see, for example, Baddeley 1990).

7.5.5.1 *Goal Management*

The fact that there seem to be many executive processes may make one wonder whether they have *anything* in common—that is, whether there is any value in arguing that they all belong to a single category of executive processes rather than each being different from the others. If the processes had no common characteristics, then the label "executive processes" would be more gratuitous than real. Analyzing the many processes that can be performed on information held in working memory reveals, however, that they share some features.

One has to do with doing more than one thing at once. Often, various goals confront a person simultaneously. Think about driving a car when you have a passenger with whom you are having a conversation. In this case, you have two goals at the highest level of analysis: keeping the car heading where you intend, and keeping up your end of the conversation. Each of these, in turn, has subgoals. On the driving end, you not only want to get to your destination, but you want to do so by observing the law, keeping up a decent level of speed, allowing other drivers their turn at a stop sign, and so on. On the conversation end, you want not only to spew out a series of words when it's your turn to speak, but you want the words to form sentences, convey your thoughts, allow you to develop your arguments, and so on. This example and others illustrate that there are many times when we have goals and subgoals which have to be kept in mind, and which have to control our behavior in a changing fashion from one moment to the next. One function of central executive processes is to keep the goals of the current situation in memory and to allow each to control behavior in a manner that is coordinated with each of the other goals. Also, of course, there is the need to update the goal list as time passes so that new ones can be added and defunct ones can be deleted. All this activity requires significant coordination.

The empirical analysis of this sort of goal-tracking behavior has relied on fairly spare tasks, but ones in which two or more goals have to be monitored and respected. In such tasks, one finds that the more complicated or difficult each task associated with a goal, the more difficult it is to switch from honoring one goal to honoring another. This is true even for tasks that are quite familiar to us. Let's return to the mental arithmetic example. Consider this: Suppose you are given a series of simple addition problems to do mentally, or a series of subtraction problems. Now consider being given a series of problems that alternate between addition and subtraction. If goal setting were automatic and simply a function of the task at hand, it should take no longer to do the mixed series of problems than the average of each individual series. But Rubenstein and colleagues (1993; Rubenstein, Meyer, and Evans, submitted) showed that this is not remotely the case. In their experiment, the time to do a set of addition problems was 37.50 seconds, and the time to do subtraction was 44.33 seconds, but the time to do a mixed series of the same length as the addition and subtraction series was 46.50 seconds. On average, they calculated, it took about .51 second to switch from each addition to subtraction problem and back in the mixed series. Furthermore, if the comparison was between multiplication and division (more complex mathematical calculations), the switching time increased to 1.27 seconds. This is consistent with the view that one function of central executive processes is to monitor task goals, and this monitoring trades off in its processing resources with the tasks at hand. The more complex the task, the more time it takes to disengage from it and switch to another.

Given this result, you won't find it surprising that if one of the tasks involved in a two-task situation is the Raven Matrix task, switching between it and another task will be quite taxing. Hunt (1980) discovered this difficulty in examining performance on a motor guidance task while subjects tackled Raven's problems of varying difficulty. As the difficulty of the Raven problems increased, performance on the guidance task suffered, indicating that the increased Raven difficulty made it more difficult to switch from it to the guidance task. This overall result may be due to the increased difficulty in switching, or to the decreased availability of processing resources as they are stretched ever more thinly with more demanding tasks. In either case, executive processes must balance one set of goals against another.

7.5.5.2 *Scheduling*

Another of the functions of executive processes is to schedule the subcomponent processes that are required to follow through on any task that is aimed at a single goal. As discussed, any complex cognitive task—mental arithmetic being just one—is best described in terms of a set of processes that must be engaged to arrive at a task goal. Sometimes these processes are engaged in turn, sometimes in parallel with one another, but there are multiple ones nonetheless. This assumption of multiple subcomponent processes makes clear that there must be executive control over scheduling as well as executive control over goal management, as we saw in the preceding section. Scheduling involves assigning priority to one or another mental operation so that it has control at any given time, as well as switching priorities among different mental operations as they are needed. Thus, for example, in solving a Raven's matrix problem, scheduling would coordinate among feature identification, feature comparison within a row or column, and extrapolation to the missing item, among other processes. In working on a mental-addition problem, scheduling is critical so that the units digits are added before the tens digits, that the carrying operation is done before the next column of digits is processed, and so on. Most tasks that face us in our daily lives involve some element of scheduling, in that most tasks have identifiable components, and these components need to be coordinated one with the other to reach a successful outcome (see chapter 8).

There are many occasions when we have learned some skill well and can apply it to a situation easily, with little depth of analysis of the variables in that situation. In such cases, scheduling processes for working on a task is considered to be automatic. Scheduling the order of strokes when brushing your teeth might be an example. Most people have a quite stereotyped order in which they attack the different parts of the mouth, going from left to right and top to bottom, for example. This, of course, is not usually a matter for deep thought in the morning. Quite the contrary: one can think about the plan for the day quite effectively and still do a good job of getting around the mouth. More complex tasks such as driving a car might qualify as well. Sometimes drivers find that they have driven for some miles with little memory of how they negotiated the drive. To be sure, decisions had to be made along the way, including how much to press on the accelerator, whether to apply the brakes, whether to turn the steering wheel to remain in the center of one's lane, and so on. But once driving becomes a well-learned skill, these sorts of operations can be handled with little effort.

Substantial research has been conducted to determine the conditions under which automaticity develops for skills, and it is impressive to find that even complex skills such as reading and taking dictation can be done together after they have become automatic (see, for example, Spelke, Hirst, and Neisser 1976). Research has also shown that the critical variable in the development of automaticity is the regularity of the relationships that one is practicing. When there is a consistent relationship between stimuli and responses to those stimuli, automaticity in processing develops nicely. By contrast, when the relationship between stimuli and responses is variable, automaticity never develops. Apparently, consistency in learning conditions coupled with extensive practice can automate the scheduling of even complex tasks, making the work of executive processes relatively effortless (Schneider and Shiffrin 1977).

Of course, many of the mental tasks that occupy our time are not automatic. It is these that tax the scheduling function of executive processes. Norman and Shallice (1986) recognized this in devising a model of executive control over scheduling that includes a component responsible for scheduling in relatively automatic contexts and a component that dominates when scheduling is required for novel or unpracticed behaviors. They argue that when faced with tasks that can be accomplished by well-learned sequences of processes, we call up from memory processes that can be strung together to reach the task goal. For example, in driving to work, you might retrieve a representation for a standard route. This choice, in turn, would cause lower-level representations or subroutines to be engaged to sequence the various parts of the drive. These, in turn, would engage the processes necessary to start the car, press the accelerator, hit the brake, and so on. In many cases, Norman and Shallice (1986) argue, we function by virtue of having a large number of these processes in memory, and we can engage them in the proper sequence, having done so many times previously. Once triggered, a representation will then compete with similar representations for other actions, inhibiting ones that will conflict with the ongoing activity if it is sufficiently powerful in its control of action. Success in completing a routine task, then, will depend on the strength of its representations versus the strengths of others. This establishes a goal dominance of the sort we examined above.

Going beyond automatic routines, according to Norman and Shallice (1986), involves engaging another process, which they call the Supervisory Attentional System (SAS). This system is engaged whenever two competing tasks must be completed, or when a novel behavior is needed in a task. In such cases, the SAS gains control over scheduling of processes and can engage a memory representation even if its strength to control behavior is low. In short, the SAS acts as an executive process, recruiting whatever processing operations it deems necessary to accomplish some goal. It can also trade off between different processes if multiple task goals have to be met.

Thinking of scheduling as a supervisory process that organizes component processes as needed recognizes two important functions of the central executive. One is planning. If the SAS is to organize component processes to meet a behavioral goal that cannot be met by exercising some routine skill, then it must have the capability to plan a line of attack on a problem to be solved. The other function of central executive processes highlighted by Norman and Shallice (1986) is selective attention. What, after all, does it mean to schedule a set of mental component processes so that they can meet some new goal? It means that each process must be attended to in turn so that its prominence is highlighted sufficiently for it to have priority. In this way, the SAS goes beyond routine processing to engage and disengage mental representations as needed in some novel combination.

Selective attention to component processes (that is, scheduling) is a function that is not well understood at present in terms of brain function. However, there is some reason to believe that the sort of attention required for executive functioning may be controlled by the frontal lobes of the brain (Posner and Petersen 1990), in contrast to selective attention to stimulus attributes such as color or position. This view is also consistent with observations on the effect of frontal damage in planning, the other function of executive processes. Luria (1973) recognized this effect in his characterization of one of the deficits that accompanies damage to the frontal lobes of the brain. He argued that, "As a rule patients with lesions of the frontal lobes with their distinctive impulsiveness never start with a preliminary analysis of the task's conditions but immediately attempt to solve. This leads to typical errors in planless solving attempts that usually remain uncorrected" (Luria 1973, 15). Although the full scope of frontal function is not in sight at this time, certain functions of this area of the brain have made themselves apparent in patients with damage to the frontal lobes. One is concentration on a task, without being interrupted by other stimuli present in the visual array. Another is being able to adopt new strategies as needed to solve problems with which one is faced (see chapter 8 for more on the role of the frontal lobes in cognition).

One symptom that has been cited frequently as a sign of frontal damage is high susceptibility to interruption. Many tasks require sustained attention to a task, something that patients with frontal damage often find difficult (see, for instance, McCarthy and Warrington 1990, for a description). Their symptoms are characterized by relative inability to ignore irrelevant stimulation in the environment. This condition seems most prevalent when the task at hand does not itself contain stimuli that capture attention. In such cases, of course, concentration on the task is made more difficult because it must be internally generated, rather than relying on the salience of stimuli that occur. There are many illustrations of this general difficulty to resist interruption. For example, it appears in tasks that require vigilance to infrequently appearing stimuli, a task that is difficult if attention is not concentrated on the stimuli for long periods (for example, Salamaso and Denes 1982). Difficulty with tasks such as this in the face of frontal damage indicates a disruption of the scheduling function of executive processes, a disruption that interrupts the normal flow of information processing when irrelevant stimuli intrude.

Another symptom of frontal damage is the tendency to perseverate. Perhaps the most frequently cited evidence of this difficulty comes from use of the Wisconsin card-sorting task (Milner 1964). In this task, subjects are given four target cards, each bearing a design in which shape is one dimension of variation (for example, cross or triangle), color is another, and number of figures is the third. The subjects are then given a stack of cards to sort, placing each card in front of one of the four target cards. The cards can be sorted according to one of the dimensions, but the subjects do not know which. All they are told with each card placement is whether their sorting is right or wrong. Subjects continue sorting until they are correct in placing cards according to the dimension the experimenter has in mind, and then the criterion dimension is changed without notice. Subjects then must reach criterion with this new dimension, and so on with another dimension. Normal subjects can learn to adopt one or another dimension as the critical one within a few trials, but patients with frontal damage may continue to use an incorrect dimension for as many as 100 trials without switching. This behavior indicates quite graphically how patients with frontal damage can perseverate in their behavior. They can do so even when they realize that what they are doing is incorrect, moreover, suggesting a certain lack of control over strategic processes. It is as if they can set up a routine to pay attention to one dimension, but they cannot switch attention to another dimension even when they know that they must. This inability to switch from one dimension to another is symptomatic of a difficulty in arranging goals properly in the face of changing task demands.

The results of studies of central executive processes paint a picture of a coordinating mechanism. Its repertoire of functions can vary from mental arithmetic, to logical analysis, to spatial problem solving, and beyond. But whatever the particular processing required, there remains a need to coordinate the various goals that must be attained moment by moment, as well as a need to organize the component processes that will be scheduled to meet these goals. Although much remains to be understood about how this coordination is accomplished, viewing processing requirements in terms of a central set of principles such as goal management and scheduling will help organize a variety of findings about executive processes.

7.6 Summary

As the discussion in this chapter lays out, it can be fairly argued that working memory is the engine of cognition. It is intimately involved in the complex cognitive processes that underlie reasoning, problem solving, and, perhaps, certain aspects of language processing. It participates in all these activities of our cognitive lives by allowing us to execute a large array of cognitive routines and by temporarily storing information on which these routines operate. Although limited in capacity to store and compute, working memory nonetheless enjoys considerable horsepower by virtue of fine coordination between the storage buffers and the computing operations. This architecture, though not an inevitable design for powerful computing devices, serves human beings quite handsomely.

Suggestions for Further Reading

Many textbooks about cognition and memory can provide introductory material about working memory and about the thinking processes that it serves. Among them are Baddeley 1990, Medin and Ross 1992, and Best 1992. These texts provide an overview of the topics in cognition that may be helpful not only to one interested in working memory, but also to one who would like to place the role of working memory in the context of a functioning cognitive system. Those with an interest in the breakdown of this system that accompanies brain injury might be advised to consult a text by McCarthy and Warrington 1990. Even more focused material on deficits accompanying damage to the particular systems that affect working memory can be found in Vallar and Shallice 1990.

Research about working memory populates the major journals in the field of cognitive psychology, and the journals that publish research about brain injury and its effects on cognitive processes. Many of these journals are represented in the reference list that accompanies this chapter. An overview of a theory of working memory that includes memory buffers and a central executive can be found in Baddeley 1986, 1992. This theory has been subject to test in a variety of ways: using behavioral tests of dual-task performance, studies of individual differences in working memory and the relation of these differences to other cognitive skills, and studies of patients with lesions. Discussion of each of these lines of research will be found in the reference sections of these works by Baddeley 1986, 1992.

Realize that aspects of the view of working memory presented here are not without controversy. Some, for example, question its role in language function (Martin 1993). Some question the arguments about the nature of the codes stored in working memory (Reisberg, Rappaport, and O'Shaughnessy 1984). Some question whether what we know about working memory relates to its role in thinking (Potter 1993). Yet others question the appropriateness of various tasks for measuring working memory (Klapp, Marshburn, and Lester 1983). In addition, the view presented here is different from the classical view of working memory (then called "short-term memory") that is exemplified in Atkinson and Shiffrin (1971). These arguments and others are worth considering to evaluate the promise of the present view of working memory and to decide the crucial issues for further study; a student who wishes to examine this topic further should consult these sources.

Problems

7.1 Carpenter et al. 1990 found a substantial correlation between performance on Raven's problems and the Tower of Hanoi problem. This they interpreted as indicating that both tasks tapped working memory insofar as goal and subgoal management are features of working memory. Goal management has been identified as one of the hallmarks of the central executive in working memory. In view of this finding, if you were to search for patients who had a deficit in working memory that would reveal itself in either Raven's problems or the Tower of Hanoi, what patients would you seek? That is, where would you expect to find damage in the brain that interfered with tasks such as Raven's? How would you doubly dissociate a deficit in goal management from a deficit in other tasks dependent on working memory, such as memory span? If you could establish such a double dissociation, what would this tell you about the relationship of central executive processes to the memory buffers of working memory?

7.2 Baddeley 1986 and others have found that having subjects store a number of items in working memory while they also engage in a task that requires sentence comprehension does not seem to have profoundly damaging effects on performance in the sentence-comprehension task. Does this result critically wound the hypothesis that working memory plays an important role in language comprehension?

7.3 The evidence reviewed in this chapter strongly supports the hypothesis that phonological coding is critical to the storage of verbal material. One might wonder, then, what code is used by people who are congenitally deaf. Given that they cannot code information phonologically, do they have working-memory spans for verbal material of zero? Design an experiment to examine the nature of the code used by congenitally deaf subjects.

7.4 Neurobiological studies of cognitive processes have been criticized on occasion for offering little evidence beyond what one can gain from strictly behavioral experiments. As the criticism goes, the only new information offered by neurobiological studies is an indication of where information processing takes place in the brain. Critics argue that knowing about the localization of processes tells us relatively little about the functioning of the cognitive system. Is this true of research on working memory? What else is offered by neurobiological studies in this domain?

References

Atkinson, R. C., and R. M. Shiffrin (1971). The control of short-term memory. *Scientific American* 225, 82–90.

Baddeley, A. D. (1986). *Working memory*. Oxford: Oxford University Press.

Baddeley, A. D. (1990). *Human memory: Theory and practice.* Needham Heights, MA: Allyn & Bacon.

Baddeley, A. D. (1992). Working memory. *Science* 255, 556–559.

Baddeley, A. D., and G. J. Hitch (1974). Working memory. In G. Bower, ed., *Recent advances in learning and motivation,* vol. VIII. New York: Academic Press.

Baddeley, A. D., N. Thomson, and M. Buchanan (1975). Word length and the structure of short-term memory. *Journal of Verbal Learning and Verbal Behavior* 14, 575–589.

Basso, A., H. Spinnler, G. Vallar, and E. Zanobio (1982). Left hemisphere damage and selective impairment of auditory verbal short-term memory: A case study. *Neuropsychologia* 20, 263–274.

Best, J. B. (1992). *Cognitive psychology.* St. Paul, MN: West Publishing.

Brooks, L. R. (1968). Spatial and verbal components of the act of recall. *Canadian Journal of Psychology* 22, 349–368.

Byrne, R. M. J., and P. N. Johnson-Laird (1989). Spatial reasoning. *Journal of Memory and Language* 28, 564–575.

Carpenter, P. A., M. A. Just, and P. Shell (1990). What one intelligence test measures: A theoretical account of the processing in the Raven Progressive Matrices Test. *Psychological Review* 97, 404–431.

Conrad, R. (1964). Acoustic confusions in immediate memory. *British Journal of Psychology* 55, 75–84.

Conrad, R. (1970). Short-term memory processes in the deaf. *British Journal of Psychology* 61, 179–195.

Conrad, R. (1972). Short-term memory in the deaf: A test for speech coding. *British Journal of Psychology* 63, 173–180.

Dale, H. C. A., and M. Gregory (1966). Evidence of semantic encoding in short-term memory. *Psychonomic Science* 5, 153–154.

Daneman, M., and P. A. Carpenter (1980). Individual differences in working memory and reading. *Journal of Verbal Learning and Verbal Behavior* 19, 450–466.

Daneman, M., and P. A. Carpenter (1983). Individual differences in integrating information between and within sentences. *Journal of Experimental Psychology: Learning, Memory and Cognition* 9, 561–584.

Deese, J., and R. A. Kaufman (1957). Serial effects in recall of unorganized and sequentially organized verbal material. *Journal of Experimental Psychology* 54, 180–187.

Ellis, N. C., and R. A. Hennelly (1980). A bilingual word-length effect: Implications for intelligence testing and the relative ease of mental calculation in Welsh and English. *British Journal of Psychology* 71, 43–52.

Funahashi, S., C. J. Bruce, and P. S. Goldman-Rakic (1989). Mnemonic coding of visual space in the monkey's dorsolateral prefrontal cortex. *Journal of Neurophysiology* 61, 331–349.

Gilhooly, K. J., R. H. Logie, N. E. Wetherick, and V. Wynn (1993). Working memory and strategies in syllogistic-reasoning tasks. *Memory and Cognition* 21, 115–124.

Glanzer, M., and A. R. Cunitz (1966). Two storage mechanisms in free recall. *Journal of Verbal Learning and Verbal Behavior* 5, 351–360.

Goldman-Rakic, P. S. (1987). Circuitry of primate prefrontal cortex and regulation of behavior by representational memory. *Handbook of physiology,* sec. 1, vol. V, 373–417.

Hardyck, C. D., and L. R. Petrinovich (1970). Subvocal speech and comprehension level as a function of the difficulty level of reading material. *Journal of Verbal Learning and Verbal Behavior* 9, 647–652.

Hintzman, D. L. (1965). Classification and aural coding in STM. *Psychonomic Science* 3, 161–162.

Hitch, G. J. (1978). The role of short-term working memory in mental arithmetic. *Cognitive Psychology* 10, 302–323.

Hitch, G. J., and A. D. Baddeley (1976). Verbal reasoning and working memory. *Quarterly Journal of Experimental Psychology* 28, 603–621.

Huey, E. B. (1908). *The psychology and pedagogy of reading*. New York: Macmillan.

Hunt, E. (1980). Intelligence as an information processing concept. *British Journal of Psychology* 71, 449–474.

Jacobsen, C. F. (1936). Studies of cerebral function in primates. *Comparative Psychology Monographs* 13, 1–68.

Johnson-Laird, P. N., and B. G. Bara (1984). Syllogistic inference. *Cognition* 16, 1–61.

Jonides, J., E. E. Smith, R. A. Koeppe, E. Awh, S. Minoshima, and M. A. Mintun (1993). Spatial working memory in humans as revealed by PET. *Nature* 363, 623–625.

Klapp, S. T., E. A. Marshburn, and P. T. Lester (1983). Short-term memory does not involve the "working memory" of information processing: The demise of a common assumption. *Journal of Experimental Psychology: General* 112, 240–264.

Koeppe, R. A., S. Minoshima, J. Jonides, E. E. Smith, E. S. Awh, and M. A. Mintun (1993). PET studies of working memory in humans: Differentiation of visuospatial and articulatory buffers. Paper presented to the Meeting of the Society of Nuclear Medicine.

Kosslyn, S. M. (1980). *Image and mind*. Cambridge, MA: Harvard University Press.

Kosslyn, S. M. (1981). The medium and the message in mental imagery: A theory. *Psychological Review* 88, 46–66.

Kosslyn, S. M., N. M. Alpert, W. L. Thompson, V. Maljkovic, S. B. Weise, C. F. Chabris, S. E. Hamilton, and F. S. Buonanno (1993). Visual mental imagery activates topographically organized cortex: PET investigations. *Journal of Cognitive Neuroscience* 5, 263–287.

Kyllonen, P. C., and R. E. Christal (1990). Reasoning ability is (little more than) working-memory capacity?! *Intelligence* 14, 389–433.

Larson, G. E., C. R. Merritt, and S. E. Williams (1988). Information processing and intelligence: Some implications of task complexity. *Intelligence* 12, 131–147.

Larson, G E., and D. P. Saccuzzo (1989). Cognitive correlates of general intelligence: Toward a process theory of g. *Intelligence* 13, 5–31.

Longoni, A. M., J. T. E. Richardson, and A. Aiello (1993). Articulatory rehearsal and phonological storage in working memory. *Memory and Cognition* 21, 11–22.

Luria, A. R. (1973). *The working brain*. New York: Basic Books.

Martin, R. C. (1993). Short-term memory and sentence processing: Evidence from neuropsychology. *Memory and language* 21, 176–183.

McCarthy, R. A., and E. K. Warrington (1990). *Cognitive neuropsychology: A clinical introduction*. San Diego: Academic Press.

Medin, D. L., and B. H. Ross (1992). *Cognitive psychology*. New York: Harcourt Brace Jovanovich.

Miller, G. A. (1956). The magical number seven, plus or minus two: Some limits on our capacity for processing information. *Psychological Review* 63, 81–97.

Milner, B. (1964). Some effects of frontal lobectomy in man. In J. M. Warren and K. Akert, eds., *The frontal granular cortex and behaviour* 313–331. New York: McGraw-Hill.

Milner, B. S., S. Corkin, and H.-L. Teuber (1968). Further analysis of the hippocampal amnesic syndrome: 14-year follow-up study of H. M. *Neuropsychologia* 6, 215–234.

Murray, D. J. (1968). Articulation and acoustic confusability in short-term memory. *Journal of Experimental Psychology* 78, 679–684.

Naveh-Benjamin, M., and T. J. Ayres (1986). Digit span, reading rate, and linguistic relativity. *Quarterly Journal of Experimental Psychology* 38, 739–751.

Norman, D. A., and T. Shallice (1986). Attention to action: Willed and automatic control of behavior. In R. J. Davidson, G. E. Schwarts, and D. Shapiro, eds., *Consciousness and self-regulation: Advances in research and theory* 4, 1–18. New York: Plenum Press.

Paulesu, E., C. D. Frith, and R. S. J. Frackowiak (1993). The neural correlates of the verbal component of working memory. *Nature* 362, 342–344.

Posner, M. I., and S. Petersen (1990). The attention system of the human brain. *Annual Review of Neuroscience* 13, 25–42.

Postman, L, and L. W. Phillips (1965). Short-term temporal changes in free recall. *Quarterly Journal of Experimental Psychology* 17, 132–138.

Potter, M. C. (1993). Very short-term conceptual memory. *Memory and Cognition* 21, 156–161.

Potts, G. R. (1974). Storing and retrieving information about ordered relationships. *Journal of Experimental Psychology* 103, 431–439.

Raven, J. C. (1962). *Advanced progressive matrices, Set II.* London: H. K. Lewis. (Distributed in the United States by The Psychological Corporation, San Antonio, TX.)

Reisberg, D., I. Rappaport, and M. O'Shaughnessy (1984). Limits of working memory: The digit digit-span. *Journal of Experimental Psychology: Learning, Memory, and Cognition* 10, 203–221.

Roy, C. S., and C. S. Sherrington (1890). On the regulation of the blood supply of the brain. *Journal of Physiology* 11, 85–109.

Rubenstein, J. S. (1993). Executive control of cognitive processes in task switching. Doctoral dissertation, University of Michigan.

Rubenstein, J. S., D. E. Meyer, and J. Evans (submitted). Executive control of cognitive processes in task switching. *Journal of Experimental Psychology: General.*

Salamaso, D., and G. Denes (1982). Role of the frontal lobes on an attention task: A signal detection analysis. *Perception and Motor Skills* 55, 1147–1150.

Salame, P., and A. D. Baddeley (1982). Disruption of short-term memory by unattended speech: Implications for the structure of working memory. *Journal of Verbal Learning and Verbal Behavior* 21, 150–164.

Salthouse, T. A. (1990). Working memory as a processing resource in cognitive ageing. *Developmental Review* 10, 101–124.

Salthouse, T. A. (1992). Influence of processing speed on adult age differences in working memory. *Acta Psychologica* 79, 155–170.

Salthouse, T. A. (1992). Reasoning and spatial abilities. In F. I. M. Craik and T. A. Salthouse, eds., *Handbook of aging and cognition.* Hillsdale, NJ: Erlbaum.

Salthouse, T. A. (1993). Influence of working memory on adult age differences in matrix reasoning. *British Journal of Psychology* 84, 171–199.

Schacter, D. L., C.-Y. P. Chiu, and K. N. Ochsner (1993). Implicit memory: A selective review. In W. M. Cowan, E. M. Shooter, C. F. Stevens, and R. F. Thompson, eds., *Annual review of neuroscience,* Vol. 16. Palo Alto, CA: Annual Reviews, Inc.

Schneider, W., and R. M. Shiffrin (1977). Controlled and automatic information processing I: Detection, search and attention. *Psychological Review* 84, 1–66.

Scholz, K. W., and G. R. Potts (1974). Cognitive processing of linear orderings. *Journal of Experimental Psychology* 102, 323–326.

Schwartz, F. (1966). Morphological coding in short-term memory. *Psychological Reports* 18, 487–492.

Shulman, H. G. (1971). Similarity effects in short-term memory. *Psychological Bulletin* 75, 399–415.

Smith, E. E., and J. Jonides (1994). Working memory in humans: Neuropsychological evidence. In M. Gazzaniga, ed., *The cognitive neurosciences.* Cambridge, MA: MIT Press.

Spelke, E., W. Hirst, and U. Neisser (1976). Skills of divided attention. *Cognition* 4, 215–230.

Squire, L. R. (1992). Memory and the hippocampus: A synthesis from findings with rats, monkeys, and humans. *Psychological Review* 99, 195–231.

Turner, M. L., and R. W. Engle (1989). Is working memory task dependent? *Journal of Memory and Language* 28, 127–154.

Vallar, G., and A. D. Baddeley (1984). Fractionation of working memory: Neuropsychological evidence for a phonological short-term store. *Journal of Verbal Learning and Verbal Behavior* 23, 151–161.

Vallar, G., and A. D. Baddeley (1987). Phonological short-term store and sentence processing. *Cognitive Neuropsychology* 4, 417–438.

Vallar, G., and T. Shallice, eds. (1990). *Neuropsychological impairments of short-term memory*. Cambridge: Cambridge University Press.

Warrington, E. K., and T. Shallice (1969). The selective impairment of auditory verbal short-term memory. *Brain* 92, 885–896.

Waters, G., D. Caplan, and N. Hildebrandt (1991). On the structure of verbal short-term memory and its functional role in sentence comprehension: Evidence from neuropsychology. *Cognitive Neuropsychology* 8, 81–126.

Wickens, D. D., D. G. Born, and C. K. Allen (1963). Proactive inhibition and item similarity in short-term memory. *Journal of Verbal Learning and Verbal Behavior* 2, 440–445.

Wilson, F. A. W., S. P. O Scalaidhe, and P. S. Goldman-Rakic (1993). Dissociation of object and spatial processing domains in primate prefrontal cortex. *Science* 260, 1955–1958.

Chapter 8

Problem Solving

Keith J. Holyoak

The ability to solve problems is one of the most important manifestations of human thinking. The range of problems people encounter is enormous: planning a dinner party, tracking deer, diagnosing a disease, winning a game of chess, solving mathematical equations, managing a business. This radical diversity of problem domains contrasts with the relative specificity of many human cognitive activities, such as vision, language, basic motor skills, and memory activation, which have a relatively direct biological basis and which all normal individuals accomplish with substantially uniform proficiency. In the course of normal development we all learn, for example, to speak a native language, but without specialized experience we will never acquire competence in deer tracking or chess playing.

On the other hand, all normal people do acquire considerable competence in solving at least some of the particular types of problems they habitually encounter in everyday life. We might therefore suspect that problem solving depends on general cognitive abilities that can potentially be applied to an extremely broad range of domains. We will see, in fact, that such diverse cognitive abilities as perception, language, sequencing of actions, memory, categorization, judgment, and choice all play important roles in human problem solving.

The ability to solve problems is clearly a crucial component of intelligence. Furthermore, the phenomena of problem solving present many intriguing puzzles that must be accounted for by a successful theory of problem solving. For example, consider the differences between the best computer programs for playing chess and the performance of the very best human players. Before selecting its next move, a top-ranked chess-playing program is likely to assess billions of alternative possible continuations of the game. In contrast, the human grand master may consider a mere dozen alternatives—and then proceed to select a better move than the program did. What mechanisms allow the best move to so readily "come to mind"

Preparation of this chapter was supported by NSF Grant SBR-9310614. The chapter benefitted from the comments of John Jonides and Edward Smith on an earlier draft. Nina Robin provided suggestions for the section on the brain basis of problem solving.

for the grand master? And what kind of learning processes allow this sort of expertise to be acquired from problem-solving experience? These and other questions about human problem solving are the focus of this chapter.

In order to understand the nature of human problem solving, it is useful to first consider the nature of problems. We can often learn a great deal about how problems are solved by considering how they *could* be solved. That is, a *task analysis* of problems can provide information about constraints that the nature of the problem imposes on the nature of the problem solver. We will also see that task analysis suggests that problem solving is intimately connected with *learning*. An intelligent problem solver uses the results of solution attempts to acquire new knowledge that will help solve similar problems more readily in the future.

We begin by characterizing the nature of problem solving and the fundamental theoretical issues the topic raises for cognitive science. We introduce the topic using a problem that has been investigated by psychologists over the past several decades. In addition, we briefly consider the implications of neuropsychological evidence regarding the basic components of problem-solving skill. We then examine in more detail one of the major concerns of recent research, the acquisition of expertise in particular problem-solving domains, such as chess or physics. Finally, we examine aspects of problem solving that seem to involve parallel and unconscious information processing.

8.1 The Nature of Problem Solving

8.1.1 Problem Solving as Search

The Gestalt psychologist Karl Duncker (1945) performed a series of experiments in which he recorded what university students said as they "thought aloud" while attempting to solve the "radiation problem":

> Suppose you are a doctor faced with a patient who has a malignant tumor in his stomach. To operate on the patient is impossible, but unless the tumor is destroyed, the patient will die. A kind of ray, at a sufficiently high intensity, can destroy the tumor. Unfortunately, at this intensity the healthy tissue that the rays pass through on the way to the tumor will also be destroyed. At lower intensities the rays are harmless to healthy tissue but will not affect the tumor, either. How can the rays be used to destroy the tumor without injuring the healthy tissue?

As well as stating the problem verbally, Duncker showed his subjects the sketch in figure 8.1, which illustrates a ray passing through a cross-section of the body with the tumor in the middle. Obviously, this arrangement

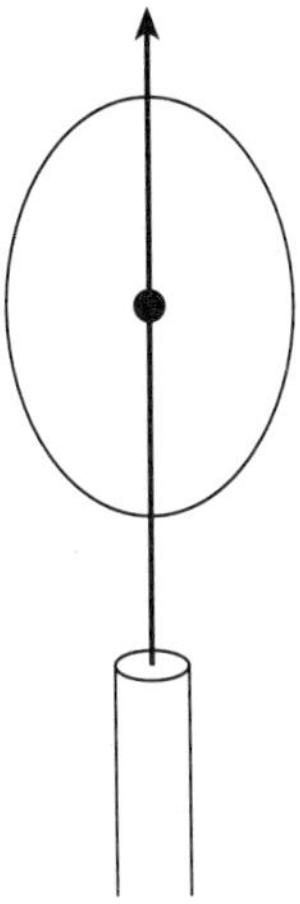

Figure 8.1
A sketch of the initial problem situation in Duncker's radiation problem. From Duncker 1945.

will not do. You may want to pause here for a few moments to try to think of possible solutions to the radiation problem.

What makes the doctor's situation a "problem"? In general, a problem arises when we have a *goal*—a state of affairs that we want to achieve—and it is not immediately apparent how the goal can be attained. Thus the doctor has the goal of destroying the tumor with the rays, without damaging the surrounding healthy tissue. Some valuable clues to the nature of problem solving can be found in the everyday metaphors we use to talk about it (Lakoff and Turner 1989). It is conventional to think of abstract states such as goals as metaphorical spatial locations, and event sequences as metaphorical paths leading from one state to another. This spatial conception permeates descriptions of problem solving. We speak of "searching for a way to reach a goal," "getting around roadblocks" encountered along the way, finding a "shortcut" solution, "getting lost" in the middle of a solution, "hitting a dead end" and being forced to "backtrack," "approaching the problem from a different angle," and so on.

This conception of problem solving as search in a metaphorical space, which underlies our common-sense understanding, has been elaborated to provide a rigorous theoretical framework for the analysis of problem solving. Although some of the theoretical ideas can be traced back to Gestalt psychologists such as Duncker (1945), the modern formulation of a general theory of problem solving as search through a space is due to Newell and Simon (1972). In their problem-space formulation, the representation of a problem consists of four kinds of elements: a description of

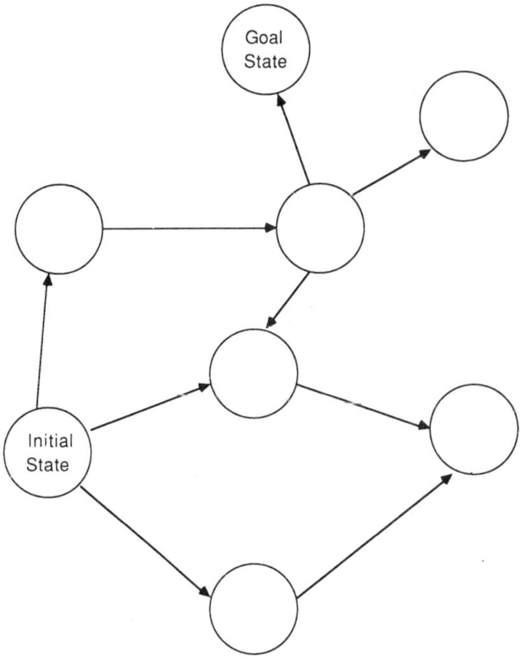

Figure 8.2
A graphical illustration of a search space for a problem.

the *initial state* at which problem solving begins; a description of the *goal state* to be reached; a set of *operators,* or actions that can be taken, which serve to alter the current state of the problem; and *path constraints* that impose additional conditions on a successful path to solution, beyond simply reaching the goal (for instance, the constraint of finding the solution using the fewest possible steps).

The *problem space* consists of the set of all states that can potentially be reached by applying the available operators. A *solution* is a sequence of operators that can transform the initial state into the goal state in accord with the path constraints. A problem-solving *method* is a procedure for finding a solution. Problem solving is thus viewed as search: methods are used to find a solution path among all the possible paths emanating from the initial state and goal state. Figure 8.2 provides a graphical illustration of a search space. Each circle represents a possible state of affairs, and the arrows represent possible transitions from one state to another that can be effected by applying operators. A sequence of arrows leading from the initial state to the goal state constitutes a solution path.

How might search proceed in attempting to solve the radiation problem? In his analyses of subjects' think-aloud protocols, Duncker identified three general "paths" toward solutions. One approach is to alter the direction from which the rays are applied so as to *avoid contact* with the healthy tissue. For example, people often suggested sending the rays down the esophagus, taking advantage of an "open passage" through the healthy tissue. This solution is impracticable, since the esophagus is not straight, but nonetheless represents a serious attempt to achieve the doctor's basic goal. A second approach is to *desensitize* or immunize the healthy tissue so that it will not be harmed by the rays. A third approach is to *reduce the intensity* of the rays along their path to the tumor. Duncker observed that subjects often developed increasingly refined solutions that could be reached by following one or more of these basic search paths.

8.1.2 Heuristic Search

The problem-space analysis yields a mathematical result with brutal implications for the feasibility of solving many problems, such as the problem of winning a chess game. If at each step in the search any of F operators might be applied, and a solution requires applying a sequence of D steps (that is, D is the "depth" of the search), then the number of alternative operator sequences is F^D. As F and D get even modestly large, F^D becomes enormous. A typical game of chess, for example, might involve a total of 60 moves, with an average of 30 alternative legal moves available at each step along the way. The number of alternative paths would thus be 30^{60}, a number so astronomical that not even the fastest computer could play chess by exploring every possible move sequence. The fact that the size of the search space increases exponentially with the depth of the search is termed *combinatorial explosion,* a property that makes many problems impossible to solve by exhaustive search of all possible paths.

Human beings, with their limited working memory, are actually far less capable of "brute-force" search than are computers. (See chapter 7.) For example, human chess players are unable to "look ahead" more than three or four moves. Yet a human grand master can play superlative chess, better than any computer program yet devised. How can this be? The answer is that human beings use problem-solving methods that perform *heuristic search*—rather than attempting the impossible task of examining all possible operator sequences, people consider only a small number of alternatives that seem most likely to yield a solution. Intelligent problem solving, in fact, consists largely of using methods for heuristic search. Some heuristic search methods are very general and can be applied to virtually any problem; others are much more specific and depend on detailed knowledge of a particular problem domain. As we will see, the development of expertise is largely the acquisition of knowledge that restricts the need for extensive search.

The efficacy of heuristic search depends in part on the nature of the problem to be solved. A major distinction is whether the *best possible* solution is required, or whether any reasonable solution that achieves the goal will suffice. Heuristic methods are seldom of much use in solving "best-solution" problems. An example is the notorious "traveling-salesman" problem. This problem involves taking the locations of a number of cities (say, ten) and trying to find the shortest possible route that passes through each of the cities exactly once. Due to combinatorial explosion, this problem has an enormous search space of possible routes once the number of cities grows at all large. No one has found a method other than "brute-force" search of all possible routes that guarantees finding the shortest route. However, if the goal is simply to find a route that is reasonably short by some criterion, heuristic search methods may be useful. Human problem solvers are particularly good at what Simon (1981) calls *satisficing*: finding reasonably good but not necessarily optimal solutions.

8.1.3 Means-Ends Analysis

Search for a problem solution can proceed in either of two directions: forward from the initial state to the goal state, or backward from the goal state to the initial state. Forward search involves applying operators to the current state to generate a new state; backward search involves finding operators that could produce the current state. Duncker observed both forward and backward search in his studies with the radiation problem. For example, a subject might first seek a free path to the stomach, and then realize that the esophagus could serve this function. This procedure would exemplify backward search from a goal to a way of achieving it. In contrast, other subjects seemed to make a relatively "planless" survey of the situation, thinking of various body parts associated with the stomach. In this process the solver might "stumble upon" the esophagus, and then search forward to find a possible way to put it to use in generating an attempted solution. In general, it is most efficient to search in whichever direction requires fewest choices at each decision point. For example, if there is only one way to reach the goal state, it may be easiest to work backward from the goal. (Rips, chapter 9, also distinguishes between forward and backward strategies.)

Newell and Simon (1972) suggested a small number of general heuristic search methods. One of the most important of these, *means-ends analysis*, involves a mixture of forward and backward search. The key idea underlying means-ends analysis is that search is guided by detection of differences between the current state and the goal state. Specifically, means-ends analysis involves these steps:

1. Compare the current state to the goal state and identify differences between the two. If there are none, the problem is solved; otherwise, proceed.
2. Select an operator that would reduce one of the differences.
3. If the operator can be applied, do so; if not, set a new *subgoal* of reaching a state at which the operator could be applied. Means-ends analysis is then applied to this new subgoal until the operator can be applied or the attempt to use it is abandoned.
4. Return to step 1.

Suppose, for example, that you have the goal of trying to paint your living room. The obvious difference between the current state and the goal state is that the room is unpainted. The operator "apply paint" could reduce this difference. However, to apply this operator you need to have paint and a brush. If these are lacking, you now set the subgoal of getting paint and brush. These could be found at a hardware store. Thus you set the subgoal of getting to a hardware store. And so on, until the conditions for applying the operator are met, and you can finally reduce the difference in the original problem.

Duncker observed the use of a form of means-ends analysis in his studies of the radiation problem. For example, a subject might first think of the possibility of desensitizing the healthy tissue. But how is this to be done? The person might then form the new subgoal of finding some chemical that could be used to alter the sensitivity of the tissue.

Means-ends analysis illustrates several important points about intelligent heuristic search. First, it is explicitly guided by knowledge of the goal. Second, an initial goal can lead to subsequent subgoals that effectively decompose the problem into smaller parts. Third, methods can be applied *recursively*; that is, in the course of applying a method to achieve a goal, the entire method may be applied to achieve a subgoal. Thus, in step 3 of means-ends analysis, the method may be reapplied to the subgoal of reaching a state in which a desirable operator is applicable.

8.1.4 Planning and Problem Decomposition

The idea that the process of problem solving is a kind of search suggests a separation between the initial *planning* of a solution and its actual *execution*. It is usually advantageous to perform at least a partial search by "looking ahead" for a solution before actually applying any operators. The obvious advantage of planning is that by anticipating the consequences of possible actions, one can avoid the unfortunate consequences of making overt errors. To the extent that errors are irreversible, or reversible only with difficulty, planning is especially important. A doctor would not attempt to treat a malignant tumor without careful planning. By imagining the consequences of actions prior to an overt solution attempt, one can identify dead ends without actually executing actions. In addition, planning provides information that can be used to monitor and learn from an overt solution attempt. By explicitly anticipating the consequences of applying operators, the problem solver generates expectations that can be compared to what actually happens when the operators are applied. If the actual effects of operators differ from their expected effects, this may trigger revision of the plan as well as revision of beliefs about what will happen in similar future applications of the relevant operators. Problem solving thus provides valuable information that can guide learning (Holland et al. 1986).

Planning often is combined with a process of *problem decomposition,* in which an overall problem is broken into parts, such that each part can be achieved separately. Suppose, for example, that you need to select a slate of officers to run a club. Rather than try to select people to fill the entire slate at once, it makes more sense to decompose this goal into several subgoals: select a president, a treasurer, and so on. Each of these subgoals defines a problem that can be attacked independently. Finding a solution to each subgoal will require fewer steps than solving the overall compound goal. Because search increases exponentially with the number of steps, solving all the subgoals, each of which requires a relatively small number of steps, is likely to require far less total search than would have been needed to solve the entire problem at once. Thus the sum of the steps required to solve the subgoals of selecting a good person to fill each of the officer positions, considered separately, is likely to be less than the number of steps that would be required to make an equally good selection of the entire slate, treating the task as a single undecomposed problem.

Unfortunately, realistic problems are seldom perfectly decomposable into parts that can be solved completely independently. For example, choices of officers for the various positions in a club interact in various ways. The same person cannot be both president and treasurer, and the various officers need to get along with each other—Sally might make a fine president and Joe a good treasurer, but if they dislike each other they would make a poor combination. But despite this lack of complete independence, total search may be minimized by first making some tentative decisions about each subgoal and then later working on integrating the components into a workable overall plan. That is, the problem solver can take advantage of the fact that some problems are *partially decomposable* (Simon 1981). This can best be done if foresight is used to form a coherent overall plan before actually beginning an overt solution attempt. Thus, before actually proposing a slate of officers, we could check for compatibility of the tentative list of choices and make corrections where needed. The general strategy is to first try to solve each subgoal independently, but to note constraints on how the individual decisions interact, and then to check that these constraints are satisfied before finalizing the overall solution attempt. Planning is thus particularly important in effectively reducing search for partially decomposable problems.

8.1.5 Production-System Models of Problem Solving

Newell and Simon's problem-space analysis is highly abstract and is potentially compatible with a variety of specific representations and algorithms. In practice, however, their approach has been closely tied to a particular type of formal model, the *production system* (Newell 1973, 1990). The central component of a production system is a set of *production rules* (also termed *condition-action rules*). A typical production rule might be

IF you have a paint roller
  and you have paint
  and you have a surface ready to paint
  and the surface is large
  and your goal is to paint the surface
THEN roll the paint onto the surface
  and expect the surface to be painted.

This rule represents the knowledge required for appropriate application of a problem-solving operator. The "then" portion of the rule specifies the action to be taken and the expected state change it will bring about; the "if" portion consists of a set of clauses describing when the operator could and should be invoked. Notice that the clauses in the condition of this rule are of two types. The first four describe *preconditions* that must be met before the operator can be applied—you need a roller before you can roll. The fifth clause specifies a *goal* for which the operator is useful—if you want to paint, consider using a roller. The goal restriction helps to limit search, because it means this rule will be considered only when the relevant goal has arisen.

A typical production system operates by cycling through these steps:

1. The conditions of rules are matched against the currently active contents of working memory (for instance, the representation of the current problem state) to identify those rules with conditions that are fully satisfied.
2. If more than one rule is matched, procedures for *conflict resolution* select one of the matched rules.
3. The selected rule is *fired*; that is, its action is taken.
4. Return to step 1.

Production-system models of problem solving have been extremely influential in the development of modern cognitive science. For example, Rips in chapter 9 shows how a production-system model of deduction can be used to account for many findings regarding human deductive reasoning. Within artificial intelligence such models have been used to develop expert systems that help perform such tasks as medical diagnosis and mineral exploration. In cognitive psychology, Anderson's ACT* model (1983) is predicated on the claim that human cognition is fundamentally a production system. The knowledge in a production system is encoded in a highly modular fashion. It is relatively easy to add new rules to the system without unduly disrupting the operation of the older rules. Production systems are therefore capable of modeling learning from problem-solving experience (Anderson 1983; Rosenbloom and Newell 1986).

8.1.6 The Brain and Problem Solving

Our discussion so far has focused on computational analyses (for example, the size of search spaces) and types of representations and processes (for example, production systems), rather than on evidence regarding the way problem solving is actually performed by the brain. As is the case for other major cognitive activities, however, it is valuable to consider the implications of neuropsychological evidence in characterizing the basic components of human problem solving. (See chapter 7 on working memory and chapter 1 on categorization.) We can attempt to understand the functional decomposition of problem-solving skills in terms of the functions of relatively localized brain areas, as has been done for language, vision, memory, and categorization.

This is not an easy task. Noninvasive imaging techniques are only beginning to be applied to the study of problem solving. Localization of functions is more often inferred either from lesion experiments with animals, which obviously differ radically from humans in their cognitive abilities, or from clinical studies of brain-damaged individuals, who seldom have injuries confined to a single clear anatomical region. Given its integrative nature, problem-solving ability is likely to be impaired to some degree whenever any major cognitive function, such as working memory, is disturbed. (See chapter 7.) It is therefore especially difficult to identify brain areas that are selectively implicated in problem solving or planning per se.

Nonetheless, there is some evidence that implicates the *frontal lobes* of the cerebral cortex as an area of special importance in problem solving (Stuss and Benson 1986). This large area at the front of the cortex appears to play a role in a broad range of cognitive and emotional responses. However, careful clinical observations and a few experimental studies have revealed some interesting selectivity in the deficits that result from damage to this area. Part of the selectivity concerns what is *not* seriously affected. People with frontal lesions typically are not intellectually impaired as measured by traditional IQ tests. In some cases they are able to function reasonably well in professions in which they were experienced prior to incurring the injury. Nonetheless, some major decrements in cognitive abilities can be identified. A major source of difficulty is novelty: frontal-lobe patients may be able to perform well-learned tasks using old information, yet have great difficulty solving new types of problems. As the great Russian psychologist A. R. Luria put it, "When intellectual operations demand the creation of a program of action and a choice between several equally probable alternatives, the intellectual activity of patients with a marked 'frontal syndrome' is profoundly disturbed" (1969, 749).

Based on an extensive review of the literature on the effects of frontal lesions, Stuss and Benson (1986, 222) suggested several classes of deficits. Frontal damage leads to deficits in the ordering or handling of sequential behaviors; impairment in establishing, maintaining, or changing a mental "set"; decreased ability to monitor personal behavior; dissociation of knowledge from the direction of action; and various changes in normal emotional and motivational responses. Each of these classes of deficits is linked to problem solving. The ability to plan and execute sequences of actions is, of course, essential. Establishing, changing, and maintaining a set requires the ability to selectively attend and respond to goal-relevant information. On a categorization task, frontal-lobe patients are likely to repeat errors despite corrective feedback and be unable to shift from one basis of classification to another. For example, a person who has learned to sort a set of objects by color will have great difficulty sorting by shape instead. (See Delis et al. 1992 for a careful analysis of the deficits observed in sorting performance by frontal patients.) Some of these impaired functions appear to involve working memory. (See chapter 7 for a discussion of the role of the frontal cortex in working memory.)

In addition, frontal patients have difficulty monitoring their own behavior. They may behave in socially unacceptable ways even though they appear to understand that their behavior is wrong. Similarly, they have trouble translating verbal instructions into appropriate actions. A patient may be told to return to work, may express a desire to return to work, and yet fail to do so. Finally, abnormal emotional responses and attitudes are revealed by failure to set goals or care about the future. The person appears to lack "drive" or "motivation."

Shallice (1982) conducted a study that specifically examined the manner in which frontal-lobe patients approach novel problems requiring planning and organized sequential action. He tested patients with various forms of brain damage, as well as control subjects, on their ability to solve various

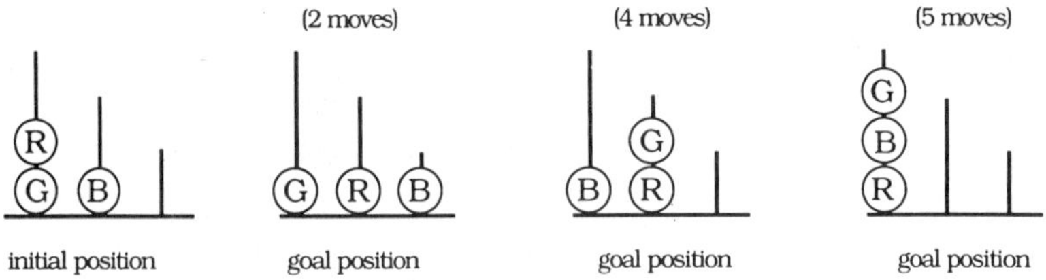

Figure 8.3
The "Tower of London" puzzle. The three goal states represent three levels of difficulty, given the initial state. From Shallice 1982.

versions of the "Tower of London" puzzle (see figure 8.3). This puzzle consists of three differently colored beads and three pegs of different lengths. The experimenter places the beads in a starting configuration, and the subject must then move them into a new configuration defined by the experimenter, in a minimum number of moves. (The related "Tower of Hanoi" puzzle is discussed in chapters 7 and 9.) The number of moves required to achieve the goal defines the level of difficulty. Although all the groups of brain-damaged subjects in Shallice's study were impaired in their performance relative to the control subjects, those with damage to the left frontal lobe showed the greatest decrement, particularly for the more difficult versions of the puzzle. The nature of the errors made by the frontal-lobe subjects indicated that they had difficulty in planning; they could not establish an appropriate order of subgoals. The deficit was not due to a general limitation of short-term memory, for variations in the patients' performance on a digit-span test could not account for the differences in problem-solving success.

More recent evidence suggests that we should be cautious in interpreting the findings above (see Shallice 1988). In particular, although the overall frontal deficit on the Tower of London task has been replicated (Owen et al. 1990), the selective effect of left-hemisphere damage has not been found in other experiments. However, the role of the frontal cortex in problem solving has been confirmed for another task—chess playing—using PET activation measures (Nichelli et al., 1994). When chess players are asked to decide whether it is possible to achieve checkmate in one move (a task requiring planning), brain activity was selectively increased in regions of both the left and the right frontal cortex. This same study found that several posterior regions of the brain, especially those associated with generation of visual images, also play significant roles in chess playing.

Stuss and Benson (1986) argue that the frontal lobes are crucial in *executive control* of cognition. The frontal-lobe syndrome in large part appears to involve a loss in ability to control cognitive processes: the ability to select and maintain goals, to plan sequential activities, to anticipate the consequences of actions, to monitor the effects of actions, and to revise plans on the basis of feedback. (See chapter 7 for a related discussion of executive processes.) These neuropsychological observations have several implications for theories of problem solving and planning, most of which are consistent with other evidence obtained with normal subjects. The crucial importance of selective attention and of the ability to organize sequential action would be expected on the basis of task analysis. The fact that the deficits are primarily observed when the patient faces novel problems suggests that expertise leads to a reduction in the requirements for executive control. The gap between verbal knowledge and action is consistent with the claim that developing skill in solving new problems involves a process of *proceduralization*: translating verbal knowledge into procedures, perhaps encoded as production rules (Anderson 1983). It appears that proceduralization is impaired by frontal-lobe damage.

The motivational component of the syndrome emphasizes the significance of an aspect of problem solving that is often neglected in computational approaches to problem solving. Unless the organism cares about the future, there is no clear basis for establishing or maintaining goals; and without goals, problem solving simply disintegrates.

8.2 Development of Expertise

Our survey of the nature of problem solving has raised a number of issues that an adequate theory must explain: namely, how goals are formed; how heuristic methods develop; how problems can be decomposed; and how planning is conducted. In addition, a theory must explain how learning takes place during problem solving, and how knowledge acquired in one problem situation is transferred to another. Many of these issues are related to central questions that have been addressed by research on problem solving. How does a novice problem solver become an expert? What makes expert problem solvers better than novices? Clearly, experts in a domain have had more training and practice than have novices, but what exactly is it that experts have learned? Have they learned how to reason better in general, or perhaps to become more skilled in applying heuristic search methods, such as means-ends analysis? Let us look at two domains in which a considerable amount of research has examined differences in the problem-solving methods of experts and novices: playing chess and solving textbook physics problems.

8.2.1 Expertise in Chess

The pioneering work on expertise in chess playing was reported by De Groot (1965). In order to determine what makes a master chess player better than a weaker player, De Groot had some of the best chess players in the world "think out loud" as they selected chess moves. By analyzing these problem-solving protocols—transcripts of what the players said as they reached a decision—De Groot was able to observe some distinct differences in the ways in which masters and novices selected moves.

His results did not support any of the obvious hypotheses about the masters having superior general reasoning ability or greater proficiency in means-ends analysis. Nor was it that the masters performed more extensive search through the vast space of alternative possible moves. In fact, if anything the masters considered fewer alternative moves than did the weaker players. However, the master players spent their time considering relatively good moves, whereas the weaker players spent more time exploring bad moves. It appeared that the masters were able to exploit knowledge that led them very quickly to consider the best moves possible, without extensive search.

The most striking difference between the two classes of players was observed in a test of their perceptual and memory abilities. Chase and Simon (1973) extended De Groot's results. In the test the player saw a chess position, drawn from the middle portion of an actual chess game, which was presented for just 5 seconds. An example board position is depicted in figure 8.4a. After the board was removed, the player was asked to reconstruct it from memory. In Chase and Simon's experiment the subject was either an expert master player (M), a very good class A player (A), or a beginning player (B). The number of pieces correctly recalled over seven trials by each player is depicted in figure 8.5a. The results showed that the greater the expertise of the player, the more accurately the board was recalled.

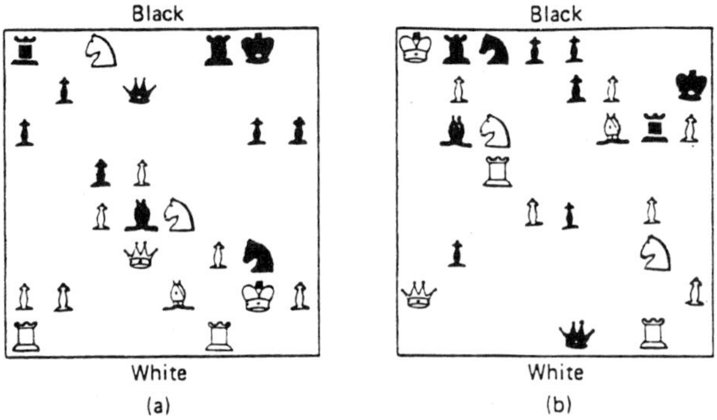

Figure 8.4
Examples of chess configurations: (a) real middle game; (b) random counterpart. From Chase and Simon 1973.

One might suppose that this result indicates that master chess players have particularly good memories. However, this is not generally the case. To assess this possibility, Chase and Simon also performed the test using random board positions such as the one illustrated in figure 8.4b. As the results shown in figure 8.5b indicate, the master player's advantage was entirely eliminated in this condition.

On the basis of these and other related findings, Chase and Simon argued that master players have learned to recognize large, meaningful perceptual units corresponding to board configurations that tend to recur in real chess games. These units are stored as unitary *chunks* in long-term memory. Such chunks can be used to encode quickly and accurately the configuration of a novel but realistic board. They are useless, however, in encoding random positions, in which meaningful patterns are unlikely to occur. Chunks also serve as the conditions of production rules that suggest good moves. These rules would have the form, "IF Pattern P is present on the board, THEN consider Move M." Such specific rules would direct the master player quite directly to the relatively small number of alternative moves that are serious candidates, without having to search through large numbers of highly implausible possibilities. It seems likely that the development of specialized rules that are cued by perceptual units contributes to the acquisition of expertise in many domains other than playing board games.

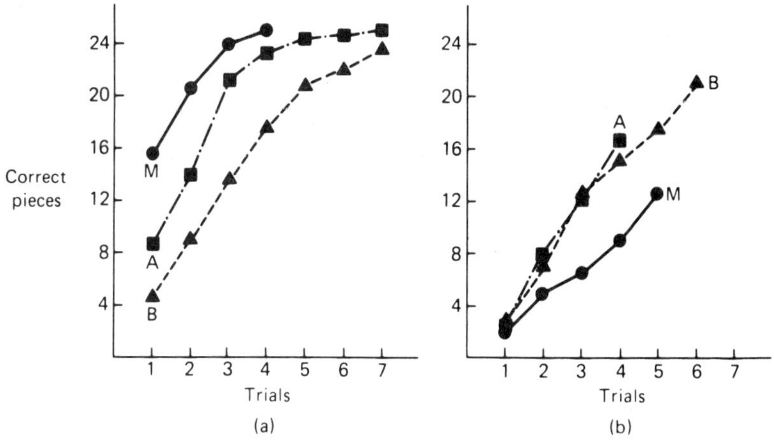

Figure 8.5
Number of pieces recalled correctly by master (M), class A player (A), and beginner (B) over trials: (a) for actual board positions; (b) for random board positions. From Chase and Simon 1973.

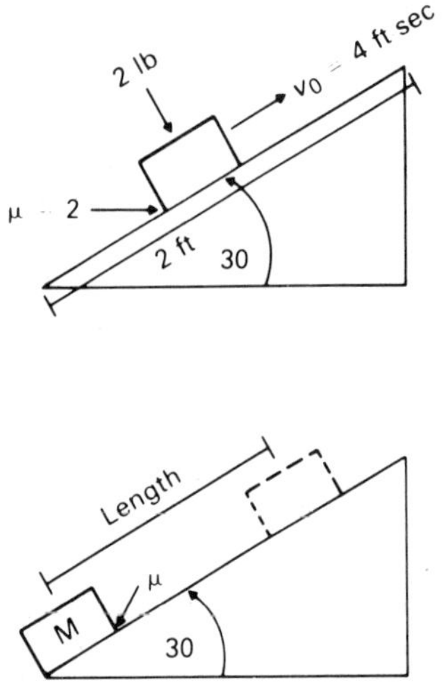

Novice 1: "These deal with blocks on an incline plane."
Novice 2: "Inclined plane problems, coefficient of friction."
Novice 3: "Blocks on inclined planes with angles."

Figure 8.6
Diagrams of two problems categorized together by novices, and samples of explanations given. From Chi, Feltovich, and Glaser 1981.

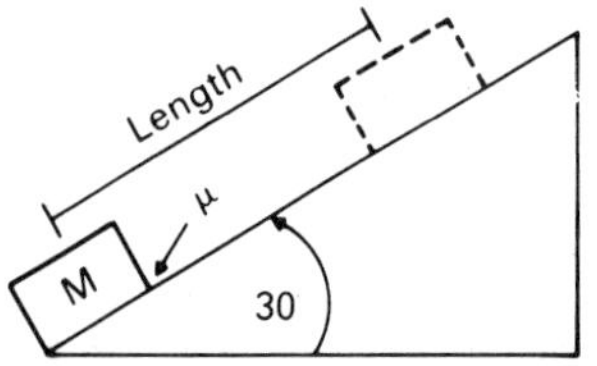

Expert 1: "Conservation of energy."
Expert 2. "Work-energy theorem: They are all straightforward problems.
Expert 3: "These can be done from energy considerations. Either you should know the principle of conservation of energy, or work is lost somewhere."

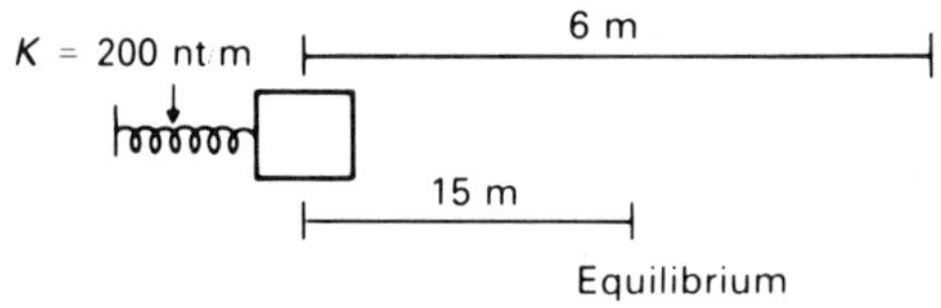

Figure 8.7
Diagrams of two problems categorized together by experts, and samples of explanations given. From Chi, Feltovich, and Glaser 1981.

8.2.2 Expertise in Physics

The conclusions derived from studies of chess have been confirmed and extended by work on expert–novice differences in solving physics problems. A study by Chi, Feltovich, and Glaser (1981) provided especially interesting results. These investigators asked experts and novices to sort physics problems into clusters on the basis of similarity. Novices tended to base their sortings on relatively superficial features of the problem statements. (See chapter 1 for a discussion of the role of perceptual similarity in categorization.) For example, figure 8.6 depicts the diagrams for two problems that were often grouped together by novices. A glance at the diagrams associated with each problem indicates that they look very similar; the novices explained that both are "inclined-planes" problems. In fact, although both of these problems involve inclined planes, very different procedures are required to solve them. By contrast, figure 8.7 shows two problem diagrams that experts classified as belonging together. These look very different; however, the experts explained that both problems can be solved by the law of "conservation of energy."

In general, the work of Chi, Feltovich, and Glaser (1981) and others indicates that experts have learned *schemas* for identifying important categories of problems. Problem schemas represent complex categories that are defined in part by patterns of relations between problem elements, rather than by the specific elements (such as inclined planes) themselves. Problem schemas in physics are based on more abstract relations than those included in the perceptual chunks available to the chess master; but like perceptual chunks, abstract problem schemas function to vastly reduce the amount of search required to find appropriate solutions. In general, expertise in problem solving is in large part the result of the development of sophisticated mental representations for categorizing problems in the domain.

8.2.3 How Does Expertise Develop?

Research comparing the performance of expert and novice problem solvers tells us a great deal about how to characterize the differences in the knowledge used by people at different skill levels; however, it tells us less about how an initially unskilled problem solver can eventually become an expert. A number of theoretical efforts have, however, attempted to describe learning mechanisms that might allow some combination of direct problem-solving experience, instruction, and exposure to solved examples —the obvious types of environmental inputs available to the learner—to produce increased expertise. (See also the discussion of knowledge reorganization in chapter 4.)

Most models of learning have assumed a production-system representation for procedural knowledge; accordingly, learning is mainly treated as the acquisition of new production rules. The general idea is that by inspecting the results of a solution attempt, learning mechanisms can encode important regularities into new rules. For example, Larkin (1981) has developed a computer simulation that can learn to solve physics problems more efficiently. The program starts by using means-ends analysis to find unknown quantities by using equations. For example, to find the value of acceleration, a, it might use the equation $V_f = V_i + at$ (final velocity equals initial velocity plus acceleration times time). The learning mechanism could then form a new production rule that checks to see whether V_i, V_f, and t are known (the condition), and if so asserts that a can be found (the action). This new rule will then eliminate the need to apply means-ends analysis to solve future problems with this form. The result of this learning mechanism is a shift from a novice strategy of working backward from the goal, using means-ends analysis and subgoaling, to a more expert strategy of working forward from the givens to the unknown goal quantity. Protocol studies with human experts and novices in physics have found evidence for such a shift from backward to forward search (Larkin et al. 1980).

This type of change in strategy may not always result from forming new rules based on solutions initially found by means-ends analysis. In fact, Sweller, Mawer, and Ward (1983) found that use of a means-ends strategy can actually impair acquisition of expertise in solving mathematics problems. They argue that means-ends analysis focuses attention on the specific features of the problem situation required to reach the stated goal, reducing the degree to which other important aspects of problem structure are learned. Sweller et al. found that a forward-search strategy developed more rapidly when learners were encouraged to explore the problem statements more broadly, simply calculating as many variables as possible. They suggested that less directed exploration of the problems facilitated acquisition of useful problem schemas.

In addition to acquiring new rules and schemas, expertise may be improved by combining old rules in more efficient ways. For example, if two rules apply one after another, it may be possible to construct a single rule that combines the effects of both. This process is termed *composition* (Anderson 1983; Lewis 1978). As mentioned earlier, Anderson (1983, 1987) also stresses the role of a process of *proceduralization,* which uses very general productions for following verbal instructions to construct more specific productions to execute a solution procedure.

Finally, learning mechanisms can also make use of solved examples that are provided to illustrate solution procedures. Learners can use examples when they are first presented to actively construct useful rules and schemas. Chi et al. (1989) have found that good and poor learners use solved examples of physics problems in radically different ways. Good learners generate inferences that serve to explain why the examples can be solved in the illustrated manner, whereas poor learners encode them in a much more passive manner (for instance, they fail to ask questions while studying the examples). The development of expertise clearly depends not only on the nature of environmental inputs provided to problem solvers but also on the learning skills they bring to the task.

8.3 Restructuring and Parallelism in Problem Solving

8.3.1 Ill-Defined Problems

The search metaphor for problem solving, as elaborated into formal models by Newell and Simon and others, has clearly been extremely useful in understanding human problem solving. However, neither the metaphor nor the models derived from it capture the full richness of the mental processes that underlie problem-solving skill. The search perspective seems most appropriate when the problem solver has a clear goal, understands the initial state and constraints, and knows exactly what operators might be useful. Given an appropriate method, finding a solution is then indeed a search through a well-defined space of possibilities; if a solution path exists, it will eventually be found by patiently "grinding it out."

Many of the most difficult problems that beset us, however, have a very different quality. For example, if your goal is to find a career that will bring you happiness, it may be very difficult to specify the state from which you are starting, the operators that might be applicable, or even to recognize when your goal has been achieved. Reitman (1964) observed that many problems are *ill defined* in that the representations of one or more of the basic components—the goal, initial state, operators, and constraints—are seriously incomplete. Ill-defined problems are usually hard, and not simply because the search space is large. Indeed, many ill-defined problems seem difficult, not because we are swamped by the task of searching through an enormous number of alternative possibilities, but because we have trouble thinking of even one idea worth pursuing.

Duncker's radiation problem is in some ways quite ill defined. Very few subjects suggest the idea of irradiating the tumor from multiple directions simultaneously with low-intensity rays, focusing the rays so that the tumor receives a higher dosage than does the surrounding healthy tissue. Yet most people will agree that this is a rather good solution to the problem, once it is pointed out to them. To actually discover the solution, however, usually requires more than dogged search, because the operator "create multiple ray sources" is unlikely to even be considered. In fact, Duncker found that the sketch he usually provided to his subjects (figure 8.1) actually impeded discovery of the idea of using multiple rays, for the diagram shows only a single ray source. In this case the solution can be achieved only by first inventing a new operator.

8.3.2 Restructuring, Insight, and Analogies

To understand how ill-defined problems can be solved, it is useful again to look at everyday language. We speak of "looking at the problem in a new light," having the solution "just pop out," and realizing the answer was "staring me in the face all along." These metaphors suggest that a solution may not always be reached by a gradual serial-search process; rather, it may be achieved suddenly as the result of "seeing" the problem differently. The notion that problem solving shares certain important properties with perception was a major theme of the Gestalt psychologists such as Duncker (1945) and Maier (1930), who proposed that solutions sometimes require insight based on a restructuring of the problem representation. People do not always simply establish a representation of a problem and then perform search; rather, they sometimes change their representations in major ways. Although Newell and Simon's treatment of search and means-ends analysis was foreshadowed by Duncker's ideas, the Gestalt emphasis on the importance of restructuring has been less prominent in their theory (see Newell 1985).

There has been very little firm experimental evidence to support the notion that some problems are solved by restructuring and sudden insight. However, work by Metcalfe (1986a,b; Metcalfe and Wiebe 1987) has established several criteria that distinguish the process of solving "insight" problems from the process of solving "routine" problems. Her experiments compared people's performance in predicting their own ability to solve algebra problems (routine) versus a variety of insight problems, such as this:

> A landscape gardener is given instructions to plant four special trees so that each one is exactly the same distance from each of the others. How could the trees be arranged?[1]

One major distinction involved subjects' ability to predict whether they would eventually be able to solve the problem, for those problems they could not solve immediately. For algebra problems, subjects' "feelings of knowing" accurately predicted their eventual success; that is, people were able to tell which algebra problems they would be able to solve if they tried, and which would prove intractable. In contrast, subjects were completely unable to predict which insight problems they would be able to solve (Metcalfe 1986b).

A second major distinction was apparent in a measure of subjects' changes in expectations during problem solving. Metcalfe and Wiebe (1987) had subjects rate how "warm" they felt as they worked on each problem: that is, how close they believed they were to finding a solution. If people were using means-ends analysis, or any heuristic-search method involving a comparison of the current state and the goal state, they should

1. The gardener could build a hill, plant one tree at the top, and plant three others in an equilateral triangle around the base of the hill. Assuming the hill is built to the appropriate height, the four trees will form a tetrahedron in which each of the four corners is equidistant from every other corner.

be able to report getting "warmer" as they approached the goal (because they would know that the difference between the current state and the goal was being progressively reduced). On the other hand, if a solution was discovered on the basis of a rapid restructuring of the problem, the problem solver would not be able to report increased warmth prior to the insight.

Figure 8.8 depicts the striking difference that emerged between the patterns of warmth ratings obtained for insight and for algebra problems. Each of the histograms in the figure shows the distribution of subjects' warmth ratings at a particular time prior to achieving a solution. A rating of 1 indicates least warmth (feeling nowhere close to a solution), whereas a rating of 7 indicates maximal warmth (the problem seems virtually solved). The histograms in each column are ordered in time from bottom to top, from 60 seconds prior to the solution to the time a solution was actually found. For the algebra problems (right-hand column), the ratings shift gradually to the right of the histogram as the time of solution approaches, indicating that subjects accurately reported getting warmer and warmer as they neared a solution. For the insight problems (left-hand column), the results are utterly different. The ratings do not shift as the time of solution approaches. Rather, most subjects rate themselves as "cold" until they suddenly solve the problem, at which time their rating jumps from maximally cold to maximally warm.

Metcalfe's results thus provide empirical evidence that insight is a real psychological phenomenon. For a problem that requires insight, people are unable to assess how likely they are to solve it, either in advance of working on the problem or as they actually are working on it. If they eventually succeed in finding a solution, they are genuinely surprised.

Although restructuring and insight do play a role in problem solving, we are far from a full understanding of the mechanisms involved. In some cases restructuring may be triggered by finding an *analogy* between the target problem at hand and some other situation (the *source* analog) from a very different domain. For example, Gick and Holyoak (1980, 1983) performed a series of experiments in which subjects first read a story about a general who wished to conquer a fortress located in the middle of a country. Many roads radiated out from the fortress, but these were mined so that although small groups of men could pass over them safely, any large group would detonate the mines. Yet the general needed to get his entire army to the fortress to capture it. He accomplished this by dividing his men into small groups, dispatching each to the head of a different road, and having all the groups converge simultaneously on the fortress.

Does this story remind you of any of the problems we have discussed? It is, of course, an analog to Duncker's radiation problem. When college students were asked to use the fortress problem to help solve the radiation

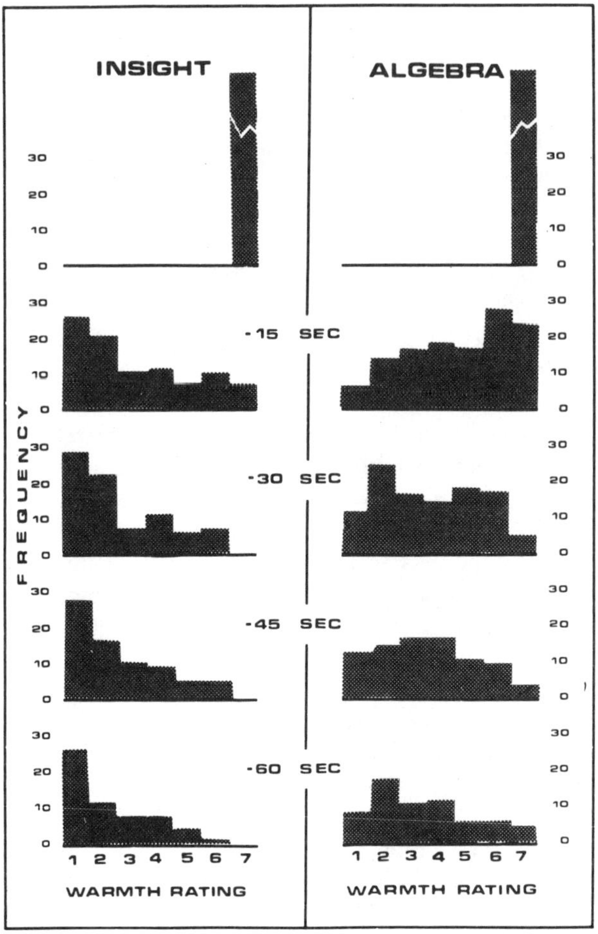

Figure 8.8
Frequency histograms of warmth ratings for correctly solved insight and algebra problems. The panels, from bottom to top, give the ratings 60, 45, 30, and 15 seconds before solution. As shown in the top panel, a 7 rating was always given at the time of solution. From Metcalfe and Wiebe 1987.

problem, most of them came up with the idea of using converging low-intensity rays. In the absence of the source analog, very few subjects tested by either Duncker or by Gick and Holyoak proposed this variation of the "reduced-intensity" type of solution. Providing the analogy allowed subjects to restructure their representation of the target problem so that the operator of creating multiple ray sources was constructed and used. (Of course, analogies may also be used to help solve problems that do not require restructuring.)

How can a useful analogy be found? It is often difficult. Gick and Holyoak found that many subjects would fail to notice on their own that the fortress story was relevant to solving the radiation problem even when the analogs were presented in immediate succession. Accessing a source analog from a different domain than the target is yet more difficult when the source has been encoded into memory in a different context (Spencer and Weisberg 1986). In the absence of guidance from a teacher, analogical access requires that elements of the target problem must serve as retrieval cues, which will activate other related situations as the result of activation spreading through semantic memory along the paths that link similar concepts. The greater the similarity of the elements of the two analogs, the more likely it is that the source will be retrieved (Holyoak and Koh 1987).

Of course, there is no guarantee that a source analog will help rather than hinder solving the target problem. For example, Duncker suggested that people may sometimes be misled by a false analogy to the radiation problem: seeing the rays as analogous to a syringe that produces an injection only after the needle is inserted. This source analog might suggest that the rays could be turned on at full strength only *after* they had reached the tumor. But of course, the intensity of rays cannot be altered once they have been emitted by the ray source. Analogy can provide ideas about how to solve a novel problem, but these ideas are only plausible conjectures, not firm deductions.

8.3.3 Parallel Constraint Satisfaction

One of the hallmarks of Newell and Simon's approach to problem solving is an emphasis on the serial nature of the solution process. A problem is typically decomposed into subproblems; then each subgoal is solved, one by one. For any particular subgoal, alternative operators are tried sequentially in the search for a solution path. Parallel processing is certainly not entirely excluded; in particular, the process of matching the current problem state against the conditions of production rules is typically assumed to be performed in parallel. Nonetheless, the serial aspects of the solution process are theoretically most central.

The notion of restructuring, in contrast, suggests that parallel (and largely unconscious) information processing may have a major impact on problem solving. The role of spreading activation in the retrieval of potential source analogs is one example of how parallel access to information stored in long-term memory may redirect conscious problem solving. It is also possible that the way in which active information is used to construct a solution may sometimes involve parallel integration of knowledge rather than strictly sequential processing. Indeed, this is the intuition that appears to have led the Gestalt psychologists to claim that problem solving was similar to perception. The following quotation from Maier (1930, 116) illustrates this connection (as well as the notorious vagueness that left Gestalt theories of problem solving in ill repute):

> First one has one or no gestalt, then suddenly a new or different gestalt is formed out of the old elements. The sudden appearance of the new gestalt, that is, the solution, is the process of reasoning. How and why it comes is not explained. It is like perception: certain elements which one minute are one unity suddenly become an altogether different unity.

One of the major advances of modern cognitive science has been to build much more explicit models of how parallel processes are used in perception; consequently, we can now begin to delve more deeply into what it might mean for problem solving to have the perceptionlike quality that a unified interpretation of an input typically emerges from parallel integration of information at an unconscious level. A key idea is the concept of *parallel constraint satisfaction,* which is illustrated in the work of Marr and Poggio (1976) on vision, and described in more general terms by Rumelhart et al. (1986).

The idea of finding a solution that satisfies the constraints of the problem is, of course, familiar by now. For example, in section 8.1.4 we looked at the problem of selecting a slate of officers, in which it is necessary to consider interactions between the decisions about each position (for instance, the person selected as president must get along with the treasurer). We saw that the overall problem of choosing a slate can be decomposed into the subproblems of filling each position. These subproblems can be solved separately, with a subsequent check to make sure no interactive constraints are violated. This form of constraint satisfaction is not inherently parallel.

Sometimes, however, the interactive constraints are so pervasive that it is not feasible to solve each subgoal separately and only then check that all constraints are satisfied. In addition, satisfying a constraint is not always an all-or-nothing matter. For example, a possible president-treasurer pair may be compatible to some degree; if each person is individually an excellent choice for the position, the pair may be satisfactory despite some interpersonal tension. When the solution of each subgoal depends in a major way

Figure 8.9
The top word has a clear interpretation even though each of its constituent letters is ambiguous, as illustrated by the three lower words. From McClelland, Rumelhart, and Hinton 1986.

on the solution of other subgoals, and the best solution requires trade-offs between competing constraints, it is most efficient to solve all the subgoals incrementally in parallel, allowing information about the results accruing in each subproblem to affect the emerging decisions about the other subproblems. The problem can still be decomposed, but the solution process is interactive.

Figure 8.9 depicts a striking perceptual example of when parallel constraint satisfaction is important. If our problem is to recognize a word, search can be sharply reduced if the problem is decomposed into the subproblems of recognizing each constituent letter. But as figure 8.9 illustrates, the subgoals of identifying the individual letters cannot always be solved independently. You probably recognize the top word in the figure as RED, even though each of the letters is partially obscured. In fact, as the other three words in the figure show, each letter in RED is ambiguous: the R could be a P, the E could be an F, and the D could be a B. Clearly, our interpretation of each individual letter is affected by the interpretations we give the others.

At first glance, the recognition of RED in figure 8.9 seems to create a paradoxical "chicken-and-egg" problem: you need to identify the letters to recognize the word, but you need to identify the word to recognize the letters. This recognition problem can, however, be solved by parallel constraint satisfaction (McClelland et al. 1986). Each subgoal of identifying a letter is influenced not only by the constraints provided by the visual input at that position but also by the constraints imposed by the surrounding letters. The solution process is highly interactive, with information about possible letters at each position being integrated to form the optimal "gestalt."

Although it is clear that perception involves parallel constraint satisfaction, we need to consider whether similar processes might be involved in higher-level problem solving. Is there any reason, beyond Gestalt intuitions, to suppose that parallel constraint satisfaction also plays a role in the kinds of restructuring we discussed earlier? In fact, there is. One clear possibility arises in the process of solving a target problem by analogy, as discussed earlier. For example, how could a person make use of the fortress problem to help solve the radiation problem? Clearly, part of the person's task will be to find the best *mapping,* or set of correspondences, between the elements of the source and target. That is, the person must realize that the general's goal of capturing the fortress corresponds to the doctor's goal of destroying the tumor and that the army's ability to do the capturing is like the rays' capacity to destroy. How can this mapping be established? The problem of finding the best overall mapping can be decomposed into the subproblems of finding the best mapping for each of the constituent elements (just as the problem of word recognition can be decomposed into the subproblems of identifying the constituent letters). But as in the perceptual example in figure 8.9, the subgoals of mapping elements cannot be accomplished in isolation. Why, for example, should we map the fortress onto the tumor, rather than, say, onto the rays? After all, neither pair is highly similar in meaning.

Holyoak and Thagard (1989) have proposed a model of how analogical mappings can be constructed by parallel constraint satisfaction. The basic idea is simple, as illustrated in figure 8.10. The nodes in this figure represent some possible mappings between elements of the radiation and fortress problems, and the arrows represent positive and negative relations between possible decisions. One major constraint on analogical mappings is that each pair of mapped elements in the source and target should play consistent roles. This constraint is termed *structural consistency* (Falkenhainer, Forbus, and Gentner 1989). Suppose, for example, that "capturing" maps onto "destroying." If the analogy is structurally consistent, then the capturer in the fortress problem would have to map onto the destroyer in the radiation problem ("army = rays"), and the object of capturing would map onto the object of destruction ("fortress = tumor"). In fact, as illustrated in figure 8.10, the intuitively correct mappings between elements in the two problems form a mutually consistent set and hence support each other.

A closely related constraint on mapping is that the mapping should be *one to one:* if an element of one analog maps onto a particular element in the other analog, it probably doesn't also map onto a different element. Thus, the mapping "fortress = tumor" contradicts "fortress = rays" (as

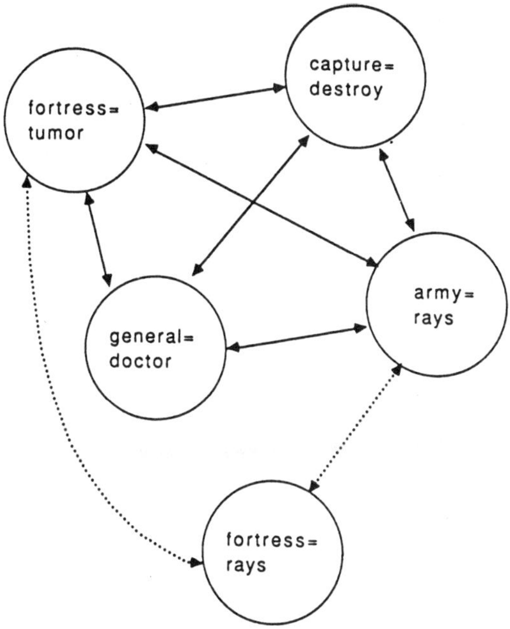

Figure 8.10
A simplified constraint-satisfaction network for finding an analogical mapping between elements of the "fortress" and "radiation" problems.

does "army = rays"). The structurally consistent mappings thus not only support each other but tend to discredit alternative mappings as well. Holyoak and Thagard found that a constraint-satisfaction model of analogical mapping provided a good account of a wide range of data regarding when people find the mapping process easy or difficult. Although many hurdles remain, there is reason to hope that work in cognitive science is beginning to establish a firmer basis for the Gestalt intuition that human perception and thinking have a fundamental unity.

Suggestions for Further Reading

A number of books can be explored for more detailed discussions of aspects of problem solving. Newell and Simon (1972) is a classic, but difficult. Ginsberg (1993) provides a good introduction to artificial intelligence that includes a discussion of problem solving and search. The most highly developed production-system models of cognition are ACT* (Anderson 1983) and SOAR (Newell 1990); both of these books include chapters on learning in the context of problem solving. Klahr, Langley, and Neches (1987) is a collection of papers on learning within production systems, and Michalski, Carbonell, and Mitchell (1983, 1986) are two volumes of papers on machine learning, several of which involve problem solving. A thorough treatment of the analysis of verbal protocols as a method of studying problem solving is provided in Ericsson and Simon (1984). Ericsson and Smith (1991) have edited a book with chapters on expertise in many domains, including chess and physics.

A detailed survey of frontal-lobe functions is provided in Stuss and Benson (1986). Polya (1957) and Wickelgren (1974) discuss useful problem-solving heuristics in an informal manner. A discussion of relations among learning, categorization, analogy, and problem solving is contained in Holland et al. (1986). The Gestalt notion of restructuring is articulated in Duncker (1945). Holyoak and Thagard (1995) provide a general discussion of the role of analogy in thinking. There are many books on creative thinking; among the best is that of Boden (1992). The papers cited in section 8.3.3 can be consulted for a general introduction to parallel constraint satisfaction.

Problems

8.1 Can you think of any way in which means-ends analysis might lead a problem solver away from the goal in some situations?

8.2 How does problem decomposition reduce the size of the search space?

8.3 What qualities make a problem suitable for solution by parallel constraint satisfaction?

8.4 A robot in an office can perform a small number of actions: it can PUSH an object, PICK-UP an object, CARRY an object, PUT-DOWN an object, or WALK by itself. It can PICK-UP an object only if that object has nothing else on it and if its own arm is empty. It can PUSH an object even if that object has something else on it.

a. Write a production rule appropriate for using the operator PICK-UP. Include relevant preconditions and a goal.

b. Suppose the robot is in room B and a table with a typewriter on it is in room A. The robot is instructed to move the table into room B. List the subgoals that would be established by means-ends analysis in the course of solving this problem, using the fewest possible operators.

8.5 A problem can be solved in five steps. At each step any one of ten operators can be applied. How many possible paths are there in the search space?

Questions for Further Thought

8.1 Does research on expertise provide any useful suggestions about how best to teach novices?

8.2 What defines an "insight" problem?

References

Anderson, J. R. (1983). *The architecture of cognition.* Cambridge, MA: Harvard University Press.

Anderson, J. R. (1987). Skill acquisition: Compilation of weak-method problem solutions. *Psychological Review* 94, 192–210.

Boden, M. A. (1992). *The creative mind: Myths and mechanisms.* New York: Basic Books.

Chase, W. G., and H. A. Simon (1973). The mind's eye in chess. In W. G. Chase, ed., *Visual information processing*. New York: Academic Press.

Chi, M. T. H., M. Bassok, M. Lewis, P. Reimann, and R. Glaser (1989). Self-explanations: How students study and use examples in learning to solve problems. *Cognitive Science* 13, 145–182.

Chi, M. T. H., P. J. Feltovich, and R. Glaser (1981). Categorization and representation of physics problems by experts and novices. *Cognitive Science* 5, 121–152.

De Groot, A. D. (1965). *Thought and choice in chess.* The Hague: Mouton.

Delis, D. C., L. L. Squire, A. Bihrle, and P. Massman (1992). Componential analysis of problem-solving ability: Performance of patients with frontal lobe damage and amnesic patients on a new sorting task. *Neuropsychologia* 30, 683–697.

Duncker, K. (1945). On problem solving. *Psychological Monographs* 58 (Whole No. 270).

Ericsson, K. A., and H. A. Simon (1984). *Protocol analysis: Verbal reports as data.* Cambridge, MA: MIT Press.

Ericsson, K. A., and J. Smith (1991). *Toward a general theory of expertise: Prospects and limits.* Cambridge: Cambridge University Press.

Falkenhainer, B., K. D. Forbus, and D. Gentner (1989). The structure-mapping engine: Algorithm and examples. *Artificial Intelligence* 41, 1–63.

Gick, M. L., and K. J. Holyoak (1980). Analogical problem solving. *Cognitive Psychology* 12, 306–355.

Gick, M. L., and K. J. Holyoak (1983). Schema induction and analogical transfer. *Cognitive Psychology* 15, 1–38.

Ginsberg, M. (1993). *Essentials of artificial intelligence.* San Mateo, CA: Kaufmann.

Holland, J. H., K. J. Holyoak, R. E. Nisbett, and P. R. Thagard (1986). *Induction: Processes of inference, learning, and discovery.* Cambridge, MA: MIT Press.

Holyoak, K. J., and K. Koh (1987). Surface and structural similarity in analogical transfer. *Memory and Cognition* 15, 332–340.

Holyoak, K. J., and P. Thagard (1989). Analogical mapping by constraint satisfaction. *Cognitive Science* 13, 295–355.

Holyoak, K. J., and P. Thagard (1995). *Mental leaps: Analogy in creative thought.* Cambridge, MA: MIT Press.

Klahr, D., P. Langley, and R. Neches, eds. (1987). *Production system models of learning and development.* Cambridge, MA: MIT Press.

Lakoff, G., and M. Turner (1989). *More than cool reason: The power of poetic metaphor.* Chicago: University of Chicago Press.

Larkin, J. H. (1981). Enriching formal knowledge: A model for learning to solve textbook physics problems. In J. R. Anderson, ed., *Cognitive skills and their acquisition.* Hillsdale, NJ: L. Erlbaum Associates.

Larkin, J. H., J. McDermott, D. P. Simon, and H. A. Simon (1980). Expert and novice performance in solving physics problems. *Science* 208, 1335–1342.

Lewis, C. H. (1978). Production system models of practice effects. Doctoral dissertation, University of Michigan, Ann Arbor.

Luria, A. R. (1969). Frontal lobe syndromes. In P. J. Vinken and G. W. Bruyn, eds., *Handbook of clinical neurology,* vol. 2. Amsterdam: North Holland.

McClelland, J. L., D. E. Rumelhart, and G. E. Hinton (1986). The appeal of parallel distributed processing. In D. E. Rumelhart, J. L. McClelland, and the PDP Research Group, *Parallel distributed processing: Explorations in the microstructure of cognition. Vol. 1: Foundations.* Cambridge, MA: MIT Press.

Maier, N. R. F. (1930). Reasoning in humans. 1. On direction. *Journal of Comparative Psychology* 10, 115–143.

Marr, D., and T. Poggio (1976). Cooperative computation of stereo disparity. *Science* 194, 283–287.

Metcalfe, J. (1986a). Feeling of knowing in memory and problem solving. *Journal of Experimental Psychology: Learning, Memory, and Cognition* 12, 288–294.

Metcalfe, J. (1986b). Premonitions of insight predict impending error. *Journal of Experimental Psychology: Learning, Memory, and Cognition* 12, 623–634.

Metcalfe, J., and D. Wiebe (1987). Intuition in insight and noninsight problem solving. *Memory and Cognition* 15, 238–246.

Michalski, R., J. G. Carbonell, and T. M. Mitchell, eds. (1983). *Machine learning: An artificial intelligence approach.* Palo Alto, CA: Tioga Press.

Michalski, R., J. G. Carbonell, and T. M. Mitchell, eds. (1986). *Machine learning: An artificial intelligence approach,* vol. 2. Los Altos, CA: Kaufmann.
Newell, A. (1973). Production systems: Models of control structures. In W. G. Chase, ed., *Visual information processing.* New York: Academic Press.
Newell, A. (1985). Duncker on thinking: An inquiry into progress in cognition. In S. Koch and D. Leary, eds., *A century of psychology as science.* New York: McGraw-Hill.
Newell, A. (1990). *Unified theories of cognition.* Cambridge, MA: Harvard University Press.
Newell, A., and H. A. Simon (1972). *Human problem solving.* Englewood Cliffs, NJ: Prentice-Hall.
Nichelli, P., J. Grafman, P. Pietrini, D. Alway, J. C. Carton, and R. Miletich (1994). Brain activity in chess playing. *Nature* 369, 191.
Owen, A. M., J. J. Downes, B. J. Sahakian, C. E. Polkey, and T. W. Robbins (1990). Planning and spatial working memory following frontal lobe lesions in man. *Neuropsychologia* 28, 1021–1034.
Polya, G. (1957). *How to solve it.* Garden City, NY: Doubleday/Anchor.
Reitman, W. (1964). Heuristic decision procedures, open constraints, and the structure of ill-defined problems. In W. Shelley and G. L. Bryan, eds., *Human judgments and optimality.* New York: Wiley.
Rosenbloom, P. S., and A. Newell (1986). The chunking of goal hierarchies: A generalized model of practice. In Michalski, Carbonell, and Mitchell (1986).
Rumelhart, D. E., P. Smolensky, J. L. McClelland, and G. E. Hinton (1986). Schemata and sequential thought processes in PDP models. In J. L. McClelland, D. E. Rumelhart, and the PDP Research Group, *Parallel distributed processing: Explorations in the microstructure of cognition. Vol. 2: Psychological and biological models.* Cambridge, MA: MIT Press.
Shallice, T. (1982). Specific impairment of planning. In D. E. Broadbent and L. Weiskrantz, eds., *The neuropsychology of cognitive function.* London: The Royal Society.
Shallice, T. (1988). *From neuropsychology to mental structure.* Cambridge: Cambridge University Press.
Simon, H. A. (1981). *The sciences of the artificial.* 2nd ed. Cambridge, MA: MIT Press.
Spencer, R. M., and R. W. Weisberg (1986). Is analogy sufficient to facilitate transfer during problem solving? *Memory and Cognition* 14, 442–449.
Stuss, D. T., and D. F. Benson (1986). *The frontal lobes.* New York: Raven Press.
Sweller, J., R. F. Mawer, and M. R. Ward (1983). Development of expertise in mathematical problem solving. *Journal of Experimental Psychology: General* 112, 639–661.
Wickelgren, W. A. (1974). *How to solve problems.* San Francisco: W. H. Freeman.

Chapter 9

Deduction and Cognition

Lance J. Rips

In trying to explain deductive reasoning, psychologists seem to be in much the same unpleasant position as Lewis Carroll's (1895) Achilles in the fable, "What the Tortoise Said to Achilles." Achilles' friend the Tortoise claimed to believe both (1a) and (1b), but did not accept (1z).

(1) a. Things that are equal to the same are equal to each other.

b. The two sides of this Triangle are things that are equal to the same.

z. The two sides of this Triangle are things that are equal to each other.

To convince the Tortoise that he must also accept (1z), Achilles asked him to accept sentence (1c).

c. If (1a) and (1b) are true, then (1z) must be true.

The Tortoise replied that he was only too happy to accept (1c), but did not quite understand why if (1a–c) were true, he must also accept (1z). Achilles responded that it is obvious that if (1a–c) are true then (1z) must be true. But although the Tortoise said he was ready to accept this sentence too (that is, (1d)), he wasn't sure why accepting (1a–d) meant having to accept (1z).

d. If (1a) and (1b) and (1c) are true, (1z) must be true.

And so on. Achilles was left wearily formulating ever-longer sentences on the pattern of (1c) and (1d) to try to clinch the case for (1z).

Inferences like the one from (1a–b) to (1z) have a rock-bottom quality that makes it difficult to explain them to logical skeptics like the Tortoise. To take a second example, why is the inference from (2a) to (2b) correct, but the inference from (3a) to (3b) dubious?

I'm grateful to Daniel Osherson and Edward Smith for very helpful comments on an earlier draft of this chapter. NIMH grant MH39633 help supported its preparation.

(2) a. Martha is majoring in Astronomy and Calvin is majoring in Gastronomy.

b. Martha is majoring in Astronomy.

(3) a. Martha is majoring in Astronomy or Calvin is majoring in Gastronomy.

b. Martha is majoring in Astronomy.

You might try to explain that the first inference is right because (2a) means that both Martha is majoring in Astronomy and Calvin is majoring in Gastronomy, whereas (3a) means that one or the other is true but not necessarily both. But saying this won't be very helpful, for it relies on an understanding of the same principles it purports to explain.

Similarly, explaining how children learn the concepts expressed by words such as "and" and "or" quickly runs into the problem of how such learning could ever get started (Fodor 1975). Of course, they could learn that the English word "and" maps onto their concept of conjunction if they already have one, but how do they acquire the concept itself? Explaining the concept by means of a paraphrase is unlikely to be helpful, because the paraphrase is probably no more likely to be understood than *and* itself. Nor can they learn the concept by learning that sentences of the form "X and Y" are true just in case both X is true *and* Y is true, for this also relies on a previous understanding of an equivalent concept. It is difficult to imagine a person or a device capable of learning the concept *and* that doesn't already possess the logical skill for grasping *and*.

Recognizing the correctness of simple inferences, such as that from (1a–b) to (1z) or that from (2a) to (2b), appears to be a primitive cognitive ability—one that is not easy to explain or to justify in simpler terms. Realizing that the conclusion follows from the initial sentences is a mental event which happens quickly and which can't be reduced to the acceptance of further sentences. It's clear that inferences of this sort are crucial for mathematics—the Tortoise borrowed (1a–b) and (1z) from Euclid—and it is also tempting to suppose that they may have a more general role to play in human thinking. In fact, one strategy for cognitive science is to posit that people have a basic repertoire of inferences of this sort, which they use to deal with more complicated problems (McCarthy 1988). To prove a complex theorem or even to solve more mundane problems of planning, language understanding, and classifying, people may string together these basic inferences into chains that produce the result they want. Later in this chapter, we'll look at a minitheory of this type as a case study of what deduction can do (and what it can't do).

It would be wrong, however, to suppose that all cognitive scientists have embraced the idea of explaining general mental activities as streams of elementary logical inferences. There are many reasons for doubting that this strategy is correct (see chapter 6 for some of these). From a psychological point of view, the most serious obstacle to understanding cognition in this way comes from experiments suggesting that people are prone to errors in reasoning about seemingly simple problems. If people can't deal with even easy inferences in a reliable way, then there's little support for the view that they solve more complex problems by combining these simpler ones. Examples of error-prone tasks appear below.

There appears to be a dilemma, then, about the nature of logical intuition. On one hand, inferences like (2) appear too obvious to doubt or to explain, and people hardly ever get them wrong. They seem good candidates for cognitive primitives. On the other hand, certain inferences that also appear quite simple give people real difficulty, and this threatens to undermine the idea that logical inferences play a significant role in human thinking. Reconciling these contrary ideas is the central problem in the psychology of deductive reasoning. To tackle it, we need some background on deduction in order to be precise about its relation to thought. We take up this logic background in the following section and then proceed to explore possible relations between deduction and cognition in section 9.2. Section 9.3 briefly surveys one way of developing this connection—a framework based on mental models. The rest of the chapter is focused on a second possible way of viewing the deduction–cognition relation that gives the notion of proof a central role. Section 9.4 lays out this framework, and section 9.5 applies it to a standard example (the Towers of Hanoi puzzle) from the literature on problem solving. This task is not ordinarily considered an example of deductive reasoning; and so if the deduction framework can help us understand its solution, we can claim some generality for the proposal. Finally, section 9.6 returns to empirical findings on how people make decisions about logic type problems, using these findings to illustrate some of the strengths and weaknesses of the deduction framework.

9.1 Deduction Basics

The central concept in deduction is the relation that Achilles and the Tortoise were struggling over. We can call this the *entailment* relation, and it holds between a set of statements and a single further statement. For example, the entailment relation holds between the set {(1a), (1b)} and (1z), setting aside the Tortoise's doubts about it. It also holds between {(2a)} and (2b) in our earlier example, but not between {(2b)} and (2a) or between {(3a)} and (3b). When the entailment relation is in place, we can say that the set *entails* the further statement (for example, {(1a), (1b)} entails (1z)).

We can also schematize the entailment relationship as a list consisting of the entailing sentences, followed by an *inference line* (a horizontal bar), followed by the entailed sentence. In the case of (1a–b) and (1z), the scheme looks like this:

Things that are equal to the same are equal to each other.
The two sides of this Triangle are things that are equal to the same.

The two sides of this Triangle are things that are equal to each other.

It's usual to refer to this scheme as a (formal) *argument*. We also call the entailing sentences (the ones above the line) the *premises* and the final sentence the *conclusion*.

The entailment relation is a very strong one, in the sense that the entailing statements provide maximal support for the entailed statement. If a set of statements X entails a statement y, then the support that X lends y is equivalent to the support that y lends itself. For example, the support that *Martha is majoring in Astronomy and Calvin is majoring in Gastronomy* gives to *Martha is majoring in Astronomy* is as strong as the support that *Martha is majoring in Astronomy* gives to itself. The following subsections explore more rigorous ways of characterizing the entailment relation; but the notion of maximal support can help differentiate entailment from other relations among statements that also play a role in human inference. Consider, for example, the support that (4a) and (4b) give to (4c):

(4) a. 98 percent of students at the Culinary Institute of America major in Gastronomy.

b. Calvin is a student at the Culinary Institute of America.

c. Calvin is majoring in Gastronomy.

Clearly, (4a–b) give us a good reason to suppose that (4c) is true, but the degree of support in (4) falls short of that in examples (1) and (2). There's always the chance that Calvin is among the 2 percent of non-Gastronomy majors at the Institute. The support relationship in (4) is less than maximal, and {(4a), (4b)} do not entail (4c). In problem solving and decision making, we often have to work with evidence that doesn't maximally support our conclusions; and so the study of inferences based on such evidence has obvious importance in cognitive science (see chapters 2, 3, and 8). In section 9.2.2 we consider the possibility that both sorts of reasoning are handled by the same mental mechanism, but the focus in this chapter is entailment.

9.1.1 Proof and Deducibility

So far we have been vague about the entailment relation, relying on intuition to decide when a set of statements entails another. Logic provides us with two ways of making this relation more rigorous. The first of these methods approaches the entailment relation in terms of proofs. If it is possible to prove sentence *y* on the basis of the sentences in X, then *y* is said to be *deducible* from X, and deducibility is one criterion of entailment. The notion of proof that lies behind this definition is similar to the one familiar in mathematics; however, logic is quite precise about what counts as a proof in order to explore the limits of this concept. Many formal proof techniques are available in logic (see, for example, Quine 1972). But I describe the "natural-deduction" method here, because there are claims in the literature that natural deduction provides a good fit to human inferencing (Braine, Reiser, and Rumain 1984; Osherson 1974–1976; Rips 1994).

Natural-deduction proofs take as given the premise sentences X and apply designated inference rules to these sentences to generate further proof sentences. The inference rules can be applied again to the expanded set of sentences (that is, X plus the newly generated ones) to produce more sentences, and so on. If this process eventually produces the conclusion sentence *y*, then there is a proof of *y* from X, and *y* is thus deducible from X. For example, consider a natural-deduction system containing the rule in (5), called AND Elimination.

(5) a. If one of the sentences in the proof has the form "p AND q" then "p" can be the next sentence of the proof.

b. If one of the sentences in the proof has the form "p AND q" then "q" can be the next sentence of the proof.

In the statement of the rule, *p* and *q* stand for arbitrary sentences. The word AND is capitalized to signal that it is a special part of our logical system and may differ in some ways from the "and" of English. (We ignore these differences for the moment, but see subsection 9.1.3.) With rule (5) we can easily give a proof of (2b) from (2a); in fact, the proof just consists of (2a) followed by (2b), because the latter sentence follows from the former by rule (5a). Thus, (2b) is deducible from (2a).

To produce more interesting proofs, we have to introduce more inference rules. Let's supplement our fledgling system with the rule in (6), AND Introduction, and the rule in (7), IF Elimination (or *modus ponens*).

(6) If the proof contains a sentence "p" and a sentence "q", then "p AND q" can be the next sentence of the proof.

(7) If the proof contains a sentence "p" and a sentence "IF p THEN q" then "q" can be the next sentence of the proof.

With these new rules it is possible to prove (8d) from (8a–c).

(8) a. Martha is majoring in Astronomy.

b. Calvin is majoring in Gastronomy.

c. IF Martha is majoring in Astronomy AND Calvin is majoring in Gastronomy THEN Ted is majoring in Phlebotomy.

d. Ted is majoring in Phlebotomy.

The proof is shown in (9).

(9) a. Martha is majoring in Astronomy.

b. Calvin is majoring in Gastronomy.

c. Martha is majoring in Astronomy AND Calvin is majoring in Gastronomy.

d. IF Martha is majoring in Astronomy AND Calvin is majoring in Gastronomy THEN Ted is majoring in Phlebotomy.

e. Ted is majoring in Phlebotomy.

In this proof, (9a), (9b), and (9d) are the original premises from (8a–c). Sentence (9c) follows from (9a–b) by the AND Introduction rule in (6). The final sentence, (9e), is the one we wanted to prove, and it follows from (9c) and (9d) by the IF Elimination rule in (7). Thus, (8d) is deducible from (8a–c) in this system. Of course, this proof is still extremely simple; but even so you can begin to see that by combining rules and applying them iteratively, you can build up more complex proof structures. In section 9.4 we take up a psychological system for deduction that is based on proof.

There are some theoretical limitations on the search for proofs. For example, standard proof systems that appear in texts on elementary predicate logic (systems that are capable of handling all the entailments that we have discussed so far) do not guarantee that the search will terminate. If a proof exists for an entailment, these systems will eventually find it and stop. If no proof exists, however, the search may continue indefinitely, and the system will never stop to report that no proof exists. This property holds, not just for the type of natural-deduction system described here, but for any mechanically realizable system within broad limits, whether or not it employs formal rules of proof. The limitation can be avoided only at the cost of reducing the number of entailments that the system can recognize.

9.1.2 Truth and Semantic Entailment

A second criterion for entailment in logic makes use of relations among the truth values of statements. The statement *Martha is majoring in Astronomy* can be either true or false depending on circumstances. Although Martha might in fact be an Astronomy major, in other possible circumstances—for example, if her university's president had axed the Astronomy Department before Martha had arrived—this might not have been the case. In any circumstance, however, in which it is true that *Martha is majoring in Astronomy AND Calvin is majoring in Gastronomy*, it is also true that *Martha is majoring in Astronomy*. This relation between the truth of (2a) and (2b) is constant across shifting circumstances. In general, a set of statements X *semantically entails* a statement *y* if *y* is true in all possible circumstances in which each statement in X is true. Notice that this means it is possible for X to semantically entail *y* even if *y* is false in our current circumstance. Even if Martha is not majoring in Astronomy, it is still the case that in all circumstances in which (2a) is true so too is (2b).

Semantic entailment provides the second criterion for the basic entailment relation. As just defined, however, semantic entailment relies on the idea of truth in all possible circumstances, a notion that may not be clear. What is a possible circumstance? How can we tell one possible circumstance from another? How do we know when a statement is true in an arbitrary possible circumstance? To help with these questions, logic has formalized the notion of a circumstance, just as it has formalized the notion of proof. Using the tools of set theory, we can define a mathematical structure, called a "model," that takes the place of a circumstance in the definition of semantic entailment. A set of statements X semantically entails a statement *y* if and only if *y* is true in all models in which each statement in X is true. For the sorts of entailments in (2) and (8), a model might consist of the set of all true *atomic sentences* (Chang and Keisler 1973). Here an atomic sentence, such as *Martha is majoring in Astronomy*, is one that does not contain sentence connectives such as AND, IF, OR, and NOT. We can then distinguish one model from another if they contain different atomic sentences. By definition, an atomic sentence will be true in a model if and only if it is a member of the model.

Compound sentences with ANDs, IFs, ORs, and NOTs will be true in the model if they are composed in the right way from the atomic sentences. For example, *Martha is majoring in Astronomy AND Calvin is majoring in Gastronomy* will be true in a model if and only if both the atomic sentences *Martha is majoring in Astronomy* and *Calvin is majoring in Gastronomy* are members of that model. This means that in any model in which *Martha is majoring in Astronomy AND Calvin is majoring in Gastronomy* is true, *Martha is majoring in Astronomy* is true as well. Thus, by the definition of semantic entailment, {(2a)} semantically entails (2b).

Similarly, elementary logic represents the sentence *IF Martha is majoring in Astronomy THEN Ted is majoring in Phlebotomy* as true in a model in either of two cases: (a) *Martha is majoring in Astronomy* is *not* in the model, or (b) *Ted is majoring in Phlebotomy* is in the model. (This representation of IF is called the *material conditional*.) With this definition in mind, suppose that both the sentences *IF Martha is majoring in Astronomy THEN Ted is majoring in Phlebotomy* and *Martha is majoring in Astronomy* are true in a model. Because *Martha is majoring in Astronomy* is true in the model, case (a) cannot hold. But because *IF Martha is majoring in Astronomy THEN Ted*

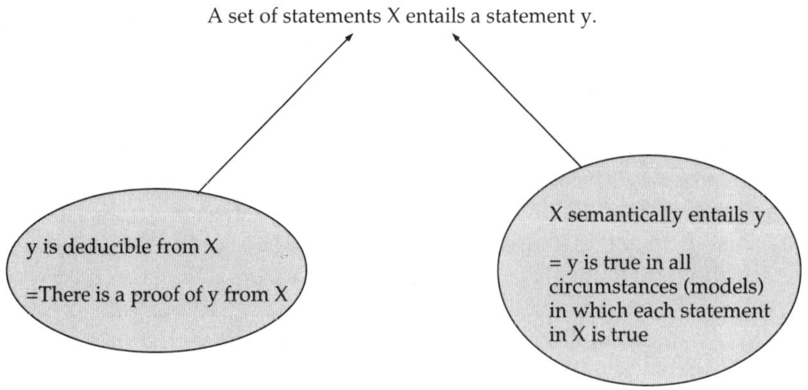

Figure 9.1
Deducibility and semantic entailment as dual criteria for the basic entailment relation.

is majoring in Phlebotomy is also true in the model, case (b) must obtain. Hence, the sentence *Ted is majoring in Phlebotomy* must be in the model as well. This is consistent with the IF Elimination rule in (7). Textbooks on elementary logic (for example, Bergmann, Moor, and Nelson 1980) describe the general conditions under which compound statements with AND, OR, IF, and NOT are true, as well as models for the types of statements in (1) above. Johnson-Laird and Byrne (1991) suggest that mental representations analogous to models are useful in understanding human inferences. We survey this point of view in section 9.3 below.

Figure 9.1 summarizes our two logical criteria for entailment. On one hand, we can establish an entailment relation between X and *y* by offering a proof of *y* from X. On the other, there is an entailment between X and *y* if *y* is true in all circumstances (or models) in which each X sentence is true. For simple systems, such as those discussed in most elementary logic textbooks, these two criteria coincide, and *y* will be deducible from X if and only if X semantically entails *y*. In more complex logical systems, however, the number of semantic entailments outstrip the possibility of proving all of them, even in theory. Such logical systems are said to be *incomplete*. In this chapter, however, we are concerned only with the simpler portions of logic for which there are complete proof systems, and our aim is to develop a sample cognitive system based on proof. We give less attention to semantic entailment.

9.1.3 Gricean Pragmatics

We noticed earlier that there is no entailment from {(3a)} to (3b), but what about the reverse direction? Does {(3b)} entail (3a)? If we interpret the *or* in (3a) as the inclusive OR of elementary logic, then this entailment does hold. In this system, *Martha is majoring in Astronomy OR Calvin is majoring in Gastronomy* is true in a model if and only if *Martha is majoring in Astronomy* is true in the model or *Calvin is majoring in Gastronomy* is true in the model (or both). It follows that if (3b) (that is, *Martha is majoring in Astronomy*) is true in a model, so too is (3a), and the entailment holds. However, people who have had no training in formal logic differ in their intuitions about this case (Rips and Conrad 1983), some consistently agreeing that such arguments are correct and others consistently disagreeing.

One way to account for this clash of intuitions is to recognize two different OR's: an inclusive and an exclusive one. People who went along with the entailment from {(3b)} to (3a) might have had the inclusive meaning in mind, whereas people who denied the entailment were thinking of the exclusive meaning. According to the exclusive interpretation, *Martha is majoring in Astronomy OR Calvin is majoring in Gastronomy* is true in a model if and only if *Martha is majoring in Astronomy* is true in the model or *Calvin is majoring in Gastronomy* is true in the model, but not both. Thus, even if *Martha is majoring in Astronomy* is true in a model, the larger sentence may not be, for *Calvin is majoring in Gastronomy* may also be true in the model. Rips and Conrad argue, however, that the difference between inclusive and exclusive *or* can't explain the results, because people who reject the entailment from {(3b)} to (3a) often accept others that would be equally invalid if *or* is exclusive. An example is the entailment from a sentence of the form: "If p or q then r" to "If p then r."

H. P. Grice (1989) has suggested a second way of explaining the difference of opinion about the {(3b)}–(3a) relation. Suppose the meaning of *or* in (3a) is the inclusive meaning above. Nevertheless, in the everyday situations in which a speaker uses such statements, *or* seems to signal that the speaker doesn't happen to know which of the component sentences, *Martha is majoring in Astronomy* or *Calvin is majoring in Gastronomy*, is true. Normally, we try to make our contributions to a conversation as informative as possible. (Grice calls this the conversational Maxim of Quantity.) Hence, if the speaker uses (3a) instead of one of its component sentences, this signals that the speaker isn't in a position to tell us which of the component sentences holds. It is possible, then, that some of the people in Rips and Conrad's experiment rejected the entailment from {(3b)} to (3a) because of this everyday expectation about the use of *or*. It may have seemed quite odd to them that anyone who had just stated *Martha is majoring in Astronomy* would go on to assert the larger sentence, and this odd quality may have led them to deny the entailment. The remaining people may have thought that the context of a psychology experiment is enough to cancel the normal restrictions on the use of *or* and responded on the basis of the meaning of *or* alone. (See Fillenbaum 1977 and chapter 10 in this volume for a discussion of other effects of conversational contexts on people's understanding of sentences.)

9.2 What Role, If Any, Does Deduction Play in Cognition?

The entailment relation, as we've described it, is a relation among statements and has no clear counterpart in the psychological realm. {(1a), (1b)} would entail (1z) and {(2a)} would entail (2b) even if no one had thought of them (or so it seems to many logicians, for example, Frege 1893/1964). This distinction between logical and psychological relations also enters into Lewis Carroll's story. The Tortoise was right to point out that you can accept (or believe) each statement in a set X without necessarily accepting all statements y that X entails (see Cherniak 1986; Stroud 1979; and chapter 6 in this volume); a particular y may be too long for you to comprehend or other matters may distract you before you can attend to y.[1] It is therefore uncertain whether entailment has any role to play in cognition. Of course, we can contemplate the entailment relation, just as we can contemplate the relation of being west of Saskatoon or being the fourth root of some integer; but this isn't enough to establish that entailment is an important part of our cognitive processes. It's easy to be misled on this point, for the word *deduction* (or the phrase *deductive reasoning*) encourages us to look for a mental process—the process of deducing something—that directly embodies entailment. Perhaps there is such a mental deduction process, but it would be unwise to assume it without a good reason.

9.2.1 Deduction as Heuristics

Let's consider some ways in which entailment could fit into cognition, beginning with views in which there are no mental processes devoted exclusively to deductive reasoning. One such view is analogous to probability judgment. As discussed in chapter 2, estimations of chance often rely on mental mechanisms that have little or nothing to do with the principles of probability (Tversky and Kahneman 1983). From this perspective, there may likewise be no psychological process that computes entailment relations. Instead, what passes for deductive reasoning may be the result of simple cognitive assessments based on the similarity or the salience of the entailing and the entailed statements. For example, people may decide that an argument is a good one if they believe that its conclusion is true, and may decide that an argument is bad if they believe that its conclusion is false (Morgan and Morton 1944). It is difficult to tell this story convinc-

1. Which is not to say that the Tortoise was right in thinking that you can believe a statement without believing *any* of its entailments. What makes the Tortoise's statements seem so disingenuous is how unlikely it is that one could believe (1a–b) without believing obvious entailments like (1z). Black (1970, ch. 2), Davidson (1970), and Dennett (1981) have pointed out that part of what it means to believe (or to understand) a proposition is to believe (understand) some of its entailments.

ingly for entailments that are as simple as those in (1) and (2), but for more complicated cases these factors may be important (Pollard 1982). As an illustration, ask yourself whether the conclusion of argument (10a) follows from its premises.

(10) a. No addictive things are inexpensive.
Some cigarettes are inexpensive.
____
Some cigarettes are not addictive.

b. No cigarettes are inexpensive.
Some addictive things are inexpensive.
____
Some addictive things are not cigarettes.

There's a fairly strong tendency for people to believe that the conclusion of (10a) cannot be "logically deduced" from the premises (Evans, Barston, and Pollard 1983). But consider a particular inexpensive cigarette of the sort that the second premise describes. Because that cigarette is inexpensive, it must not be addictive (according to the first premise); and so it follows that some cigarettes are not addictive, just as the conclusion states. The tendency to regard (10a) as nondeducible seems to be due to the fact that people believe the argument's conclusion to be false on the basis of their previous beliefs about addictive things and cigarettes. When the positions of *cigarettes* and *addictive things* are interchanged in the argument, as in (10b), the conclusion is deducible as before; however, more people regard the conclusion as true and are more likely to agree that it follows from the premises. This difference is shown as the top line in figure 9.2. As we noticed in the preceding section, the premises of an argument semantically entail the conclusion just in case the conclusion is true in any circumstance rendering the premises true. An entailment can hold even if the conclusion is false in the present circumstance, as (10a) demonstrates. But people's tendency to use their belief in the conclusion in evaluating arguments may constitute a heuristic or short-cut strategy that is analogous to those which appear in the literature on probabilistic judgment.

It is difficult, however, to defend the idea that people use *only* their belief in the conclusion in judging entailments. Studies that have independently varied the truth of the conclusions and the presence of entailments across a set of arguments have turned up effects of both factors (Evans et al. 1983; Newstead, Pollard, Evans, and Allen 1992). For example, in the Evans et al. study, people were more likely to judge an argument correct when an entailment was present (top line in figure 9.2) than when no entailment was present (bottom line in the figure). Thus, belief in the conclusion can't be the only method people use to evaluate arguments. It is possible, of course, that other heuristics are responsible for the difference

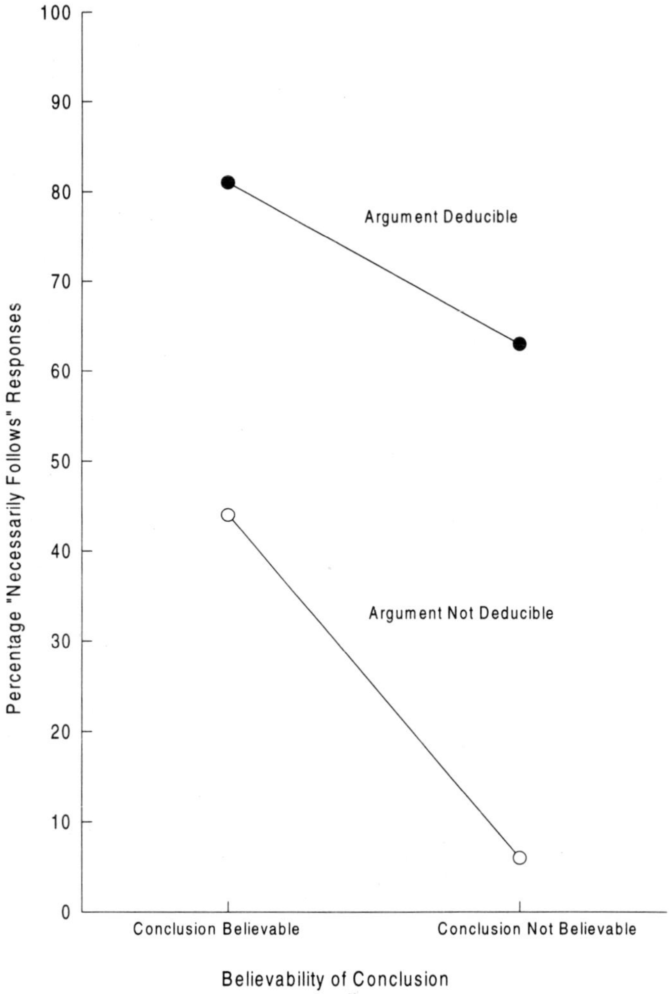

Figure 9.2
Percentage of "necessarily follows" responses as a function of the deducibility of an argument and the believability of its conclusion (from Evans et al. 1983).

between entailments and nonentailments in figure 9.2, but it is unclear which heuristics these could be.[2]

9.2.2 Deduction as a Limiting Case of Other Inference Forms

Probabilistic judgment suggests a second way to view the relation between entailment and thought that also avoids positing special mental processes devoted exclusively to deductive reasoning. According to this view, people are able to recognize entailments, but they do so by means of a general mechanism that covers entailment as a special or limiting case. Imagine a mental process, for example, that is able to assess the degree of support that the premises of an argument give to its conclusion. Such a process would identify some premises as lending negligible support to their conclusion, other premises as providing stronger support for their conclusion (as in (4)), and yet others as providing maximal support for their conclusion (as in (1) and (2) above). If people possessed such a mechanism there would be no need for a special-purpose entailment recognizer; entailment would simply be one end point on a continuum of strength of support. One apparent source of evidence for such a mechanism comes from studies showing that, even in nominally deductive tasks, people are sensitive to degree of support, not just the presence of an entailment. As one example, Staudenmayer (1975) asked separate groups of people whether the conclusions of arguments (11a) and (11b) were true given their premises.

(11) a. If the switch is turned on then the light will go on.
The light is on.
___
The switch was turned on.

b. If I turn on the switch then the light will go on.
The light is on.
___
I turned the switch on.

2. Evans et al. assessed the believability of the conclusions by asking an independent group of people to rate how believable they were. One difficulty in interpreting "believability" effects in other studies is that investigators often use conclusions that are not only believable but also true "by definition," such as *All rabbits are mammals* or *No apples are grapefruit.* If such statements are true in all circumstances, then the arguments that include them are semantic entailments in the sense of section 9.1.2: The conclusion is true in all circumstances in which the premises are true, because the conclusion is always true. Thus, these studies confound believability with entailment. This confounding does not affect arguments such as (10a) and (10b), however, because the conclusion of (10a) is not false in all circumstances and the conclusion of (10b) is not true in all circumstances. (For a discussion of the fact that arguments can be entailments even though they are instances of an invalid inference form, see Massey 1981.)

Neither of these arguments is deducible when the *if* of the first premise is interpreted as the IF of elementary logic (that is, the material conditional).[3] In fact, textbooks in logic sometimes call arguments of this type "fallacies of affirming the consequent." (The "then" part of a conditional sentence is its *consequent*; the "if" part its *antecedent*.) Notice, however, that the premises of (11a) give its conclusion more support than do the premises of (11b). When the light is on it is probably also true that the switch was turned on; however, when the light is on it need not be true that *I* turned it on (because someone else might have turned it on). We can summarize this idea by saying that the probability that the conclusion is true when the premises are true is greater for (11a) than for (11b), and this probability is one measure of support (Haviland 1974). In accord with this difference between the arguments, people in Staudenmayer's experiment more often agreed that the conclusion was true on the basis of the premises for (11a) than for (11b).[4] (It's worth noticing that the conclusion of (11a) does not seem any more believable on its own than that of (11b); and so the "believability heuristic" of subsection 9.2.1 cannot explain this result.)

If there is a special mental process that can detect entailments, then people might be able to reject both (11a) and (11b), ignoring the probability difference between them. Staudenmayer's finding implies that people don't ignore the probabilities, and this fact may militate against a special deduction process. We need to be careful, of course, in interpreting the experiment in this way, for some of the features of the experimental setup may

3. As mentioned earlier, the material conditional sentence "IF p THEN q" is true if and only if "p" is false or "q" is true. Hence, when "IF p THEN q" is true and "p" is true as well, "q" must also be true. However, when "IF p THEN q" is true and "q" is true as well, "p" could be either true or false; thus {"IF p THEN q", "q"} does not semantically entail "p". Does the material conditional provide a faithful representation of the *if* of ordinary language? See Grice (1989) for a defense and Adams (1965) and Anderson and Belnap (1975) for critiques.

4. Staudenmayer (1975) pooled his results over several types of arguments that shared the same conditional premise in order to determine how his subjects were interpreting this conditional sentence. He does not report data for (11a) and (11b) separately. However, among subjects who responded in a statistically consistent manner to all problems, at least 76.7 percent consistently accepted (11a), whereas at least 52.6 percent consistently *rejected* (11b).

Other investigators have reported similar findings, but the results are sometimes difficult to interpret. Some studies obtain ratings of confidence in the conclusion rather than judgments of entailment. A rating scale, however, invites people to attend to quantitative variations, and this by itself may lead them to consider the difference in probability. Similarly, in some experiments the instructions may not be clear enough to get people to view the task as one where entailment is relevant. In an earlier paper (Rips 1990), I've reviewed other findings in the deduction literature that are susceptible to a probability explanation.

have led people to think of the task as one in which probabilities were relevant (see note 4). Nevertheless, if we can account for people's judgments on both deduction and probabilistic tasks by positing just one mental mechanism, then parsimony suggests that we prefer such an explanation to one that requires two or more different processes. What would such a unified process look like? One plausible candidate is a device that could compute the conditional probability of a conclusion given that the premises of an argument are true, which we can denote *P*(*Conclusion* | *Premises*). (See chapter 2 for a definition of conditional probability.) Such a device would tell us that *P*(*The switch was turned on* | *If the switch is turned on then the light will go on AND The light is on*) is greater than *P*(*I turned the switch on* | *If I turn on the switch then the light will go on AND The light is on*), consistent with the difference between (11a) and (11b). Such a device would also determine that the conditional probabilities associated with (1) and (2) are maximal (that is, equal to 1), as it should.

The possibility of a unified theory of deductive and probabilistic reasoning is obviously attractive, but it encounters some major obstacles. First, there are problems with directly identifying entailment with *P* (*Conclusion* | *Premises*) = 1. When the premises entail the conclusion, this conditional probability will equal 1, but it seems that the conditional probability can be 1 even when no entailment is present. It is a matter of empirical fact that all creatures with backbones have hearts. Then *P* (*Fred has a heart* | *Fred has a backbone*) equals 1, but it is not the case that {*Fred has a backbone*} entails *Fred has a heart*. People seem to appreciate this distinction; and so in order to get a closer correlation between probabilities and entailment, we have to find some way of strengthening the conditional probability relationship or finding a new probabilistic relationship to take its place.[5] The need to do this, however, makes it less likely that we will be able to view deduction as a limiting case of probabilistic reasoning. A second obstacle to such a prospect is that research on probabilistic reasoning (reviewed in chapters 2 and 3) suggests that no single psychological mechanism is responsible for all such inferences. Thus, if probabilistic thinking is itself the result of disparate processes, the hope for a single probabilistic-deductive mechanism may be ephemeral.

5. One way to strengthen the probability relationship is to generalize over other sentences in the language. Thus, in a system proposed by Popper (1968, Appendixes *iv and *v), X entails y if and only if $P(X \mid z) \leq P(y \mid z)$ for all statements z. A related approach, advocated in Field (1977), generalizes over both probability functions and statements: X entails y if and only if $P(X \mid z) \leq P(y \mid z)$ for all statements z and all probability assignments P. Although it's possible to relate entailment to conditional probabilities in these ways, the adaptations make it less likely that recognizing entailments is psychologically a special case of recognizing probabilistic dependencies.

9.2.3 Deduction as a Special-Purpose Cognitive Component

A more common way to locate deduction in the space of mental processes is to view it as a relatively self-contained system for checking or producing entailments. According to this view, when a person has a problem to solve that calls for deductive reasoning, he or she represents the specifics of the problem in some sort of memory structure (say, a conceptual working memory like that described in chapter 7), applies deduction procedures to the representation, and uses the output of these procedures to respond to the query. There is room for disagreement as to how powerful the deduction component is: Some theorists believe that human beings typically possess only rudimentary inference abilities, whereas others advocate much more sophisticated reasoning skills. There is also a great deal of disagreement as to the operating principles that govern such a component (see Johnson-Laird and Byrne 1991 and Rips 1994, ch. 9–10, for a taste of the debate). It seems fair to say, however, that most investigators give people credit for deduction abilities that are at least up to the task of evaluating entailments such as (1) and (2). Of course, the output of such a component is liable to interference from external factors, such as limitations of memory and attention; thus this position is not forced to predict that people's performance on deduction problems is perfect, even within the range of problems to which the component applies. Similarly, it is possible that heuristics and probabilistic principles coexist with the deduction component. Heuristics or probabilistic inference may take over when things get tough for the deduction process, producing effects such as those we glimpsed in (10) and (11).

This way of thinking of deduction as a specific ability is probably consistent with the experimental results, but it raises questions for cognitive theory. Many higher cognitive processes, such as planning, categorization, language understanding, question answering, problem solving, and decision making, appear to involve mechanisms that have a deductive character. For example, all cognitive theories of these activities rely on procedures that relate general sentences or operations to specific instances that fall under them. In the case of planning, problem solving, and decision making, there must be a way to relate a specific situation to the general conditions that invoke one strategy rather than another. Suppose, for example, that you have resolved to go to graduate school next year if you get into a school on the West Coast, and to take a year off otherwise. When Berkeley calls to offer you admission, you need to recognize it as a specific instance of a West-Coast school in order to take advantage of their invitation and to fulfill your resolution. According to most theories of cognition, this connection between general forms and specific instances is accomplished by *instantiating* or *binding* the general forms stored in memory to the specific cases in ways that we explore in section 9.4. But instantiation in these mental processes appears quite similar to the step that allows us to plug *The two sides of this Triangle are things that are equal to the same* into the general statement *Things that are equal to the same are equal to each other* in (1). It's difficult to imagine a Tortoiselike cognizer who is unable to carry out this step, probably because instantiation is a prerequisite to so many basic cognitive skills. Likewise, other simple patterns of entailment, such as the one embodied in (2), may be parts of a wide range of mental abilities and may not be limited to solving problems in logic and math.

We can regard the deduction component as supplying logical processes, such as instantiation, to other mental operations; in doing so, though, we have elevated the component to a role that psychologists have usually ignored. According to the more traditional way of thinking, deduction plays a part in cognition that is analogous to that of other specialized skills, such as mental multiplication, which are useful under certain conditions, but don't influence many other procedures. It is obvious that children can categorize and plan quite well long before they're able to perform much mental multiplication; thus mental multiplication can't be necessary for these abilities. A deduction component might have a similar status as a special-purpose device; but the possibility that instantiation and other inference patterns are crucial to other abilities suggests that deduction may have a more general part to play. It is possible, of course, that each mental ability has its own means for carrying out instantiation—instantiation for comprehension, instantiation for planning, and so on—and similarly for other deductionlike operations; but a more elegant theory would avoid replicating processes in this way. In the next two sections, we review two fairly general theories of deductive reasoning that may be able to supply the cognitive underpinnings for other processes.

9.3 Deduction by Mental Models

We noticed earlier that we can define semantic entailment in terms of models: Statements X semantically entail y just in case y is true in all models in which each of the statements in X is true. In logic these models are sets—for instance, sets of atomic sentences in the example we considered in subsection 9.1.2. Let's consider, however, a psychological analogy to semantic entailment. Perhaps, in deductive reasoning, we decide whether statements X entail y according to whether all mental representations of X contain y. We might proceed, for example, by considering an initial mental representation of X and inspect it to determine whether this representation contains (a representation of) y as a part. If not, we immediately reject the entailment. If so, we consider a second representation of *X*, inspect it for *y*, and continue in this way until we're either satisfied that all representations of *X* contain *y* or have found a counterexample of an *X*-representation with no *y*.

Johnson-Laird and Byrne (1991) have developed a mental-model theory that illustrates this analogy to models in logic. For example, this theory represents sentence (2a), *Martha is majoring in Astronomy and Calvin is majoring in Gastronomy*, as two horizontally arrayed tokens:

m c

where *m* stands for *Martha is majoring in Astronomy* and *c* stands for *Calvin is majoring in Gastronomy*. Sentence (2b), *Martha is majoring in Astronomy*, holds in this mental model, because *m* is part of the model. Furthermore, according to Johnson-Laird and Byrne, there is no alternative mental model for (2a); hence every mental model for (2a) is also a model for (2b). Thus {(2a)} entails (2b) in mental-model theory. By contrast, sentence (3a), *Martha is majoring in Astronomy or Calvin is majoring in Gastronomy* has two different models, indicated by placing the tokens *m* and *c* on separate lines.

m
    c

Because *m* is part of only one of these models, *Martha is majoring in Astronomy* does not hold in all models of (3a), and {(3a)} does not entail (3b). Johnson-Laird and Byrne hypothesize that people have more difficulty in drawing conclusions when they must consult more than one model. This means that arguments based on conjunctions (that is, sentences connected by *and*) will tend to be easier than ones based on disjunctions (that is, sentences connected by *or*).

Johnson-Laird and Byrne (1991) have developed other types of mental models to handle more complex deduction problems, such as those in (10). Mental-model theory is a promising research direction, developed with great ingenuity, but it is not the line that we explore in the remainder of the chapter (for reasons discussed, for example, in Bonatti 1994, Hodges 1993, and Rips 1994).

9.4 A Case Study: Deduction as a Psychological Operating System

What would a mind be like that operated by deduction? This section develops a miniature general-purpose deduction mechanism that can direct other forms of cognition. The framework is highly speculative, for it would require a great deal more experience with the theory before we would be

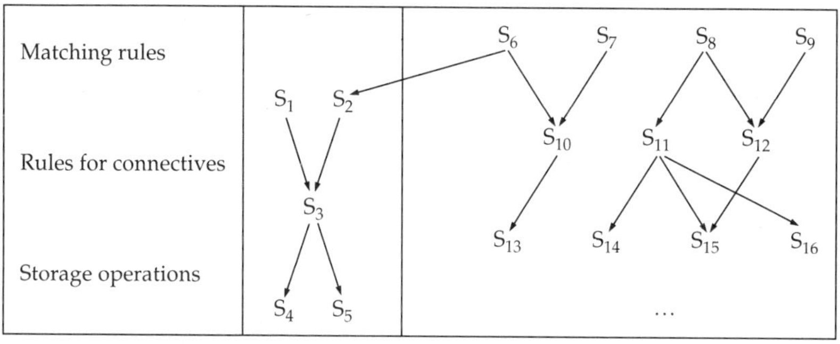

Figure 9.3
Memory structure for the sample deduction system of section 9.4.

confident of its merits. It is offered here mainly as an example of a working deduction theory, based on natural-deduction proofs, which may provide a springboard for further development.[6] After sketching the theory and some of its applications, we will return to the question of how well it fits with current ideas and data.

As a start, let's assume that the system's memory is organized along fairly standard lines, such as that in figure 9.3. Two of the slices of memory in the figure store sentencelike entities (the S's) that record information of interest to the system. These two slices, working memory and long-term declarative memory, differ in their capacity, with working memory containing only a limited set of sentences—roughly the set we are pondering at a given moment. Limited capacity implies that if a reasoning problem becomes too complicated, information may be forgotten and reasoning performance will degrade (Gilhooly, Logie, Wetherick, and Wynn 1993; Hitch and Baddeley 1976; and Toms, Morris, and Ward 1993). We can also assume that pointers interconnect sentences within both working and long-term memory, as the arrows in the figure indicate. These pointers represent a wide variety of meaningful relations that hold among sentences. We are concerned here mainly with the entailment relation that obtains when the system has deduced one sentence from others. Although the figure segregates working memory and long-term memory, it is reasonable to think of working memory as the active portion of an encompassing long-term memory, with both memories containing conceptual information (see Anderson 1993 and Potter 1993, and the discussion of working memory in chapter 7). This means that there will often be pointers interconnecting sentences in working memory and sentences in long-term

6. The theory is part of a larger one that is implemented in a Prolog program; for details about the program, see Rips (1994).

memory, as the figure shows. Sentences in working memory can then activate related information in long-term memory, making this information part of working memory in turn and displacing earlier information. An interesting aspect of this setup, which differentiates it from most formal theorem-proving systems, is that the premises or axioms of a particular problem need not be fixed, but will fluctuate with changes in the content of working memory.

The third or leftmost slice in figure 9.3 contains mental processes that inspect and operate upon the sentences in working memory. Thus, working memory provides a kind of interface between these processes and the rest of the system. Depending on the nature of these sentences, the processes can create new working-memory sentences and new pointers between them. In the present system these processes are of just three types: matching rules that instantiate or generalize sentences, rules for connectives similar to those in (5)–(7), and simple storage operations on working-memory sentences. The idea is that the rules create mental proofs by producing newly deduced sentences in working memory and stringing them together with entailment pointers. The proofs might be solutions to logical or mathematical problems, but they will more usually concern everyday tasks that the system is undertaking. To find out how the system works, we can begin by looking at its structural assumptions and then at the way it produces inferences.[7]

9.4.1 Representations

The basic unit in our system is a mental sentence, and these sentences display important logical properties. An atomic sentence in our notation will have a two-part structure, consisting of a descriptor or *predicate* followed by one or more *arguments* (a different sense of "argument" from that introduced in section 9.1). For example, we might phrase *Martha is majoring in Astronomy* as *Majoring-in* (*Martha, Astronomy*), where *Majoring-in* is the predicate, and *Martha* and *Astronomy* are the arguments. Intuitively, the predicate refers to a property or relation, and the arguments refer to entities over which the property or relation holds.

Arguments like *Martha* and *Astronomy* are names, referring to specific entities (a specific person and a specific field of study). However, we sometimes need to express general information that is true of unnamed entities, and for this reason we will allow two other types of arguments in

7. The assumptions embodied in figure 9.3 are quite similar to those of some production-system theories, except that we are dealing with a much smaller set of productions (and a correspondingly larger set of sentences). See chapter 8 in this volume for a description of production systems, and Anderson 1993; Holland, Holyoak, Nisbett, and Thagard 1986; and Newell 1990 for specific models.

our sentences, called *constants* and *variables*. These arguments are similar to the symbolic constants and variables that you've encountered in elementary algebra. For example, in the equation $y = 3x + k$, the numeral 3 functions as a name that refers to an individual number, but k and x have a different status, though of course they ultimately refer to numbers too. This equation means that there is some number or other k which is such that, for any number x, y will equal $3x + k$. Here the k functions as a constant, and the x functions as a variable. We will use constants and variables in a similar manner in our sentences in order to achieve generality. For example, to express the fact that there is someone or other majoring in Astronomy, we will use a constant as *Majoring-in*'s first argument: *Majoring-in(a, Astronomy)*. To express the idea that everyone is majoring in Astronomy, we will use a variable as the first argument: *Majoring-in(x, Astronomy)*. In general, a sentence containing a variable will be true if the sentence is true no matter which entity the variable refers to, and a sentence containing a constant will be true if the sentence is true for some entity or other that the constant might refer to. In our notation, constants will start with lowercase letters from the beginning of the alphabet, and variables will start with lowercase letters from the end of the alphabet. Names start with a capital letter. Sentences will often contain a mix of constants, variables, and proper names.[8]

We can also create compound sentences from our atomic ones by combining them with AND, OR, IF ... THEN, and NOT. As examples, (1a′) translates (1a) into our notation, (2a′) translates (2a), and (3a′) translates (3a).

8. We need to observe a further convention when a sentence includes both constants and variables. Consider the sentence *Everyone is majoring in something*. One meaning of this sentence is that there is a specific field (Computer Science, say) that everyone is majoring in, and we can express this as *Majoring-in(x,a)*. However, there is a second meaning of the sentence, perhaps the more natural one for this sentence, in which everyone is majoring in some field or other, but not necessarily the same one. Martha may be majoring in Astronomy, Calvin in Gastronomy, and so on, without there being any one field in which everyone is majoring. In this second meaning, the *something* of the original sentence refers to a potentially different major depending on the "major-er," and to distinguish this meaning from the earlier one, we mark this dependence explicitly by writing *Majoring-in* (x,a_x). (We can't use a second variable in this case because *Majoring-in(x,y)* would mean that everyone is majoring in everything.) The subscript on the constant serves as a reminder that what a_x refers to depends on what x refers to. Constants that have no subscripts are said to have *wide scope*; constants with subscripts *narrow scope* (with respect to the variable).

This representation for sentences is similar to that found in textbooks on predicate logic (for example, Bergmann et al. 1980), except that we are using variables and constants to do the work that is normally assigned to quantifiers. The present notation is due to Skolem (1928/1967) and is sometimes called *Skolem normal form* or *Skolem function form*. We use Skolem form in preference to a notation with quantifiers because it simplifies the deduction process.

(1) a′. IF Equals (x, z) AND Equals (y, z) THEN Equals (x, y).

(2) a′. Majoring-in (Martha, Astronomy) AND
Majoring-in (Calvin, Gastronomy).

(3) a′. Majoring-in (Martha, Astronomy) OR
Majoring-in (Calvin, Gastronomy).

To complete our representation, we need a way to record in memory that the system has deduced a sentence from certain others. As mentioned earlier, memory pointers will serve this purpose, and we will depict these pointers with arrows that run from the entailing sentences to the entailed one. We can also label an entailment pointer with the name of the inference rule that is responsible for the new sentence. Thus, the simple proof in (9) will appear in our system's working memory in the form shown in figure 9.4. The figure shows that sentence c comes from a and b via the AND Introduction rule and that sentence e (the conclusion of the argument) comes from c and d via IF Elimination. The arcs connecting the arrows indicate that the sentences at the base of the arrows jointly entail

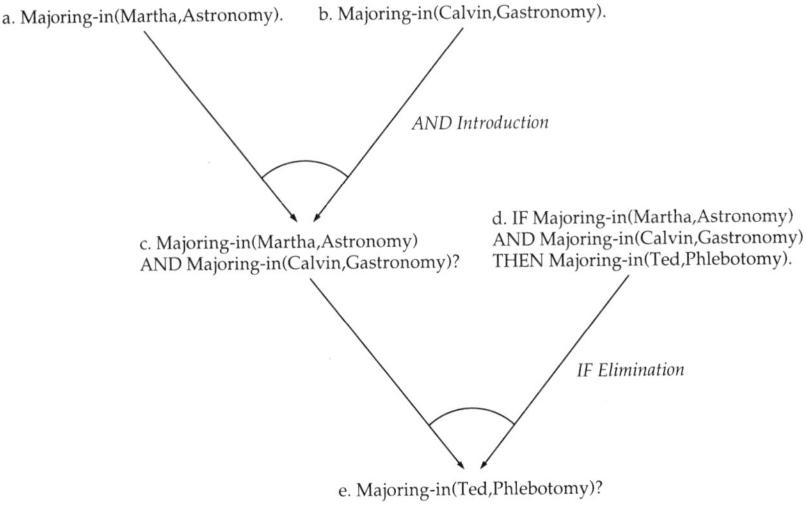

Figure 9.4
Proof of the argument:

Martha is majoring in Astronomy
Calvin is majoring in Gastronomy
IF Martha is majoring in Astronomy AND Calvin is majoring in Gastronomy
THEN Ted is majoring in Phlebotomy

Ted is majoring in Phlebotomy

using the inference rules of the sample deduction system.

the sentence at the end. (The periods and question marks following the sentences are explained in the following subsection.)

9.4.2 Inference Processes

To carry out a proof, such as the one in figure 9.4, the system uses rules for connectives and rules for matching arguments. The connective rules are similar to the AND Introduction, AND Elimination, and IF Elimination rules that we encountered in (5)–(7), but include additional constraints to keep them on the track of the proof. The matching rules decide when one sentence entails another on the basis of its arguments (variables, constants, and names). For example, the sentence *Majors-in(x, Computer Science)* (that is, everyone majors in Computer Science) entails *Majors-in(Fred, Computer Science)*, and we'd like the system to draw this inference in appropriate circumstances. In the opposite direction, however, *Majors-in(Fred, Computer Science)* does not entail *Majors-in(x, Computer Science)*; thus the rules must specify which matches are legitimate.

9.4.2.1 *Rules for connectives*

Some of the connective rules create massive inefficiencies if we allow them to produce all possible entailments from a set of premises. For example, the AND Introduction rule, as stated in (6), joins any two sentences *p* and *q* to create a new sentence *p AND q*. But notice that this rule applies to its own output in a way that can yield an infinite number of sentences. Once it gets *p AND q*, it can join this sentence to the earlier ones (or to itself); thus in successive steps, it could produce (for example) *p AND (p AND q)*, *p AND (p AND (p AND q))*, and so on. Obviously, we can't let the system get sidetracked in this maze of sentences, because most of them will be irrelevant to the task at hand.

One way to avoid this problem is to distinguish two types of sentences that can appear in a mental proof. The first type, *assertions*, consists of the premises of a problem (possibly including other temporary assumptions) and the sentences that the system has deduced from the premises at a given stage in the proof. The second type, *subgoals*, consists of the conclusion of the problem and other sentences that, if proved, would entail the conclusion. The trick to constraining AND Introduction and similar rules is to use them only when they can produce a subgoal. Compare our old AND Introduction rule in (6) (repeated below) to the new formulation in (6′). In (6) AND Introduction applied to assertions and produced new assertions, which then became fodder for the same rule. In (6′), however, a reformulated AND Introduction applies to subgoals.

(6) If the proof contains a sentence "p" and a sentence "q", then "p AND q" can be the next sentence of the proof.

(6′) If the current subgoal in a proof is "p AND q," then make "p" the next subgoal. If the latter subgoal succeeds, make "q" the next subgoal.

The idea is that if we ever need to prove "p AND q," we do so by proving "p" and "q" separately. Thus, (6′) allows us to work backward from the sentence we want to establish. The important feature is that the system will never apply this rule unless "p AND q" is already needed in the proof; so (6′) will never produce arbitrary sentences with AND. The old IF Elimination rule in (7) can similarly be amended, as shown in (7′).

(7) If the proof contains a sentence "p" and a sentence "IF p THEN q," then "q" can be the next sentence of the proof.

(7′) If the current subgoal in a proof is "q" and "IF p THEN q" is an assertion, then make "p" the next subgoal.

Some rules, such as IF Elimination, work well both as forward and as backward rules, and so we will keep both (7) and (7′). The forward version of IF Elimination is helpful, for it is often useful to be able to draw an inference as soon as we are in a position to do so (for example, to anticipate upcoming situations). We can get away with this in the case of (7), because applying this rule does not lead to further, snowballing opportunities for IF Elimination. The forward version of AND Introduction is a disaster, however, as we've seen, and this means discarding (6) while retaining (6′). We discuss evidence for this forward/backward distinction in subsection 9.6.1.

To see why these modifications are helpful, let's return to the proof in figure 9.4. At the beginning of this proof, working memory contains the premises of the argument, labeled a, b, and d in the figure, and the conclusion, e. The premises end in a period to indicate their status as assertions, and the conclusion ends in a question mark to show that it is the goal we'd like to prove. In this situation, rule (7′) applies, because the current (sub)goal is *Majoring-in(Ted, Phlebotomy)* and one of the assertions is *IF Majoring-in(Martha, Astronomy) AND Majoring-in(Calvin, Gastronomy) THEN Majoring-in(Ted, Phlebotomy)*. Rule (7′) advises us to make the next subgoal *Majoring-in(Martha, Astronomy) AND Majoring-in(Calvin, Gastronomy)*: If we can prove this sentence, then the conclusion follows. The system then places this subgoal in working memory as sentence c in the figure. But notice that this new sentence is of the form "p AND q," and so we can now use our backward AND Introduction rule (6′). AND Introduction tells us that the subgoal follows if we can prove both "p" and "q" (that is, *Majoring-in(Martha, Astronomy)* and *Majoring-in(Calvin, Gastronomy)*). This is easy to do, however, for these two sentences are already among the assertions. We've now fulfilled Subgoal c, which in turn fulfills

Subgoal e, completing the proof. The system never contemplates proving irrelevant sentences with AND (for example, *Majoring-in(Calvin, Gastronomy) AND (IF Majoring-in(Martha, Astronomy) AND Majoring-in(Calvin, Gastronomy) THEN Majoring-in(Ted, Phlebotomy)))*, because these never become subgoals.

9.4.2.2 *Matching rules*

In the proof of figure 9.4 we didn't have to worry about variables and constants, for the sentences contained only names. To deal with problems such as (1), however, the system needs principles for comparing names, variables, and constants. In general, a sentence containing a variable entails the sentence formed by replacing the variable with a name or a constant (for example, *Majoring-in(x, Computer Science)* entails *Majoring-in(Fred, Computer Science)* and *Majoring in(a, Computer Science)*—if everyone majors in Computer Science then Fred majors in Computer Science and someone majors in Computer Science). Similarly, a sentence containing a proper name entails the sentence formed by replacing the proper name with a constant (for example, *Majoring-in(Fred, Computer Science)* entails *Majoring-in(a, Computer Science)*—if Fred majors in Computer Science then someone majors in Computer Science). An argument can occur more than once in a given sentence, however, meaning that the rules that match arguments have to observe some distribution requirements. For example, it's not the case that *Equals(x,x)*—everything is identical to itself—entails *Equals(Martha, Calvin)*. Table 9.1 spells out the restrictions on the matching rules that we need for cases like (1).[9] For more on why these restrictions are necessary, see problem 9.3 at the end of this chapter.

In addition to instituting these rules for matching, we must modify the connective rules to enable them to handle variables and constants. In the case of AND Introduction, we need to be sure that any matching that we've done in fulfilling the first part of the rule carries over to the second. For example, suppose we have the goal of proving that Side1 and Side2 of a triangle are equal to the same: *Equal(Side1, b) AND Equal(Side2, b)*. If we are able to show that Side1 is equal to some line segment L in carrying out the first part of (6′), then we must make sure that we show that Side2 is also equal to L. The goal wouldn't be fulfilled by matching *Equal(Side1, b)* to *Equal(Side1, L)* and then matching *Equal(Side2, b)* to *Equal(Side2, M)*. Similar restrictions apply to our backward IF Elimination rule in (7′). We can use the assertion *IF Equal(x,z) AND Equal(y,z) THEN Equal(x,y)* from

9. Table 9.1 simplifies the matching rules and the rules for connectives by omitting conditions on subscripted constants (for example, a_x), as mentioned in the preceding footnote. For a complete statement of rules that includes these conditions, see Rips (1994, ch. 6).

Table 9.1
A partial list of inference rules for mental proof finding. (These rules omit conditions imposed on subscripts of constants; see Note 8.)

Backward AND Introduction:

If the current subgoal is "p AND q", then make "p" the next subgoal.
If the latter subgoal succeeds,
then:
  If "p" and "q" share constants and these constants matched names in fulfilling "p", then substitute the names for the same constants in "q".
  Make "q" the next subgoal.

Backward IF Elimination:

If the current subgoal "q" can be matched to "q′" in an assertion "IF p THEN q′",
then:
  If "p" and "q′" share variables and arguments in "q" matched these variables, then substitute the matched arguments for the same variables in "p".
  If "p" contains variables or constants not in "q′",
  then change these old variables to new constants and change the old constants to new variables.
  Make "p" the next subgoal.

Matching proper names in subgoals to variables in assertions:

If "p" is a subgoal and "q" is an assertion,
  and "p" and "q" are identical except for their arguments,
  and a name "m" appears in "p" at each position occupied by a variable "x" in "q",
then "m" matches "x".

Matching constants in subgoals to proper names in assertions:

If "p" is a subgoal and "q" is an assertion,
  and "p" and "q" are identical except for their arguments,
  and a proper name "m" appears in "q" in each position occupied by a constant "c" in "p",
then "c" matches "m".

(1a′) to try to fulfill the goal *Equal(Side1, Side2)*. This involves matching the goal to the THEN part of the assertion and attempting to prove the IF part. But this means proving, not *Equal(x,z) AND Equal(y,z)*, but *Equal (Side1, b) AND Equal(Side2, b)*. We must substitute *Side1* and *Side2* for the two variables *x* and *y*, and we must change the remaining variable *z* to a constant. That is, we want to show that Side1 and Side2 are both equal to the same constant item. Table 9.1 gives the final forms of the connective rules that implement these modifications. A full-blown, psychologically plausible deduction system would include many more rules than those in the table, but this sample will get us surprisingly far in our illustrations.

To see how these rules work together, let's consider a slightly modified version of (1), shown here as (12).

(12) a. IF x = z AND y = z THEN x = y.

b. Side1 = L.

c. Side2 = L.

---

d. Side1 = Side2.

The first premise of (12) represents the Tortoise's *Things that are equal to the same are equal to each other* as we did earlier, except that (12) uses "=" as an abbreviation for the predicate *Equal* to make the argument easier to read. Premises b and c assert that Side1 of "this triangle" is equal to some specific line segment L, and Side2 is also equal to L. These assertions appear as separate premises to make the proof more interesting and to bring out the similarity to the earlier proof in figure 9.4.

Figure 9.5 shows how the system we've been designing would prove argument (12). At the beginning of the proof, working memory would contain just the premises and conclusion, sentences a–d. Because the conclusion/goal is to prove *Side1 = Side2,* the backward IF Elimination rule notices that sentence a may be helpful (see the statement of the rule in table 9.1). The goal matches to the THEN part of this sentence, with *Side1*

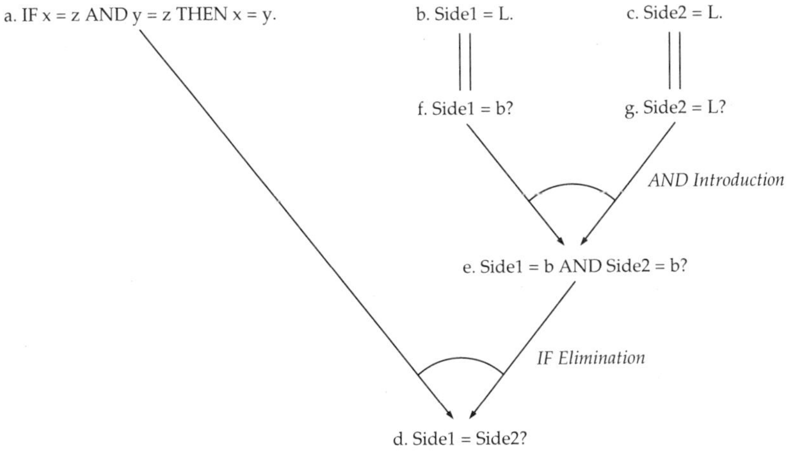

Figure 9.5
Proof of the argument:

IF x = z AND y = z THEN x = y
Side1 = L
Side2 = L

Side1 = Side2

using the inference rules of the sample deduction system.

matching *x* and *Side2* matching *y*; and so IF Elimination tells us that we can prove the goal if we can show that *Side1* = *b* *AND* *Side2* = *b*. In producing this subgoal—sentence e in the figure—IF Elimination substitutes *Side1* and *Side2* into the IF part of sentence a and changes variable *z* to a constant *b*, as discussed earlier. At this point, AND Introduction can apply, for the new subgoal e has the "p AND q" format. This rule first tries the (sub)subgoal *Side1* = *b* in order to find something to which Side1 is equal. This subgoal succeeds easily, because it matches *Side1* = *L*, one of the original assertions. A double line in the figure represents this matching step. AND Introduction then substitutes *L* for *b* as the last step of the rule (table 9.1) and tries to prove *Side2* = *L*. (As mentioned above, we need to substitute because the constant *b* will match any name. Thus, if we try to prove *Side2* = *b* and succeed by matching to *Side2* = *M*, with *M* ≠ *L*, we would not have shown that *Side1* and *Side2* are "equal to the same".) This subgoal also succeeds because it is a copy of another of the assertions, and this last match suffices to finish the proof. Notice that the same two rules, IF Elimination and AND Introduction, are responsible for the proofs of both figures 9.4 and 9.5. The only substantive addition in 9.5 lies in the processing of variables and constants.

9.5 An Illustration of Problem Solving by Deduction

We can apply the psychological deduction system of the preceding section, not only to determine whether or not the premises of an argument entail its conclusion, but also to accomplish more general-purpose cognitive tasks. It's important to see how we can use the system in this way, for our motive in developing the theory was to have a system that could guide other forms of thinking. We can't, of course, survey all such domains, but it is possible to illustrate the system's generality by showing how it can solve a puzzle that cognitive scientists don't ordinarily think of as requiring deduction.

The example we use is a chestnut from the literature on problem solving: the Towers of Hanoi puzzle. The props in this puzzle are three pegs—one on the left, one at the center, and one on the right—and a group of disks of different sizes that stack on the pegs. The problem can include any number of disks, but we focus on three disks in this illustration. (The solution we will develop extends very easily to larger numbers of disks.) At the start of the problem the disks are on the left peg, in order of increasing size from top to bottom. Figure 9.6 shows this starting state in the picture that is inserted at the bottom of the diagram. (We will explore the rest of this figure later.) The aim of the puzzle is to restack the disks in the same order on the right peg, subject to two restrictions on moving

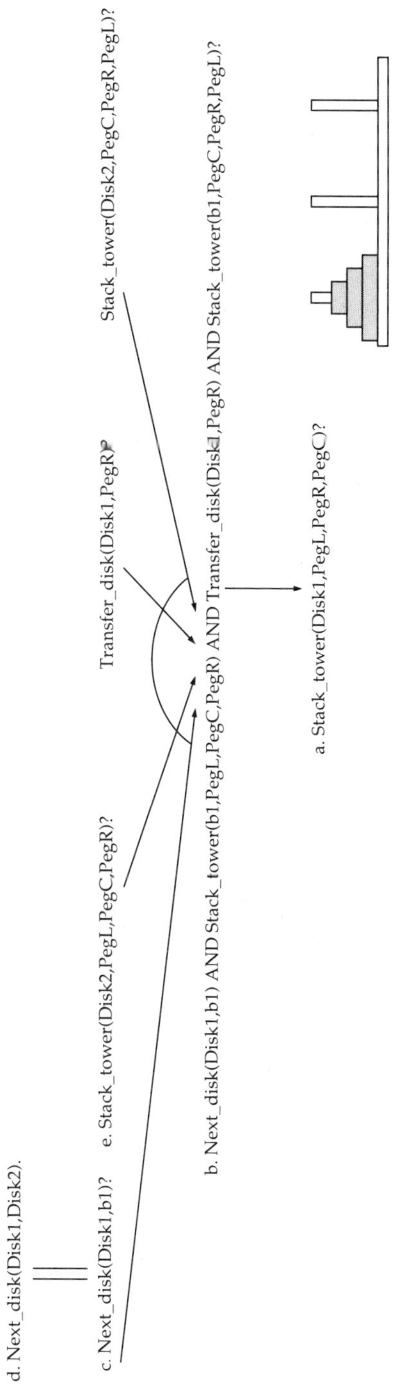

Figure 9.6
Initial part of the solution to the 3-peg Towers of Hanoi problem (see text for explanation).

the disks: First, you can move only one disk at a time from one peg to another, and second, you cannot place a larger disk on top of a smaller one.

Problem-solving theorists have extensively analyzed the Towers of Hanoi and have described several strategies that are able to solve it with a minimum number of moves (Anderson 1993; Simon 1975). For example, Simon (1975) outlines one method consisting of these three steps: To stack a tower currently on Peg A to Peg C, (1) stack the tower consisting of all except the largest disk onto Peg B, (2) transfer the largest disk to Peg C, and (3) stack the tower on B to C. As Simon states,

> Only the second stage, of course, corresponds to a legal move. The first stage, which clears A and C for move (2), and the third stage, which brings the remaining disks to C, are themselves Tower of Hanoi problems with one less disk than the original problem; hence they can be solved by decomposing them into the same three stages, for the location of the largest disk places no constraints on the movement of smaller disks. Since the original number of disks is finite, say *n*, we can continue to decompose each problem into smaller problems until, after $n - 1$ recursions, the "pyramids" to be moved have been reduced to single disks—that is, to goals of making single legal moves.

Egan and Greeno (1974) present evidence that people do follow such a strategy, based on numbers of erroneous moves and on recognition memory for the different states of the problem.

We can easily express this "goal-recursion" strategy in our notation. Let the predicate *Stack_tower(disk,source-peg,destination-peg,spare-peg)* mean that the tower whose largest disk is *disk* moves from *source-peg* to *destination-peg* with *spare-peg* as the remaining peg. Thus, if *Disk1* is the largest disk, *PegL* is the left peg, *PegR* is the right peg, and *PegC* is the center peg, the goal of the entire problem is *Stack_tower(Disk1,PegL,PegR,PegC)*. Let's also use the predicate *Transfer_disk(disk,peg)* to mean that the single disk, *disk*, is moved to *peg*. A legal move will then correspond to a Transfer-disk operation under the proper circumstances. Finally, we need the predicate *Next_disk(xdisk,ydisk)* to record the fact that *ydisk* is one size smaller than *xdisk* in order to keep our place in the serial order. With these three predicates, we can represent the entire goal-recursion strategy as in (13).

(13) a. Next_disk(Disk1,Disk2).

b. Next_disk(Disk2,Disk3).

c. IF Transfer_disk(Disk3,ypeg) THEN
Stack_tower(Disk3,xpeg,ypeg,zpeg).

d. IF Next_disk(xdisk,ydisk)
AND Stack_tower(ydisk,xpeg,zpeg,ypeg)
AND Transfer_disk(xdisk,ypeg)
AND Stack_tower(ydisk,zpeg,ypeg,xpeg)
THEN Stack_tower(xdisk,xpeg,ypeg,zpeg).

---

e. Stack_tower(Disk1,PegL,PegR,PegC).

The conclusion of this argument is the goal just discussed. Premises (13a–b) simply name the three disks in order from largest (Disk1) to smallest (Disk3). The real workhorse of the strategy is (13d), which formalizes Simon's description. As we will see momentarily, when the system tries to prove the conclusion of (13), it matches this conclusion to the THEN part of (13d) and then attempts to prove the IF part, according to the backward IF Elimination rule (table 9.1). Thus, (13d) says that we can stack the tower whose largest disk is *xdisk* from *xpeg* to *ypeg* IF: (1) *ydisk* is one size smaller than *xdisk*, (2) we can stack the tower whose largest disk is *ydisk* on *zpeg*, (3) we can transfer *xdisk* to *ypeg*, and (4) we can stack the tower we've just put on *zpeg* onto *ypeg*. In addition to this general method of stacking towers, we also need to specify the special case that arises when the "tower" consists of just the smallest disk, Disk3. Premise (13c) asserts that we can do this just by transferring Disk3 to the desired peg. When a person actually carries out the goal-recursion strategy, fulfilling a *Transfer_disk* goal would produce a motor command that physically moved the disk. In our simulation of the strategy, we will simply allow all such goals to succeed immediately. Because these goals arise only in the contexts created by (13c) and (13d), this policy will not get us into trouble. The proof of (13) will be more efficient if the system considers (13c) before (13d), and we will assume that pointers in working memory enforce this ordering. The remaining pairs of premises can appear in any order. (See Clocksin and Mellish 1981 for a similar solution in the Prolog programming language.)

Figures 9.6–9.8 illustrate the steps in the solution that occur when our system proves (13). To keep the figures simple, I have shown only the sequence of subgoals that the system produces, omitting the assertions from (13) except when they directly match a subgoal. (Double lines indicate the exceptions in the figures.) The inset pictures of the Towers of Hanoi disks and pegs illustrate the actions that the system performs in response to the *Transfer_disk* subgoals. The starting configuration appears near Subgoal a in figure 9.6. As usual, the system starts with the conclusion of (13), shown in this first figure as Subgoal a. As just mentioned, the backward IF Elimination rule is relevant here, for Subgoal a matches the THEN part of (13d). Carrying out this IF Elimination strategy means trying to prove the IF part of the same premise, which appears as Subgoal b. This second subgoal is a long conjunction, and so the backward AND Introduction rule (table 9.1) applies to it, instructing the system to prove each part of the conjunction in turn.[10] The resulting *Next_disk, Stack_tower, Transfer_disk,* and *Stack_tower* subgoals appear directly above Subgoal b in figure 9.6. The first of these subgoals, *Next_disk(Disk1, b1)?*, is satisfied by matching against (13a), *Next_disk(Disk1, Disk2)*, and AND Introduction then substitutes *Disk2* for *b1* in the remaining subgoals currently on the agenda.

As figure 9.7 shows, the system next attempts Subgoal e, *Stack_tower(Disk2, PegL, PegC, PegR)?*, which requests that the two-disk tower consisting of the two smaller disks be moved out of the way onto the center peg. Notice that this second *Stack_tower* goal has the same form as the original Goal a. Thus, the very same strategy of plugging into (13d) is available. The system again uses a combination of IF Elimination and AND Introduction to generate the four subgoals in g, i, k, and l in the figure. This "decomposes [the] problem into smaller problems until ... the 'pyramids' to be moved have been reduced to single disks—that is to goals of making single legal moves." Subgoal g checks to see which disk is the next size smaller than Disk2 (*Next_disk(Disk2, b2)?*) and immediately determines that the next disk is Disk3 by matching to (13b). Subgoal i requests that the tower whose largest disk is Disk3 be moved to PegR. This subgoal, *Stack_tower(Disk3, PegL, PegR, PegC)?*, is exactly the special case for which we envisioned premise (13c): The tower consisting of just the smallest disk can be transferred immediately. This is put into action when IF Elimination matches Subgoal i to the THEN part of (13c), and the resulting *Transfer_disk* operation appears at j. This is the first actual move in the solution: Disk 3 is picked up from the left peg and placed on the right peg, resulting in the configuration that appears above Subgoal j in figure 9.7. Having transferred Disk3, the system can similarly transfer Disk2 to the center peg (Subgoal k), and then place Disk3 on top of Disk2 (Subgoal m). At this point, then, the system has completed its mission of stacking the tower whose largest disk is Disk2 onto the center peg; that is,

10. One slight simplification in figures 9.6–9.8 is that it treats Subgoals b, f, and p as four-part conjunctions, rather than the two-part conjunctions of the AND Introduction rule of table 9.1. To translate the problem into the two-part format, we could simply rewrite (13d) as

```
IF Next_disk(xdisk, ydisk)
   AND (Stack_tower(ydisk, xpeg, zpeg, ypeg)
      AND (Transfer_disk(xdisk, ypeg)
         AND Stack_tower(ydisk, zpeg, ypeg, xpeg)))
THEN Stack_tower(xdisk, xpeg, ypeg, zpeg).
```

This would increase the total number of subgoals that occur during the solution process, but has no other effect on the proof.

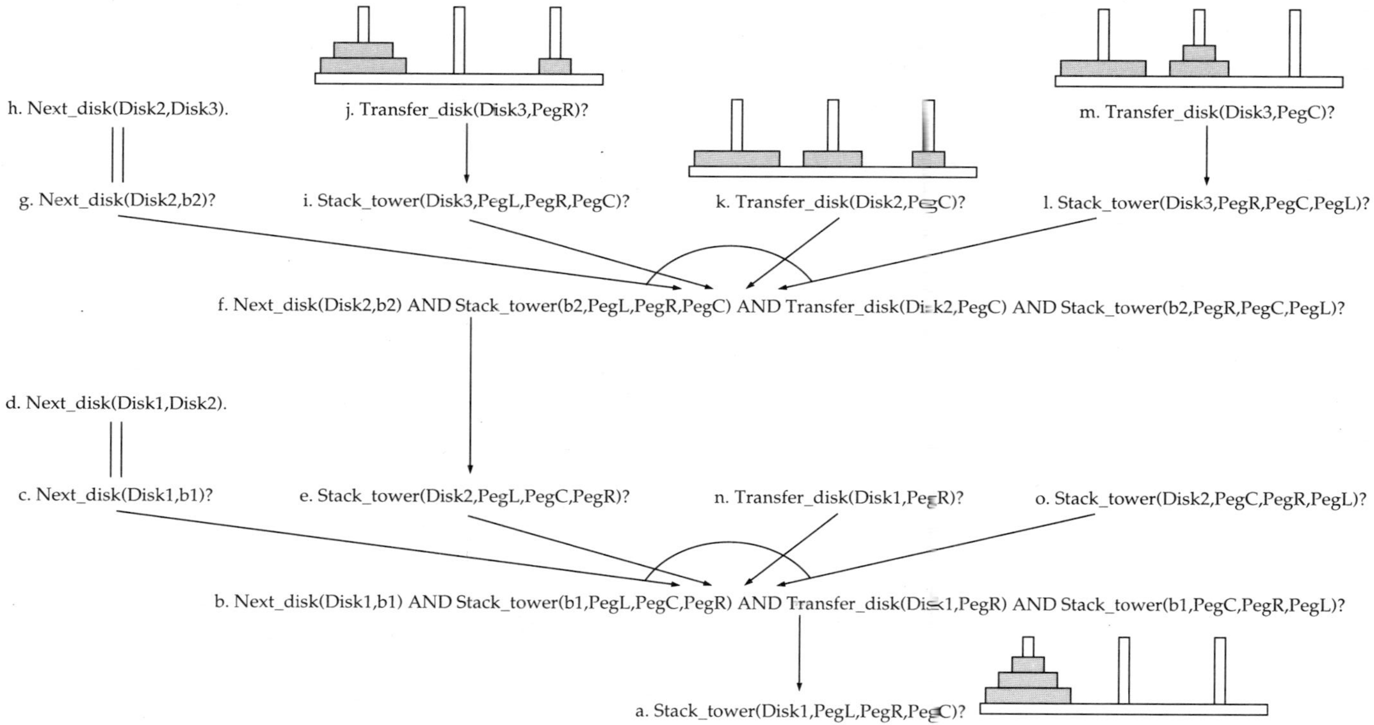

Figure 9.7
Solution to the 3-peg Towers of Hanoi problem, continued.

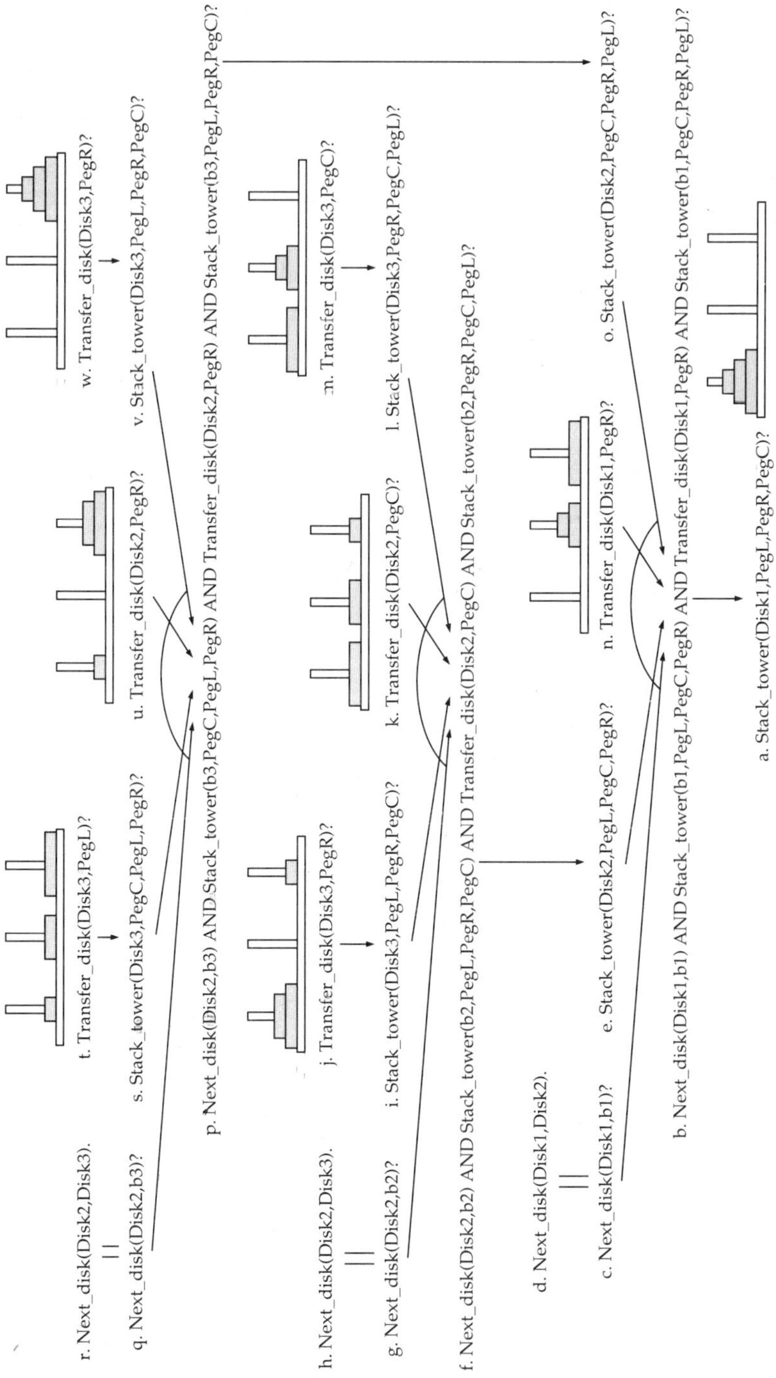

Figure 9.8
Final part of the solution to the 3-peg Towers of Hanoi problem.

it has now fulfilled Subgoal e. The disks and pegs now look like the picture above Subgoal m, and the system can return to the still unfulfilled subgoals n and o.

The rest of the Towers of Hanoi problem is solved through a combination of the same steps, as you can trace in figure 9.8. This figure shows the final steps that lead to the solution state at Subgoal w. Notice that there are a variable number of intermediate subgoals that the system must process before it can make the next move. For example, only one intermediate goal occurs between the move at k and the move at m in figure 9.8. However, four intermediate goals occur between move n and move t. Egan and Greeno (1974) found that people's errors increase with the number of intervening goals, which is what we would expect if more goals consume more memory and more processing resources.

This example should help clarify how it is that a system based on deduction rules can guide cognition in tasks that aren't specifically deductive. The key point is that the system can insert in working memory information that is not necessarily an entailment of the premises. In the Towers of Hanoi example, the *Transfer_disk* goals that move the disks are cases in point. It's easy to imagine other examples in which the system adds sentences to memory under conditions that support these sentences but don't entail them. (See Rips 1994, ch. 8, for an illustration of how such a system can classify objects from inductive evidence.) This does not mean that cognition is nothing but deductive reasoning. It is simply that a deduction system is rich enough to support and to coordinate a variety of procedures, some of which may not directly deal with entailments.

9.6 Applications to Experimental Findings

Let's go back to some results from psychological studies to see whether the deduction system that we've just developed can shed any light on them. We first review a number of studies which investigators have designed to test models like the one in section 9.4 and which seem to support some of the models' basic predictions. We then consider possible problems for these models that arise from the belief bias and the probabilistic effects that we met in subsections 9.2.1 and 9.2.2.

9.6.1 An Empirical Brief for the Deduction System

Results supporting our approach to deduction fall into several classes. Most of the support comes from experiments in which people inspect a series of arguments and judge whether each of these arguments is logically correct (whether "the conclusion follows logically from the premises" or whether "the conclusion must be true whenever the premises are true").

The number of correct responses for an argument, the average time that it takes to evaluate the argument, or the average rating of the difficulty of evaluating the argument constitute the dependent variables. This procedure has the advantage of gathering data on a fairly broad range of arguments in an efficient way. A smaller number of more labor-intensive experiments, however, have looked at what people say when they think aloud while solving a deduction puzzle. Still others have examined people's ability to follow or to remember text that embodies certain inferences.

9.6.1.1 *Argument evaluation*

The object of the game in argument-evaluation experiments is to predict the relative difficulty of each of a group of arguments from a theory such as the one in section 9.4. As we have just seen, argument difficulty is generally measured in terms of the percentage of people who get the wrong answer, their difficulty ratings, or the amount of time it takes them. The key idea is that those problems which require a small number of steps, according to the theory, should be easier than those which require many. This consequence follows from the general consideration, common to many studies in cognitive psychology, that executing a large number of steps in solving a problem consumes more time and leaves more room for error. Investigators have usually counted the number of steps as the number of times the system applies its rules in trying to prove the argument. (This total might include rule applications that occur during false starts, as well as those which occur in a correct proof.) And so if the theory constructs the proof of an argument by means of a single application of a rule, but needs two rule applications for the proof of a second argument, then people should take less time to solve the first than the second, they should rate the first easier than the second, and more of them should get the correct answer for the first than for the second (other things being equal).

As an example of this method, Braine et al. (1984) asked people to evaluate the conclusion and to rate the difficulty of 85 separate arguments. Arguments (14)–(16) were among these problems, which were said to be about the presence or absence of letters on an imaginary blackboard:

(14) There is a G.
There is an S.
___
There is a G and an S?

(15) If there is an E, then there is not a K.
There is an E.
___
There is a K?

(16) If there is both an A and an M, then there's not an S.
There is an A.
There is an M.

There is an S?

We can deduce the conclusion of argument (14) merely by applying the AND Introduction rule (see table 9.1); thus this argument should be relatively easy. Likewise, in argument (15), we can use IF Elimination to deduce that there is not a K. Because this contradicts the conclusion of (15), it is easy to see that this conclusion does not follow. Argument (16), however, combines the steps of (14) and (15). We need AND Introduction to get *There is both an A and an M* and then IF Elimination to deduce *There's not an S*, as we have seen in the proof in (9) and in figure 9.4. This last sentence contradicts the conclusion of (16); hence, this conclusion does not follow. The important point is that (16) requires more steps than either (14) or (15) alone; and so we would expect people to rate (16) as more difficult than either of the other problems, which is what Braine et al. found.[11] Across the entire set of arguments, the correlation between number of rule applications and rated difficulty was .79.

Other predictions follow from the type of rules that appear in a proof. Other things being equal, an argument whose proof requires a smaller variety of rules should be easier than one whose proof needs a wider variety. For example, we'd expect people to have less difficulty with an argument whose proof uses three applications of the same rule than with an argument whose proof uses one application of each of three *different* rules. In addition, individual rules can vary in their complexity, and proofs that require simpler rules will be easier than proofs that require complex ones. When Braine et al. (1984) included an index of the complexity of each rule in their predictions of argument difficulty, the correlation between predictions and ratings increased from .79 to .92. Investigators have proposed and substantiated predictions based on rule complexity and number of rules for many logic domains—for example, arguments based on sentence connectives (Braine et al. 1984; Osherson 1974–1976; Rips 1994), on single variables or constants (Osherson 1974–1976; Rips 1994), on multiple variables or constants (Rips 1994), on constructs such as necessity/possibility and obligation/permission (Osherson 1974–1976), and on liar/truth-teller problems (Rips 1989).

11. Argument (16) is also somewhat longer than either (14) or (15), and length could also contribute to the difficulty of evaluating it. However, Braine et al. (1984) found that statistically controlling the length of the problems did not eliminate the effect of number of rules.

9.6.1.2 Inferences in understanding text

The distinction we have made between forward and backward rules (see subsection 9.4.2) leads to some further tests of the theory. Recall that forward rules, such as the forward IF Elimination rule in (7), depend only on assertions that are already in the proof. Once the system knows that "p" and "IF p THEN q," it can deduce "q" automatically. However, backward rules, such as the backward AND Introduction rule in (6′) require subgoals before they can apply. If the system encounters "p" and "q," it does not automatically draw the conclusion "p AND q"; it needs a subgoal to prove "p AND q" in order to motivate that inference. This difference gives rise to a number of related predictions. Consider a situation in which you are reading a prose passage:

(a) Suppose you come to a group of sentences (for example, "p" and "IF p THEN q") that permit a forward inference. According to the theory just discussed, you should make the inference ("q") immediately. Thus if you then come across the same conclusion later in the passage, you should be quite fast in recognizing that it follows. By contrast, if the initial sentences are premises of a backward inference (for example, "p" and "q"), you will not automatically draw the conclusion ("p AND q"). Hence, if you later read that conclusion in the passage, you should be relatively slow in appreciating that it follows, for you must now stop and perform the necessary backward reasoning. This difference in reaction times for forward versus backward conclusions has been confirmed in an experiment reported in Rips (1994, ch. 5).

(b) In situation (a) we assumed that the passage includes an explicit statement of the conclusion. But imagine instead that the passage omits the conclusion entirely. The theory predicts that from the premises of a forward inference (for example, "p" and "IF p THEN q") you will draw the conclusion ("q") on your own. From the premises of a backward inference (for example, from "p" and "q"), however, you may never draw the conclusion ("p AND q"). Hence, if you are later asked whether the conclusion appeared in the passage, you should be more likely to say "yes" for the forward conclusion than for the backward conclusion. In line with this idea, Lea, O'Brien, Fisch, Noveck, and Braine (1990) found larger false-alarm rates in recognition memory (that is, more cases in which people incorrectly stated that they had seen a sentence in the text) for forward conclusions than for backward conclusions across a number of inference types.

(c) Finally, consider a situation similar to (a), except that before reading the passage you receive a question about the upcoming inference. For example, before reading the passage containing "p" and "IF p THEN q," the experimenter asks you to decide whether "q" follows from the passage. Similarly, before reading the passage with "p" and "q," the experimenter asks whether "p AND q" follows. Because these questions invoke subgoals, you should be prepared to apply backward rules during reading. In the passage with "IF p THEN q" and "p," backward IF Elimination in (7′) (as well as forward IF Elimination in (7)) will allow you to deduce "q"; and likewise in the passage with "p" and "q," backward AND Introduction in (6′) will allow you to deduce "p AND q." Thus, the preliminary question should eliminate the difference between the two passage types that appeared in (a). A result like this one (using categorical sentences such as *All exhibits in the Nelson museum are paintings* rather than IF's and AND's) was obtained by Carlson, Lundy, and Yaure (1992).

9.6.1.3 Protocol results

A third type of evidence for systems like that of section 9.4 comes from the mumblings of people that occur when they must think aloud while solving a problem. The transcripts of this verbalizing are called *protocols* (see the discussion in chapter 8). Table 9.2 contains an example of this sort from a study of how people solve liar/truth-teller puzzles, such as the one that appears at the top of the table (from Smullyan 1978). In this problem, *knights* are characters who tell only the truth, and *knaves* are characters

Table 9.2
A liar/truth-teller puzzle from Smullyan (1978) and its solution by a student asked to think aloud while solving it (Rips 1989).

Problem:

Suppose there are three individuals, A, B, and C, each of whom is either a knight or a knave.
Also, suppose that two people are of the same *type* if they are both knights or both knaves.
A says, "B is a knave."
B says, "A and C are of the same type."
Question: Is C a knight or a knave?

Solution by Subject 3:

Well, the *type* introduction, that's a little confusing.
If A is a knight, then B has to be lying.
So A and C are of, are not of the same type.
That would mean that B and C are knaves.
So that's one possibility.
If A is a knave, then B is a knight, and A and C are both knaves.
Now I've forgotten my first possibility.
If A is a knight, then B ... if A is a knight, B is a knave, and C is a knave.
So my first possibility is C is a knave.
Second possibility is if A is a knave.... Wait a minute....
If A is a knight, no, if A is a knight, then C is a knave.
Uh, if A is a knave ... then C is a knave.
So, either way, C is a knave.

who only lie. Using this information, together with the facts stated in the problem, you should be able to answer the question shown at the top. You may want to solve the problem on your own and compare your strategy to that of the person whose answer appears in table 9.2. (At the time of the study, this person was a freshman who had no training in formal logic.)

Perhaps not too much should be claimed for this thinking-aloud evidence, because it is possible that people actually solve the problem in a way that is not fully reflected in their verbal statements (Nisbett and Wilson 1977). Still, this individual's solution exhibits a common pattern of reasoning that is interesting in its own right. Her solution progresses by assuming that speaker A is a knight and deducing consequences about the knight or knave status of B and C. She concludes that if A is a knight, then B and C must be knaves. She then turns to the possibility that A might be a knave and quickly determines that in this case, too, C would be a knave. Although at one point she loses track of one of these possibilities and has to go back to recompute it, she eventually determines that no matter whether A is a knight or a knave, C must be a knave, which is the right answer to the puzzle. This pattern of making assumptions and deducing entailments from them in a step-by-step fashion is quite consistent with the natural-deduction method of section 9.4. In fact, it is possible to produce a theory along these lines that accounts for the general shape of the thinking-aloud evidence, as well as for response times and errors in solving knight/knave puzzles (Rips 1989). The theory includes rules such as forward IF Elimination, along with more specific rules for the knight–knave domain (for example, "A is a knight" and "A says P" entail "P"). (See Johnson-Laird and Byrne 1991 for an alternative account of knight/knave problems based on mental models.)

9.6.2 Belief Bias, Probabilistic Effects, and "Errors" in Reasoning

The evidence we have just considered supports some of the assumptions of our deduction system. However, there are also a number of findings that appear to pose a challenge or define some limits for a system of this type. Most of this evidence comes from experiments in which people seem to be reasoning incorrectly—where the conclusions they draw depart from those they would give if they were strictly following logical rules. We should therefore take a closer look at the nature of these errors, for it is not always an easy matter to convict someone of a mistake in reasoning (Cohen 1981).

When a psychologist analyzes the number of errors on a reasoning problem, the errors that she counts are cases in which the answer deviates from the one she obtained by translating the problem into some logical formalism (for example, classical logic). This means that some of the "errors" could be due to inappropriate analysis on the psychologist's part rather than to any failure of the subject. Because there are rival logic systems that differ in the entailments they sanction, the psychologist would have to justify one system over another before correctly blaming the subject for an erroneous response to one of the disputed arguments. Similarly, there is usually more than one way to translate the English sentences that appear in the experiment into the logic-based representation. Translation differences could also give rise to spurious errors.

Even if we grant that the psychologist can justify the choice of correct answers, there are still many potential causal factors underlying people's responses, and some of these we might be hesitant to classify as errors of reasoning (Henle 1962). Some of these factors are highlighted in the system of section 9.4. A person's answer might differ from the approved one because: (1) the problem exceeded the capacity of working memory; (2) activation placed in working memory sentences that were associated with, but not strictly part of, the problem; (3) the person didn't possess an inference rule that was necessary for the solution; (4) the person failed to apply an inference rule when it was appropriate to do so (perhaps due to the complexity of the problem sentences); (5) the person applied an inference rule when it was inappropriate to do so (perhaps because he or she relaxed one of the conditions on the rule); (6) the output of the rule was garbled; (7) the person incorrectly took failure to find a proof as evidence of his or her inability rather than as evidence for the absence of an entailment. Other deduction theories would, of course, have alternative explanations of error. In addition, many peripheral factors could also cause errors, such as (8) misunderstanding the experimental instructions, (9) misunderstanding the problem statements, (10) time limits, or (11) failure to attend to important features of the problem. Not all these factors apply in any given situation, of course, but usually several of them are possible causes. In such cases we may have a choice as to whether the error is due to factors connected with reasoning (for example, misapplying a rule), to factors connected with interference from other processes (such as distractions), or to borderline factors that we may or may not want to call "reasoning" (including comprehension problems, such as (8) and (9), or decision problems such as (7)).

It seems clear that a deduction system, such as the one we developed earlier, is consistent with errors arising from the factors just listed. As we've seen, some of the strongest evidence in favor of such a system comes from error data. However, what about the systematic trends due to belief bias or to probabilistic effects that we ran into earlier? Don't these show that there's something wrong with the system's assumptions?

Belief bias occurs when people base their judgment of an argument's correctness on belief in its conclusion, as in examples (10a–b). Figure 9.2

shows that this is not simply a matter of people forsaking the entailment relation, because the degree of belief bias depends on whether an entailment is present or not; larger belief-bias effects occur when the argument is nondeducible. This suggests one possible way of reconciling belief bias with the deduction system, based on factor (7) above: Perhaps people use their belief in the conclusion when their own deduction abilities give out. If they are unable to find a mental proof for an argument, this may be due (from their point of view) either to the fact that the premises do not entail the conclusion or to their own inability to find a proof. Because people are not ordinarily in a position to determine which of these alternatives is correct, they may resort to other cues, such as whether the conclusion seems sensible. (This is like answering a math problem on the basis of the plausibility of an answer when you're stuck in finding a formal solution.) Because this uncertainty typically occurs when the premises fail to entail the conclusion (these arguments never have proofs), this scenario explains why figure 9.2 shows a bigger effect of belief when the argument is not deducible.[12] Notice, too, that acknowledging such a heuristic mechanism does not necessarily imply that such heuristics exist outside the domain of the deduction system. It is conceivable that the deduction system implements them in the same way as it implements that Towers of Hanoi solution in section 9.5.

We could also explain probabilistic effects, such as that in (11a–b), in terms of a similar fall-back mechanism. If people are uncertain about the outcome of an attempted proof, they may decide on the basis of how likely the conclusion is, given the premises. In the case of (11a), it seems likely that the switch was turned on, given that the light is on; thus people may be willing to gamble that the conclusion of (11a) follows. On the other hand, it is less likely that I turned on the switch, given that the light is on, and people may place less trust in (11b) for this reason. There are other potential explanations, however, based on some of the factors mentioned earlier. It is possible that people interpret their task as one of evaluating degree of support for the conclusion rather than entailment per se, in line with factor (8). This is consistent with the finding that probabilistic effects increase when the experimental instructions deemphasize the logical nature of the task or when the instructions ask people for their confidence in the conclusion (rather than for a simple "follows" versus "doesn't follow" answer). (See Cummins, Lubart, Alksnis, and Rist

12. For very easy arguments, people will tend to be more successful in obtaining a proof when the argument is deducible and less likely to blame failure to find a proof on their own inabilities. Under mild assumptions, this should increase the difference due to deducibility, decrease the difference due to believability, and decrease the size of the interaction between them, relative to the results shown in figure 9.2. Newstead et al. (1992) obtained these effects, though their account of them differs from the one offered here.

1991; Fillenbaum 1977.) It is also possible that mention of switches and lights in arguments (11a) and (11b) evokes additional information from long-term memory (factor (2) above). The representational assumptions of the theory provide a mechanism for this retrieval in the links that run between working memory and long-term memory, as in figure 9.3. Long-term information might specify that a light normally goes on if and only if its switch is turned on, providing warrant for (11a). The same information might indicate that a light goes on if (but not only if) I turn on the switch, which would undercut (11b). At this point, it is unclear which of these explanations—a probabilistic inference process or retrieval of associatively related information—provides the best account of the results.

9.7 Summary

The discussion of errors in the preceding section takes us back to our original puzzle about logical intuition: How can we reconcile the primitive character of the entailment relation with evidence for human mistakes on deduction problems? On one hand, IF Elimination, AND Introduction, and the matching rules license inferences that are obvious to everyone. Although formulating the rules may take some ingenuity, the inferences that these rules produce seem decisive to people. No special training in logic or math is necessary to appreciate them. Furthermore, many cognitive processes presuppose instantiation (that is, matching) and other logical operations that these same rules provide. We've seen how it is possible to construct a deduction system by means of these rules that is capable, not only of proving simple theorems, but also of solving problems such as the Towers of Hanoi and other higher cognitive tasks.

On the other hand, people's judgment about deduction problems isn't always what we would expect on the basis of textbook logic. People often fail to make inferences that embody logical entailments. We've seen, however, that there are many ways in which deduction "errors" can materialize even in a system that operates strictly in accord with logical rules. Although the individual parts of a problem may be obvious, the correct judgment may fail to occur, due to the number or the variety of component steps, to memory or time limits, to interference from related information in memory, and to many other factors. In such cases, people may base their answers on simple procedures built around believability or probability, perhaps implemented within the same deduction framework. If current philosophical theories are correct (for example, Davidson 1970), errors like these are only identifiable against a background of correct reasoning; and so we must balance descriptions of errors with theories of correct judgment.

Suggestions for Further Reading

There's no shortage of introductory surveys of psychological research on deduction. Among the most recent are Galotti (1989) and Evans, Newstead, and Byrne (1993). Braine and Rumain (1983) is a review of the literature on logical reasoning in children and is written from the perspective of a rule-based account, similar to the one developed in section 9.4. Johnson-Laird and Byrne (1991) is the book to read for the mental-model theory of deduction. (As mentioned in the text, Johnson-Laird and Byrne develop a psychological proposal based on the notion of semantic entailment.) Braine, Reiser, and Rumain (1984), Osherson (1974–1976), and Rips (1994) provide specific theories of deduction based on logical rules. Much recent work has been directed to explanations of a task in which people must determine whether specific instances are consistent or inconsistent with conditional sentences. See Evans et al. (1993) and Wason and Johnson-Laird (1972) for reviews, and Cheng and Holyoak (1985), Cosmides (1989), Griggs and Cox (1982), and Manktelow and Over (1991) for original research.

For background on logic, you could start with Bergmann, Moor, and Nelson (1980) or Enderton (1972), among many other introductory textbooks. You can find more advanced treatments in Smullyan (1968) or van Fraassen (1971). A good place to look for special topics in logic is the *Handbook of Philosophical Logic* (Gabbay and Guenthner 1983–1989), which has chapters on modal logic, presupposition, quantifiers, and many other areas. Genesereth and Nilsson (1987) provide an introduction to the role of deduction in artificial intelligence.

Problems

9.1 a. Using the rules of section 9.1.1, prove that *Ted is majoring in Phlebotomy* follows from (a) *Martha is majoring in Astronomy* and (b) *IF Martha is majoring in Astronomy THEN (Calvin is majoring in Gastronomy AND Ted is majoring in Phlebotomy).*

b. Using the rules of section 9.1.1, prove that *Ted is majoring in Phlebotomy AND Calvin is majoring in Gastronomy* follows from (a) *IF Calvin is majoring in Gastronomy THEN Ted is majoring in Phlebotomy* and (b) *Calvin is majoring in Gastronomy.*

9.2 Suppose that a sentence of the form *p OR q* is true in a model **M** iff either *p* is true in **M** or *q* is true in **M**. Let $\mathbf{M}_1$ = {*Dewey is majoring in Cosmetology, Louie is majoring in Cosmogony*}. Which of these sentences are true in $\mathbf{M}_1$? Which of these sentences are true in $\mathbf{M}_2$ = {*Huey is majoring in Cosmology, Dewey is majoring in Cosmetology*}?

a. Huey is majoring in Cosmology OR Dewey is majoring in Cosmetology.

b. Huey is majoring in Cosmology AND Dewey is majoring in Cosmetology.

c. (Huey is majoring in Cosmology AND Dewey is majoring in Cosmetology) OR Louie is majoring in Cosmogony.

d. Huey is majoring in Cosmology AND (Dewey is majoring in Cosmetology OR Louie is majoring in Cosmogony).

e. (Huey is majoring in Cosmology OR Dewey is majoring in Cosmetology) AND Louie is majoring in Cosmogony.

9.3 For each of the following pairs, let the left-hand sentence be an assertion and the right-hand sentence be a subgoal. Decide in each case whether the arguments of the paired sentences match according to the rules of table 9.1.

a. Contemplates(Fred,Martha)	Contemplates(a,b)
b. Contemplates(Fred,Fred)	Contemplates(a,b)
c. Contemplates(Fred,Martha)	Contemplates(a,a) (that is, someone contemplates him- or herself)
d. Contemplates(Fred,Fred)	Contemplates(a,a)
e. Contemplates(x,y)	Contemplates(Fred,Martha)

f. Contemplates(x,x) (that is, everyone contemplates him- or herself) — Contemplates(Fred,Martha)
g. Contemplates(x,y) — Contemplates(Fred,Fred)
h. Contemplates(x,x) — Contemplates(Fred,Fred)

Do the matching pairs correspond to your intuition about whether the assertion entails the subgoal?

9.4 Consider a modification to the Towers of Hanoi program of section 9.5 that omits the second *Stack_tower* predicate in line (13d). That is, (13d) would now appear as:

IF Next_disk(xdisk,ydisk)
AND Stack_tower(ydisk,xpeg,zpeg,ypeg)
AND Transfer_disk(xdisk,ypeg)
THEN Stack_tower(xdisk,xpeg,ypeg,zpeg).

If the rest of (13) is unchanged, would the system still be able to prove the conclusion? What moves of the disks would be made during the attempted proof?

References

Adams, E. (1965). The logic of conditionals. *Inquiry* 8, 166–197.

Anderson, A. R., and N. D. Belnap, Jr. (1975). *Entailment: The logic of relevance and necessity*, vol. 1. Princeton, NJ: Princeton University Press.

Anderson, J. R. (1993). *Rules of the mind.* Hillsdale, NJ: Erlbaum.

Bergmann, M., J. Moor, and J. Nelson (1980). *The logic book.* New York: Random House.

Black, M. (1970). *Margins of precision.* Ithaca, NY: Cornell University Press.

Bonatti, L. (1994). Why should we abandon the mental logic hypothesis? *Cognition* 50, 17–39.

Braine, M. D. S., B. J. Reiser, and B. Rumain (1984). Some empirical justification for a theory of natural propositional reasoning. In G. H. Bower, ed., *Psychology of learning and motivation*, vol. 18. New York: Academic Press.

Braine, M. D. S., and B. Rumain (1983). Logical reasoning. In P. H. Mussen, ed., *Handbook of child psychology*, vol. 3. New York: Wiley.

Carlson, R. A., D. H. Lundy, and R. G. Yaure (1992). Syllogistic inference chains in meaningful text. *American Journal of Psychology* 105, 75–99.

Carroll, L. (1895). What the Tortoise said to Achilles. *Mind* 14, 278–280.

Chang, C. C., and H. J. Keisler (1973). *Model theory.* Amsterdam: North-Holland.

Cheng, P. W., and K. J. Holyoak (1985). Pragmatic reasoning schemas. *Cognitive Psychology* 17, 391–416.

Cherniak, C. (1986). *Minimal rationality.* Cambridge, MA: MIT Press.

Clocksin, W. F., and C. S. Mellish (1981). *Programming in Prolog.* New York: Springer-Verlag.

Cohen, L. J. (1981). Can human irrationality be experimentally demonstrated? *Behavioral and Brain Sciences* 4, 317–370.

Cosmides, L. (1989). The logic of social exchange: Has natural selection shaped how humans reason? *Cognition* 31, 187–276.

Cummins, D. D., T. Lubart, O. Alksnis, and R. Rist (1991). Conditional reasoning and causation. *Memory and Cognition* 19, 274–282.

Davidson, D. (1970). Mental events. In L. Foster and J. W. Swanson, eds., *Experience and theory.* Amherst: University of Massachusetts Press.

Dennett, D. (1981). True believers: The intentional strategy and why it works. In A. F. Heath, ed., *Scientific explanation.* Oxford: Clarendon.

Egan, D. E., and J. G. Greeno (1974). A theory of rule induction: Knowledge acquired in concept learning, serial pattern learning, and problem solving. In L. W. Gregg, ed., *Knowledge and cognition*. Hillsdale, NJ: Erlbaum.

Enderton, H. B. (1972). *A mathematical introduction to logic*. New York: Academic Press.

Evans, J. St. B. T., J. L. Barston, and P. Pollard (1983). On the conflict between logic and belief in syllogistic reasoning. *Memory and Cognition* 11, 295–306.

Evans, J. St. B. T., S. E. Newstead, and R. M. J. Byrne (1993). *Human reasoning: The psychology of deduction*. Hillsdale, NJ: Erlbaum.

Field, H. H. (1977). Logic, meaning, and conceptual role. *Journal of Philosophy* 74, 379–409.

Fillenbaum, S. (1977). Mind your *p*'s and *q*'s: The role of content and context in some uses of *and, or,* and *if*. In G. H. Bower, ed., *Psychology of learning and motivation* (vol. 11). New York: Academic Press.

Fodor, J. A. (1975). *The language of thought*. New York: Crowell.

Frege, G. (1893/1964). *The basic laws of arithmetic*. Berkeley: University of California Press.

Gabbay, D., and F. Guenthner (1983–1989). *Handbook of philosophical logic*, vols. 1–4. Dordrecht: Reidel.

Galotti, K. M. (1989). Approaches to studying formal and everyday reasoning. *Psychological Bulletin* 105, 331–351.

Genesereth, M. R., and N. J. Nilsson (1987). *Logical foundations of artificial intelligence*. Palo Alto, CA: Morgan Kaufmann.

Gilhooly, K. J., R. H. Logie, N. E. Wetherick, and V. Wynn (1993). Working memory and strategies in syllogistic reasoning. *Memory and Cognition* 21, 115–124.

Grice, H. P. (1989). *Studies in the way of words*. Cambridge, MA: Harvard University Press.

Griggs, R. A., and J. R. Cox (1982). The elusive thematic materials effect in the Wason selection task. *British Journal of Psychology* 73, 407–420.

Haviland, S. E. (1974). *Nondeductive strategies in reasoning*. Ph.D. thesis. Stanford University.

Henle, M. (1962). On the relation between logic and thinking. *Psychological Review* 69, 366–378.

Hitch, G. J., and A. D. Baddeley (1976). Verbal reasoning and working memory. *Quarterly Journal of Experimental Psychology* 28, 603–621.

Hodges, W. (1993). The logical content of theories of deduction. *Behavioral and Brain Sciences* 16, 353–354.

Holland, J. H., K. J. Holyoak, R. E. Nisbett, and P. R. Thagard (1986). *Induction: Processes of inference, learning, and discovery*. Cambridge, MA: MIT Press.

Johnson-Laird, P. N., and R. M. J. Byrne (1991). *Deduction*. Hillsdale, NJ: Erlbaum.

Lea, R . B., D. P. O'Brien, S. M. Fisch, I. A. Noveck, and M. D. S. Braine (1990). Predicting propositional logic inferences in text comprehension. *Journal of Memory and Language* 29, 361–387.

Manktelow, K. I., and D. E. Over (1991). Social roles and utilities in reasoning with deontic conditionals. *Cognition* 39, 85–105.

Massey, G. J. (1981). The fallacy behind fallacies. In P. A. French, T. E. Uehling, and H. K. Wettstein, eds., *Midwest studies in philosophy*, vol. VI. Minneapolis, MN: University of Minnesota Press.

McCarthy, J. (1988). Mathematical logic in artificial intelligence. In S. R. Graubard, ed., *The artificial intelligence debate*. Cambridge, MA: MIT Press.

Morgan, J. J. B., and J. T. Morton (1944). The distortion of syllogistic reasoning produced by personal convictions. *Journal of Social Psychology* 20, 39–59.

Newell, A. (1990). *Unified theories of cognition*. Cambridge, MA: Harvard University Press.

Newstead, S. E., P. Pollard, J. St. B. T. Evans, and J. L. Allen (1992). The source of belief bias effects in syllogistic reasoning. *Cognition* 45, 257–284.

Nisbett, R. E., and T. D. Wilson (1977). Telling more than we can know: Verbal reports on mental processes. *Psychological Review* 84, 231–259.

Osherson, D. N. (1974–1976). *Logical abilities in children,* vols. 2–4. Hillsdale, NJ: Erlbaum.
Pollard, P. (1982). Human reasoning: Some possible effects of availability. *Cognition* 12, 65–96.
Popper, K. R. (1968). *The logic of scientific discovery.* New York: Harper and Row.
Potter, M. C. (1993). Very short term conceptual memory. *Memory and Cognition* 21, 156–161.
Quine, W. V. (1972). *Methods of logic.* 3rd ed. New York: Holt, Rinehart & Winston.
Rips, L. J. (1989). The psychology of knights and knaves. *Cognition* 31, 85–116.
Rips, L. J. (1990). Reasoning. *Annual Review of Psychology* 41, 321–353.
Rips, L. J. (1994). *The psychology of proof: Deductive reasoning in human thinking.* Cambridge, MA: MIT Press.
Rips, L. J., and F. G. Conrad (1983). Individual differences in deduction. *Cognition and Brain Theory* 6, 259–285.
Simon, H. A. (1975). The functional equivalence of problem solving skills. *Cognitive Psychology* 7, 268–288.
Skolem, T. (1967). On mathematical logic. In J. van Heijenoort, ed., *From Frege to Godel: A source book in mathematical logic, 1879–1931.* Cambridge, MA: Harvard University Press. (Original work published 1928.)
Smullyan, R. M. (1968). *First-order logic.* New York: Springer-Verlag.
Smullyan, R. M. (1978). *What is the name of this book? The riddle of Dracula and other logical puzzles.* Englewood Cliffs, NJ: Prentice-Hall.
Staudenmayer, H. (1975). Understanding conditional reasoning with meaningful propositions. In R. J. Falmagne, ed., *Reasoning: Representation and process.* Hillsdale, NJ: Erlbaum.
Stroud, B. (1979). Inference, belief, and understanding. *Mind* 88, 179–196.
Toms, M., N. Morris, and D. Ward (1993). Working memory and conditional reasoning. *Quarterly Journal of Experimental Psychology* 46A, 679–699.
Tversky, A., and D. Kahneman (1983). Extensional versus intuitive reasoning: The conjunction fallacy in probability judgment. *Psychological Review* 90, 292–315.
van Fraassen, B. C. (1971). *Formal semantics and logic.* New York: Macmillan.
Wason, P. C., and P. N. Johnson-Laird (1972). *The psychology of reasoning.* Cambridge, MA: Harvard University Press.

Chapter 10

Social Cognition: Information Accessibility and Use in Social Judgment

Norbert Schwarz

10.1 Introduction

When we interpret new information, or form a judgment about some person or social situation, what knowledge do we draw on? For example, when we learn that someone we have just met enjoys skydiving and whitewater rafting, do we identify these hobbies as adventurous or as reckless? And when asked how life is going these days, which aspects of our life do we consider? Do we review the many facets of life, or do we simply rely on whatever happens to come to mind? In more general terms, when a variety of information may potentially be relevant to a judgment, which information are we most likely to use? This is the key issue addressed in the present chapter. This issue has fascinated psychologists for many decades and is a main topic of research in an area called social cognition.

What, however, is *social cognition*? As Martin and Clark (1990, 265) put it, "Social cognition is an approach to the understanding of human social behavior. It involves the investigation of the mental processes that come into play when people interact with one another." This approach addresses topics that have traditionally been of interest to social psychologists, such as person perception, stereotyping, social interaction, group behavior, and attitude formation and change (see Fiske and Taylor 1991 for a textbook-length review of social cognition research). In all these areas, social psychologists have traditionally been guided by the assumption that individuals do not react to the world per se, but to the world as they see it. Hence, understanding how people make sense of their social environment has been a major focus of social psychological research, even in times when research in other areas of psychology was dominated by behaviorist approaches that paid little attention to "nonobservables," such as cognitive processes (see Markus and Zajonc 1985). Following the "cognitive revolution" in experimental psychology, social psychologists borrowed theoretical insights and methodological tools (such as reaction-time measurement) from cognitive psychologists to gain a better understanding of the cognitive processes underlying social judgment and behavior. The emerging area of research at the interface of cognitive and social psychology has been named *social cognition.* This approach has stimulated enormous research productivity and has become the dominant metatheoretical approach in social psychology since early in the 1980s, contributing numerous new insights to classic areas of research. However, social cognition research is not restricted to applying cognitive psychology's information-processing paradigm to social stimuli. Rather, social psychologists' attention to social processes has also uncovered how the social context in which human beings do their thinking in turn influences cognitive processes (see McCann and Higgins 1992, Schwarz 1994, for reviews).

Thus, whereas authors of the preceding chapters in this volume address specific cognitive tasks—including remembering, categorization, judgment, deductive reasoning, and problem solving—social cognition as the topic of the present chapter does not pertain to a specific cognitive task. Rather, social cognition denotes a broad domain of research at the interface between cognitive and social psychology. In line with the case-study approach taken in the present series, however, this chapter is focused on one of the key topics in social cognition research, namely accessibility and use of information.

Specifically, I review how fortuitous events may influence what comes to mind later on. As we shall see, what happens to come to mind strongly affects the judgments we form at the time, ranging from our impressions of other people to evaluations of the quality of our life. The processes involved are somewhat different depending on whether we acquire new information or base the judgment solely on information recalled from memory. Moreover, the specific outcome of the judgment process depends not only on what comes to mind, but also on what we do with the information that comes to mind. Accordingly, I review research on the accessibility and subsequent use of information stored in memory, focusing on how we make sense of ambiguous events in our social environment and how we form evaluative judgments about ourselves and others.

10.2 Information Accessibility: Some Basic Assumptions

Most obviously, we can recall information from memory only if it has been stored there at some time. Following terminology introduced by Tulving and Pearlstone (1966; see Higgins, in press, for a more extended discussion of terminology), social cognition researchers usually refer to information stored in memory as *available* information. That a given piece of information is stored somewhere in memory, however, does not necessarily imply that we can recall, or *access,* it at any given time—as we all realize when we search memory without success, only to have the information pop to mind on some other occasion. How likely it is that some piece of information does come to mind, is referred to as that information's *accessibility*. Thus, information that is not available in memory can never be accessed; but information that is available, and may be accessed in principle, varies in its degree of accessibility at any given time.

How accessible information is in memory depends on a number of factors, most notably the recency and frequency of its use (see Higgins 1989, in press, for reviews). Thus, information that has just been used for some other purpose is particularly likely to come to mind later on, when we form a judgment to which it may be relevant. Suppose that you just talked with a friend about a particularly good psychology class. When asked later on how satisfied you are with the education you receive at your university, information bearing on this class would be especially likely to come to mind. As a result, you would probably arrive at a more positive judgment than if you had not thought of this class. In this case, its recent use rendered information about this class *temporarily accessible*. However, the accessibility of this information will decline as time goes on and other information is brought to mind. Information that is used very frequently is also highly accessible in memory, in part because the frequency of its use implies that little time has elapsed since it was last activated. If it is used very frequently, in particular over extended periods, it may eventually become *chronically accessible*. In this case, it is likely to come to mind under many circumstances, independent of temporary influences. Thus, information about a class which you find annoying every time you attend it, and which is the topic of frequent discussion with friends, may become chronically accessible. If so, this information may come to mind when you are asked to evaluate the education you receive, even if you haven't just thought about it. That the accessibility of information varies with the recency and frequency of its use is compatible with different formal models of memory, which provide somewhat different accounts of the underlying processes (see Higgins, in press). These differences are of little concern for the purposes of the present chapter, and are not elaborated here.

Why is it that social cognition researchers consider accessibility of information to be of crucial importance? Shouldn't a field concerned with human social behavior leave these issues to cognitive psychologists, who have traditionally dealt with memory research? In fact, social cognition researchers are not interested in memory per se, but in the role of memory in our thinking about the social world. One of the key assumptions in social cognition research holds that individuals rarely retrieve all the information that may be relevant in forming an impression of another person or a judgment about some social issue, such as the state of the economy or the quality of the education one receives. Given the large amount of information that may potentially be relevant to these tasks, this behavior is no surprise. If we tried to recall all potentially relevant information on each occasion, we might well spend our life lost in thought. Rather, individuals truncate the search for relevant information as soon as enough information has come to mind to form the judgment with sufficient subjective certainty. Accordingly, the judgment is based on the subset of potentially relevant information that comes to mind most easily (see Bodenhausen and Wyer 1987 for a review). This simply reflects that the search process is truncated before less accessible information has been retrieved. In terms of the example above, you would be unlikely to recall and consider all classes you attended when asked to evaluate the quality of your education. Rather, you would truncate the search as soon as some classes had been retrieved, resulting in more positive judgments when these highly accessible classes happened to be good rather than bad.

Of course, we do not always rely on the first few pieces of information that come to mind. If the judgment is very important, or if a mistake would have dramatic consequences, we are likely to engage in a more thorough search of the available information, extending beyond what is highly accessible (see Kruglanski 1989). Thus, if you considered switching majors, for example, you would probably engage in a more thorough information search than if a friend asked you how good your college is. Under most conditions of daily life, however, our judgments are primarily based on the information that is most accessible at the time, which explains social cognition researchers' interest in information accessibility.

In the following sections I review the key influences of information accessibility. The first section addresses how we form an impression of other persons and make sense of their behavior. The subsequent section is focused on evaluative judgments and explores how we determine if life is going well or not. Whereas both of these sections focus on *what* comes to mind, and what we *do* with the information that comes to mind, the final section explores the role of subjective experiences that may accompany the recall process. Specifically, the accessibility of information in memory not only determines what comes to mind but also how easy or difficult we find it to recall some information. These *accessibility experiences*, however, may influence our judgments in their own right.

10.3 Information Accessibility and the Interpretation of Ambiguous Information: Making Sense of the Social Environment

10.3.1 Interpreting Ambiguous Information in Terms of Accessible Concepts: Assimilation Effects

Many aspects of our social environment are inherently ambiguous and need interpretation. Suppose, for example, that a friend describes an old acquaintance with these words: "Once Donald made up his mind to do something it was as good as done, no matter how long it might take or how difficult the going might be. Only rarely did he change his mind, even when it might well have been better if he had."

What kind of person is this Donald? Does he strike you as STUBBORN or as PERSISTENT? As discussed in chapter 1, we make sense of a stimulus by categorizing it. Thus, an object becomes a CHAIR if it resembles our mental representation of the category CHAIR. The more features the object shares with our representation of CHAIR, the more likely we are to consider the object a chair. In much the same way, social psychologists assume that we interpret information about another person in terms of the trait category with which it shares most features. In many cases, however, different trait categories may be applicable to the same behavior. In fact, when Higgins, Rholes, and Jones (1977) developed the ambiguous-person description from which the excerpt above is taken, they observed that their subjects were equally likely to characterize Donald as STUBBORN or as PERSISTENT.

What determines in such a case which concept is used to interpret Donald's behavior? If several alternative concepts are applicable, we are likely to use the one that comes to mind first, that is, the one that is most accessible in memory, as Bruner (1957) assumed four decades ago. One of the key determinants of the accessibility of a concept is the recency of its use; the less time elapsed since we last used a concept, the more easily it comes to mind. Higgins et al. (1977) demonstrated this in their Donald study by asking subjects to participate in two purportedly unrelated experiments. In the first of these experiments, subjects had to memorize different trait words, which were said to serve as distractor words in an alleged perception task. This task was designed to *prime* different trait concepts, that is, to increase their temporary accessibility. Following this priming manipulation, subjects participated in a supposedly unrelated study on "reading comprehension," in which they read an ambiguous description of Donald and were asked to characterize Donald's behaviors in trait terms. As expected, subjects who had to memorize the word STUBBORN as part of the alleged first experiment were more likely to interpret the behavioral description above as indicating that Donald was "stubborn," whereas subjects who had to memorize the word PERSISTENT were more likely to interpret the same behavior as indicating "persistence."

This finding reflects that the activation of the respective trait term in the first experiment increased the cognitive accessibility of the trait concept and thus increased the likelihood that this, rather than the competing concept, was used in interpreting the ambiguous behavioral description. Thus, whether we construe another person's behavior as reflecting persistence, a desirable trait, or stubbornness, an undesirable trait, may depend on fortuitous influences, such as whether one or the other trait concept was rendered accessible in memory by an unrelated event.

This basic finding has been replicated in many studies, using a variety of procedures (see Higgins 1989, in press; Wyer and Srull 1989, for reviews). Throughout, these studies demonstrated that ambiguous information is interpreted in terms of the concept that is most accessible at the time, resulting in what is usually called an *assimilation effect*. That is, the interpretation assimilates the behavior to the meaning of the primed concept. However, these studies have also documented a number of important limiting conditions. Most important, an effect of the primed concept can be observed only if the behavior is ambiguous and hence open to interpretation. Moreover, the primed concept must be applicable to the behavior. Thus, priming the concept FRIENDLY, for example, would not influence our interpretation of the description above. Whereas these conditions need to be satisfied to observe any effect of the primed concepts at all, other conditions determine if the priming manipulation results in the usually observed assimilation effect or its opposite, a *contrast effect*.

10.3.2 Beyond Assimilation: Concept Priming and the Emergence of Contrast Effects

Following the Higgins et al. (1977) initial demonstration of priming effects in impression formation, social cognition researchers assumed for about a decade that increasing the accessibility of a trait concept would always result in assimilation effects, provided that the behavior was ambiguous and the trait concept applicable. All studies that demonstrated assimilation effects, however, were based on very subtle priming manipulations. In most studies, researchers designed procedures that disguised the nature of the priming task by introducing this task as an unrelated experiment (as we have seen above; Higgins et al. 1977), or even by presenting the primes subliminally—that is, outside of subjects' conscious awareness (for example, Bargh and Pietromonaco 1982). This strategy reflects social cognition researchers' interest in avoiding demand effects in experiments. If a trait concept were introduced blatantly one could argue, for example, that subjects use it not because it is highly accessible in memory, but because they infer from the experimental procedures that the experimenter wants them to use this concept (see Orne 1962; Bless, Strack, and Schwarz 1993, for a discussion of demand effects). However, subsequent research demonstrated that the subtlety of the priming procedure is not only of methodological importance but bears in important ways on the underlying cognitive processes.

Specifically, when the trait concept is primed in a subtle manner, subjects are not aware that this concept may come to mind because it has been rendered accessible by the experimental procedures. Rather, they operate on the default assumption that all of us employ in daily life: the thoughts that come to mind in response to an observed behavior presumably reflect our reaction to the behavior. Thus, if STUBBORN comes to mind, it presumably does so because the behavior we observe or read about elicits this reaction. Hence, we characterize the behavior as stubborn and base our evaluation of the person on that characterization. Not so, however, when we have reason to assume, for example, that STUBBORN comes to mind because of the preceding task. In that case, it does not seem to reflect our reaction to the behavior itself and is therefore not used to characterize it. As Martin and his colleagues (for example, Martin 1986; Martin, Seta, and Crelia 1990) suggested, this reflects that we are usually motivated to form an independent and unbiased impression of other persons. Hence, if we are aware that our impression may be unduly influenced by an irrelevant source, we are likely to correct it, as first demonstrated by Martin (1986).

This correction usually results in an impression that is biased in the direction *opposite* to the primed concept. Thus, if STUBBORN comes to mind but we assume it does so for the wrong reason, we may be likely to characterize the person as PERSISTENT. Such contrast effects have been observed in studies that used a blatant priming task, thus ensuring that subjects were aware of the possible influence (Martin 1986; Martin et al. 1990), as well as in studies that reminded subjects of the priming episode before they were asked to form a judgment (Strack, Schwarz, Kübler, Bless, and Wänke 1993). The exact mechanism that underlies these contrast effects, however, is still an open issue and three different accounts have been offered.

As one possibility, Martin (1986; Martin and Achee 1992; Martin et al. 1990) suggested that people try to avoid the concept that seems to come to mind for an extraneous reason. Hence, they search for another concept that is applicable to the ambiguous information they have to interpret. In many cases, this concept will have opposite evaluative implications, as in switching from STUBBORN to PERSISTENT. As a result, our interpretation of the ambiguous information will be opposite to the implications of the concept that was initially primed. As a second possibility, Strack et al. (1993) suggested that we may not use another concept to interpret the ambiguous information—for example, we do not use PERSISTENT instead of STUBBORN—but may only adjust our inferences based on this interpretation. Thus, assuming that our interpretation has been influenced by the primed concept, we may hesitate to characterize the person as very stubborn and may try to provide a more moderate judgment. Given that it is difficult to tell how strong the unwanted influence was, however, we are likely to go overboard in correcting our judgment. As a result, we may "overcorrect" and may characterize the person as even less stubborn than we would have decided even in the absence of any priming manipulation (see Strack 1992 for more extended discussion). Finally, Higgins (1989) suggested that although we may not use the primed trait concept in interpreting the ambiguous behavior, the trait may still come to mind when we have to evaluate the target person. If the trait STUBBORN comes to mind, however, it may also increase the accessibility of extremely stubborn behaviors. To the extent that these behaviors serve as a standard of comparison, the target person may seem less stubborn by comparison than would otherwise be the case, again resulting in a contrast effect.

At present, it is difficult to decide between these different explanations for the emergence of contrast effects as a function of trait priming. Whichever of these processes operates, however, making a correction requires cognitive effort. When individuals' cognitive capacity is taxed by some other task, or when they are not motivated to invest the necessary effort, they proceed on the basis of the default assumption that what comes to mind reflects their reaction to the target. If so, we should typically see assimilation effects under these conditions. In line with this assumption, Martin et al. (1990) observed contrast effects when subjects were aware of the possible influence of the priming manipulation and were motivated and able to process the information in sufficient detail. However, when subjects were distracted by working on a different task (Experiment 1) or were unmotivated (Experiments 2 and 3), an assimilation rather than a contrast effect emerged. This pattern of findings suggests that making a correction is a somewhat effortful process that requires sufficient motivation and cognitive resources. If these conditions are not met, individuals use the concepts that come to mind in forming an impression, even under conditions where the priming manipulation is blatant enough to allow for awareness of its possible influence.

In combination, these studies demonstrate that the accessibility of a concept that is applicable to the information at hand does not always result in concept-consistent interpretations. If we assume that the concept comes to mind for the wrong reason, we try not to be influenced by it. To do so, we try to "correct" our judgment, provided that we have the necessary motivation and cognitive resources. Ironically, however, these correction attempts will typically not eliminate the unwanted influence, but will bias our judgment in the opposite direction.

Section Summary

The research we have reviewed indicates that our interpretation of newly acquired information is strongly influenced by the concepts that are most accessible at the time. When exposed to ambiguous information, we are unlikely to try several categorizations, applying a number of potentially applicable concepts. Rather, we use the first applicable concept that comes to mind and interpret the ambiguous information in terms of that concept. This results in interpretations consistent with the concept, reflecting an assimilation effect. If we are aware that the concept may not reflect our reaction to the target but may come to mind for some extraneous reason, we try to avoid undue influences by "correcting" our judgment. Such correction attempts typically result in contrast effects, that is, a judgment that is biased in the direction opposite to the implications of the primed concept. Correcting our judgments, however, requires some effort and we are likely to do so only when we are sufficiently motivated and have the necessary cognitive resources. If these conditions are not met, we are likely to use the most accessible concept in making sense of ambiguous information, even under conditions where we could be aware that the concept may come to mind for the wrong reason.

Whereas the research above pertained to how we interpret newly acquired ambiguous information, the research reviewed below indicates that similar principles hold for judgments of things we are very familiar with, such as our own life.

10.4 Information Accessibility and Context Effects in Memory-Based Judgment: Evaluating One's Environment

Before you read on, please answer this question, which has been asked of hundreds of thousands of survey respondents around the world (see Campbell 1981):

> Taking all things together, how would you say things are these days? Would you say you are very happy, pretty happy, not too happy?

To answer this question, you presumably drew on some mental representation of how your life is going these days. But did you really "take all things together"? And if not, which of the myriad aspects of your life did you draw on? Chances are that you relied on the ones that came to mind most easily at this time, suggesting that your answer may look quite different at some other time. In fact, a large body of research demonstrates that judgments of life-satisfaction are very susceptible to subtle situational influences, ranging from momentary moods, the weather of the day, events in the news, to questions asked earlier in a questionnaire (Schwarz and Strack 1991a).

As may be expected on the basis of the preceding discussion, our assessments of the quality of life, as well as our evaluations of any other target, depend on which information is most accessible at the time of judgment. This, of course, reflects social cognition researchers' assumption that people rarely retrieve all information that may potentially be relevant to the judgment at hand, but truncate the search as soon as enough information has come to mind to form a judgment. In a research situation, this is often the information that has been used to answer a preceding question, or, more technically, the information that has been activated most recently. How that information influences the judgment depends on whether it is used to form a representation of the target, in this case, a representation of "your life these days," or a representation of a standard, against which the target is compared. In the following sections we explore these processes in more detail.

10.4.1 Constructing a Representation of the Target: Assimilation Effects

Several studies on judgments of life-satisfaction may illustrate the influence of information accessibility on evaluative judgments. In all these studies, subjects were first induced to think either about positive or about negative aspects of their life and subsequently reported their general life-satisfaction. For example, Strack, Schwarz, and Gschneidinger (1985, experiment 1) asked subjects to write down three recent events that were either particularly positive and pleasant or particularly negative and unpleasant. This was done under the pretext of collecting life-events for a life-event inventory, and the dependent variables, among them "happiness" and "satisfaction," were said to be assessed in order to "find the best response scales" for that instrument. As expected, subjects who had been induced to think about positive aspects of their life described themselves as happier and more satisfied with their life as a whole than subjects who had been induced to think about negative aspects.

In two other studies, the same idea was tested with a somewhat subtler priming manipulation. Respondents were led to think about a relevant life-domain simply by asking a specific question before they had to report their general happiness. Generating an answer should render this specific information more accessible for subsequent use and therefore influence the judgment. In one of these studies, Strack, Martin, and Schwarz (1988) explored the influence of dating frequency on college students' general life-satisfaction. Not surprisingly, previous research (Emmons and Diener 1985) suggested that frequent dating might be a particularly important contributor to college students' general happiness. However, the apparent relevance of dating frequency depended on the order in which the questions were asked in the Strack et al. (1988) study. When respondents had to answer the general-happiness question before they were asked a question about their dating frequency, both measures correlated only $r = -.12$. This correlation is not significantly different from zero, suggesting that dating frequency may not be a major determinant of happiness for college students, in contrast to what Emmons and Diener (1985) assumed. When the general-happiness question was asked *after* the dating frequency question, however, the correlation increased to $r = .66$, suggesting that dating frequency is indeed a very important determinant of general happiness. Similarly, Schwarz, Strack, and Mai (1991) asked German respondents to report their marital satisfaction and their general life-satisfaction. Again, both measures correlated only $r = .32$ when the general life-satisfaction question preceded the marital-satisfaction question, but correlated $r = .67$ when the question order was reversed. Moreover, the order in which both questions were asked also affected subjects' mean reported life-satisfaction. Specifically, happily married respondents reported higher, and unhappily married respondents lower, general life-satisfaction when the marital-satisfaction question was asked before rather than after the general question.

Obviously, we would draw very different conclusions about the relevance of dating frequency or marital satisfaction for people's overall life-satisfaction, depending on the order in which we happened to ask these questions. Not surprisingly, such question-order effects have received considerable attention in social science research because they suggest that the substantive conclusions drawn may depend on the specific context in which the questions were presented in a questionnaire (see Schwarz and Strack 1991b; Schwarz and Sudman 1992; Tourangeau and Rasinski 1988, for reviews and research examples). Hence, the processes underlying the emergence of context effects in social judgment are not only of interest to social and cognitive psychologists. Rather, they are relevant to all researchers who use evaluative judgments as data in their investigations of substantive issues, ranging from public-opinion polls (for example, Schuman and Presser 1981) to market research (for example, Feldman and Lynch 1988) or decision making (for example, Plous 1993).

But how are we to account for findings of this type? When asked to form an evaluative judgment, we have to retrieve relevant information from memory to form a mental representation of the target—in the present case, a mental representation of how life is going these days. As mentioned repeatedly, however, we are unlikely to retrieve all information that may potentially be relevant, but truncate the search when enough information has come to mind to form a judgment. That is, we construct a representation of the target on the basis of the information that is most accessible at the time. Thus, when we have just been asked to report a positive or a negative life-event (as in the Strack et al. 1985 study), the reported event is particularly likely to come to mind and will be included in the representation that we form of our life. Because our judgment of life-satisfaction, for example, is based on this representation, we arrive at a more positive judgment when the preceding task rendered a positive rather than a negative event highly accessible. Similarly, college students may draw on a wide range of aspects of their life in assessing their general life-satisfaction, and the aspects that come to mind may or may not include dating frequency. But having just answered a question about dating frequency, information bearing on this life-domain is highly accessible and hence will influence the judgment (Strack et al. 1988).

In the examples above, information about specific life-events, dating, or one's marriage was rendered *temporarily accessible* by the specific questions asked. The actual impact of an accessible piece of information, however, depends not only on its own implications but also on the amount and implications of other information that may come to mind. Other information may be temporarily accessible due to other temporary influences, unrelated to the questions asked, such as events of the day, what happened to be in the news (for example, Iyengar 1990), and so on. Moreover, some information is likely to be *chronically accessible* (Higgins and King 1981). For example, individuals who are unemployed or suffer from a severe illness are likely to frequently think about this aspect of their life, thus rendering information related to their problem chronically accessible in memory, independent of whether it is addressed in a preceding question or not. Chronically or temporarily accessible information that is unrelated to the information primed by preceding questions is likely to limit the size of question-order effects.

In more general terms, including highly accessible information in the representation of the target results in assimilation effects, as we have seen above. The size of these assimilation effects increases with the amount and extremity of the primed information that is included in the representation of the target. Other things being equal, the more positive events we include in the representation of our life, and the more extreme these events are, the more positive is our judgment of life-satisfaction. However, adding one positive event to a representation that already includes ten other events, for example, will change our overall evaluation less than adding one positive event to a representation that includes only one other event. Accordingly, the size of assimilation effects decreases with the amount and extremity of other information that is temporarily or chronically accessible (Schwarz and Bless 1992a).

In line with the latter assumption, Schwarz, Strack, et al. (1991) observed that asking subjects about other life domains, in addition to their marriage, decreased the impact of marital satisfaction on overall life-satisfaction. Specifically, they asked some respondents to report their satisfaction with their jobs and their leisure time in addition to their marriage, before they answered the life-satisfaction question. Under this condition, the correlation between marital satisfaction and general life-satisfaction still increased from $r = .32$, when the life-satisfaction question was asked before the domain-specific questions, to $r = .46$, when it was asked after the domain-specific questions. However, this increase is significantly less pronounced than the increase to $r = .67$, which was obtained when marital satisfaction was the only domain-specific question asked. This pattern of findings reflects that the questions about other life-domains brought additional information to mind, which reduced the effect of marriage-related information.

In summary, our judgments depend on the information we include in the mental representation that we form of the target. Information included in that representation of the target results in assimilation effects. However, the impact of any given piece of information depends not only on the implications of that information itself, but also on the implications of other information that is included in the representation, as seen above. To form a judgment, however, we need not only a representation of the target, but also a representation of a standard against which we can evaluate the target. This issue is addressed next.

10.4.2 Constructing a Representation of a Standard: Contrast Effects

To evaluate a target, we need some relevant standard against which the target is compared. And much as the representation of the target depends on what happens to come to mind at the time, so too does the representation that we form of a relevant standard. In constructing a standard, we again do not draw on all information that may potentially be relevant, but truncate the search early, relying on what is most accessible in memory.

The Strack et al. (1985, experiment 1; see also Tversky and Griffin, 1991) study on life-satisfaction may again serve as an example. As noted above, subjects in this study reported higher satisfaction with their current life when they were induced to recall three *recent* positive, rather than negative life-events. However, other subjects were not asked to recall three recent events, but to recall either three positive or three negative events that happened to them at least five years ago. Figure 10.1 shows the full pattern of results.

As can be seen, subjects who had to recall three *distant* positive events reported lower life-satisfaction than subjects who had to recall three distant negative events. Thus, thinking about positive or negative events that occurred several years ago resulted in a contrast effect, whereas thinking about three positive or negative events that happened recently resulted in an assimilation effect. What drives this reversal of the impact of life-events, depending on their temporal distance?

Recall that the judgment that subjects are asked to make is an evaluation of their *current* life-satisfaction. Hence, the target of judgment is the current

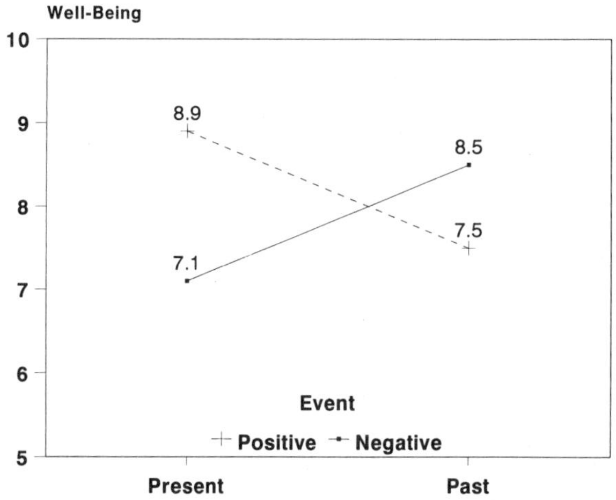

Figure 10.1
Current life-satisfaction: the impact of valence of event and time perspective.

Note. Mean score of happiness and satisfaction questions is given; range is 1 to 11, with higher values indicating reports of higher well-being. Adapted from Strack, Schwarz, and Gschneidinger (1985, experiment 1).

period of their life and recent events should obviously be included in the representation of this target. And as discussed in the preceding section, including these events in the representation of the target resulted in an assimilation effect. Events that happened several years ago, however, do not pertain to the current period of one's life, but bear on some previous period. Accordingly, they may not be included in the representation formed of one's current life. Nevertheless, they are highly accessible in memory and are now used in constructing a standard of comparison against which the period is compared. And relative to the bad things that happened several years ago, life now is pretty good, whereas relative to the good events of that time, life now is pretty bland.

As this example illustrates, highly accessible information that is not included in the representation formed of the target (in this case, the current period of one's life) may be used in constructing a standard of comparison. If the implications of the primed information are more extreme than the implications of other temporarily or chronically accessible information used in constructing a standard, this results in a more extreme standard, eliciting a contrast effect. And much as the size of assimilation effects depends on the implications of other information used in constructing a representation of the target, so too does the size of contrast effects depend on the implications of other information used in constructing a representation of the standard. Specifically, the size of comparison-based contrast effects increases with the extremity and amount of the primed information used in constructing the standard, and decreases with the amount and extremity of other temporarily or chronically accessible information used in this construction (Schwarz and Bless 1992a).

That highly accessible information can be used to construct a representation of the target or a representation of a standard raises an obvious question: What determines if we use information to construct one or the other representation? An answer to that question is offered by Schwarz and Bless's (1992a) inclusion/exclusion model of assimilation and contrast in evaluative judgment. According to this model, the default operation is to include information that comes to mind in the representation of the target, resulting in assimilation effects. However, we do not always operate on this default. Rather, a host of factors may induce us to exclude information that comes to mind from the representation of the target, rendering it available for constructing a standard. The relevant factors can be conceptualized as bearing on three global decisions: Does the information come to mind for the wrong reason? Does it bear on the target? And am I supposed to use it?

The first of these decisions is already familiar from the discussion above of priming effects in impression formation. As seen in this context, we try to form unbiased judgments and avoid using information that may not reflect our reaction to the target, but the influence of some other source (for example, Martin 1986; Martin et al. 1990; Strack et al. 1993). The other two decisions are discussed in more detail below.

10.4.2.1 Does the Information Belong to the Target Category?

As we have seen in discussing the Strack et al. (1985) life-satisfaction study, information that comes to mind is included in the representation of the target—in that case, the current period of one's life—only if it bears on it. If the information that came to mind pertained to a previous period in the subject's life, it was used as a standard of comparison, resulting in a contrast effect. Whereas the inclusion or exclusion of information from the representation of the target was determined by the temporal distance of the recalled events in that study, numerous other variables may have the same effect (see Schwarz and Bless 1992a). In essence, any variable that influences the categorization of information may also determine if accessible information is included in, or excluded from, the representation formed of some target. Two of the most interesting variables are the salience of category boundaries and the width of the target category.

Category Boundaries In the Strack et al. (1985) study, past life-events could presumably be used as a standard of comparison because they fell outside the boundaries of the target category "the present period of my life." If so, any variable that affects how we chunk the stream of life into discrete periods should have similar effects. Empirical findings support this assumption.

For example, Schwarz and Hippler (unpublished data) asked first-year students to report a positive or a negative event that happened to them "two years ago." Under this condition, subjects subsequently reported higher current life-satisfaction after recalling a positive rather than a negative event, reflecting that they included the recalled events in the mental representation of the current period of their life. For other subjects, however, Schwarz and Hippler increased the salience of a major role-transition that could serve as a boundary marker. These subjects were asked to report an event "that happened two years ago, *that is, before you entered college*." Except for the reminder that they were not yet in college two years ago, the instructions were identical. This reminder, however, reversed the pattern of results obtained. In this case, subjects reported higher life-satisfaction after recalling a negative rather than positive event.

Thus, drawing subjects' attention to a major change in their life, namely entering college, apparently induced them to chunk their life into a "high-school period" and a current "college period." And given this chunking, the events recalled from two years ago pertained to the "high-school period" rather than to their current life as college students. As a result, these events were not included in the representation formed of the target, but served as standards of comparison, resulting in contrast effects. As these findings illustrate, the same negative as well as positive past life-events may either increase or decrease current life-satisfaction, depending on their use in constructing representations of the past and the present, which may be determined by the events' temporal distance as well as by salient boundary markers. In more general terms, findings of this type indicate that the use of accessible information in constructing a representation of the target or a standard depends on the temporarily salient boundaries of the target category (Schwarz and Bless, 1992a).

Category width. Another variable that determines the use of accessible information is the width of the target category. Suppose, for example, that you are asked to evaluate the trustworthiness of politicians in the United States. In that case, the target category includes all politicians in the United States, and you may include any American politician who comes to mind in the representation that you form of American politicians in general. On the other hand, if you were asked to evaluate the trustworthiness of politicians of the Democratic Party, this target category would allow the inclusion of only Democrats. Finally, if asked to evaluate the trustworthiness of President Clinton, the target category would be restricted to one person.

> In general, wider target categories allow for inclusion of a wider range of information than narrower categories. This has important implications for the impact of accessible information on the evaluation of targets of differential category width.

For example, how should thinking of politicians who were involved in a scandal influence the judgments of trustworthiness above? According to the logic of the inclusion/exclusion model, the politicians involved in the scandal are members of the wide target category "politicians" and are therefore likely to be included in the temporary representation formed of that category. If so, evaluations of the trustworthiness of politicians in general should decrease, reflecting an assimilation effect. Not so, however, when the judgment pertains to a specific politician, let us say Bill Clinton, who was not involved in the scandal. In evaluating a specific person, this person makes up a category by him- or herself. Hence, the scandal-ridden politicians cannot be included in the representation formed of this narrow target category. But if they are highly accessible in memory, they can be used in constructing a standard against which Bill Clinton is evaluated, resulting in a contrast effect. Thus, we may expect a rather counterintuitive pattern of findings: Thinking about politicians who were involved in a scandal should decrease judgments of trustworthiness for politicians in general, but should increase judgments of trustworthiness for each individual politician, provided that this individual was not involved in the scandal.

Schwarz and Bless (1992b) tested this prediction by asking German subjects to recall the names of some politicians who were involved in a political scandal in Germany, either before or after they answered questions about trustworthiness. As expected, thinking about politicians who were involved in a scandal resulted in decreased judgments of the trustworthiness of German politicians in general. This assimilation effect reflects that subjects could include the politicians who were involved in the scandal in their representation of German politicians in general. Other subjects, however, were asked to evaluate the trustworthiness of three specific politicians, whom pretests had shown to be not particularly trustworthy to begin with, although they were not involved in the scandal under study. As expected, thinking about the scandal *increased* judgments of trustworthiness of these specific politicians. This contrast effect reflects that subjects used the politicians who were rendered accessible by the scandal question in constructing a standard of comparison, relative to which these otherwise not so trustworthy individuals didn't look so bad after all.

From a theoretical perspective, these findings once again indicate that the same information may affect related judgments in opposite directions, depending on whether the respective target category invites inclusion or exclusion of the information that comes to mind. From an applied perspective, it comes as no surprise that political scandals are typically accompanied by attempts to channel the public's categorization of scandal-related information (Ebbighausen and Neckel 1989). To the extent that individual politicians, or groups of politicians, can dissociate themselves from the scandal, they may actually benefit from the misbehavior of their peers, although the impact on the perception of the profession as a whole is likely to be negative.

Section Summary

The studies above illustrate how features of the target category, such as the salience of relevant boundaries or the category's width, determine the inclusion or exclusion of accessible information in the representation formed of the target. These inclusion/exclusion operations, in turn, determine the emergence of assimilation or contrast effects in judgment. Information that is included in the representation formed of the target results in assimilation effects, whereas information that is excluded from the representation of the target may be used in constructing a representation of the standard, resulting in contrast effects (Schwarz and Bless 1992a).

10.4.2.2 Am I Supposed to Use the Information? The Impact of Conversational Norms

The cognitive processes considered so far were not particularly "social" in nature. In contrast to what the label "social cognition" may suggest, one may argue that the only feature that renders the reviewed research on information accessibility and use "social" is the nature of the stimuli and dependent variables employed in these studies. After all, impression formation and political attitudes, for example, have traditionally been of interest to social psychologists. But as mentioned in the introduction, social cognition research does not imply only the application of theoretical principles borrowed from cognitive psychology to social stimuli. Although this application accounts for a large part of social cognition research, as many critics state (see Forgas 1981; Schneider 1991), social cognition researchers are also interested in how the social context in which we form a judgment affects cognitive processes (see McCann and Higgins 1992; Schwarz 1994 for more detailed discussions). With respect to information accessibility and use, a particularly relevant aspect of social influences is the impact of conversational norms on the use of accessible information (Clark and Schober 1992; McCann and Higgins 1992; Schwarz 1994; Strack and Schwarz 1992).

One of the principles that govern the conduct of conversation in everyday life requests speakers to make their contribution as informative as is required for the purpose of the conversation, but not more informative than is required (Grice 1975). In particular, speakers are not supposed to be redundant and provide information that the respondent already has. In psycholinguistics, this principle is known as the *given-new contract*, which emphasizes that speakers should provide "new" information rather than information that has already been "given" (Clark 1985; Haviland and Clark 1974). As an illustration, consider these two question–answer sequences (from Strack and Martin 1987):

Sequence A
Question: How is your family?
Answer: . . .

Sequence B
Question: How is your spouse?
Answer: . . .
Question: And how is your family?

What does the term "family" refer to in these two sequences? In sequence A, the term "family" seems to include the spouse, whereas this is not the case in sequence B. This reflects that including the spouse in answering the question about the family's well-being in sequence B would violate the given-new contract, because relevant information about the spouse's well-being has already been given in response to the first question. Hence, the question about the family is now interpreted as referring to other members of the family, much as if it were worded, "Aside from your spouse, how are the other members of your family?"

As Strack and Martin (1987) commented, following related suggestions by Bradburn (1982) and Tourangeau (1984), this process may influence the use of accessible information in forming a judgment. The previously discussed study on the relationship of marital satisfaction and general life-satisfaction (Schwarz, Strack, et al. 1991) bears on this prediction. As reviewed above, marital satisfaction and life-satisfaction were correlated $r = .32$ when the life-satisfaction question preceded the marital-satisfaction question, but $r = .67$ when the question order was reversed. This increase reflects that answering the marital satisfaction question increased the accessibility of marriage-related information and that this information was used in answering the subsequent life-satisfaction question. However, would that information *not* be used if the conversational norm of nonredundancy is activated? Schwarz, Strack, et al. (1991) tested this possibility in another condition of their study. In that condition, the marital-satisfaction question again preceded the life-satisfaction question, but both questions were placed in the same conversational context by a joint lead-in. This lead-in informed respondents that they would be asked two questions about their life, one pertaining to their marital satisfaction and one to their general life-satisfaction. Under this condition, the same question order that resulted in a correlation of $r = .67$ without a lead-in, now produced a correlation of only $r = .18$ with the lead-in.

This finding suggests that respondents deliberately ignored information that they had already provided in response to a specific question when making a subsequent general judgment, despite the fact that it was easily accessible in memory. Apparently, they interpreted the general question as if it referred to aspects of their life that they had not yet reported on. Consistent with this interpretation, a condition in which respondents were explicitly asked how satisfied they were with "other aspects" of their life, "aside from their relationship," yielded a nearly identical correlation of $r = .20$.

Moreover, these manipulations did also affect respondents' reported mean life-satisfaction. For example, in the condition without a joint lead-in, unhappily married respondents reported lower life-satisfaction when the marital-satisfaction question preceded the general life-satisfaction question, than when it followed this question. As discussed above, this response reflects that the marital question brought information bearing on their poor marriage to mind, which was included in the representation that they formed of their life as a whole. However, when the joint lead-in prompted them to exclude the information that they had already provided in response to the earlier question, unhappily married respondents reported higher life-satisfaction when the marital-satisfaction question preceded rather than followed the general one. This response reflects that they excluded the negative information about their marriage from the representation that they formed of their life in general, resulting in a more positive judgment. The reports of happily married respondents provided a mirror image of these findings.

As this and related studies (Strack et al. 1988; Strack, Schwarz, and Wänke 1991) illustrate, the social context in which we form a judgment may influence the use of highly accessible information. In the present case, highly accessible information was excluded from the representation formed of the target because its repeated use would have violated the conversational norm of nonredundancy, which requests speakers to provide information that is new to the recipient rather than to reiterate information that the recipient already has. Accordingly, conversational norms can trigger inclusion or exclusion processes, which, in turn, result in assimilation or contrast effects.

10.4.3 Summary

The research reviewed in the preceding sections illustrates that our evaluative judgments depend on the information that is most accessible at the time. How this information influences the judgment, however, depends on whether we include it in the representation that we form of the target or not. Information that is included in the representation of the target results in assimilation effects. Information that is excluded from this representation may be used in forming a standard against which the target is compared, resulting in contrast effects. Numerous different variables may determine inclusion or exclusion of accessible information and in the present chapter we can address only a few of them (see Schwarz and Bless 1992a). What renders these context effects in social judgment important for many areas of research is that they may greatly affect the conclusions that we draw about the substantive issue under investigation, as the examples above illustrate.

10.5 Accessibility Experiences

The preceding discussion of information accessibility is focused on *what* comes to mind. That a given piece of information is highly accessible in memory, however, does not imply only that it is more likely to come to mind than less accessible information. Rather, the recall of highly accessible information may also be *experienced* as easier than the recall of less accessible information. The experience that something comes to mind easily, or needs to be searched for with some effort, is informative in its own right and may itself influence our judgments. In this final section we explore this possibility by reviewing how the experience of ease or difficulty of recall may affect judgments of frequency, and may sometimes lead us to draw inferences that actually contradict the implications of recalled content.

10.5.1 Ease of Recall and Judgments of Frequency

The role of the subjective experience of ease of recall was first explored by Tversky and Kahneman (1973). They assumed that individuals estimate the frequency of an event, or the likelihood of its occurrence, "by the ease with which instances or associations come to mind" (Tversky and Kahneman 1973, 208). They called this inference rule the *availability heuristic,* although in the terminology employed in the present chapter it might better be called the accessibility heuristic (see section 10.2).

The reliance on this heuristic in making frequency judgments reflects the correct insight that instances of frequent events should be easier to recall than instances of rare events. Hence, when we think of some class of events and relevant examples come to mind easily, this presumably implies that the event is frequent. Unfortunately, however, how easily examples come to mind may reflect other influences than the actual frequency of the class of events, such as how recently we encountered a relevant example or how vivid and memorable the example was. To this extent, reliance on this heuristic is likely to lead us astray, as Tversky and Kahneman (1973) showed in several experiments (see Sherman and Corty 1984 for an extended review).

For example, in one of Tversky and Kahneman's studies (1973, experiment 8) subjects were read two lists of names, one presenting 19 famous men and 20 less famous women, and the other presenting 19 famous women and 20 less famous men. When asked, subjects reported that there were more men than women in the first list, but more women than men in the second list, even though the opposite was the case (by a difference of one). Presumably, the famous names were easier to recall than the nonfamous ones, resulting in an overestimate. In fact, subjects were able to recall about 50 percent more of the famous than of the nonfamous names. Unfortunately, it remained unclear in this and related studies what actually drives the overestimate: Are subjects' judgments indeed based on the phenomenological *experience* of the ease or difficulty with which they could bring the famous and nonfamous names to mind, as Tversky and Kahneman's interpretation suggests? Or are their judgments based on the *content* of their recall, with famous names being overrepresented in the recalled sample?

In a related study (Tversky and Kahneman 1973, experiment 3), subjects were found to overestimate the number of words that begin with the letter *r*, but to underestimate the number of words that have *r* as the third letter. Again, this finding may reflect either that subjects recalled more words of the first type, resulting in a biased sample, or that they relied on the ease with which relevant exemplars came to mind. Similar ambiguities apply to other studies (see Sherman and Corty 1984; Taylor 1982; Taylor and Thompson 1982, for reviews). Typically, the manipulations that have been introduced to increase the subjectively experienced ease of recall are also likely to affect the amount and detail of subjects' recall. This ambiguity renders it difficult to determine if the estimates of frequency obtained are based on subjects' subjective experiences or on a biased sample of recalled information. In the latter case, there wouldn't be anything special to the availability heuristic—after all, "one's judgments are always based on *what* comes to mind," as Taylor (1982, 199) noted and as we have seen in the preceding sections of this chapter. Thus, the final issue to be addressed in this chapter is: Does the subjective experience of ease or difficulty of recall influence our judgments over and above the impact of *what* comes to mind? Several studies bear on this issue.

In an extended replication of Tversky and Kahneman's (1973, experiment 3) letter study, Wänke, Schwarz, and Bless (in press) attempted to manipulate the informative value of the ease with which words with a certain letter could be brought to mind. In their control condition, they provided subjects with a blank sheet of paper and asked them to first write down ten words with the letter *t* in the third position, and subsequently ten words with the letter *T* in the first position. Following this listing task, subjects estimated the extent to which words beginning with *T* are more or less frequent than words that have *t* as the third letter. As in Tversky and Kahneman's (1973) study, they reported that it was easier to recall words that had *T* as the first, rather than as the third letter. Moreover, they estimated that words that begin with *T* are much more frequent than words having a *t* in the third position.

As in the original study, however, this estimate may either be based on the experience that words beginning with a *T* came to mind more *easily*, or on the observation that they could recall a *larger number* of these words (although they were asked to record only ten). To disentangle the role of experienced ease, subjects assigned to the experimental conditions were asked to complete the same listing task. However, they had to record ten words that begin with *T* on a sheet of paper that was imprinted with pale but visible rows of *t*'s. Some of them were told that this background made it easy to recall *t*-words, whereas others were told that this background interfered with the recall task, thus rendering it difficult to bring *t*-words to mind. These manipulations were designed to affect the perceived informational value of the experienced ease of recall. If it is easy to recall words beginning with *T* despite the fact that the background of one's worksheet allegedly renders recall difficult, there must be many of them. On the other hand, if one's worksheet allegedly renders it easy to recall these words, finding the recall task easy is not very informative. In line with this reasoning, subjects who could attribute the experienced ease of recalling words beginning with *T* to the impact of their worksheet, assumed that there are fewer of these words than subjects in the control condition. Conversely, subjects who expected their worksheet to interfere with recall, but found recall easy nevertheless, estimated that there are more words beginning with *T* than did subjects in the control condition. Thus, subjects' estimates depended on the perceived informational value of the experienced ease of recall, much as has been observed for other phenomenal experiences (see Clore 1992; Schwarz 1990 for reviews). This pattern of results renders it unlikely that subjects' frequency estimates were solely based on the *number* of words they could recall. Whatever the actual impact of the pale rows of *t*'s, or of writing down ten *t*-words, might have been, this influence was the same in all conditions. The only difference between conditions was the information provided about the alleged impact of the worksheet, which rendered the *subjective experience* of ease or difficulty of recall differentially informative.

In summary, this research illustrates that the subjective experience of the ease with which some information can be brought to mind is informative in its own right. The more easily examples come to mind, the higher the frequency that we infer. On the other hand, the more difficulty we experience in recalling relevant examples, the less frequent and typical they seem to be, as the next study will illustrate.

10.5.2 Qualifying the Implications of Recalled Content

Suppose that you are asked to describe six examples of situations in which you behaved assertively and felt at ease, or six examples of situations in which you behaved unassertively and felt insecure. How would that affect your assessment of how assertive you are? Based on the research reviewed in section 10.4, one may assume that recalling these experiences renders them highly accessible in memory and results in assimilation effects on subsequent judgments of assertiveness. Thus, you would presumably describe yourself as more assertive after recalling examples of your own assertive rather than unassertive behaviors. And this effect should be the more pronounced the more examples you recall. But what if recalling these examples is difficult? Suppose you try to come up with twelve examples of assertive behaviors—and find it difficult to bring them to mind? It seems that this experience would suggest that you can't be that assertive after all, or else recalling relevant examples shouldn't be so hard. Schwarz, Bless, Strack, Klumpp, Rittenauer-Schatka, and Simons (1991) tested this possibility in several studies.

In one of these studies, subjects were asked to report either six or twelve examples in which they behaved either assertively or unassertively. Although all subjects could complete this task, pretests had shown that recalling six examples was experienced as easy, whereas recalling twelve examples was experienced as difficult. Following their reports, subjects had to evaluate their own assertiveness. Figure 10.2 shows the results.

As expected, subjects reported higher assertiveness after recalling six examples of assertive behaviors than after recalling six examples of unassertive behaviors. This difference reflects that the recall task rendered these examples accessible in memory. However, the difference did not increase as subjects had to recall more examples. On the contrary, subjects who had to recall assertive behaviors reported lower assertiveness after recalling twelve rather than six examples. Similarly, subjects who had to recall unassertive behaviors reported higher assertiveness after recalling twelve rather than six examples. In fact, the subjects actually reported higher assertiveness after recalling twelve unassertive, rather than twelve assertive behaviors, in contrast to what one would expect on the basis of recall content. It seems that the experience that it was difficult to bring twelve examples to mind suggested to them that they couldn't be that assertive (or unassertive) after all. Thus, the experienced difficulty of recall apparently induced subjects to draw inferences opposite to the implications of the content that they recalled.

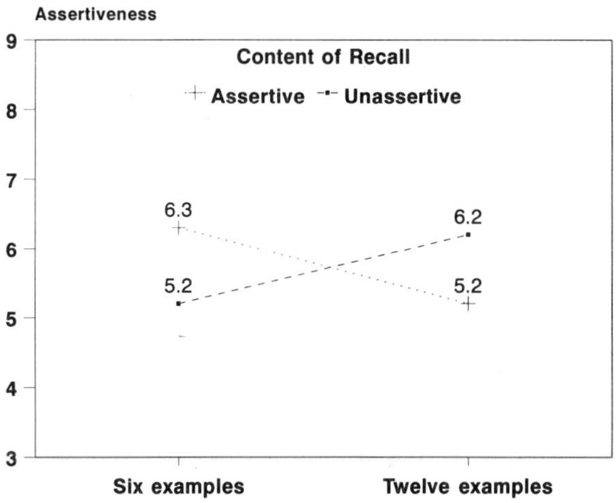

Figure 10.2
Assessments of assertiveness: the impact of accessible content and experienced ease of recall

Note. Mean score of three questions is given; range is 1 to 10, with higher values reflecting higher assertiveness. Adapted from Schwarz, Bless, Strack, Klumpp, Rittenauer-Schatka, and Simons (1991, experiment 1).

There may, however, be a plausible alternative explanation. Although all subjects who were asked to do so did in fact report twelve examples, it is conceivable that their examples were getting worse. Thus, they may have been able to recall some examples of clearly assertive behavior, but as the requested number increased, they had to include less and less convincing examples of assertiveness. If so, these less convincing examples, reported toward the end of the list, may have been more accessible later on than the examples reported earlier. Hence, if subjects based their judgments on the last few examples generated, one would obtain the same pattern of results. Schwarz, Bless, et al. (1991, experiment 1) tested this possibility by analyzing the examples that subjects reported. This content analysis provided no evidence that the extremity of the examples decreased toward the end. If anything, the last two examples reported were somewhat more extreme than the first two examples reported. Thus, this alternative explanation can be discarded. Yet, one would like to see more direct evidence that it is really the *subjective experience* of ease or difficulty of recall that drives the observed effects than has been provided by the first experiment.

To provide this more direct test of the experience hypothesis, Schwarz, Bless, et al. (1991, experiment 3) manipulated the perceived informational value of the experienced ease or difficulty of recall. To accomplish this, they had subjects listen to meditation music while they worked on the recall task. Moreover, they told subjects that this music would facilitate the recall of a certain kind of autobiographical memories, namely either memories of situations in which one behaved assertively and felt at ease, or behaved unassertively and felt insecure. This manipulation renders subjects' experiences of ease or difficulty of recall uninformative under conditions where their accessibility experiences could be due to the alleged influence of the music. For example, finding it easy to bring six examples of assertive behavior to mind is not very informative with regard to one's own assertiveness when the experienced ease of recall may actually be due to the music. Similarly, finding it difficult to recall twelve examples of assertive behavior is also not very informative when the music allegedly facilitates recall of the opposite behavior. In this case, one's difficulty may be due to the fact that the music interferes with one's recall task. On the other hand, subjects' experiences of ease or difficulty of recall are rendered particularly diagnostic when they contradict the alleged side effects of the music. Thus, when the music is said to make recall of assertive behaviors easy, finding it difficult to recall twelve assertive behaviors should provide food for thought. Given these manipulations, we may expect that subjects will rely on their subjective experiences of ease or difficulty of recall only when their informational value is not called into question. If these experiences may be due to the alleged effect of the music, however, subjects may disregard their subjective experiences and may solely rely on recalled content instead.

The findings supported these predictions. When the informational value of subjects' experienced ease or difficulty of recall was not called into question, the previously obtained results were replicated. Thus, subjects evaluated themselves as less assertive after recalling twelve rather than six examples of assertive behavior, and as more assertive after recalling twelve rather than six examples of unassertive behavior. As in the previous study, they apparently concluded from the experienced difficulty of recall that they couldn't be that assertive (or unassertive) if it was so difficult to recall twelve relevant examples. Not so, however, when the informational value of their accessibility experiences was called into question. In that case, subjects reported higher assertiveness after recalling twelve rather than six examples of assertive behavior, and lower assertiveness after recalling twelve rather than six examples of unassertive behavior. In other words, their judgments reflected the content of the examples they recalled, and the more so the more examples were brought to mind.

In combination, this pattern of findings demonstrates that our judgments do not depend only on *what* comes to mind. Rather, the subjective experience of the ease or difficulty with which something may be brought to mind is a source of information in its own right. As suggested by

Tversky and Kahneman's (1973) availability heuristic, we estimate the frequency, likelihood, or typicality of an event by the ease with which we can bring relevant examples to mind. Hence, finding it difficult to recall relevant examples, we are likely to conclude that there can't be many and that behaving assertively (or unassertively) may not be so typical for us. Accordingly, our subjective accessibility experience may qualify the implications of the content that comes to mind, as the studies above illustrate.

10.5.3 Summary

The research reviewed in this section extends the preceding discussion of information accessibility and use by drawing attention to the fact that the accessibility of information in memory doesn't just determine *what* comes to mind, but also affects our *phenomenal experiences* of ease or difficulty of recall. The phenomenal experiences that accompany our reasoning processes are a fascinating issue in their own right, and have received considerable attention in social cognition research (see Clore 1992; Jacoby and Kelley 1987; Schwarz 1990; Strack 1992, for reviews). Throughout, this work has shown that accessibility experiences of the type discussed above, feelings of familiarity, or our apparent affective reactions to a target can profoundly influence judgmental processes.

10.6 Concluding Remarks

In the introduction to this chapter we raised the question of which knowledge we draw on when we interpret new information or form a judgment about something we are familiar with. As the reviewed research indicates, it is the subset of potentially relevant knowledge that is most accessible at the time of judgment. Thus, we interpret newly acquired ambiguous information in terms of the most accessible concept that is applicable to it, without considering alternative interpretations in terms of less accessible concepts. Similarly, we base our evaluative judgments on the information that comes to mind most easily, truncating the search process before less accessible information has been retrieved. Although we may engage in more extended recall processes when the judgment is of great importance to us, many of our daily judgments depend on the information that is most accessible at the time. This is often the information that we happened to use most recently, for some other purpose, rendering our judgments susceptible to the influence of fortuitous events. How accessible information affects our judgment depends on what we do with it; most notably, whether we use it in constructing a representation of the target of judgment or a representation of the standard to which the target is compared. Moreover, the subjective experience of ease or difficulty of recall is a source of information in its own right, influencing which conclusions we draw from the content that we recall. All these aspects of information accessibility and use can profoundly influence how we see the world around us, and hence, how we behave in it. Accordingly, these aspects of human thinking have greatly interested researchers working at the interface of social and cognitive psychology to which this chapter on *social cognition* provides an introduction.

Suggestions for Further Reading

This chapter provides a very selective review of social cognition research, focusing on a small subset of the issues addressed in this field. Fiske and Taylor (1991) offer an excellent undergraduate-level introduction to the field that covers the full range of issues addressed by social cognition researchers. At present, this is the best introductory source available. A short but comprehensive review, geared toward the interests of cognitive psychologists, is provided by Martin and Clark (1990). Detailed, but highly technical, reviews of different domains of social cognition research are provided in the *Handbook of social cognition* (Wyer and Srull 1994). In addition, the *Annual Review of Psychology* covers recent developments in social cognition every few years.

Comprehensive reviews of information accessibility and use are offered by Higgins (1989, in press). Martin and Achee (1992) discuss how processing objectives affects the use of accessible information, and Schwarz and Bless (1992a) offer a comprehensive model of assimilation and contrast in social judgment, which is partially presented in this chapter. Strack (1992) discusses the processes involved when we try to correct a judgment to avoid undue influences, and reviews the limited literature currently available on this topic. Finally, Clore (1992) and Schwarz and Clore (in press) discuss the role of phenomenal experiences in judgment, focusing on experiences of ease or difficulty of recall as well as moods and emotions.

That we are likely to rely on the most accessible information in forming a judgment violates normative rules of rational decision making. Nisbett and Ross (1980) explore the implications of these processes for assumptions about human rationality in a highly readable book that has become a classic in the field.

In addition to addressing theoretical issues of information accessibility and use, the present chapter touches on a number of substantive domains of research. Research on person perception and impression formation is thoroughly covered in Fiske and Taylor's (1991) textbook. The cognitive processes involved in judgments of life-satisfaction are addressed in Schwarz and Strack (1991a); Schwarz, Wänke, and Bless (1994) explore how we determine if life is getting better or worse. Finally, the emergence of context effects in social research is reviewed by Tourangeau and Rasinski (1988) and in the contributions to Schwarz and Sudman (1992).

Problems

10.1 Suppose that undergraduates are asked to describe the best (worst) class they had in college. Next, they are asked either (a) to evaluate the quality of the college education they receive, or (b) the quality of their introductory psychology class. What are your predictions?

10.2 Common sense suggests that we feel better about our life when we expect positive rather than negative things to happen in the future. But this may not always be the case. Use the research reviewed in this chapter to derive conditions under which (a) positive or

(b) negative expectations about the future will result in *increased* or in *decreased* current life-satisfaction.

10.3 This chapter emphasizes the context dependency of evaluative judgments. However, the process assumptions reviewed allow us to predict the conditions under which evaluative judgments change as a function of the context of judgment; they also specify the conditions under which evaluative judgments should be stable over time. Suppose that the same question, let us say, about the quality of life, is asked at two points in time. Under which conditions would you predict (a) that the report at t_2 differs from the report at t_1, and (b) that the report at t_2 is very similar to the report at t_1? That is, when would you predict change or stability over time? Consider situational (for example, questionnaire) as well as individual difference variables in your predictions.

References

Bargh, J. A., and P. Pietromonaco (1982). Automatic information processing and social perception: The influence of trait information presented outside of conscious awareness on impression formation. *Journal of Personality and Social Psychology* 35, 303–314.

Bless, H., F. Strack, and N. Schwarz (1993). The informative functions of research procedures: Bias and the logic of conversation. *European Journal of Social Psychology* 23, 149–165.

Bodenhausen, G. V., and R. S. Wyer (1987). Social cognition and social reality: Information acquisition and use in the laboratory and the real world. In H. J. Hippler, N. Schwarz, and S. Sudman, eds., *Social information processing and survey methodology*, 6–41. New York: Springer-Verlag.

Bradburn, N. (1982). Question wording effects in surveys. In R. Hogarth, ed., *Question framing and response consistency*, 65–76. San Francisco: Jossey-Bass.

Bruner, J. S. (1957). Going beyond the information given. In H. Gruber et al., eds., *Contemporary approaches to cognition*. Cambridge, MA: Harvard University Press.

Campbell, A. (1981). *The sense of well-being in America*. New York: McGraw-Hill.

Clark, H. H. (1985). Language use and language users. In G. Lindzey and E. Aronson, eds., *Handbook of social psychology*, vol. 2, 179–232. New York: Random House.

Clark, H. H., and M. F. Schober (1992). Asking questions and influencing answers. In J. M. Tanur, ed., *Questions about questions*, 15–48. New York: Russell Sage.

Clore, G. L. (1992). Cognitive phenomenology: Feelings and the construction of judgment. In L. L. Martin and A. Tesser, eds., *The construction of social judgment*, 133–163. Hillsdale, NJ: Erlbaum.

Ebbighausen, R., and S. Neckel, eds. (1989). *Anatomie des politischen Skandals* (*The anatomy of political scandals*). Frankfurt: Suhrkamp.

Emmons, R. A., and E. Diener (1985). Factors predicting satisfaction judgments: A comparative examination. *Social Indicators Research* 16, 157–167.

Feldman, J. M., and J. G. Lynch (1988). Self-generated validity and other effects of measurement on belief, attitude, intention, and behavior. *Journal of Applied Psychology* 73, 421–435.

Fiske, S. T., and S. E. Taylor (1991). *Social cognition*. 2nd ed. New York: McGraw-Hill.

Forgas, J. P. (1981). What is social about social cognition? In J. P. Forgas, ed., *Social cognition: Perspectives on everyday understanding*, 1–26. New York: Academic Press.

Grice, H. P. (1975). Logic and conversation. In P. Cole and J. L. Morgan, eds., *Syntax and semantics*, vol. 3: *Speech acts*, 41–58. New York: Academic Press.

Haviland, S. E., and H. H. Clark (1974). What's new? Acquiring new information as a process of comprehension. *Journal of Verbal Learning and Verbal Behavior* 13, 512–521.

Higgins, E. T. (1989). Knowledge accessibility and activation: Subjectivity and suffering from unconscious sources. In J. S. Uleman and J. A. Bargh, eds., *Unintended thought,* 75–123. New York: Guilford Press.

Higgins, E. T. (in press). Knowledge activation: Accessibility, applicability, and salience. In E. T. Higgins and A. Kruglanski, eds., *Social psychology: A handbook of basic principles.* New York: Guilford Press.

Higgins, E. T., and G. King (1981). Accessibility of social constructs: Information processing consequences of individual and contextual variability. In N. Cantor and J. F. Kihlstrom, eds., *Personality, cognition, and social interaction,* 69–121. Hillsdale, NJ: Erlbaum.

Higgins, E. T., W. S. Rholes, and C. R. Jones (1977). Category accessibility and impression formation. *Journal of Experimental Social Psychology* 13, 141–154.

Iyengar, S. (1990). The accessibility bias in politics: Television news and public opinion. *International Journal of Public Opinion Research* 2, 1–15.

Jacoby, L. L., and C. M. Kelley (1987). Unconscious influences of memory for a prior event. *Personality and Social Psychology Bulletin* 13, 314–336.

Kruglanski, A. W. (1989). *Lay epistemics and human knowledge: Cognitive and motivational bases.* New York: Plenum.

Markus, H., and R. B. Zajonc (1985). The cognitive perspective in social psychology. In G. Lindzey and E. Aronson, eds., *The handbook of social psychology,* vol. 1, 137–230. New York: Random House.

Martin, L. L. (1986). Set/reset: Use and disuse of concepts in impression formation. *Journal of Personality and Social Psychology* 51, 493–504.

Martin, L. L., and J. W. Achee (1992). Beyond accessibility: The role of processing objectives in judgment. In L. L. Martin and A. Tesser, eds., *The construction of social judgments,* 195–216. Hillsdale, NJ: Erlbaum.

Martin, L. L., and L. F. Clark (1990). Social cognition: Exploring the mental processes involved in human social interaction. In M. W. Eysenck, ed., *Cognitive psychology: An international review,* 265–310. Chichester: Wiley.

Martin, L. L., J. J. Seta, and R. A. Crelia (1990). Assimilation and contrast as a function of people's willingness to expend effort in forming an impression. *Journal of Personality and Social Psychology* 59, 27–37.

McCann, C. D., and E. T. Higgins (1992). Personal and contextual factors in communication: A review of the 'communication game.' In G. R. Semin and K. Fiedler, eds., *Language, interaction, and social cognition,* 144–172. Newbury Park, CA: Sage.

Nisbett, R., and L. Ross (1980). *Human inference: Strategies and shortcomings of social judgment.* Englewood Cliffs, NJ: Prentice-Hall.

Orne, M. T. (1962). On the social psychology of the psychological experiment: With particular reference to demand characteristics and their implications. *American Psychologist* 17, 776–783.

Plous, S. (1993). *The psychology of judgment and decision making.* New York: McGraw-Hill.

Schneider, D. (1991). Social cognition. *Annual Review of Psychology* 42, 527–561.

Schuman, H., and S. Presser (1981). *Questions and answers in attitude surveys.* New York: Academic Press.

Schwarz, N. (1990). Feelings as information: Informational and motivational functions of affective states. In E. T. Higgins and R. M. Sorrentino, eds., *Handbook of motivation and cognition: Foundations of social behavior,* vol. 2, 527–561. New York: Guilford.

Schwarz, N. (1994). Judgment in a social context: Biases, shortcomings, and the logic of conversation. In M. Zanna, ed., *Advances in experimental social psychology,* vol. 26, 123–162. San Diego, CA: Academic Press.

Schwarz, N., and H. Bless (1992a). Constructing reality and its alternatives: Assimilation and contrast effects in social judgment. In L. L. Martin and A. Tesser, eds., *The construction of social judgment,* 217–245. Hillsdale, NJ: Erlbaum.

Schwarz, N., and H. Bless (1992b). Scandals and the public's trust in politicians: Assimilation and contrast effects. *Personality and Social Psychology Bulletin* 18, 574–579.

Schwarz, N., H. Bless, F. Strack, G. Klumpp, H. Rittenauer-Schatka, and A. Simons (1991). Ease of retrieval as information: Another look at the availability heuristic. *Journal of Personality and Social Psychology* 61, 195–202.

Schwarz, N., and G. L. Clore (in press). Feelings and phenomenal experiences. In E. T. Higgins and A. Kruglanski, eds., *Social psychology: A handbook of basic principles.* New York: Guilford Press.

Schwarz, N., and F. Strack (1991a). Evaluating one's life: A judgment model of subjective well-being. In F. Strack, M. Argyle, and N. Schwarz, eds., *Subjective well-being. An interdisciplinary perspective,* 27–47. Oxford: Pergamon.

Schwarz, N., and F. Strack (1991b). Context effects in attitude surveys: Applying cognitive theory to social research. In W. Stroebe and M. Hewstone, eds., *European review of social psychology,* vol. 2, 31–50. Chichester: Wiley.

Schwarz, N., F. Strack, and H. P. Mai (1991). Assimilation and contrast effects in part-whole question sequences: A conversational logic analysis. *Public Opinion Quarterly* 55, 3–23.

Schwarz, N., and S. Sudman, eds. (1992). *Context effects in social and psychological research.* New York: Springer-Verlag.

Schwarz, N., M. Wänke, and H. Bless (1994). Subjective assessments and evaluations of change: Some lessons from social cognition research. In W. Stroebe and M. Hewstone, eds., *European review of social psychology,* vol. 5, 181–210. Chichester: Wiley.

Sherman, S. J., and E. Corty (1984). Cognitive heuristics. In R. S. Wyer and T. K. Srull, eds., *Handbook of social cognition,* vol. 1, 189–286. Hillsdale, NJ: Erlbaum.

Strack, F. (1992). The different routes to social judgments: Experiential versus informational strategies. In L. Martin and A. Tesser, eds., *The construction of social judgment,* 249–275. Hillsdale, NJ: Erlbaum.

Strack, F., and L. Martin (1987). Thinking, judging, and communicating: A process account of context effects in attitude surveys. In H. J. Hippler, N. Schwarz, and S. Sudman, eds., *Social information processing and survey methodology,* 123–148. New York: Springer-Verlag.

Strack, F., L. L. Martin, and N. Schwarz (1988). Priming and communication: The social determinants of information use in judgments of life-satisfaction. *European Journal of Social Psychology* 18, 429–442.

Strack, F., and N. Schwarz (1992). Communicative influences in standardized question situations: The case of implicit collaboration. In K. Fiedler and G. Semin, eds., *Language, interaction and social cognition,* 173–193. Beverly Hills, CA: Sage.

Strack, F., N. Schwarz, and E. Gschneidinger (1985). Happiness and reminiscing: The role of time perspective, mood, and mode of thinking. *Journal of Personality and Social Psychology* 49, 1460–1469.

Strack, F., N. Schwarz, A. Kübler, and M. Wänke (1993). Awareness of the influence as a determinant of assimilation versus contrast. *European Journal of Social Psychology* 23, 53–62.

Strack, F., N. Schwarz, and M. Wänke (1991). Semantic and pragmatic aspects of context effects in social and psychological research. *Social Cognition* 9, 111–125.

Taylor, S. E. (1982). The availability bias in social perception and interaction. In D. Kahneman, P. Slovic, and A. Tversky, eds., *Judgment under uncertainty: Heuristics and biases,* 190–200. Cambridge: Cambridge University Press.

Taylor, S. E., and S. Thompson (1982). Stalking the elusive vividness effect. *Psychological Review* 89, 155–181.

Tourangeau, R. (1984). Cognitive science and survey methods: A cognitive perspective. In T. Jabine, M. Straf, J. Tanur, and R. Tourangeau, eds., *Cognitive aspects of survey methodology: Building a bridge between disciplines,* 73–100. Washington, DC: National Academy Press.

Tourangeau, R., and K. A. Rasinski (1988). Cognitive processes underlying context effects in attitude measurement. *Psychological Bulletin* 103, 299–314.

Tulving, E., and Z. Pearlstone (1966). Availability versus accessibility of information in memory for words. *Journal of Verbal Learning and Verbal Behavior* 5, 381–391.

Tversky, A., and D. Griffin (1991). On the dynamics of hedonic experience: Endowment and contrast in judgments of well-being. In F. Strack, M. Argyle, and N. Schwarz, eds., *Subjective well-being*. Oxford: Pergamon.

Tversky, A., and D. Kahneman (1973). Availability: A heuristic for judging frequency and probability. *Cognitive Psychology* 5, 207–232.

Wänke, M., N. Schwarz, and H. Bless (in press). The availability heuristic revisited: Experienced ease of retrieval in mundane frequency estimates. *Acta Psychologica.*

Wyer, R. S., and T. K. Srull (1989). *Memory and cognition in its social context.* Hillsdale, NJ: Erlbaum.

Wyer, R. S., and T. K. Srull, eds. (1994). *Handbook of social cognition.* 2nd ed., 2 vols. Hillsdale, NJ: Erlbaum.

Chapter 11

The Mind as the Software of the Brain

Ned Block

Cognitive scientists often say that the mind is the software of the brain. This chapter is about what this claim means.

11.1 Machine Intelligence

In this section, we start with an influential attempt to define "intelligence," and then we consider how human intelligence is to be investigated on the machine model. In the last part of the section we discuss the relation between the mental and the biological.

11.1.1 The Turing Test

One approach to the mind has been to avoid its mysteries by simply *defining* the mental in terms of the behavioral. This approach has been popular among thinkers who fear that acknowledging mental states that do not reduce to behavior would make psychology unscientific because unreduced mental states are not intersubjectively accessible in the manner of the entities of the hard sciences. "Behaviorism," as the attempt to reduce the mental to the behavioral is called, has often been regarded as refuted, but it periodically reappears in new forms.

Behaviorists don't define the mental in terms of just plain *behavior*, for after all something can be intelligent even if it has never had the chance to exhibit its intelligence. Behaviorists define the mental not in terms of behavior, but rather behavioral *dispositions*, the tendency to emit certain behaviors given certain stimuli. It is important that the stimuli and the behavior be specified nonmentalistically. Thus, intelligence could not be defined in terms of the disposition to give sensible responses to questions, because that would be to define a mental notion in terms of another mental notion (indeed, a closely related one). To see the difficulty of behavioristic analyses, one has to appreciate how mentalistic our ordinary behavioral descriptions are. Consider, for example, *throwing*. A series of motions that constitute throwing if produced by one mental cause might be a dance to get the ants off if produced by another.

An especially influential behaviorist definition of intelligence was put forward by A. M. Turing (1950). Turing, one of the mathematicians who cracked the German code during World War II, formulated the idea of the universal Turing machine, which contains, in mathematical form, the essence of the programmable digital computer. Turing wanted to define intelligence in a way that applied to both men and machines, and indeed, to anything that is intelligent. His version of behaviorism formulates the issue of whether machines could think or be intelligent in terms of whether they could pass this test: A judge in one room communicates by teletype (this was 1950!) with a computer in a second room and a person in a third room for some specified period (let's say an hour). The computer is intelligent if and only if the judge cannot tell the difference between the computer and the person. Turing's definition finessed the difficult problem of specifying nonmentalistically the behavioral dispositions that are characteristic of intelligence by bringing in the discrimination behavior of a human judge. And the definition generalizes. *Anything* is intelligent if, and only if, it can pass the Turing test.

Turing suggested that we replace the concept of intelligence with the concept of passing the Turing test. But what is the replacement *for*? If the purpose of the replacement is practical, the Turing test is not a big success. If one wants to know if a machine does well at playing chess or diagnosing pneumonia or planning football strategy, it is better to see how the machine performs in action than to subject it to a Turing test. For one thing, what we care about is that it do well at detecting pneumonia, not that it do so in a way indistinguishable from the way a person would do it. And so if it does the job, who cares if it doesn't pass the Turing test?

A second purpose might be utility for theoretical purposes. But machines that can pass the Turing test, such as Weizenbaum's ELIZA (see below), have been dead ends in artificial intelligence research, not exciting beginnings. (See "Mimicry versus Exploration" in Marr 1977, and Shieber 1994.)

A third purpose, the one that comes closest to Turing's intentions, is the purpose of *conceptual clarification*. Turing was famous for having formulated a precise mathematical concept that he offered as a replacement for the vague idea of mechanical computability. The precise concept (computability by a Turing machine) did everything one would want a precise concept of mechanical computability to do. No doubt, Turing hoped that the Turing-test conception of intelligence would yield everything one would want from a definition of intelligence without the vagueness of the ordinary concept.

Construed as a proposal about how to make the concept of intelligence precise, there is a gap in Turing's proposal: we are not told how the judge is to be chosen. A judge who was a leading authority on genuinely intelligent machines might know how to tell them apart from people. For example, the expert may know that current intelligent machines get certain problems right that people get wrong. Turing acknowledged this point by jettisoning the claim that being able to pass the Turing test is a necessary condition of intelligence, weakening his claim to: passing the Turing test is a sufficient condition for intelligence. He says, "May not machines carry out something which ought to be described as thinking but which is very different from what a man does? This objection is a very strong one, but at least we can say that if, nevertheless, a machine can be constructed to play the imitation game satisfactorily, we need not be troubled by this objection" (p. 435). In other words, a machine that *does pass* is necessarily intelligent, even if some intelligent machines fail.

But the problem of how to specify the qualities of the judge goes deeper than Turing acknowledges, and ruins the Turing test as a sufficient condition too. A stupid judge, or one who has had no contact with technology, might think that a radio was intelligent. People who are naive about computers are amazingly easy to fool, as demonstrated in the First Turing Test at the Boston Computer Museum in 1991. (See Shieber 1994.) A version of Weizenbaum's ELIZA (described in the next paragraph) was classified as human by five of ten judges. The test was "restricted" in that the computer programmers were given specific topics that their questions would be restricted to, and the judges were forbidden to ask "tricky" questions. For example, if the topic were Washington, D.C., a judge was not supposed to ask questions like, "Is Washington, D.C. bigger than a breadbox?" However, the winning program's topic was "whimsical conversation," a "smart-aleck" way of interacting that all the judges fell in with immediately, and one that would have had the same effect, even without set topics. Further, the restrictions to nontricky questions weren't enforced. (I speak as one of the referees who failed to enforce them.) For the most part, the computer-naive judges didn't really know how to formulate a tricky question. Thus the variant of ELIZA may be regarded as having done well in an unrestricted Turing test. Variants on ELIZA (all written by Joseph Weintraub) also were victorious in the Second and Third Turing Tests. The upshot is that a completely stupid computer program has *already* been shown to pass a reasonable facsimile of a Turing test.

ELIZA is a simple program written by Joseph Weizenbaum that in one version imitates a psychiatrist. See Weizenbaum (1976). It employs a group of simple but effective strategies. For example, it looks for "key words" on a list supplied by the programmer, for example, "I," "you," "alike," "father," and "everybody." The words are ordered; for example, "father" comes before "everybody," and so if you type in "My father is afraid of everybody," the machine will spit back one of its "father" responses, such as "WHAT ELSE COMES TO MIND WHEN YOU THINK OF YOUR FATHER?" If you type in "Everybody laughed at me," you will get one of its responses to "everybody," such as "WHO IN PARTICULAR ARE YOU THINKING OF?" It also has techniques that simultaneously transform "you" into "I," and "me" into "you" so that if you type in "You don't agree with me," it can reply: "WHY DO YOU THINK THAT I DON'T AGREE WITH YOU?" It also *stores* sentences including certain key words such as "my." If your *current* input includes no key words, but if you earlier said, "My boyfriend made me come here," the program will say "DOES THAT HAVE ANYTHING TO DO WITH THE FACT THAT YOUR BOYFRIEND MADE YOU COME HERE?" It also has stock responses to "Parlez-vous francais?" (or any other sentence with "francais" in it), namely "I SPEAK ONLY ENGLISH." If all else fails, the machine has a list of last-ditch responses such as "WHO IS THE PSYCHIATRIST HERE, YOU OR ME?"

This type of program is easy to trip up if you know how it works. For example, in the First Turing Test, one judge said, "You're trying to make this difficult for me, aren't you?" and the program replied roughly as follows: "Would you prefer it if it was not true that you're trying to make this difficult for you aren't you?" As Shieber points out, the pronoun-transposition rules can't handle "tag questions" that end with, for example, "aren't you?"

The point that this program illustrates is that a simple program can be extraordinarily successful in activities akin to passing the Turing test. Weizenbaum's program is not sophisticated or complex by current standards (there is a PC version that is only 200 lines in BASIC) yet this type of program is better at passing the Turing test than anything else written to date, as shown by the three victories in a row in the Turing tests mentioned above. Imagine how convincing a program would be produced if the Defense budget were devoted to this task for a year! But even if a high-budget government initiative produced a program that was good at passing the Turing test, if the program was just a bundle of tricks like the Weizenbaum program, with question types all thought of in advance, and canned responses placed in the machine, the machine would not be intelligent.

One way of dealing with the problem of specifying the judge is to make some characterization about the judge's mental qualities part of the formulation of the Turing test. For example, one might specify that the judge be moderately knowledgeable about computers and good at thinking, or better, good at thinking about thinking. But including a specification of the judge's mental qualities in the description of the test will ruin the test as a way of *defining* the concept of intelligence in nonmentalistic terms. Further, if we are going to specify that the judge must be good at thinking about thinking, we might just as well give up on having the judge judge which contestants are human beings or machines and just have the judge judge which contestants *think*. And then the idea of the Turing test would amount to: A machine thinks if our best thinkers (about thinking) think it thinks. Although this sounds like a platitude, it is actually false. For even our best thinkers are fallible. The most that can be claimed is that if our best thinkers think that something thinks, then it is rational for us to believe that it does.

I've made much of the claim that judges can be fooled by a mindless machine that is just a bag of tricks. "But," you may object, "how do we know that *we* are not just a bag of tricks?" Of course, in a sense perhaps we are, but that isn't the sense relevant to what is wrong with the Turing test. To see this point, consider the ultimate in unintelligent Turing test passers, a hypothetical machine that contains *all conversations of a given length* in which the machine's replies make sense. Let's stipulate that the test lasts one hour. Because there is an upper bound on how fast a human typist can type, and because there are a finite number of keys on a teletype, there is an upper bound on the "length" of a Turing test conversation. Thus there are a finite (though more than astronomical) number of different Turing test conversations, and there is no contradiction in the idea of *listing them all*.

Let's call a string of characters that can be typed in an hour or less a "typable" string. In principle, all typable strings could be generated, and a team of intelligent programmers could throw out all the strings that cannot be interpreted as a conversation in which at least one party (say the second contributor) is making sense. The remaining strings (call them the sensible strings) could be stored in a hypothetical computer (say, with marks separating the contributions of the separate parties), which works as follows. The judge types in something. Then the machine locates a string that starts with the judge's remark, spitting back its next element. The judge then types something else. The machine finds a string that begins with the judge's first contribution, followed by the machine's, followed by the judge's next contribution (the string will be there because all sensible strings are there), and then the machine spits back its fourth element, and so on. (We can eliminate the simplifying assumption that the judge speaks first by recording *pairs* of strings; this would also allow the judge and the machine to talk at the same time.) Of course, such a machine is only logically possible, not physically possible. The number of strings is too vast to exist, and even if they could exist, they could never be accessed by any sort of a machine in anything like real time. But because we are considering a proposed definition of intelligence that is supposed to capture the *concept* of intelligence, conceptual possibility will do the job. If the concept of intelligence is supposed to be exhausted by the ability to pass the Turing test, then even a universe in which the laws of physics are very different from ours should contain exactly as many unintelligent Turing-test passers as married bachelors, namely zero.

Notice that the choice of one hour as a limit for the Turing test is of no consequence, for the procedure just described works for *any* finite Turing test.

The following variant of the machine may be easier to grasp. The programmers start by writing down all typable strings, call them $A_1 \ldots A_n$. Then they think of *just one* sensible response to each of these, which we may call $B_1 \ldots B_n$. (Actually, there will be fewer *B*'s than *A*'s because some of the *A*'s will take up the entire hour.) The programmers may have an easier time of it if they think of themselves as simulating some definite personality, say my Aunt Bubbles, and some definite situation, say Aunt Bubbles being brought into the teletype room by her strange nephew and asked to answer questions for an hour. Thus each of the B's will be the sort of reply Aunt Bubbles would give to the preceding A. For example, if A_{73} is "Explain general relativity," B_{73} might be "Ask my nephew, he's the professor." What about the judge's replies to each of the B's? The judge can give any reply up to the remaining length limit, and so below each of the B's, there will sprout a vast number of C's (vast, but fewer than the number of B's, for the time remaining has decreased). The programmers' next task is to produce just one D for each of the C's. Thus if the B just mentioned is followed by a C that is "xyxyxyxyxyxyxy!" (Remember, the judge doesn't have to make sense), the programmers might make the following D "My nephew warned me that you might type some weird messages."

Think of conversations as paths downward through a tree, starting with an A_i from the judge, a reply, B_i from the machine, and so on. See figure 11.1. For each A_i–B_i–C^i_j that is a beginning to a conversation, the pro-

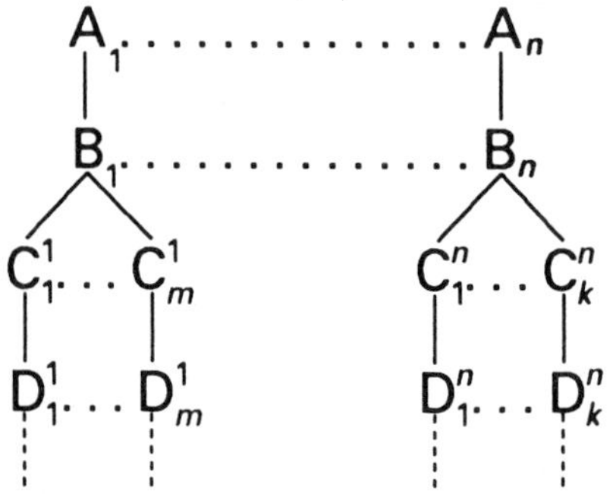

Figure 11.1
A conversation is any path from the top to the bottom.

grammers must produce a D that makes sense given the A, B, and C that precede it.

The machine works as follows. The judge goes first. Whatever the judge types in (typos and all) is one of $A_1 \ldots A_n$. The machine locates the particular A, say A_{2398}, and then spits back B_{2398}, a reply chosen by the programmers to be appropriate to A_{2398}. The judge types another message, and the machine again finds it in the list of C's that sprout below B_{2398}, and then spits back the prerecorded reply (which takes into account what was said in A_{2398} and B_{2398}). And so on. Though the machine can do as well in the one-hour Turing test as Aunt Bubbles, it *has the intelligence of a jukebox*. Every clever remark it produces was specifically thought of by the programmers as a response to the previous remark of the judge in the context of the previous conversation.

Though this machine is too big to exist, there is nothing incoherent or contradictory about its specification, and so it is enough to refute the behaviorist interpretation of the Turing test that I have been talking about.[1]

Notice that there is an upper bound on how long any particular Aunt Bubbles machine can go on in a Turing test, a limit set by the length of the strings it has been given. Of course *real people* have their upper limits too, given that real people will eventually quit or die. However, there is a very important difference between the Aunt Bubbles machine and a real person. We can define "competence" as idealized performance. Then, relative to appropriate idealizations, it may well be that real people have an infinite competence to go on. That is, if human beings were provided with unlimited memory and with motivational systems that gave passing the Turing test infinite weight, they could go on forever (at least according to conventional wisdom in cognitive science). This is definitely not the case for the Aunt Bubbles machine. But this difference provides no objection to the Aunt Bubbles machine as a refutation of the Turing-test conception of intelligence, because the notion of competence is not behavioristically acceptable, requiring as it does for its specification a distinction among components of the mind. For example, the mechanisms of thought must be distinguished from the mechanisms of memory and motivation. do they?

"But," you may object, "isn't it rather chauvinist to assume that a machine must process information in just the way *we* do to be intelligent?"

1. The Aunt Bubbles machine refutes something stronger than behaviorism, namely the claim that the mental "supervenes" on the behavioral; that is, that there can be no mental difference without a behavioral difference. (Of course, the behavioral dispositions are finite —see the next paragraph in the text.) I am indebted to Stephen White for pointing out to me that the doctrine of the supervenience of the mental on the behavioral is widespread among thinkers who reject behaviorism, such as Donald Davidson. The Aunt Bubbles machine is described and defended in detail in Block (1978, 1981a), and was independently discovered by White (1982). It has been dubbed the "Blockhead" in Jackson (1993).

Answer: Such an assumption would indeed be chauvinist, but I am not assuming it. The point against the Turing-test conception of intelligence is not that the Aunt Bubbles machine wouldn't process information in the way we do, but rather that the way in which it does process information is unintelligent despite its performance in the Turing test.

Ultimately, the problem with the Turing test for theoretical purposes is that it focuses on performance rather than on competence. Of course, performance is evidence for competence, but the core of our understanding of the mind lies with mental competence, not behavioral performance. The behaviorist cast of mind that leads to the Turing-test conception of intelligence also leads to labeling the sciences of the mind as "the behavioral sciences." But as Chomsky (1959) has pointed out, that is like calling physics the science of meter readings.

11.1.2 Two Kinds of Definitions of Intelligence

We have been talking about an attempt to define intelligence using the resources of the Turing test. However, there is a very different approach to defining intelligence.

To explain this approach, it will be useful to contrast two kinds of definitions of water. One might be better regarded as a definition of the word *'water'*. The word might be defined as the colorless, odorless, tasteless liquid that is found in lakes and oceans. In this sense of "definition," the definition of "water" is available to anyone who speaks the language, even someone who knows no science. But one might also define water by saying what water really is—that is, by saying what physicochemical structure in fact makes something pure water. The answer to this question involves its chemical constitution: H_2O. Defining a **word** is something we can do in our armchair, by consulting our linguistic intuitions about hypothetical cases, or, bypassing this process, by simply stipulating a meaning for a word. Defining (or explicating) the *thing* is an activity that involves empirical investigation into the nature of something in the world.

What we have been discussing so far is the first kind of definition of intelligence, the definition of the word, not the thing. Turing's definition is not the result of an empirical investigation into the components of intelligence of the sort that led to the definition of water as H_2O. Rather, he hoped to avoid muddy thinking about machine intelligence by stipulating that the word "intelligent" should be used in a certain way, at least with regard to machines. Quite a different way of proceeding is to investigate intelligence *itself* as physical chemists investigate water. We consider how this might be done in the next section, but first we should recognize a complication.

There are two kinds (at least) of kinds: *structural* kinds such as *water* or *tiger*, and *functional* kinds such as *mousetrap* or *gene*. A structural kind has a "hidden compositional essence"; for water, the compositional essence is a matter of its molecules consisting of two hydrogen molecules and one oxygen molecule. Functional kinds, by contrast, have no essence that is a matter of composition. A certain sort of function, a causal role, is the key to being a mousetrap or a carburetor. (The full story is quite complex: Something can be a mousetrap because it is made to be one even if it doesn't fulfill that function very well.) What makes a bit of DNA a gene is its function with respect to mechanisms that can read the information that it encodes and use this information to make a biological product.

Now the property of being intelligent is no doubt a functional kind, but it still makes sense to investigate it experimentally, just as it makes sense to investigate genes experimentally. One topic of investigation is the role of intelligence in problem solving, planning, decision making, and so on. Just what functions are involved in a functional kind is often a difficult and important empirical question. The project of Mendelian genetics has been to investigate the function of genes at a level of description that does not involve their molecular realizations. A second topic of investigation is the nature of the realizations that have the function in us, in humans: DNA in the case of genes. Of course, if there are Martians, their genes may not be composed of DNA. Similarly, we can investigate the functional details and physical basis of human intelligence without attention to the fact that our results will not apply to other mechanisms of other hypothetical intelligences.

11.1.3 Functional Analysis

Both types of projects just mentioned can be pursued via a common methodology, which is sometimes known as *functional analysis*. Think of the human mind as represented by an intelligent being in the head, a "homunculus." Think of this homunculus as composed of smaller and stupider homunculi, and each of these being composed of still smaller and still stupider homunculi until you reach a level of completely mechanical homunculi. (This picture was first articulated in Fodor 1968; see also Dennett 1974 and Cummins 1975.)

Suppose one wants to explain how we understand language. Part of the system will recognize individual words. This word-recognizer might be composed of three components, one of which has the task of fetching each incoming word, one at a time, and passing it to a second component. The second component includes a dictionary, that is, a list of all the words in the vocabulary, together with syntactic and semantic information about each word. This second component compares the target word with words in the vocabulary (perhaps executing many such comparisons simultaneously) until it gets a match. When it finds a match, it sends a signal to a third component whose job it is to retrieve the syntactic and semantic

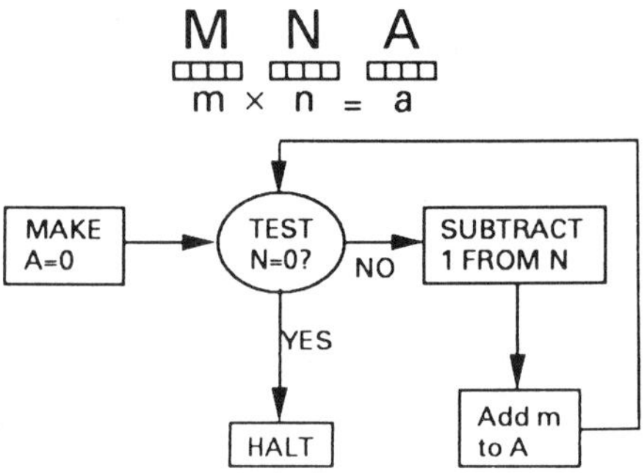

Figure 11.2
Program for multiplying. The user begins the multiplication by putting representations of *m* and *n*, the numbers to be multiplied, in registers M and N. At the end of the computation, the answer will be found in register A. See the text for a description of how the program works.

information stored in the dictionary. This speculation about how a model of language understanding works is supposed to illustrate how a cognitive competence can be explained by appeal to simpler cognitive competences, in this case the simple mechanical operations of fetching and matching.

The idea of this kind of explanation of intelligence comes from attention to the way in which computers work. Consider a computer that multiplies *m* times *n* by adding *m* to zero *n* times. Here is a program for doing this computation. Think of *m* and *n* as represented in the registers M and N in figure 11.2. Register A is reserved for the answer, *a*. First, a representation of 0 is placed in the register A. Second, register N is examined to see if it contains (a representation of) 0. If the answer is yes, the program halts and the correct answer is 0. (If $n = 0$, m times $n = 0$.) If no, N is decremented by 1 (and so register N now contains a representation of $n - 1$), and (a representation of) *m* is added to the answer register, A. Then the procedure loops back to the second step: register N is checked once again to see if its value is 0; if not, it is again decremented by 1, and again *m* is added to the answer register. This procedure continues until N finally has the value 0, at which time *m* will have been added to the answer register exactly *n* times. At this point, the answer register contains a representation of the answer.

This program multiplies via a "decomposition" of multiplication into other processes, namely addition, subtraction of 1, setting a register to 0, and checking a register for 0. Depending on how these things are themselves done, they may be further decomposable, or they may be the fundamental bottom-level processes, known as *primitive processes*.

The cognitive-science definition or explication of intelligence is analogous to this explication of multiplication. Intelligent capacities are understood via decomposition into a network of less intelligent capacities, ultimately grounded in totally mechanical capacities executed by primitive processors.

The concept of a primitive process is very important; the next section is devoted to it.

11.1.4 Primitive Processors

What makes a processor primitive? One answer is that for primitive processors, the question, "How does the processor work?" *is not a question for cognitive science to answer*. The cognitive scientist answers "How does the multiplier work?" for the multiplier described above by giving the program or the information-flow diagram for the multiplier. But if components of the multiplier, say the gates of which the adder is composed, are primitive, then it is not the cognitive scientist's business to answer the question of how such a gate works. The cognitive scientist can say, "That question belongs in another discipline, electronic circuit theory." Distinguish the question of *how something works* from the question of *what it does*. The question of *what* a primitive processor does is part of cognitive science, but the question of *how* it does it is not.

This idea can be made a bit clearer by looking at how a primitive processor actually works. The example involves a common type of computer adder, simplified so as to add only single digits.

To understand this example, you need to know these simple facts about binary notation:[2] 0 and 1 are represented alike in binary and normal (decimal) notation, but the binary representation that corresponds to decimal '*2*' is '*10*'. Our adder will solve these four problems:

$$0 + 0 = 0$$

$$1 + 0 = 1$$

$$0 + 1 = 1$$

$$1 + 1 = 10$$

The first three equations are true in both binary and decimal, but the last is true only if understood in binary.

The second item of background information is the notion of a gate. An AND gate is a device that accepts two inputs, and emits a single output. If both inputs are '*1*'s, the output is a '*1*'; otherwise, the output is a '*0*'. An EXCLUSIVE-OR (either but not both) gate is a "difference detector": it

2. The rightmost digit in binary (as in familiar decimal) is the 1s place. The second digit from the right is the 2s place (corresponding to the 10s place in decimal). Next is the 4s place (that is, 2 squared), just as the corresponding place in decimal is the 10 squared place.

emits a '*0*' if its inputs are the same (that is, '*1*'/'*1*' or '*0*'/'*0*'), and it emits a '*1*' if its inputs are different (that is, '*1*'/'*0*' or '*0*'/'*1*').

This talk of '*1*' and '*0*' is a way of thinking about the "bistable" states of computer representers. These representers are made so that they are always in one or the other of two states, and only momentarily in between. (This is what it is to be bistable.) The states might be a 4-volt and a 7-volt potential. If the two input states of a gate are the same (say 4 volts), and the output is the same as well (4 volts), and if every other combination of inputs yields the 7-volt output, then the gate is an AND gate, and the 4-volt state realizes '*1*'. (Alternatively, if the 4-volt state is taken to realize '*0*', the gate is an "inclusive or" (either or both) gate.) A different type of AND gate might be made so that the 7-volt state realized '*1*'. The point is that '*1*' is conventionally assigned to *whatever* bistable physical state of an AND gate it is that has the role mentioned, that is, '*1*' is conventionally assigned to whatever state it is such that two of them as inputs yield another one as output, and nothing else yields that output. And all that counts about an AND gate from a computational point of view is its input-output function, not how it works or whether 4 volts or 7 volts realizes a '*1*'. Notice the terminology I have been using: one speaks of a physical state (4-volt potential) as "realizing" a computational state (having the value '*1*'). This distinction between the computational and physical levels of description will be important in what follows, especially in section 11.3.

Here is how the adder works. The two digits to be added are connected both to an AND gate and to an EXCLUSIVE-OR gate, as illustrated in figures 11.3a and 11.3b. Let's look at 11.3a first. The digits to be added are '*1*' and '*0*', and they are placed in the input register, which is the top pair of boxes. The EXCLUSIVE-OR gate, which, you recall, is a difference detector, sees different things, and so outputs a '*1*' to the rightmost box of the answer register, which is the bottom pair of boxes. The AND gate outputs a '*0*' except when it sees two '*1*'s, and so it outputs a '*0*'. In this way, the circuit computes '$1 + 0 = 1$'. For this problem, as for '$0 + 1 = 1$' and '$0 + 0 = 0$', the EXCLUSIVE-OR gate does all the real work. The role of the AND gate in this circuit is *carrying*, and that is illustrated in figure 11.3b. The digits to be added, '*1*' and '*1*', are placed in the top register again. Now, both inputs to the AND gate are '*1*'s, and so the AND gate outputs a '*1*' to the leftmost box of the answer (bottom) register. The EXCLUSIVE-OR gate puts a '*0*' in the rightmost box, and so we have the correct answer, '*10*'.

The borders between scientific disciplines are notoriously fuzzy. No one can say *exactly* where chemistry stops and physics begins. Because the line between the upper levels of processors and the level of primitive processors is the same as the line between cognitive science and one of the

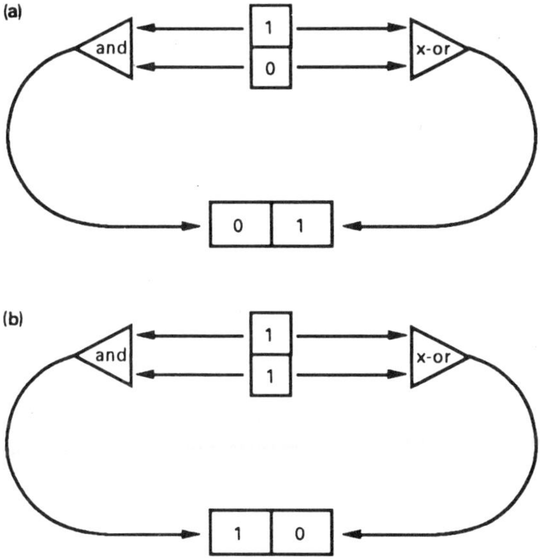

Figure 11.3
(a) Adder doing 1 + 0 = 1 (b) Adder doing 1 + 1 = 10.

"realization" sciences such as electronics or physiology, the boundary between the levels of complex processors and the level of primitive processors will have the same fuzziness. Nonetheless, in this example we should expect that the gates are the primitive processors. If they are made in the usual way, they are the largest components whose operation must be explained, not in terms of cognitive science, but rather in terms of electronics or mechanics or some other realization science. Why the qualification, "If they are made in the usual way"? It would be *possible* to make an adder each of whose gates were *whole computers,* with their own multipliers, adders, and normal gates. (We could even make an adder whose gates were people!) It would be silly to waste a whole computer (or a person) on such a simple task as that of an AND gate, but it could be done. In that case, the real level of primitives would not be the gates of the original adder, but rather the (normal) gates of the component computers.

Primitive processors are the only computational devices for which *behaviorism is true.* Two primitive processors (such as gates) count as computationally equivalent if they have the same input-output function, that is, the same actual and potential behavior, even if one works hydraulically and the other electrically. But computational equivalence of *non*primitive devices is not to be understood in this way. Consider two multipliers that work via different programs. Both accept inputs and emit outputs only in decimal notation. One of them converts inputs to binary, does the computation in binary, and then converts back to decimal. The other does the computation directly in decimal. These are not computationally equivalent multipliers despite their identical input-output functions.

If the mind is the software of the brain, then we must take seriously the idea that the functional analysis of human intelligence will bottom out in primitive processors in the brain.

11.1.5 The Mental and the Biological

One type of electrical AND gate consists of two circuits with switches arranged as in figure 11.4. The switches on the left are the inputs. When only one or neither of the input switches is closed, nothing happens, because the circuit on the left is not completed. Only when both switches are closed does the electromagnet go on, and that pulls the switch on the right closed, thereby turning on the circuit on the right. (The circuit on the right is only partially illustrated.) In this example, a switch being closed realizes '1'; it is the bistable state that obtains as an output if and only if two of them are present as an input.

Another AND gate is illustrated in figure 11.5. If neither of the mice on the left is released into the right-hand part of their cages, or if only one of the mice is released, the cat does not strain hard enough to pull the leash. But when both are released, and are therefore visible to the cat, the cat strains enough to lift the third mouse's gate, letting it into the cheesy part of its box. And so we have a situation in which a mouse getting cheese is output if and only if two cases of mice getting cheese are input.

The point illustrated here is the irrelevance of hardware realization to computational description. These gates work in very different ways, but they are nonetheless computationally equivalent. And of course it is possible to think of an indefinite variety of other ways of making a primitive AND gate. How such gates work is no more part of the domain of cognitive science than is the nature of the buildings that hold computer factories. This question reveals a sense in which the computer model of the mind is profoundly *unbiological*. We are beings who *have* a useful and interesting biological level of description, but the computer model of the mind aims for a level of description of the mind that abstracts away from the biological realizations of cognitive structures. As far as the computer model goes, it does not matter whether our gates are realized in gray matter, switches, or cats and mice.

Of course, this is not to say that the computer model is in any way incompatible with a biological approach. Indeed, cooperation between the biological and computational approaches is vital to *discovering* the program of the brain. Suppose one were presented with a computer of alien design

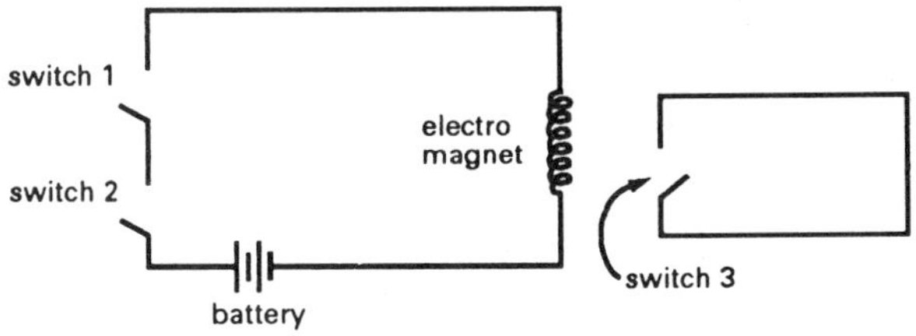

Figure 11.4
Electrical AND gate.
Open = 0, *closed* = 1

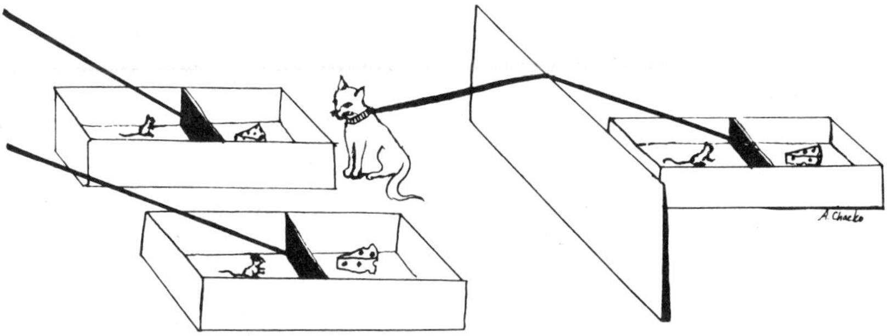

Figure 11.5
Cat and mouse AND gate.
Hungry mouse = 0, *mouse fed* = 1

and set the problem of ascertaining its program by any means possible. Only a fool would choose to ignore information to be gained by opening the computer up to see how its circuits work. One would want to put information at the program level together with information at the electronic level, and likewise, in finding the program of the human mind, one can expect biological and cognitive approaches to complement each other.

Nonetheless, the computer model of the mind has a built-in antibiological bias, in the following sense. If the computer model is right, we should be able to create intelligent machines in our image—our *computational* image, that is. And the machines we create in our computational image may not be biologically similar to us. If we can create machines in our computational image, we will naturally feel that the most compelling theory of the mind is one that is general enough to apply to both them and us, and this will be a computational theory, not a biological theory. A biological theory of the *human* mind will not apply to these machines, though the biological theory will have a complementary advantage: namely, that such a biological theory will encompass us together with our less intelligent biological cousins, and thus provide a different kind of insight into the nature of human intelligence. Both approaches can accommodate evolutionary considerations, though for the computational paradigm, evolution is no more relevant to the nature of the mind than the programmer's intentions are to the nature of a computer program.

Some advocates of connectionist computer models of the mind claim that they are advocating a biological approach. But examining typical connectionist models shows that they are firmly within the computationalist paradigm. For example, the popular backpropagation models allow weights of network connections to shift between positive and negative, something that cannot happen with neural connections. It would be a simple matter to constrain the network models so that connections could not change between excitatory and inhibitory, but no one wants to do this because then the models would not work. Thus, although these models are biologically inspired, biological fidelity is rejected when it does not make computational sense.

11.2 Intelligence and Intentionality

Our discussion so far has centered on the computational approach to one aspect of the mind, intelligence. But the mind has a different aspect that we have not yet discussed, one that has a very different relation to computational ideas, namely *intentionality*.

For our purposes, we can take intelligence to be a capacity for various intelligent activities such as solving mathematics problems, deciding whether to go to graduate school, and figuring out how spaghetti is made. (Notice that this analysis of intelligence as a capacity to solve, figure out, decide, and the like, is a mentalistic, not a behaviorist analysis.)

Intentionality is aboutness. Intentional states represent the world as being a certain way. The thought that the moon is full and the perceptual state of seeing that the moon is full are both about the moon and they both represent the moon as being full. Thus both are intentional states. (See volume 2, chapter 9.) We say that the *intentional content* of both the thought and the perceptual state is *that the moon is full*. A single intentional content can have very different behavioral effects, depending on its relation to the person who has the content. For example, the fear that there will be nuclear war might inspire one to work for disarmament, but the belief that there will be nuclear war might influence one to emigrate to Australia. (Don't let the spelling mislead you: intending is only one kind of intentional state. Believing and desiring are others.) Intentionality is an important feature of many mental states, but many philosophers believe it is not "the mark of the mental." There are bodily sensations, the experience of orgasm, for example, that are genuine mental states but have no intentional content. (Well, maybe there is a bit of intentional content to this experience, for example, locational content, but the phenomenal content of the experience, what it is like to have it, is clearly not exhausted by that intentional content.)

The features of thought just mentioned are closely related to features of language. Thoughts represent, are about things, and can be true or false; and the same is true of *sentences*. The sentence "Bruce Springsteen was born in the USSR" is about Springsteen, represents him as having been born in the Soviet Union, and is false. It would be surprising if the intentional content of thought and of language were independent phenomena, and so it is natural to try to reduce one to the other or to find some common explanation for both. We pursue this idea below, but before we go any further, let's try to get clearer about just what the difference is between intelligence and intentionality.

One way to get a handle on the distinction between intelligence and intentionality is to recognize that in the opinion of many writers on this topic you can have intentionality without intelligence. Thus John McCarthy (creator of the artificial-intelligence language LISP) holds that thermostats have intentional states in virtue of their capacity to represent and control temperature (McCarthy 1980). And there is a school of thought that assigns content to tree rings in virtue of their representing the age of the tree (see the references below in section 11.3). But no school of thought holds that the tree rings are actually intelligent. An intelligent system must have certain intelligent capacities, capacities to *do* certain sorts of things, and tree rings can't do these things. Less controversially, words on a page and images on a television screen have intentionality. For example, my remark earlier in this paragraph to the effect that McCarthy created LISP is about McCarthy. But words on a page have no intelligence. Of course, the intentionality of words on a page is only derived intentionality, not original intentionality. (See Searle 1980 and Haugeland 1980.) Derived intentional content is inherited from the original intentional contents of intentional systems such as you and me. We have a great deal of freedom in giving symbols their derived intentional content. If we want to, we can decide that "McCarthy" will now represent Minsky or Chomsky. Original intentional contents are the intentional contents that the representations of an intentional system have *for* that system. Such intentional contents are not subject to our whim. Words on a page have derived intentionality, but they do not have any kind of intelligence, not even derived intelligence, whatever that would be.

Conversely, there can be intelligence without intentionality. Imagine that an event with negligible (but, and this is important, nonzero) probability occurs: In their random movement, particles from the swamp come together and by chance result in a molecule-for-molecule duplicate of your brain. The swamp brain is arguably intelligent, because it has many of the same capacities that your brain has. If we were to hook it up to the right inputs and outputs and give it an arithmetic problem, we would get an intelligent response. But there are reasons for denying that it has the intentional states that you have, and indeed, for denying that it has any intentional states at all. For because we have not hooked it up to input devices, it has never had any information from the world. Suppose the swamp brain and your brain go through an identical process, which in your case is the thinking of the thought that Bernini vandalized the Pantheon. The identical process in the swamp-brain has the phenomenal features of that thought, in the sense of "phenomenal content" indicated in the discussion of orgasm above. What it is like for you to think the thought is just what it is like for the swamp-brain. But, unlike you, the swamp-brain has no idea who Bernini was, what the Pantheon is, or what vandalizing is. No information about Bernini has made any kind of contact with the swamp-brain; no signals from the Pantheon have reached it, either. Had it a mouth, it would merely be mouthing words. Thus no one should be happy with the idea that the swamp-brain is thinking the thought that Bernini vandalized the Pantheon.

The upshot: what makes a system intelligent is what it can do, what it has the capacity to do. Thus intelligence is future oriented. What makes a system an intentional system, by contrast, is in part a matter of its causal history; it must have a history that makes its states represent the world, that is, have *aboutness*. Intentionality has a past-oriented requirement. A system can satisfy the future-oriented needs of intelligence while flunking the past-oriented requirement of intentionality. (Philosophers disagree about just *how* future-oriented intentionality is, whether thinking about something requires the ability to "track" it; but there should be little disagreement that there is *some* past-oriented component.)

Now let's see what the difference between intelligence and intentionality has to do with the computer model of the mind. Notice that the method of functional analysis that explains intelligent processes by reducing them to unintelligent mechanical processes *does not explain intentionality*. The parts of an intentional system can be just as intentional as the whole system. (See Fodor 1981.) In particular, the component processors of an intentional system can manipulate symbols that are about just the same things that the symbols manipulated by the whole system are about. Recall that the multiplier of figure 11.2 was explained via decomposition into devices that add, subtract, and the like. The multiplier's states were intentional in that they were about numbers. The states of the adder, subtractor, and so on, are also about numbers and are thus similarly intentional.

There is, however, an important relation between intentionality and functional decomposition that is explained in the next section. As you will see, though the multiplier's and the adder's states are about numbers, the gate's representational states represent *numerals*, and in general the subject matter of representations shifts as we cross the divide from complex processors to primitive processors.

11.2.1 The Brain as a Syntactic Engine Driving a Semantic Engine

To see the idea of the brain as a syntactic engine it is important to see the difference between the number 1 and the symbol (in this case, a numeral or digit) '*1*'. (The convention in this book is that italics indicate symbols, but in this chapter, numerals are indicated by italics plus single quotation marks.) Certainly, the difference between the city, Boston, and the word '*Boston*' is clear enough. The former has bad drivers in it; the latter has no people or cars at all, but does have six letters. No one would confuse a city with a word, but it is less obvious what the difference is between the number 1 and the numeral '*1*'. The point to keep in mind is that many different symbols, such as '*II*' (in Roman numerals), and '*two*' (in alphabetical writing) denote the same number, and one symbol, such as '*10*', can denote different numbers in different counting systems (as '*10*' denotes one number in binary and another in decimal).

With this distinction in mind, one can see an important difference between the multiplier and the adder discussed earlier. The algorithm used by the multiplier in figure 11.2 is notation *in*dependent: *Multiply n by m by adding n to zero m times* works in any notation. And the program described for implementing this algorithm is also notation independent. As we saw in the description of this program in section 11.1.3, the program depends on the properties of the numbers represented, not the representations themselves. By contrast, the internal operation of the adder described in figures 11.3A and 11.3B depends on binary notation, and its description in section 11.1.4 speaks of numerals (notice the quotation marks and italics) rather than numbers. Recall that the adder exploits the fact that an EXCLUSIVE-OR gate detects symbol differences, yielding a '*1*' when its inputs are different digits, and a '*0*' when its inputs are the same digits. This gate gives the right answer all by itself so long as no carrying is involved. The trick used by the EXCLUSIVE-OR gate depends on the fact that when you add two digits of the same type ('*1*' and '*1*' or '*0*' and '*0*') the rightmost digit of the answer is the same. This result is true in binary, but not in other standard notations. For example, it is not true in familiar decimal notation. ($1 + 1 = 2$, but $0 + 0 = 0$.)

The inputs and outputs of both the multiplier and the adder must be seen as referring to numbers. One way to see this fact is to notice that otherwise one could not see the multiplier as exploiting an algorithm involving multiplying numbers by adding numbers. What are multiplied and added are numbers. But once we go *inside* the adder, we must see the binary states as referring to *symbols themselves*. For as just pointed out, the algorithms are notation dependent. This change of subject matter is even more dramatic in some computational devices, in which there is a level of processing in which the algorithms operate over *parts* of decimal numerals. Consider, for example, a calculator, in which the difference between an *'8'* and a *'3'* is a matter of two small segments on the left of the *'8'* being turned off to make a *'3'*. In calculators, there is a level at which the algorithms concern these segments.

This fact gives us an interesting additional characterization of primitive processors. Typically, as we functionally decompose a computational system, we reach a point where there is a shift of subject matter from abstractions like numbers or from things in the world to the symbols themselves. The inputs and outputs of the adder and multiplier refer to numbers, but the inputs and outputs of the gates refer to numerals. Typically, this shift occurs when we have reached the level of primitive processors. The operation of the higher-level components such as the multiplier can be explained in terms of a program or algorithm that is manipulating numbers. But the operation of the gates cannot be explained in terms of number manipulation; it must be explained in symbolic terms (or at lower levels, for example in terms of electromagnets). At the most basic computational level, computers are symbol crunchers, and for this reason the computer model of the mind is often described as the symbol-manipulation view of the mind.

Seeing the adder as a syntactic engine driving a semantic engine requires noticing two functions: one maps numbers onto other numbers, and the other maps symbols onto other symbols. The symbol function is concerned with the numerals as symbols—without attention to their meanings. Here is the symbol function:

'0', '0' → *'0'*

'0', '1' → *'1'*

'1', '0' → *'1'*

'1', '1' → *'10'*

The idea is that we interpret something physical in a machine or its outputs as symbols, and some other physical aspect of the machine as indicating that the symbols are inputs or outputs. Then given that interpretation, the machine's having some symbols as inputs causes it to have other symbols as outputs. For example, having the pair *'0', '0'* as inputs causes having *'0'* as an output. And so the symbol function is a matter of the causal structure of the machine under an interpretation.

This symbol function is mirrored by a function that maps the numbers represented by the numerals on the left onto the numbers represented by the numerals on the right. This function will thus map numbers onto numbers. We can speak of this function that maps numbers onto numbers as the *semantic* function (semantics being the study of meaning), because it is concerned with the meanings of the symbols, not the symbols themselves. (It is important not to confuse the notion of a semantic function in this sense with a function that maps symbols onto what they refer to; the semantic function maps numbers onto numbers, but the function just mentioned, which often goes by the same name, would map symbols onto numbers.) Here is the semantic function (in decimal notation—you must choose *some* notation to express a semantic function):

$0, 0 \rightarrow 0$

$0, 1 \rightarrow 1$

$1, 0 \rightarrow 1$

$1, 1 \rightarrow 2$

Notice that the two specifications just given differ in that the first maps quoted entities onto other quoted entities. The second has no quotes. The first function maps symbols onto symbols; the second function maps the numbers referred to by the arguments of the first function onto the numbers referred to by the values of the first function. (A function maps arguments onto values.) The first function is a kind of linguistic "reflection" of the second.

The key idea behind the adder is that of an isomorphism between these two functions. The designer has found a machine that has physical aspects that can be interpreted symbolically, and under that symbolic interpretation, there are symbolic regularities: some symbols in inputs result in other symbols in outputs. These symbolic regularities are isomorphic to rational relations among the semantic values of the symbols of a sort that are useful to us, in this case the relation of addition. It is the *isomorphism between these two functions* that explains how it is that a device that manipulates symbols manages to add numbers.

Now the idea of the brain as a syntactic engine driving a semantic engine is just a generalization of this picture to a wider class of symbolic activities, namely the symbolic activities of human thought. The idea is that we have symbolic structures in our brain, and that nature (evolution and learning) has seen to it that there are correlations between causal interactions among these structures and rational relations among the meanings of the symbolic structures. A crude example: the way in which we avoid swimming in shark-infested water is that the brain-symbol structure *'shark'* engenders the brain-symbol structure *'danger'*. (What makes *'danger'* mean *danger* is discussed below.)

The primitive mechanical processors "know" only the "syntactic" forms of the symbols they process (for example, what strings of zeroes and ones they see), and not what the symbols mean. Nonetheless, these meaning-blind primitive processors control processes that "make sense"—processes of decision, problem solving, and the like. In short, there is a correlation between the meanings of our internal representations and their forms. And this explains how it is that our syntactic engine can drive our semantic engine.[3]

In the last paragraph I mentioned a correlation between causal interactions among symbolic structures in our brain and rational relations among the meanings of the symbol structures. This way of speaking can be misleading if it encourages the picture of the neuroscientist opening the brain, just *seeing* the symbols, and then figuring out what they mean. Such a picture inverts the order of discovery, and gives the wrong impression of what makes something a symbol.

The way to discover symbols in the brain is first to map out rational relations among states of mind, and then identify aspects of these states that can be thought of as symbolic in virtue of their functions. Function is what gives a symbol its identity, even the symbols in English orthography, though this relation can be hard to appreciate because these functions have been rigidified by habit and convention. In reading unfamiliar handwriting we may notice an unorthodox symbol, someone's weird way of writing a letter of the alphabet. How do we know which letter of the alphabet it is? By its function! Th% function of a symbol is som%thing on% can appr%ciat% by s%%ing how it app%ars in s%nt%nc%s containing familiar words whos% m%anings w% can gu%ss. You will have little trouble figuring out, on this basis, what letter in the last sentence was replaced by '%'.

11.2.2 Is a Wall a Computer?

John Searle (1990a) argues against the computationalist thesis that the brain is a computer. He does not say that the thesis is false, but rather that it is trivial, because, he suggests, everything is a computer; indeed, everything is *every* computer. In particular, his wall is a computer computing

3. The idea described here was first articulated to my knowledge in Fodor (1975, 1980); see also Dennett (1981) to which the terms "semantic engine" and "syntactic engine" are due, and Newell (1980). More on this topic can be found in Dennett (1987) by looking up "syntactic engine" and "semantic engine" in the index.

Wordstar. (See also Putnam 1988, for a different argument for a similar conclusion.) The points in the preceding section allow easy understanding of the motivation for this claim and what is wrong with it. In that section we saw that the key to computation is an isomorphism. We arrange things so that, if certain physical states of a machine are understood as symbols, then causal relations among those symbol-states mirror useful rational relations among the meanings of those symbols. The mirroring is an isomorphism. Searle's claim is that this sort of isomorphism is cheap. We can regard two aspects of the wall at time *t* as the symbols '*0*'and '*1*', and then we can regard an aspect of the wall at time $t + 1$ as '*1*', and so the wall just computed $0 + 1 = 1$. Thus, Searle suggests, everything (or rather everything that is big or complex enough to have enough states) is every computer, and the claim that the brain is a computer has no bite.

The problem with this reasoning is that the isomorphism that makes a syntactic engine drive a semantic engine is more full-bodied than Searle acknowledges. In particular, the isomorphism has to include not just a particular computation that the machine *does perform,* but also all the computations that the machine *could have* performed. The point can be made clearer by a look at figure 11.6, a type of X-OR gate. (See O'Rourke and Shattuck, forthcoming.)

The numerals at the beginnings of arrows represent inputs. The computation of $1 + 0 = 1$ is represented by the path $A \rightarrow C \rightarrow E$. The computation of $0 + 1 = 1$ is represented by the path $A \rightarrow B \rightarrow E$, and so on. Now here is the point. In order for the wall to be this computer, it isn't enough for it to have states that correspond to '*0*' and '*1*' followed by a state that corresponds to '*1*'. It must also be such that *had* the '*1*' input been replaced by a '*0*' input, the '*1*' output *would have been* replaced by the '*0*' output. In

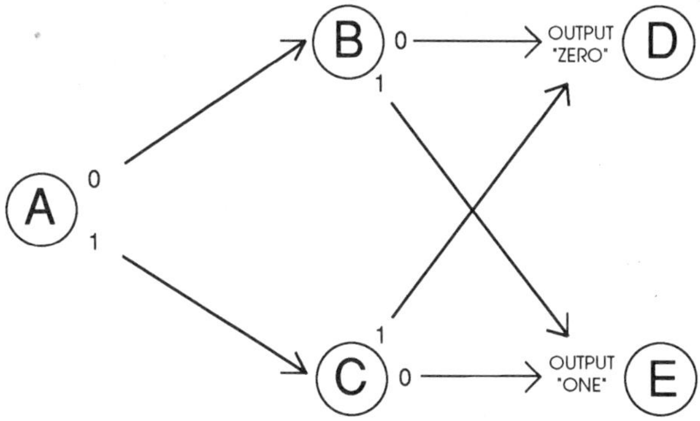

Figure 11.6
The numerals at the beginnings of arrows indicate inputs.

other words, it has to have symbolic states that satisfy not only the *actual* computation, but also the *possible* computations that the computer *could* have performed. And this is nontrivial.

Searle (1992, 209) acknowledges this point, but insists nonetheless that there is no fact of the matter of whether the brain is a specific computer. Whether something is a computer, he argues, depends on whether we decide to interpret its states in a certain way, and that is up to us. "We can't, on the one hand, say that anything is a digital computer if we can assign a syntax to it, and then suppose there is a factual question intrinsic to its physical operation whether or not a natural system such as the brain is a digital computer." Searle is right that whether something is a computer and what computer it is is *in part* up to us. But what the example just given shows is that it is not *totally* up to us. A rock, for example, is not an X-OR gate. We have a great deal of freedom as to how to interpret a device, but there are also very important restrictions on this freedom, and that is what makes it a substantive claim that the brain is a computer of a certain sort.

11.3 Functionalism and the Language of Thought

Thus far we have (1) considered functional analysis, the computer model of the mind's approach to intelligence, (2) distinguished intelligence from intentionality, and (3) considered the idea of the brain as a syntactic engine. The idea of the brain as a syntactic engine explains how it is that symbol-crunching operations can result in a machine "making sense." But so far we have encountered nothing that could be considered the computer model's account of intentionality. It is time to admit that although the computer model of the mind has a natural and straightforward account of intelligence, there is no account of intentionality that comes along for free.

We will not survey the field here. Instead, let us examine a view that represents a kind of orthodoxy, not in the sense that most researchers believe it, but in the sense that the other views define themselves in large part by their response to it.

The basic tenet of this orthodoxy is that our intentional contents are simply meanings of our internal representations. As mentioned earlier, there is something to be said for regarding the content of thought and language as a single phenomenon, and this is a quite direct way of so doing. There is no commitment in this orthodoxy on the issue of whether our internal language, the language in which we think, is the same or different from the language with which we speak. Further, there is no commitment as to a direction of reduction, that is, as to which is more basic, mental content or meanings of internal symbols.

For concreteness, let us talk in terms of Fodor's (1975) doctrine that the meaning of external language derives from the content of thought, and the content of thought derives from the meaning of elements of the language of thought. (See also Harman 1973.) According to Fodor, believing or hoping that grass grows is a state of being in one or another computational relation to an internal representation that means that grass grows. This doctrine can be summed up in a set of slogans: believing that grass grows is having 'Grass grows.' in the Belief Box, desiring that grass grows is having this sentence (or one that means the same) in the Desire Box, and so on.

Now, if all content and meaning derives from meaning of the elements of the language of thought, we immediately want to know how the mental symbols get their meaning.[4] This is a question that gets wildly different answers from different philosophers, all equally committed to the cognitive-science point of view. We briefly look at two of them. The first point of view, mentioned earlier, takes as a kind of paradigm those cases in which a symbol in the head might be said to covary with states in the world in the way that the number of rings in a tree trunk correlates with the age of the tree. (See Dretske 1981, Stampe 1977, Stalnaker 1984, and Fodor 1987, 1990.) On this view, the meaning of mental symbols is a matter of the correlations between these symbols and the world.

One version of this view (Fodor 1990) says that T is the truth condition of a mental sentence M if and only if: M is in the Belief Box if and only if T, in ideal conditions. That is, what it is for 'Grass is green' to have the truth condition that grass be green is for 'Grass is green' to appear in the Belief Box just in case grass really is green (and conditions are ideal). The idea behind this theory is that there are cognitive mechanisms that are designed to put sentences in the Belief Box when and only when they are true, and if those cognitive mechanisms are working properly and the environment cooperates (no mirages, no Cartesian evil demons), these sentences will appear in the Belief Box when and only when they are true.

One problem with this idea is that even if this theory works for "observation sentences" such as 'This is yellow', it is hard to see how it could work for "theoretical sentences." A person's cognitive mechanisms could be working fine, and the environment could contain no misleading evidence, and still one might not believe that space is Riemannian or that some quarks have charm or that one is in the presence of a magnetic field.

4. In one respect, the meanings of mental symbols cannot be semantically more basic than meanings of external symbols. The name "Aristotle" has the reference it has because of its causal connection (via generations of speakers) to a man who was called by a name that was an ancestor of our external term 'Aristotle.' And so the term in the language of thought that corresponds to 'Aristotle' will certainly derive its reference from and thus will be semantically less basic than the public-language word.

For theoretical ideas, it is not enough to have one's nose rubbed in the evidence: you also have to have the right theoretical idea. And if the analysis of ideal conditions includes "has the right theoretical idea," that would make the analysis circular because having the right theoretical idea amounts to "comes up with the true theory." And appealing to truth in an analysis of 'truth' is to move in a very small circle. (See Block 1986, 657–660.)

The second approach is known as functionalism (actually, "functional role semantics" in discussions of meaning) in philosophy, and as procedural semantics in cognitive psychology and computer science. Functionalism says that what gives internal symbols (and external symbols too) their meanings is how they function. To maximize the contrast with the view described in the last two paragraphs, it is useful to think of the functionalist approach with respect to a symbol that doesn't (on the face of it) have *any* kind of correlation with states of the world, say the symbol 'and'. Part of what makes 'and' mean what it does is that if we are sure of 'Grass is green and grass grows', we find the inference to 'Grass is green' and also 'Grass grows' compelling. And we find it compelling "in itself," not because of any other principle (see Peacocke 1993). Or if we are sure that one of the conjuncts is false, we find compelling the inference that the conjunction is false too. What it is to mean *and* by 'and' is to find such inferences compelling in this way, and so we can think of the meaning of 'and' as a matter of its behavior in these and other inferences. The functionalist view of meaning applies this idea to all words. The picture is that the internal representations in our heads have a function in our deciding, deliberating, problem solving—indeed in our thought in general—and that is what constitutes their meanings.

This picture can be bolstered by considering what happens when one first learns Newtonian mechanics. In my own case, I heard a large number of unfamiliar terms more or less all at once: *'mass'*, *'force'*, *'energy'*, and the like. I never was told definitions of these terms in terms I already knew. (No one has ever come up with definitions of such "theoretical terms" in observation language.) What I did learn was how to *use* these terms in solving homework problems, making observations, explaining the behavior of a pendulum, and the like. In learning how to use the terms in thought and action (and perception as well, though its role there is less obvious), I learned their meanings, and this fits with the functionalist idea that the meaning of a term just *is* its function in perception, thought, and action. (See chapter 4 for a discussion of the restructuring of concepts that goes on in learning a new theory.) A theory of what meaning is can be expected to jibe with a theory of what it is to acquire meanings, and so considerations about acquisition can be relevant to semantics.

An apparent problem arises for such a theory in its application to the meanings of numerals. After all, it is a mathematical fact that truths in the familiar numeral system *'1'*, *'2'*, *'3'* are preserved, even if certain nonstandard interpretations of the numerals are adopted (so long as nonstandard versions of the operations are adopted too). For example, *'1'* might be mapped onto 2, *'2'* onto 4, *'3'* onto 6, and so on. That is, the numerals, both "odd" and "even," might be mapped onto the *even* numbers. Because *'1'* and *'2'* can have the *same* functional role in different number systems and still designate the very numbers they usually designate in normal arithmetic, how can the functional role of *'1'* determine whether *'1'* means 1 or 2? It seems that all functional role can do is "cut down" the number of possible interpretations, and if there are still an infinity left after the cutting down, functional role has gained nothing.

A natural functionalist response would be to emphasize the *input* and *output* ends of the functional roles. We say "two cats" when confronted with a pair of cats, not when confronted with one or five cats, and our thoughts involving the symbol *'3'* affect our actions toward triples in an obvious way in which these thoughts do not affect our actions toward octuples. The functionalist can avoid nonstandard interpretations of *internal* functional roles by including in the semantically relevant functional roles external relations involving perception and action (Harman 1973). In this way, the functionalist can incorporate the insight of the view mentioned earlier that meaning has something to do with covariation between symbols and the world.

The picture of how cognitive science can handle intentionality should be becoming clear. Transducers at the periphery and internal primitive processors produce and operate on symbols so as to give them their functional roles. In virtue of their functional roles (both internal and external), these symbols have meanings. The functional role perspective explains the mysterious correlation between the symbols and their meanings. It is the activities of the symbols that give them their meanings, and so it is no mystery that a syntax-based system should have rational relations among the meanings of the system's symbols. Intentional states have their relations by virtue of these symbolic activities, and the contents of the intentional states of the system, thinking, wanting, and so on, are inherited from the meanings of the symbols. This is the orthodox account of intentionality for the computer model of the mind. It combines functionalism with commitment to a language of thought. Both views are controversial, the latter both in regard to its truth and its relevance to intentionality even if true. Notice, incidentally, that in this account of intentionality, the source of intentionality is computational structure, independently of whether the computational structure is produced by software or hardware. Thus the title of this chapter, in indicating that the mind is the software of the brain, has the potential to mislead. If we think of the computational structure of a computer as coming entirely from a program put into a structureless general-purpose machine, we are very far from the facts about the human brain—which is not such a general-purpose machine.

At the end of this chapter we discuss Searle's famous Chinese Room argument, which is a direct attack on this theory. The next two sections are devoted to arguments for and against the language of thought.

11.3.1 Objections to the Language-of-Thought Theory

Many objections have been raised to the language-of-thought picture. Let us briefly look at three objections made by Dennett (1975).

The first objection is that we all have an infinity of beliefs (or at any rate a very large number of them). For example, we believe that trees do not light up like fireflies, and that this book is probably closer to your eyes than the President's left shoe is to the ceiling of the Museum of Modern Art gift shop. But how can it be that so many beliefs are all stored in the rather small Belief Box in your head? One line of response to this objection involves distinguishing between the *ordinary* concept of belief and a *scientific* concept of belief toward which one hopes cognitive science is progressing. For scientific purposes, we home in on cases in which our beliefs *cause* us to *do* something, say throw a ball or change our mind, and cases in which beliefs are caused by something, as when perception of a rhinoceros causes us to believe that there is a rhinoceros in the vicinity. Science is concerned with causation and causal explanation, and so the protoscientific concept of belief is the concept of a *causally active* belief. It is only for these beliefs that the language-of-thought theory is committed to sentences in the head. This idea yields a very simple answer to the infinity objection, namely that on the protoscientific concept of belief, most of us did not *have* the belief that trees do not light up like fireflies until they read this paragraph.

Beliefs in the protoscientific sense are explicit, that is, recorded in storage in the brain. For example, you no doubt were once told that the sun is 93 million miles away from the earth. If so, perhaps you have this fact explicitly recorded in your head, available for causal action, even though until reading this paragraph, this belief hadn't been conscious for years. Such explicit beliefs have the potential for causal interaction, and thus must be distinguished from cases of belief in the ordinary sense (if they are beliefs at all), such as the belief all normal people have that trees do not light up like fireflies.

Being explicit is to be distinguished from other properties of mental states, such as being conscious. Theories in cognitive science tell us of mental representations about which no one knows from introspection, such as mental representations of aspects of grammar. If this is right, there is much in the way of mental representation that is explicit but not conscious, and thus the door is opened to the possibility of belief that is explicit but not conscious.

It is important that the language-of-thought theory is not meant to be a theory of all possible believers, but rather only of *us*. The language-of-thought theory allows creatures who can believe without explicit representation at all, but the claim of the language-of-thought theory is that they aren't us. A digital computer consists of a central processing unit (CPU) that reads and writes explicit strings of zeroes and ones in storage registers. One can think of this memory as in principle unlimited, but of course any actual machine has a finite memory. Now any computer with a finite amount of explicit storage can be simulated by a machine with a much larger CPU and *no* explicit storage, that is, no registers and no tape. The way the simulation works is by using the extra states as a form of implicit memory. So, in principle, we could be simulated by a machine with no explicit memory at all.

Consider, for example, the finite automaton diagrammed in figure 11.7. The table shows it as having three states. The states, S_1, S_2, and S_3, are listed across the top. The inputs are listed at the left side. Each box is in a column and a row that specifies what the machine does when it is in the state named at the top of the column, and when the input is the one listed at the side of the row. The top part of the box names the output, and the bottom part of the box names the next state. This is what the table says: when the machine is in S_1, and it sees a '*1*', it says "1", and goes to S_2. When it is in S_2, if it sees a '*1*' it says "2" and goes into the next state, S_3. In that state, if it sees a '*1*' it says "3" and goes back to S_1. When it sees nothing, it says nothing and stays in the same state. This automaton counts "modulo" three, that is, you can tell from what it says how many

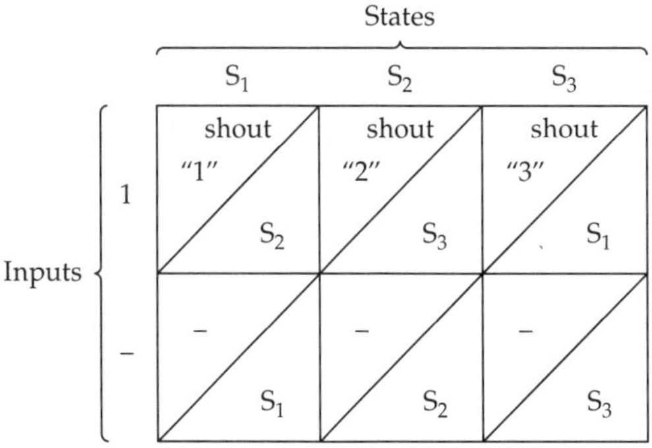

Figure 11.7

ones it has seen since the last multiple of three. But what the machine table makes clear is that this machine need have no memory of the sort that involves writing anything down. It can "remember" solely by changing state. Some theories based on neural-network models assume that we are such machines.

Suppose, then, that we are digital computers with explicit representations. We could be simulated by finite automata that have many more states and no explicit representations. The simulators will have just the same beliefs as we do, but no explicit representations (unless the simulators are just jukeboxes of the type of the Aunt Bubbles machine described in section 11.1.1). The machine in which remembered items are recorded explicitly has an advantage over a computationally equivalent machine that "remembers" by changing state, namely that the explicit representations can be part of a combinatorial system. This point is explained in the next section.

Time to sum up. The objection was that an infinity of beliefs cannot be written down in the head. My response was to distinguish between a loose and ordinary sense of 'belief' in which it may be true that we have an infinity of beliefs, and a protoscientific sense of 'belief' in which the concept of belief is the concept of a causally active belief. In the latter sense, I claimed, we do not have an infinity of beliefs.

Even if you agree with this response to the infinity objection, you may still feel dissatisfied with the idea that, because the topic has never crossed their minds, most people don't believe that zebras don't wear underwear in the wild. Perhaps it will help to say something about the relation between the protoscientific concept of belief and the ordinary concept. It is natural to want some sort of reconstruction of the ordinary concept in scientific terms, a reconstruction of the sort we have when we define the ordinary concept of the weight of a person as the force exerted on the person by the earth at the earth's surface. To scratch this itch, we can give a first approximation to a definition of a belief in the ordinary sense as anything that is either (1) a belief in the protoscientific sense, or (2) naturally and easily follows from a protoscientific belief.

A second objection to the language-of-thought theory is provided by Dennett's example of a chess-playing program that "thinks" it should get its queen out early, even though there is no explicitly represented rule that says anything like "Get your queen out early." The fact that it gets its queen out early is an "emergent" consequence of an interaction of a large number of rules that govern the details of play. But now consider a human analog of the chess-playing machine. Shouldn't we say that she believes she should get her queen out early despite her lack of any such explicit representation?

The reply to this challenge to the language-of-thought theory is that in the protoscientific sense of belief, the chess player simply does not believe that she should get her queen out early. If this idea seems difficult to accept, notice that there is no additional predictive or explanatory force to the hypothesis that she believes she should get her queen out early beyond the predictive or explanatory force of the explicitly represented strategies from which getting the queen out early emerges. (Though there is no additional predictive force, there may be some additional predictive utility, just as there is utility in navigation to supposing that the sun goes around the earth.) Indeed, the idea that she should get her queen out early can actually conflict with her deeply held chess principles, despite being an emergent property of her usual tactics. We could suppose that if you point out to her that her strategies have the consequence of getting her queen out early, she says, "Oh no, I'd better revise my usual strategies." Thus, postulating that she believes that she should get her queen out early could lead to mistaken predictions of her behavior. In sum, the protoscientific concept of a causally active belief can be restricted to the strategies that really are explicitly represented.

Perhaps there is a quasi-behaviorist ordinary sense of belief in which it is correct to ascribe the belief that the queen should come out early simply because she behaves as if she believes it. Even if we agree to recognize such a belief, it is not one that ever causally affects any other mental states or any behavior, and so it is of little import from a scientific standpoint.

A third objection to the language-of-thought theory is provided by the "opposite" of the "queen out early" case—Dennett's sister in Cleveland case. Suppose that a neurosurgeon operates on someone's Belief Box, inserting the sentence, "I have a sister in Cleveland." When the patient wakes up, the doctor says "Do you have a sister?" "Yes," the patient says, "In Cleveland." Doctor: "What's her name?" Patient: "Gosh, I can't think of it." Doctor: "Older or younger?" Patient: "I don't know, and by golly I'm an only child. I don't know why I'm saying that I have a sister at all." Finally, the patient concludes that she never really believed she had a sister in Cleveland, but rather was a victim of some sort of compulsion to speak as if she did. The upshot is supposed to be that the language-of-thought theory is false because you can't produce a belief just by inserting a sentence in the Belief Box.

The objection reveals a misleading aspect of the "Belief Box" slogan, not a problem with the doctrine that the slogan characterizes. According to the language-of-thought theory, believing that one has a sister in Cleveland is a computational relation to a sentence, but this computational relation shouldn't be thought of as simply *storage*. Rather, the computational relation must include some specification of relations to other sentences to which one also has the same computational relation, and in that sense the computational relation must be holistic. This point holds both for the ordinary notion of belief and the protoscientific notion. It holds for the ordinary notion of belief because we don't count someone as believing just because she mouths words as our neurosurgery victim mouthed the words, "I have a sister in Cleveland." And it holds for the protoscientific notion of belief because the unit of explanation and prediction is much more likely to be groups of coherently related sentences in the brain than single sentences all by themselves. If one is going to retain the "Belief Box" way of talking, one should say that for a sentence in the Belief Box to count as a belief, it should cohere sufficiently with other sentences so as not to be totally unstable, disappearing on exposure to the light.

11.4 Arguments for the Language of Thought

So it seems that the language-of-thought hypothesis can be defended from these a priori objections. But is there any positive reason to believe it? One such reason is that it is part of a reasonably successful research program. But there are challengers (mainly, some versions of the connectionist program mentioned earlier), and so a stronger case will be called for if the challengers' research programs also end up being successful.[5]

A major rationale for accepting the language of thought has been one form or another of *productivity* argument, stemming from Chomsky's work (see Chomsky 1975). The idea is that people are capable of thinking vast numbers of thoughts that they have not thought before—and indeed that no one may ever have thought before. Consider, for example, the thought mentioned earlier that this book is closer to you than the President's shoe is to the museum gift-shop ceiling. The most obvious explanation of how we can think such new thoughts is the same as the explanation of how we can frame the sentences that express them: namely, via a combinatorial system in which we think. Indeed, abstracting away from limitations on memory, motivation, and length of life, there may be no upper bound on the number of thinkable thoughts. The number of sentences in the English language is certainly infinite (see volume 1). But what does it mean to say that sentences containing millions of words are "in principle" thinkable?

5. Notice that the type of success is important to whether connectionism is really a rival to the language-of-thought point of view. Connectionist networks have been successful in various pattern-recognition tasks, for example discriminating mines from rocks. Of course, even if these networks could be made to do pattern-recognition tasks much better than we can, that wouldn't suggest that these networks can provide models of higher cognition. Computers that are programmed to do arithmetic in the classic symbol-crunching mode can do arithmetic much better than we can, but no one would conclude that therefore these computers provide models of higher cognition.

Those who favor productivity arguments say this: The explanation for the fact that we cannot actually think sentences containing millions of words would have to appeal to such facts as that, were we to try to think sufficiently long or complicated thoughts, our attention would flag, or our memory would fail us, or we would die. They think that we can idealize away from these limitations, because the mechanisms of thought themselves are unlimited. But this claim that if we abstract away from memory, mortality, motivation, and the like, our thought mechanisms are unlimited, is a doctrine for which there is no *direct* evidence. The perspective from which this doctrine springs has been fertile, but it is an open question what aspect of the doctrine is responsible for its success.

After all, we might be finite beings, essentially. Not all idealizations are equally correct, and contrary to widespread assumption in cognitive science, the idealization to the unboundedness of thought may be a bad one. Consider a finite automaton naturally described by the table in figure 11.7.[6] Its only form of memory is change of state. If you want to get this machine to count to 4 instead of just to 3, you can't just add more memory, you have to give it another state by changing the way the machine is built. Perhaps we are like this machine.

An extension of the productivity argument to deal with this sort of problem has recently been proposed by Fodor (1987), and Fodor and Pylyshyn (1988). Fodor and Pylyshyn point out that it is a fact about human beings that, if someone can think the thought that Mary loves John, then she can also think the thought that John loves Mary. And likewise for a vast variety of pairs of thoughts that involve the same conceptual constituents, but are put together differently. There is a *systematicity* relation among many thoughts that begs for an explanation in terms of a combinatorial system. The conclusion is that human thought operates in a medium of "movable type."

However, the most obvious candidate for the elements of such a combinatorial system in many areas are the *external* symbol systems themselves. Perhaps the most obvious case is arithmetical thoughts. If someone is capable of thinking the thought that $7 + 16$ is not 20, then presumably she is capable of thinking the thought that $17 + 6$ is not 20. Indeed, someone who has mastered the ten numerals plus other basic symbols of Arabic notation and their rules of combination can think any arithmetical thought that is expressible in a representation that he or she can read. (Notice that false propositions can be thinkable—one can think the thought that $2 + 2 = 5$, if only to think that it is false.)

6. This table could be used to describe a machine that does have a memory with explicit representation. I say "naturally described" to indicate that I am thinking of a machine that does not have such a memory, a machine for which the table in figure 11.7 is an apt and natural description.

One line of a common printed page contains eighty symbols. There are a great many different arithmetical propositions that can be written on such a line—about as many as there are elementary particles in the universe. Though almost all of them are false, all are arguably thinkable with some work. Starting a bit smaller, try to entertain the thought that 695,302,222,387,987 + 695,302,222,387,986 = 2. How is it that we have so many possible arithmetical thoughts? The obvious explanation is that we can string together—either in our heads or on paper—the symbols (numerals, pluses, and so on) themselves, and simply read the thought off the string of symbols. Of course, this does not show that the systematicity argument is *wrong*. Far from it, for it shows *why* it is right. But this point does *threaten the value* of the systematicity argument considerably. For it highlights the possibility that the systematicity argument may apply only to *conscious* thought, and not to the rest of the iceberg of unconscious thought processes that cognitive science is mainly about. Thus Fodor and Pylyshyn are right that the systematicity argument shows that there is a language of thought. And they are right that if connectionism is incompatible with a language of thought, so much the worse for connectionism. But where they are wrong is with respect to an unstated assumption: that the systematicity argument shows that languagelike representations pervade cognition.

To see this point, notice that much of the success in cognitive science has been in our understanding of perceptual and motor modules (see volume 2). The operation of these modules is neither introspectible—accessible to conscious thought—nor directly influencible by conscious thought. These modules are "informationally encapsulated" (see Pylyshyn 1984, and Fodor 1983). The productivity in conscious thought that is exploited by the systematicity argument certainly does not demonstrate productivity in the processing inside such modules. True, if someone can think that if John loves Mary, then he can think that Mary loves John. But we don't have easy access to such facts about pairs of representations of the kind involved in unconscious processes. Distinguish between the conclusion of an argument and the argument itself. The conclusion of the systematicity argument may well be right about unconscious representations. That is, *systematicity itself* may well obtain in these systems. My point is that the systematicity *argument* shows little about encapsulated modules and other unconscious systems.

The weakness of the systematicity argument is that, resting as it does on facts that are so readily available to conscious thought, its application to unconscious processes is more tenuous. Nonetheless, as the reader can easily see by looking at the other chapters in these volumes, the symbol-manipulation model has been quite successful in explaining aspects of perception thought and motor control. So, although the systematicity argument is limited in its application to unconscious processes, the model it supports for conscious processes appears to have considerable application to unconscious processes nonetheless.

To avoid misunderstanding, I add that the point just made does not challenge all the thrust of the Fodor and Pylyshyn critique of connectionism. Any neural-network model of the mind will have to accommodate the fact of our use of a systematic combinatorial symbol system in conscious thought. It is hard to see how a neural-network model could do this without being in part an implementation of a standard symbol-crunching model.

In effect, Fodor and Pylyshyn (1988, 44) counter the idea that the systematicity argument depends entirely on conscious symbol manipulating by saying that the systematicity argument applies to animals. For example, they argue that the conditioning literature has no cases of animals that *can* be trained to pick the red thing rather than the green one, but *cannot* be trained to pick the green thing rather than the red one.

This reply has some force, but it is uncomfortably anecdotal. The data a scientist collects depend on his or her theory. We cannot rely on data collected in animal conditioning experiments run by behaviorists—who, after all, were notoriously opposed to theorizing about internal states.

Another objection to the systematicity argument derives from the distinction between linguistic and pictorial representation that plays a role in the controversies over mental imagery. (See chapter 7 in volume 2.) Many researchers think that we have two different representational systems, a languagelike system—thinking in words—and a pictorial system—thinking in pictures. If an animal that can be trained to pick red instead of green can also be trained to pick green instead of red, that may reflect the properties of an imagery system shared by human beings and animals, not a properly languagelike system. Suppose Fodor and Pylyshyn are right about the systematicity of thought in animals. That may reflect only a combinatorial pictorial system. If so, it would suggest (though it wouldn't show) that human beings have a combinatorial pictorial system too. But the question would still be open whether humans have a *languagelike* combinatorial system that is used in unconscious thought. In sum, the systematicity argument certainly applies to conscious thought, and it is part of a perspective on unconscious thought that has been fertile, but there are difficulties in its application to unconscious thought.

11.5 Explanatory Levels and the Syntactic Theory of the Mind

In this section, let us assume that the language-of-thought hypothesis is correct in order to ask another question: Should cognitive-science explanations appeal only to the syntactic elements in the language of thought (the

'*0*'s and '*1*'s and the like), or should they also appeal to the content of these symbols? Stich (1983) has argued for the "syntactic theory of mind," a version of the computer model in which the language of thought is construed in terms of uninterpreted symbols, symbols that may *have* contents, but whose contents are irrelevant for the purposes of cognitive science. I shall put the issue in terms of a critique of a simplified version of the Stich (1983) argument.

Let us begin with Stich's case of Mrs. T, a senile old lady who answers, "What happened to McKinley?" with "McKinley was assassinated," but cannot answer questions like, "Where is McKinley now?" "Is he alive or dead?" and the like. Mrs. T's logical facilities are fine, but she has lost most of her memories, and virtually all the concepts that are normally connected to the concept of assassination, such as the concept of death. Stich sketches the case so as to persuade us that though Mrs. T may know that something happened to McKinley, she doesn't have any real grasp of the concept of assassination, and thus cannot be said to believe that McKinley was assassinated.

The argument that I will critique concludes that purely syntactic explanations undermine content explanations because a syntactic account is superior to a content account. The syntactic approach is said to be superior in two respects. First, the syntactic account can handle Mrs. T, who has little in the way of intentional content, but plenty of internal representations whose interactions can be used to explain and predict what she does, just as the interactions of symbol structures in a computer can be used to explain and predict what it does. And the same holds for very young children, people with weird psychiatric disorders, and denizens of exotic cultures. In all these cases, cognitive science can (at least potentially) assign internal syntactic descriptions and use them to predict and explain, but there are problems with content ascriptions (though, in the last case at least, the problem is not that these people have no contents, but just that their contents are so different from ours that we cannot assign contents to them in *our terms*). In sum, the first type of superiority of the syntactic perspective over the content perspective is that it allows for the psychology of the senile, the very young, the disordered, and the exotic, and thus, it is alleged, the syntactic perspective is far more *general* than the content perspective.

The second respect of superiority of the syntactic perspective is that it allows more *fine-grained* predictions and explanations than the content perspective. To take a humdrum example, the content perspective allows us to predict that if someone believes that all men are mortal, and that he is a man, he can conclude that he is mortal. But suppose that the way in which this person represents the generalization that all men are mortal to himself is via a syntactic form of the type "All nonmortals are nonmen";

then the inference will be harder to draw than if he had represented it without the negations. In general, what inferences are hard rather than easy, and what sorts of mistakes are likely will be better predictable from the syntactic perspective than from the content perspective, in which all the ways of representing one belief are lumped together.

The upshot of this argument is supposed to be that because the syntactic approach is more general and more fine-grained than the content approach, content explanations are therefore undermined and shown to be defective. And so cognitive science would do well to scrap attempts to explain and predict in terms of content in favor of appeals to syntactic form alone.

But there is a fatal flaw in this argument, one that applies to many reductionist arguments. The fact that syntactic explanations are better than content explanations in some respects says nothing about whether content explanations are not *also* better than syntactic explanations in some respects. A dramatic way of revealing this fact is to notice that if the argument against the content level were correct, *it would undermine the syntactic approach itself*. This point is so simple, fundamental, and widely applicable that it deserves a name: let's call it the Reductionist Cruncher. Just as the syntactic objects on paper can be described in molecular terms, for example as structures of carbon molecules, so too the syntactic objects in our heads can be described in terms of the viewpoint of chemistry and physics. But a physicochemical account of the syntactic objects in our head will be more general than the syntactic account in just the same way as the syntactic account is more general than the content account. There are possible beings, such as Mrs. T, who are similar to us syntactically but not in intentional contents. Similarly, there are possible beings who are similar to us in physicochemical respects, but not syntactically. For example, creatures could be like us in physicochemical respects without having physicochemical parts that function as syntactic objects—just as Mrs. T's syntactic objects don't function so as to confer content upon them. If neural-network models of the sort that antilanguage-of-thought theorists favor could be bioengineered, they would fit this description. The bioengineered models would be like us and like Mrs. T in physicochemical respects, but unlike us and unlike Mrs. T in syntactic respects. Further, the physicochemical account will be more fine-grained than the syntactic account, just as the syntactic account is more fine-grained than the content account. Syntactic generalizations will fail under some physicochemically specifiable circumstances, just as content generalizations fail under some syntactically specifiable circumstances. I mentioned that content generalizations might be compromised if the syntactic realizations included too many syntactic negations. The present point is that syntactic generalizations might fail when syntactic objects interact on the basis of certain physicochemical properties. To take a slightly silly example, if a token of '*s*' and a token of '*s* → *t*' are both positively charged so that they repel each other, that could prevent logic processors from putting them together to yield a token of '*t*'.

In sum, if we could refute the content approach by showing that the syntactic approach is more general and fine-grained than the content approach, then we could also refute the syntactic approach by exhibiting the same deficiency in it relative to a still deeper theory. The Reductionist Cruncher applies even within physics itself. For example, anyone who rejects the explanations of thermodynamics in favor of the explanations of statistical mechanics will be frustrated by the fact that the explanations of statistical mechanics can themselves be "undermined" in just the same way by quantum mechanics.

The same points can be made in terms of the explanation of how a computer works. Compare two explanations of the behavior of the computer on my desk, one in terms of the programming language, and the other in terms of what is happening in the computer's circuits. The latter level is certainly more general in that it applies not only to programmed computers, but also to nonprogrammable computers that are electronically similar to mine—for example, certain calculators. Thus the greater generality of the circuit level is like the greater generality of the syntactic perspective. Further, the circuit level is more fine-grained in that it allows us to predict and explain computer failures that have nothing to do with program glitches. Circuits will fail under certain circumstances (for example, overload, excessive heat or humidity) that are not characterizable in the vocabulary of the program level. Thus the greater predictive and explanatory power of the circuit level is like the greater power of the syntactic level to distinguish cases of the same content represented in different syntactic forms that make a difference in processing.

However, the computer analogy reveals a flaw in the argument that the "upper" level (the program level in this example) explanations are defective and should be scrapped. The fact that a "lower" level like the circuit level is superior in some respects does not show that "higher" levels such as the program levels are not themselves superior in other respects. Thus the upper levels are not shown to be *dispensable*. The program level has *its own* type of greater generality—namely, it applies to computers that use the same programming language, but are built in different ways, even computers that don't have circuits at all (but, say, work via gears and pulleys). Indeed, there are many predictions and explanations that are simple at the program level, but would be absurdly complicated at the circuit level. Further (and here is the Reductionist Cruncher again), if the program level could be shown to be defective by the circuit level, then the circuit level could itself be shown to be defective by a deeper theory, such as the quantum field theory of circuits.

The point here is *not* that the program level is a convenient fiction. On the contrary, the program level is just as *real* and *explanatory* as the circuit level.

Perhaps it will be useful to see the matter in terms of an example from Putnam (1975). Consider a rigid, round peg 1 inch in diameter and a square hole in a rigid board with a 1-inch diagonal. The peg won't fit through the hole for reasons that are easy to understand via a little geometry. (The side of the hole is 1 divided by the square root of 2, which is a number substantially less than 1.) Now if we went to the level of description of this apparatus in terms of the molecular structure that makes up a specific solid board, we could explain the rigidity of the materials, and we would have a more fine-grained understanding, including the ability to predict the incredible case where the alignment and motion of the molecules is such as to allow the peg to actually go through the board. But the "upper"-level account in terms of rigidity and geometry nonetheless provides correct explanations and predictions, and applies more generally to *any* rigid peg and board, even one with quite a different sort of molecular constitution, say one made of glass—a supercooled liquid—rather than a solid.

It is tempting to say that the account in terms of rigidity and geometry is only an approximation, the molecular account being the really correct one. (See Smolensky 1988 for a dramatic case of yielding to this sort of temptation.) But the cure for this temptation is the Reductionist Cruncher: the reductionist will also have to say that an elementary-particle account shows the molecular account to be only an approximation. And the elementary-particle account itself will be undermined by a still deeper theory. The point of a scientific account is to cut nature at its joints, and nature *has real joints* at many levels, each of which requires its own kind of idealization.

Further, those which are counted as elementary particles today may be found to be composed of still more elementary particles tomorrow, and so on, ad infinitum. Indeed, contemporary physics allows this possibility of an infinite series of particles within particles. (See Dehmelt 1989.) If such an infinite series obtains, the reductionist would be committed to saying that there are no genuine explanations because for any explanation at any given level, there is always a deeper explanation that is more general and more fine-grained that undermines it. But the existence of genuine explanations surely does not depend on this recondite issue in particle physics!

I have been talking as if there is just one content level, but actually there are many. Marr distinguished among three levels: the computational level, the level of representation and algorithm, and the level of implementation. At the computational or formal level, the multiplier discussed earlier is to be understood as a function from pairs of numbers to their products, for example, from {7,9} to 63. The most abstract characterization at the level of representation and algorithm is simply the algorithm of the multiplier, namely: multiply *n* by *m* by adding *m n* times. A less abstract characterization at this middle level is the program described earlier, a sequence of operations including subtracting 1 from the register that initially represents *n* until it is reduced to zero, adding *m* to the answer register each time. (See figure 11.2.) *Each of these levels is a content level rather than a syntactic level.* There are many types of multipliers whose behavior can be explained (albeit at a somewhat superficial level) simply by referring to the fact that they are multipliers. The algorithm mentioned gives a deeper explanation, and the program—one of many programs that can realize that algorithm—gives a still deeper explanation. However, when we break the multiplier down into parts such as the adder of figures 11.3a and 11.3b, we explain its internal operation in terms of gates that operate on syntax, that is, in terms of operations on numerals. Now it is crucial to realize that the mere possibility of a *description* of a system in a certain vocabulary does not by itself demonstrate the existence of a genuine explanatory level. We are concerned here with cutting nature at its joints, and *talking* as if there is a joint does not make it so. The fact that it is good *methodology* to look first for the function, then for the algorithm, then for the implementation, does not by itself show that these inquiries are inquiries at different levels, as opposed to different ways of approaching the same level. The crucial issue is whether the different vocabularies correspond to genuinely distinct laws and explanations, and in any given case, this question will be answerable only empirically. However, we already have good empirical evidence for the reality of the content levels just mentioned—as well as the syntactic level. The evidence is to be found in this very book, where we see genuine and distinct explanations at the level of function, algorithm, and syntax.

A further point about explanatory levels is that it is legitimate to use different and even *incompatible* idealizations at different levels. See Putnam (1975). It has been argued that because the brain is analog, the digital computer must be incorrect as a model of the mind. But even digital computers are analog at one level of description. For example, gates of the sort described earlier in which 4 volts realizes '*1*' and 7 volts realizes '*0*' are understood from the digital perspective as always representing either '*0*' or '*1*'. But an examination at the electronic level shows that values intermediate between 4 and 7 volts appear momentarily when a register switches between them. We abstract from these intermediate values for the purposes of one level of description, but not another.

11.6 Searle's Chinese Room Argument

As we have seen, the idea that a certain type of symbol processing can be what *makes* something an intentional system is fundamental to the computer model of the mind. Let us now turn to a flamboyant frontal attack on this idea by John Searle (1980, 1990b; Churchland and Churchland 1990; the basic idea of this argument stems from Block 1978). Searle's strategy is one of avoiding quibbles about specific programs by imagining that cognitive science in the distant future can come up with the program of an actual person who speaks and understands Chinese, and that this program can be implemented in a machine. Unlike many critics of the computer model, Searle is willing to grant that perhaps this can be done so as to focus on his claim that *even if this can be done, the machine will not have intentional states.*

The argument is based on a thought experiment. Imagine yourself given a job in which you work in a room (the Chinese Room). You understand only English. Slips of paper with Chinese writing on them are put under the input door, and your job is to write sensible Chinese replies on other slips, and push them out under the output door. How do you do it? You act as the CPU (central processing unit) of a computer, following the computer program mentioned above that describes the symbol processing in an actual Chinese speaker's head. The program is printed in English in a library in the room. This is how you follow the program. Suppose the latest input has certain unintelligible (to you) Chinese squiggles on it. There is a blackboard on a wall of the room with a "state" number written on it; it says '*17*'. (The CPU of a computer is a device with a finite number of states whose activity is determined solely by its current state and input, and because you are acting as the CPU, your output will be determined by your input and your "state." The '*17*' is on the blackboard to tell you what your "state" is.) You take book 17 out of the library, and look up these particular squiggles in it. Book 17 tells you to look at what is written on your scratch pad (the computer's internal memory), and given both the input squiggles and the scratch-pad marks, you are directed to change what is on the scratch pad in a certain way, write certain other squiggles on your output pad, push the paper under the output door, and finally, change the number on the state board to '*193*'. As a result of this activity, speakers of Chinese find that the pieces of paper you slip under the output door are sensible replies to the inputs.

But you know nothing of what is being said in Chinese; you are just following instructions (in English) to look in certain books and write certain marks. According to Searle, because you don't understand any Chinese, the system of which you are the CPU is a mere Chinese simulator, not a real Chinese understander. Of course, Searle (rightly) rejects the Turing test for understanding Chinese. His argument, then, is that because the program of a real Chinese understander is not sufficient for understanding Chinese, no symbol-manipulation theory of Chinese understanding (or any other intentional state) is correct about what *makes* something a

Chinese understander. Thus the conclusion of Searle's argument is that the fundamental idea of thought as symbol processing is wrong even if it allows us to build a machine that can duplicate the symbol processing of a person and thereby duplicate a person's behavior.

The best criticisms of the Chinese Room argument have focused on what Searle—anticipating the challenge—calls the systems reply. (See the responses following Searle 1980, and the comment on Searle in Hofstadter and Dennett 1981.) The systems reply has a positive and a negative component. The negative component is that we cannot reason from "Bill has never sold uranium to North Korea" to "Bill's company has never sold uranium to North Korea." Similarly, we cannot reason from "Bill does not understand Chinese" to "The system of which Bill is a part does not understand Chinese." (See Copeland 1993b.) Hence there is a gap in Searle's argument. The positive component goes further, saying that the whole system—man + program + board + paper + input and output doors—does understand Chinese, even though the man who is acting as the CPU does not. If you open up your own computer, looking for the CPU, you will find that it is just one of the many chips and other components on the mother board. The systems reply reminds us that the CPUs of the thinking computers we hope to have someday will not *themselves* think—rather, they will be *parts* of thinking systems.

Searle's clever reply is to imagine the paraphernalia of the "system" *internalized* as follows. First, instead of having you consult a library, we are to imagine you *memorizing* the whole library. Second, instead of writing notes on scratch pads, you are to memorize what you would have written on the pads, and you are to memorize what the state blackboard would say. Finally, instead of looking at notes put under one door and passing notes under another door, you just use your *own body* to listen to Chinese utterances and produce replies. (This version of the Chinese Room has the additional advantage of generalizability so as to involve the complete behavior of a Chinese-speaking system instead of just a Chinese note exchanger.) But as Searle would emphasize, when you seem to Chinese speakers to be conducting a learned discourse with them in Chinese, all you are aware of doing is thinking about what noises the program tells you to make next, given the noises you hear and what you've written on your mental scratch pad.

I argued above that the CPU is just one of many components. If the whole system understands Chinese, that should not lead us to expect the CPU to understand Chinese. The effect of Searle's internalization move—the "new" Chinese Room—is to attempt to destroy the analogy between looking inside the computer and looking inside the Chinese Room. If one looks inside the computer, one sees many chips in addition to the CPU. But if one looks inside the "new" Chinese Room, all one sees is *you*, for you have memorized the library and internalized the functions of the scratch pad and the blackboard. But the point to keep in mind is that although the non-CPU components are no longer easy to see, they are not gone. Rather, they are internalized. If the program requires the contents of one register to be placed in another register, and if you would have done so in the original Chinese Room by copying from one piece of scratch paper to another, in the new Chinese Room you must copy from one of your mental analogs of a piece of scratch paper to another. You are implementing the system by doing what the CPU would do and you are simultaneously simulating the non-CPU components. Thus if the positive side of the systems reply is correct, the total system that you are implementing does understand Chinese.

"But how can it be," Searle would object, "that you implement a system that understands Chinese even though *you* don't understand Chinese?" The systems-reply rejoinder is that you implement a Chinese understanding system without yourself understanding Chinese or necessarily even being aware of what you are doing under that description. The systems reply sees the Chinese Room (new and old) as an English system implementing a Chinese system. What you are aware of are the thoughts of the English system, for example your following instructions and consulting your internal library. But in virtue of doing this Herculean task, you are also implementing a real, intelligent Chinese-speaking system, and so your body houses two genuinely distinct intelligent systems. The Chinese system also thinks, but though you implement this thought, you are not aware of it.

The systems reply can be backed up with an addition to the thought experiment that highlights the division of labor. Imagine that you take on the Chinese simulating as a 9-to-5 job. You come in Monday morning after a weekend of relaxation, and you are paid to follow the program until 5:00 P.M. When you are working, you concentrate hard on working, and so instead of trying to figure out the meaning of what is said to you, you focus your energies on working out what the program tells you to do in response to each input. As a result, during working hours you respond to everything just as the program dictates, except for occasional glances at your watch. (The glances at your watch fall under the same category as the noises and heat given off by computers: aspects of their behavior that are not part of the machine description but are due rather to features of the implementation.) If someone speaks to you in English, you say what the program (which, you recall, describes a real Chinese speaker) dictates. So if during working hours someone speaks to you in English, you respond with a request in Chinese to speak Chinese, or even an inexpertly pronounced "No speak English," which was once memorized by the Chinese speaker being simulated, and which you the English-speaking system may even fail to recognize as English. Then, come 5:00 P.M., you stop working and react to Chinese talk just as any monolingual English speaker would.

Why is it that the English system implements the Chinese system rather than, say, the other way around? Because you (the English system whom I am now addressing) are following the instructions of a program in English to make Chinese noises and not the other way around. If you decide to quit your job to become a magician, the Chinese system disappears. However, if the Chinese system decides to become a magician, he will make plans that he would express in Chinese, but then when 5:00 P.M. rolls around, you quit for the day, and the Chinese system's plans are on the shelf until you come back to work. And of course you have no commitment to doing *whatever* the program dictates. If the program dictates that you make a series of movements that leads you to a flight to China, you can drop out of the simulating mode, saying "I quit!" The Chinese speaker's existence and the fulfillment of his plans depends on your work schedule and your plans, not the other way around.

Thus, you and the Chinese system cohabit one body. In effect, Searle uses the fact that you are not aware of the Chinese system's thoughts as an argument that it has no thoughts. But this is an invalid argument. Real cases of multiple personalities are often cases in which one personality is unaware of the others.

It is instructive to compare Searle's thought experiment with the string-searching Aunt Bubbles machine described at the beginning of this paper. This machine was used against a behaviorist proposal of a behavioral *concept* of intelligence. But the symbol-manipulation view of the mind is not a proposal about our everyday concept. To the extent that we think of the English system as implementing a Chinese system, that will be because we find the symbol-manipulation theory of the mind plausible as an empirical theory.

There is one aspect of Searle's case with which I am sympathetic. I have my doubts as to whether there is anything "it is like" to be the Chinese system, that is, whether the Chinese system is a *phenomenally conscious* system. My doubts arise from the idea that perhaps consciousness is more a matter of implementation of symbol processing than of symbol processing itself. Though surprisingly Searle does not mention this idea in connection with the Chinese Room, it can be seen as the argumentative heart of his position. Searle has argued independently of the Chinese Room (Searle 1992, ch. 7) that intentionality requires consciousness. (See the replies to Searle (1990c) in *Behavioral and Brain Sciences* 13, 1990.) But this doctrine, if correct, can shore up the Chinese Room argument. For if the Chinese system is not conscious, then, according to Searle's doctrine, it is not an intentional system, either.

Even if I am right about the failure of Searle's argument, it does succeed in sharpening our understanding of the nature of intentionality and its relation to computation and representation.

Suggestions for Further Reading

For book-length treatments of the computer model of the mind, see Pylyshyn (1984) and Copeland (1993a). There are a number of excellent anthologies: Block (1980, 1981b), Haugeland (1981), Lycan (1990), Rosenthal (1991), Beakley and Ludlow (1992), and Goldman (1993). These anthologies include many of the papers discussed here. In addition, I recommend Guttenplan (1994), which has short summaries of the state of play on these and many other issues about the mind.

On internal representation and its semantics, Fodor (1985) provides a good but dated guide. Cummins (1989) and Sterelny (1990) are readable books with chapters on all the major views. Haugeland (1990) looks at the major views from a phenomenological perspective. See also Dreyfus (1979). Putnam (1988) is a critique of the notions of meaning and content implicit in the computer model. See also the articles in the first section of Block (1980), especially Field (1978), which is the classic article on the relation between internal representation and functionalism. This book, and Lycan (1990) as well, have sections on imagery that cover the issue of whether mental images are coded in representations like the '*1*'s and '*0*'s in computers, or in representations that are "pictorial." For a book-length treatment, see Tye (1991). Stich and Warfield (1994) covers a wide range of issues about mental representation.

The best books to date on philosophical issues surrounding connectionism are Clark (1993) and Ramsey, Stich, and Rumelhart (1991). See also Smolensky (1988).

The discussion here of issues of reduction and levels of description is very one-sided. The best presentation of the other side is Kim (1992). See also Churchland (1986).

Philosophers are increasingly concerned with the reality of content and its role in cognitive science. The place to start is with Churchland (1981) and Stich (1983). Sterelny (1985) is an interesting review of Stich. Dennett (1987) takes a view somewhere between Churchland's eliminativism and the realism espoused here. The case against content from the point of view of issues in the philosophy of language is discussed in detail in Schiffer (1987), a difficult work. Horwich (1990) argues that deflationary views of truth are irrelevant to these issues about content.

Discussions of the Turing test are to be found in Moor (1987) and Block (1981a).

The discussion in this chapter has omitted all mention of consciousness except at the very end. This neglect reflects limitations of space, not ideology. See the entries on "Consciousness" and "Qualia" in Guttenplan (1994) and Davies and Humphreys (1993). See also Block (1995).

Problem

11.1 Schwartz (1988) argues for connectionism and against standard computational models on the ground that the brain is slow, squishy, and error-prone, whereas computers execute an intricate parallel dance of interlocking reliable processes. The conclusion is that computer models of the mind cannot be right, and that we must seek biological approaches to the mind. Can you find anything wrong with this argument?

Questions

11.1 Recall the example of the molecule-for-molecule duplicate of your brain that happened by chance to come together from molecules from the swamp. You disapprove of the

Supreme Court, and the swamp-brain, if hooked up to a mouth, mouths all the same anti–Supreme Court slogans as you do. But as I argued earlier, the swamp-brain, never having read about the Supreme Court or heard anyone talk about it or anything of the kind, should not be regarded as having any intentional states that are *about* it. Still, all the swamp-brain's states are the same as yours "from the inside," and so the question naturally arises: "Is there *some* kind of content you share with him (it)?" Philosophers who answer Yes have named the kind of content you (putatively) share with the swamp-brain "narrow" content, and there is a raging debate about whether there is such a thing. The case against it is presented in Burge (1979, 1986), Putnam (1988), and Pettit and McDowell (1986). A defense is to be found in Fodor (1987), ch. 2.

11.2 Our beliefs certainly influence what we do, and it seems that our beliefs do so by virtue of their content. If my belief that the American political system is rotten caused me to speak out, my action was due to the content of my belief. Had I believed our political system was great, I wouldn't have spoken. But how can content be causally efficacious when the primitive processors in our heads are sensitive only to the syntactic properties of representations, and not their semantic properties? The issue is further discussed in Lepore and Loewer (1987), Dretske (1988), and Block (1990b).

11.3 Suppose you had an identical twin raised from birth with color-"inverting" lenses in his eyes. Isn't it possible that things that you both call "green" look to him the way things you both call "red" look to you? If this sort of spectrum inversion is possible, does it show that there can be no computer model of this "qualitative" content? A good case for the possibility of spectrum inversion is provided by Shoemaker (1981). For the opposing view, see Dennett (1988) and Harman (1989); Block (1990a) is a reply to Harman. Comprehensive studies are Lycan (1987) and Dennett (1991).

16.4 Many philosophers have followed Dennett (1969) in adopting an *evolutionary* approach to intentionality. Papineau (1984) and Millikan (1984) have argued that what makes the frog's fly representation represent flies is that this representation fulfills its biological function when flies are present. But if evolution is essential to intentionality, how could a computer, being a nonevolved device, have intentionality?[7]

References

Beakeley, B., and P. Ludlow, eds. (1992). *Philosophy of mind: Classical problems/contemporary issues.* Cambridge, MA: MIT Press.

Block, N. (1978). Troubles with functionalism. In C. W. Savage, ed., *Minnesota studies in philosophy of science,* IX, 26–325. Minneapolis, MN: University of Minnesota Press. Reprinted in Rosenthal (1991) and Lycan (1990).

Block, N. (1980, 1981b). *Readings in philosophy of psychology,* vols. 1, 2. Cambridge, MA: Harvard University Press.

Block, N. (1981a). Psychologism and behaviorism. *The Philosophical Review* 90, 1, 5–43.

Block, N. (1986). Advertisement for a semantics for psychology. In P. A. French et al., eds., *Midwest studies in philosophy,* vol. X. Minneapolis, MN: University of Minnesota Press, 615–678.

Block, N. (1990a). Inverted earth. In J. Tomberlin, ed., *Philosophical perspectives,* vol. 4, Atascadero: Ridgeview.

Block, N. (1990b). Can the mind change the world? In G. Boolos, ed., *Essays in honor of Hilary Putnam.* Cambridge: Cambridge University Press.

7. I am indebted to Ken Aizawa, George Boolos, Susan Carey, Willem DeVries, Jerry Fodor, and Steven White for comments on an earlier draft. This work was supported by the National Science Foundation (DIR8812559)

Block, N. (1995). On a confusion about a function of consciousness. *The Behavioral and Brain Sciences* 18, 227–247.

Block, N., O. Flanagan, and G. Guzeldere (1995). *The nature of consciousness.* Cambridge, MA: MIT Press.

Burge, T. (1979). Individualism and the mental. In P. A. French et al., eds., *Midwest studies in philosophy* IV, 73–121. Minneapolis, MN: University of Minnesota Press.

Burge, T. (1986). Individualism and psychology. *The Philosophical Review* 95, 1, 3–45.

Chalmers, D. (1994). On implementing a computation. *Minds and Machines* 4, 4, 391–402.

Chomsky, N. (1959). Review of B. F. Skinner's *Verbal Behavior. Language* 35, 1, 26–58.

Chomsky, N. (1975). *Reflections on language.* New York: Pantheon.

Churchland, P. M. (1981). Eliminative materialism and the propositional attitudes. *The Journal of Philosophy* 78, 67–90.

Churchland, P. M., and P. S. Churchland (1990). Could a machine think? *Scientific American* 262, 1, 26–31.

Churchland, P. S. (1986). *Neurophilosophy.* Cambridge, MA: MIT Press.

Clark, A. (1993). *Associative engines.* Cambridge, MA: MIT Press.

Copeland, J. (1993a). *Artificial intelligence: A philosophical introduction.* Oxford: Blackwell.

Copeland, J. (1993b). The curious case of the Chinese gym. *Synthese* 95, 173–186.

Cummins, R. (1975). Functional analysis. *Journal of Philosophy* 72, 741–765. Partially reprinted in Block (1980).

Cummins, R. (1989). *Meaning and mental representation.* Cambridge, MA: MIT Press.

Davies, M., and G. Humphreys (1993). *Consciousness.* Oxford: Blackwell.

Dehmelt, H. (1989). Triton, ... electron, ... cosmon, ...: An infinite regression? *Proceedings of the National Academy of Sciences* 86, 8618.

Dennett, D. (1969). *Content and consciousness.* London: Routledge and Kegan Paul.

Dennett, D. C. (1974). Why the law of effect will not go away. *Journal of the Theory of Social Behavior* 5, 169–187.

Dennett, D. C. (1975). Brain writing and mind reading. In K. Gunderson, ed., *Minnesota studies in philosophy of science,* vol. VII. Minneapolis, MN: University of Minnesota Press.

Dennett, D. C. (1981). Three kinds of intentional psychology. In R. Healy, ed., *Reduction, time and reality.* Cambridge: Cambridge University Press.

Dennett, D. C. (1987). *The intentional stance.* Cambridge, MA: MIT Press.

Dennett, D. C. (1988). Quining qualia. In A. Marcel and E. Bisiach, eds., *Consciousness in contemporary society.* Oxford: Oxford University Press.

Dennett, D. C. (1991). *Consciousness explained.* Boston: Little, Brown.

Dretske, F. (1981). *Knowledge and the flow of information.* Cambridge, MA: MIT Press.

Dretske, F. (1988). *Explaining behavior: Reasons in a world of causes.* Cambridge, MA: MIT Press.

Dreyfus, H. L. (1979). *What computers can't do.* New York: Harper and Row.

Field, H. (1978). Mental representation. *Erkenntnis* 13, 1, 9–61. Reprinted in Block (1980).

Fodor, J. (1968). The appeal to tacit knowledge in psychological explanation. *The Journal of Philosophy* 65, 20.

Fodor, J. (1975). *The language of thought.* New York: Crowell.

Fodor, J. (1980). Methodological solipsism considered as a research strategy in cognitive psychology. *The Behavioral and Brain Sciences* 3, 417–424. Reprinted in Haugeland (1981).

Fodor, J. (1981). Three cheers for propositional attitudes. In Fodor's *RePresentations.* Cambridge, MA: MIT Press.

Fodor, J. (1983). *The modularity of mind: An essay on faculty psychology.* Cambridge, MA: MIT Press.

Fodor, J. (1983). *The modularity of mind.* Cambridge, MA: MIT Press.
Fodor, J. (1985). Fodor's guide to mental representation. *Mind* 94, 76–100.
Fodor, J. (1987). *Psychosemantics.* Cambridge, MA: MIT Press.
Fodor, J. (1990). Psychosemantics, or where do truth conditions come from? In Lycan (1990).
Fodor, J., and Z. Pylyshyn (1988). Connectionism and cognitive architecture: A critical analysis. *Cognition* 28, 3–71.
Goldman, A., ed. (1993). *Readings in philosophy and cognitive science.* Cambridge, MA: MIT Press.
Guttenplan, S., ed. (1994). *A companion to philosophy of mind.* Oxford: Blackwell.
Harman, G. (1973). *Thought.* Princeton, NJ: Princeton University Press.
Harman, G. (1990). The intrinsic quality of experience. In J. Tomberlin (1990).
Haugeland, J. (1978). The nature and the plausibility of cognitivism. *The Behavioral and Brain Sciences* 1, 215–226. Reprinted in Haugeland (1981).
Haugeland, J. (1980). Programs, causal powers, and intentionality. *The Behavioral and Brain Sciences* 3, 432–3.
Haugeland, J., ed. (1981). *Mind design.* Cambridge, MA: MIT Press.
Haugeland, J. (1990). The intentionality all-stars. In Tomberlin (1990).
Hofstadter, D., and D. Dennett (1981). *The mind's I: Fantasies and reflections on mind and soul.* New York: Basic Books.
Horwich, P. (1990). *Truth.* Oxford: Blackwell.
Jackson, F. (1993). Block's challenge. In J. Bacon, K. Campbell, and L. Reinhardt. *Ontology, causality and mind.* Cambridge, MA: Cambridge University Press, 235–246.
Kim, J. (1992). Multiple realization and the metaphysics of reduction. *Philosophy and Phenomenological Research* 52, 1.
LePore, E., and B. Loewer (1987). Mind matters. *The Journal of Philosophy* 84, 11, 630–641.
Lycan, W., ed. (1987). *Consciousness.* Cambridge, MA: MIT Press.
Lycan, W. (1990). *Mind and cognition.* Oxford: Blackwell.
Marr, D. (1977). Artificial intelligence: A personal view. *Artificial Intelligence* 9, 37–48. Reprinted in Haugeland (1981).
McCarthy, J. (1980). Beliefs, machines and theories. *The Behavioral and Brain Sciences* 3, 435.
Millikan, R. G. (1984). *Language, thought and other biological categories: New foundations for realism.* Cambridge, MA: MIT Press.
Moor, J. (1987). Turing Test. In S. Shapiro, ed., *Encyclopedia of artificial intelligence.* New York: John Wiley and Sons, 1126–1130.
Newell, A. (1980). Physical symbol systems. *Cognitive Science* 4, 2, 135–183.
O'Rourke, J., and J. Shattuck (1993). Does a rock realize every finite automaton? A critique of Putnam's theorem. TR #030 Smith College.
Papineau, D. (1984). Representation and explanation. *Philosophy of Science* 51, 4, 550–572.
Peacocke, C. (1993). *A study of concepts.* Cambridge, MA: MIT Press.
Pettit, P., and J. McDowell (1986). *Subject, thought, and context.* Oxford: Oxford University Press.
Putnam, H. (1975). Philosophy and our mental life. In *Mind, language and reality: Philosophical papers,* vol. 2. London: Cambridge University Press. Reprinted in Block (1980), and, in somewhat different form, in Haugeland (1981). Originally published in *Cognition* 2 (1973) with a section on IQ that is omitted from both of the reprinted versions.
Putnam, H. (1988). *Representation and reality.* Cambridge, MA: MIT Press.
Pylyshyn, Z. (1984). *Computation and cognition: Issues in the foundations of cognitive science.* Cambridge, MA: MIT Press.
Ramsey, W., S. Stich, and D. Rumelhart (1991). *Philosophy and connectionist theory.* Hillsdale, NJ: Erlbaum.

Rosenthal, D. M., ed. (1991). *The nature of mind.* Oxford: Oxford University Press.
Schiffer, S. (1987). *Remnants of meaning.* Cambridge, MA: MIT Press.
Schwartz, J. (1988). The new connectionism: Developing relationships between neuroscience and artificial intelligence. *Daedalus* 117, 1, 123–142.
Searle, J. (1980). Minds, brains, and programs. *The Behavioral and Brain Sciences* 3, 417–424. Reprinted in Haugeland (1981).
Searle, J. (1990a). Is the brain a digital computer? *Proceedings and Addresses of the American Philosophical Association* 64, 21–37.
Searle, J. (1990b). Is the brain's mind a computer program? *Scientific American* 262, 1, 20–25.
Searle, J. (1990c). Consciousness, explanatory inversion and cognitive science. *The Behavioral and Brain Sciences* 13: 4, 585–595.
Searle, J. (1992). *The rediscovery of the mind.* Cambridge, MA: MIT Press.
Shieber, S. (1994). Lessons from a restricted Turing test. *Communications of the ACM* 37, 6, 70–78.
Shoemaker, S. (1981). The inverted spectrum. *The Journal of Philosophy* 74, 7, 357–381.
Smolensky, P. (1988). On the proper treatment of connectionism. *Behavioral and Brain Sciences* 11, 1–23. See also the commentary that follows and the reply by the author.
Stalnaker, R. (1984). *Inquiry.* Cambridge, MA: MIT Press.
Stampe, D. W. (1977). Toward a causal theory of linguistic representation. In P. A. French et al., eds., *Midwest studies in philosophy* II. Minneapolis, MN: University of Minnesota Press, 42–46.
Sterelny, K. (1985). Review of Stich (1983). *Australasian Journal of Philosophy* 63, 4, 510–519.
Sterelny, K. (1990). *The representational theory of the mind.* Oxford: Blackwell.
Stich, S. (1983). *From folk psychology to cognitive science: The case against belief.* Cambridge, MA: MIT Press.
Stich, S., and T. Warfield (1994). *Mental representation: A reader.* Cambridge, MA: Blackwell.
Tomberlin, J. (1990). *Philosophical perspectives,* IV: *Philosophy of mind and action theory.* Atascadero, CA: Ridgeview Publishing Co.
Turing, A. M. (1950). Computing machinery and intelligence. *Mind* 59, 433–460.
Tye, M. (1991). *The imagery debate.* Cambridge, MA: MIT Press.
Weizenbaum, J. (1976). *Computer power and human reason.* San Francisco: W. H. Freeman.
White, S. (1982). Functionalism and propositional content. Doctoral dissertation, University of California, Berkeley.

Index

Note: Italicized page numbers indicate illustrations.